Contents

P9-CQC-753

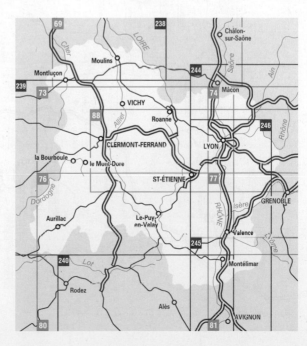

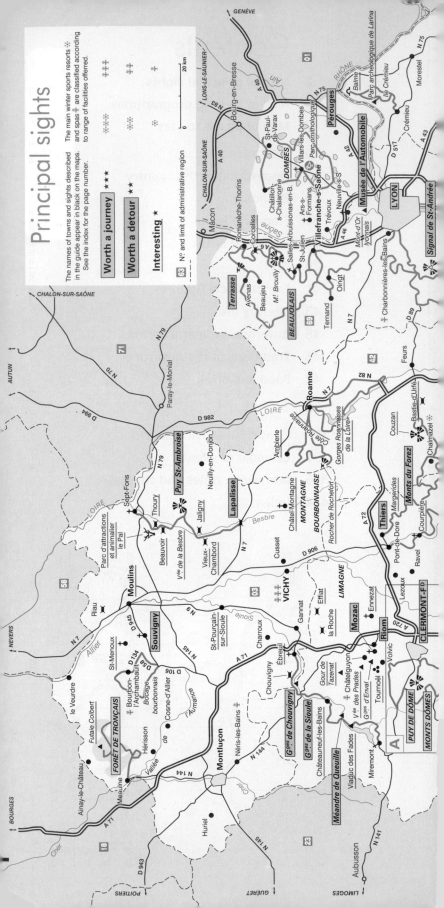

Principal sights

The names of towns and sights described in the guide appear in black on the maps.
See the index for the page number.

Worth a journey	★★★
Worth a detour	★★
Interesting	★

The main winter sports resorts ※ and spas ‡ are classified according to range of facilities offered.

	※※※	‡‡‡
	※※	‡‡
	※	‡

63 Nº and limit of administrative region

0   20 km

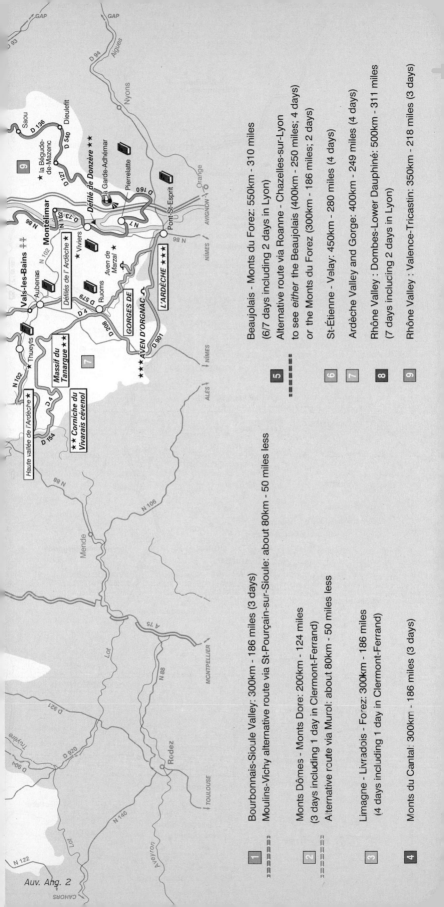

1 Bourbonnais-Sioule Valley: 300km - 186 miles (3 days)
Moulins-Vichy alternative route via St-Pourçain-sur-Sioule: about 80km - 50 miles less

2 Monts Dômes - Monts Dore: 200km - 124 miles (3 days including 1 day in Clermont-Ferrand)
Alternative route via Murol: about 80km - 50 miles less

3 Limagne - Livradois - Forez: 300km - 186 miles (4 days including 1 day in Clermont-Ferrand)

4 Monts du Cantal: 300km - 186 miles (3 days)

5 Beaujolais - Monts du Forez: 550km - 310 miles (6/7 days including 2 days in Lyon)
Alternative route via Roanne - Chazelles-sur-Lyon to see either the Beaujolais (400km - 250 miles; 4 days) or the Monts du Forez (300km - 186 miles; 2 days)

6 St-Étienne - Velay: 450km - 280 miles (4 days)

7 Ardèche Valley and Gorge: 400km - 249 miles (4 days)

8 Rhône Valley : Dombes-Lower Dauphiné: 500km - 311 miles (7 days including 2 days in Lyon)

9 Rhône Valley : Valence-Tricastin: 350km - 218 miles (3 days)

Auv. Ang. 2

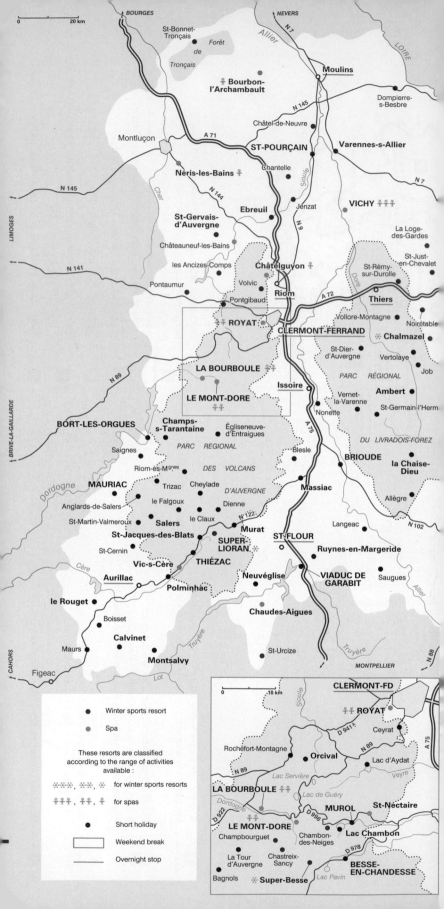

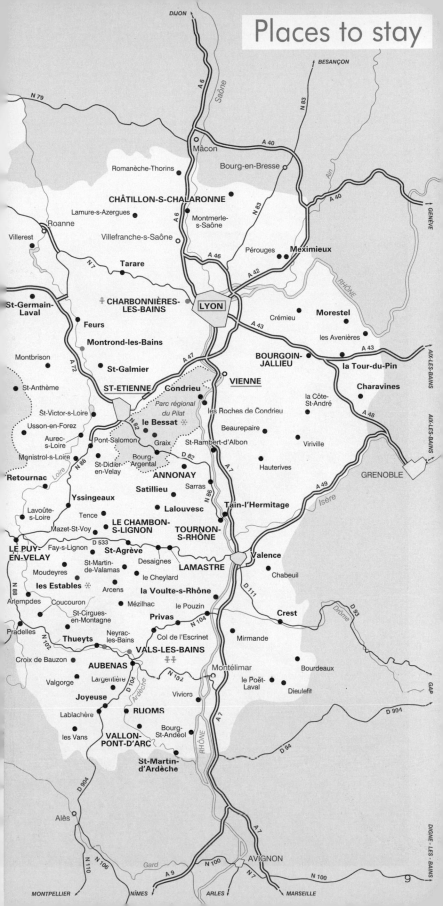

DIJON

BESANÇON

Saône

N 79

A 6

N 83

Mâcon

A 40

Bourg-en-Bresse

Romanèche-Thorins

CHÂTILLON-S-CHALARONNE

Ain

A 40

GENÈVE

Lamure-s-Azergues

A 6

N 83

Montmerle-s-Saône

Roanne

Villefranche-s-Saône

Villerest

A 46

Pérouges

Meximieux

N 7

Tarare

A 42

RHÔNE

St-Germain-Laval

CHARBONNIÈRES-LES-BAINS

LYON

A 43

Crémieu

Morestel

Feurs

Montrond-les-Bains

les Avenières

A 43

Montbrison

A 72

St-Galmier

A 47

BOURGOIN-JALLIEU

la Tour-du-Pin

AIX-LES-BAINS

St-Anthème

ST-ETIENNE

Condrieu

VIENNE

Charavines

St-Victor-s-Loire

Parc régional du Pilat

la Côte-St-André

A 48

AIX-LES-BAINS

Usson-en-Forez

N 82

le Bessat ✳

les Roches de Condrieu

Beaurepaire

Aurec-s-Loire

Pont-Salomon

Graix

St-Rambert-d'Albon

Viriville

GRENOBLE

Monistrol-s-Loire

N 88

St-Didier-en-Velay

Bourg-Argental

D 82

Hauterives

A 7

Retournac

Loire

ANNONAY

A 49

Isère

Yssingeaux

Satillieu

Lalouvesc

Sarras

N 86

Tain-l'Hermitage

Lavoûte-s-Loire

Tence

LE CHAMBON-S-LIGNON

TOURNON-S-RHÔNE

Mazet-St-Voy

LE PUY-EN-VELAY

Fay-s-Lignon

D 533

St-Agrève

Desaignes

LAMASTRE

Valence

Moudeyres

St-Martin-de-Valamas

le Cheylard

Chabeuil

D 111

les Estables ✳

Arcens

la Voulte-s-Rhône

Arlempdes

Coucouron

Mézilhac

le Pouzin

D 93

Pradelles

St-Cirgues-en-Montagne

Privas

N 104

Crest

Drôme

N 88

Thueyts

Neyrac-les-Bains

Col de l'Escrinet

Mirmande

N 102

VALS-LES-BAINS

✳✳

Croix de Bauzon

AUBENAS

Montélimar

Bourdeaux

GAP

Valgorge

Largentière

N 102

le Poët-Laval

Dieulefit

D 104

Ardèche

Joyeuse

Viviers

Lablachère

RUOMS

Bourg-St-Andéol

D 994

les Vans

VALLON-PONT-D'ARC

RHÔNE

A 7

St-Martin-d'Ardèche

D 94

D 904

D 994

DIGNE-LES-BAINS

Alès

Gard

A 7

AVIGNON

D 904

N 110

N 106

A 9

N 100

N 7

N 100

MONTPELLIER

NÎMES

ARLES

MARSEILLE

9

Puy de Pariou and Puy de Dôme

Introduction

Description of the country

The name **Auvergne** conjures up a vision of a superb natural environment of outstanding beauty, a rugged landscape of mountain ranges and volcanoes, lakes and springs at the heart of France. The area has been cut off from the rest of the country since time immemorial because of a lack of roads or railways. The local people are proud and austere, and there is a preponderance of agriculture.

The **Rhône valley**, on the other hand, is long and wide. It is an important through route for road and rail, a melting-pot of different cultures and an area at the forefront of industrial progress, which seems destined to play an increasingly important role within Europe in the future. The region is dominated by Lyon, the second largest city in France, which has the lively cultural life of any major conurbation, with museums, a new opera house and a long-standing tradition of good food.

RHONE VALLEY
The Rhône Corridor

La Dombes – This is a clay plateau dotted with lakes which ends in the fairly sheer "côtières" of the Saône to the west and the Rhône to the south. In the north, the plateau runs into Bresse.

The waters of the melting glacier in the Rhône valley dug shallow dips into the surface of the land and left moraines, an accumulation of debris swept along by the glacier, on the edge of the dips. It is on these **poypes** or slight rises that the villages were built. The **Dombes** is now a charming area of tranquil countryside, with lines of trees, countless birds, and calm lakes reflecting the sky above.

Lower Dauphiné – The countryside in Lower Dauphiné is a succession of stony plateaux, plains and hills.

L'Île Crémieu is a limestone plateau separated from the Jura to the north by the Rhône and to the west by an unusual cliff. The water that infiltrated the soil created a series of caves, the best-known of which are the Grottes de la Balme.

The **Balmes area** west of Vienne is partly covered in vineyards. It consists of granite and shale hills separated from Mont Pilat by the Rhône. It extends into the **Terres Froides plateau** which is slashed into strips by narrow valleys filled with fields of vegetables.

The **Bonnevaux and Chambaran plateaux** are vast expanses of woodland stretching south from Vienne and almost totally devoid of human habitation.

The wide fertile **Blèvre and Valloire plains** specialise in cereal crops. They indicate the course once followed by the Isère but abandoned after the ice had receded.

The **Isère valley** itself opens out onto the Valence plateau; its well-cultivated terraces are covered with magnificent walnut groves.

Valence and Le Tricastin – From Tain to the Donzère gorge, the Rhône valley widens to the east of the river, forming a patchwork of plains until it reaches the foothills of the pre-Alps. The **Valence plain** consists of a series of alluvial terraces built up in steps. Its irrigated fields and its climate are a foretaste of the south of France and the Mediterranean. It was here that the "Tree of Gold", the mulberry, was first planted

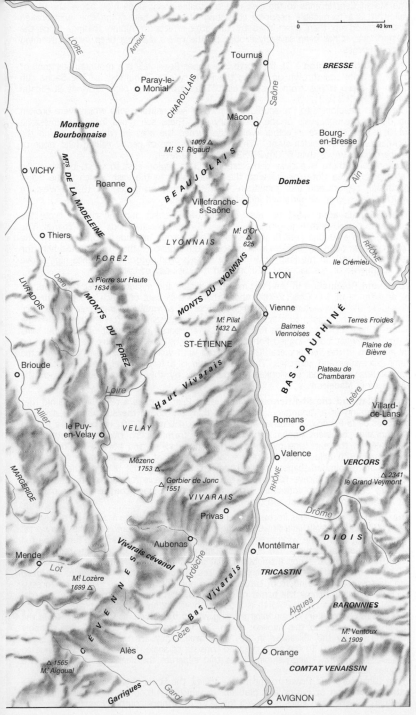

in the 17C and provided the local inhabitants with a reasonable living from the cultivation of silkworms. Nowadays, the many orchards have maintained the old-fashioned appearance of the countryside where hedgerows abounded.

The **Montélimar basin**, south of the Cruas gorge, is similar to but narrower than the Valence plain; olive trees grow on the south-facing slopes.

The **Tricastin area**, crossed by the rivers Lauzon and Lez, is a succession of arid hills covered with vineyards and olive trees. Its old villages perched on defensive sites form remarkable lookout posts. That flat irrigated land is divided into small fields protected from the wind by rows of cypress trees.

The edge of the Massif Central

The Massif Central ends to the east in a crystalline scarp slope high above the Rhône valley. It is a formidable precipice consisting of a mountain range that was broken down, raised up then overturned by the after-effects of Alpine folding. Since the Tertiary era, it has been severely eroded by the rivers that dig deep into it, forming narrow gorges.

The Beaujolais region – To the north, the upper Beaujolais is a mountainous zone of mainly granite soil thrown up during the Primary era. Tributaries of the Saône run down its steep slopes from west to east. The highest local peak is Mont St-Rigaud (alt 1 009m/3 310ft).

The lower Beaujolais, to the south, is formed of sedimentary soils which were broken up during the upheavals of the Secondary era. These soil types include a limestone which is almost ochre in colour which has earned the area in which it is found the nickname "land of golden stone". The landscape is one of gently rolling hills, none of which reaches more than 650m/2 133ft above sea level.

Economically, there is a clear demarcation of this region east to west, between the "escarpment" (La Côte) overlooking the Saône valley in the east, which is the wine-producing region, and the "mountain" (La Montagne) or hinterland to the west, in which forests, crop-farming and industry predominate.

The Lyonnais area – Set between the St-Étienne basin and the city of Lyon, the plateau is dotted with high grassy hills, pine forests, beech woods and orchards. The Mont d'Or is a rugged area (highest peak: Mont Verdun, altitude 625m/2 050ft). The Lyonnais area owes its uniform appearance to the industries that have existed here for centuries. It ends in the Fourvière hill, the superb promontory that stands high above the confluence of the Saône and Rhône and the vast city of Lyon.

Forez and Roannais – In the **Forez mountains**, fields and meadows cover the slopes up to an altitude of 1 000m/3 280ft. Above them are carpets of beech and pine forests, providing the raw material for a large number of sawmills. In summer, animals are taken up for the season to graze on the scrubby mountain tops (on the land called the Hautes Chaumes) rising to the Pierre-sur-Haute moors. At the foot of the mountains is the somewhat water-logged Forez plain crossed by the River Loire; it was silted up by alluvium in the Tertiary era. This is dotted with volcanic hillocks on which are the ruins of castles and churches. The **Roanne basin** is a fertile rural area specialising in animal husbandry and overlooked, to the west, by the vine-covered slopes of the Monts de la Madeleine.

Mont Pilat and the St-Étienne basin – Mont Pilat forms a forest-clad pyramid that has something of a mountainous air about it, rising above the surrounding dales; at the Crêt de la Perdrix, it reaches an altitude of 1 432m/4 698ft. Its peaks are topped with granite boulders known as *chirats* which form superb observation platforms, especially on the east side overlooking the Rhône valley and Lower Dauphiné some 1 200m/3 937ft below. The St-Étienne basin at the foot of the mountain follows the outline of the almond-shaped coalfield that stretches from the Loire to the Rhône. It corresponds to a concave fold in the carboniferous layers formed at the end of the Primary era. The basin contains a string of factories, a stark contrast to the pastures on the slopes of Mont Pilat and the Monts Lyonnais.

The Vivarais area – This forms the largest part of the eastern edge of the Massif Central. Its huge basalt lava flows running down from the volcanoes in the Velay area, its shale ridges, and the widespread erosion of its limestone make this a landscape full of strange natural features that are a constant source of surprise and amazement.

The **Upper Vivarais** stretches from Mont Pilat and the Velay area to the Rhône valley. People in the dark, austere countryside in Les Boutières, where the gullies are deep and narrow, earn a living from cattle farming and cutting timber in its pine forests. Further downhill, nearer the banks of the Rhône, there are fruit trees and vineyards. The Annonay plateau to the north is a terrace overlooking the Rhône plain.

The **Vivarais Cévenol** (part of the Vivarais lying within the Cévennes range) runs from the Upper Allier valley to the Aubenas basin. To the west, the "uplands" are strongly characterised by the volcanoes in the Velay area. They are covered in pines, beech trees and meadows. To the east, the land consists of shale, forming narrow elongated ridges *(serres)* with steeply-sloping sides that separate the deep valleys in what is a complex landscape.

From Lablachère and Privas to the Rhône valley, the **Lower Vivarais** is a limestone area with a succession of basins and plateaux in which scrub, olive trees, almond trees, blackberry bushes and vines provide a foretaste of a more southerly environment.

To the north it is separated from the **Upper Vivarais** by the Coiron plateau and its black basalt cliffs. The unusual features of the vast plains *(planèzes)* grazed by flocks of sheep are the **dikes** and **necks** (pinnacles), the most famous of which is the one in Rochemaure. The limestone plateaux of Gars form a stretch of whitish stone, with swallowholes, deep narrow gullies and rocks shaped like ruined buildings.

AUVERGNE

Granite and volcanic mountains – In the region to the east, the climate is hard and the landscape rugged. From north to south, the **Monts de la Madeleine, Forez and Livradois areas** consist of valleys, rounded hilltops, forest plateaux and pastures on which flocks of sheep graze. The area is covered with forests that provide timber. Further south, the **Velay area** is a succession of vast basalt plateaux lying at altitudes of more than 1 000m/3 280ft beneath skies that are a foretaste of the Riviera. Dotted across the countryside are **outcrops of rock** formed by lava. Crops are generally so rare that the basin around Le Puy, which is irrigated by the Loire, looks almost like an oasis. The mountains in the **Devès area** form one vast plateau where basalt lava flows are covered with pasture and fields of barley or lentils. Along the watershed between the Loire and Allier basins are deep lakes which fill volcanic craters. The *planèze* (sloping plateau) is dotted with some 150 cinder cones consisting of black or reddish ash often capped with pine trees. The **Margeride plateau** is gashed by deep valleys and its climate and vegetation are reminiscent of the Forez mountains.

Limagnes – The *limagnes* are low-lying, fertile, sunny plains drained by the Dore and, more particularly, by the Allier and its tributaries. The plains consist almost entirely of arable land. To the east are the "poor Limagnes" or "Varennes", a hilly area of marshes, woodland, fields of crops and lush pastures where alluvium has been washed down from the crystalline mountains of the Forez area. To the west, the soil in the "fertile Limagnes" is dark brown, almost black. It has been enriched by the mixture of decomposed lava and volcanic ash. This is very fertile land, producing tobacco, wheat, sugar beet, vegetable crops, seed crops and fruit.

Volcanic uplands – To the west of the region, the **Monts Dômes, Monts Dore** and the mountains in the **Cézallier** and **Cantal** areas form a striking landscape of extinct volcanoes rising to an altitude of 1 885m/6 185ft at the highest peak, the Puy de Sancy. Around the Puy de Dôme, Puy Mary, Puy de Sancy, La Bourboule and St-Nectaire, forests, woods and pastures alternate with lakes and waterfalls. The **Artense**, which backs onto the Monts Dore, is a rocky plateau worn away by glaciers; it now provides grazing land for sheep and cattle. The cultivated areas represent land that has been slowly and painfully clawed back from the moors by the few people living there.

The Bourbonnais area – The scenery in the Bourbonnais area is like the people who live there – calm and temperate. It marks the northern edge of the Massif Central, and the gently-rolling countryside is covered with a patchwork of small fields hemmed in by hedges which give the landscape a wooded appearance.
The Besbre, Cher and Aumance valleys are wide and well-drained, forming open, fertile areas crossed by major road and rail links. It is here that the main towns are to be found. The St-Pourçain vineyards, the impressive Tronçais forest, and the conifers on the mountainsides in the Bourbonnais area add a touch of variety to a landscape that is otherwise dominated by grassland.

The volcanoes of the Auvergne

What makes the Auvergne so unusual is the presence of a large number of volcanoes which, although extinct, are a major feature of the landscape. They vary in appearance depending on their formation, type and age.

Inverse composite volcanoes (Stromboli-type) – In the depths of the earth, magma is subjected to enormous pressure and infiltrates through cracks in the Earth's crust *(see diagram)*. When the pressure becomes too great, there is a sudden eruption accompanied by a sudden eruption of incandescent matter. A huge column of gas, smoke and vapour rises into the sky, spreading out like a parasol, while the matter in fusion (spindle-shaped volcanic bombs, gas-swollen "pozzolana" looking like a very lightweight, dark reddish-coloured stone) falls back to earth and accumulates around the mouth of the volcano, gradually building up a **cinder cone**. At the top is a **crater**. The most typical of all can be seen on the Puy des Goules and the Pariou *(see below)*.
When the pressure inside the Earth's crust decreases and the matter thrown up by the eruption is more fluid, lava flows are created, running from the crater or down the mountainsides. Depending on the type of rock, these **lava flows** *(cheires)* may cool to form a fairly smooth surface

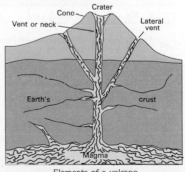

Elements of a volcano

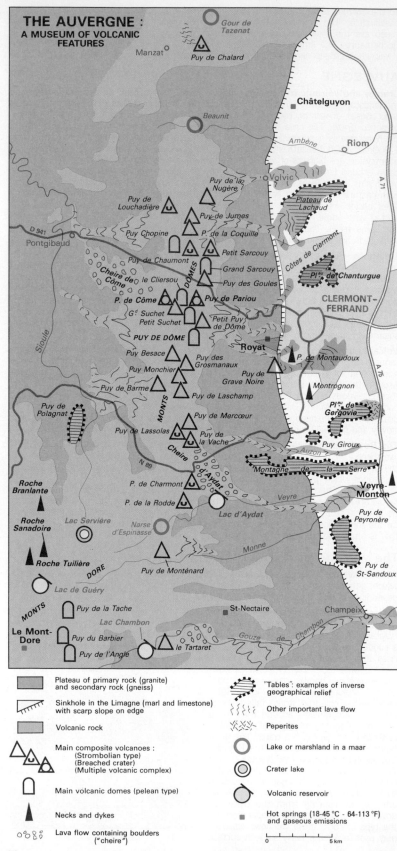

THE AUVERGNE:
A MUSEUM OF VOLCANIC FEATURES

Gour de Tazenat

Manzat

Puy de Chalard

Châtelguyon

Beaunit

Ambène

Riom

A 71

Puy de la Nugère

Volvic

Plateau de Lachaud

Puy de Louchadière

Puy de Jumes

D 941

Puy Chopine

P. de la Coquille

Pontgibaud

Petit Sarcouy

Côtes de Clermont

Puy de Chaumont

Grand Sarcouy

Pl.au de Chanturgue

Cheire de Côme

le Cliersou

DÔMES

Puy des Goules

CLERMONT-FERRAND

P. de Côme

Puy de Pariou

Stoule

Gd Suchet

Petit Suchet

Petit Puy de Dôme

PUY DE DÔME

Royat

P. de Montaudoux

Puy Besace

Puy des Grosmanaux

Puy Monchier

Puy de Grave Noire

Montrognon

A 75

Puy de Barme

MONTS

Puy de Laschamp

Puy de Polagnat

Pl.au de Gergovie

Puy de Mercœur

Puy Giroux

Puy de Lassolas

Puy de la Vache

Auzon

Cheire

d'Aydat

Montagne de la Serre

N 89

Veyre-Monton

Roche Branlante

P. de Charmont

Veyre

Roche Sanadoire

P. de la Rodde

Lac d'Aydat

Puy de Peyronère

Lac Servière

Narse d'Espinasse

Monne

Roche Tuilière

DORE

Puy de Monténard

Puy de St-Sandoux

Lac de Guéry

MONTS

Puy de la Tache

St-Nectaire

Champeix

Le Mont-Dore

Lac Chambon

Puy du Barbier

Gouze de Chambon

Puy de l'Angle

le Tartaret

	Plateau of primary rock (granite) and secondary rock (gneiss)		"Tables": examples of inverse geographical relief
	Sinkhole in the Limagne (marl and limestone) with scarp slope on edge		Other important lava flow
	Volcanic rock		Peperites
	Main composite volcanoes: (Strombolian type) (Breached crater) (Multiple volcanic complex)		Lake or marshland in a maar
	Main volcanic domes (pelean type)		Crater lake
	Necks and dykes		Volcanic reservoir
	Lava flow containing boulders ("cheire")		Hot springs (18-45 °C - 64-113 °F) and gaseous emissions

0   5 km

16

Breached volcano – Le Puy de la Vache

Multiple volcanic complex –
Le Puy de Pariou

or, alternatively, be rough and full of boulders. When the mass of lava is very thick, it contracts as it cools, breaking into prisms or "columns" (very much like organ pipes, hence their French name *orgues*) such as those in Bort-les-Orgues or Murat.

Sometimes a lava flow or an explosion carries away a piece of the volcanic cone, as it did in the Puy de Louchardière or the Puy de la Vache; in this case, the crater is described as "**breached**" and is shaped like a half-funnel.

In Le Pariou and the Puy de Dôme, a new cinder cone was formed inside the crater of an older volcano. This led to the formation of a **multiple volcanic complex.**

Volcanic domes (Mount Pelée-type composite volcano) – Sometimes, the volcanic eruption throws up a lava paste which solidifies upon contact with the ground. It then forms a dome with steep sides but has no crater at the summit. The Puy de Dôme is a good example of this type of volcano.

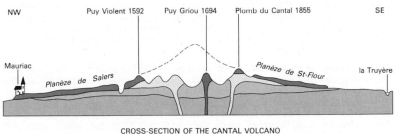

CROSS-SECTION OF THE CANTAL VOLCANO

	Primary rock		Ash and Breccia		Andesite
	Phonolite		Basalt		

Volcanoes with planèzes – When the Cantal volcano was active more than 20 000 000 years ago, it would have been a formidable sight: it had a circumference of 60km/37mi and rose to an altitude of 3 000m/9 843ft. Formed by a succession of layers of lava and ash, it was dissected by erosion which cut its sides into **planèzes** (sloping plateaux) with a tip pointing towards the centre of the volcano *(see diagram)*. The Monts Dore, which are younger than the Cantal volcano (2-3.5 million years), also consist of successions of layers of lava and ash but the **planèzes** are less well-developed.

Necks and dikes – Scattered across the Limagne in total disorder are volcanic systems which penetrated, and were consolidated within, a mass of sedimentary rock that has since been worn away. All that remain are a few spurs of rock called "necks" or ridges known as "dikes", which no longer have their covering of soil. The Puy de Monton near Veyre, and Montrognon near Ceyrat, are typical necks. Montaudoux to the south of Royat is a good example of a "dike".

Tables – Ancient lava flows originally spread out across the valleys, protecting the underlying soil from the erosion that cleared the area between rivers and caused an "inversion relief". These lava flows now jut up above the surrounding countryside *(see diagram overleaf)*, forming tables such as the Gergovie and Polignac plateaux, the Serre "Montagne" etc.

Lahars and Peperites – Volcanic eruptions are often accompanied by torrential rain and enormous emissions of water vapour. They then cause *lahars* (an Indonesian word) or flows of mud and boulders which progress at astonishing speed, destroying everything in their path. The Pardines plateau near Issoire owes its existence to this type of phenomenon. South of Clermont-Ferrand, some of the small plateaux and hillocks in the Limagne area consist of peperites, rock formations created by underwater volcanic eruptions. Their "peppery" appearance is due to the mixing of lava and sediment from the bed of the lake.

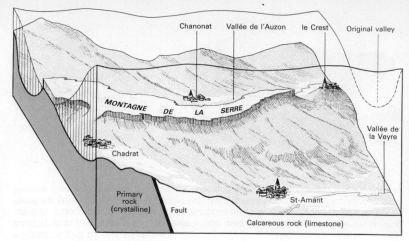

An example of inversion relief: Montagne de la Serre.
This simplified diagram shows the original valley in red.

Lakes of volcanic origin – The volcanoes have given the landscape of the Auvergne its very particular relief and the magnificent stretches of water that reflect the surrounding countryside. Many of the lakes in the Auvergne owe their existence to volcanic eruptions. In some places, a lava flow closed off a valley, holding back the waters of a river upstream; examples of this are lakes Aydat and Guéry (the latter was also formed by the action of glaciers). In other places, a volcano erupted in the middle of a valley, blocking it with its cone, as was the case in Chambon and Montcineyre. Still elsewhere, subsidence caused by underground volcanic activity was filled with run-off water (Lake Chauvet). "Maars" are lakes which were formed in craters.

The volcanoes of the Auvergne at present – The volcanoes are now more or less well-preserved depending on their age and the hardness of their rocks. The **Dômes range**, with its eighty volcanoes that became extinct less than 4 000 years ago, has a strikingly fresh-looking relief. The **Monts Dore** are older and have a more fragmented appearance. The lava flows on Sancy, Aiguiller and Banne d'Ordanche are heaped up to a height of more than 1 000m/3 280ft but water, snow and glaciers have worn away the sides. With its 60km/37mi circumference and altitude of 3 000m/9 843ft, the **Cantal volcano** was even more impressive in its day. The landscapes visible today reveal only a fraction of the original; it is difficult to imagine the initial size of the range.

Economy

INDUSTRY

Industry came into being in the 16C with the introduction of silk working around Lyon, paid for by the capital earned from fairs. Later, the coalfields in the area were one of the factors that led to the expansion of industry. Once the seams had been worked out, the energy supply was provided by the hydroelectric plants and, since the 1970s and 1980s, by the nuclear power plants along the Rhône valley. Around Clermont-Ferrand the major industry is tyre making.

Metal working – After the gradual shut-down of the coal mines in the area around St-Étienne, the metal working sector began to specialise in the production of steels, rare metals, fissile products for use in the nuclear industry, and smelting, a sector that benefits from the high demand for moulded components (boiler-making, pipes). The region along the Rhône ranks second to the Paris basin in the field of mechanical engineering (machine tools, precision engineering, car manufacture). Electrical and electronic engineering are well represented with companies producing high-voltage equipment, communications equipment and domestic appliances. Until the 19C, tin and copper were the two main materials used in the Auvergne.

Textiles – After the silk workers' revolts in 1831 and 1834 in the streets and alleyways of Lyon, the textile industry relocated to villages and manufacturers distributed the jobs (weaving and dyeing) to a rural work force. This was the "outworker" system which has lasted to the present day though in a more flexible and improved form. The importance of silk has decreased greatly in the face of competition from manmade fibres but the weaving of "artificial silks" (a combination of fibres and threads of all types) has remained famous. The new products have benefited from the wealth of inventiveness and the excellent taste that won it its original reputation.

The production and weaving of manmade textiles is carried out in Valence (nylon and polyester) and Roanne (viscose). The manmade textile industry has many offshoots such as dyeing and dressing, and clothing (ready-to-wear, sportswear, lingerie, hosiery, curtains, net curtains, ribbons, elastic, lace).

Chemicals– A major chemical industry developed in Lyon in order to meet the needs of the textile industry. It was here that one of Europe's petro-chemical centres was established. In Feyzin, there is a large oil refinery and the Institut Français du Pétrole has set up its largest research centre here. The region currently leads the field in certain areas of the chemical industry: fungicides, paint, varnish and, in particular, pharmaceuticals.

Additional industries – Other industrial activities in the region include tyre making, food processing (dairy products, pork meat products, health foods), building materials and glass, wires and cables, leather and shoemaking, paper, jewellery, tobacco, cabinet-making, quarrying (Volvic), enamelled lava (signposts, viewing tables) and bottling mineral waters (Vichy, Volvic). Thiers is one of France's major cutlery-making centres. Traditionally, industry in the Auvergne has centred around specialist crafts, production frequently operating on a cottage-industry scale, such as coppersmithing (Cantal), lace-making (Velay) and papermaking (Livradois).

Administration offices (local authority and government offices etc) and tourism also play an important part in the local economy; traditional industries (eg cheese making) no longer do any more than "top it up".

Lace-makers

AGRICULTURE

The Auvergne is first and foremost a rural area, in contrast to the Rhône valley where industry predominates. Life on farms has undergone profound change over the course of the 20C. The introduction of motor vehicles and the destruction of hedgerows ended the subdivision of property into small fields and, in many places, the traditional landscape of fields and narrow lanes lined with walnut trees has given way to wide, open fields. Farmers, who are decreasing in number, have also had to comply with the milk quotas imposed upon them by the EU; despite these difficulties, animal breeding and crop farming remain an important part of the economy of the region.

Stock breeding – The high plateaux and mountains are popular with cattle breeders and, to a lesser extent, sheep farmers. The pastures on the slopes of the Monts Dômes and Monts Dore provide grazing land for the **Salers** breed of cattle (of which it is said that its fiery red coat turns pale if it leaves the basalt areas of Cantal), the French black and white Friesian, and the Montbéliarde. Dairy herds predominate in every part of the region.

Towards the middle of May the animals leave their byres and, for the five months of summer, live in the open air on the mountain pastures which are now fenced so that there is no need for a herdsman to be in attendance. In days gone by, cowherds had a squat, low summer hut called a *buron*, built to withstand the wind, in which cheese was often made.

The **fairs** give visitors an opportunity to enjoy the busiest moments of rural life. They are held in most of the centrally-situated localities and in other places that lie in the heart of the stock-breeding areas. The largest fairs are held in late summer and in autumn.

Crops – In the Auvergne, wheat, barley and oats have traditionally been grown on the fertile black soil of the Limagnes, and now also sugar beet, tobacco, sunflowers and fodder or maize crops from selected strains of seeds.

Towards the southern end of the Rhône valley the dampness and cold of maritime or continental climates gives way to the heat and radiant skies of the south of France: almond and olive trees and a few mulberry bushes can be seen in the countryside.

The natural environment here is both crop- and farmer-friendly. The land is fertile and easy to irrigate; the soil is light and siliceous; well-sheltered corries and dales benefit from the spring sunshine.

Orchards – It was in 1880 that fruit production took over from wine, after the vineyards had been blighted by phylloxera. The long fruit-producing season made possible by careful selection of varieties and the differences in exposure or altitude enable the orchards in the Rhône valley to produce one-third of all French fruit. Every type of fruit can be found here – raspberries, redcurrants and blackcurrants in Isère, sweet chestnuts in Ardèche, cherries, apricots, apples and pears and, in particular, peaches, the fruit that has made the Eyrieux valley famous.

In the Auvergne the orchards are declining but they continue to supply the main ingredients for local candied fruit and fruit jelly factories.

Vineyards – The vineyards in the Rhône valley, which were already popular in Roman times, underwent massive expansion after the crisis in the silkworm-breeding industry in the mid 19C. At present, the vineyards cover an area of more than 160 000ha/ 774 sq mi, one-third of which produce high-quality wines. The best are the **Côtes du Rhône**. Châteauneuf-du-Pape, St-Joseph, Crozes-Hermitage, Hermitage, Côte-Rôtie, Château-Grillet and Condrieu are wines that age well, and it is they that brought the area its reputation for excellence. With an annual output of 2 500 000 hecto-litres of *appellations contrôlées*, the Rhône valley vineyards account for 14% of the total French production of fine wines.

The vineyards stretch over a distance of 200km/124mi producing a variety of wines thanks to the **types of vines** selected: Marsanne and Viognier for the whites, Syrah and Grenache for the reds. The wines also vary depending on the **different types of soil** on which the vines are planted – the crumbly granite of the gorges, and the sands, pebbles or marl that predominate in alluvial plains. There are climatic differences in the basins and, finally, the terraces that climb the hillsides between this area and the Alps face in different directions.

Further north, the vineyards of the **Beaujolais** – which are usually grouped with those of neighbouring Burgundy in wine guides – produce wines which go very well indeed with the traditional cuisine of Lyon, where they are to be found in every local brasserie or *bouchon*. The third Thursday in November is a red letter day locally (and further afield, now that the reputation of Beaujolais wines has spread abroad!) as it marks *"l'arrivée du Beaujolais Nouveau"*, or the release for sale to the public of the latest Beaujolais vintage *(vin primeur)*. *For further details on Beaujolais wines, see under BEAUJOLAIS in the alphabetical section of the guide.*

The limestone hillsides to each side of the Limagnes used to be covered with vineyards. Nowadays, some of the wines fall within the all-enveloping name "Côtes d'Auvergne", among them Châtaugay, Corrent, Boudes and St-Pourçain.

Respect the life of the countryside
Drive carefully on country roads
Protect wildlife, plants and trees

Flora and fauna

RHÔNE VALLEY

The Rhône valley is not only a major road and rail route and intersection of geographical areas, it also combines differing natural environments which have resulted in a huge variety of flora and fauna. Almost 3 000 species of plant, some sixty wild mammals and more than 200 birds have been observed in the forests, plains and lakes. The Pilat regional nature park alone boasts some 90 species of bird.

Flora – In addition to the plants ordinarily found in the centre of France, the area also has mountain plants which have come down from the Alps and the Jura, and Mediterranean plants which have spread up from the south. Because of this, it is possible to find, in the mountains in the Forez area for example, gentians, monkshood, or the superb Martagon (or Turk's Cap) lily. This is a very rare plant, a hardy annual growing to a height of 30-80cm/12-30in or even, on occasions, to more than 1.10m/3ft 6in, with clusters of reddish-orange flowers spotted with black growing on a tall stem. Nor is it unusual, on the lower plateaux and hillsides in the Saône and Rhône valleys, to see evergreen oaks, Montpellier aphyllantes, lavender, purple orchids or other varieties of orchid growing in the month of April on dry grasslands.

Fauna – Just like the flora, Mediterranean species of fauna are found in the Rhône valley as the northernmost habitats are sited in the Rhône basin. Among them is the Provençal field mouse, a tiny rodent, and the mouse-eared bat. Deer are very adaptable creatures and can be seen throughout the region in forested areas. The Rhône valley is a major point along the migratory routes followed by **birds** flying between Northern Europe and the Mediterranean basin. The banks of the Saône and Rhône are full of larks, buntings, quail, plovers and curlews. It is the **Dombes**, though, that boasts the largest numbers of birds, because of its many lakes. In addition to the numerous web-footed friends, partridges, herons, and song thrushes, birds from all over the world can be seen at the bird sanctuary in Villars-les-Dombes where toucans and parrots rub shoulders with rare species such as the black-tailed godwit, or the corncrake, which is an endangered species.

The wels, the largest freshwater fish – Before it was introduced into France in the second half of the 19C by fish farmers, this species of large catfish was found mainly in the waters of the Caspian Sea and the River Danube. The fish living in the Rhône and Saône can grow to a length of more than 2m/6ft 6in and weigh more than 50kg/110lb (7 stone). It feeds on bream, moorhens, ducks and rats; to kill its prey, it grabs their paws and drags them down to the river-bed until they drown. This little aquatic monster is however short-sighted and dislikes the light, so it waits until nightfall before seeking to catch its food; it is therefore unlikely to be seen, except perhaps on a dinner plate as it is becoming increasingly popular with fishermen.

Beavers of Île du Beurre – The beaver is a hard-working animal, continuously cutting, felling and nibbling branches of trees in order to build dams and dikes which it cements with mud to create a lodge. These days, though, lodges are no longer built because beavers have changed their habits and they now live in burrows dug into the river banks. They are particularly fond of the banks of the Île du Beurre (in old French, *beurre* meant "beaver"). This island to the south of Lyon is the last place in France in which beavers live in the wild and, because of this, it has been covered by a preservation order since 1988.

AUVERGNE

The Auvergne has all sorts of landscapes and soils, each with its own particular flora and fauna. Forests, peat bogs and salmon are just some of its many characteristics.

Vegetation at different altitudes – The **forests** in the Auvergne grow in very specific tiers. The hillsides are covered in oak woods with pedunculate oaks on clay soil and sessile oaks on well-drained ground. On the mountains, there are beeches and pines although the conifers predominate only in cold, damp areas (Bois-Noirs, Monts Dore). The beech is the commonest tree in the forests of the Auvergne and can grow to a height of 30-40m/97-130ft after 150 to 300 years. It is easily recognisable for its smooth, grey bark and leaf colouring – red in winter and soft green in spring. Natural pine groves cover the driest hillsides like those in Upper Loire.

The **moors** of the Margeride area often mark the abandonment of pastures or farmland. In fact, moorland precedes the stage at which land is overrun by forest. Ferns, calluna, gorse, myrtle and redcurrants grow here. Gradually, however, the forest takes over, with birches, hazelnut trees and pines being the first trees to appear.

The **mountain pastures** above an altitude of 1 000m/3 250ft provide a natural environment for species which have been observed here for many centuries, such as the three-coloured violet, the scented wild pansy which blooms from April to October, the red-purple sawwort which is used to produce a yellow dye, and the globe flower, a large, golden flower which seems to be closed in upon itself. The gentian, a delightful yellow flower, is used to make the liqueur that bears its name; other species of gentian produce blue flowers.

The **subalpine stage** of vegetation begins at altitudes of more than 1 400-1 500m/4 550-4 875ft; plantlife varies depending on the exposure of the slopes. Calluna and myrtle grow on moorland, and ground-cover plants on grassland, rocks and scree. It is here, from May to July, that the spring anemone blooms, a rare plant with delicately indented leaves and flowers with huge white petals tinged with purple. Mountain arnica, a downy plant with yellow flowers, is used to make creams that prevent bruising. The blue carnation, which is actually a very unusual bluish green in colour, can be seen in tufts only a few inches high on the peaks in the Monts Dore and Cantal ranges.

Peat bogs – Peat bogs are natural environments created by an accumulation of organic matter in damp areas. There are a number of features which lead to the formation of peat bogs, eg a break in a slope along the course of streams and cold springs as is the case in the mountains of Cantal. They also tend to form on valley floors, along meanders and streams like the ones in the Upper Forez area, in the bases of volcanic craters that have been rendered impermeable by clay deposits, or over-deepening caused by glacial erosion as was the case in the Margeride, Forez and Artense regions. Maars (lakes in the bottom of craters) can also be overrun by vegetation. Examples of this can be seen in the Devès range and the Velay area.

Peat is formed from a range of spongy mosses called sphagnum, which ensure photosynthesis and store water. These mosses can retain up to 30 times their dry weight of water. The bogs are exceptional because some of them have survived for more than 5 000 years and have developed a unique form of plant and animal life.

Mountain arnica

The herbaceous willow is the smallest tree in the world, the lycopode has remained unchanged for 300 million years, and the dwarf birch is typical of more northerly climes.

There are countless carnivorous plants which have adapted to this environment because they suffer from a nitrogen deficiency; they capture small insects by secreting a sticky substance. Two such plants are sundew and drosera which produce droplets that act as multiple mirrors reflecting the light.

The animals are also extraordinary. There are flies and mosquitoes which, because they have had to adapt to cold environments in which they cannot fly, have no wings. Common frogs live on land and only enter the water to spawn. The meadow pippit is a northern bird that is a frequent sight in peat bogs.

The odyssey of the salmon – The life cycle of the salmon is surprising. Born in a river, it stays in the area where it was born for two years (at this stage, it is known as a smelt or parr) before letting the river carry it down to the sea tail-first, during the period known as downstream migration. At this stage its scales turn white.

Certain salmon travel as far as the seas off Greenland. Here, they grow and acquire their more familiar appearance – it is the shrimps on which they feed that give them their "salmon pink" colouring.

Two years later the salmon swims up the Loire to return to its spawning grounds in Allier or Upper Loire, in particular around Brioude which is famous as the "salmon's paradise"; the trip can take several months. It is said that salmon return to the place of their own birth thanks to an olfactory memory and the return is known as **homing**. When the fish arrives, it is exhausted and very thin, because it has had to overcome a number of obstacles, quite apart from the fact that it does not feed in rivers. The female burrows into the gravel on the river bed with her tail and lays the eggs that the male covers with his milt. The salmon then usually die. Sometimes, however, a salmon will make the journey twice.

In the Auvergne, this extraordinary fish is the subject of many a tale or anecdote. One of them recounts how, at the turn of the century when the railway line was being built through the Allier gorge, the workmen went on strike because they had nothing to eat – nothing, that is, but salmon!

REGIONAL NATURE PARKS

Parc naturel régional des Volcans d'Auvergne

This park is the largest of all France's regional nature parks, covering more than 395 000ha/987 500 acres along a north-south axis of about 120km/75mi. It encompasses 153 localities in the *départements* of Puy-de-Dôme and Cantal and has a resident population of 91 000. Five main natural regions make up the park: the **Monts Dômes** range of volcanic hills *(puys)*; the **Monts Dore** massif, the vast grass-covered basalt plains of **Cézallier**; the **Artense** with its granite hills, moorland and valleys dotted with lakes and peat bogs; and the **Cantal** mountains.

The main aim of the park is to protect the region's exceptional natural and architectural heritage, which it does by running nature reserves and making good any sites which have fallen into disrepair. It is also involved in boosting the local rural economy – based largely on agriculture and handicrafts – and developing tourism in the region.

Parc naturel régional Livradois-Forez

This park was founded in 1986 and covers nearly 300 000ha/ 741 000 acres (175 localities and about 110 000 inhabitants). It stretches along the line of the Dore valley, from the Bois Noirs (Puy-de-Dôme) in the north to the Velay border (Haute-Loire) in the south, and encompasses six main regions: the area around **Thiers**; the **Lower Livradois**; the **Upper Livradois**; the Monts du **Forez**; the **Ambert** plain; and the area around **Chaise-Dieu**.

Like France's other regional parks, the Livradois-Forez was founded to preserve the local natural environment and educate visitors to the area about the region's natural and traditional heritage. The park's cultural programme includes the music festivals of Chaise-Dieu and Thiers. The residents of the areas encompassed by the park are proud of their history and the craftsmanship they have practised over the centuries, reflected in various local museums: cutlery making (Thiers); lace-making (Arlanc); paper making (Richard-de-Bas); agriculture and cheese-making (Ambert).

There are a number of waymarked paths which cover the park, enabling visitors to explore it to the full. Those fond of sports will appreciate the facilities for water sports, riding and paragliding.

Parc naturel régional du Pilat

See Mont PILAT in the alphabetical section of the guide.

Gentians on the shores of Lac de Guéry

Historical notes

Words in italics indicate a few major events in this chronological look at history.

The Auvergne appears to have some of the oldest human settlements in France.

BC	Prehistory
1500000	**Lower Palaeolithic era:** beginnings of human settlement in the Massif Central (sites of Châtelperron in the Allier, and of Enval and Cheix in Puy-de-Dôme).
7500-2800	**Neolithic Era: Stone Age.** The volcanoes in the Puy range cease to erupt. Farmer-stock breeders settle in the Rhône valley and the Massif Central, leaving some fifty dolmens and twenty or more menhirs.
c2000-700	**Bronze Age.** Human settlements become denser and the Rhône valley is the major amber and tin route. The Celts settle in Gaul. The Helvians settle on the right bank of the Rhône, the Allobroges on the left and the Arverni in the Auvergne.

Arverni domination of the Auvergne – The main expansion of the Celtic people occurred during the 5C BC, probably as a result of the push southwards by Germanic tribes fleeing the increasingly rigorous climate of Northern Europe. Little is known about them for they had no written literature and they were divided into several different peoples in accordance with criteria that have remained mysterious. What is known beyond a shadow of doubt is that the Celts in Gaul, such as the **Allobroges** in Lugdunum (Lyon), were subject to the authority of the **Arverni** in the Massif Central. They traded with their own coinage. In order to ensure the submission of other peoples, their sovereigns acted as demagogues throughout the region, in much the same way as Greek tyrants. King Luern,

V. d'Amboise/PIX

Vercingetorix

who reigned in the 2C, is famous for his gifts of gold. Rome, worried by his power, launched a military campaign against his son, Bituit, who died in battle with Roman forces near Bollène in 121 BC. The Roman legions settled in Vienne, the capital of the Allobroges. The Arverni monarchy was no more. The great Celtic families took power and, thereafter, were forced to share it with the Aedui of Burgundy who were allied to Rome. In 52 BC, however, in one last attempt to revive Arverni authority, **Vercingetorix**, head of the Gauls' resistance to Caesar, recruited an army and defeated the Romans at **Gergovia**. Later, though, besieged in Alésia, he surrendered in order to save his people. This marked the end of Arverni independence.

43	Lyon founded soon after Caesar's conquest of Gaul by one of his lieutenants, Munatius Plancus. Roman settlers arrive and build houses on the hillsides above the Saône.
27	Lyon, capital of the Gauls (Aquitaine, Lyon area, Belgium); the Rome and Augustus Altar is built on the hill at La Croix Rousse.
AD	
1C	The beginnings of Christianity. Preachers come to spread the gospel in the Auvergne and the Rhône Valley.
177	Marcus Aurelius instigates persecution. Christians are martyred in Lyon.
280	Emperor Probus removes the monopoly on sales of wine in Gaul previously enjoyed by the people of Lyon. This marks the start of Lyon's decline and, during the reign of Diocletian (284-305), the city is nothing more than the capital of the Lyon province.
406	After the invasion of the Vandals, the emperor introduces a federation of barbarian states in Gaul with the Visigoths in the Auvergne and the Burgundians on the left bank of the Rhône.

Sidonius Apollinaris stands up to the Visigoths — Sidonius Apollinaris was born in Lyon in AD 432 to a wealthy family of senators; later, his father-in-law, Avitus, was one of the last emperors of the Western world. Sidonius remained in Rome after the death of Avitus in AD 456 and wrote tributes to the emperors. His poetry pleased them and when he returned to the Auvergne, he was elected Bishop of Clermont. Although initially not a very committed Christian, Sidonius realised that the Church was, in those troubled times, the only solidly-based institution in the Roman world. Like other aristocrats, he made it the final bastion of the Roman way of life. Euric, King of the Visigoths, who already owned a large part of Aquitaine, threatened the Auvergne. Sidonius headed the resistance and withstood a siege lasting several years in the walled town of Clermont. Eventually the province was transferred to the barbarians in exchange for Provence and Sidonius was sent into exile. Twenty years later, the province passed into the hands of the Franks after the Battle of Vouillé.

5-9C	Founding of the first abbeys — in Lyon, Vienne, Romans, in the Vivarais, the Lyonnais and the Velay...
761-767	Pepin the Short attempts to gain power over the noblemen of the Auvergne by means of military expeditions.
781	The Auvergne is subject to the Carolingian kingdom of Aquitaine; the Rhône Valley is subject to Burgundy.
800	Charlemagne is crowned in Rome.
843	Treaty of Verdun. Charlemagne's empire is divided into three kingdoms (West, Central, and East). The Auvergne is ruled by Charles the Bald (West Francia); the Rhône Valley by Lothair I (Lotharingia).
9-10C	Power is actually held by the many castle owners, all of them difficult to control. Safe on their feudal mottes, they war against their neighbours, devastate the countryside, attack churches and pillage monasteries.
999	Gerbert, a former monk from Aurillac, is elected to the papacy as Sylvester II. He is the first French pope and he occupies the papal throne at the end of the first millennium.
1095	Pope Urban II preaches the First Crusade in Clermont. The wave of popular faith aroused by his call arrives just at the right time to channel the warring energies of the turbulent feudal lords. The Pope has a chance to gauge the vitality of the Church in the Auvergne. The Gregorian Reform purges the parishes by removing the power of the layman. The influence of a few of the great monasteries begins to spread. The Counts of Albon, who come from Vienne, extend their territory and their lands, stretching from the Rhône to the Alps, become known as Dauphiné.
11-12C	Founding of new abbeys in the Vivarais area.

Royal intervention in the Auvergne — Divided between their position as vassals to the King of France and their allegiance to the Duke of Aquitaine, the great lords of the Auvergne failed to come to an agreement that would enable them to set up their own state. These feuding lords of mixed loyalties governed large estates with no clearly defined borders, which eventually enabled the sovereign to annex sections of the region, little by little over the 12C and 13C: first Riom and the Limagne, then Montferrand and the area subsequently known as Dauphiné and finally Lower Auvergne.

13-14C	The development of towns leads to the granting of numerous municipal charters. Royal authority gains a foothold and is strengthened in Auvergne and the Rhône Valley: -1213: Philip Augustus annexes the Auvergne to his kingdom. -1292: Nomination of a royal "guardian" in Lyon. -1307: The so-called "Philippine" conventions strengthen Philip the Fair's hold on Lyon. -1308: The Bishop of Viviers recognises royal sovereignty. -1349: Dauphiné is annexed to France as the States of Dauphiné.
1229	The Treaty of Paris ends the Albigensian Crusade and the influence of the Counts of Toulouse in the Vivarais area.
1241-71	The Auvergne is part of the appanage with which Alphonse of Poitiers, St Louis' brother, is endowed. He dies childless and the region is returned to the royal estate.
1262	Marriage of St Louis' son, Philip, to Isabella of Aragon in Clermont.
1337-1453	Hundred Years War.
1348	The Black Death ravages France.
1360	The Auvergne becomes a duchy and is given to John the Good's son, Jean, Duc de Berry.
15C	The first firearms are made in St-Étienne.
1416-25	The Auvergne and the Bourbonnals region are united for one hundred years under the authority of the House of Bourbon.

| 1419 | The first fairs in Lyon, instituted by the heir to the throne, the future Charles VII, make the town one of the largest warehouses in the world. |
| 1450 | Charles VII grants Lyon a monopoly on the sale of silk throughout the kingdom. |

Auvergne, held in appanage by Jean de Berry – The sovereign's hold on the Auvergne took it out of the sphere of influence of southern France. It was divided in two with the creation of a bailiwick in the mountainous region corresponding to Upper Auvergne. The Church proceeded to follow suit, setting up the bishopric of Saint-Flour. While the Bourbons continued to increase their power, with a barony that was raised to a duchy in 1327 (the Bourbonnais area), the Auvergne was granted in appanage to Jean, Duc de Berry in 1360. War and epidemics combined with the heavy fiscal pressures imposed by a spendthrift lord. In order to get round the rules on land held in appanage, Jean de Berry transferred the Duchy of Auvergne to his son-in-law, the Duke of Bourbon, an action which the monarchy, by then in a weakened position, was obliged to accept formally in 1425. The Bourbons were then at the head of a huge feudal state which continued to exist until the Constable of Bourbon's treachery in 1527.

1473	The first book is printed in Lyon by Barthélémy Buyer.
1494	The start of the Italian Campaign. Charles VIII brings his court to Lyon. The bank in Lyon enjoys a period of rapid development.
1527	After the Constable of Bourbon's treachery, the Auvergne and the Bourbonnais region are confiscated by François I.
1528	The Reformation is preached in Annonay.
1536	A silkmaking factory is opened in Lyon.
1546	The first Reform Church is opened in the Lyon area.
1562	Protestants led by Baron des Adrets ransack the Rhône Valley and Forez area.
1572	After the St Bartholomew's Day Massacre, the Auvergne enters a period of chaos. Bloody battles are won in turn by the Huguenots, the royal army, and members of the Catholic League.
1598	Promulgation of the Edict of Nantes which grants freedom of conscience to the Protestants along with limited rights to hold church services, and gives them political equality.

The Reformation and the Wars of Religion – In 1525, the Reformation spread right across the Cévennes thanks to travelling Bible salesmen and merchants. It also spread along the Rhône Valley, through the Vivarais area and along the Durance Valley. Printers in Lyon produced and distributed the doctrines preached in Basle and Geneva over a very wide area. The Auvergne, perhaps partially because of the mountainous lie of the land, was little concerned by the Reformed Religion, except in Issoire and the paper-making areas of Ambert and Aurillac.

The preachers began their work in Annonay. The local people were attracted to Calvinist ideas which complied with their taste for independence. The concepts were spread by craftsmen in the villages, carders and silk merchants travelling to Montpellier via Le Puy-en-Velay and Alès. The ideas were also spread by shoemakers whose shops, like the tanneries, often served as centres of propaganda. By 1550-60, the Reformed Religion had conquered the locality. The property belonging to the Catholic Church was sold and, by the end of the century, Mass was generally no longer being celebrated.

However, Catholics and Protestants were soon to become locked in conflict. The eight wars fought over a period of almost three decades coincided with a period of political instability. Interspersed with ceasefires and edicts aimed at pacifying both sides, they never totally appeased the people's passion. In 1562 the murder of a group of Protestants in Champagne led to the Huguenot uprising, and Catholic resistance was led by the Parliament of Toulouse. The conflict was particularly bitter in the Dauphiné and Vivarais regions where the warring factions laid waste to entire towns and committed massacres. The Baron des Adrets captured the main towns in Dauphiné, where he was the leader of the Huguenot movement, before moving on to decimate the Rhône Valley with his troops and marching to the Forez area where he took Montbrison. After the tragic St Bartholomew's Day massacre (24th August 1572), the conflict took on a more markedly political character and, paradoxically, it led to forms of cooperation between Huguenots and Catholics (united under the banner of the **Catholic League**, who sought political as much as religious power) in the face of royal authority and power.

Peace was not re-established until the Edict of Nantes was signed.

1629	Siege and destruction of Privas by the King's troops. Richelieu orders the dismantling of fortresses.
17C	Counter-Reformation: founding of a large number of convents.
1643	Accession of Louis XIV.
1685	Revocation of the Edict of Nantes. The dragoons sweep through the Vivarais area, ill-treating and massacring the people.
1704	First edition of the Trévoux Dictionary by the Jesuits in reaction against the Age of Enlightenment.
1783	First public ascent by the Montgolfier brothers in a hot-air balloon.

Auvergne's finest hours – Although the aristocracy in the Auvergne was careful not to become involved in the Fronde Revolt against the monarchy, the King brought the hand of royal justice to bear on the region in order to ensure its submission for all time.

In September 1665 Louis XIV sent commissioners vested with full judicial authority to the Auvergne, in order to provide an exemplary display of royal authority. The return to law and order included the repression of the often tyrannical behaviour and excessive violence used by the local nobility to stamp out revolt among the country people. In the Auvergne as elsewhere, the rural uprisings had resulted from the constraints imposed by a central authority that had not yet acquired its finality.

The Court heard 1 360 cases and passed 692 sentences, of which 450 were handed down by default for the suspects had fled as soon as the first of the 23 executions was carried out. Thereafter, offenders were sentenced in their absence and effigies were hung in their place. This simulation of justice "without any spilling of blood" **(Esprit Fléchier)** nevertheless allowed for the return of a large amount of property and the destruction of castles that had been spared by Richelieu 40 years earlier. The authority of the State and royal justice could be felt by all throughout France. The magistrates also tried to remedy abuses of the system by drawing up regulations on statute labour, weights and measures. The **Intendants** began to check the titles held by the nobility and laid the foundations for a fiscal reform in order to share the burden of taxation more fairly.

1789	Start of the French Revolution. 14th July: capture of the Bastille Prison. France is subdivided into *départements*.
1790	The first town council is set up in Lyon.
1793	A Resistance movement is set up in Lyon to fight the Convention: the town is subject to vicious reprisals as a result. In the Auvergne, **Georges Couthon**, a member of the Committee of Public Salvation, orders the demolition of bell towers in the Auvergne on grounds of equality. Non-juring priests seek refuge in the mountains.
Early 19C	Mining begins in the coalfields around St-Étienne.
1804	The Jacquard loom is invented.
1820	Silk production becomes a boom industry in the Vivarais area.
1825	The Seguin brothers build the first suspension bridge over the Rhône.
1832	The St-Étienne-Lyon railway line is inaugurated. Barbier and Daubrée open a factory in Clermont and begin working with rubber; this is the embryo of the future Michelin group.
1831-34	The silk workers revolt in Lyon.
1850	Pebrine, a disease that attacks silkworms, causes a crisis in the silk industry. There is a sudden sharp drop in the number of silkwormfarms.
1855	The railway is extended as far as Clermont.
1870-71	The Fall of the Second Empire; the Second Republic is founded.
1880	Phylloxera destroys half of the vineyards in Ardèche. Orchards are planted in the Rhône and Eyrieux Valleys.
1889	Phylloxera devastates the vineyards in the Limagne.
Late 19C	The chemical industry is set up in Lyon and metal-working enjoys a period of expansion.
1895	The cinematograph is invented by the Lumière brothers in Lyon.

The birth of the cinematograph – In 1882 a photographer from Besançon named Antoine Lumière opened a workshop in a shed in Lyon and began to produce dry silver bromine plates to a formula that he had invented himself. Within four years he had sold over one million plates under the brand name *Étiquette bleue*. The former photographer's two sons, Louis and Auguste **Lumière**, worked with their father on a new device; the equipment, invented in 1895 and exhibited in Lyon in June 1896, was to be known as the cinematograph.

The general public, after initial indifference, rushed to see the first 10 films – short farces whose humour has withstood the test of time. The first film, *Workers Leaving the Lumière Factory* was followed by *The Arrival of a Train in the Station*, *The Gardener* (including the famous scene of the gardener being doused with water from the garden hose) and *Baby Food*. The prodigious adventure of the motion picture had just begun.

1939-45	Second World War.
1940	Vichy becomes the capital of France.

The Vichy government – The armistice signed in Compiègne on 22 June 1940 marked the defeat of France, which was divided into two zones – the North was occupied by Nazi Germany and the South was declared a free zone. Parliament, tolling the death knell of the Third Republic, vested all power in **Maréchal Pétain**, the victor of Verdun in 1916. The choice of a seat for the new government fell on the prosperous spa town of Vichy *(see VICHY in the alphabetical section)*.

The years 1940-44 were dark days indeed. Two films about this period – *L'œil de Vichy*, directed by Claude Chabrol, and *Pétain* directed by Jean Marbœuf – were produced in 1993 and, since the summer of 1987, there have been organised tours in Vichy to the places occupied by Pétain's government.

1942-44	Lyon is the "capital" of the Resistance Movement.
1944	Battles are fought in the Rhône Valley as part of the liberation of France. The Germans blow up the bridges over the Rhône.
1946	Founding of the Fourth Republic.
1957	The Treaty of Rome leads to the setting up of the EEC.
1958	Founding of the Fifth Republic.
1969	Georges Pompidou, who was born in Cantal, is elected President of the Republic.
1974	Valéry Giscard d'Estaing, Mayor of Chamalières (Puy de Dôme), is elected President of the Republic.
1981	The first high-speed train service (TGV) is run between Paris and Lyon (journey time: 2hr 40min).
1986	**Superphénix**, Europe's first fast-breeder reactor to operate on an industrial scale, is brought into service in Creys-et-Pusignieu (Isère).
1989	Completion of the motorway link (A 71) between Clermont-Ferrand and Paris (Orléans).
1992	Opening of several sections of the new motorway (A 75) linking Clermont-Ferrand with the south of France (Montpellier and Béziers).
1993	The EU introduces the Single Market.
1994	The opening of the ultra-modern Lyon-Satolas airport/TGV station with its distinctive metal bird designed by Calatrava means Lyon can play an increasingly international role.

Lyon, a centre of the Resistance Movement – Lyon, a city in the southern zone, found itself near the demarcation line after the signing of the armistice in 1940. Countless Parisians sought refuge here and initially it became the intellectual heart of France. The city was one of the major centres for the printing of literature, tracts, posters, and journals, many of them more popular with readers than the press that supported Vichy.

Lyon was also a major centre of intelligence work through "Marco Polo", "Electra" and "Alliance" who had connections at the very core of the Vichy administration. Important Resistance movements took action in Lyon but they were badly organised until the arrival of **Jean Moulin**, sent by General de Gaulle; the various groups then joined together in 1943 to form the Mouvements Unis de la Résistance (Unified Resistance Movements). Moulin set up an administrative structure for the Resistance, organising services that were common to all the networks and a secret army operating in the south of France and the Rhône Valley. Georges Bidault, who took over after Moulin's arrest, created the Forces Françaises de l'Intérieur (FFI). This is why, when France was finally liberated, General de Gaulle called Lyon the "Capital of the Resistance Movement".

Use the Index to find more information about a subject mentioned in the guide – towns, places of interest, isolated sights, historical events or natural features.

Art

ABC OF ARCHITECTURE

To assist readers unfamiliar with the terminology employed in architecture, we describe below the most commonly used terms, which we hope will make their visits to ecclesiastical, military and civil buildings more interesting.

Ecclesiastical architecture

illustration I ►

Ground plan: The more usual Catholic form is based on the outline of a cross with the two arms of the cross forming the transept: ① Porch – ② Narthex – ③ Side aisles (sometimes double) – ④ Bay (transverse section of the nave between 2 pillars) – ⑤ Side chapel (often predates the church) – ⑥ Transept crossing – ⑦ Arms of the transept, sometimes with a side doorway – ⑧ Chancel, nearly always facing east towards Jerusalem; the chancel often vast in size was reserved for the monks in abbatial churches – ⑨ High altar – ⑩ Ambulatory: in pilgrimage churches the aisles were extended round the chancel, forming the ambulatory, to allow the faithful to file past the relics – ⑪ Radiating or apsidal chapel – ⑫ Axial chapel. In churches which are not dedicated to the Virgin this chapel, in the main axis of the building, is often consecrated to the Virgin (Lady Chapel) – ⑬ Transept chapel.

◄ Illustration II

Cross-section: ① Nave – ② Aisle – ③ Tribune or gallery – ④ Triforium – ⑤ Barrel vault – ⑥ Half-barrel vault – ⑦ Pointed vault – ⑧ Buttress – ⑨ Flying buttress – ⑩ Pier of a flying buttress – ⑪ Pinnacle – ⑫ Clerestory window.

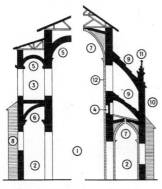

Romanesque   Gothic

◄ illustration III

Gothic cathedral: ① Porch – ② Gallery – ③ Rose window – ④ Belfry (sometimes with a spire) – ⑤ Gargoyle acting as a waterspout for the roof gutter – ⑥ Buttress – ⑦ Pier of a flying buttress (abutment) – ⑧ Flight or span of flying buttress – ⑨ Double-course flying buttress – ⑩ Pinnacle – ⑪ Side chapel – ⑫ Radiating or apsidal chapel – ⑬ Clerestory windows – ⑭ Side doorway – ⑮ Gable – ⑯ Pinnacle – ⑰ Spire over the transept crossing.

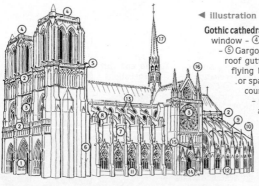

◄ illustration IV

Groined vaulting:
① Main arch –
② Groin –
③ Transverse arch.

illustration V ►

Oven vault: termination of a barrel vaulted nave.

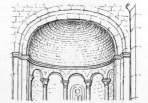

illustration VI
Lierne and tierceron vaulting: ① Diagonal – ② Lierne – ③ Tierceron – ④ Pendant – ⑤ Corbel.

illustration VII
Quadripartite vaulting: ① Diagonal – ② Transverse – ③ Stringer – ④ Flying buttress – ⑤ Keystone.

▼ **illustration VIII**

Doorway: ① Archivolt. Depending on the architectural style of the building this can be rounded, pointed, basket-handled, ogee or even adorned by a gable – ② Arching, coving (with string courses, mouldings, carvings or adorned with statues). Recessed arches or orders form the archivolt – ③ Tympanum – ④ Lintel – ⑤ Archshafts – ⑥ Embrasures. Arch shafts, splaying sometimes adorned with statues or columns – ⑦ Pier (often adorned by a statue) – ⑧ Hinges and other ironwork.

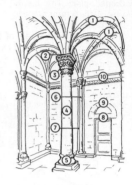

illustration IX ▶
Arches and pillars: ① Ribs or ribbed vaulting – ② Abacus – ③ Capital – ④ Shaft – ⑤ Base – ⑥ Engaged column – ⑦ Pier – ⑧ Lintel – ⑨ Discharging or relieving arch – ⑩ Frieze.

Military architecture

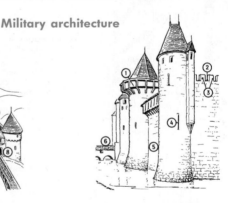

illustration X
Fortified enclosure: ① Hoarding (projecting timber gallery) – ② Machicolations (corbelled crenellations) – ③ Barbican – ④ Keep or donjon – ⑤ Covered watchpath – ⑥ Curtain wall – ⑦ Outer curtain wall – ⑧ Postern.

illustration XI
Towers and curtain walls: ① Hoarding – ② Crenellations – ③ Merlon – ④ Loophole or arrow slit – ⑤ Curtain wall – ⑥ Bridge or drawbridge.

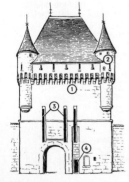

◀ **illustration XII**
Fortified gatehouse:
① Machicolations – ② Watch turrets or bartizan – ③ Slots for the arms of the drawbridge – ④ Postern.

illustration XIII ▶
Star fortress: ① Entrance – ② Drawbridge – ③ Glacis – ④ Ravelin or half-moon – ⑤ Moat – ⑥ Bastion – ⑦ Watch turret – ⑧ Town – ⑨ Assembly area.

ART AND ARCHITECTURAL TERMS USED IN THE GUIDE

Acroterion: ornaments placed at the apex and ends of a pediment of a temple.

Aedicule: a small house or room; a niche.

Aisle: illustration I.

Altarpiece or retable: illustration XX.

Ambulatory: illustration I.

Apsidal or radiating chapel: illustration I.

Archivolt: illustration VIII.

Axial or Lady Chapel: illustration I.

Barrel vaulting: illustration II.

Basket arch: depressed arch common to late-medieval and Renaissance architecture.

Bas-relief: low relief, or sculpture in which forms project only slightly from their background.

Bay: illustration I.

Bishop's throne: Gothic chair with a high back.

Buttress: illustrations II and III.

Capital: illustration IX.

Cardo maximus: main street of Roman town running north-south.

Caryatid: female figure used as a column (atlantes are male caryatids).

Chevet: French term for the east end of a church; illustration I.

Cippus (-i): small pillar used to mark a burial place or serve as a sepulchral monument.

Coffered ceiling: vault or ceiling decorated with sunken panels.

Corbel: illustration VI.

Crypt: underground chamber or chapel.

Curtain wall: illustration XI.

Decumanus maximus: main street of Roman town running east-west.

Depressed arch: three-centred arch sometimes called a basket arch.

Diagonal arch: illustrations VI and VII.

Dome: illustrations XIV and XV.

Exedra: niche, usually semi-circular, with a bench around the wall.

Flamboyant: latest phase (15C) of French Gothic architecture; name taken from the undulating (flame-like) lines of the window tracery.

Flame ornament: ornamentation used in classical art representing a vase spewing flames.

Foliated scrolls: sculptural or painted ornamentation depicting foliage, often in a frieze.

Fresco: mural paintings executed on wet plaster.

Gable: triangular part of an end wall carrying a sloping roof; the term is also applied to the steeply pitched ornamental pediments of Gothic architecture: illustration III.

Gallery: illustrations II and III.

Gargoyle: illustration III.

Génoise: decorative frieze under the eaves, composed of a double or triple row of tiles embedded end-on in the wall.

Groined vaulting: illustration IV.

Haut-relief: high relief, or sculpture in which forms project sharply from their background, while nonetheless remaining attached to it.

Hypocaust: an underground furnace to heat the water for the baths or rooms of a house.

Keystone: illustration VII.

Lintel: illustrations VIII and IX.

Lombard arcades: decorative blind arcading composed of small arches and intervening pilaster strips; typical of Romanesque architecture in Lombardy.

Machicolations: illustration X.

Modillion: small console supporting a cornice.

Mullion: a vertical post dividing a window.

Oppidum (-a): Latin word for a fortified agglomeration, usually set on a hill or height.

Oven vaulting: illustration V.

Overhang or jetty: overhanging upper storey.

Ovolo moulding: egg-shaped decoration.

Peribolus (-os): sacred enclosure or court around a temple.

Peristyle: a range of columns surrounding or on the façade of a building.

Pier: illustration III.

Pietà: Italian term designating the Virgin Mary with the dead Christ on her knees.

Pilaster: engaged rectangular column.

Pinnacle: illustrations II and III.

Piscina: basin for washing the sacred vessels.

Portico: a colonnaded space in front of a façade or in an interior courtyard.

Postern: illustrations X and XII.

Quadripartite vaulting: illustrations VII.

Recessed arches: see voussoir.

Recessed tomb: funerary niche.

Rood screen: illustration XVI.

Rose or wheel window: illustration III.

Rustication: large blocks of masonry often separated by deep joints and given bold textures (rock-faced, diamond-pointed...); commonly employed during the Renaissance.

Segment: part of a ribbed vault; compartment between the ribs.

Semicircular arch: round-headed arch.

Spire: illustration III.

Splay: a slope; applied usually to the sides of a door or a window; illustration VIII.

Stalls: illustration XIX.

Stucco: mixture of powdered marble, plaster and strong glue; used for decoration.

Tracery: intersecting stone ribwork in the upper part of a window.

Transept: illustration I.

Triforium: illustration II.

Triptych: three panels hinged together, chiefly used as an altarpiece.

Twinned or paired: columns, pilasters, windows... grouped in twos.

Voussoir: wedge-shaped masonry in an arch or a vault.

Watchpath or wall walk: illustration X.

◄ illustration XIV
Dome on squinches:
① Octagonal dome –
② Squinch – ③ Arches of
transept crossing

illustration XV ►
Dome on pendentives:
① Circular dome – ② Pendentive –
③ Arches of transept crossing

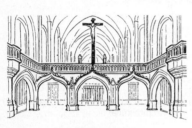

illustration XVI
Rood screen – This replaced the rood beam in larger churches and was used for the preaching and reading the Epistle and Gospel. From the 17C onwards many were removed as they tended to hide the altar.

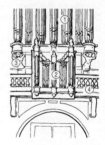

illustration XVII
Organ
① Great organ case
② Little organ case
③ Caryatids – ④ Loft

illustration XVIII
Renaissance ornament

① Shell – ② Vase – ③ Foliage –
④ Dragon – ⑤ Nude child –
⑥ Cherub – ⑦ Cornucopia –
⑧ Satyr

illustration XIX
Stalls

① High back – ② Elbow rest –
③ Cheek-piece – ④ Misericord

illustration XX
Altar with retable or altarpiece
① Retable or altarpiece – ② Predella –
③ Crowning piece – ④ Altar table –
⑤ Altar front
Certain Baroque retables consisted of several altars; contemporary liturgy tends to eliminate them.

Roman architecture in the Rhône valley

By the 1C, the region had become the starting point for the conquest of Germany and this, in addition to the building of the Rome and Augustus altar at the confluence of the Rhône and Saône, made Lyon the capital of Gaul. In the 2C, major road building and town planning work was undertaken in Vienne and Lyon, which were then at the height of their power. However, the fires, pillaging and devastations by the Barbarians, coupled with the later destruction during the Middle Ages – when the ancient public buildings were used as quarries and the marble statues were used to stoke the limestone kilns – destroyed the remains of the old civilization.

From 1922 in Vienne and 1933 in Lyon, archaeologists began to uncover a number of outstanding groups of buildings, in particular small theatres adjacent to smaller buildings or odeons. The digs are continuing today. Some of the buildings are still being unearthed and large areas remain to be explored, in particular in St-Romain-en-Gal on the right bank of the Rhône where part of a residential district has been uncovered.

Theatres – These consisted of tiers of seats ending in a colonnade known as the **cavea**, an orchestra pit, a dais used by dignitaries and a raised stage *(scena)*. The actors performed in front of a wall with doors in it through which they made their entrances. Behind the wall at the back of the stage were the richly-decorated actors' dressing rooms and the stores. Beyond that was a portico opening onto gardens where the actors walked before entering the stage. Spectators could come and stroll there during the intervals or take shelter from the rain. The acoustics in Roman theatres are still a source of amazement, even in buildings that have been half destroyed; it is easy to imagine how perfect they must have been 2 000 years ago.

Temples – These consisted of a closed sanctuary containing the effigy of a god or the emperor in the form of a god, and an open vestibule. They were partially or totally surrounded by a colonnade. The Temple of Augustus and Livia in Vienne is one of the best-preserved anywhere.

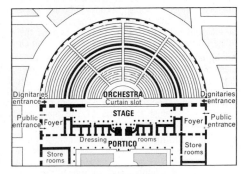

Roman theatre

Roman baths – Roman baths were public and free of charge. They were both not only public baths but also fitness centres, meeting places and a centre where people could enjoy games and entertainment. The way in which the baths operated shows that the Romans had acquired extensive knowledge concerning water supplies and heating. Water was brought to the baths by an aqueduct, stored in tanks then piped through a system of lead and mortar ducts. Waste water was carried away through a sewage system. The water and rooms were heated by a system of hearths and hypocausts in the basement. The hot air obtained by the burning of coal and wood circulated through a conduit built into the walls. The buildings were vast, sumptuous and extremely luxurious. There were columns and capitals decorated with vivid colours, mosaic facing on the walls, coloured marble floor and wall coverings, richly-coffered ceilings, and frescoes and statues like those found in the remains of the Roman baths in Ste-Colombe near Vienne.

Amphitheatres – Shows were staged in the arena, which was usually oval in shape. There were fights between wild beasts or gladiators, and people sentenced to death were executed here. Around the arena were tiers of seats for the audience. Lyon, the official centre for the worship of Rome in Gaul, had its own amphitheatre. It was here, in AD 177 during the reign of Marcus Aurelius, that the Christians of Lyon were martyred.

Circus – The circus attracted crowds of people who enjoyed watching chariot racing. In the middle of the track was a long rectangular construction – the **spina** – marked at each end by huge, semicircular stones. The horses and drivers wore white, blue, red or green, the colours of the rival factions organising the competitions. Built partly of timber, the circus was, despite its impressive size (several hundred yards long and over one hundred yards wide), particularly vulnerable to destruction. Two circuses in France have been the subject of an archaeological dig – one in Arles and one in Vienne where the **pyramid** that marked the centre of the **spina** is still visible.

Aqueducts – On the plateau to the southwest of Lyon stand well-preserved sections of aqueduct (Arches de Chaponost, *see LYON: Mont du Lyonnais*). Aqueducts were one of the essential features of any town. The tall arches built to maintain the level of the pipes were monuments in their own right. Indeed, the aqueduct, more than any other construction, is a striking illustration of the building skills of the Romans who attached very great importance to the quality of the water supplied to their towns and cities.

Decorative arts – The large, delicately-coloured mosaics found in Lyon (circus games, Bacchus etc.) prove that mosaic makers were particularly active in Lyon. The medallions that decorated the sides of vases were made by potters from Lyon and Vienne who excelled in illustrations of scenes from mythology or everyday life.

Romanesque Architecture

There is no Romanesque school inherent to the Rhône valley for the region, situated as it is at the junction of countless roads, was influenced by artists from Italy, Burgundy, Provence – and the Auvergne. In the Auvergne a Romanesque school developed which is considered one of the most unusual in the history of the architecture of the Western world, giving the churches an air of similarity that is immediately apparent. It originated in the 11C. After the great invasions and the establishment of the Capetian kingdom, the Auvergne enjoyed a period of prosperity. The local people undertook land clearance, acquiring new areas of land and instigating new building projects. In the 11C this movement was amplified by the Gregorian Reform and the desire on the part of men of the Church for independence from lay authorities. Gradually, countless churches and chapels were built across the countryside and, even today, they reveal something of the soul of the Auvergne and its people, for they are all built with an economic use of resources and an immense simplicity. This is what gives the architecture its strength.

The churches in Clermont-Ferrand (Notre-Dame-du-Port), Issoire, Orcival, St-Nectaire and St-Saturnin are just some of the finest examples of this Romanesque style in which the beauty is both austere and logical. Yet it is also worth seeking out churches that are almost forgotten because they are less well-known or because they are lost in the depths of the countryside. They include treasures such as the coloured spire on St-Julien in Brioude, the frescoes in Ébreuil, the capitals in Mozac, and the domes of Notre-Dame-du-Puy which are redolent of the Orient.

An unusual school – It developed in the 11C and 12C within the large diocese of Clermont. The churches, often small but always beautifully-proportioned, give an impression of being much bigger than they actually are. Paul Bourget describes the appearance of these churches which are powerful and rugged like the people who created them: "Seen from the east end, especially with the tight semicircle of chapels huddled up against the mass of the main building, these churches give a striking impression of aplomb and unity".

Volcanic building materials – In Limagne, arkose, a yellowish metamorphic sandstone, was used until the 13C. Volcanic lavastone was first used for bonding beneath load-bearing arches, in the upper sections of buildings which did not support the weight of the vaulting and to which they added a touch of colour. In the 13C improvements to the quality of tools made it possible to cut the hard blocks of lavastone and developments in stone-cutting techniques made it the commonest building material available.

Great churches in Lower Auvergne – The layout of the churches slowly changed to meet new needs arising out of pilgrimages. The basic layout is the one seen in Clermont cathedral, which was consecrated in AD 946 and was the first one to have an ambulatory and radiating chapels. Today, all that remains is the crypt. Yet it took a period of trial and error (churches in Ennezat, Glaine-Montaigut) to achieve the perfection of the 12C buildings.

Exterior

West Front – Exposed to the weather and almost devoid of decoration, the west front – which includes a porch – forms a stark contrast to the east end because of its austerity. In some cases, it is topped by a central bell tower and two side towers.

Bell towers – Two-storey, traceried, octagonal bell towers were a source of light, emerging from the mass of the building around the dome. They stood high above the chancel and ambulatory. In Auvergne, there are a large number of bellcotes (*clocher à peigne*): gable walls with openings in which the bells are hung in one or two tiers.

Bellcote

D'après photo A. Roux/EXPLORER

Side walls – The windows in the side aisles are built inside enormous load-bearing arches that support the walls. Beneath these arches, the stone often has a decorative role through its colour or layout. Above them is the line of the clerestory in which the windows are linked by arcading. A few portals include the pentagonal lintel that is particular to the Auvergne school.

East end – The magnificent layout of the various levels at the east end makes it the most beautiful and most characteristic part of the Auvergne churches. This masterpiece of austerity counterbalances the thrust from the octagonal bell tower. It stands like a carefully combined pyramid, giving an impression of harmony and security through the perfection of each of its elements and the regularity of the design.

Interior

The nave is usually strikingly sturdy in appearance. The only decorative features are the capitals and they are not immediately apparent because most of these buildings are very dark.
The narthex lies beyond the porch and constitutes the first span of the church. Huge arches support the gallery and the weight of the bell tower if it has been built above the west front.

Nave and vaulting – The wide naves lined with side aisles providing extra support were designed to cater for large numbers of pilgrims. Heavy Romanesque barrel vaulting replaced roof rafters which were too susceptible to fire and which, between the 5C and 11C, led to the loss of many churches. Above the side aisles with their ribbed vaulting were vaulted galleries that were designed to provide direct support for the nave and to let light into the upper section of the church from the small windows they contained.

Chancel – This part of the church was reserved for the clergy and it was here that Mass was celebrated. By raising it up a few steps and lowering the vaulting, perspective made it appear larger than it actually was and drew attention to it. It was here that sculptors gave free rein to their talent and the beautifully designed and carved capitals in the chancel are often the finest in the church.
In large churches, the chancel included a straight bay. Behind it was a semicircle around which tall columns, set out in such a way as to avoid blocking the light, extended into small raised arches forming a sort of crown. The capitals here were often the most complex and intricate in the church.

Ambulatory – In large churches, an ambulatory extended beyond the side aisles and skirted the chancel. An even number of radiating chapels formed a crown around the ambulatory so that, on major feast days, several Masses could be celebrated simultaneously. The chapels were separated from each other by windows. In churches dedicated to other saints, a side chapel was dedicated to the Blessed Virgin Mary (the Lady Chapel).

Transept and dome – The construction of the transept posed a difficult problem for architects; they had to design large ribbed vaulting capable of supporting the entire weight of the central bell tower and which was formed by the interpenetration of the vaulting in the nave and the arms of the transept.
In Issoire and Notre-Dame-du-Port, for example, the vaulting in the arms of the transept has been built at the same height as the vaulting in the nave. Then half-barrel vaulting buttresses the upper sections, forming an initial tier leading on to the second level including the dome and supporting the bell tower.
Squinches were built in order to pass from the square layout of the transept to the dome mounted on an octagonal base.

Crypt – Beneath the chancel in large churches, there is often a crypt laid out like the church above it. The chancel in the crypt, like the one in the upper church, is flanked by an ambulatory decorated with radiating chapels. The crypt never extends westwards beyond the transept. It is used for worship of the Blessed Virgin Mary or the relics of saints.

Decorative features

Capitals – The capitals are magnificently carved with fanciful scenes. Most of them are to be found around the chancel *(see above)*. Many artists did not merely illustrate scenes from the Bible; they introduced an entire portrait gallery of figures that were as numerous as they were varied: figures from Antiquity rub shoulders with eagles, mermaids, centaurs, minotaurs, telamones, snakes, genies, figures from the Orient, griffons and birds drinking out of a chalice. Beside them are the heroes of medieval epics, the founders of the church, knights in armour dating from the period of the First Crusade and local saints. The sculptors included animals and figures, some from a fantasy world, such as monkeys wearing chains, donkeys playing musical instruments, angels and devils. Finally, the Virtues and Vices are depicted, with a certain degree of humour, in caricatures such as the one illustrating Anger or a miser storing his money away in a pot.

Often the subjects are grouped in sequences so that the entire building, or part of it, centres on a single theme. There is the sacred character of the church emphasised by an illustration of the Temple or Jerusalem the Celestial City; there is religious symbolism, with scenes from the Old Testament paving the way for scenes from the New Testament, signs of the Zodiac etc.

Statues of the Virgin Mary in Majesty and statue-reliquaries – Worship of the Blessed Virgin Mary has always been an important part of religion in the Auvergne for, in Celtic countries, the Christian religion was grafted onto worship of a mother-goddess. These statues are striking for their hieratic attitudes, attractive for the honesty of the faces, modelled on those of country women, and admirable for the symbolism of their long, protective hands. The best of these statues can be seen in Mozac, Notre-Dame-du-Port, Orcival and Marsat.

Statue-reliquaries are original creations from the Auvergne and they combined the artistry of the carver with the skill of the enamellers of Limoges. Together, they produced superb pieces in gold and silver ornamented with precious stones. These statues dating from the 12C represent the earliest stages of sculpture in France. The most famous are the bust of St Baudime,

Virgin Mary in Majesty, Issoire

the arm-reliquary of St Nectaire in St-Nectaire, and the bust of St Césaire in Maurs.

From Gothic to the present day

Gothic architecture came from the north and took some time to spread further south in France. It reached Lyon in the early 13C but the Rhône valley has none of the great churches of which northern France is so proud and it continued to be subject to the influence of the south as is evident in the width of the buildings and the horizontal line of the roofs.

The Auvergne, strong in its own Romanesque school, resisted change for a long time. Not until the language of northern France, *langue d'oïl*, was introduced in place of the southern French *langue d'oc*, after the province had been conquered by Philip Augustus, and began to spread during the days of Alphonse of Poitiers did the Rayonnant Gothic style gain a foothold on the rebellious region, to the detriment of the sources of inspiration from further south which had been predominant until that time. This change of style marked the seizure of the province by the Capetians. There were, though, two main currents in the architectural style – Northern French Gothic and Languedoc Gothic.

Northern French Gothic – Clermont cathedral, dating from the 13C and 14C, is only very vaguely reminiscent of the great buildings of the Paris basin and not until the 19C was Gothic architecture introduced into its west front and spires designed by the architect Viollet-le-Duc. Lavastone from Volvic, a building material that was too hard to be carved but which architects liked for its strength, resistance and permanence, gave the cathedral an austerity that even the sun cannot brighten up. The roofs on the chapels and side aisles consist of stone slabs forming a terrace beneath the flying buttresses, a very unusual design that was totally unknown in the north of France.

Clermont cathedral's flying buttresses

The same stylistic movement can be seen in the Ste-Chapelle in Riom, which was designed by the Dammartin brothers who had worked on the Louvre during the reign of Charles V, the Ste-Chapelle in Aigueperse and the chancel in Moulins Cathedral.

Languedoc Gothic – Characterised by a wide nave devoid of side aisles, side chapels inserted between the piers and the absence of flying buttresses, this was the commonest style in the area. The abbey church at La Chaise-Dieu, a masterpiece of monastic architecture, is a fine example, as are other churches commissioned by the mendicant orders such as Le Marthuret church in Riom or Notre-Dame-des-Neiges in Aurillac.

Painting – A vast selection of medieval painting has been preserved within the Auvergne. The frescoes in St-Julien church in Brioude, for instance, date from the 12C; there is the 13C representation of the legend of St George in one of the ambulatory chapels in Clermont cathedral, and the 14C Assumption and Coronation of the Virgin Mary in Billom. From the 15C are the Last Judgement in Issoire, St George slaying the dragon in Ébreuil, the Dance of Death in La Chaise-Dieu, and the frescoes in Ennezat. The triptych painted on wood by the Maître de Moulins is considered to be one of the last masterpieces of Gothic painting in France.

Defensive castles – During the days of the feudal system, the country was dotted with castles; by building fortresses, lords, viscounts and barons could display their power and authority compared to that of the king. This is why there are so many castles, with outlines that adapt to the shape of the rock beneath them. From the 13C, they were subject to successive attacks by the troops under Philip Augustus, who conquered 120 of them from 1210 onwards, to destruction during the Hundred Years War and, at the end of the conflict, to destruction by villagers who, at enormous cost, succeeded in routing the mercenaries and captains who were using them as a source of building material for their own houses. The castles were again damaged during the Wars of Religion, dismantled on the orders of Richelieu and Louis XIV then, later, further damaged by the French Revolution.

It is not difficult to imagine, despite their often ruined state today, how these great castles once looked.

The gentler architecture of the Renaissance – The influence of the Italian Renaissance travelled to Northern France via the Rhône corridor and in the 15C it slowly penetrated the Auvergne where a certain taste for well-being made itself apparent after the end of the war. The fortresses were turned into charming residences in which ornamentation supplanted systems of defence, even if, in the Auvergne, the austerity of the building in lavastone remained intact. Numerous castles were bought up by gentlemen of the robe or members of the middle classes who had recently acquired wealth through trade. Alterations softened the severity of older buildings; Cordès castle was endowed with arbours and gardens designed by the famous 17C landscape architect Le Nôtre, for example, and Ravel was extended by three new wings. In the Rhône valley, the same phenomenon can be seen today in the Maison des Chevaliers in Viviers, some of the houses in the St-Jean and St-Nizier districts of Lyon and the Château de la Bastié d'Urfé which is decorated with a superb gallery.

Château de Cordès

R. Claquin/EXPLORER

Town planning during the Classical period – In Lyon this manifested itself in a new form of town planning, which can be seen mainly in the 17C Terreaux District around the town hall. In the 18C, a new concept of urban layout was introduced, based on speculation. The Bellecour and Perrache Districts were built on the site of former marshes. The main feature of these areas is the Place Bellecour, laid out during the reign of Louis XIV and flanked by Louis XVI residences.

Soufflot, designer of the Panthéon church in Paris, was one of the architects who, along with A-M Perrache and A Morrand, accelerated the development of urban planning so that it was launched on a bigger and grander scale. In his desire to pay homage to the buildings of Antiquity, and using his position as a leader in the Louis XVI style, he built bridges, houses along quaysides and the majestic hospice (Hôtel-Dieu) with its multi-faceted dome.

The 19C and the architecture of the Auvergne spas: a fantasy world – In the spa towns of the 19C, "taking the waters" was not a new idea but it was during this period that it became fashionable. On the pretext of taking the waters and enjoying a rest, members of high society, and those with power or money, flocked to spa towns. Their visits were an opportunity to lead an active social life and it was this that governed the architectural style. In the centre of the town were the pump rooms, a veritable palace to which the architects paid particular attention; around them were the park and springs built to resemble Ancient Greek or Roman temples and providing the bucolic environment for the casino and the luxury hotels where the interiors were decorated with an exuberance that was almost Baroque. In the streets of the town, troubadour-style castles stood next to Venetian palaces, and Henri IV residences rubbed shoulders with Art Nouveau mansions.

The history of this architecture, designed for enjoyment and pleasure, is a history of intermingling. The eclectic mix was the result of ideas by the most fashionable urban architects of the day combined with those of the architects of the Auvergne who were inspired by a long tradition based on Early Romanesque architecture and the volcanic and granite rocks available locally; these ideas were also influenced by the mixture of water and a natural environment with a town of stone, including its culture and its social events. Even the railway stations were not forgotten, since they provided the first impression for visitors who had just arrived. The result was a luxurious style of architecture full of exuberance and voluptuousness in the dream world constituted by the resorts in the heart of the Auvergne.

The new opera house in Lyon, a fine example of 20C architecture – Throughout the 19C and 20C Lyon was considered an ideal place for architectural experiments. In 1825 iron suspension bridges were built over the Rhône, using new techniques. In 1896 the basilica on Fourvière hill was completed in an eclectic Byzantine-cum-medieval style.

In the 1970s, with a view to the launch of the high-speed train service which would bring Lyon to within 2 hours of Paris, a major development was begun in the La Part-Dieu district: a new business centre that was to take the city to the forefront of Europe's business world. In 1993 the latest architectural feat was completed; the old opera house designed in 1831 had to be renovated and it was **Jean Nouvel** who took up the gauntlet. All that remains of the old building are the four walls and an old foyer decorated with gold leaf and stucco work; the interior of the building has been gutted. Inside, a vast glass vault, high-tech lighting systems and a suspended auditorium are just some of the innovative features in the building. The outer shell of the opera house was retained, however, since the 19C architects had designed the ideal size for song and music (1 300 seats). The U-shape common to Italian opera houses was also kept.

TRADITIONAL RURAL HOUSING

Ecomusée de la Margeride, Ruynes-en-Margeride

Farm interior with boxbed in the Margeride

Over the centuries, changes in rural housing have kept pace with changes in agricultural work. Housing has also been subject to the influence of neighbouring regions and new building techniques.

Auvergne

Roofs – Owing to its geographical situation the Auvergne is in contact with two civilizations, "the northern French one in which roofs are built with a 45° slope and flat tiles, and that from the Mediterranean Basin in which the roofs have a slope of 30° and rounded tiles" (Max Derruau). In the mountains, thatch is replaced by slate or corrugated iron. The most attractive roofs are those made of stone slabs called *lauzes* that look like gigantic tortoise shells. They can only be mounted on a steeply-sloping roof with a very strong set of rafters. On the plains, the old round tiles and rows of guttering once common in the countryside are beginning to lose ground in the face of competition from more stable mass-produced tiles.

Housing in the Limagne – The houses with upper storeys, which belong to wine-growers or farmers specialising in mixed agriculture, are commonplace in the old villages huddling on the hillsides. The ground floor is used for work (stables, cellars) and the upper floor is the house, reached by an outside flight of steps leading to a balcony sheltered by a porch roof.

Freestone, in particular Volvic stone, was used mainly for the houses of the bourgeoisie.

Housing in the mountains – These houses are sturdy buildings, constructed from large blocks of basalt. The heavy roofs extend below the top of the walls. The single building contains both dwelling and byre side by side. They always face south, and are sheltered from bad weather by the haybarn. Doors and windows are narrow and the roof drops down to the ground at the rear of the building. In the Upper Livradois area, the house is raised and is separate from the farm buildings.

A "buron"

Housing in the Velay area – Houses in this area are unusual as their walls are made of ash-lar, with a predominance of grey or dark red lavastone in volcanic areas, light-coloured granite in areas of older soil, and yellow arkose in areas of sedimentary rock. The blocks of stone are cemented together using a mortar that is often mixed with pozzolano, a reddish volcanic gravel. In the villages, a bell turret indicates the village hall *(assemblée)* or *"maison de la béate"*.

Shepherds' and cowherds' huts – A **buron** is a squat, stone-roofed temporary dwelling high up in the mountains, used by cowherds during periods of transhumance. This was where the cheese and butter was made which the *cantalès*, or master of the *buron*, then sent down to the valleys from time to time. A small number of these huts are still in use. In the Livradois and Forez areas, and on the slopes of Mont Pilat, there are **"jasseries"** or "mountain farms" used during the summer months. Solidly built of stone with thatched roofs, they consist of a living room, a byre and a cheese cellar below.

Rhône valley

Housing in the Forez and Lyonnais areas – Houses in the Forez area are farmsteads enclosed by high walls around a central courtyard. The walls are often made of rows of stones set at a slant. In the Dombes area, the farmhouses are elongated and have an upper storey. External pebbledash protects the walls made of terracotta bricks or cob.

Housing in the Rhône valley – On the **Valence and Montélimar plains**, the walls often have no doors or windows on the north side since this is where the mistral wind blows. Additional protection is often provided by a row of thuyas, cypress and plane trees. Large, iso-lated farmsteads consist of a group

A farm in the Forez

of buildings around a walled courtyard, and their external walls, devoid of doors or windows, make them look like fortresses.

Housing in Lower Dauphiné – Between Bourbe and Isère, pebbles or **"rolled stones"** were often used as a building material because they were commonplace in this area of moraine and alluvial deposits. The stones are assembled end on, on a bed of mortar, and the angle changes from one level to the next.

In some areas (eg Morestel and Creys) there is a style of roofing that has been imported from the pre-Alps: **crow-stepped or corbie-stepped gabling**. The flat-tiled roofs are supported by the gables of the side walls on which the rise is set back. The "steps" are roofed with an overhanging stone slab, giving the houses their own, very special appearance.

House in the Upper Vivarais

Housing in the Upper Vivarais area – On the edges of the Velay area, along the Mézenc range and on the high plateaux above the upper reaches of the Ardèche and Eyrieux rivers, the houses are low and squat with stone-slabbed roofs, seeming almost weighed down by this shell designed to withstand bad weather. The houses have granite or basalt walls with few doors or windows and most of the farmers specialise in stock breeding. The first room was the cowshed with an earth or stone-slabbed floor. A wooden partition separated it from the kitchen where hole-in-the-wall beds were built into the thickness of the walls. Above the byre was the hayloft which was equipped with trap doors so that, in winter, the animals could be fed without the farmer having to brave the weather outside.

In the Vernoux area, farmsteads were built in a horseshoe shape around the courtyard. The farmhouse was set at right angles to the byre which was topped by the hayloft. The yard was lined with sheds, including the *calabert*, the shed built on timber posts in which the farm implements were stored.

On the St-Agrève plateau, the granite farmhouses have an upper storey and bedrooms next to the hayloft. Access is via a ramp on the side facing the mountain.

Farmhouse, St-Agrève plateau

Housing in the Lower Vivarais area – Houses here have an upper storey and are built in a square, like southern French houses. The gently-sloping roofs have half-round tiles. At the top of the wall, between wall and roof, there is usually a double or triple row of guttering made with fragments of tiles mounted in mortar. The south-facing wall is usually decorated with a trellis. Access to the first floor, the living quarters, is by way of a flight of stone steps leading to a patio *(couradou)* that is usually roofed. Beyond it is the kitchen which has a stone-slabbed or terracotta-tiled floor.

House in the Lower Vivarais

The **silk wormery** often opened onto the *couradou*. Until 1850, it was an essential part of the house and a vital feature of life in the Vivarois area.

In addition to the farmhouses themselves, there are often outbuildings such as the bread oven, the barn and the chestnut-drying room *(clède)*.

In the middle Ardèche valley, most of the houses are built of limestone.

The Practical information section at the end of the guide lists :
– information on travel, motoring, accommodation, recreation
– local or national organisations providing additional information;
– calendar of events
– admission times and charges for the sights described in the guide.

Famous local figures

THE RHÔNE VALLEY – A LAND OF INNOVATORS

Few regions in France have given the country so many scientists and engineers as the Lyonnais, Vivarais and Forez areas – the engineer Marc **Seguin** (steam boiler), the physicist André-Marie **Ampère** (electrodynamics), the physiologist Claude **Bernard**, and cinematographers the **Lumière** brothers, to name but a few.

The Montgolfier brothers and the first flight – In the last few years before the French Revolution, the brothers Joseph and Étienne de Montgolfier, descendants of one of the oldest paper-making families in Europe, became famous by successfully achieving the first flights in a hot-air balloon.

Tirelessly continuing his research into a gas that was lighter than air, Joseph completed his first successful experiment with a taffeta envelope which he filled with hot air by burning a mixture of damp straw and wool. His brother joined him in his research and, after a few successful attempts, one of which was carried out in the gardens of the family estate in Vidalon-les-Annonay, they triumphantly launched their first aerostat on the Place des Cordeliers in Annonay on 4 June 1783. It was so successful that Louis XVI asked them to repeat it in his presence, and so it was that, on 19 September of that same year, the first "manned" flight took place in Versailles, under the control of Étienne and in the presence of the amazed royal family and Court. Attached beneath the balloon was a latticework cage containing the first passengers – a cockerel, a duck and a sheep. In just a few minutes, the **Réveillon** bearing the king's cipher on a blue background rose into the air and then came to rest in Vaucresson woods.

One month later, at the Château de la Muette in Paris, Marquis d'Arlandes and Pilâtre de Rozier completed the first human flight in a hot-air balloon.

The trials and tribulations of an inventor: Jacquard and the weaving loom – Jacquard was born in Lyon in 1752. His father, a small-time figured material manufacturer, employed his son as a drawboy to work the cords that operate the complicated machinery used to form the pattern in silk. The child was in poor

The Montgolfier brothers

health and he was unable to stand the work; he was placed with a bookbinder then with a type founder. However, in a silk worker's family, leaving the trade was seen as a form of failure.

After his father's death, Jacquard tried to set up a fabric factory but his lack of commercial experience and the experiments he undertook to try and perfect the weaving of the fabric left him financially ruined. In 1793 he enlisted with a military regiment. On returning to Lyon, he worked for a manufacturer. He spent his nights working on the design of a new loom and on a machine to manufacture fishing nets. He registered his first patent in 1801. The officers of the Republic were looking for inventors and so Jacquard was brought to Paris where he earned a salary of 3000FF. At the newly created **Conservatoire**, he perfected a machine invented by a man from Grenoble named Vaucanson, who had also installed a new type of mill in Aubenas. In 1804 Jacquard returned to Lyon to complete the work on the loom with which his name has remained linked ever since. In place of the ropes and pedals that required the work of six people, Jacquard substituted a simple mechanism based on perforated cards laid on the loom to define the pattern. A single worker, in place of five in earlier times, could make the most complicated fabrics as easily as plain cloth. In a town that had 20 000 looms, tens of thousands of workers found themselves under threat of losing their jobs. They immediately protested against the new loom which deprived them of work. Despite this, Jacquard succeeded in convincing them of the utility of his invention. By decreasing the production costs, it would be possible to withstand foreign competition and increase sales. Manufacturers set an example and, in 1812, several Jacquard looms were brought into service in Lyon. The experiment worked so well that the name is still in use today – the "jacquard" technique is usually known in Britain as "fair isle".

Ciselé velvet
(Lyon, Second Empire)

Embroidery
(France, Régence period)

Silk and linen brocatelle
(Lyon, 1867)

Silk lampas
(France, early 18C)

Embroidered satin
(France, late 19C)

Corded figured silk
(France, 18C)

Thimonnier, the unfortunate inventor of the sewing machine – Unlike Jacquard, Thimonnier did not have the good fortune to see his invention being used in his native country. His father was a dyer from Lyon who had fled the town and its upheavals during the French Revolution. In 1795 the family settled in Amplepuis where the young Thimonnier was apprenticed to a tailor. In 1822 he left the region to set up in business as a tailor near St-Étienne. Haunted by the idea of sewing clothes mechanically, and taking inspiration from the hooks used by embroiderers in the Monts Lyonnais, he secretly built a wooden and metal device that would produce chain stitch. This was the first sewing machine.

In order to register a patent, the inventor entered a partnership with Auguste Ferrand, a teacher at the Miners' School in St-Étienne. An application was filed on 13 April 1830 in the names of both partners. Ferrand, for his part, succeeded in interesting a man named Beaunier in the idea, an engineer who had already invented the first animal-drawn railway.

Thimonnier then left St-Étienne for Paris where the first mechanical sewing shop soon saw the light of day. In it, 80 sewing machines produced goods six times quicker than manual workers, thereby arousing the hatred of Parisian tailors who feared that their profession was on the point of ruin. On the night of 20 to 21 January 1831, 200 workers employed in the sewing and tailoring business ransacked the Parisian workshop. Thimonnier was ruined and he returned to Amplepuis where, in order to feed his large family, he again began work as a tailor. In 1834 he was back in Paris but nobody was interested in mechanical sewing. Two years later, utterly destitute, he travelled south again on foot, carrying his machine on his back and using it to pay for his board and lodging on the way. In 1848, through a man named Magnin, a company from Manchester expressed an interest in his *"couso-brodeur"*. Worn out by 30 years of work and struggle, Thimonnier died at the age of 64 – without seeing the extraordinary success enjoyed by the sewing machine.

LEADING LIGHTS FROM THE AUVERGNE

538-594	**Gregory of Tours** (born in Clermont-Ferrand), churchman and historian
938-1003	**Gerbert d'Aurillac**, theologian and scholar who went on to become Pope Sylvester II
1555-1623	**Henri de La Tour d'Auvergne**, Marshal of France under Henri IV and Calvinist leader
1623-1662	**Blaise Pascal** (Clermont-Ferrand), academic, writer and philosopher
1652-1719	**Michel Rolle** (Ambert), mathematician and author of a treaty of algebra
1757-1834	**Marquis de La Fayette** (Chavaniac), general and politician
1851-1914	**Fernand Forest** (Clermont-Ferrand), inventor (four-stroke engine)
1853-1929	**André Messager** (Montluçon), composer
1853-1931 and 1859-1940	**André and Édouard Michelin** (Clermont-Ferrand), industrialists (rubber tyres and tourist publications)
1884-1932	**Albert Londres** (Vichy), journalist and writer
1911-1974	**Georges Pompidou**, politician and President of the French Republic (1969-74)
b 1926	**Valéry Giscard d'Estaing**, politician and President of the French Republic (1974-1981)

Literary life

The language

Like all the regions in France the Auvergne has its own language, which has undergone continual development since the days of Antiquity, in accordance with historical and political upheaval and, more especially, as a result of local experiences. This means that the borders of the area in which the dialect of the Auvergne is spoken do not correspond to the historical and administrative borders of the province.

Auvergnat, the dialect of the Auvergne, which is considered to be similar to North Occitan, is said to have developed from a "Medio-Roman" language used in the part of Central France occupied by the Romans and which gradually died out in the face of competition from *oïl*, the language of Northern France and, therefore, the language of power and authority which was usually concentrated on the Paris Basin. The dialect spoken in and around Aurillac is closer to the Guyennais dialect spoken in the southwest of France (Aquitaine), which was under English domination for a considerable time, but it has nevertheless been influenced by Auvergnat. Bourbonnais is a Northern French language. Nowadays there are very few people who know the local dialect well and fewer still who actually use it, though linguistic studies of Auvergnat are continuing and a complete dictionary is now available.

A few great writers from the Auvergne

Local writers have brought fame to a few of the Auvergne's prelates among them Sidonius Apollinaris, Gerbert (10C) and Massillon who gave Louis XIV's funeral oration in the 18C. The Auvergne also had poets such as Théodore de Banville (1823-91) who founded the Parnassian school of poetry and philosophers such as Pierre Teilhard de Chardin (1881-1955). In the 20C, Henri Pourrat and the chronicler Alexandre Vialatte have both described their native land, each in his own style. Of all the Auvergne authors, the best-known is Blaise Pascal though Gregory of Tours, the medieval chronicler, is almost equally important.

Gregory of Tours – He was born c 583 in Clermont-Ferrand into a rich family of Senators. He spent most of his life in Tours, to which he was appointed Bishop in 573, yet he never forgot the place of his birth. His *History of the Franks* which retraces the reigns of the Merovingian kings and their ancestors is one of the main sources of historical information about the Auvergne during the Dark Ages and not until the 14C was there any chronicle about the region.

Gregory of Tours tells, for example, how, when Clovis' son, Thierry, took possession of the region, the people of the Auvergne, who already had a strong regional identity, rebelled against annexation to Austrasia which was situated at the easternmost tip of Gaul. He also described the Church's hold on the province, the building of the monasteries and the life of the monks.

Yet Gregory of Tours was not only concerned with the Auvergne. His work covers the whole of Gaul and is one of the only sources of information about that time. Indeed, it is the first historical work concerning the kingdom of the Franks that has survived to this day. As a Christian, Gregory of Tours interpreted signs of divine intervention in order to explain changes in the world but he was also a careful observer of the real world. He had a marked visual sense and he enjoyed describing things he saw, while carefully seeking the truth through differing sources of information which he had no hesitation in comparing and contrasting.

J.-D. Sudres/SCOPE

Blaise Pascal

Blaise Pascal – It was in 1623 that Pascal, undoubtedly the most famous native of the Auvergne, was born in Clermont-Ferrand. His mother died when he was three years old and it was his father, President of the Court of Aids (forerunner of the Customs & Excise) in Clermont, who brought him up. In 1631 Pascal senior came to Paris to devote all his time to his son who was already showing signs of extraordinary intelligence. Châteaubriand described him as a "terrifying genius". At the age of 11 he wrote a treatise on sound and, at 19, he invented his first mathematical machine to assist him in his calculations. In 1646 Pascal entered Port-Royal, the abbey where he wrote his treatises on Physics and Philosophy. He then left the abbey to lead a life among high society where he discovered that "the heart has its reasons". It was at this time that he wrote his *Discourse on the Passions of Love*. Soon, though, he began to suffer from the "emptiness" of his life. In 1664 he survived a carriage accident and believed that this was a sign from on high. He retired to Port-Royal, which he was never again to leave, and continued his writings. It was because his memory played tricks on him that he began noting his *Thoughts*, with a view to writing an *Apology of the Christian Religion*. This was his most famous work, but was never completed. Pascal died in 1662, at the age of 39.

*With this guide, use the appropriate **Michelin Maps** (scale 1 : 200 000) shown below the contents table on page 3. The common symbols will make planning easier.*

Auvergne's mineral springs

Whether naturally-carbonated or still, water is one of the main sources of wealth in the Auvergne and it has been exploited here since the days of Antiquity. The *département* of Puy-de-Dôme and the Vichy Basin alone account for one-third of all French mineral springs and their output exceeds 90 000 hectolitres a day.

Origins – Ordinary springs are created by water that seeps into permeable land and eventually meets an impermeable layer down which it runs. When the impermeable layer rises to the surface, the water follows suit. **Mineral springs** are either springs of infiltrated water or springs rising from the depths of the Earth's crust. In this case, substances or gases that have therapeutic properties are added naturally to the water as it flows underground. The adjective **"thermal"** is used more particularly to describe springs with water at a temperature of at least 35°C/95°F when it comes out of the ground.

In the Auvergne, the heat in the soil increases by 1°C every 13m/42ft instead of the average 30m/97ft. Vichy water can have a temperature of 66°C/150°F and the water in Chaudes-Aigues rises to as much as 85°C/185°F.

Resurgent springs – The water in these springs only flows at regular intervals, for example every eight hours. The column of water rising from the depths of the Earth is subjected, at some point along its course, to a very high increase in temperature. The steam produced at this point acquires sufficient pressure to project the upper part of the column of water above the surface of the ground. The projection is interrupted for as long as it takes to heat a second column, then the whole process begins again. This type of spring can be found in Bellerive, near Vichy.

Thermal springs are located in places where the Earth's crust is weak, for instance in areas of volcanic rock that have been dislocated by fissuring.

Mineral spring (iron), Vallée de Chaudefour

Properties of thermal springs – When thermal water rises to the surface, it gives off a very low level of radioactivity which stimulates the human organism. However, the water is very unstable and it deteriorates as soon as it comes out of the ground. This is why, for therapeutic purposes, it is so important to take full advantage of the water where it rises to the surface and why spa towns were built. The composition of the water varies greatly, depending on the type of rocks through which it has passed and the volcanic fissuring that created the spring. This means that people visit Vichy to treat disorders of the digestive system, Royat for heart and arterial disease, Châtel-guyon for intestinal problems, Le Mont-Dore for asthma, La Bourboule for respiratory diseases, St-Nectaire for liver complaints, Chaudes-Aigues for rheumatism etc.

Spa towns lost some of their popularity in the aftermath of the Second World War but are now enjoying a revival. The medical aspect of "taking the waters" has been maintained but people also come to keep fit, stay slim, and enjoy a round of golf, a day at the races, or a night at the opera, almost as they did last century.

Mineral water, a boom industry – The French drink more mineral water than any other nationality. This is why the Auvergne is so popular – it has everything they could ask for. Bottling has required the development of modern techniques, for water is one of the most difficult commodities to package. It is, though, a source of employment for small towns such as Volvic which has become famous not only in France but far beyond its borders.

Traditions in the Auvergne

Because of the isolated nature of much of the Auvergne countryside, many ancient traditions have survived; today, the inhabitants are doing their utmost to preserve the special character of this region and the cultural heritage.

Fêtes and festivals – Some of the old customs are upheld on the most important occasions. Bonfires are still lit on the mountain tops to celebrate the summer solstice (Feast of St John) and local fêtes have kept up the tradition of the music and songs played to young girls by the young men of the village. There has also been a revival of country festivals to celebrate haymaking, cheese making, harvesting, grape harvests...

Costume – Originally, there was a difference between the costumes worn by the people who lived in the mountains and those from the plains but nowadays every folk group has its own interpretation of traditional costume. The men wear the *biaude,* a voluminous dark blue smock, over a pair of coarse black trousers, with a brightly-coloured scarf, a wide-brimmed, black felt hat and the clogs or hob-nailed boots that are so vital when tapping out the dance rhythm. The women are dressed in long, waisted, multicoloured dresses with an embroidered apron and a head-dress that varies depending on the region; they also wear jewellery.

The bourrée – This dance dates back a long way but it is since the 18C that it has become synonymous with the Auvergne. The *bourrée* enacts the chasing of a coquettish young girl by an enterprising young man, whom she alternately runs away from and beckons to. The dance has precise figures and gives rise to shouts, hand-clapping and loud stamping of the clogs. Traditional village dances are currently undergoing something of a revival.

Processions and pilgrimages – Worship of the Virgin Mary is very important in the Auvergne. Countless churches and chapels have been dedicated to Her ever since; it is said St Austremoine dedicated a chapel to Her in Clermont in the 3C. Indeed, the statues of the Virgin Mary in the Auvergne are among the oldest in France.

Processions and pilgrimages in honour of the Blessed Virgin remain very much alive and are quite spectacular. The processions to Notre-Dame-du-Port (Clermont-Ferrand) or Orcival, and the pilgrimages to Mauriac and Thiézac in Cantal and to Marset and Monton in Puy de Dôme are the most popular. However, worship of the Virgin is also associated with work in the fields and with farm animals. Notre-Dame-de-Vassivière in the Monts Dore accompanies the animals during the transhumance: at the beginning of the summer the statue is carried from Besse to the chapel further up the mountainside; it is carried down again early in the autumn.

Though the worship of the saints is a less solemn affair, it too remains important, as can be seen from a study of place-names. The saints with healing powers have fallen victim to the progress of medicine but sometimes people pray to them as a last resort.

Salers cow in summer pastures, Monts du Cantal

Food and drink

The Rhône valley abounds in good food because it is situated at the heart of various regions containing an outstanding wealth of local produce. Bresse is famous for its poultry, the Charolais area produces beef, the Dombes region abounds in game, the lakes of Savoy teem with fish and the Forez and Rhône valley specialise in fruit.

The Auvergne, a rugged area of countryside, is not the place for complex, sophisticated cuisine; it specialises in family cooking – good food and plenty of it. This is an area where the speciality foods are as diverse as they are appetising.

LYON

In the 19C silk workers ate, like their employers, in small family-run restaurants; there was no snobbery in Lyon when it came to good food. The dishes served were based on cheap cuts of meat and offal but the food was plentiful and tasty. Diners could eat sausages, potted pork, black sausage, pigs' trotters, knuckle of veal and other stewed meats.

The tradition of good food remains unchanged. Today, local specialities include spicy saveloy sausage with truffles and pistachio nuts, pigs' trotters and tails, cardoons with marrow bone jelly, pork brawn in vinaigrette, and gently-stewed tripe. Other dishes include braised, stuffed trout, fish in Burgundy wine, poultry – especially chicken cooked in stock with thin slivers of truffle inserted between the skin and the meat, and chicken in cream.

Gratinée lyonnaise

Forez – Hunting, shooting, fishing and stock breeding provide the basic ingredients for a delicate, tasty type of cooking. Among the local dishes are crayfish and trout from the River Lignon, or poultry or meat of quite outstanding quality. Also on offer may be a local form of pork pie, a dish of duck, a delicious local ham, Feurs sausage or, in the autumn, game paté; sometimes even woodcock.

Vivarais – Food here is rustic; this is the land of chestnuts and wild mushrooms such as St George's agaric and boletus. Among the filling, tasty specialities are partridge with cabbage, thrush with grapes, chicken cooked in a bladder, chicken with crayfish, goose and turkey with chestnuts, hare with *poivrade* (a highly-seasoned sauce), and pork meat products from Ardèche. During the summer, the cherries, apricots, peaches, pears, plums and apples are among the finest such fruits found anywhere in France.

Lower Dauphiné – The Rhône Valley area of Lower Dauphiné marks the transition between the Lyonnais area and Provence. This is the land of *gratin dauphinois* (potatoes sliced and baked in milk), veal with leeks, *pognes* (brioches, a sort of sweet bread) in Romans and Valence, cheese from St-Marcellin, Grignan-style braised beef and the inimitable Montélimar nougat.

AUVERGNE

The food in the Auvergne has traditionally been farm cooking, and as a result it has been accused of lacking any appreciable local specialities; this criticism is, though, totally unfounded.

The people of the Auvergne have taken the great national specialities and adapted them to suit local taste so that, in the Auvergne, the food is rich and sometimes heavy but it is always extremely good.

Potée (Pork stew) – Vermenouze, a poet born in Cantal, left a recipe for this traditional dish containing an impressive list of ingredients:

"Take a cabbage, a large succulent cabbage, firm and close and not too damaged by frost, a knuckle of local pork with its bristle just singed, two lumps of pork fat, two good lumps, some fat and thin bacon on the turn but only just, turnips from the Planèze, Ussel or Lusclade. Add to the pot a well-stuffed cockerel or an old hen, a knuckle of veal, a rib of beef. Put the meat in the pot, a goodly amount, don't be afraid..."

All the ingredients are left to stew gently for four to five hours over a wood fire until the kitchen is filled with a mouth-watering aroma.

Meat and fish – The *coq au vin* (chicken casserole) is delicious, especially when flavoured with a good local wine. The *tripoux* from Aurillac, St-Flour and Chaudes-Aigues are also wonderful: sheep's feet stuffed and folded up in pieces of sheep's stomach. There is also ham from Maur, local sausages, fried gudgeon, trout from mountain streams, eels from the Dore and salmon from the Allier.

Vegetables – The *truffado* from Aurillac is a smooth blend of fresh *tomme* cheese and mashed potatoes; seasoned with garlic in Chaudes-Aigues and Aubrac, it is called *aligot*. Potato paté, a light pastry browned in the oven with a lot of fresh cream and potatoes, is one of the specialities of the Montluçon and Gannat area. Morel mushrooms are cooked with cream and used to fill omelettes and stuff poultry. Peas from the Planèze and green lentils from Le Puy are well-known to gourmets.

Cheeses – This is one of the region's main specialities. The round, flat St-Nectaire is a delight when well matured. There is also Fourme d'Ambert and Fourme de Montbrison, a blue cheese with an orange-tinted rind, Bleu d'Auvergne and Cantal. These are the best-known of the local cheeses but there is in addition Murol, a variant of St-Nectaire, or the garlic-flavoured Gaperon, made on the plains and shaped like a rounded cone. "Cabecou" goat's cheese is made in the Margeride area, around Aurillac and Salers.

Locally, the cheese usually known as "Cantal" is called "Fourme", named after the wooden mould (or "form") used to hold it together. This word gave the French language the word *formage* ("forming") which later became *fromage* (cheese). It takes the milk of twenty to thirty cows to make a 40kg/88lb Cantal cheese. The milk is collected in a narrow, deep vat called a *gerle*. The rennet is then added before the mixture is heated and allowed to drain. The curd is then known as *tomme*. After being left to stand for three days, it is crumbled and salted, then placed in a mould where it is pressed in order to extract the whey. The *fourme* placed in the cellar below the mountain hut is periodically turned until it matures. Among the cheeses still made on farms are St-Nectaire and Fourme d'Ambert but these days most of the milk is processed in co-operatives or dairies to make Cantal Laitier (indicated by a square label) or Bleu d'Auvergne, a cow's milk cheese with a fermented curd to which mould is added; it is reminiscent of Roquefort.

Some cheeses of the Auvergne:
(left to right) Cantal, Bleu d'Auvergne, Fourme d'Ambert, St-Nectaire

Desserts – In Lower Auvergne and the Ambert Plain, two of the specialities are *milliards*, tarts made with unstoned cherries or grapes, and *pompes*, large, heavy cakes filled with fruit. Cantal has the *fouasse* which is a type of sweet bread. A *picoussel* is a buckwheat flour flan filled with plums and seasoned with herbs. *Cornets de murat* are filled with fresh cream and there are also cream tarts in Vic-sur-Cère. In Salers, the speciality is the *carré*.

The production of fruit jellies, glacé fruits and jams is an old tradition. In the 15C, important visitors were offered "dry jams" – apple or apricot jellies. There are countless orchards in the Auvergne. The area around Clermont specialises in apricots; the Limagne produces mainly peaches and apples, including the much-prized Canada variety. The Courpière area grows red fruits.

WINES

The Auvergne still boasts a few wines produced on the slopes of the Limagne such as St-Pourçain, Châtaugay and Corent but the best wine-growing areas are to be found in the Rhône Valley, where Beaujolais and Côtes du Rhône are produced.

Côtes du Rhône – The vineyards on the Côtes du Rhône are thought to be the oldest in France and the stock is said to have been brought here by the Greeks several centuries BC. They stretch along both banks of the river like a narrow ribbon, producing wines whose quality and balance are guaranteed by a skilful blend of varieties of grape. The reds should be drunk at room temperature, the whites well chilled. Côte Rôtie wines have a bouquet reminiscent of violets; the wines from l'Hermitage distil the scent of raspberries. Château-Condrieu and Château-Grillet are among the greatest of all French white wines. If drunk young, they are a marvellous accompaniment to a crayfish gratin. Cornas was much appreciated by Charlemagne. St-Péray and the fresh, bubbling, musky Clairette-de-Die are both sparkling wines. Finally, further south where the valley enters Provence, the vineyards produce the warm, friendly Châteauneuf-du-Pape, a powerful wine with a purple robe, Gigondas, the sweet, suave and flavoursome Muscat from Beaumes-de-Venise and, on the other bank of the Rhône, the rosés from Tavel and the reds and rosés from Lirac and Chusclan.

Gratin dauphinois

Ingredients (for 4-6 people):
- 60g/2oz butter
- 900g/2lb potatoes, peeled and cut into thin slices
- 110g/4oz Cantal cheese, grated
- 2 cloves garlic, crushed
- 300ml/10fl oz milk/stock
- salt and pepper to taste

Preheat the oven to 160°C/325°F or gas mark 3. Grease a large, shallow round or oval dish (about 30cm/12in across) fairly lavishly with some of the butter. Layer the potato slices with the grated cheese, garlic and seasoning, ending with a layer of potatoes. Pour on the milk or stock, sprinkle a couple of tablespoons of grated cheese on the top and dot with the remaining butter. Bake for about 1hr 30min, until the potatoes are cooked through and the top is golden brown. Delicious served with roast or grilled meat and accompanied by red wine.

Bon appetit!

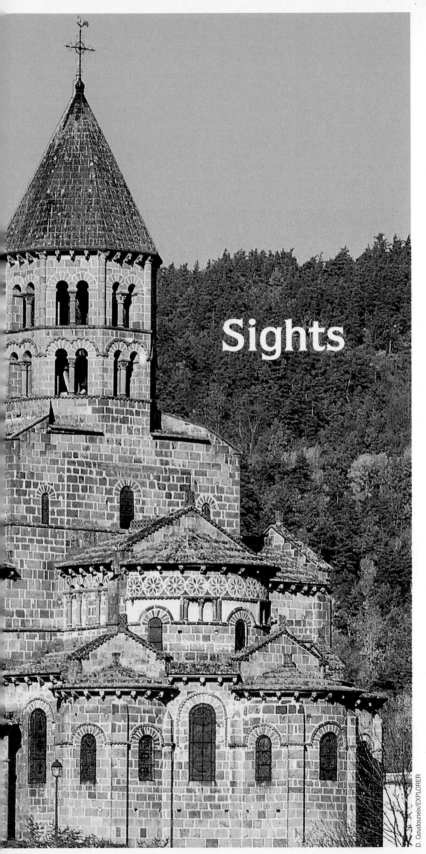

Sights

Château d'ALLEUZE★★

Michelin map 76 fold 14 or 239 fold 43 – Local map under Gorges de la TRUYÈRE

There can scarcely be another beauty spot in the Auvergne as romantic as the site of this castle.

The fortress was built in the 13C by the Constables of the Auvergne but belonged to the Bishops of Clermont when, during the Hundred Years War, Bernard de Garlan – an adventurer who supported the English side – took it by storm and set up camp. For seven years he terrorised the region, pillaging a wide area and holding it to ransom. In order to ensure that Garlan was not the first of many, the inhabitants of St-Flour burnt the castle down in 1405.

The castle can be reached from the north, via the D 40 and D 48 from St-Flour, or from the south by following the route described under Gorges de la TRUYÈRE, between Garabit viaduct and Chaudes-Aigues. The D 48 leads right down to the ruins.

Near the hill topped by the castle is a modern Calvary which stands next to the old church (12C-15C) of Alleuze and the graveyard.

Château d'Alleuze

★★**Site** – The D 48 west of Barry skirts the narrow Alleuze valley, providing some breathtaking views of the castle and its ruins, a vast keep flanked by four round towers standing on a spur of barren rock, almost 30m/97ft above Grandval reservoir.

An even better view of the site may be had from the village of **La Barge**. Park beside the war memorial and turn left towards the church and the Calvary. From here it is possible to follow a path marking the Stations of the Cross laid out along the ridge of a rocky promontory *(15min Rtn on foot)*.

Gorges de l'ALLIER★★

Michelin map 76 folds 5, 6, 16 or 239 folds 32, 33, 45, 46

The River Allier rises in the south of the Auvergne, on the southern slopes of the Mourre de la Gardille (alt 1 053m/3 422ft) between Châteauneuf-de-Radon and La Bastide. The upper reaches cross the Lozère plateau at an altitude of some 1 000m/3 250ft before the river flows through Langogne. Lower down, before reaching the Langeac plain, the Allier cuts an almost uniformly narrow valley forming magnificent gorges that can be seen from some of the roads. In all, there are some 40km/25 miles of gully between Le Pont d'Alleyras and Langeac but only the railway line runs alongside the river all the way from Langogne (upstream of Chapeauroux) to Langeac.

Downstream of Langogne, although still little more than a large mountain stream, the Allier has carved out a valley that digs deeper and deeper into the crystalline rocks covering the lava flows produced by the volcanoes in the Dèves or western Velay area. The limpid waters of the river running over a bed bristling with rocks and boulders are flanked by scarp slopes of granite or gneiss interspersed in some places with columnar basalt. The dark tones of the rocks and woodland covering the hillsides lend the Allier gorge a certain atmosphere of brooding.

★★SOUTH OF THE "PETITES LIMAGNES"

① From Brioude to Monistrol-d'Allier

105km/65mi – allow half a day – local map below

Most of the small region around Brioude consists of fertile plains known as *limagnes*.

★★**Brioude** – *See BRIOUDE.*

Leave Brioude on the N 102 towards Le Puy-en-Velay.

★**Lavaudieu** – *See LAVAUDIEU.*

Return to Vieille-Brioude and the west bank of the Allier. Take the D 585 towards Lavoûte-Chilhac.

St-Ilpize – This medieval town clinging to a basalt rock is crowned by the ruins of a castle. The castle walls enclose a 14C **chapel** with an apse of polychrome tufa and a basalt gable wall containing the church bells.

Rejoin the D 585.

Blassac – The **church** ⊘ in this village is built on a flow of basalt. Its chancel contains a set of 14C frescoes depicting Christ in Glory, St Michael slaying the Dragon and scenes from the life of the Virgin Mary.

Rejoin the D 585.

Lavoûte-Chilhac – This village is built on the banks of the Allier, which washes up against the walls of the houses. It has an elegant 11C bridge, restored in the 15C, and a Gothic **church** surrounded by the buildings of an 18C Benedictine abbey. The church has a single, wide nave. Note the large 12C Crucifix opposite the pulpit and the beautiful carved wooden door of the original 11C church.

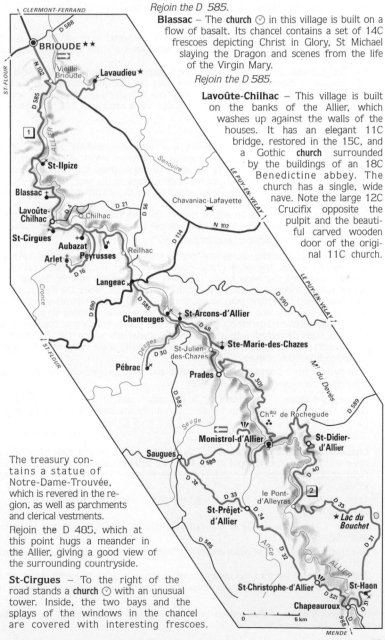

The treasury contains a statue of Notre-Dame-Trouvée, which is revered in the region, as well as parchments and clerical vestments.

Rejoin the D 585, which at this point hugs a meander in the Allier, giving a good view of the surrounding countryside.

St-Cirgues – To the right of the road stands a **church** ⊘ with an unusual tower. Inside, the two bays and the splays of the windows in the chancel are covered with interesting frescoes.

Note the springing of the chancel vaulting, which rests on pilasters carved in human forms which are themselves supported on consoles shaped like human faces.

Carry on along the D 585.

Aubazat – This village in a pleasant setting has a **church** ⊘ containing a Pietà and interesting polychrome wooden statues representing an Entombment (15C).

Rejoin the D 585 for a further 500yds, and at the crossroads turn right onto the D 41, and then right again onto the D 16.

Arlet – This tiny hamlet nestling at the bottom of the Cronce valley has a small Romanesque **church** ⊘ containing a remarkable 12C Byzantine Crucifix, an 11C statue of St Peter and a beautiful 15C painted wooden triptych, reminiscent of those produced by the Rhenish school.

From the D 585, there is a view of the steep basalt cliffs on the opposite river bank and the village of Chilhac built on a terrace of columnar basalt.

Peyrusses – The **church** ⊘ here contains an interesting Virgin Mary in Majesty and fine – if somewhat faded – frescoes depicting the Dormition of the Virgin.

Follow the D 585 through Reilhac.

Langeac – This busy little town lies in a wide cultivated 'corridor' at the downstream end of the Allier gorge. One or two old houses are still to be seen along its streets.

The Gothic **church** contains choir stalls and a pulpit dating from the 16C. Note the 12C font, in a chapel left of the chancel, and the 15C Entombment in another chapel, in which the wall is decorated with two 15C paintings showing an Annunciation and a Virgin and Child. The church also has a handsome 14C wrought-iron grille.

Carry on along the D 585.

Chanteuges – This village on a basalt spur between the Allier and one of its tributaries boasts an attractive Romanesque **church** from a local abbey which used to be the summer residence of the abbots of La Chaise-Dieu. The church is built of warm-coloured volcanic stone. Note the large window in the west front (16C); the pretty sculpted capitals in the nave, especially on the south side; and the well-carved Renaissance choir stalls.

North of the church is the arcade of the old cloisters from where there is a good view of the Allier valley. The 16C Abbot's chapel has a finely-carved door frame.

Turn right under a railway bridge onto the D 30.

Pébrac – After running along the pretty little valley of the Desges between pine-covered slopes, the road brings you to this quiet hillside village with red-roofed houses and the ruins of an 11C **abbey** ⊘. The abbey church, flanked by a square tower, underwent extensive alteration in the 15C when the height of the nave was raised by adding pointed vaulting. Beautiful carved capitals survive from the Romanesque era, one of which shows two large heads vomiting serpents.

The **treasury** contains interesting items of church plate, including a chased copper box with sides decorated with scenes from everyday life in the 13C (troubadour, tournament), clerical vestments and the Pébrac Nativity scene with its finely-carved and painted wooden statues.

Turn back to the crossroads with the D 585 and carry straight on along the D 30, crossing to the opposite bank of the Allier.

St-Arcons-d'Allier – The **church** ⊘ in the upper part of the village has a very classic Romanesque nave with basalt columns. Its arcades are roofed by sturdy relief arches.

Take the D 48.

Chapelle Ste-Marie-des-Chazes – This isolated chapel on the east bank of the Allier stands on a peaceful spot at the foot of a striking basalt rock. A monumental flight of 30 steps leads to a porch-belfry (rebuilt in the 19C) crowned by a conical lantern.

Cross the Allier once more before going through St-Julien-des-Chazes and carrying on along the D 48.

Prades – This small village is situated in a splendid **setting**★ hemmed in by the valley sides.

The D 48 crosses the river again and climbs to the junction with the D 301, where you turn right.

The D 301, half cut into the valley slopes, commands some beautiful views. After dropping downhill a little, it runs along at the foot of the ruins of the Château de Rochegude.

Monistrol-d'Allier – This village lies in a very impressive **setting**★ in the Allier valley.

★★BETWEEN THE DEVÈS AND THE MARGERIDE

② Round trip from Monistrol-d'Allier to Chapeauroux

95km/59mi – about 3hr – local map above

Monistrol-d'Allier – *See above.*

Leave Monistrol east on the D 589, and turn right in St-Privat-d'Allier onto the D 40.

St-Didier-d'Allier – This small village occupies a precarious site on a steep-sided rock.

Take the D 40 as far as Pont-d'Alleyras, then turn left into the D 33.

★**Lac du Bouchet** – *A woodland footpath leads round the lake; allow 45min. See Le PUY-EN-VELAY: Excursions.*

On the road leaving the lakeside heading towards Le Bouchet-St-Nicolas, at the edge of the forest, there is a beautiful view of the volcanic Velay countryside and more particularly the Meygal and Mézenc mountain ranges.

St-Haon – The village built on the edge of the plateau has a **church** ⊘ with a remarkable late 12C apse.

Follow the D 31.

Chapeauroux – This hamlet is built on the confluence of the Allier and the Chapeauroux in an attractive valley crossed by a sweeping railway viaduct with 28 arches.

On leaving Chapeauroux, turn right onto the D 321.

St-Christophe-d'Allier – From the road leading up the steep slope to this village there is a broad view of the Allier gorge.

Rejoin the D 32 and just before it crosses the Allier, turn right into the D 34.

St-Préjet-d'Allier – This village on the eastern flank of the Margeride has two dams across the Ance: La Valette and Pouzas.

Take the D 33 alongside the graveyard.

Saugues – *See SAUGUES.*

The D 589 back to Monistrol gives incredible views of the gorge carved out of the granite by the Allier and from time to time also of the enormous basalt boulders on the river's banks.

Michelin Green Guides for North America:

California
Canada
Chicago
Florida
New England
New York City
Quebec
San Francisco
Washington DC

AMBERT

Population 7 420
Michelin map 73 fold 16 or 239 fold 22
Local maps under Le LIVRADOIS and Monts du FOREZ
Town plan in the current Michelin Red Guide France

The small, seemingly-isolated town of Ambert lies in the middle of a low, wide plain between the Livradois and Forez mountains. Formerly known for the production of paper and religious artefacts, Ambert is nowadays a centre of more diversified economic activity.

Papermaking and the Wars of Religion – Ambert's origins are obscure but the town began to make a name for itself in the 15C, when the paper industry here came into its own; in the 16C this area boasted more than 300 paper mills, each jealously protecting its own manufacturing secrets. The main market was Lyon with its many printers. The church of St-Jean, the "cathedral" of the Livradois area, was built during this prosperous period.

However, Ambert was not safe from national political upheavals and became involved in the Wars of Religion. On 15 February 1577 the town was taken by **Merle**, the formidable Huguenot leader, who massacred all prisoners. Catholic armies rushed to the rescue. Lacking the manpower to defend the town, Merle thought of a brilliant stratagem: statues were taken from the local churches, given helmets and posted on the city walls. Astonished to see the defendants maintain their position under enemy fire and believing them to be invulnerable, the besiegers finally withdrew. The city subsequently came under the control of members of the Catholic League, who did not surrender until 1596.

Industrial diversification – The manufacture of braiding – today the major industry in Ambert – saved the town. During the 17C clothmaking began to decline in favour of the production of braiding and trimmings, and Ambert quickly became the capital of this industry. The making of shoe-laces, braids, ribbons etc further flourished in the 18C while the papermaking industry now went into decline, as did the production of religious articles (rosaries, medals). The braidings and trimmings industry has expanded to include cable- and ropemaking and the production of elasticated braiding for clothing.

Papermaking was badly hit by the effects of the Industrial Revolution and today it plays only a minor role in the local economy. Local agriculture is also in difficulties, but a thriving dairy industry exports its products to the USA and Switzerland, where Ambert is one of the leading suppliers of raclette cheese.

The Athens of the Auvergne – Ambert has produced a long line of outstanding personalities: in the 17C the theory of equations took a giant step forward through the work of mathematician **Michel Rolle**; in the 19C the composer Emmanuel Chabrier and the erudite poet Maurice Faucon showed an unusually high degree of sensitivity in their respective fields.

In the early 20C Ambert became a hotbed of intellectuals who included philosophers, writers and geographers (Pierre de Nolhac, Alexandre Vialatte, Cécile Sauvage, Antoine Sylvère, Claude Dravaine, Lucien Gachon) who all focused their intellect on their native or adoptive Livradois area. Another famous son of the Livradois area was **Henri Pourrat**(1887-1959), who formed a link between the rural and industrial worlds, and who in his novels, short stories and historical works wrote chiefly about country life in the Auvergne, expressing "the poetry of the soil, Man's purposes and the spirit of civilizations" *(A Vialatte)*. The municipal and university library at Clermont-Ferrand runs an Henri-Pourrat centre containing the author's archives and library.

SIGHTS

In summer, rides may be taken on the **Livradois-Forez tourist railway** ⊘, which operates between Ambert and Courpière *(see Vallée de la DORE)*.

★St-Jean – *Place St-Jean*. The church of St-Jean, built between 1471 and 1518, is a typical example of Flamboyant Gothic architecture, except for the upper part of the tower and a chapel which both date from the Renaissance. The flights of fancy of the Gothic sculptor were restrained by the hard granite used to build the church. The tower is surrounded by machicolations; the southern façade has a fine portal. Inside, note the irregular size of the arch spans. In the first chapel on the left is a 16C painted wooden Pietà known as Our Lady of Layre. The gilded lead altar in the transept crossing was designed by Philippe Kaeppelin.

Hôtel de ville – *Boulevard Henri IV*. The town hall, an unusual circular building, has been immortalised in literature by Jules Romains; the "large rotunda" is the meeting-place of the heroes of his novel *Copains ("Chums")*, who visit Ambert in order to mystify the inhabitants by playing practical jokes on them.

Musée de la Fourme et des Fromages ⊘ – *Off Rue du Château*. This museum of **cheese making** is housed in a 15C building. Guided tours describe the manufacture of Fourme (a local blue cheese) and the discovery by accident, 10 000 years ago, of the process of cheese making. In a laboratory the four fundamental stages of production are revealed – curdling the milk, pouring it into a mould, leaving it to drain, drying it. Two upper rooms concentrate on cheesemaking in detail, and explain the precise conditions needed to make Fourme d'Ambert in particular. In the cellar various local cheeses are maturing, which takes a minimum of 28 days.

Granite needle – *Place Charles-de-Gaulle*. This beautiful granite block comes from the Job area.

Musée de la Machine agricole et à vapeur (Agrivap) (**Museum of Agricultural and Steam-powered Machinery**) ⊘ – *Rue de l'Industrie. South of Ambert via the D 269*. This museum installed in an old sawmill boasts a large collection of steam-powered machines from the early 20C.

Pride of place is given to an SACM-Pinguet micro-power plant, designed to power the former sawmill. It consists of a steam-powered generator dating from 1906 and a boiler built in 1909 that is heated by wood chips and offcuts. The agricultural implements in the harvesting and threshing section clearly show the evolution from horse-power to engine-power. The tractor hall displays many different models from various countries, including a wooden tractor (never used).

The Agrivap museum now shares part of its premises with another museum, on the subject of braiding **(Musée de la Tresse).**

EXCURSIONS

*★**Moulin Richard-de-Bas** – 5.5km/3mi east via the D 996, and left turn into the D 57 which runs up the Lagat valley. See under Moulin RICHARD-DE-BAS.*

Parc zoologique du Bouy ⊘ – 8.5km/5 mi south via the D 906 and right onto the D 56 to Champetières.
The zoo covers an area of 50ha/123 acres planted with beautiful Scotch firs, spruce, Douglas firs and sequoias which blend into the surrounding forest. Many species of animal, whose habits and characteristics are explained on information panels, live here in semi-liberty: birds, monkeys, lions, lynx, jackals, hyenas, wolves, kangaroos, camels, bison, white deer, emus etc. A children's playground completes the zoo's attractions.

This guide, which is revised regularly,
is based on tourist information provided at the time of going to press.
Changes are however inevitable owing to improved facilities and fluctuations in the cost of living.

Château d'ANJONY★

Michelin map 76 south of fold 2 or 239 south of fold 29
Local map under Monts du CANTAL

This castle of reddish basalt is one of the most remarkable castles in Upper Auvergne. Strategically located on the tip of the Tournemire promontory, it dominates the lush landscape of the Doire valley with its four tall towers (height 40m/130ft). The castle was built in the 15C by Louis II of Anjony, the companion of Dunois and Joan of Arc, near the towers of Tournemire which had been held in joint fief by his family and the Tournemires since 1351. This dual ownership led to three centuries of bloody rivalry between the families, one of old feudal stock, the other having prospered through business and service to the royal family. The feud ended around 1650 when the Tournemires left the area for pastures new. While pursuing their military career, the Anjonys set their sights on Versailles.

Tour ⊘ – The castle, a keep with four corner towers, has only one room on each floor. In the 18C the owners added a small wing in the style of the day. The low, vaulted cellar in the basement has been turned into a vast entrance hall.
The main hall on the first floor boasts a coffered ceiling with three tiers of beams, and throughout the castle there are some fine furnishings and furniture: a vast fireplace in the kitchen, tapestries from Aubusson and Flanders, a tester bed, a reclining seat. The chapel in the southeastern tower is decorated with 16C **frescoes** showing scenes from the Life of Christ. An alcove contains the statue of Our Lady of Anjony, a Black Virgin and Child of painted and gilded wood. The Knights' Hall on the

Château d'Anjony

Le Naviose-IMAGES PHOTOHÈQUE

57

second floor has **frescoes★** of Michel of Anjony and his wife Germaine of Foix in late 16C dress, and scenes illustrating the legend of the Nine Valiant Knights from a medieval poem. Note the beautiful Florentine table with ivory inlay, the secretaire in Mudejar style, the engraved silver dishes and the Renaissance *objets d'art*. The 3rd-floor audience chamber with diagonal vaulting has walls hung with two large tapestries, including a Flemish *verdure* (hunting scene). The loopholes along the watchpath overlook the Doire valley. From the top of the last tower (splendid oak rafters), there is an attractive view of the whole castle and of the surrounding countryside.

EXCURSIONS

St-Cernin – *7km/4mi west*. This small town is a pleasant base from which to explore the western Monts du Cantal. The 12C **church** of St-Louis, dominated by its bell tower, was altered in the 15C and boasts some fine **woodwork★** (note in particular the misericords on the choir stalls, from the chapter house at St-Chamant), a handsome Louis XIV lectern near the pulpit and lovely corbels carved into the basalt of the church's east end.

St-Chamant – *12km/8mi north*. The **church** here contains eight choir stalls decorated with painted **panels★**. The **château** ⊙ is 17C with a 15C square machicolated keep; inside are wonderful **tapestries★**, in very good condition, decorated with themes including spring, mythological events and the crusades. The castle chapel houses a lovely gilded wooden altarpiece (18C) depicting the Holy Family.

★Gorges de la Maronne – *14km/9mi northwest*. A trip down the valley takes in **St-Martin-Valmeroux**, a small glovemaking centre with a Gothic church, an old fountain and the ruins of a castle; **Château de Branzac** – a massive keep with corner towers – is now just a picturesque ruin on the end of a promontory; **Notre-Dame-du-Château** chapel is an attractive building roofed with *lauzes*, sitting in a lovely **setting★** overlooking a double meander of the river; **St-Martin-Cantalès** has a **church** ⊙ with a Romanesque doorway; the **Gorges de la Bertrande** is an attractive canyon through which the river meanders; **St-Illide** has a small Romanesque church (enlarged in the 15C) with interesting choir stalls (from St-Chamant) and a fine lectern.

Michelin Maps which cover the area described in this guide are nos 69, 73, 74, 76, 77, 80, 81 and 88.

ANNONAY

Population 18 525
Michelin map 76 fold 10 or 246 fold 18
Local map under Moyenne vallée du RHÔNE

Annonay is located in a deep cleft of the Vivarais plateau, at the confluence of the Deûme and Cance rivers. In the Middle Ages, the exceptional quality of the water here encouraged a leather and wool industry to be established which then flourished.
Being one of the first towns to side with the principles of the Reformation, Annonay suffered greatly during the Wars of Religion. In the 17C, however, following the establishment in the town of the Johannot and Montgolfier families' paperworks, Annonay once again began to prosper.
Today, traditional industries around the town are complemented by a wide array of other activities including coach building, mechanical engineering, the production of industrial felts, wool, shoes, health food and pharmaceutical products. These modern businesses located in the surrounding uplands form a striking contrast with the façades of historic Annonay.
The native city of the Montgolfier brothers *(see below)*, Annonay was also the home of one of their descendants, **Marc Seguin** (1786-1875), the engineer who improved the steam boiler. His model, used in 1830 for Stephenson's Rocket, increased the train's speed from 9kph/5.6mph to a maximum of 60kph/37mph.

An aerostatic experiment – Observing that hot air rises, the **Montgolfier brothers** decided to harness this energy; after several successful experiments, they were ready to test their process in public. On 4 June 1783, in the presence of the States General of the Vivarais area, they launched a balloon of 769m³/27 157ft³. The strips forming the balloon itself were made of packaging fabric and paper, held together by some 1 800 buttons. Rising in nine and a half minutes to its maximum height – from 1 000-2 000m/3 250-6 500ft, according to different eyewitness accounts – the balloon remained in the air for half an hour and finally landed more than 2km/1mi from its launch site. The aerostat, the forerunner of the aeroplane, was born.
This feat is commemorated by an obelisk at the roundabout in Avenue Marc-Seguin, a plaque on Place des Cordeliers, where the experiment was conducted, and an annual reconstruction of the historic first flight *(see Calendar of events at the end of the guide)*.

OLD TOWN *1hr 30min*

The old neighbourhoods on the hills overlooking the two rivers are currently benefiting from a major restoration project.

Start from Place de la Libération.

On this square stands a statue of the Montgolfier brothers, erected in 1883 to commemorate the first centenary of their aerostatic experiments.

A little lookout point opposite the post office offers a **view** of the Cance valley and Mignot park.

Turn into Rue Boissy-d'Anglas.

Chapelle de Trachin – This Gothic chapel is all that remains of a priory founded in 1320 by Guy Trachin, a wealthy resident of Annonay. Having escaped destruction during the Wars of Religion, it served in turn as a brotherhood chapel and a parish church. The tall stone spire dates from the 16C. The north porch bears a bust of the founder, and is topped by a 17C Madonna and Child.

From the bottom of Place de la Liberté turn into Montée du Château.

Fortified gates (Portes fortifiées) – Montée du Château forms a steep incline up to the old machicolated gate (**B**); a second gate also survives, at the end of Rue de Bourgville (**D**).

Rue Montgolfier leads to the bridge of the same name.

Pont Montgolfier (**26**) – This bridge spans the Deûme. Upstream, the view is of the humpback **Valgelas bridge** (14C) and the convent of Ste-Marie (16C). Downstream, the Deûme flows into the **Défilé des Fouines**, a dark and narrow rocky gorge overlooked by abandoned taweries.

Place des Cordeliers (**10**) – The square is named after a Franciscan convent which once occupied the site of the theatre. A plaque on the right of the tourist office commemorates the Montgolfier brothers' first public experiment.

Walk to Valgelas bridge and follow Voûtes Soubise, a vaulted passageway, to the steps of Rue Barville. Turn right into Rue de Deûme and continue to Avenue de l'Europe.

Avenue de l'Europe partly covers the Deûme. From the intersection with Rue de la Valette there is a **view** west over the **Tour des Martyrs** (12-13C), the last remnant of the old ramparts, and the former convent of Ste-Marie.

Place de la Liberté (**19**) – This square located in the centre of the old town becomes a bustling hub of trade on market days *(Wednesdays and Saturdays)*. The northwestern side of the square is graced by a statue of Marc Seguin. The square provides an attractive view of Trachin chapel.

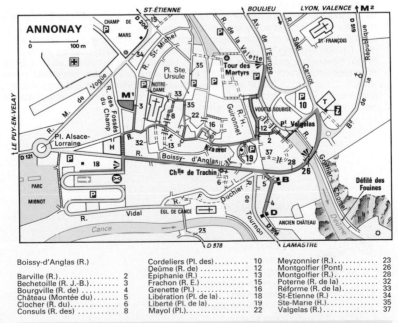

Boissy-d'Anglas (R.)

Barville (R.)	2
Bechetoille (R. J.-B.)	3
Bourgville (R. de)	4
Château (Montée du)	6
Clocher (R. du)	—
Consuls (R. des)	8

Cordeliers (Pl. des)	10
Deûme (R. de)	12
Épiphanie (R.)	13
Frachon (R. E.)	15
Grenette (Pl.)	16
Libération (Pl. de la)	18
Liberté (Pl. de la)	19
Mayol (Pl.)	22

Meyzonnier (R.)	23
Montgolfier (Pont)	26
Montgolfier (R.)	28
Poterne (R. de la)	32
Réforme (R. de la)	33
St-Étienne (R.)	34
Ste-Marie (H.)	35
Valgelas (R.)	37

B, D Portes fortifiées	**M²** Musée des Papeteries
M¹ Musée Vivarois César-Filhol	Canson et Montgolfier

Rue Franki-Kramer – Annonay's old high street, like the nearby Place Grenette and Place Mayol, is flanked by picturesque 16C, 17C and 18C houses. A plaque on the left commemorates Marc Seguin's birthplace. The house on the next corner still shows iron cladding designed to protect its walls.

Walk through Place Grenette and return to Rue Franki-Kramer.

The 17C alms church at no 15 is now used as a Protestant church.

Follow the passage, cross Place Mayol, then take Rue Ste-Marie to Rue des Consuls.

On the left stands an old mansion with mullioned windows.

Musée vivarois César-Filhol (M¹) ⊘ – This ancient royal bailiwick dating from 1700 contains interesting collections on old Annonay, its famous citizens and the folklore of the Vivarois area. Local works of art include a beautiful 16C wooden Crucifix and a touching 17C wooden Pietà. The museum also has a reconstruction of a kitchen from the Ardèche region and a wide range of documentation on the Montgolfier brothers, Marc Seguin (model of his 1828 locomotive) and on the Seguin brothers, inventors in 1908 of the "Gnome" rotating aircraft engine.

ADDITIONAL SIGHT

Musée des Papeteries Canson et Montgolfier (Canson and Montgolfier Paperworks Museum) (M²) ⊘ – *2.5km/1mi northeast. Leave Annonay on the Boulevard de la République, following signs to Valence. Turn left just before the Davézieux industrial estate; the road goes downhill and is marked "Musée des Papeteries Canson et Montgolfier". Park in the car park in front of the church.*

The museum is laid out in the house where the brothers Joseph and Étienne de Montgolfier, the inventors of the hot-air balloon, were born; it retraces the history of the paperworks established on the banks of the Deûme, particularly the Vidalon paperworks, appointed purveyors to the court in 1784 for its quality products. The museum presents a traditional papermaking workshop with a vat, a set of moulds, a stretcher and a wooden press. Many documents, explanatory panels and

Musée Vivarois – Marc Seguin's locomotive

tools show the development of techniques used in Vidalon from the time of the first papermill, established by the Chelles family from Beaujeu. The display provides a fascinating glimpse of papermaking techniques used in the Far East. The museum also focuses on daily life and customs in the papermaking industry before the French Revolution, and there is a reconstruction of an old laboratory and the office of a paper manufacturer at the turn of the century. The vast workshop in the vaulted cellar houses large machines including a cylinder mould papermaking machine, the link between manual and contemporary techniques. Here, visitors can watch traditional manual manufacturing techniques.

MICHELIN GREEN GUIDES

Architecture
Fine Art
Ancient monuments
History
Geography
Picturesque scenery
Scenic routes
Touring programmes
Places to stay
Plans of towns and buildings
A collection of regional guides for France.

Gorges de l'ARDÈCHE ★★★

Michelin map 80 folds 9 and 10 or 246 fold 23

The Ardèche gorge, overlooked by an audaciously-engineered road, ranks among the most impressive sites of natural beauty in the south of France; a large part of the gorge is now a nature reserve. Since 1993, this exceptional stretch of landscape has been designated a major national site (Grand Site d'intérêt national).

Spates and droughts – The Ardèche rises in the Mazan massif (alt 1 467m/4 813ft). After a 119km/74mi journey, it flows into the Rhône, just upstream from Pont-St-Esprit *(see Michelin Green Guide Provence)*. In the upper valley *(see Vallée de l'ARDÈCHE below)* the Ardèche cuts a steep downhill course, but it is in the lower valley that some of the more interesting formations due to erosion are to be seen. Here the river has carved a passage through the limestone strata of the plateau, which had already been undermined from the inside by subterranean streams. The Ardèche's tributaries flowing down from the mountain accentuate its sporadic yet typically Mediterranean flow; autumn spates give way to a shallow stream in winter, then swell into spring torrents, before subsiding to a comparative trickle during the summer. During the autumn spates, when the river's volume can increase by as much as 3 000 times its norm, there is a tremendous convergence of flood waters at Vallon-Pont-d'Arc. A powerful wall of water can sweep down the valley at between 15-20km/9-12mi an hour! The strength of these erratic flood waters is such that the river pushes the (by no means weak) flow of the Rhône eastwards and deposits a pile of alluvial debris in its river bed. In 1890, the force of the Ardèche spate was so strong that it cut right across the course of the Rhône and broke through the Lauzon dike on the opposite bank. The level of the Ardèche drops as suddenly as it rises.

FROM VALLON-PONT-D'ARC TO PONT-ST-ESPRIT
(NORTH BANK)

58km/36mi – allow a day – local map overleaf

On leaving the Vallon basin, the Ardèche crosses the limestone plateau of the Lower Vivarais, cutting between the Gras plateau to the east and the Orgnac plateau to the west, covered with thickets of evergreen oaks and pitted with caves.

The D 290, a **panoramic road**, overlooks the gorge from the clifftops at the edge of the Gras plateau, giving breathtaking views from the many lookout points (*belvédères*) along the way.

Vallon-Pont-d'Arc – This town is the departure point for boat trips down the gorge. Southeast of the town, on the slope of a hill, stand the ruins of Vieux Vallon castle, a reminder of the old medieval village here. On the ground floor of the **Mairie** ⊘ (town hall housed in a Louis XIII mansion) are seven 17C Aubusson **tapestries** in a remarkable state of preservation, with their colours still extremely fresh.

Head for Pont-d'Arc (D 290 southeast).

The road skirts the foot of hill with the ruins of Vieux Vallon castle *(undergoing restoration)* and after crossing the Ibie, comes to the Ardèche. On the left is the **Grotte des Tunnels**, a cave through which an underground torrent once ran, and then **Grotte des Huguenots** ⊘, which houses an exhibition on speleology and prehistory.

★★**Pont-d'Arc** – *Park in one of the car parks on either side of the viewing point.* The river flows under this natural arch (34m/111ft high, 59m/193ft wide at water level). At one time the river meandered around this promontory, following the route now taken by the road; the arch would have been just a gulley through which underground waters drained. General erosion and the undermining activities of the river must have worn away the land around the arch, and then the river itself, during some particularly large spate, abandoned its old meander to slip through the passage, which it has subsequently made larger *(the arch can be reached along a footpath starting 150m/165yds on the Vallon side of the viewing point).*

Beyond Pont-d'Arc the landscape becomes more impressive still. The river follows a series of gentle meanders, interspersed with rapids, at the bottom of a deserted gorge, 30km/18mi long. The height of the surrounding cliffs – some of them reaching 300m/984ft – together with their rich colouring and dramatic appearance leave a lasting impression.

After Chames the road veers round in a deep curve to the left, at the bottom of Tiourre valley which forms an impressive, rocky **cirque★**, before reaching the edge of the plateau.

★★**Belvédère du Serre de Tourre** – Poised almost vertically above the Ardèche, which flows 200m/656ft below, this viewing point offers a superb **view** of the meander known as the **Pas du Mousse**, with the ruins of the 16C Château d'Ebbo clearly visible on the rocky promontory.

Opposite, the rounded clifftops of the Falaises de Saleyron can be seen. Towering on the horizon, to the right, is the impressive Mont Lozère peak, while to the left stretches the Orgnac plateau.

The broad tourist road follows the tortuous relief of the cliffs on the east bank, running through forests of evergreen oaks, first the Bois Bouchas and then the Bois Malbosc.

★★Belvédères de Gaud – This viewpoint gives a fine view of the upstream sweep of the Gaud meander and the turrets of its small 19C castle.

★Belvédères d'Autridge – To reach the two viewpoints, take the panoramic curve. The needle of rock known as the Aiguille de Morsanne soars up from the Ardèche like the prow of a ship.

500m/550yds beyond a majestic coomb (Combe d'Agrimont), there are splendid **vistas★★** back upriver of the magnificent meander with the Morsanne needle in the foreground.

★Belvédères de Gournier – These viewing points are well situated, 200m/656ft above the Ardèche. Below, Le Gournier farm lies in ruins in a small meadow beside the river, which finds a way through the rocks of la Toupine (*toupine* means "cooking pot").

★Grotte de la Madeleine ⊙ – This cave (discovered in 1887) was carved out by an underground river which once drained part of the Gras plateau. Enter through the Grotte Obscure, then follow a tunnel hewn out of the rock *(steep stairway)*, which leads to the Salle du Chaos, a vast chamber divided into two by a mass of columns coming down from the cave roof. Beyond this lies a vast gallery full of magnificent rock formations: draperies (note the white rock "cascade" between two red drapery stacks), 30m/98ft high sets of "organ pipes", horn-shaped eccentrics, coral-like concretions on the cave walls etc.

Continue to Marzal chasm along the road across the Gras plateau.

★Aven de Marzal ⊙ – *Interior temperature 14°C/57°F; 743 steps.* The chasm is a natural well, which leads to a number of caves. Near the first, the Salle du Tombeau, are the bones of animals which fell into the chasm (bear, deer, bison). The caves are rich in magnificent stalagmites, stalactites and other limestone formations, ranging from brown-ochre to snow-white in colour.

Return to the La Madeleine junction and leave the car in one of the car parks by the Belvédère de la Madeleine.

★★★La Haute Corniche – This, the most outstanding section of the drive, offers breathtaking views of the gorge from a series of viewing points in quick succession.

★Belvédère de la Madeleine – From here there is an imposing view of the Madeleine "fortress", a rocky outcrop blocking the view of the rest of the gorge downstream. These are the highest cliffs of the entire gorge, towering 300m/984ft above the river valley.

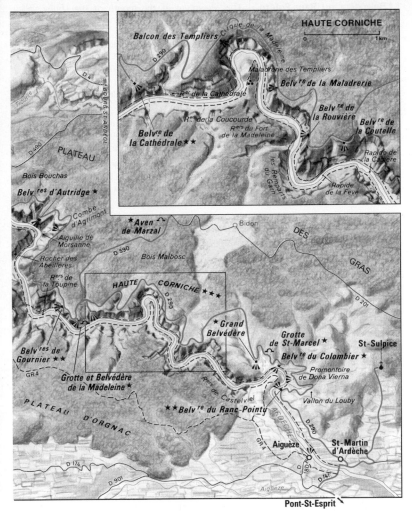

★★Belvédère de la Cathédrale – *15min on foot Rtn*. This lookout point gives an unparalleled view of one of the most fascinating sights along the gorge: an immense jagged rock known as the "Cathédrale", whose rocky spires rise sheer above the river.

Balcon des Templiers – From the "Templars' Balcony" there are striking views of a tight loop in the river, cut deep into the surrounding, magnificent rock walls. Down below, a small spur is crowned by the ruins of a leper hospital *(maladrerie)* established by the Knights Templar.

Belvédère de la Maladrerie – From here there is a good view of the "Cathedral" rock upstream.

Belvédère de la Rouvière – This overlooks the Garn "ramparts" opposite.

Belvédère de la Coutelle – This viewpoint overlooks the Ardèche from a dizzying height of 180m/590ft. To the right is the end of the Garn ramparts; to the left, along the axis of the gorge, are the Castelviel rocks. The Fève and Cadière rapids can also be seen up- and downriver.

★Grand Belvédère – The view from here takes in the exit of the gorge and the final meander of the river.

★Grotte de St-Marcel ⊙ – A tunnel dug through the rock leads into chambers and passageways lined with stalagmites and stalactites in diverse shapes and colours, tinted by calcite, iron oxide, manganese...

★Belvédère du Colombier – From here, there is a lovely view over a meander enclosed by walls entirely of rock.

The road follows a loop along a dry valley, skirts the Dona Vierna promontory and makes a long detour along the Louby valley.

★★Belvédère du Ranc-Pointu – This viewpoint at the mouth of the Louby valley overlooks the last incised meander of the Ardèche. Note the various phenomena caused by erosion: striation, potholes and caves.

From here the landscape changes dramatically on the way down to St-Martin; the bare defile gives way to a cultivated valley which opens out as it gets nearer the Rhône. On the opposite bank, the village of **Aiguèze** *(see below)* can be seen clinging to a rocky crest.

St-Martin-d'Ardèche – This is the first settlement since Vallon.

Chapelle St-Sulpice – *4km/2.5mi northeast via Trignan.* This dazzling white Romanesque chapel (12C-17C) stands isolated on a slight hillock amidst a sea of vines. The south wall is built of re-used stones carved with interlacing designs.

Return to St-Martin and cross the Ardèche via the suspension bridge (pont suspendu).

Pont-St-Esprit – This town owes its name to the 13C-14C bridge, nearly 1 000m/3 280ft long, which spans the Rhône *(see Michelin Green Guide Provence).* Pont-St-Esprit became an important stopping place along the Rhône.

Cirque de la Madeleine

PLATEAU D'ORGNAC (SOUTH BANK)

Local map previous page

Aiguèze – A medieval village with a church with a 16C north doorway and brightly coloured interior decoration typical of the late 19C religious art. The 14C fort has a watchpath which offers fine **views★** of the mouth of the gorge, with Mont Ventoux in the distance and the suspension bridge linking Aiguèze and St-Martin-d'Ardèche in the foreground.

Les Crottes – This ruined village *(partly restored)* was destroyed during the Second World War. A stele commemorates the inhabitants, who were shot by the Nazis on 3 March 1944.

★Aven de la Forestière ⊘ – This cavern, first explored by A. Sonzogni in 1966, was opened to tourists in 1968. It is not far below ground and is easily accessible. The cleverly-lit chambers contain a wealth of fine concretions in interesting shapes and subtle colours. A small underground zoo is home to a variety of fish, shellfish, frogs, toads and insects.

Labastide-de-Virac – This fortified village on the boundary between the Languedoc and Vivarais regions is an ideal departure point for outings to the Aveyron gorge or the Orgnac plateau. Just north of the village stands a 15C castle, the **Château des Roure** ⊘, which guarded the passage through the gorge at the Pont-d'Arc. The two round towers were pulled down in 1629 during the Wars of Religion. Since 1825, the castle has belonged to the family of sculptor James Pradier (1795-1825; he carved the statues representing Lille and Strasbourg on the Place de la Concorde in Paris), whose forebears were tenant farmers to the Counts of Roure. The tour takes in the Florentine courtyard, a spiral staircase and the great hall with its fine chimneypiece. The castle watchpath overlooks the Ardèche and Gras plateaus, and in clear weather Mont Lozère and Mont Mézenc can be seen to the north. The tour ends with an exhibition of hand-made silk goods. A working silkworm farm illustrates traditional methods of silkworm breeding.

★★Belvédère du Méandre de Gaud – This promontory commands an excellent **view★★** of the Ardèche and the Gaud cirque.

★★★Aven d'Orgnac – See Aven d'ORGNAC.

A new shrine to Prehistory

At the end of 1994, a set of cave paintings and engravings of exceptional interest was discovered on the site of the Combe-d'Arc in the Ardèche gorge. Part of a vast network of underground galleries, the cave (named the **Grotte Chauvet** after the man who discovered it) features almost 300 black or red paintings and as many engravings on its walls. These depict a variety of animals, including horses, mammoths, bears, woolly rhinoceroses, cats and aurochs; figures of a hyena and an owl are also portrayed, which is exceptionally rare. Geometrical motifs and outlines of hands – both positive and reversed-out – appear alongside these figures, in which the artists' skill is reflected by the accuracy of their draughtsmanship and the way they have managed to portray movement and relief.

Initial studies of these works of art date them from the Upper Palaeolithic Age, about 30 000 years before our time. The number, quality and originality of these animal paintings place the Vallon-Pont-d'Arc on a level with the Cosquer cave discovered in the *calanques* east of Marseille and the Lascaux cave in the Dordogne, in terms of the importance of their contribution to the study of cave paintings worldwide. Furthermore, as the cave has remained untouched since the Palaeolithic Age, it constitutes an enormous potential site of investigation for palaeontologists, who will analyse the bones of bear-like mammals found scattered in the cave, and for archaeologists, who will use the numerous artefacts and other evidence (fire-places, chipped flints, footprints etc.) to be found on the site to learn more about the activities of our ancestors.

For the time being, only specialists are allowed into the cave; but eventually some kind of reproduction is planned (much as at Lascaux) so that the cave's hidden treasures can be admired by all interested parties. In the mean time, there is an exhibition on the wonders to be found in Grotte Chauvet and other caves of the Ardèche valley in the Rue Miarou in Vallon-Pont-d'Arc.

★★★FOLLOWING THE ARDÈCHE ON FOOT OR BY BOAT

From Pont-d'Arc to St-Martin-d'Ardèche

On foot ⊙ – Only the south bank, leaving from Salavas or Aiguèze, offers the possibility of a "dry" walk. Taking the path along the north bank, leaving from St-Martin or Chames, involves crossing two fords, passable only when the water level is low.

By boat or canoe ⊙ – The river can be explored by boat or canoe from March to late November, although the best time is in May and June.
After a long, calm stretch, the river flows into a bend and enters the gorge. To the right, the entrance to the Ebbo cave comes into sight, followed by the Pas du Mousse rock, a narrow passage in the cliff leading to the plateau; to the left stands the Aiguille rock. After passing the foot of the tall Saleyron cliffs, the river forms some rapids, the Rapide de la Dent Noire, before reaching the sweeping Gaud meander and cirque marked by the small castle. Rapids alternate with smooth-flowing stretches beneath impressive cliffs. Note the Morsanne needle to the left and the jagged red and black Rocher des Abeillières to the right. After negotiating the boulders and cauldrons of the Toupine de Gournier – where the river bed is 18m/60ft deep in places – the Rocher de la Cathédrale comes into view in the distance *(after about 4hr on the river)*. Just before you actually pass this rock, the river takes you past one of the natural openings into La Madeleine cave.
The stretch of river at the foot of the Rochers de la Madeleine, passing beneath towering cliffs, is one of the most beautiful along the river. The river forms straits, rapids and limpid reaches as it passes between bare rock faces which contrast strongly with the evergreen oaks of the surrounding countryside. Downriver of the strange-looking Coucourde rock (Provençal for "crane") and the Castelvieil cliff, the opening of St-Marcel cave comes into sight on the left and, as you round a bend,

the Dona Vierna promontory and the Belvédère du Ranc-Pointu can be seen. The cliffs melt away as the valley finally widens out, overlooked by the tower of Aiguèze on the edge of the rocky outcrop to the right.

Some tips for those exploring the gorge on foot or by boat:

Canoeists should note that hire of canoes is withdrawn if the water level rises above 0.8m/3ft beneath the Salavas bridge. Before embarking upon a walk along the gorge, it is advisable to check the water levels to be sure of being able to cross the fords safely.

The Ardèche nature reserve is a conservation area, so every effort should be made to protect its ecosystem. In particular, visitors are forbidden to light a fire, leave behind garbage, pick plants and stray from the waymarked footpaths. Camping or bivouacking are prohibited outside authorised camp sites.

Vallée de l'ARDÈCHE ★

Michelin maps 76 south of folds 17 to 19 and 80 folds 8 and 9, or 239 folds 47 and 48 and 240 folds 4 and 8

The upper and middle valley of the River Ardèche offers a wide variety of landscapes and sights, including rocky slopes, flows of basalt, sun-drenched basins planted with orchards and vineyards, medieval ruins, hilltop villages and steep passes. Further downriver, the impetuous Ardèche has carved its famous gorge in the limestone of the lowlands *(see Gorges de l'ARDÈCHE)*.

Profile of the River – From its source in the Mazan hills, the Ardèche flows downhill particularly steeply along its upper reaches. Over the first 24km/15mi of its course, the Ardèche drops a massive 40m per km/220ft per mile. Initially heading southeast, the Ardèche turns south just east of Aubenas. There is evidence that the Ardèche originally flowed straight on to the Rhône along the southern edge of the Coiron plateau, but after the last volcanic eruptions in the Quaternary era, it seems to have been displaced to its current course by a more southerly river. The original course of the Ardèche valley is still visible between Mirabel and St-Jean-le-Centenier.

The Ardèche starts life as a mountain stream tumbling downhill at the foot of forbidding cliffs. The scenery changes at Thueyts; a vast orchard blossoms on a thick flow of basalt which once flowed down from Gravenne de Montpezat, at the foot of which the river enters a gorge. After this the Ardèche crosses the Aubenas basin, where the quality of the light, the colours and the flora bring a foretaste of the south of France. The Vogüé cliffs, eroded into strange shapes, mark the start of a series of limestone gorges interspersed by basins.

★HAUTE VALLÉE DE L'ARDÈCHE

① From Col de la Chavade to Aubenas

42km/26mi – allow 1 day – local map opposite

Col de la Chavade – Alt 1 266m/4 115ft. This pass marks the watershed between the Atlantic Ocean and the Mediterranean. A few mountain farms are to be found nearby.

The N 102 between Le Puy and Viviers follows the traditional route from the Velay area to the Rhône valley. The horizontal lines of the sloping plateau *(planèze)* are abruptly broken by the dip down into the Ardèche valley. Just over a mile beyond the pass, the road crosses the Ardèche river, which cascades down on the left.

The drive, which is quite hilly, offers particularly beautiful views down the valley, overlooked from the right by the rounded summit of the Croix de Bauzon and the jagged outline of Abraham's rock.

The harshness of this mountain valley is softened by a few sunny orchards surrounding the villages, by rambling plants on house fronts and retaining walls, and by ancient humpback bridges used by travellers in the Middle Ages. Adding to the interest of the drive, the road passes the ruins of feudal castles: **Château des Montlaur** upstream of Mayres, the tall round tower of **Château de Chadenac** downstream of Mayres and, on reaching Pont-de-Labeaume, **Château de Ventadour**, a medieval fortress in ruins, part of which have now been restored.

Mayres – This village lies in a wooded gorge.

1km/0.6 mile downstream of Mayres, a footbridge over the Ardèche offers an attractive **view★** of the village and the upper valley.

★**Thueyts** – This small town surrounded by orchards lies on a thick and impressive basalt flow, the remains of an ancient volcanic eruption. Business locally consists mainly of a fruit market, various workshops, and quarrying building stone. The **viewpoint** off the N 102 to the east of town *(car park)* offers a good view of the lava flow and the Pont du Diable ("Devil's Bridge") in the valley below. A **waymarked footpath★** *(1hr 30min Rtn; follow the red arrows)* leads along the edge of the lava flow. Just upstream of the Pont du Diable, the Ardèche flows through a narrow gorge, making an interesting **scene★** against the dark backdrop of the basalt cliffs. Two sets of steps – the **Échelle du Roi** *(narrow, steep and can be slippery)* and the **Échelle de la Reine** *(easier, allow an extra 30min Rtn)* – lead up to the top of the basalt cliffs, from where there is a good view of the river valley.

On leaving Thueyts on the N 102, there is a view of the valley and the Montagne Ste-Marguérite towering to the north.

✦ **Neyrac-les-Bains** – This small spa town known to the Romans backs onto the slopes of the Soulhiol volcano. In the Middle Ages its bicarbonated hot springs were thought to cure leprosy.

At the exit of Pont-de-Labeaume turn left following signs to Notre-Dame de Niègles; the road drops into a valley before reaching a plateau. Park the car down on the right.

Notre-Dame de Niègles – The church stands on a hill overlooking the river. Little remains of the original 10C building owing to subsequent additions and alterations. The building has an 18C doorway and an 11C apse. The church interior *(under restoration)* is lit through circular windows, or oculi. There is a pretty little graveyard in front of the church.

The road back to Pont-de-Labeaume gives some good views of the medieval fortress of Ventadour *(under restoration)*.

✦✦ **Vals-les-Bains** – *See VALS-LES-BAINS.*

Labégude – The Ardèche flows right by a glassworks in this village.

The D 104 leads to Aubenas.

Aubenas – *See AUBENAS.*

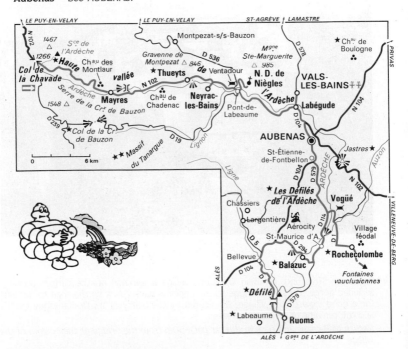

★DÉFILÉS DE L'ARDÈCHE

② From Aubenas to Ruoms

44km/27mi – about 2hr – local map above

The light-filled Ardèche valley forms a wide dip stretching to the basin of the lower Chassezac in the west. The river flows through a succession of fertile basins, in which its green waters contrast strikingly with the light-coloured gravel and golden sand of the river banks, and steep-sided ravines.

Aubenas – *See AUBENAS.*

Take the D 104 from Aubenas to St-Étienne-de-Fontbellon, then turn left into the D 579.

Here the road runs close to the river, in between orchards and vineyards.

Vogüé – The village of ancient, arch-spanned streets dominated by a castle is built against a cliff overlooking the Ardèche. The vast 16C **château** ⊘, which still belongs to the Vogüé family, replaced the original medieval fortress and now houses exhibitions on the Vivarais region throughout the ages, as well as cultural events.

★**Rochecolombe** – *5.5km/3mi south of Vogüé.* The medieval village of Roche-colombe occupies a secluded **site**★ overlooking a small, clear stream rising from the bottom of a limestone corrie. There are in fact two villages of Rochecolombe; the upper one is the first reached by road, with houses grouped around a church built in 1858. From the square in the upper village, turn left into a small tarmacked road down towards a bridge across the stream. Park a little further along, just before a bend, and follow the footpath down to the water's edge. On the right stands the **medieval village**, at the foot of the ruins of a square tower and the charming bell tower of a Romanesque chapel. At the bottom of the corrie, which is enclosed by tall limestone cliffs with wild scrub clinging to their ledges, are two vauclusian **springs**.

Return towards Vogüé on the D 579 and turn left onto the D 114 after crossing the Ardèche.

In Lanas, the road crosses the river over a narrow bridge, offering an attractive view of the point where the Auzon flows into the Ardèche.

In St-Maurice-d'Ardèche turn right onto the D 579, then right onto the D 294 just after the station in Balazuc.

The road climbs uphill, giving a **view**★ of the basin in the shadow of the Coiron.

Balazuc

★**Balazuc** – This once-fortified limestone village is perched on the clifftop above a secluded gorge. Cross the bridge to the opposite bank *(park by the road to the left)* for a good view of the village, dominated by the belfry of its Romanesque church and the remains of its watchtowers.

Return to Balazuc and park in the car park 50m from the bridge at the bottom of the village.

Like many other villages in the Lower Vivarais area, Balazuc was settled by a Saracen colony in the 8C and 9C. It now makes a pleasant place for a stroll, particularly in the old streets leading up to the castle, which are bright with flowers in season. For a pleasant walk downstream along the banks of the Ardèche, take the dirt track to the left of the bridge at the foot of the village. Here the river flows through a narrow passage between walls of rock. On the cliffs on the right bank stand the ruins of Reine Jeanne tower.

From the road up to the top of the plateau on the west bank there is a **view**★ of the entire gorge. From the arid, rocky plateau (where only boxwood and juniper thrive) the road winds its way down to Uzer in the valley; opposite, the hills around Largentière and one of the towers in the village of Montréal can be seen, against a backdrop of the Cham du Cros and Tanargue ranges to the northwest and Mont Lozère summit just visible to the southwest.

Take the D 104 to Uzer; on reaching Bellevue, take the D 4 to Ruoms.

The entrance to the Ligne gorge is marked by a narrow rocky passage. A beautiful **view** unfolds upstream of the Ardèche at the confluence of the two rivers in the shadow of cliffs almost 100m/325ft high. The regularity of the rock strata makes them a particularly striking sight.

The Ligne gorge is followed by the **Défilé de Ruoms★**, alongside which the road passes through picturesque tunnels in the rock. In between, it looks down onto the clear green waters of the river. Just beyond the tunnels, straight ahead further along the valley, the domed outline of the Sampzon rock comes into view.

Take the bridge on the left to Ruoms.

Ruoms – The old walled centre of this town lies within a quadrilateral of ramparts flanked by seven round towers. The Romanesque church has an unusual arcaded belfry decorated with inlaid motifs made of volcanic rock.

West of Ruoms lies **Labeaume★**, an attractive village at the edge of a gorge, with arcaded streets and galleried houses.

The fascinating countryside along the Ardèche valley can be explored in a number of ways. It is possible to hire a canoe from Aubenas or Vogüé to Vallon-Pont-d'Arc, and footpaths have been laid out for ramblers and cross-country cyclists. Alternative amusements include parks like that of Aérocity near Aubenas.

ARLEMPDES ★

Population 142
Michelin map 76 fold 17 or 239 fold 46
Local map under Gorges de la LOIRE

Arlempdes occupies one of the most striking **sites★★** in the Velay area. Perched on a spur of volcanic rock, the ruins of a medieval castle overlook the Loire gorge from a height of 80m/260ft.

Village – The village huddling below the castle boasts a fortified 11C gate and a charming **church** ⊙. On the small square in front of the church stands a beautiful 15C cross decorated with figures.

Castle ⊙ – *15min Rtn on foot. Follow the path to the left of the church, leading under an arch to the entrance gate.*

Arlempdes

The castle was built by the lords of Montlaur in the 13C and, despite its impregnable position, has been sacked on numerous occasions. At the very top of the rock outcrop are the remains of a small chapel built of red volcanic rock. From the east end of the chapel there is an impressive **view**★★ over the Loire gorge.

The north wall with its well-preserved merlons and battlements overlooks the magnificent basalt lava flows on the opposite bank. From the foot of the right-hand tower there is a view down into the Loire valley lying at the foot of a striking basalt needle.

★VOLCANIC PLATEAUX

Various local villages are built on or of volcanic stone. A half-day tour of this region would take in **St-Paul-de-Tartas** *(south via the D 54 and D 500)* with its Romanesque church built of purplish volcanic rock; the attractive, once-fortified village of **Pradelles** *(south)*, with a **local museum** ⊘ in one of the houses with Renaissance windows on the market square, and the **Musée Vivant du Cheval de Trait** ⊘ (draught-horse museum) housed in a 19C inn; the Romanesque church at **Lespéron** *(south-west of Pradelles)*, an interesting example of a mountain sanctuary; the **Auberge de Peyrebeille** *(northeast, via Lavillatte, on the N 102)*, an inn with a gruesome history; and the church with a Romanesque doorway at **Coucouron** *(north of the inn via the D 16)*.

Return to Arlempdes on the D 298 as far as the D 500, onto which you turn right and then immediately left onto the D 54.

ARS-SUR-FORMANS

Population 851
Michelin map 88 fold 7 or 244 south of fold 3 – Local map under La DOMBES

This tiny Dombes village was once the spiritual charge of the priest **Jean-Marie Vianney** (1786-1859), who was canonised in 1925. The "priest of Ars" subsequently became the patron saint of parish priests and the village has therefore become a popular place of pilgrimage *(see Calendar of events at the end of the guide)*.

Pilgrimage – The small village church is now abutted by a basilica built in 1862 to plans by Pierre Bossan. Inside, the saint's body reposes in a magnificent shrine. The bare concrete crypt, built half underground and 55m/179ft long, is the work of one of the architects of the basilica dedicated to St Pius X in Lourdes.

The old **presbytery** ⊘ has been kept as it was when the priest of Ars died. Visitors can see the kitchen, the priest's bedroom and the "relics room", containing mementoes of the priest. An audio-visual show in a room by the presbytery gives an insight into the saint's personality. The **Chapelle du Cœur** houses a repository which contains the priest's heart, and a marble statue by the sculptor Emilien Cabuchet (1819-1902) showing the priest at prayer.

The largest annual pilgrimage takes place on 4 August, the anniversary of the priest's death.

L'Historial ⊘ – Thirty-five waxworks figures, made by the workshops of the Musée Grévin (Paris's answer to Madame Tussaud's), are displayed in a series of 17 tableaux illustrating scenes from the life of the saintly priest.

L'ARTENSE

Michelin maps 73 folds 12 and 13 and 76 folds 2 and 3 or
239 folds 17, 18, 29 and 30

The Artense, a granite plateau southwest of the Monts Dore in the wedge formed by the Dordogne and Rhue rivers, is cut across by the Tarentaine, a tributary of the Rhue which rises in the Puy de Sancy. Early in the Quaternary era the plateau was covered with vast glaciers which slid down from the Monts Dore and from the mountains in Cantal and the Cézallier region. The glaciers left behind marked reminders of their existence, giving this region its highly unusual appearance: a greatly varied relief with peaks some 50-100m/1 612-3 250ft high separated by small basins that are now lakes, peat bogs or marshy grasslands; and large rocks in which the weight of the slow-moving mass of ice carved deep grooves. The Artense is graced by charming copses in a landscape typical of the Auvergne, although the region was long known for the poverty of its soil. Local inhabitants continue to cultivate rye as they did in the past but new methods have enabled them to introduce barley and oats and, more recently, maize. The marshes are gradually being drained, making it possible to breed red Salers cattle, more and more frequently sharing their pastures with black-and-white Friesians. Most of the milk produced by these cattle is used to make Cantal cheese and particularly the local blue cheese, Bleu d'Auvergne. Farm production of St-Nectaire cheese is another major source of income.

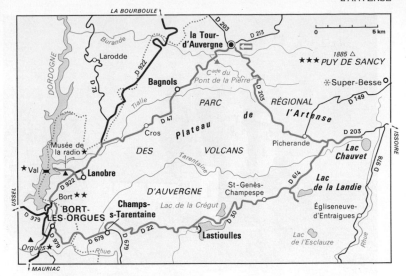

IN BETWEEN THE DORES AND CANTAL MOUNTAINS

Round trip leaving from La Tour-d'Auvergne

85km/53mi – allow 3hr – local map above

La Tour-d'Auvergne – *See Monts DORE.*

The road to Bagnols passes the foot of the tumultuous Pont-de-la-Pierre waterfall on the left.

Bagnols – This village lies in the Tialle valley, an undulating region of meadows and copses.

Beyond Cros, the road winds down into the Tialle valley.

Lanobre – The 12C church here is a good example of the Romanesque style typical of the Upper Auvergne.

At the junction of the D 922 and the road to the Château de Val stands a radio museum.

★Musée de la Radio et du Phonographe ⊙ – This Radio and Phonograph Museum displays more than 400 working appliances: late-19C cylinder phonographs, record players from 1898 to 1930, cylinder recorders, radios (coherer and crystal sets, receivers with external lamps dating from 1895 to 1930, "mains" radios from 1928 to 1940 etc) and such items as Grenet's cell battery (1845), barrel organs, harmoniums, bar pianos...

The collection is accompanied by information panels *(in French)*, posters and documents. A few of the old appliances are switched on to give visitors a chance to compare the developments and progress in audio techniques.

★Château de Val ⊙ – Since the reservoir and dam at Bort became operational, the **setting★★** in which the Château de Val stands is extremely picturesque. When the reservoir is full, the castle stands fairly and squarely on a rocky island which can only be reached across a narrow dike *(photograph overleaf)*.

Walk a little way to the left for a charming view of the château, which dates from the 15C. The exterior, with its charming pepper-pot towers, is highly evocative of the elegance of the period the château was built.

The interior *(paintings displayed on the 2nd floor)* features some fine staircases and two magnificent Renaissance fireplaces. The chapel of St-Blaise houses a regional tourist information centre. A watchpath runs beneath the eaves.

At the foot of the castle are a beach *(lifeguards in attendance)*, a watersports centre and an embarkation point for **boat trips** ⊙ along the Dordogne valley.

Bort-les-Orgues – *See BORT-LES-ORGUES.*

Turn left onto the D 979 which, as it climbs the hillside, provides some wonderful views of the columnar basalt around Bort.

Champs-sur-Tarentaine – This holiday resort huddles in a wooded valley near the confluence of the Rhue and Tarentaine rivers.

Turn left into the D 22, a pretty road winding across the plateau.

Château de Val

Barrage de Lastioulles – This huge arch-dam is part of the hydroelectrical engineering works along the upper Tarentaine.

The road runs alongside the reservoir, passes La Crégut lake on the left and then goes through St-Genès-Champespe.

Lac de la Landie – This lake is surrounded by peaceful meadows and woodlands.

Continue along the D 614 then take the D 203 on the right to Lac Chauvet.

Lac Chauvet – *See Monts DORE.*

Return to La Tour-d'Auvergne via Picherande, the starting point of a picturesque route up to Super-Besse (winter sports resort) on the right.

AUBENAS

Population 11 105
Michelin map 76 fold 19 or 246 fold 21
Local map under Vallée de l'ARDÈCHE
Town plan in the current Michelin Red Guide France

Aubenas stands in an impressive **setting★**, perched on a spur of rock overlooking the Ardèche. The roads hugging the Coiron cliffs to the east reveal a wonderful **view** of the valley below. Aubenas is known for its *marrons glacés* (candied chestnuts) and jam.

A local peasant revolt – Following the bitter winter of 1669-70 which killed all the local olive trees, rumours of new taxes fuelled deep-seated dissatisfaction. On 30 April 1670 a farm inspector was stoned in Aubenas; the ringleader of the attackers was thrown into prison, but the rioters, led by a country squire from Chapelle-sous-Aubenas, **Antoine du Roure**, effected his release the very next day. While the governor of Languedoc played for time by holding negotiations, Roure's men captured Aubenas. Towards the end of July, the rebels fought the royal army at Lavilledieu. The peasants were massacred, and Roure was subsequently executed in Montpellier. Aubenas and La Chapelle were condemned to pay heavy fines, as a reflection of royal wrath.

SIGHTS

Château ⊙ – *Place de l'Hôtel-de-Ville.* The oldest parts of this fine building date from the 12C. The castle was gradually enlarged and embellished by a succession of illustrious families, among them the Montlaurs, the Ornanos and the Vogüés.
The main façade, flanked by machicolated round towers, became the main entrance in the 18C following the addition of two large, pedimented doorways. Decorative glazed tiles (such as those found in Burgundy) brighten up the building, which is crowned by a 12C keep with bartizans. The inner courtyard is adorned with 15C turrets, encasing spiral staircases, and a beautiful 18C staircase; the **panelled and furnished rooms** exude the charming atmosphere of an 18C mansion. In one room, works by the Symbolist painter Chaurand-Neyrac (1878-1948) are on display.

Dôme St-Benoît ⊙ – *Place de la Grenette, northwest of town centre.* This hexagonal building is the former Benedictine chapel of Aubenas (17C-18C). The marshal of Ornano and his wife are buried in the mausoleum inside (dating from 1640).

Old houses – The 16C "House of Gargoyles" stands opposite the château; its tall polygonal turret is decorated with magnificent gargoyles and there are attractive, mullioned windows adorning the façade. There is a charming 16C staircase-turret in the courtyard of the "Maison de Castrevieille" in Place Parmentier; handsome town houses line Rue Jourdan. Delightful little arches span Rue Delichères.

Église St-Laurent – *Rue Delichères, far end from Château.* The chancel contains a group of three carved wooden altarpieces in the Jesuit style. The church also boasts a beautifully-carved wooden pulpit dating from the 17C.

Viewing table – *Near the Tourist Office.* The view extends over Mont Ste-Marguerite, the Vals gap, Gourdon rock, Escrinet pass and the mountain ridges of the Coiron.

EXCURSIONS

★**Jastres panorama** – *7.5km/5mi via the N 102 southeast. 4km/2.5mi beyond the bridge over the Ardèche, turn left into the access road to an industrial estate. After 200m, turn right into a tarred road. After 1km/0.6mi turn left into a rocky uphill road. Park at the top.*
The edge of the plateau *(30min Rtn on foot)* was the site of a prehistoric settlement. Where the road ends, the view encompasses the entire Lower Ardèche, the Aubenas valley, and the Coiron range to the northeast.

Aérocity ⊙ – *10km/6mi south via the D 104.* This amusement park has numerous attractions including trails, games areas and rides on the theme of flight.

AURILLAC ★

Population 30 773
Michelin map 76 fold 12 or 239 fold 41 – Local map under Monts du CANTAL

Aurillac, the business and tourist capital of Upper Auvergne, is a modern town that has grown up around an old neighbourhood with narrow, winding streets.

Gerbert, the first French Pope (10C-11C) – Aurillac's Gallo-Roman origins were brought to light by the discovery of a 1C temple (Rue Jacques-Prévert, reached from Avenue Milhaud, **AZ**). In the 9C St Gerald, Count of Auvergne, built an abbey, laying the foundations for the city's future prosperity; this abbey gave Christianity its first French Pope. Gerbert, a shepherd in the Aurillac area, attracted the attention of the monks of St-Géraud, who quickly taught this unusually bright student everything they knew. After completing his studies at the abbey, Gerbert left for Spain where he studied medicine and mathematics at the Moorish universities. According to certain authors, it was Gerbert who introduced the use of Arabic numerals into the western world. He built the first pendulum clock, invented an astrolabe for sailors and improved the church organ. His extensive knowledge brought him to the attention of Emperor Otto, who appointed him private tutor to his son. Gerbert, a theologian steeped in classical culture, was the driving force behind the Ottonian renaissance. In AD 999 he became Pope under the name Sylvester II. He was the "Pope of the Millenium", who managed to impose the "Truce of God" – whereby hostilities were suspended on certain days and during certain seasons – on the feudal classes.

Gold-washers – According to Gerbert's contemporaries, his knowledge smacked of witchcraft. The gold flakes found in the River Jordanne were popularly ascribed to his spells.
The gold industry was born, but remained fairly primitive: flakes of gold were collected by holding a fleece in the water to trap them.
In the 14C a new process was invented by a certain **Jean de la Roquetaillade**, who had been brought up as a child by a gold-washer and has then taken Holy Orders at the abbey of St-Géraud: he covered slanted boards with coarse cloth which then caught the gold flakes in its weave.
Brother Jean, besides being an inspired preacher, also possessed powers of prophecy. Four centuries in advance, he forecast the ruin of the clergy and nobility, and the fall of the monarchy. The church authorities did not appreciate predictions of this kind and Brother Jean was jailed by his bishop. When he nonetheless reoffended, the Pope imprisoned him for four years in the dungeons of Avignon.

Baron des Adrets (16C) – The people of Aurillac remained at odds with their lord, the abbot, but finally managed to obtain administrative autonomy, as the consuls' residence (Maison consulaire) proves.

AURILLAC

The town was flourishing when it became swept up in the Wars of Religion. In 1561 the governor ordered the slaughter of the large local Protestant population. They were avenged eight years later by the Baron des Adrets, a Protestant leader notorious for his brutality. His men began by swooping down on the monasteries on the outskirts of the town, burning or flaying the monks alive. On the night of 6 September 1569 the Huguenots blew up the town gate and burst their way in on the slumbering citizens, who were caught entirely unawares and so put up minimal resistance. All the town's main buildings were burned to the ground.

In 1581 the Protestants returned but were repelled, so the story goes, by the miraculous intervention of the Virgin Mary. To commemorate this event, the towns-people built the Chapelle d'Aurinques *(see below)*.

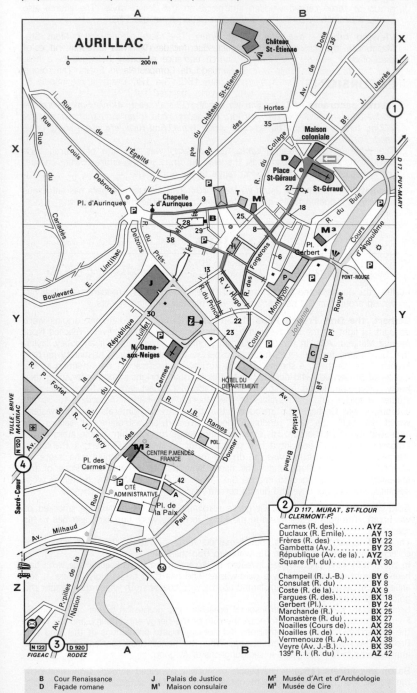

Carmes (R. des) .... **AYZ**
Duclaux (R. Émile)....... **AY** 13
Frères (R. des) .... **BY** 22
Gambetta (Av.).......... **BY** 23
République (Av. de la).. **AYZ**
Square (Pl. du) .... **AY** 30

Champeil (R. J.-B.) ..... **BY** 6
Consulat (R. du)........ **BY** 8
Coste (R. de la)......... **AX** 9
Fargues (R. des)........ **BX** 18
Gerbert (Pl.)............ **BY** 24
Marchande (R.) .... **BX** 25
Monastère (R. du) ...... **BX** 27
Noailles (Cours de) ..... **AX** 28
Noailles (R. de) .... **AX** 29
Vermenouze (R. A.)...... **AX** 38
Veyre (Av. J.-B.)........ **BX** 39
139ᵉ R. I. (R. du) .... **AZ** 42

B	Cour Renaissance	J	Palais de Justice	M²	Musée d'Art et d'Archéologie
D	Façade romane	M¹	Maison consulaire	M³	Musée de Cire

74

From lace to umbrellas – Aubenas was struggling to recover from these events for many years, until Colbert founded a laceworks which doubled as a gold and silver smithy. This entrepreneur also encouraged other industries, such as boiler-making and tanning, which have since declined. Modern Aurillac's economy is based on agriculture and the manufacture of furniture, cheese, plastics and umbrellas.

In the last two centuries Aurillac has contributed several major figures to history: General Delzons, who fought in Napoleon's Russian campaign; de Parieu, a government minister; Emile Duclaux, the biochemist who was Pasteur's assistant; Arsène Vermenouze, an author who wrote in the dialect of Southern France; Paul Doumer, the French President assassinated in 1934; and, more recently, the surgeon and writer Professor Henri Mondor.

OLD TOWN

Place St-Géraud (**BX**) – The Romanesque façade (**D**) with arcades and colonettes which stands opposite the church entrance probably belonged to a hospice for pilgrims on their way to Santiago de Compostela in Spain. The colonial house on the left dates from the late 15C. The 12C basin in the middle of the square is made of serpentine, a dark, marbled rock. The east end of the church overlooks the old graveyard where some ancient sarcophagi can be seen.

Église Saint-Géraud (**BX**) – This old abbey church shows traces of a long and complex architectural evolution. It was founded in the late 9C by Count Gerald and became a stop-over for pilgrims on their way to Santiago de Compostela. Enlarged in the 10C and again in the 11C, it then underwent extensive alteration from 1530 to 1536. In 1569 it was destroyed by the Protestants, at that time the masters of Aurillac. Charles de Noailles, Bishop of St-Flour, rebuilt it in the first half of the 17C. Its walls were made higher and Gothic vaulting was added. The remains of the earlier Romanesque constructions were hidden under a roughcast finish. In 1794 the Romanesque tower over the narthex was demolished. 19C architects added the last two bays in the nave and the steeple. The restoration work carried out from 1965 to 1972 revealed some interesting Romanesque remains.

The nave has a balanced and unified appearance owing to its size and the perspective created by its pillars, rising straight to the lierne and tierceron vaulting. The stoups are made of two Romanesque capitals. The organ loft contains a large 18C organ.

In the north transept, a walled-up Romanesque window has been discovered; an 18C Pietà stands in a niche at the back. The **chapel of St-Géraud** contains beautiful stone fragments: two carved Romanesque slabs, one of which is decorated with animals back to back, capitals with with palm-leaf and interlaced motifs; a pre-Romanesque sculpture supporting a reliquary is decorated with a scene from the story of Samson. The 18C statue of St Gerald is made of gilded wood.

On the end wall in the south arm of the transept is a major decorative feature from the 11C building – a triple arch with a pointed arch in the centre. The chapel of Notre-Dame-du-Cœur (Our Lady of the Heart) has 15C vaulting and beautiful wooden panelling from the early 20C.

The canopied high altar in the chancel is made of multi-coloured marble and dates from 1762.

Walk down Rue du Monastère and Rue des Forgerons and turn right into Rue Victor-Hugo.

On reaching the 19C Hôtel de Ville (**BY H**), follow Rue Vermenouze to Place d'Aurinques. The **Chapelle d'Aurinques** (**AX**), built at the end of the 16C in a tower in the city wall, was completed in the 19C by an upper chapel.

Follow Rue de la Coste.

No 7 in Rue de Noailles on the right has a Renaissance courtyard (**B**) *(access through Cours de Noailles).*

Return to Rue de la Coste.

No 4 in Rue du Consulat has a staircase tower.

Maison consulaire (**BX M¹**) – This Renaissance building has been restored and turned into an exhibition hall. Note the sculptures adorning the door on Rue de la Coste.

Continue to Place Gerbert.

Musée de cire (Waxworks museum) (**BY M³**) ⊙ – A dozen or so scenes bring to life the events and personalities who left their mark on the history of Aurillac.

View of the Jordanne (**BY**) – The old houses along the River Jordanne can be seen from a spot near Pont Rouge bridge and Cours d'Angoulême. The square boasts a statue of Pope Silvester II by David d'Angers.

Houses on the banks of the Jordanne

ADDITIONAL SIGHTS

Château St-Étienne (BX) – The castle keep dates from the 13C; the rest of the buildings date mostly from the late 19C. The upper terrace offers a magnificent view of the Jordanne valley and the Cantal mountains, as well as of Aurillac in its valley. An exhibition centre and a museum have been set up in the château.

Musée des Sciences de la Maison des Volcans ⊘ – During restoration work, this museum is nonetheless hosting an exhibition on ecology and its implications for the flora, fauna, summer pastures and cheese-making huts of the Cantal mountains.

The castle also houses a permanent information centre on the environment of the Upper Auvergne.

Musée d'Art et Archéologie (AZ M²) ⊘ – The **Art and Archaeology Museum**, housed in the former Visitandines convent (17C), is part of the Carmelite Cultural Centre.

First floor – The museum evokes lifestyles and housing in Cantal from the earliest days of human settlement until the 19C. The visit begins with a reconstruction of the inside of a typical Cantal house, complete with a light and sound display. The museum collections built up from local excavations include a remarkable series of Palaeolithic bifaces, and tools from the Mesolithic (from the site at Cuze de Neussargues) and Neolithic (notably polished bifaced axes and flints from Mur-de-Barrez) Ages. There are also objects from burial mounds (painted ceramics and arms from the Iron Age).

The collection from the Gallo-Roman period includes objects found during the excavation of the Aron temple in Aurillac, including a 1C **tomb** with a glass urn in perfect condition. The collection from medieval times includes all the furnishings found at Chastel-sur-Murat, a settlement that was occupied continuously from the Neolithic Age until the Renaissance. An information centre contains computer records on the museum collections which can be consulted.

Second floor – This floor is given over to art collections.

Paintings: 17C French, Dutch and Italian schools, French painters from the second half of the 18C (Nattier, Joseph Vernet, Verhulst), "official" 19C painters (Cabanel, Richard, Couture) and contemporary painters (Boutet de Monvel, Lebourg and Lebasque).

Sculpture: *Napoleon* by Chaudet, *Victor Hugo* by Rodin (plaster), *Rodin* by Camille Claudel (bronze), *A Peasant from Abruzzi* by Landowski (bronze).

Two rooms are reserved for rotating exhibitions by well-known international photographers (Callahan, Fontana, Sandek).

A museum annexe in the stables (*Écuries*) houses exhibitions on painting, sculpture and photography.

Église Notre-Dame-aux-Neiges (AY) – This chapel, once part of a 14C Franciscan monastery, was rebuilt in the 17C. A chapel on the left contains a widely revered Black Virgin from the 18C. The sacristy in the Gothic style is in the old chapter house, where the pointed vaulting is supported by two columns. This room gives access to an elegant 15C chapel; note the fine Renaissance lectern.

Palais de Justice (AY J) ⊘ – The Assizes Chamber in the Law Courts contains three 17C Flemish tapestries.

Église du Sacré-Cœur ⊘ – *Reached via Avenue de la République, ④ on the town plan.* This church was built from 1935 to 1937 and is remarkable for the simplicity of its architecture and the harmony of its proportions. Note the unusual Stations of the Cross, forming a frieze along a white stone string-course.

EXCURSION

Château de Conros – *5km/3mi southwest. Leave Aurillac by ③ on the town plan, the N 122, and turn left beyond the airfield onto the D 17 to Marcolès. See Château de CONROS.*

AUZON

Population 920
Michelin map 76 fold 5 or 239 fold 32

Auzon's dramatic **setting★** on a sheer-sided spur of rock overlooking the valley of the river which shares its name is best appreciated when seen from the D 5 coming from the Allier valley. This old fortified town still has many traces of its ramparts and castle.

Church – *30min.* The narrow streets and alleys of the old town lead to an open square on which a fortified church stands, built on a rock, on the site of a 5C church from which the stone altar and font have survived.

The building has a beautiful Romanesque east end and a solid porch with sculpted capitals. The gate still has its 12C iron strap hinges and strips of leather. Inside, on the right of the nave, is an interesting white stone statue of St Peter (late 15C). To the left of the entrance to the chancel is a 12C wooden reliquary of Christ. A small two-storey chapel opposite the entrance, entirely decorated with 14C murals, houses a graceful 15C statue of **Our Lady of the Portal★★**, made of white stone. The church contains many old statues and an unusual 15C organ loft.

Écomusée du pays d'Auzon ⊘ – All the items in this regional museum (exhibitions on traditional arts and crafts, minerals etc) have been given or lent by people living in Auzon or in the region.

Gorges d'AVÈZE★

Michelin map 73 fold 12 or 239 folds 17, 18

This rocky gorge offers breathtaking views.

FROM TAUVES TO MESSEIX *19km/12mi – allow 2hr*

Tauves – Tauves is built along the River Mortagne, a tributary of the Dordogne. The town has a fortified 14C Romanesque church, a squat building with massive buttresses and a belfry-porch with machicolations. The exterior is decorated with carved corbels. Inside, the first four bays of the nave are spanned by ribbed barrel vaults, the fifth bay and the chancel by diagonal vaults. There are some interesting capitals, both foliated and narrative, several Baroque altarpieces and a 17C Pietà. Note also a 16C bell.

The cliff road runs along overlooking the valley before entering the sheer-sided, thickly wooded gorge carved by the Dordogne through the granite rock. Here and there loom large boulders. Beyond the "iron bridge", the road rises through a pine forest, providing further views of the gorge.

Messeix – This little town was once famous for its coal mines. The Romanesque church here was altered in the Gothic period but has retained its attractive 13C entrance.

Gourmets...
The annual Michelin Red Guide France
offers a selection of good restaurants.

Lac d'AYDAT ★

Michelin map 73 fold 14 or 239 fold 19

This lake, situated at an altitude of 825m/2 681ft, is a perfect example of a volcanic reservoir; its waters were retained by the Aydat lava flow *(see Monts DÔMES* ② *and Introduction: Volcanoes of the Auvergne)*. This tranquil stretch of water, reaching a maximum depth of 15m/49ft, is ideal for boating and angling. It lies in a wooded setting and is a delightful destination for an outing.

Near the north bank is a small island called St-Sidoine in memory of the country house that **Sidonius Apollinaris**, Bishop of Clermont in the 5C, is said to have had built for himself on the shores of the lake.

THE LAVA TRAIL

Round trip from Aydat

60km/37mi – allow 1 day – local map opposite

Aydat – Note the church and its unusual buttresses in the shape of adjacent turrets.

Leave Aydat on the D 90 towards Sauteyras. Turn right towards Rouillas then left onto the D 145. There are numerous views of the Serre mountain range.

Montagne de la Serre – The long backbone of the Serre juts out like a promontory into the Limagne plain. It is a typical example of "inversion relief".

At Nadaillat, a fine example of a village built of black lavastone, turn right onto the D 96 then left onto the D 213 towards Le Crest.

Le Crest – This wine-growers' village built at the very tip of the Serre mountain range has a 13C church with 14C and 15C alterations.

There is a superb **panoramic view★** from the old tower – northwards over the Gergovie and Limagne plateaux around Clermont, eastwards over the Allier valley and the mountains in the Livradois area, southwards and to the southwest over the Monts Dore and Sancy range, and to the west and northwest over the Dômes range.

Take the D 3 through Chanonat.

★Château de la Batisse ⊘ – This château built of pale stone exudes an atmosphere of tranquillity and gracious living which forms a stark contrast to the feudal fortresses of Auvergne. It is flanked by a pepperpot tower and two corner towers crowned with red-tiled domes and lantern turrets, all that remain of the original 15C castle. The flat roofs, terraces, and 18C wings with their wide windows give the château a welcoming appearance.

The interior *(enter through the east tower and the former kitchens)* contains a number of interesting pieces of Louis XIII and Louis XVI furniture, tapestries, weapons, a 16C Pietà, and the workshop of Jean de Chasteauneuf, a painter from the Auvergne.

The gardens, laid out by Le Nôtre in the 17C, are being returned to their design with the help of an 18C watercolour which is displayed in the Le Nôtre room. A delightful avenue runs alongside the labyrinth of greenery at the end of the park, leading to the **waterfalls** on the Auzon.

Continue northwards to Opme.

Château d'Opme ⊘ – This old fortress (11C) stands high above a mountain pass which was once the route taken by the Roman road from Clermont to Le Puy-en-Velay. It originally belonged to the Counts of Auvergne and was modernised into an elegant Renaissance château by Antoine de Ribeyre, Treasurer of France under Louis XIII. The new owner built the interior staircase, let more light into the old building through wide mullioned windows set at regular intervals, and relieved the austerity of its appearance by adding a courtyard, balustraded balconies, terraced gardens, and statues and colonnettes of Ancient Greek and Roman inspiration.

In the lower room of the keep, a small museum retraces highlights from the life of great French Field Marshall De Lattre de Tassigny, who was resident here at the time he founded the Opme military cadet school.

The upper terrace is laid out as a formal French garden around an ornamental basin with a fountain, the whole shaded by two avenues of antique lime trees. On the lower terreace, a 17C kitchen garden has been recreated, with a vase fountain attributed to Androuet de Cerceau in the centre.

★Plateau de Gergovie – *See CLERMONT-FERRAND: Excursions.*

Access – *To get to the plateau, drive up a road off the D 3 between Opme and Romagnat. As the road climbs it offers a superb* **view★** *over Clermont, the hills around the city, and the Dômes range to the left. Beyond the Col des Goules, the road runs along the southern ridge of the plateau. To the right, in the distance, is the Monts Dore range with the long backbone of the Serre range in the middle distance and the volcanic peaks of the Comté in the foreground.*

★★Panoramic view – A memorial erected in 1900 stands at the end of the road; it consists of a group of rustic columns topped by a winged helmet. From the terrace in front of the Maison de Gergovie *(see CLERMONT-FERRAND: Excursions)* 200m away,

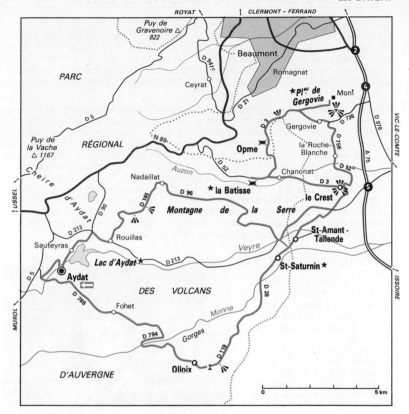

there is a wonderful view of the Limagne around Clermont, closed off on the horizon by the mountains in the Forez and Livradois areas, and of the Allier valley with the extinct volcanoes of the Comté in the distance.

Turn back the way you came up and take the narrow road to the left towards the village of Gergovie. Go through La Roche-Blanche and head back to Le Crest on the D 52⁰. Take the D 3, cross straight over the D 213 and head for St-Amant-Tallende.

St-Amant-Tallende – This village and its shops form an attractive sight seen from the medieval bridge. Note the fortified house in the old town.

★St-Saturnin – *See ST-SATURNIN.*

The D 28 and D 119 go through an austere landscape of cropped grass dotted with rocks, but they provide some extensive views before reaching Olloix. Stop near the polylobed Cross on the roadside to enjoy the panoramic view.

Olloix – This village consists of a string of old houses stretching out along the road. It was once the seat of a commandery of the Knights of St John of Jerusalem (Order of Malta) and one of its daughter-houses was the Knights Hospitallers' commandery in La Sauvetat. The **church** ⊙ contains the tomb and recumbent figure of Odo of Montaigu.

The road down into the Monne gorge (the D 794) provides a number of delightful views. Turn left into the D 788 after Fohet and return to Aydat.

Join us in our constant task of keeping up-to-date.
Please send us your comments and suggestions.

Michelin Tyre PLC
Tourism Department
The Edward Hyde Building
38 Clarendon Road
WATFORD – Herts WD1 1SX
Fax: 01923 415250/052

Château de la BASTIE-D'URFÉ ★

Michelin map 88 fold 5 or 239 fold 23 – 7km/4mi east of Boën

In the 15C, the rough lords of Urfé built a manor on the banks of the River Lignon. The family's rise to power was rapid. During the Italian Wars Claude d'Urfé spent several years in Rome as ambassador, and on his return to France he converted Bastie manor into a Renaissance château. **Honoré d'Urfé** (1567-1625), grandson of the ambassador and author of the first French novel, *Astrée*, grew up in these refined surroundings.

Unhappy in love – After graduating from Tournon College, Honoré d'Urfé returned to Bastie, where he stayed as the guest of his older brother. The latter's wife, the beautiful Diane de Châteaumorand, a passionate woman disappointed by her husband, aroused burning passion in the young man. After obtaining the annulment of her first marriage, which had never been consummated, Diane wed her former brother-in-law in 1600. The couple moved to her castle in Châteaumorand, northwest of La Pacaudière. This second marriage was no more successful than the first. Honoré d'Urfé fled from Châteaumorand and started writing *Astrée*, for which he had already begun to draft out a few ideas on his return from Tournon. Published from 1607 to 1628, this extraordinarily successful saga, 5 000 pages long, set the fashion in France for the novel and all things pastoral. The interminable love affair of a shepherd, Céladon, and his shepherdess, Astrée, became a bible for the 17C "honest man".

TOUR ⏱ *allow 1hr*

The original manor (14C-15C) was enlarged in the 16C by Claude d'Urfé, who brought artists from Italy to help with the decoration.

The main courtyard is flanked on the left by a wing reserved for the guard and on the right by an Italian-style construction consisting of two superposed galleries linked by a stairway with a crouching sphinx on a pedestal at the bottom. The ground floor of the central building includes the famous **Rockwork Grotto**, or Cool Room, richly decorated with pebbles, shells and multi-coloured sand which form the background from which figures stand out in relief. The pagan decoration of this room gives way to the Biblical scenes adorning the adjacent chapel which has a very fine coffered **ceiling**★ of gilded stucco.

Honoré d'Urfé

La Diana – Société historique et archéologique du Forez

The rooms on the first floor have beautifully painted ceilings and most of the rooms have retained their original furnishings and panelling. There are also many fine tapestries in the château.

The rotunda in the enclosure on the west of the château houses a statue of Bacchus. The gardens have been restored following plans from the period they were originally laid out.

*The **Michelin Maps** for this region are shown
in the diagram below the table of contents on page 1.
The text refers to the maps which, owing to their scale or coverage,
are the clearest and most appropriate in each case.*

BEAUJOLAIS★★

Michelin map 73 folds 8, 9 and 10 or 244 folds 1, 2, 3, 13 and 14

According to an old French saying, Lyon is fed by three rivers, the Rhône, the Saône and ... the Beaujolais. It is true that the Beaujolais is renowned both within and beyond French borders largely as a wine-growing region but, although this industry makes a considerable contribution to local economy, it is by no means the region's only source of income.

The Beaujolais region owes its name to the aristocratic **Beaujeu** family, who were at the height of their power from the 9C to 11C, founding Villefranche-sur-Saône and Belleville abbey. In 1400, Édouard de Beaujeu gave his estate to the House of Bourbon-Montpensier, one of whose members, Pierre de Bourbon, married Louis XI's daughter, thereafter known as Anne de Beaujeu. The Beaujolais passed briefly into the hands of the French Crown under François I, who confiscated it among other territory from the Connétable de Bourbon as punishment for his somewhat negative attitude towards his monarch, but by 1560, the Bourbon-Montpensiers had been reinstated as landlords. Anne-Marie-Louise d'Orléans, Duchesse de Montpensier, who was known as "**La Grande Mademoiselle**" (she was renowned for her love affairs and her active support of the Roman Catholic Fronde movement), bequeathed the Beaujolais to the House of Orléans, who remained its owners until the Revolution.

GEOGRAPHICAL NOTES

The Beaujolais is a mountain range which stretches between the Loire and Rhône valleys, on the line where the Atlantic and Mediterranean watersheds meet. The region is clearly delimited to the west and east, but less so to the north and south, where it gradually gives way to the Charollais region and the Lyonnais mountain range.
With a maximum altitude of 1 009m/3 310ft at St-Rigaud, the Beaujolais is best qualified as hilly, rather than truly mountainous. Its distinguishing features are nonetheless numerous mountain plateaux criss-crossed by narrow sinuous valleys, and an asymmetrical relief from east to west. To the east the land drops sharply down to the river plain of the Saône, while to the west it slopes gently away. The cliffs formed by the subsidence of the Saône river bed are home to the vineyards of the "Côte beaujolaise", while the rest of the region forms "la Montagne".

La Montagne – Picturesque hills and valleys, and landscapes which are as varied as they are appealing, make this a region well worth exploring. Vast panoramic views unfold from the crests of ridges or from the many lookout points over the Saône valley as far as the foothills of the Jura and the snow-capped Alpine peaks on the horizon. The upper slopes of the mountain slopes are covered in pine forest and broom, while lower down there are stands of oak separated by wide open clearings. Geographically, the area is well placed for trade and transport, situated as it is near Lyon between the Loire and Rhône valleys. A number of industries have blossomed here.
A textile industry has evolved gradually in and around the mountain towns. Labours undertaken a century ago, when the areas around Monsols and the upper valley of the Azergues were planted with conifers, are also bearing fruit, as magnificent plantations of Douglas firs supply a thriving timber industry. Thus the timber and textile industries of La Montagne, together with the vineyards of the lower slopes, constitute a rich source of income for the Beaujolais.

BEAUJOLAIS WINE

Beaujolais vineyards and the wine they produce have broadcast the region's reputation far beyond the borders of France.
The vine has been cultivated here since Roman occupation, with varying degrees of success; having flourished during the Middle Ages, it was virtually abandoned during the 17C, but then taken up again in the 18C, when Lyon, the "Beaujolais syphon", ceased to be the only market and Beaujolais wines began to be transported to Paris. The market expanded still further as the road and rail networks evolved, and vine-growing became a monoculture in the region.
Nowadays, the vineyards stretch from the mountain slopes near Mâcon in the north to the Azergues valley towards Lyon in the south, covering the sides of the hills which are exposed to the sun, overlooking the course of the Saône. A single grape variety – the Gamay – is used to produce the light and fruity red Beaujolais wines with their characters determined by the soil in which the grapes were grown. Beaujolais vineyards can in fact be divided into two distinct areas of production.

Coteaux de Beaujolais – North of Villefranche, the soil, granitic in origin, is gritty and clay-based – the perfect terrain for the Gamay vine. This is the region of **Beaujolais-Villages** and the ten officially recognised "vintage" Beaujolais wines, or *crus*: Moulin-à-Vent, Fleurie, Morgon, Chiroubles, Juliénas, Chénas, Côte de Brouilly, Brouilly, St-Amour and Régnié (the most recent *appellation* granted in 1988).

Gaudeamus in vino

Pays des Pierres Dorées – Between Villefranche and the Azergues valley in the "land of golden stone", the soil is composed more of sedimentary rocks which alter the flavour of the wine produced from grapes grown in this ground. The wines produced here are the more ordinary "Beaujolais" and "Beaujolais supérieur" labels.

Unlike most other red wines, Beaujolais is best drunk while young, and should be served chilled. It is possible to taste local wines in many places—look out for signs advertising *dégustations* in wine cellars large or small *(caveaux, celliers, châteaux)*. There are several local wine-tasting brotherhoods *(confreries)*, of which the "Compagnons du Beaujolais", the "Gosiers secs de Clochemerle" and the "Grappilleurs des Pierres Dorées" are perhaps the most active in promoting the glories of Beaujolais wine.

★BEAUJOLAIS VINEYARDS

① From Villefranche-sur-Saône to St-Amour-Bellevue
98km/61mi – allow 5hr – local map opposite

The road winds its way through the vineyards, at first climbing the granite escarpments, then dropping down towards the Saône valley.

Villefranche-sur-Saône – *See VILLEFRANCHE-SUR-SAÔNE.*
Leave Villefranche on the D 504, take the D 19 on the right, then the D 44 on the left.

Montmelas-St-Sorlin – Drive round to the north of the feudal castle *(not open to the public)*, which was restored in the 19C by Dupasquier, a student of Viollet-le-Duc. The castle, complete with high crenellated walls, turrets and a keep, looks most imposing, perched in solitary splendour on a rocky crag.
Carry on from Montmelas as far as the Col de St-Bonnet. From the pass, an unsurfaced track leads off to the right to the St-Bonnet beacon (30min Rtn on foot).

Signal de St-Bonnet – From the east end of the chapel there is a broad view of Montmelas in the foreground, set against the hills and vineyards of the Beaujolais and beyond them the Saône valley. To the southwest lie the mountains of the Lyonnais and Tarare regions.
From the pass, take the D 20 on the right.

St-Julien – This pretty little wine-growing village is the birthplace of the doctor **Claude Bernard** (1813-78). He was born the son of a wine-grower and earned part of the money for his studies by working in a chemist's. He became a professor at the Collège de France and a member of the Académie Française. The **Musée Claude Bernard** ⊘ recalls his work in the field of physiology, in particular on the absorption of fats and sugars by the liver. The museum garden leads to the house where Claude Bernard was born.
Take the D 19 as far as Salles.

Salles-Arbuissonnas-en-Beaujolais – The monks of Cluny founded a **priory** in Salles as early as the 10C. This was taken over by nuns of the Benedictine Order in the 14C, who ran it until they were replaced by "aristocratic" canonesses in the 18C. The 11C chancel contains the prior's chair (16C) and the choir stalls (18C). The 15C chapter house *(reached through the garden and the cloisters to the south of the church; light switch near the door on the left)* has been converted into a **museum** ⊘; note its vaulting, supported on a central pillar, and the elegant keystones decorated with the symbols of the four Evangelists. An elegantly arcaded gallery is all that remains of the Romanesque **cloisters** *(reached through the little Flamboyant Gothic doorway to the south of the church's west front)*. Around the **Place du Chapitre**, shaded by plane trees, stand the houses once inhabited by the canonesses. There is a good view of the plain east end of the church and of the Romanesque tower with a pyramidal roof, a very common feature of churches of this period in the Beaujolais region.

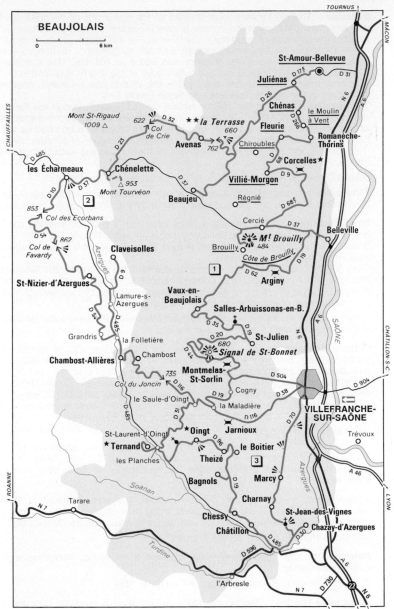

The wine-producing area is shown in green – Names of *grands crus* are underlined in red

From Salles, take the D 35, then the D 49ᴱ to the right.

Vaux-en-Beaujolais – This wine-growing village and the ribaldry of its wine-tippling inhabitants in the 1920s inspired **Gabriel Chevallier** (1895-1969) to write his satirical novel *Clochemerle*.

Carry on along the D 49ᴱ through Le Perréon and then take the D 62 to Charentay.

The unusual shape of the Château d'Arginy comes into sight 1km/0.6mi east of Charentay.

Château d'Arginy – All that remains of the castle is the great red brick tower known as the Tour d'Alchimie. This is shrouded in mystery; some say it was used by the Knights Templar to hide their treasure, brought here by Guichard de Beaujeu, the nephew of Jacques de Molay, the Grand Master of the Order who was burned at the stake in Paris in 1314.

Follow the D 68, turn left into the D 19, then right into the D 37 to Belleville.

Belleville – This old fortified town situated on the crossroads of the north-south and east-west communications routes is now a centre of wine-production and industry (manufacture of agricultural machinery). The 12C **church** ⊘ was once part of an abbey run by Augustinian canons, founded by the lords of Beaujeu. The square belfry above the south transept was added in the 13C. The handsome Romanesque doorway leading into the Gothic body of the church is decorated with geometric motifs on the outer arch. Inside the church, the naïve-style sculpted decoration on the capitals represents the Seven Deadly Sins.

The **Hôtel-Dieu** ⊘, built in the 18C to replace the old hospital, was in use for the care of the sick until 1991. The three large rooms are divided into characteristic alcoves with white curtains, and are connected to the chapel through openings with finely wrought iron railings. The dispensary contains a collection of porcelain dating from the 17C and 18C, which is set off well by the surrounding walnut woodwork fittings.

Beyond Cercié *(carry on along the D 37)*, the road skirts Mont Brouilly.

Those wishing to climb Mont Brouilly should take the D 43, turn left into the D 43ᴱ, then 100m further on take the road signposted "la Côte de Brouilly" again to the left.

Mont Brouilly – Côte de Brouilly, a fruity wine with a fragrant bouquet, comes from the grapes harvested on the sunny slopes of Mont Brouilly. Together with Brouilly, also produced by the villages around Mont Brouilly, this is the southern-most of the Beaujolais appellations.

From the esplanade, there is a marvellous **view**★ of the vineyards, the Beaujolais hills, the Saône valley and the Dombes region. A chapel at the summit (alt 484m/1 588ft) is the object of an annual autumn pilgrimage by local wine-growers *(see the Calendar of events at the end of the guide)*.

Return to Cercié. On leaving the village turn left into the D 68ᴱ towards the old village of Corcelles, then continue on the D 9 to the left.

★**Château de Corcelles** ⊘ – This fortress was built in the 15C to protect the border between Burgundy and the Beaujolais. It was converted in the 16C, and took on a more comfortable, genteel air. Above the entrance to the keep is the family coat of arms of Madeleine de Ragny. The inner courtyard is surrounded by Renaissance arcades and contains a fountain with an ornate piece of 15C wrought-iron work on top. The chapel houses some remarkable Gothic woodwork. The huge 17C wine vat is one of the most handsome in the Beaujolais.

Rejoin the D 9 to the right.

The road goes through vineyards of some of the most famous *grands crus* of the Beaujolais, giving pretty views of the Saône valley on the way. Most of the wine-producing villages en route offer the opportunity to taste their product *(dégustations)*.

Villié-Morgon – Unusually for Beaujolais wines, the wine produced in Villié-Morgon matures well. It has a particularly fruity taste because of the broken-up schist soil in which the vines are cultivated. Interesting wine-cellars *(wine-tasting)*.

Leave Villié-Morgon on the D 68 heading north.

Fleurie – The fine, light Fleurie wines are best drunk young. Interesting wine-cellars *(wine-tasting)*.

In Fleurie take the D 32 east, then turn left ino the D 186.

Romanèche-Thorins – The famous Moulin-à-Vent wine is produced here and in the neighbouring village of Chénas. The **Maison de Benoît Raclet** ⊘ makes an interest-ing visit. Raclet's empirical discovery of a preventative measure against the pyralis worm, namely by pouring boiling water over the vines *(échaudage)*, was used until 1945. There is a wine museum located in the railway station—"**Le Hameau du vin**" **S. A. Dubœuf**★ ⊘. The **Musée du compagnonnage Guillon** ⊘ displays exhibits from the days of itinerant craftsmen; there are some particularly fine examples of their work.

Take the D 266, which goes through the hamlet of Moulin-à-Vent, to the D 68.

Chénas – Home of robust, top quality Moulin-à-Vent and the lighter, no less excellent Chénas.

Juliénas – The strong wines from this locality can still be tasted in the **Cellier de la Vieille Église** ⊘, tasting cellars in an old deconsecrated church converted for this purpose. The church walls are covered with pictures of Bacchanalian revels. By the exit to the village, taking the D 137; there is a beautiful 16-17C tithe house *(Maison de la Dîme)*, easily recognised by its arcaded façade.

Drive on to St-Amour-Bellevue.

St-Amour-Bellevue – This village at the northerly tip of the Beaujolais produces dark red wines with plenty of body and high quality white wines.

★"LA MONTAGNE"

② From St-Amour-Bellevue to Villefranche sur-Saône

134km/83mi – allow 6hr – local map above

This pretty drive climbs through vine-clad hills to dark pine forests, then drops down to the Azergues valley, in which a number of sawmills have been set up.

St-Amour-Bellevue and Juliénas – *See above.*

From Juliénas, take the D 26 uphill, going through two passes one after the other (Col de Durbize at 550m/1 804ft and Col du Truges at 445m/1 460ft).

Beaujeu – The capital of the Beaujolais lies amidst vine-covered hillsides.

Musée des traditions populaires Marius-Audin ⊘ – Audin (1872-1951) was a printer from Beaujeu who founded this museum of traditional folk art in 1942. The first floor houses a collection of dolls, some dressed in 19C French fashions and others in folk costumes from French and Italian regions. Doll's furniture, toys and knick-knacks surround this miniature society. The section on folklore contains the reconstructed interior of a 19C farmer's house, as well as the various tools used by cobblers, tanners, coopers, wine-growers and farmers, and furniture and other objects from the hospital at Beaujeu: bed, enamel ware, porcelain nightlights and enema syringes. Above the entrance to the wine cellar, called the "Temple of Bacchus", where there is the opportunity of tasting some Beaujolais-Villages wine, a handsome Antique head of the Roman wine god watches over the proceedings.

St-Nicolas ⊘ – The Romanesque church tower is the only remaining original feature of this unusual-looking church built in 1130 from uneven blocks of black rock.

★★**La Terrasse** – Alt 660m/2 165ft. *Viewing table.* The broad **view** from a bend in the D 18 about half a mile after the Col du Fût d'Avenas takes in the Saône valley, with behind it the Bresse plateaux, the Jura peaks and (in clear weather) the Alps, with Mont Blanc, the Vanoise massif and the Pelvoux.

Avenas – The Roman road from Lyon to Autun once passed through this village. The late 12C church contains a lovely 12C white limestone **altar★**, which depicts Christ seated in Majesty in a mandorla, surrounded by the symbols of the Evangelists and six seated Apostles on either side. The altar sides show scenes from the life of the Virgin Mary *(left)* and King Louis, the donor *(right)* – this is assumed to be Louis VII, although the inscription does not clarify this.

Take the D 18^E, then the D 32.

Shortly before the pass (Col de Crie), there is a beautiful view north down the Grosne Orientale valley. As the road carries on downhill, it passes Mont Rigaud on the right, the highest peak in the region at 1 009m/3 310ft above sea level.

Chénelette – This small village lies in a charming wooded setting. The **Tourvéon** (alt 953m/3 127ft) towers above it. This summit was once the site of the great fortress of Ganelon. According to the *Chanson de Roland*, Ganelon betrayed Charlemagne's army, bringing about its defeat and the death of Roland at Roncevaux. For this, he was put into a barrel lined with nails and cast off the Tourvéon peak. His castle *(to visit the ruins, 45min Rtn on foot)* was probably destroyed on the orders of the Louis the Pious.

Les Écharmeaux – This summer holiday resort is set against a backdrop of pine forests and meadows near the mountain pass of the same name, which is an important junction for several of the main roads through the Beaujolais (alt 720m/2 632ft). From the pass, there is a fine view of the steep slopes of the Haut Beaujolais to the north.

From Les Écharmeaux, the D 10 towards Ranchal crosses the Aillets and, after a stretch through forest, the Écorbans passes. Between Ranchal and St-Nizier-d'Azergues, there are some charming **views★** of the Azergues valley from the D 54. After the **Col de Favardy** (alt 862m/2 828ft) there is a lookout point over an impressive **panorama★** to the northeast: in the foreground lies the Azergues valley, and in the distance loom the Tourvéon peak and the foothills of the Beaujolais.

St-Nizier-d'Azergues – This small town occupies a pleasant site above the Azergues valley.

The pretty road carries on to Grandris.

After Grandris, turn left onto the D 504 as far as La Folletière, then left again onto the D 485 which runs along the upper valley of the Azergues and through Lamure-sur-Azergues. In Le Gravier, turn right onto the D 9.

Claveisolles – This little village perched on a spur is well known for its plantations of coniferous trees. In the 19C, the Comte du Sablon introduced Douglas firs from America. The present forest cover is among the most beautiful in France.

Rejoin the D 485 and turn left towards Chambost-Allières.

Chambost-Allières – This is an amalgamation of two very different villages: Allières in the valley, which is quite a busy place with a lot of through traffic; and **Chambost**, a charming little rural hamlet above the valley, which is reached via the D 116.

The road from Chambost-Allières to Cogny via Le Saule-d'Oingt makes a very **pretty drive★★**. It climbs up to the Joncin pass (alt 735m/2 411ft) and then runs along the ridge, offering a lovely **view★** of the Alps in clear weather.

In Le Saule-d'Oingt, turn left onto the D 31, then left again onto the D 19.

As the road drops down to the valley, the view stretches over the Saône valley, the Bresse region and the Jura foothills.

The D 504 leads back to Villefranche.

Villefranche-sur-Saône – *See VILLEFRANCHE-SUR-SAÔNE.*

★★"LE PAYS DES PIERRES DORÉES"

③ Round tour leaving from Villefranche-sur-Saône
59km/37mi – allow 4hr – local map above

This trip explores the **Pays des Pierres Dorées** ⊘ which owes its name to the pretty ochre-coloured local stone used to build farmsteads, castles and whole villages in the region.

Villefranche-sur-Saône – *See VILLEFRANCHE-SUR-SAÔNE.*

From Villefranche, take the D 70 south.

This pretty **ridge-top road★** *(route de crête)* gives views down into the Saône valley.

Marcy – Outside this market town *(reached along a small road to the left, signposted "Tour Chappe")* stands a **telegraph tower** ⊘ built by **Claude Chappe** in 1799. The original semaphore mechanism, with moveable arms, was used to transmit visual messages until 1850.
From the foot of the tower, there is a sweeping view of the Saône valley, the Dombes and the mountains of the Lyonnais and Beaujolais regions.

Charnay – This small fortified town at the top of a hill still has the remains of its original defence-works in the shape of a 12C feudal castle. In the town square, surrounded by 15C and 16C houses built of golden stone, stands the church, which contains a beautiful Gothic statue of St Christopher in polychrome stone (12C). Higher up, the imposing 17C castle now houses the town hall.

Take a narrow road heading south from Charnay to St-Jean-des-Vignes.

St-Jean-des-Vignes – There is a good view of the countryside around Lyon from the small church perched on a hillside amidst a riot of flowers in season.

Pierres Folles ⊘ – A museum has been founded to reflect the presence of a number of important geological sites in this area. Part of the museum is given over to an exhibition on the history of the planet, as revealed by the composition of the sub-soil. Display cases, tableaux and films illustrate the slow evolution of life on Earth; the aquarium of live nautiluses (cephalopod molluscs) and the hologram of the "flight of the pterosaurs" are particularly interesting. The rest of the museum is devoted to displays on the local countryside, and the ways in which its resources are being tapped by industry and tourism.
The museum also boasts a botanical gardens containing about 400 species of herbaceous plants and shrubs indigenous to the local region.

Rejoin the D 30 to reach Chazay-d'Azergues.

Chazay-d'Azergues – All that remains of the fortified town overlooking the Azergues is the belfry, a few 15C and 16C houses and a town gateway known as the "Porte de Babouin" after a juggler who, disguised as a bear, rescued his feudal lord's wife and young daughter from a blazing tower, for which he was rewarded with the daughter's hand in marriage. The 15C castle *(not open to the public)* was once the residence of the abbots of Ainay.

Take the D 30 as far as Lozanne, then the D 485 to Châtillon.

Châtillon – A fortress built in the 12C and 13C to protect the mouth of the Azergues valley towers masterfully over this village. The **Chapelle St-Barthélémy** *(reached up a steep signposted path to the left of the parish church)*, originally part of the fortress itself, was extended in the 15C by Geoffroy de Balzac. Inside the chapel there are paintings by Lavergne and Hippolyte Flandrin. The corbelled chevet is a most unusual feature. The Esplanade du Vingtain, running below the church, gives a good view of the village. By the road (D 76) out of the village, towards Alix, there is a pretty covered well (the *Puits Sarrasin*).

J.-L. Barde/SCOPE

Châtillon

Carry on along the D 485 in between red spoil heaps.

Chessy – The Flamboyant Gothic church contains a handsome 16C font and a statue depicting St Martha subduing a dragon.
Near Chessy, a rich seam of copper which belonged to Jacques Cœur was once mined. The ore obtained was known as "Chessylite" and was a variety of azurite with a beautiful blue glint to it, highly prized by collectors.

Take the D 19 to Bagnols.

Bagnols – In this village is a 15C castle which has been restored and converted into a hotel. The **church** ⊙, dating from the same period, features a beautiful pendant keystone. There are some very pretty 15-16C houses with porches on the village square.

Go back to the D 19 and follow it to the left.

Le Boitier – As you leave this hamlet, the road takes you past the Clos de la Platière, which belonged to the Rolands, a couple who became famous during the Revolution. **Mme Roland de la Platière** stands out from her contemporaries as an exceptionally cultured, well-educated woman who forged numerous close connections with the politicians of her age. However, she made no secret of her antipathy towards Danton and Robespierre and paid for this in 1793 by being sent to the guillotine. Her husband, who as Home Secretary (since 1791) had tried to save the life of Louis XVI and had been forced to flee Paris when he failed, committed suicide on receiving the news of his wife's death.

Theizé – The village is overlooked by the robust outline of its fortress, the **Château de Rochebonne** ⊙. The Classical façade has a triangular pediment and is framed between two round towers. The building is currently being converted into an oenology centre on wine production in the Beaujolais.
The 16C **church** ⊙, which has been restored, hosts exhibitions and concerts.

In wine-growing areas such as the Beaujolais, many wine-producers offer guided tours of their cellars, enabling visitors to discover the tremendous variety of local wines, and many of these tours are accompanied by the opportunity to taste the product. Cellars such as those at the Château de la Chaize (108m/354ft long), Clochemerle or Villié-Morgon are particularly popular with visitors. It is sometimes necessary to make an appointment to visit a cellar; details are available from the "Pays Beaujolais" organisation *(see the Practical information section at the end of the guide).*

★**Oingt** – All that remains of the once mighty fortress here is the Porte de Nizy, the gateway at the entrance to the village. Narrow streets lined with beautiful houses lead to the **church** ⊙, an old castle chapel dating from the 14C. Note on the brackets supporting the arches of the chancel the carved faces of Guichard IV, his wife and their six children. From the top of the **tower** ⊘ there is a marvellous view of the Lyonnais and Beaujolais hills and the Azergues valley. In the town itself, the two pedestrian streets and the 16C Maison commune (restored) are interesting.

Carry on along the D 96.

In **St-Laurent-d'Oingt**, note the church with a porch.

At the junction with the D 485, turn right.

On the left stands the old fortified town of Ternand.

★**Ternand** – Once the bastion of the archbishops of Lyon, Ternand retains some of its earlier fortifications, such as the keep and the watchpath, from which there is a good view of the Tarare hills and the Azergues valley. The most interesting features inside the **church** ⊘ are the Carolingian capitals in the chancel and the mural paintings dating from the same period in the crypt.

Turn back through Les Planches and follow the D 31.

The **pass road**★★ over the Col du Saule-d'Oingt is extremely pretty. Picturesque farmsteads on the hillside overlook meadows below. From Le Saule-d'Oingt, heading down towards Villefranche, there is a broad view of the Saône valley.

At La Maladière turn right towards Jarnioux.

Jarnioux – The **castle** ⊘, built between the 15C and 17C, has six towers and includes a particularly charming Renaissance section. The grand entrance gateway, which still bears traces of a drawbridge, leads into two courtyards, one after the other.

Take the D 116 and the D 38 back to Villefranche.

Vallée de la BESBRE ★

Michelin maps 69 fold 15 and 73 fold 6 or 238 fold 47

The Besbre valley contains a surprising variety and number of castles. Only a few are open to visitors but they are all worth a close look. This quiet little river, which rises in the Bois Noirs (Black Woods) at the foot of the Puy de Montoncel, flows into the Loire south of Bourbon-Lancy. There are many places where anglers can fish for tench, carp, pike and roach. Trout can be found in three of its tributaries, the Têche, the Charnay and the Graveron.

FROM LAPALISSE TO DOMPIERRE 60km/37mi – allow 4hr

★★**Château de Lapalisse** – *See Château de LAPALISSE.*

Leave Lapalisse on the D 480 along the river.

Chavroches – As it climbs towards the castle, the road gives a glimpse of the 15C main building. The gate and outer walls date from the 12C and 13C.

★**Château du Vieux-Chambord** – *Private.* The 13C keep with its four watchtowers overlooks the Besbre. The main part of the building was constructed in the 14C and 16C.

Return to the D 480; at Marseigne turn right onto the D 989.

Jaligny-sur-Besbre – This little town is well known in France for being the adopted home of poet, journalist and novelist René Fallet. There is an exhibition on him in the old town hall, and a literary prize is awarded annually in his honour. Jaligny is also an agricultural centre famed for its fair; there is a cattle market and competition here every spring and a turkey market in mid-December.
Visible in the distance on the other side of a vast meadow is the **Château de Jaligny**★ *(interior not open to the public)* consisting of two sturdy towers with Renaissance windows on either side of a main building with a steep roof.

Leave Jaligny heading northeast along the D 21. Shortly after St-Léon, turn left.

Puy St-Ambroise – *Viewing table.* The **view**★★ stretches over the entire Besbre valley and, to the north and west, over the Sologne Bourbonnaise, a flat region studded with copses.

Return to St-Léon; follow the D 53 to Vaumas to rejoin the Besbre valley.

★**Château de Beauvoir** ⊘ – This ancient 13C stronghold shows traces of the 15C renovations carried out by the La Fin family. It differs from the other castles in the region because of its layout: the buildings are set at right-angles to each other. The old watchtower is a typical example of Bourbonnais architecture.
Walk up the central avenue and turn left into the path alongside the old moat to the gardens.

Continue along the D 480, then turn left onto the D 296.

* **Château de Thoury** – This is an attractive 11C, 12C and 15C stronghold, which is surrounded by a park. High curtain walls link the two main buildings and the machicolated entrance gate which has two turrets with pepperpot roofs; it is reached via a drawbridge over a moat.

The **tour** ⊙ takes in the inner courtyard (16C gallery), the guard room (display on hunting), the dining room, the salon (fine Etruscan vase dating from 450 BC), the watchtower (family mementoes) and the vaulted 11C cellar.

On leaving the château, turn right.

* **Parc d'Attractions et Animalier Le Pal** ⊙ – This 25ha/62 acre park in a forest setting is divided into two parts: an amusement park and a zoo.

The **amusement park** is laid out around Place de la Gaîté, a copy of a Parisian square in the middle of the countryside. Over a dozen different attractions include a monorail, rafting, a water train, a caterpillar, a rollercoaster etc. The **zoo** is home to more than 500 species of animals – including elephants, giraffes, big cats, monkeys, deer, waterfowl, parrots and birds of prey – which roam in semiliberty in a recreation of their natural habitat.

From the park, turn left into the road back up to the D 480. Drive through Dompierre-sur-Besbre, then turn north onto the D 55.

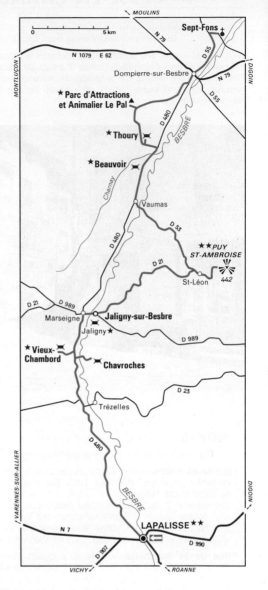

Abbaye de Sept-Fons ⊙ – This abbey is housed in 18C buildings; the church was rebuilt in 1955. An audio-visual presentation describes monastic life.

To plan a special itinerary :

– *consult the Map of touring programmes which indicates recommended routes, tourist regions, principal towns and main sights.*
– *read the descriptions in the Sights section which include Excursions from the main tourist centres.*

Michelin Maps indicate scenic routes, interesting sights, viewpoints, rivers, forests...

BESSE-EN-CHANDESSE★

Population 1 799
Michelin map 73 folds 13 and 14 or 239 south of fold 19
Local maps under Vallées des COUZES and Monts DORE

With its old houses and fortifications, Besse is a picturesque and charming town, and the beauty of its surroundings makes it a popular place to stay.

The town is the setting for a biological research centre specialising in the study of regional flora and fauna, which was set up by the Faculty of Science in Clermont-Ferrand University.

Besse-en-Chandesse

SIGHTS

NB The centre of town is closed to traffic during the summer

★**Église St André** – This Romanesque church dates from the late 12C, with side chapels built in the 17C and 18C. The chancel, originally added in 1555, was restored in the 19C.

The interior is dark with narrow aisles. The lightly-carved capitals are decorated with foliate designs or narrative scenes (eg The Rich Man's Feast, Crucifixion of St Andrew). Note the 16C choir stalls (beautiful misericords) and, behind the high altar, the revered statue of Our Lady of Vassivière.

★**Rue de la Boucherie** – This is a quaint street with black houses made of lavastone. Note the 15C shops and **Queen Margot's House** (15C), on the corner with Rue Mercière. According to local legend, Marguerite de Valois lived in this house. Its Gothic doorway, surmounted by a coat-of-arms, opens onto a beautiful spiral staircase. The interior houses a small **ski museum**.

Musée du ski ⊘ – *Rue de la Boucherie*. This ski museum is the first of its kind in France. Among the displays are 30 different pairs of skis, a 1925 bobsleigh, ski boots and shoes, and a pair of 1910 skates. Prints and photographs show Besse at the turn of the century, when this sport was first introduced here, and Super-Besse in 1958, during the early days of the new ski resort.

★**Town Gate** – *Corner of Rue de l'Abbé and Le Petit Mèze*. In the 16C this gate, which is protected by a barbican, was adapted to the use of firearms. The belfry was added at a later date.

Château du Bailli – These remains of the outer town wall are visible from the road *(northwest)* behind the church.

☀SUPER-BESSE *Alt 1 350m/4 388ft*

Located at the foot of the Puy de la Perdrix, Super-Besse – a high-altitude outpost of Besse – is first and foremost promoted as a winter sports resort, but it is popular also in summer because of the peacefulness of its surroundings.

There is a variety of chalets and holiday residences available. The vast, south-facing ski slopes are reached by ski-lift; additional facilities include a skating rink and a swimming pool.

In summer, the nearby lake (14ha/34 acres) can be used for swimming, canoeing and windsurfing. The area is ideal for rambling – all that is required is a pair of stout hiking boots.

Puy Ferrand – *15min by cable-car, then 45min Rtn on foot from Super-Besse.* The cable-car for Perdrix leaves from the Biche corrie and ends at the peak of the Puy de la Perdrix. Follow the crest to the summit of the Puy Ferrand, which offers a **view**★★ of the Monts Dore, the lakes and Chaudefour valley.

EXCURSIONS

★★**Lac Pavin** – *4.5km/3mi southwest of Besse-en-Chandesse, then 45min Rtn on foot. See Lac PAVIN.*

Chapelle de Vassivière – *7km/4mi – local map under Monts DORE. Leave Besse on the D 978 west and then turn right.*
During the summer, this 16C pilgrimage chapel in a beautiful rural setting contains a statue of Our Lady of Vassivière. On 2 July, the Feast of the Ascent, this Black Madonna, borne aloft by the "Carriers of Our Lady", solemnly leaves the church of St-André in Besse, where it returns on the first Sunday after 21 September, the Feast of the Descent *(see Calendar of events).*

Lac de Montcineyre – *8km/5mi – local map under Vallées des COUZES. Leave Besse on the D 36 south. 7km/4mi further on, turn right into the road leading to the lake.*
Crescent-shaped Montcineyre lake owes its existence to the wooded Puy Montcineyre, which dams the valley. Its water seeps into the lava and flows into the Couze de Valbeleix river. The lake lies at an altitude of 1 182m/3 842ft, covers an area of 40ha/98 acres and has a depth of 18m/59ft.
Follow the lakeshore along the foot of the volcano for an attractive view of the Monts Dore.

BILLOM ★

Population 3 968
Michelin map 73 fold 15 or 239 fold 20
Local maps under La LIMAGNE and Le LIVRADOIS

Billom is situated on the Limagne plain at the foot of the Livradois mountains. It flourished in the Middle Ages and had a university before Clermont-Ferrand. This university, transformed in the 16C, became the first Jesuit college and was well-known throughout the Auvergne.
During the "Reign of Terror" in the wake of the French Revolution, Couthon, a member of the Convention, issued a famous edict ordering the demolition of all belfries in the province on the basis that they were "contrary to equality"; this was how St-Cerneuf church lost its elegant little tower.
Modern Billom plies a wide variety of economic activities: sawmills, wood veneering, car body workshops, industrial brush and ironware works. Cultivation of the regional speciality, garlic, is declining, but many companies continue to store and sort fresh garlic for consumption or to process it for pharmaceuticals, powders and garlic paste.

OLD TOWN

Start from the Hôtel de Ville (**B H**)
Follow Quai du Terrail to Place du Creux-du-Marché, surrounded by old houses. Cross Pont du Marché-aux-Grains (Grain-Market Bridge); three troughs and gutters hewn out of Volvic stone are visible on the parapet on the right – they were used to measure grain.
Walking up Rue de l'Étézon, note the 16C belfry on the right and the 16C **Maison du Bailli** (Bailiff's House) (**B B**) at no 12.

Maison du Chapitre (**B D**) – This 15C mansion, known as the Chapter-house, was part of the medieval university and was used as a prison during the French Revolution.

★**St-Cerneuf** (**B**) ⊘ – This Gothic church was erected over an old Romanesque church from which part of the chancel, the ambulatory and a crypt remain. The doors in the front portal still have their unusual 13C strap hinges.
At the end of the nave, on the left of the entrance, note a 15C Entombment, a beautiful stone statue of an angel and 15C paintings; note also the 15C Pietà on the right.
The chancel is surrounded by a 12C **wrought-iron choirscreen**★. A carved capital in the ambulatory tells the story of Zachaeus, a topic rarely illustrated in religious art. The Rosary Chapel to the right of the chancel (formerly the chapel of the Aycelin de Montaigut family, ransacked by Couthon in 1793) is decorated with a series of 14C frescoes in which the colours and the drapery are particularly fine: they depict

B Maison du Bailli	**E** Maison de l'Échevin
D Maison du Chapitre	**F** Maison du Doyen
	K Maison du Boucher

the Assumption and the Coronation of the Virgin Mary, angels playing musical instruments, the symbols of the Evangelists and, facing each other, the Church and the Synagogue. In a niche above the tomb of an archbishop stands a naive 14C **Nativity**. The side chapel, known as the Chapel of the Precious Blood, contains two 17C wooden low-reliefs representing the Flagellation and Christ being Crowned with Thorns.

★**Crypt** – This 11C crypt, austere and extremely beautiful, is one of the oldest in the Auvergne. It follows the outline of the original east end with its ambulatory, opening out onto four radiating chapels. The first one, on the right, is decorated with 13C frescoes illustrating scenes from the life of St Margaret. The groined vaulting is supported by six sturdy columns and, in the centre, by four lighter columns. A silver reliquary decorated with instruments of the Passion is said to contain pieces of the Holy Cross.

Maison de l'Échevin (**B E**) – The entrance of this 16C alderman's house contains an attractive staircase tower and a well with its wheel.

Rue des Boucheries (**B 4**) – This narrow street paved with pointed stones, with no pavement and with a gutter running down the middle, is flanked by medieval houses including the **Maison du Doyen** (Deanery) (**F**) which has a beautiful basket-handle arch over its window and a Renaissance staircase, and the 15C **Maison du Boucher** (Butcher's House) (**K**) which has stone walls on one side, half-timbered walls on the other and two overhanging upper floors.

Espace St-Loup (**A**) – This old 14C and 15C church stands in the centre of a garden with a fountain, lawns and terraces. It has an imposing west door. The interior is used for temporary exhibitions and shows.

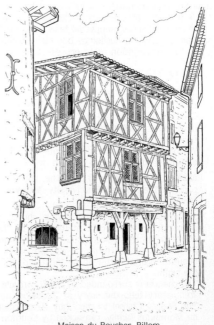

Maison du Boucher, Billom

D'après photo Arthaud Z.I.L.

EXCURSIONS

Château de Montmorin ⊙ – *4km/2mi south.*
This old stronghold used to consist of a keep flanked by round towers; it now lies largely in ruins.
Several rooms in the main building have been turned into a museum. The former stables house an interesting collection of tools from old crafts (smith, farrier, clog-maker, cooper etc) and the finds from excavations at the castle site. The guard room contains Louis XIII furniture and arms from the 15C to the 17C. Upstairs, a room has been set aside for popular arts and crafts, and includes domestic objects and furniture.
The **view** from the battlements overlooks the Livradois region on one side and the Monts range on the other.

Chauriat – *Round trip of 9km/5mi north. Leave Billom on the D 997 and turn right.*

Espirat – The village has a Romanesque **church** with a remarkably sturdy transept crossing. The great arches are topped by relief arches and a beautiful dome set on squinches. Its elegantly austere chancel is decorated with small statues.

Turn back to the D 997 and cross over it onto the D 81.

Chauriat – This village surrounded by vineyards is in the north of Comté. It has an interesting **church** in the Auvergnat Romanesque style. The exterior is striking for its very unusual marquetry of multi-coloured stones, arranged geometrically but not to any set pattern on its **gable**★ and under the arches of the right transept arm, as well as under the relief arches and in the upper parts of the nave. Inside, the large columns of the nave are topped by foliated or narrative capitals (the 3rd on the right shows the Miracle of the Loaves and the Washing of the Feet). The high dome with its octagonal base is supported by powerful Romanesque arches. Note the 12C statue of the Virgin Mary in Majesty.

Glaine-Montaigut – *6km/4mi north. Leave Billom on the D 229. After 3km/2mi turn right onto the D 212, then right again onto the D 152.*
This church marks the transition between the Carolingian and Auvergnat styles of Romanesque architecture. The 11C nave has a rounded vault with no transverse arch. While there is no visible transept, there is a dome. The narrow, dark side aisles topped by quarter-circle vaulting are separated from the nave by heavy columns. The 12C chancel has fine capitals.

The Practical information section at the end of the guide lists :
– information on travel, motoring, accommodation, recreation
– local or national organisations providing additional information;
– calendar of events
– admission times and charges for the sights described in the guide.

BORT-LES-ORGUES

Population 4 950
Michelin map 76 fold 2 or 239 fold 29 – Local map under l'ARTENSE

Situated in pleasant surroundings in the Dordogne valley, Bort owes its fame to the celebrated columnar basalt which overlooks it and to its enormous dam.
The town, straddling the boundary between the former territories of the Arverni and Lemovici tribes, flourished in the Middle Ages. Charles VII granted it the right to build a town wall, of which a few ruins survive.
For many years Bort was known for its tanning works, which are today recovering from a difficult period, but the local economy is sustained by other industries, such as clothing, leatherware, plastic injection-moulding, industrial joinery, traditional products from the Auvergne, electricity and tourism.
Every year, Bort hosts a Trade Show for Travelling Salesmen from the Massif Central, thereby keeping alive the old tradition of travellers.

★★**Barrage de Bort** – *Car parks along the D 979 (east bank) and D 922 (west bank).*
The road running along the top of the dam (390m/420yds long) overlooks the reservoir upstream dotted with **cruisers** ⊙, and the main power plant and spillway downstream. 300m/325yds away beside the D 979 on the west bank, a **viewpoint** at Les Aubazines gives a more extensive view over the 1 400ha/3 459 acres of reservoir.
A **tourist itinerary** ⊙ *(circuit visiteurs)* can be followed, starting from the foot of the dam on the west bank between the hamlet of Les Granges and Bort's tanning and leather works. This explains, through a working model and a video, the production of hydroelectricity in the Dordogne basin and its tributaries.

The Dam, Bort-les-Orgues

The dam's sheer size (700 000m³ of concrete) and its capacity of 477 million m³ makes Bort dam a showcase of hydroelectric production in the Dordogne. Its reservoir is partly filled by water from the Rhue, a tributary of the Dordogne downstream from Bort, which is then forced back through an underground passage 13.5km/8mi long. The plant at the foot of the dam is equipped with two 115 000kW generators. The Rhue power plant built on the west bank, level with the top of the Bort Dam, has a 10 700kW generator. Thanks to the generators, power production can be achieved within the space of only a few hours.

Church – The extremely simple architecture of Bort's church (12C and 15C) highlights a few fine works of art including a 15C statue of St Anne holding the Madonna and Child in her arms, beautiful modern stained-glass windows, and a bronze Crucifix by the sculptor Chavigner.
Outside, there are traces of fortifications near the east end. A 17C priory stands right by the church.

EXCURSIONS

★**Orgues de Bort** (**Bort's basalt columns**) – *Round trip of 15km/9mi – allow 2hr – local map under l'ARTENSE. Leave Bort on the D 979 towards Limoges; near the graveyard, turn uphill onto the D 127.*

As the road climbs, there is a beautiful view of the Rhue valley on the left.

Just after the last houses in Chantery, park and turn right onto some steps leading directly to the foot of the columnar basalt – signposted "Grottes des orgues".

These impressive phonolite columns stretch over a distance of about 2km/1mi and vary in height from 80-100m/260-325ft.

Return to the D 127 and, 2km/1mi further on, turn right onto a road (signposted) which leads to a car park near the television transmitter on the basalt plateau, at an altitude of 769m/2 499ft.
Park and walk (15min Rtn) to a viewing table from which there is a different view of the columnar basalt on the right.

The vast **panorama**★★ extends over the Dordogne valley, the Artense and Cantal regions and the Monts Dore. To the southwest lies lake Madic, relic of an earlier course of the Dordogne. From the spot known as the "Man's Head" (*Tête de l'homme*), reached by following the path along the ridge *(care required)*, there is an extensive view of the surrounding countryside with the town of Bort in the foreground.

Return to the car and follow the D 127 for another 500m; here a path on the left leads to a rocky outcrop (15min Rtn on foot).

From here there is a panoramic view over the Puy de Sancy, the mountains of Cantal, the Dordogne and its tributaries, the Monédières range and the Millevaches plateau.

At the pass on the Puy de Bort (alt 859m/2 792ft), there is a delightful view to the left of the vertiginous road. On the way back to Bort, the D 979 provides a view of the charming Château de Pierrefitte *(right)* and a splendid view of the Bort reservoir and dam.

Saut de la Saule – *2.5km/1mi, then 30min Rtn on foot – local maps under l'ARTENSE and Les RHUES. Leave Bort on the D 922 towards Mauriac and turn left onto the road running up to the clinic (Institut médico-pédagogique). Follow the footpath (signposted) across the Rhue, then turn left and follow the river.*

The path soon reaches the little gorge where churning pebbles caught by the waters have hollowed out the gneiss to form so-called "giant's cauldrons".

Walk on to the outcrop beyond, which overlooks the Saut de la Saule; here the Rhue crosses a threshold of rock 5-6m/16-20ft high.

★**Musée de la Radio et du Phonographe** – *6km/4mi north of Bort, near* **Lanobre**. *See L'ARTENSE.*

★**Château du Val** – *8km/5mi north of Bort. See L'ARTENSE.*

BOURBON-L'ARCHAMBAULT ⚓

Population 2 630
Michelin map 69 fold 73 or 238 fold 45
Town plan in the current Michelin Red Guide

The name of this little town serves as a reminder of the Celtic god, Borvo, protector of thermal springs, and, secondly, of the first lords of Bourbon, the Archambaults. The spring water has been appreciated since the days of Roman settlement here; it comes out of the ground at a temperature of 55°C/131°F and is recommended for the treatment of rheumatism, paralyses and functional rehabilitation.

Distinguished visitors – The waters at Bourbon, brought back into fashion by Gaston of Orléans, Louis XIII's brother, attracted many of the most famous figures of the 17C, including Madame de Montespan, Louis XIV's favourite mistress who died here in disgrace in 1707.

For thirty years, Charles-Maurice de Talleyrand-Périgord (1754-1838), Prince of Bénévent and France's Minister of Foreign Affairs, visited Bourbon-l'Archambault every August to take the waters (in showers and baths), which he considered the best guarantee of good health. His private swimming pool commemorates his visits in its name, "The Prince's Bath". His suite was visited by a host of local personalities whose company he thoroughly enjoyed. He held court, played whist, delighted in the pleasures of conversation, chatted with his barber and played pranks on his Latinist doctor. He and many other celebrities expressed their gratitude by making improvements and adding embellishments to the town.

SIGHTS

Nouveau parc – Situated to the northwest of the town, this park commands a **view**★ northeast of the promontory where there was once an awesome stronghold protected by twenty towers.

Rue de Trois-Maures links it to the park around the pump rooms. Allées Montespan, commemorating Louis XIV's mistress, run through the park.

Château ⊙ – Louis II of Bourbon turned Bourbon castle into a truly princely residence, but the destruction wrought from 1793 onwards, in the wake of the Revolution, left nothing but the three northern towers, each of which has two rooms with superb pointed vaulting. Their surroundings can be viewed from the top of the towers, reached by a spiral staircase. The roof of the left tower (Black Virgin, sundial, jack o' the clock) commands a **view**★ of the city, the lake with its mill and the Bourbonnais region.

All that remains of the 14C apartments are two huge fireplaces.

Quiquengrogne Tower – This tower in the southeast corner of the old castle wall was erected by Louis II in order to keep watch over the town. It is topped by an 18C belfry.

St-George – This church was erected in the 12C, altered and enlarged in the 15C and again in the 19C; it has beautiful capitals, including one of angels playing musical instruments in the corner of the south transept and, above the font, a 16C carving of Mary Magdalene with facial features typical of the Bourbons.

The presbytery, on the left when leaving the church, houses the church treasure including three beautiful reliquaries, one of which contains a thorn from the Crown of Thorns and a fragment of the True Cross.

Musée Augustin-Bernard ⊙ – This museum is housed in the former pump rooms, also known as the "King's House", built by Gaston of Orléans in the town centre.

The first floor includes a reconstruction of a local home and there are regional headdresses and costumes on display. Farm implements testify to the region's rural past. The mezzanine contains a 12C Virgin Mary in Majesty and a collection of 17C and 18C Nevers china *(faïence)* chemist's jars.

BOCAGE BOURBONNAIS

Round trip of 46km/29mi – allow 2hr. Leave Bourbon-l'Archambault heading north on the D 1 towards Nevers.

The Bocage Bourbonnais is a pleasantly undulating region, criss-crossed by hedges and dotted with forest groves which thrive in the heavy, clayey soil otherwise unsuited for farming.

Franchesse – Note the church with its fine bell tower.

Take the D 135 towards Ygrande.

Les Vignes – This hamlet is the home of the **Musée Émile-Guillaumin** ⊙. This farmer-writer (1873-1951) chronicled the joys and griefs of the tenant farmers of the Bourbonnais area. His books, *La Vie d'un Simple* and *Le Syndicat de Bougignoux*, give a well-documented insight into the rural world of Allier at the turn of the century.

Ygrande – The little town has a 12C church with one of the most beautiful stone spires in the region.

Forêt de Gros-Bois – Within this beautiful forest lie the ruins of the abbey of Grammont.

Continue towards Autry-Issards.

Château du Plessis – *Private.* The main part of this late-15C castle is preceded by a fortified staircase tower that gives it an unusual appearance.

Autry-Issards – The main entrance to the **church** is topped by a signed lintel. Inside, on the right of the chancel, there is a fine Deposition from the Cross, a late-15C work by the Flemish school.

La BOURBOULE⧺⧺

Population 2 113
Michelin map 73 fold 13 or 239 fold 18
Local map under Monts DORE

La Bourboule, located at an altitude of 852m/2 769ft in the lush valley of the Upper Dordogne, enjoys a climate with few seasonal variations. This well-known spa and rest resort offers many facilities for children.

The town is situated at the confluence of the Dordogne which, at this spot, is no more than a mountain stream 12km/7mi from its source, and the Vendeix, a tributary which also rises in the Sancy range. The resort's pump rooms, casino, town hall and gardens line the banks of the two rivers, which are crossed by a dozen or so bridges and footbridges.

LA BOURBOULE

Clemenceau (Bd G.) **ABY**
Féron (Quai) . . . . **BY**
Foch (Bd Mar.) . . . . . . **AY** 6

Alsace-Lorraine (Av.) **BY** 2

États-Unis
  (Av. des) . . . . **BY** 3
Gambetta (Quai) . . . . **AZ** 7
Guéneau-de-Mussy
  (Av.) . . . . **AY** 8
Hôtel-de-Ville (Q.) . . . **AY** 10
Jeanne-d'Arc (Q.) . . . **BY** 12
Jet-d'Eau (Sq. du) . . . **AY** 13

Joffre (Sq. du Mar.) . . **BY** 15
Lacoste (Pl. G.) . . . . . . **AY** 16
Libération (Q. de la) . **AZ** 17
Mangin
  (Av. du Gén.) . . . . . . **AZ** 19
République (Pl. de la) **AZ** 21
Souvenir (Pl. du) . . . . **BY** 22
Victoire (Pl. de la) . . . **AY** 23

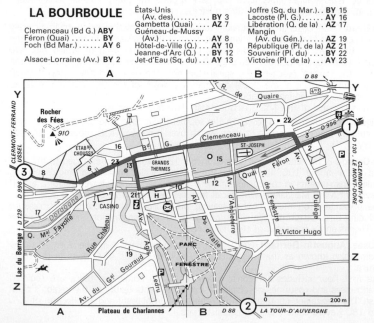

Spa town – La Bourboule's first spa was opened in 1821. At the time, its cabins were closed off with serge curtains, revealing the bathers at the whim of the wind. The bathing water was used by several patients in turn, and water for the showers was pumped manually by an elderly peasant. In 1854 Thénard, the chemist, discovered arsenic in the waters of La Bourboule; when the news spread, every house-owner in the town promptly began exploring his property in the hope of finding his own spring and each person did his utmost to excavate faster and pump harder than his neighbour. This "war of the wells" finally prompted official action. Today, the town's springs are managed by the *Société Thermale de La Bourboule* and the *Compagnie des Eaux Minérales*. There are two springs in La Bourboule – a hot spring at Choussy-Perrière (60°C/140°F), and a cold spring at Fenêstre (19°C/66°F). Their waters contain metalloid arsenic and are used to treat respiratory diseases and dermatoses (notably allergic reactions) using techniques such as inhalations, sprays and electro-sprays, baths and showers.

Treatment is available in two spa centres: Choussy and the **Grands Thermes** ⊘.
The resort has all the facilities of a major spa town including tennis courts, stables, a swimming pool, an amusement park etc.

★**Parc Fenêstre** (**ABZ**) ⊘ – This splendid wooded park – partly planted with sequoias – is a charming place for outings *(on foot or in a little train)* and relaxation. The children's play area consists of wide expanses of lawn and outdoor games. An additional attraction is the **cable-car** ⊘ linking the park with the **Charlannes plateau** *(see Excursion* ④ *below)*.

Rocher des Fées (**AY**) – *1 hour Rtn on foot. Take the footpath from Place G. Lacoste (see town plan).* This granite "Fairy Rock" rises some 50m/162ft above the spa and provides an attractive view of the town and its surroundings.

EXCURSIONS

★★★**Monts Dore** – *See Monts DORE.*

① North of La Bourboule *Trip of 10km/6mi – allow 2hr*

Leave La Bourboule on the D 88.

Murat-le-Quaire – A rocky spur, once the site of a castle, marks the entrance to this village of houses with stone-tile roofs. There is a lookout point on the spur with a pretty view of the upper Dordogne valley. Besides its role as a rural holiday destination, Murat-le-Quaire plays host to a bread festival every other year (odd numbers) as part of its preservation of local traditions.

From the church, take the D 609 towards La Banne d'Ordanche, as far as the school.

★**Musée de la Toinette** ⊘ – A gateway opens into a large courtyard in which the town hall and the museum are to be found.

The museum contains an account of rural life through the seasons in the Monts Dore region of the Auvergne during the last century, interestingly presented through the eyes of a local woman of that period, a certain Toinette Chaumard. Innovative use of technology adds sound and even smells to the four tableaux which make up this fascinating and vivid display.

A museum annexe in the neighbouring barn contains a collection of farm implements of that era, and local farm produce is on sale in season.

Carry on along the D 609 past a lake on the left, then follow it uphill round a series of hairpin bends with good views, as far as a car park at the end of the road.

★★**La Banne d'Ordanche** – *1 hour Rtn on foot.*
From the car park a footpath leads uphill *(becoming steep towards the top)* to a viewing table. La Banne d'Ordanche (in the dialect of the Auvergne *banne* means "horn") rises from a grassy hillock. From the top of this basalt outcrop (alt 1 513m/4 917ft) – the remains of the central chimney of an old volcano – there is a magnificent **panoramic view**★★ of the Dordogne valley and the surrounding mountains, the Puy de Sancy range, the Puy de l'Angle, the Monts Dômes and the Limousin area.

La Banne d'Ordanche

② East of La Bourboule *Trip of 3km/2mi – allow 45min*

Leave La Bourboule on exit ① on the town plan, taking the D 130 along the Dordogne towards Mont-Dore. 1.5km/1mi after the swimming pool a track leads off opposite the Mont-Dore water company building (left of the road). Leave the car and take the GR 30 footpath to the right. Go past a farm and continue uphill into the forest. After 15min walk, take a path to the right which cuts downhill in a series of zigzags.

★**Cascade de la Vernière** – The Vernière waterfall is formed by a large volcanic rock which obstructs the bed of the River Cliergue.

Return to the path and turn into the track leading to the Plat à Barbe refreshment kiosk. Here it is possible to go down a stepped path (dangerous except in summer) to a platform constructed opposite the Plat à Barbe waterfall.

★**Cascade du Plat à Barbe** ⊘ – This 17m/55ft high waterfall owes its name (literally "shaving dish") to the dip worn in the rock by its waters.

③ South of La Bourboule *Trip of 4km/3mi – allow 45min*

Leave La Bourboule on exit ② on the town plan, taking the D 88 towards la Tour d'Auvergne. 3.5km/2mi on past Parc Fenestre, turn right and leave the car at Verneix-Haut.

★**Roche Vendeix** – *30min Rtn on foot. See Monts DORE.*

④ West of La Bourboule *Trip of 7km/4mi – allow 1hr*

Leave La Bourboule on the D 129 towards La Tour d'Auvergne via Col de la Soeur. 500m after crossing the Dordogne, after a crossroads, leave the car and take a footpath off to the right.

Lac du Barrage – *30min Rtn on foot.* This delightful path runs through Charlet woods to the dam whose reservoir stretches for over 1km/0.6mi along the Dordogne valley.

Plateau de Charlannes – The Charlannes plateau (alt 1 250m/4 063ft) with its beautiful undergrowth is popular with spa patients for its restful scenery; it offers panoramic views of the Monts Dore and the Cantal mountains. In winter, it is popular with cross-country skiers.

The length of time given in this guide
– for touring allows time to enjoy the views and the scenery
– for sightseeing is the average time required for a visit.

BRIOUDE ★★

Population 7 286
Michelin map 76 fold 5 or 239 fold 32
Local map under Gorges de l'ALLIER

Brioude is a small, bustling town situated on a terrace overlooking the lush Allier plain.

A saint, and a bandit from the Alps – Legend has it that a tribune of the Roman Legion named Julian, who was born in the Vienne region and was converted to Christianity, sought refuge in Brioude and was martyred in the year AD 304. Pilgrims flocked to Brioude to pray at St Julian's tomb, particularly during the time of St Gregory of Tours (6C).

From the 9C onwards, the god-fearing town was subject to the authority of the Canon-Counts of St-Julien and remained so until the French Revolution, which put an end to their aristocratic tyranny.

Folk tales in Brioude still contain a reference to **Mandrin**, the infamous smuggler from Dauphiné. On 26 August 1754 he entered the town with a band of armed men, sought out the manager of the warehouse where tobacco was stored and taxed (the Farmers General held a monopoly on the sale of tobacco) and made the unfortunate man purchase a large batch of contraband "nicotine grass" at an excessively high price. Mandrin then withdrew while the people of Brioude turned a blind eye, for they were delighted at the trick played on a system which they hated. The victim, however, never recovered from the shock; he died eight days later.

★★BASILIQUE ST-JULIEN

St Julian's basilica (74.15m/243ft long) is the largest Romanesque church in the Auvergne, a "vast stone-built shrine standing over a famous tomb" (Bernard Craplet). It is typical of the Romanesque style seen in the Auvergne with its tiered east end and varying colours of masonry, though it differs in other respects: the portals, for example, are topped with smooth or carved coving or zig-zag moulding instead of the traditional string-course of billet moulding. The ornamentation at the east end is also noticeably Burgundian in style.

Exterior – Building began on the church as it stands today with the narthex in 1060, and was completed in 1180 (chancel and east end). Its nave was raised and given rib vaulting in 1259 but the west front and square bell tower above it were rebuilt in the 19C, as was the octagonal bell tower above the transept crossing. Walk round the basilica (it is particularly impressive from Rue du Chapitre and Place Grégoire-de-Tours)

Interior of Basilique St-Julien, Brioude

J.-L. Barce/SCOPE

and take a look at the attractive east end and side porches.

★★**East end** – The fine concentric layout makes this the most remarkable part of the building. It is one of the last examples of Romanesque architecture in the Auvergne. The tall apsidal nave is decorated with a string-course of wide black and white mosaics; at the base of the nave is the ambulatory opening onto five radiating chapels strengthened by buttresses. Roofed with tiers of stone slabs, the east end includes cornices with carved modillions depicting monsters, human figures, foliage and slashes, in addition to round-arched windows flanked by colonettes. The decorated capitals on the colonettes support moulded arcades. Jutting out from behind the east end are the flat walls of a false transept. Its flat machicolated roofs, side walls with loopholes and a vast pointed arch are a reminder that St-Julien's was once a fortified church.

★**Porches** – The side porches with their groin vaulting are the oldest parts of the church. They have an unusual appearance, the result of their use as chapels during the 16C and the inclusion of a gallery over the top. The north porch still contains the remains of a 12C stucco tympanum depicting the Ascension.

The south porch has fine capitals decorated with foliage. The panelled door, which was once covered in hide, still has its Romanesque strap hinges and bronze door knockers, one in the shape of a lion's head and the other shaped like the head of a monkey.

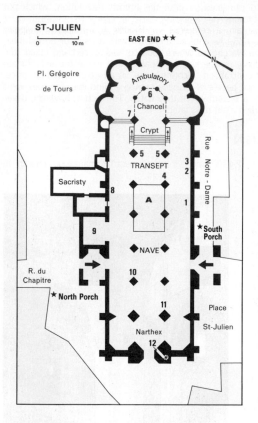

Interior – The nave is particularly striking for its size and the warm shades of the red sandstone walls and pillars. The narthex, with its three galleries opening onto the nave, and the first four bays of the nave itself are the oldest features of the church (late 11C), as shown by the magnificent huge pillars flanked by engaged columns, and the austere style. It forms a stark contrast to the abundance of architectural features in the remainder of the nave and the chancel, which were built a century later. Their upper sections were altered in the Gothic style in the 13C and 14C. The wide side aisles with groin vaulting are extremely high.

Four columns mark the entrance to the barrel-vaulted apse; the same vaulting can also be seen in four of the five apsidal chapels adjoining the ambulatory with its highly decorative traceried walls.

The delightful polychrome pebble **pavement**★ (**A**) dating from the 16C in the nave and from the pre-Romanesque era in the 5th bay in the centre, was uncovered, together with the small crypt beneath the chancel (probably on the spot of St Julian's tomb), following restoration and excavation work.

★★**Capitals** – The church contains a large number of capitals decorated with acanthus leaves, narrative scenes or themes that are commonplace in the Auvergne churches (beasts from the Classics or from imaginary worlds, human figures, masks, scenes from Hell). They are situated high on the columns which divide each pillar into sections.

Furniture, paintings – The basilica contains a number of altarpieces and old statues that are also worthy of interest. The walls and pillars in the first bays, the ambulatory and the north gallery above the narthex still contain the traces of 12C and 13C paintings, which are surprising for their diversity, "modernism" and spirited representations of human figures.

Turn to the right on entering the basilica to see:

(**1**) – (south aisle): 14C statue: Christ the Leper (Crucifix), carved in polychrome wood with canvas backing, brought here from the former leper hospital in La Bajasse near Brioude.

(**2**) – (south aisle): 14C statue: Virgin Mary in childbirth (recumbent) in polychrome wood.

(**3**) – (south aisle) 14C statue: Madonna with Bird carved in lavastone.

(**4**) – (5th bay, south pillar) capital: Christ in Majesty surrounded by the four Evangelists.

(**5**) – (first pillars of transept) carved corbels: heads of royal figures, facing each other.

(**6**) – (chancel) carved altarpiece (17C) behind the High Altar.

(**7**) – (chancel, north pillar) capital depicting the holy women.

(**8**) – (north aisle) 14C gilt wooden statue of the Madonna with Bird.

(**9**) – (Chapel of the Cross) altarpiece attributed to the 17C sculptor Vaneau.

(**10**) – (3rd bay, north pillar) two capitals: groups of soldiers around a wounded soldier or prisoner; angels and demons carrying off souls.

(**11**) – (south pillar in narthex) capital of the Punishment of the Moneylender; painting of a woman in profile, with an enlarged eye.

(**12**) – (St Michael's chapel) in the south gallery of the narthex *(access by a spiral staircase with 30 steps):* 12C frescoes depicting Christ in Glory, the Punishment of the Fallen Angels, the Triumph of the Virtues over the Vices, etc; capital depicting donkeys playing musical instruments.

BRIOUDE

H Hôtel de ville   M¹ Hôtel de la Dentelle   M² Maison du Saumon et de la Rivière

ADDITIONAL SIGHTS

Old houses – In the district around the basilica, a network of narrow streets contains a number of old buildings with remarkable façades. In Rue du 4-Septembre note the 15C building known as Mandrin's House; and at no 25, the 16C shop with arcades; and at no 29, the Lace Centre *(see below)*; note also Rue Talairat and Rue de Séguret to the north; Rue de la Chèvrerie and Place Eugène-Gilbert (Romanesque house with turret) to the south.

Hôtel de la Dentelle (M¹) ⊘ – The centre, housed in the 15C former residence of the Counts of Brioude, contains collections of old and contemporary lacework and lace making equipment.

Hôtel de Ville (H) – This is built on the site of the former castle of the Canon-Counts of St-Julien. There is a fine view over the Brioude section of the Limagne plain and the Livradois range from the neighbouring terrace.

Maison du Saumon et de la Rivière (M²) ⊘ – The Atlantic salmon or *salmo salar*, which reaches the spawning grounds of the Upper Allier at the end of its 800km/500mi journey upstream, is an integral part of Brioude's history.

Before learning about the importance of salmon fishing in the Brioude area in bygone days, visitors can see over 30 local species of river wildlife, including parr (young salmon), grayling, barbel and bream. The main attraction is the "salmon river", a curved length of glass 25m/82ft in circumference, where the migratory fish swim in simulated currents and still waters.

EXCURSIONS

★**Lavaudieu** – *9km/6mi southeast. Leave Brioude via ① on the map, the D 588. 2km/1mi further on, turn right onto the D 20, followed by the D 203 beyond Fontannes. See LAVAUDIEU.*

Beaumont – *4km/3mi via ④ on the map, the N 102, then the D 19.* The **church** ⊙ contains a very fine Romanesque Crucifix (late 12C) set against the semicircle of the chancel.

Auzon – *13km/8mi via ④ on the map, the N 102, then the D 14 and D 5. See AUZON.*

Brassac-les-Mines – *16km/10mi north via ④, the N 102 and D 76.* Coal mining here dates back to the 15C but the disused mines now house the fascinating **Musée de la Mine** ⊙. Mines, mining techniques and life as a miner are explained, and a look taken at the life in general of a mining family. A trip down the mine shows the statue of St Barbara (patron saint of miners) and the stables for the pit ponies.

★**Château de Léotoing** – *18km/11mi west on the D 20, Roche-Constant and turn right after Les Loyes.* Substantial remains of this old 14C fort overlooking the River Alagnon are still visible. There are extensive and attractive views of the surrounding landscape from here.

★**Gorges de l'Alagnon** – *14km/9mi northwest via ④, the N 102.* The road alongside the lower reaches of the River Alagnon, as it cuts its way through gneiss southwards from Lempdes, makes a very pretty drive.

★**Blesle** – *22km/13mi west via ③ on the map, the D 588.* This ancient village on the west bank of the Alagnon was founded around a once-powerful Benedictine abbey. **Église St-Pierre★** ⊙ (11-12C), which lost its belfry during the Revolution, has some interesting furniture and statues in the treasury. Other monuments of note include a great square keep, a 14C bell tower, all that remains of the church of St-Martin (destroyed in the Revolution), 15C and 16C houses, and the turret and doorway (17C) of the old hospice.

Massiac – *20km/12mi west via ③.* This is an old village in an excellent setting by the River Alagnon. There are various interesting polychrome wood statues in the church, and the **Musée-municipal Elise Rieuf** ⊙ contains portraits, landscapes and town views by this female painter (1897-1990).

Michelin Maps (scale 1 : 200 000), which are revised regularly, provide a wealth of useful information:

- *latest motorway developments and changes;*
- *vital data (width, alignment, camber, surface) of motorways or tracks*
- *the location of emergency telephones.*

*Keep current **Michelin Maps** in the car at all times.*

BURZET

Population 534
Michelin map 76 fold 18 or 239 east of fold 47

This village is renowned for its annual procession, commemorating Christ's Passion, up to a calvary overlooking the village and the River Bourges flowing beside it; the praying and chanting faithful are led by a group of figures in costume who re-enact the way of the Cross *(see Calendar of events)*.

★★VALLÉE DE LA BOURGES
Round trip of about 2hr 30min

Leave Burzet to the north along the twisting D 289.

From the bend by the calvary there is an impressive **view★★** back over the village. The route follows one of the "specials" of the Monte-Carlo rally. The narrow road continues uphill through a harsh landscape until, on reaching the top, the landscape suddenly changes as the plateau comes into view.

Turn right onto the D 122 and at Lachamp-Raphaël turn right onto the D 215.

The road drops swiftly downhill, offering a **view★** (*right*) of the top of Ray-Pic waterfall.

★★**Cascade du Ray-Pic** – *45min Rtn on foot. Park in the car park to the right of the road.* A path leads to the foot of these impressive falls, where the river gushes between two overhanging walls of basalt in an austere landscape at the bottom of a ravine.

Cascade du Ray Pic

Château de BUSSÉOL

Michelin map 73 fold 15 or 239 fold 20 – 6.5km/4mi north of Vic-le-Comte

The narrow road leading off the D 118 between St-Georges-sur-Allier and Lignat offers the best view of this medieval castle, standing on top of one of the volcanic peaks in the Comté area.

The **castle** ⊘ is one of the oldest in the province and was built in 1170 for the Counts of Auvergne. For centuries it was owned by counts and even royalty – a number of queens of France were "Ladies of Bosséol" including Joan, the wife of John the Good, Catherine de' Medici and Queen Margot.

John Stuart, Queen Catherine and Charles IX all stayed there.

In 1792 the timberwork and roof were removed on the orders of Couthon and the castle subsequently fell into disrepair. Its main façade collapsed in 1963 but has since been rebuilt with Romanesque-style windows.

Inside, note a **fireplace★** which is still used today, with a rounded Romanesque mantelpiece, the circular chamber with domed roof in the main tower and the antique furniture. A hanging garden adjoins the building.

The **view** from the parapet stretches over part of the Monts Dore and Monts Dômes and the Limagne plain: "I am Busséol, near Billom," it says on an old manuscript, "I can see far and wide".

103

Monts du CANTAL★★★

Michelin map 76 folds 2, 3, 12, 13 or 239 folds 29, 30, 31, 41, 42

The mountains of Cantal, formed by the largest extinct volcano in France, include scenery that is considered to be among the most magnificent in the Auvergne. Several of the peaks rise to more than 1 700m/5 525ft. Some of them, for instance the Puy Griou, are jagged; others such as Puy Mary are pyramid-shaped. The highest of the mountains, Plomb du Cantal, is rounded and rises to a height of 1 855m/6 029ft. Deep, picturesque valleys fan out from the mountain range, providing easy access for visitors.

GEOGRAPHICAL NOTES

The Etna of the Auvergne – In its heyday at the end of the Tertiary era the volcano in Cantal reached an altitude of 3 000m/9 750ft. It included a number of vents from which flowed the viscous lava that solidified into needles as soon as it was ejected from the crater, or the more fluid lava that spread out all round the volcano over an area some 70km/44mi in diameter. The viscous lava has given us the jagged peaks in the range such as the Puy Griou, which more or less marks the centre of the former crater. The fluid lava formed the wide open plateaux called *planèzes* which owe their lush pasturage and fertile farmland to the fertilising elements incorporated into the soil by the lava flows as they gradually decomposed.

Effects of erosion – Glaciers formed in Cantal during the Quaternary era. Their slow but powerful action, combined with that of the rivers and streams, wore down the summit of the mountain, carving deep into its sides, uncovering the lava plugs that filled the vents, digging out the corries that later became the valleys, and giving the mountain range the appearance it has today *(see illustration under Introduction: Volcanoes in the Auvergne)*.

The heart of the range is a slender crest marking the edge of a vast indented dip; this is the site of the old crater.

The most significant, and most characteristic, reminder of the gigantic volcano, which has now been worn away by erosion, is the layout of the valleys, all of which radiate out from the centre of the range.

Milk-producing mountains – The entire range was once covered by forest. In the 13C the woodland was still extensive but, gradually, land was cleared by shepherds and today it has disappeared in all but the entrance to a few valleys (Alagnon, Rhue de Cheylade, Mars). Thanks to the basalt content of the lava, which produces better quality pasture than the trachyte in the Monts Dore, Cantal has become best-known as a pastoral region. On its vast areas of pasture around the *burons* or cheesemakers' huts, where excellent mountain cheeses used to be produced *(see Introduction: Food and drink)*, herds of small Salers cattle with mahogany-red coats graze. This is one of France's foremost dairy regions.

★★ROUTE DU LIORAN
(CÈRE AND ALAGNON VALLEYS)

① From Aurillac to Murat

53km/33mi – about 4hr – local map right

★**Aurillac** – *4hr. See AURILLAC.*

Leave Aurillac by ② on the map.

From the N 122 there is a view over the Arpajon plain before the road enters the valley of a small tributary of the Cère. The moraine left by ancient glaciers filled the valley and created bosses and mounds across the hillsides.

The villages along the road have picturesque houses with hipped roofs that are typical of this area.

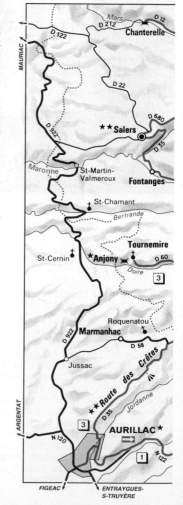

The road then runs into the wide, attractive Cère valley.

Polminhac – The houses in the village huddle round the foot of a rock topped by Pesteils castle.

Château de Pesteils – *See Château de PESTEILS.*

Comblat – Gothic manor house with alterations.

★**Vic-sur-Cère** – *See VIC-SUR-CÈRE.*

★★**Pas de Cère** – *45min Rtn on foot. The footpath leads off the N 122, 3km/2mi upstream from Vic-sur-Cère.* The path crosses a small meadow then runs down through the woods to the Cère. The river flows between high, narrow walls of rock. The bed of the river is strewn with volcanic boulders which have tumbled down from the hillsides and which are now covered with a thick growth of plant-life.

Cascade de la Roucolle – 3.5km/2mi from Vic and 500m from the start of the footpath is another path to the right leading to an observation platform only two minutes further on.

From here, there is a wonderful view of the Roucolle waterfall and the Cère gorge.

Thiézac – This is a sunny summer village with a Gothic church (**Église Notre-Dame de Consolation**) which houses a painted 15C statue of Christ seated at the Calvary, a 17C giltwood altarpiece and a fragment of a lace altar-covering given by Anne of Austria; a fish farm (**Établissement de pisciculture** ⊘) which replenishes stocks in the rivers of Cantal; and a chapel (**Chapelle Notre-Dame de Consolation**) which overlooks the village – it was after undertaking a pilgrimage here that Anne of Austria conceived, after 22 childless years of marriage, the future Louis XIV. The ceiling inside is adorned with 45 decorative paintings and roundels.

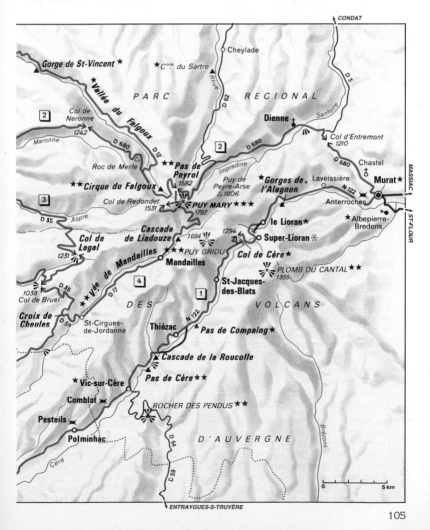

★**Pas de Compaing** – High above the road on the left are tall cliffs from which, in rainy weather or when the snow melts, drops the superb **Malbec waterfall** *(it is inadvisable to park immediately below the cliffs because of the risk of a rockfall).*
A short distance further on, the valley narrows and the road runs along the hilltop high above the deep gorge known as the Pas de Compaing.
Further on, the road enters the St-Jacques-des-Blats basin and the view extends to the end of the Cère valley, with the conical outline of the Puy Griou to the left.

St-Jacques-des-Blats – This is an ideal centre for walkers.

★**Col de Cère** – The new road (D 67) avoiding the Lioran road tunnel crosses the watershed separating the Dordogne basin into which flows the Cère, and the Loire basin into which flows the Alagnon. From this threshold (alt 1 294m/4 206ft) there are some superb views and evidence of conflicting influences from north and south. Just below the pass, the impressive pyramidal outline of Puy Griou can be seen to the left, in the distance.
Beyond the wide, light-filled Cère valley is the narrow Alagnon valley made even darker by the pine forests lining it.

★**Super-Lioran and Le Lioran** – *See Le LIORAN.*

★**Gorges de l'Alagnon** – *See BRIOUDE: Excursions.*

Beyond the Pierre-Taillade bridge which carries the N 122 across a narrow stream fanning out in its course, the hillsides to the left of the road gradually lose their covering of trees. The valley widens but the scenery is more sombre than in the Cère valley.
A few miles beyond Laveissière, the road runs along the foot of the handsome **Château d'Anterroches** (15C but restored), then the basalt rocks above Murat come into view. To the right is Bredons with its church; to the left, Bonnevie above which is a statue of the Virgin Mary.

★**Murat** – *See MURAT.*

★★PEYROL PASS

② From Murat to Salers

80km/50mi – about 6hr – local map under ① above

The D 680 which crosses the Peyrol pass is usually blocked by snow from November to June.

★**Murat** – *See MURAT.*

Leave Murat on the D 680 northwest.

As the road begins to climb, the Plomb du Cantal, Puy de Peyre-Arse and Puy Griou come into view, one after the other, to the left. The road then skirts the foot of Chastel rock, topped by a 13C chapel, and runs down from Entremont pass offering views of the Monts Dore in the distance and Puy Mary on the left. From the bridge over the Santoire there is a wonderful view of the mountains of Cantal.

Dienne – Against the north wall of the 12C Romanesque church is a 13C wooden statue of Christ with a particularly moving expression. There is also a Nativity scene in a carved giltwood frame, dating from the reign of Louis XVI, and a carved stone stoup dating from the 16C.
The road continues up the Santoire and Impradine valleys gouged out by ancient glaciers to form a trough, and now increasingly covered with pasture. The landscape takes on a truly alpine appearance.
As the road climbs up towards the Peyrol pass, it clings to the sheer sides of Puy Mary and provides superb **views★★** over the Impradine and Rhue de Cheylade Valleys, the Monts Dore and the Cézallier area; few other roads in the Auvergne provide such breathtaking views.

★★**Pas de Peyrol** – Alt 1 582m/5 141ft. This is the highest mountain pass in the Massif Central.
In the foreground, there is a magnificent view of the wooded Falgoux corrie overlooked by the Roc d'Auzière.

★★★**Puy Mary** – *Viewing table. Steep climb – 1 hour 30min Rtn on foot from the Peyrol pass – keep to the signposted track at all times.*
The footpath follows the northwest ridge of the mountain. From the summit (alt 1 787m/5 808ft) there is a breathtaking view of Cantal's gigantic extinct volcano and a superb **panoramic view** over the crystalline plateaux that form the base of the volcanic area of the Auvergne. Also visible are the jagged peaks or the gently rolling hills of the Monts Dore and the Cézallier, Livradois and Forez ranges. In the foreground is a striking view of the gigantic fan formed by the valleys radiating out

Puy Mary

from the centre of this natural water tower, separated by massive ridges with altitudes that decrease in the distance. To the north of the Plomb du Cantal is the Alagnon valley followed by the Impradine, Santoire and Rhue de Cheylade valleys to the left, then the Falgoux, Maronne and Doire valleys. To the south is the Jordanne valley and, last but not least, there is the Cère valley.

The human features added to this geological landscape are fascinating. Rural life varies with the altitude across this countryside divided by deep corries. In the depths of the valleys near the villages are fields of crops and meadows. In the less exposed areas are birch woods (which supply firewood) followed by beeches halfway up the slopes (timber for building etc), and recently-planted conifers. At higher altitudes are the alpine pastures dotted with *burons* (the huts once lived in by shepherds during the summer, where they made cheeses) surrounded by ash trees. On the descent from the Pas de Peyrol there are splendid views over the Mars valley.

**Cirque du Falgoux – The Falgoux valley, which starts here, gouges out a course for itself along the foot of Puy Mary. The corrie is flanked by rocks and forests which provide a wonderful setting.

Head northwest along the D 12.

*Vallée du Falgoux – The road follows the valley, in which there is a striking contrast between the hillside in the shade, covered in woodland but devoid of houses, and the sunny side of the valley carpeted with meadows and trees, and dotted with houses.

In the **Gorge St-Vincent*** the valley narrows and at one of the bends there is only enough room for the road and the river. Note the tall cliffs to the right, with a few examples of columnar basalt.

To the left of the road beyond the gorge is the **Château de Chanterelle**, a fortified residence dating from the 17C with later restoration. It has a parapet walkway and a stone-slabbed roof.

Return to the D 680 (or drive to Salers on the D 212 – follow signs to Anglards – and D 22).

At the pass known as the Col de Néronne, the road moves to the other side of the hill and overlooks the wide, glacial Maronne valley far below.

**Salers – *See SALERS.*

★★CREST ROAD

③ From Salers to Aurillac

60km-38 miles – about 4hr – local map under ① above

The road up to Col de Legal is usually blocked by snow from December to April.

★★Salers – *See SALERS.*

Leave Salers on the D 35 east.

Running along the western slopes of Cantal's ancient volcano, the road crosses a few of the valleys which fan out from the heart of the range. It hairpins down into the Maronne valley then crosses the river and enters the Aspre valley.

The traces left by the ancient glaciers that formed these valleys are obvious, even today. On the hillsides, covered with hillocks of moraine, are huge boulders carried there by the ice and now left lying scattered across the meadows. In some places, houses have been built between the rocks.

Fontanges – To the right, at the entrance to the village, is a **monolithic chapel** dug into a mass of volcanic rock; entry is through a wrought-iron door set between colonnettes and archivolts. From the statue of the Virgin Mary set on the rock, the view stretches right across the village. The houses are built in a style characteristic of the region, with dormer windows and stone-slabbed roofs. The **castle** here, which now lies in ruins, once belonged to the family of **Mademoiselle de Fontanges**, Louis XIV's mistress who died at the age of 20. The 15C **church** incorporates a Romanesque bell tower with eight semicircular openings. The interior includes a rib-vaulted nave with no transept, leading to a three-sided apse.

From the Aspre valley, the road enters and crosses the Bertrande valley then runs into the Doire valley.

Col de Legal – Alt 1 231m/4 001ft. From this pass there is a view in the distance over the plateaux of the Limousin area. The road runs down towards Bruel pass and provides a delightful view over the Doire valley before skirting a number of valleys.

In Le Bruel turn right onto the D 60 to Tournemire.

Tournemire – The small, Romanesque **church** ⊘ here is built of coloured volcanic tufa. It contains a number of interesting works of art and a valuable reliquary containing a thorn allegedly from the Crown of Christ.

★Château d'Anjony – *See Château d'ANJONY.*

Return to Le Bruel and take the D 35 to the right.

Beyond the Croix de Cheules, the D 35, which is called the **Route des Crêtes★★** (Crest Road) follows the long ridge that separates the Authre and Jordanne valleys, and the journey provides some very attractive views down into one or the other.

After 6km/4mi, turn right onto the D 58.

Marmanhac – Halfway along the road which drops steeply down into the Authre valley, the **Chapelle de Roquenatou**, site of a pilgrimage on 15 August, comes into view on the right. The village is home to two medieval castles barely 500m apart, competing with each other in size *(the Château de Voulte to the northeast is not open to the public)*.

Château de Sédaiges ⊘ – The castle is approached through a park with a pleasantly shaded lake.

Sédaiges was built in the 15C and modifed in the 18C and 19C and is neo-Gothic in style. The tour begins in the lower room and the chapel (18C polychrome wood Madonna). On the floor above, a room fitted with light and sound equipment displays five **Flemish tapestries**. The furnishings and decor of the two salons and the dining room reflect the standard of life of a 19C aristocratic family.

Return to the "Route des Crêtes".

As the road slopes down towards Aurillac, the broad plain at the edge of the town can be seen stretching away, while to the left there is a magnificent view of the Jordanne valley. This drive downhill is particularly rewarding at sunset.

★Aurillac – *See AURILLAC.*

★★VALLÉE DE MANDAILLES

④ From Pas de Peyrol to the Croix de Cheules

25km/15mi – about 1hr 30min – local map under ① above

★★Pas de Peyrol – *See ② above.*

Leave the pass on the D 17 southbound.

The road skirts the superb Falgoux corrie where the River Mars rises. Beyond Redondet pass there is a view of the Plomb du Cantal and Puy Griou before the road runs down into the Mandailles valley.

★★Vallée de Mandailles – The slopes that flank this picturesque valley, also known as the upper Jordanne valley, are lush and green, and carpeted with meadows screened by clumps of trees. Here and there are a few rocky escarpments dotted with caves. The River Jordanne contains gold which used to be sought by gold washers *(see AURILLAC)*, but the low value of the grains of gold-dust found in the river did not pay for the work and so the gold-washing stopped.

Cascade de Liadouze – *15min Rtn on foot. Beyond Rudez, turn left off the D 17 just beyond a bench and follow the path that leads down to the Jordanne (park by the bridge). Do not cross the river. Instead, walk about 100m along the right bank.* The waterfall drops over a threshold of rock into a narrow gorge.

Mandailles – In a particularly attractive setting lies this village which, in days gone by, raised numerous tinkers and ironmongers who left the village and settled elsewhere throughout France.

Turn right onto the D59.

The road crosses the Jordanne then climbs the hillside.

Croix de Cheules – The crossroads marks the start of the Crest Road *(see* ③ *above).*

Rocher de CARLAT★

Michelin map 76 fold 12 or 239 fold 41 – 16km/10mi east of Aurillac

The scenery here is typical of the Carlat area. The region was covered with basalt by lava flows from the volcanoes of Cantal; erosion fragmented the coating of rock, isolating a few flows which now stand, sheer-sided, at the top of steep hillsides. With its delightful valleys and its houses with steeply-sloping hipped roofs of stone slabs surrounded by gardens and orchards, the Carlat region is a pleasant place to stay or travel around.

Carlat rock itself was once topped by a castle which protected the Upper Auvergne against invasion from Aquitaine and Spain. In the 12C the turbulent Viscounts of Carlat became Counts of Rodez. During the reign of Louis XI (15C), the Lord of Carlat, **Jacques d'Armagnac**, rebelled on several occasions. He was twice pardoned by the sovereign but was finally captured in Carlat after a siege lasting eighteen months, taken to the Bastille where he was imprisoned in one of the iron cages that Louis XI was so fond of, and sentenced by a committee which had him tortured in order to make him speak "clearly". He was beheaded in the covered market in Paris.

In 1568 Carlat became a Protestant stronghold. Queen Margot lived here for thirteen months before going to stay in Ybois.

Thereafter, the castle was used on several occasions as a refuge for rebellious princes, until Henri IV had it razed to the ground in 1604.

★Carlat rock – The breach which cuts the rock in two was said to have been manmade, to isolate the western section on which the castle stood.

Cross the breach and skirt, to the left, the north side of the rock.

Climb the Queen's Staircase (Escalier de la Reine) cut into the rock to reach the northern edge of the plateau; there is a wonderful **view★** of the mountains of Cantal.

Then climb Murgat rock, topped by a statue of the Virgin Mary: the view stretches southwards beyond the village, to the Carlat region. In the distance, to the left, is the Rock and chapel at Ronesque.

Le CÉZALLIER

Michelin map 76 folds 3, 4 or 239 fold 31

The Cézallier range is situated between the Monts Dore and the mountains of Cantal; it consists of a succession of granite plateaux lying at an altitude of more than 1 200m/3 900ft, which were covered with a layer of basalt during the Tertiary era.

The volcanoes, from which the flows spread out all over the surrounding area, have neither cones nor craters. Indeed, they scarcely even jut up above the surrounding countryside because the lava thrown up by eruptions was very fluid and therefore did not build up around the vents of the volcano. The highest peak, the Signal du Luguet, reaches an altitude of 1 551m/5 041ft while the edges of the plateau descend to altitudes of 1 200m or 1 000m/3 900ft or 3 250ft. On the eastern side in particular the plateaux are gashed by impressive valleys.

The Cézallier range is one vast area of pasture dotted with former shepherd's huts *(burons)* and a few villages with huge barns and byres, and fountains made out of old drinking troughs. Here, in the summer months, thousands of heads of cattle graze on

Le CÉZALLIER

the plateaux. The Institut National de la Recherche Agronomique (National Institute for Agricultural Research) has an experimental farm in Marcenat where students and staff study stock-rearing at high altitudes.

The local people supplement their income by digging up gentian roots, which are used in the production of an alcoholic drink.

Despite its lack of hotels and places to stay, the Cézallier area is popular with those who enjoy wide open spaces, solitude and pure air, and also with winter sports enthusiasts, especially cross-country skiers because the lie of the land is ideal for this sport. Downhill skiing is also catered for, although facilities are, as yet, still limited (resorts include Parrot, Allanche and Marcenat). The area is part of a regional park, the Parc naturel régional des Volcans d'Auvergne. Two trips are described below: the first leads through the "mountains" and the second follows the valley which plunges down to the River Alagnon to the east of the range.

★ALPINE PASTURES

1 From Condat to Col de la Chaumoune

55km/34mi – about 3hr 30min – local map below

Condat – *See CONDAT.*

Marcenat – This is a modest winter sports resort.

Beyond Marcenat there are some superb views to the left of the road, over the Cézallier range.

Les Prades – Columnar basalt. From the summit, there is a delightful view of Landeyrat and the Upper Allanche Valley cutting into the *planèze*.

Turn left off the D 679 onto the D 39 then the D 23. Both of these roads cross the plateau.

Apcher – A short distance to the west of this village, an attractive waterfall drops down from the edge of the plateau.

Parrot – Small winter sports resort.

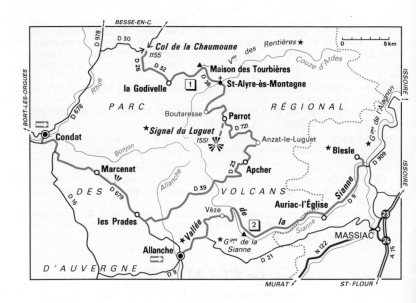

★**Signal du Luguet** – *1hr 30min Rtn on foot from Parrot. Climb up to the summit across the meadows slightly to the left of the ski lift.* The wooded summit (alt 1 551m/5 041ft) scarcely stands out above the plateaus. From it, there is a vast **panoramic view**★ over the Monts Dore and the mountains of Cantal.

Continue along the D 721 to Boutaresse then turn right onto the D 724.

The road twists and turns through picturesque scenery.

St-Alyre-ès-Montagne – On a rise a short distance from the small village is the south-facing church overlooking superb countryside lying in the shadow of Mount Gamet. The church is unusual for the strange, primitive carvings on its tympanum and for the billet-moulding on the east end.

Maison des Tourbières et du Cézallier – *See Vallées des COUZES.*

La Godivelle – This is a typical Cézallier hamlet with sturdy granite houses and a large, round fountain. Its other main feature is its geographical location, between a crater lake, the Lac d'En Haut (Upper Lake), and another, peaty lake, the Lac d'En Bas (Lower Lake), the haunt of countless migratory birds.

Col de la Chaumoune – Alt 1 155m/3 754ft. Near this mountain pass are recent conifer plantations.

From here, it is possible to drive on to Besse-en-Chandesse.

★VALLÉE DE LA SIANNE

② From Allanche to Blesle

30km/19mi – about 1hr – local map left

Allanche – Winter sports resort. The west end of the old town still has a few remnants of its ramparts.

Head eastwards from Allanche on the D 9.

Between Allanche and Vèze, the road crosses the Cézallier's great alpine meadows and then, at the top of the rise, the mountains of Cantal come into view. The hilltop road subsequently runs down to the **Sianne Gorge★**, providing some fine views of the ravine on the way. The hillsides are covered with forest.

Beyond a few gorges where huge boulders jut up from both banks of the river, the valley widens out, becoming less sombre, and fruit trees appear.

Auriac-l'Église – This village is attractively situated to the right of the road.

Turn right onto the D 8.

★**Blesle** – *See BRIOUDE: Excursions.*

Consult the Map of places to stay at the beginning of the guide to choose a suitable location.

La CHAISE-DIEU★★

Population 778
Michelin map 76 fold 6 or 239 fold 33

Set amid lush green countryside with gently-rolling hills at an altitude of more than 1 000m/3 250ft, the vast buildings and ornate architectural style of the famous abbey of La Chaise-Dieu come as a magnificent surprise. The abbey derives its name from the Latin "Casa Dei", meaning "the House of God".

HISTORICAL NOTES

Foundation of the abbey – In 1043 Robert de Turlande, a former Canon from Brioude, withdrew with a few companions to this desolate plateau. He was soon joined by increasing numbers of followers and founded a monastery under the Benedictine Rule for which, in 1052, he obtained the Pope's protection. Its success continued to grow to the extent that, at Robert's death in 1067, the monastery had 300 monks and 49 priories (including a convent, in Lavaudieu). Increasing numbers of priories continued to be founded as far away as Italy and Spain (the final total was 250) and this, taken with the flow of gifts and scope of its spiritual influence, made La Chaise-Dieu the third most important French monastic order in the mid 12C.

The Abbot was all-powerful. He was accountable to nobody but the Pope and, every year, he convened the Chapter General. In the 12C and 13C the abbots maintained the Order's independence and kept alive the spirit in which the abbey had been founded, thereby avoiding the excesses which weakened the great abbey at Cluny.

Papacy of Clement VI – The situation suddenly deteriorated in the early 14C, when the abbot's authority was weakened and several priories broke away from the mother-house. The election, however, in Avignon, of Pope Clement VI – one of the abbey's former novices and monks – brought a halt to this decline. The Pope had the church rebuilt as it is today between 1344 and 1352 to designs by an architect from southern France named Hugues Morel. The Pope's nephew, Gregory XI, completed the building (last three bays in the nave and the abbey buildings).

In the early years of the 16C, Jacques de St-Nectaire gave the abbey a dazzling set of tapestries.

Huguenot danger (16C) – The Wars of Religion struck the first blow to the abbey. On 2 August 1562 one of Baron des Adrets' lieutenants, at the head of Protestant forces, broke down the doors and took possession of the galleries and chambers. The monks sought refuge in the Clémentine tower which had been equipped for a long siege with oven, well, arsenal and a corn store. The tower also contained the abbey's title deeds, relics and treasure. The Huguenots ransacked the monastery and desecrated Clement VI's tomb. By the time the royalist army came to free the monks in the tower, the abbey was in a very sorry state.

Decline (16C-18C) – The abbey's real fall into decline came after the signing of the Concordat in 1516 by which the king was granted the power to appoint abbots. This laid the foundations of the commendatory system. Religious considerations were of very little importance; it was a monastery's income that counted. La Chaise-Dieu was therefore attributed to Henri d'Angoulême, Henri II's illegitimate son. When the abbot was killed in a duel, he was replaced by Charles d'Orléans, illegitimate son of Charles IX, who was 13 years of age.

Cardinal Richelieu, who restricted the number of monks to fifty, and the minister Mazarin, both added the abbey to their many personal sources of income. Cardinal Serroni was the exception; he donated the great organ to the abbey. In the 18C courtiers were sent into exile at La Chaise-Dieu. Among them were the Jansenist Bishop Soanen and Cardinal de Rohan, Bishop of Strasbourg, a man with a brilliant mind who spent the summer of 1786 here after a scandal involving a necklace belonging to the queen. This prelate, "who lacked devotion but was adored by the ladies", wore clothes "so luxurious that one would scarcely dare touch them". Yet he was missed here when Louis XVI gave his permission for the cardinal to move to Marmoutier near Tours.

The French Revolution struck the abbey the final blow: the monks were forced to flee.

Contemporary rebirth – The abbey was abandoned throughout the 19C but finally attracted attention in the early years of the 20C; it was not completely restored however until after the Second World War. In 1965 the pianist **Georges Cziffra** fell in love with the abbey, and founded a festival of religious music in aid of the restoration project. Restoration of the great organ was begun in 1977 and not finished until 1995. The Festival de la Chaise-Dieu continues to make a name for itself as one of the main festivals of its type in France.

Festival de la Chaise-Dieu

★★ABBEY

★★Église abbatiale St-Robert ⊘ – Solidly built of granite, the church gives an impression of grandeur and austerity which seem to reflect the personality of its founder, Clement VI.

West Front – The architecture of the west front is military in style. It overlooks a sloping square decorated with a 17C fountain and is flanked by two towers, neither of them very high. The portal, including a pier decorated with a statue of St Robert, was damaged by the Huguenots in 1562. The small house that conceals the base of the south tower is said to have been used by Cardinal de Rohan.

Nave and side aisles – The interior is an impressive sight. It has a vast nave roofed with flattened vaulting and is flanked by side aisles of the same height. Five radiating chapels open directly off the chancel. A 15C roodscreen (**1**) breaks up the

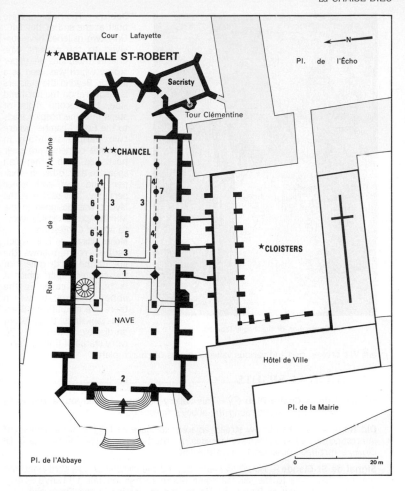

perspective and seems to reduce the height of the nave. At the top of it is a fine statue of Christ (1603) with, at the foot of the Cross, two wooden statues representing the Virgin Mary and St John (15C). The superb **organ loft★** (**2**) facing it dates from the 17C.

★★Chancel – The chancel is surrounded by 144 oak **choir stalls★★** (**3**) dating from the 15C, decorated with particularly fine carvings depicting a wide range of subjects. Above the enclosure are exquisite **tapestries★★★** (**4**) from Arras and Brussels, made of wool, linen and silk, and dating from the early 16C. The subjects are drawn from the Old and New Testaments and illustrate the theme of Salvation copied from the Poor Man's Bible that was so commonplace in the Middle Ages. They are accompanied by legends written in Gothic script.

In the middle of the chancel is Clement VI's tomb (**5**). The Pope had it made during his own lifetime and carved by Pierre Roye, Jean David and Jean de Sanholis. It was originally surrounded by 44 statues representing members of the Pope's family. The Protestants damaged the tomb and all that now remains of it is the recumbent statue on a black marble slab. In the north aisle in the chancel is the famous fresco of the **Dance of Death★** (**6**) (2m/6ft 6in high and 26m/85ft long): the three panels juxtapose the great and famous of this world and the dead; the dead are shown inviting the living to dance with them, a reminder of what lies before them. The fresco depicts the powerful to the left, the wealthy in the middle and the craftsmen to the right. Nowhere else has this theme, which was often depicted in the 15C, been treated with such realism and such a sense of movement. It was here that the composer **Arthur Honegger** (1892-1955) drew the inspiration, in 1938, for his work *The Dance of the Dead*, an oratorio with a libretto by Paul Claudel. The north aisle in the chancel contains another two tombs. In the south aisle lies the mutilated tomb of Abbot Renaud de Montclar (**7**) dating from the 14C; it still has its decoration of carved cherubs.

Sacristy – This occupies the ground floor in the Clémentine tower, a huge military-type construction.

Coronation of the Virgin Tapestry

★Cloisters – The cloisters were built at the end of the 14C. Only two galleries have survived to the present day; one of them has an upper storey which was used as a library. Beyond the cloisters is a square: on the left-hand side, the second flight of steps into the hospice leads to the Echo Chamber where two people standing in opposite corners with their backs to each other can speak to each other in whispers and hear each other perfectly. It is said that the layout was designed in the Middle Ages to enable lepers to attend Confession.

Monks' library – This sober, vaulted room follows the line of the north gallery of the cloisters upon which it is built. It contains the abbey **treasury**, in which there are magnificent Brussels tapestries (Crucifixion) on display, as well as a 17C ivory statue of Christ, Clement VI's broken ring and various valuable pieces of church plate.

ADDITIONAL SIGHTS

Historial de la Chaise-Dieu ⊘ – This gallery has been turned into a waxworks museum with displays illustrating the abbey's finest hours.

Old houses – In the narrow streets adjacent to Place de l'Église are a number of interesting houses with medieval façades. At the bottom of Rue de la Côte is La Cloze, a fortified house dating from the 15C.

Signal de St-Claude – *1km/0.6mi east.* Beyond the railway bridge, turn right into the lane that leads to the summit some 600m further on (alt 1 112m/3 614ft). Fine panoramic view of Pierre sur Haute, the mountains in the Forez and Lyon areas, Mont Pilat, the Cévennes, the mountains of Cantal and the Monts Dore.

Lac CHAMBON★★

Michelin map 73 fold 13 or 239 fold 19
Local map under Vallées des COUZES

The lake was formed by the Tartaret volcano, one of the youngest in the Auvergne, which erupted in the middle of the Couze valley and stemmed the flow of water. It is a vast (60ha/148acres) but fairly shallow lake (12m/39ft deep) lying in a very attractive setting at an altitude of 877m/2 850ft. It is dotted with tiny islands and has a very jagged shoreline, except on the north side where it is skirted by D 996 and to the southeast where there is a large beach.

Saut de la Pucelle – To the north of the lake is a slender rocky peak known as the Saut de la Pucelle (Maiden's Leap) which rises to a height of almost 100m/325ft; it is all that remains of the ancient Dent du Marais volcano. It is said that a young shepherdess who was being assiduously courted by a nobleman, against her wishes, threw herself off the top of the cliff but miraculously reached the bottom without injury. She was unwise enough to tell her disbelieving companions about the exploit and, in an effort to convince them of the truth of her tale, jumped off the cliff again; this time, she crashed to the ground and was killed.

Chambon-sur-Lac – The village lies at the end of the Couze de Chaudefour river, in a mountainous area to the west of the lake, and consists of a group of houses huddling round the church.

Church – This 12C building, which was partly engulfed by floodwater from the Couze, has a lintel over the main doorway decorated with a carving of the martyrdom of St Stephen. On the square is a haloed Cross dating from the 15C.

Lac Chambon

In the graveyard at the end of the path forking off to the left of the Murol road (some 200m from Chambon) stands a funeral chapel decorated on the outside with coloured motifs. Inside are a number of strange capitals.

Chambon-des-Neiges – The tiny ski resort of Chambon-des-Neiges (Chambon 1200 and Chambon 1400) lies high above the Chaudefour valley. The resort is equipped with snow-making facilities which are put to use in certain years; it has a number of downhill pistes and also caters for those who prefer cross-country skiing.

Le CHAMBON-SUR-LIGNON

Population 2 864
Michelin map 76 fold 8 or 239 folds 35, 36

Le Chambon lies in the upper Lignon valley and is a pleasant summer resort with a large number of sporting facilities. The mild climate, pastoral setting and altitude (960m/3 150ft) have made this an ideal location for the numerous children's holiday centres established here.

Huguenot city – The remote geographical location of Le Chambon enabled its Protestant population to survive religious persecutions and remain in the majority. In 1598 the Edict of Nantes granted religious freedom only to Le Chambon and St-Voy in this area; its Revocation in 1685 resulted in stubborn, though secret, resistance and a deep attachment to the reformed religion in both towns.
During the Second World War, the village provided many Jews with protection against persecution.
Today, Le Chambon has a number of Protestant foundations including the Collège Cévenol, a major international cultural centre which was opened in 1938.

★PROTESTANT PLATEAU
33km/20mi round trip – about 2hr

Head south from Le Chambon-sur-Lignon on the D 151, then turn onto the D 7. In Mazet-St-Voy take the 2nd road on the right to the hamlet of St-Voy. Park on the square in front of the church.

St-Voy – The tiny Romanesque **church,** dating from the 11C, is dedicated to St Évode, Bishop of Le Puy around AD 374. Its history is closely bound up with the arrival of the Reformation in the 16C: from 1560 onwards the population here followed the example set by its parish priest, Bonnefoy, and converted to the new religion, but the church was used as a Protestant place of worship only for some fifteen years.

115

The building, a granite construction with stone-slabbed roof, has all the charm of a country church. The chancel is pure in design and contains windows at different levels, raised from left to right following the rising sun. The nave with two bays (there are no aisles) opens westwards through a porch with triple semicircular coving.

Return to Mazet-St-Voy and follow the signposts for the "Foyer de ski de fond du Lizieux" (Lizieux Cross-country Ski Centre). 1.3km/nearly 1mi on, turn left into a dirt track signposted "Pic du Lizieux". 600m from the chalet there is a footpath off to the left leading to the Pic du Lizieux (park in the lay-by).

★★**Pic du Lizieux** – Alt 1 388m/4 554ft. Viewing table. *30min Rtn on foot.* The most easterly-lying volcanic cone in the Velay area overlooks a vast basaltic plain. The hillsides are ideal for cross-country skiing in winter. There is a **panoramic view** over the Yssingeaux region and the Lignon valley to the north, the Vivarais range to the east, the Boutières chain with its highest peak, Mont Mézenc, to the south and the Meygal range to the west.

Return to the car and take the minor road as far as Montbuzat. From there, turn right into the northbound forest road.

The road skirts most of the Lizieux forest and provides fine views over the pastures to the west.

Return to Le Chambon-sur-Lignon via Mazet-St-Voy and the D 151.

VALLÉE DU LIGNON

Round trip of 19km/12mi. Leave Le Chambon-sur-Lignon on the D 103 north. The River Lignon rises at the foot of the north face of Mont Mézenc and crosses the high plateaux of the Velay region before joining the Loire upstream from Monistrol.
As the Lignon flows through the Velay region, it weaves a picturesque course through a succession of wooded gorges and rolling hillsides.
On the outskirts of Tence there are views of the valley from the D 103.

Turn right onto the D 185.

Note the traditional rural granite houses. The most attractive of the houses have double sloping stone-slabbed roofs.

Return to Le Chambon-sur-Lignon on the D 157.

Tour of the Lignon valley by Le Velay Tourist Train ⊘ – This tourist train can be boarded from Le Chambon. It runs for 38km/23mi through the wooded hills and vales of the Velay and for part of the way overlooking the deep Lignon gorge.

CHAMPDIEU★

Population 1 355
Michelin map 88 north of folds 16, 17 or 239 fold 23
5km/3mi northwest of Montbrison

Champdieu lies on the edge of the Forez plain and hills. It has a remarkable Romanesque church which was built for a Benedictine priory. In the 14C the church and priory buildings were heavily fortified.

★**Church** – *30min.* The most surprising feature of this church is the extent of its system of defence. High arcading forms machicolations on the south side and the south arm of the transept. A similar system of arcading runs along the walls of the priory built on four sides of a quadrangle, with the church forming the south side. The church has two bell towers, the more outstanding being that over the transept, which dates from the Romanesque period and has fine semicircular openings. The second bell tower, by the west front, dates from the 15C; its base forms the narthex. Note, to the left of the west front's portal, the capital depicting a mermaid with two tails.

Interior – The austerity and marked influence of the Auvergne Romanesque style create a striking impression (Champdieu priory was a daughter-house of Manglieu abbey in the Auvergne). Architectural features typical of the Auvergne include the barrel-vaulted nave, and vaulted side aisles with ovolo moulding and projecting arms. The ends of the arms are decorated with arcading surrounding a pointed arch, which is characteristic of this style. Blind arcading with colonettes and carved capitals decorates the main apse. Underneath the chancel is a late 11C crypt comprising a central section divided into three aisles by colonettes with carved capitals.

Refectory – *Access via a door to the left of the church.* The former monks' refectory, on the ground floor of the western part of the priory, has retained its 15C decoration including the painted coffered ceiling and, above the fireplace, a fine mural of the Last Supper.

CHARROUX

Population 324
Michelin map 73 fold 4 or 233 folds 7, 8

Charroux is built on a hilltop and was one of the nineteen castellanies of the Barony of Bourbon. The old houses, built of dressed stone and decorated with carved mouldings, have now been restored and make the village particularly attractive.

Church – This fortified 12C building was once part of the town walls. The advanced post *(right)* is marked by the crenellated tower which formed the bastion. The bell tower rises above the transept crossing but its octagonal pyramid-shaped spire has been truncated. Inside, the nave has barrel vaulting and the aisles are roofed with rib vaults. The capitals are decorated with interlacing and foliate designs.

Leave via the north aisle.

On the square there is a medieval house with an overhanging upper storey. On the left stands the belfry, a square tower once used as a watchtower.

Rue de la Poulaillerie – An old stone well stands in the centre of this picturesque street paved with large cobblestones.

Musée de Charroux et de son canton ⊙ – This local museum is contained in a house with a façade decorated with carvings of animal heads, figures and nailhead moulding: objects and documents provide an insight into the history of the region. Downstairs there is a display of objects from the Roman era, and of Gothic and Renaissance sculptures, in addition to an exhibition on Charroux fireplaces. Jambs, mantelpieces and photographs of different designs illustrate the dexterity of the local stone cutters. A small room contains a reconstruction of the workshop of Jean-Baptiste Cailhe-Decante, a highly-reputed 19C maker of stringed instruments and hurdy-gurdies. On the first floor (18C and 19C exhibits), note the three sets of works from the town clock with their particularly complex cogwheels.
Next to the museum is the Prince of Condé's residence, a former hunting lodge; the first floor has a fine mullioned window.

Porte d'Orient – The **East Gate** was one of the bastions in the town wall. The defensive system is still visible today.

Viewpoint – *Viewing table.* A circular platform surrounded by a low wall in the shade of an oak tree offers a view over the neighbouring countryside.

Château du CHASSAN

Michelin map 76 fold 14 or 239 fold 44

In a region where medieval fortresses abound, this château provides a more peaceful addition to the landscape. In the 18C Jean-François de Ponsonnaille demolished the feudal castle of Faverolles in order to build the present house, which has remained in the family ever since.
The main building, with its austere façade, is embellished by a carved balcony and flanked by two wings, one of which is still lived in, while the other has been turned into an exhibition hall.

TOUR ⊙

The downstairs rooms contain reminders of successive generations of family members. The hallway has a stone staircase topped with a basket-handled arch. A 15C horse-blanket on the wall bears the Ponsonnaille family coat-of-arms: three bells or cow-bells flanked by two lions and topped with the count's coronet. In the dining room, the oak dresser still occupies the place for which it was made; its well-proportioned design distracts from any inherent heaviness. On the walls of the drawing room and antechamber hang fine Felletin tapestries (famous 15C Creuse manufacturer) depicting Biblical themes. The tapestries in the drawing room have been cut to size to fit into sections of wall. The rooms contain furniture in the style of Louis XIV (four-poster beds in one bedroom) and Louis XVI, and there are a number of family portraits. In the wing, the Stag Room contains exhibits relating to the folklore and country life of days gone by.

*Find the best routes in town using the plans in the **Michelin Red Guide France** which indicate:*
– through routes, by-passes, new streets, one-way systems, car parks...
All the necessary information, revised annually.

CHÂTEAUGAY ★

Population 3 050
Michelin map 73 fold 14 or 239 fold 19
9km/6mi north of Clermont-Ferrand

The town lies on the edge of a basaltic plateau and is overlooked by the squat outline of its castle. From the town, there are wide views over the Limagne plain and the surrounding mountains. The neighbouring hillsides produce a famous wine: its full-bodied flavour, reminiscent of Beaujolais, was once appreciated by Charles VI and Henri IV.

Châteaugay was built in the 14C by Pierre de Giac, Chancellor of France, and its history is a tragic one. It was in the keep that the grandson of the Chancellor poisoned his wife, Jeanne de Giac, who had won over the heart of John the Fearless, Duke of Burgundy, before she nonetheless became an accomplice to one of the duke's murderers. After being appointed minister to Charles VII, Giac himself was arrested, tortured, sewn into a sack and drowned.

Later, the beautiful Madeleine de Châteaugay fell madly in love with Charles of Valois, Charles XI's illegitimate son, and remained faithful to him even though, having been discovered to be a conspirator, he was imprisoned in the Bastille for many years. After he had abandoned her, she was stabbed to death by her vassals during a hunt.

In the years leading up to the French Revolution, **La Fayette** often came to Châteaugay to prepare "the reforms" with his friend the Marquis of Châteaugay, who appeared to be a supporter of revolutionary ideas; despite this, the marquis became one of the leaders of the Army of Émigrés in Coblenz in 1792.

Castle – Enter the inner courtyard where four out of the five wells (now blocked up) which were used as reservoirs in times of siege are still to be seen. A fine Renaissance door is decorated with the coat-of-arms of the Laqueuille family who made alterations to the castle during the 16C.

★**Keep** ⊙ – The square keep built in lavastone is the most interesting part of the castle; it is almost the only one in the Auvergne to have remained intact. Richelieu did not include it in his demolition orders, and during the French Revolution, Couthon, a member of the National Convention, was unable to raze it to the ground. It has four floors with access via a spiral staircase. Three rooms contain a collection of works by the artist Paul Trilloux based on the theme of "The Quest for the Holy Grail".

From the platform there is a fine **panoramic view**★ over the Puys range, the hills of the Livradois and Forez areas and the Limagne plain.

For historical information on the region
consult the table and notes in the Introduction.

CHÂTELGUYON ⸸

Population 4 743
Michelin map 73 fold 4 or 239 fold 19
Town plan in the current Michelin Red Guide France

Châtelguyon is situated at an altitude of 430m/1 411ft, on the edge of the regional park (Parc natural régional des Volcans d'Auvergne). It is overlooked on one side by the old town with its cluster of houses on an isolated hilltop, and on the other by the wooded slopes of Le Chalusset which have been turned into a park.

THE SPA RESORT

The resort enjoyed a massive boom in the 19C. Pipes bring water from the twelve springs up to the park on the banks of the River Sardon. The main feature of the springs is their magnesium content, the highest in Europe; their temperature varies from 27.5°C to 38°C/81°F to 100°F.

The spa itself includes the Grand Spa (1st class) and the Henry Spa (2nd class) which was completely rebuilt in 1983.

The resort specialises in the treatment of digestive and gynaecological disorders.

Today, life in the resort centres on the casino-theatre, the park at the foot of Mont Chalusset containing the Grands Thermes, and the Avenue Baraduc which is lined with cafés and souvenir gift shops.

Grands Thermes ⊙ – The foyer is a fine example of the architecture used in spas at the turn of the century. Red marble columns with Corinthian capitals support a coffered stucco vault decorated with floral designs. A double-return staircase leads to the galleries; the stairs are embellished with two colonettes topped by a lantern.

ADDITIONAL SIGHTS

Calvaire – The Calvary stands on a hilltop at the centre of town, on the site once occupied by the castle of Count Guy II of Auvergne, after whom the town was named.

From the viewing table there is a fine view over the mountains, the hillsides in the Forez area, the Limagne plain and the resort in the foreground.

Ste-Anne – The church is decorated in a very modern style. The stained-glass windows made of Baccarat crystal plate distil light onto the Byzantine-style frescoes.

EXCURSIONS

★**Vallée des Prades** – *1hr 30min Rtn on foot. From Châtelguyon take the D 78 north and turn left into the wide footpath that follows the right bank of the stream called Les Grosliers, which leads up through the Vallée des Prades (1.5km/1mi).* Scenic woodland walk.

Château de Chazeron – *See RIOM: Excursions.*

Vallée de Sans-Souci – *45min Rtn on foot. From Châtelguyon take the D 15 southwest. 200m on, after crossing the Sardon, turn right onto the signposted footpath.* Walk along the banks of the Sardon through a pleasantly fresh, wooded valley for about 2km/1.2mi, as far as the ford. The more challenging, rather rugged path continues from here to some waterfalls *(an extra 30min Rtn)*.

CHÂTEL-MONTAGNE ★

Population 400
Michelin map 73 fold 6 or 239 fold 9

The village overlooks the Besbre valley where the wooded hillsides and pastureland are typical of the scenery in the Bourbonnais area.

★**Church** ⊙ – This 12C church is part of a former Benedictine priory that was one of Cluny's daughter-houses. It is a plain but well-proportioned granite building, with an east end reminiscent of the Auvergne Romanesque style. Its two-storeyed porch (west front) with three series of semicircular bays is remarkably austere yet elegant in design.

The church interior is built in a uniform style. The nave has barrel vaulting supported by sturdy transverse ribs and is dimly-lit through windows set between blind arcades above a false triforium consisting of a row of triple bays above the main arcades. The triforium overlooks the side aisles roofed with quadripartite vaulting and gives a feeling of a lightness to the interior of the building. The capitals on the columns engaged in the piers of the nave are rough-hewn and naive in style. A 17C polychrome wood Pietà stands in the north aisle.

The chancel is surrounded by an ambulatory opening onto four radiating chapels; the second chapel on the left contains a fine 16C statue of the Madonna and Child.

EXCURSION

La Montagne Bourbonnaise – This range of mountains, with a fairly bold relief, offers extensive views from its wooded slopes, fields and pastures. To the east of Châtel-Montagne *(via the D 25)* rise the **Monts de la Madeleine★**, to the south are the **Bois Noirs★**, to the northwest lies the Bourbonnais plain. The summits barely rise above 1 000m/3 280ft (the rocky outcrop of **Pierre Charbonnière★**, from where there is a good view of the surrounding countryside, stands at 1 031m/3 381ft). The land is not much used for crop-farming; raising sheep and pale Charolais cattle takes priority, together with tending and exploiting the forests of beech, pine and spruce, and of oaks on the south-facing slopes. Tourism (both in summer and in winter) and the timber industry are the main sources of local income.

★**Puy du Roc** – *45min Rtn on foot. Head southeast from Châtel-Montagne on the D 25, towards the Croix du Sud crossroads. Immediately after a turreted house (on the right), turn right and 200m further on turn left onto a footpath which leads up to a statue of the Virgin Mary.*

The Stations of the Cross lead up to the summit of the Puy du Roc (alt 644m/2 113ft) from which there is a fine **panoramic view★** over the Bourbonnais area to the north, the Monts Dômes and Monts Dore to the west, and the Bois Noirs (Black Woods) and Madeleine hills to the south and east.

Just southwest of Châtel-Montagne *(on the D 207)* lies the capital of the Montagne Bourbonnaise, **Le Mayet-de-Montagne** (craft centre). From here it is possible to head southwest, to explore the **Vallée de la Credogne★**, a pretty little valley complete with a waterfall (Cascade du Creux-Saillant) which can be followed along the D 114. Alternatively, take the D 7 then D 177 southeast as far as the **Forêt de l'Assise★**, a forest of tall conifers and beech trees, through which the road climbs along a vertiginous hillside route. Ski-lifts testify to the area's popularity with downhill skiers in winter.

CHÂTILLON-SUR-CHALARONNE

Population 3 786
Michelin map 74 fold 2 or 244 fold 3 – Local map under La DOMBES

This pretty town, bright with flowers in season, lying in the shadow of its 11C castle on the border between the Bresse and Dombes areas, spreads along the Chalaronne valley. Coming into Châtillon from the southwest on the road from Villefranche (D 936), there is a fine **view** over the town's red rooftops with the impressive bell tower of the former almshouse rising above them.

The half-timbered houses with cob or brick walls built in the style typical of the Dombes area *(see Introduction: Traditional rural housing)* are brightened up in summer with bunches of flowers arranged in wicker baskets called *nids-de-poule* ("hens' nests"). Every Saturday, a picturesque flower and poultry market is held in the covered market, and the town is also known for making helmets for fire-fighters, soldiers and motorcyclists.

Famous sons of Châtillon – **Philibert Commerson** was born in Châtillon in 1727. As Royal Botanist, he accompanied the Count of Bougainville on his world expedition, bringing back an ornamental shrub from Japan which he called *hortensia* (hydrangea).

Châtillon is proud of the brief visit made by **St Vincent de Paul**, otherwise known as **Monsieur Vincent**. He was born into a poor peasant family in the southwest of France and decided very early on in life to join the priesthood. After becoming tutor to the children of Monsieur de Gondi, General in charge of the Galleys, he asked to be allowed to practise his ministry in a remote parish. He was appointed parish priest of Châtillon in 1617 but only stayed here for a few months. However, this was long enough for him to begin his charitable work among the poor and destitute. On 23 August he set up the first Brotherhood of Charity (Vincentian Fathers). In 1633 he founded the Society of the Sisters of Charity with St Louise de Marillac; the Order still continues its work today.

SIGHTS

Porte de Villars – All that remains of the ramparts which once protected the town is this 14C quarrystone square tower with limestone masonry courses and corners, which lies to the east. It is a fine example of military architecture, constructed during the days when Châtillon belonged to the House of Savoy (from 1272 until 1601 when the town was annexed to the Kingdom of France).

Halles – The present covered **market** dates from the 17C and replaced the market built in 1440 which was destroyed by fire. The rafters are supported on 32 pillars, each made from a single trunk of oak. Old houses with open shop fronts, an integral part of the market, can still be seen at one end of the building. Until the 1950s, from late October to mid November the covered market was used for a "servant-hiring fair".

Maison St-Vincent ⊙ – St Vincent de Paul was lodged here by a Protestant, M. Beynier, for five months while he was the incumbent of Châtillon. He founded the Order of the Sisters of Charity here. The chapel built on the spot where St Vincent's bedroom once stood contains the Foundation Deed of this institution, complete with is signature.

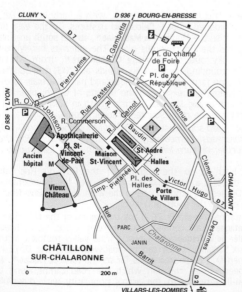

CHÂTILLON
SUR-CHALARONNE

0   200 m

VILLARS-LES-DOMBES

St-André – This church was commissioned in the 13C by Philip I of Savoy, and underwent numerous alterations during the 15C. It is a very colourful building with a brick façade and red-tiled roof which is unusually high for the Dombes area. Inside, the nave and side chapels are built of white limestone from the Mâcon region; note the restrained Flamboyant Gothic decoration. The keystone in the apse is finely traceried. The round tower, partly built into the south wall, is all that remains of the original church. At the end, there is a strikingly realistic statue of St Sebastian carved out of a single piece of walnut wood by a local artist named Jean Tarrit (1865-1950).

Place St-Vincent-de-Paul – In the centre of the square stands a bronze statue of St Vincent by Émilien Cabuchet.

Ancien hôpital – The buildings of the old hospital, commissioned by the Count of Châtelard in the 18C, now house the local cultural centre, the **Centre Culturel de la Dombes** ⊘.

Apothicairerie ⊘ – The first room contains attractive Directoire-style wood panelling and jars made of Meillonnes *faïence* (glazed earthenware). The second room displays a **triptych★** painted in 1527, which has been completely restored; the centre panel, illustrating the Deposition of Christ, is flanked by panels depicting the Apostles asleep and the Resurrection; in the bottom corners, the donor and his wife are shown kneeling. Note the balanced composition and the rich colours. The nuns' old workroom, its wardrobes decorated with beautiful wood panelling, contains a collection of local costumes.

Bridges and banks of the Chalaronne – These are a picturesque sight in the summer when the flowers are in bloom, especially around Impasse Pietanée and Rue Pasteur.

Ramparts of the Vieux Château – These are the remnants of one of the largest strongholds in Bresse. The castle was demolished at the end of the 16C, when the area was invaded by Henri IV's troops.

Vallée de CHAUDEFOUR★★

Michelin map 73 south of fold 13 or 239 southeast of fold 18
13km/8mi west of Besse-en-Chandesse
Local maps under Vallées des COUZES and Monts DORE

This interesting valley was gouged out of the granite and lava by the glaciers of the Quaternary era, which covered the slopes of the Monts Dore, and by the River Couze which flowed through the area after the glaciers had melted.
The valley floor and lower slopes boast abundant plant-life. Some of the upper slopes and peaks are gashed by ravines; others bristle with rocks which have been laid bare and carved into strange shapes by erosion. The area as a whole is of major scientific interest, with numerous peat bogs and rare flora and fauna.

Dent de la Rancune, Vallée de Chaudefour

TOUR

Geology enthusiasts will discover interesting examples of volcanic rock, and there are many good climbs for those with a keen interest in mountaineering.

Viewpoint – *Leave the Besse to Le Mont-Dore road (D 36) at the shepherd's hut and take the road through the valley. Park at the Maison de la Réserve (tourist information) and walk along the path into the valley.*
Soon a picturesque view over the valley floor forming a majestic amphitheatre becomes visible. When facing the Puy Ferrand, with the Roc de la Perdrix to the left and, opposite, the sharp pointed pyramid of the Aiguille standing out against its slopes, it is possible to see, a little further to the left, the Saut de la Biche, a slender waterfall that drops down into a deep rocky cavity.
To the right of the Puy Ferrand stand some interesting rock formations, the Crête de Coq and the Dent de la Rancune. Further right still stands the Rocher des Dents; at its foot is a natural archway known as The Gateway or The Pierced Rock.

CHAUDES-AIGUES

Population 1 110
Michelin map 76 fold 14 or 239 fold 43
Local map under Gorges de la TRUYÈRE

Chaudes-Aigues is ideally situated in the picturesque Remontalou gorge. As its name suggests, there are hot springs here, which have made it not only a spa resort but also a town where hot running water has been piped to houses since ancient times. A number of springs were tapped by the Romans. Today, 32 of the springs are tapped (they are the hottest in Europe), yielding 15 000hl/396 300 gallons of water each day at temperatures between 45°C and 82°C/113°F to 179°F. The springs were slow to find widespread popularity, largely because of the difficult access and problems with communications but now, however, they seem to be on the verge of a massive boom, firstly due to the widening of the N 9 road in 1991 and secondly thanks to the ongoing renovation work undertaken in order to turn the spa into a modern and functional place for the treatment of rheumatism, arthritis, sciatica, gout etc. Fitness breaks are also available.

Source du Par – This spring alone daily gushes out 5 000hl/132 100 gallons of water, at a temperature that can be as high as 82°C/179°F. It provides the water supply for the spa centre but its waters are also used to heat the school, the swimming pool and, above all, the local houses. It is not uncommon to see local residents filling a bucket at the spring for some immediate practical use. Tourists planning a picnic may like to test the spring's properties for themselves – it can reputedly hard-boil an egg in eight minutes! 300 out of the 450 houses in the village benefit from the heat economically-supplied by the water, which, in places, still runs through pinewood pipes with a stone slab used as a valve to regulate the flow. This ingenious system, which appears to date back many centuries, makes Chaudes-Aigues the pioneer of central heating.

Géothermia (M) ⊙ – This museum, located behind the Source du Par, unveils some of the secrets of subterranean Chaudes-Aigues. A close, warm atmosphere enfolds visitors as they enter, plunging them straight away into the world of geothermal science. On the ground floor is a description of the course taken by the water and a collection of various exhibits connected with its canalization. The first floor has a display on the fauna to be found in this abyssal zone. Eslewhere in the building there are exhibitions on geothermal science and water cures.

Église St-Martin-et-St-Blaise – This church dates from the Gothic and Renaissance periods.

Glazed Alcoves – In the streets of the town, there are several glazed alcoves containing old statues of the patron saints of each individual district.

EXCURSIONS

★★**Gorges de la Truyère** – *12km/8mi north. 2-5hr. See Gorges de la TRUYÈRE.*

Plateau de l'Aubrac – *12km/8mi south.* Beyond Chaudes-Aigues, the road offers scenic views over the Remontalou valley, then over the mountains in Cantal. It then climbs up through the Bès valley in a landscape of granite that, in most places, is harsh and rugged.

La Chaldette – This tiny old spa resort, where the water is warm with a high sulphur content, nestles in the Bès valley.
For details on excursions on the Aubrac plateau, the most southerly of the Auvergne's volcanic ranges, see the Michelin Green Guide Pyrenees Languedoc Tarn Gorges.

Château de CHAVANIAC-LAFAYETTE

Michelin map 76 fold 6 or 239 fold 33

The residence where Marie-Joseph-Gilbert, **Marquis de La Fayette**, was born on 6 September 1757, stands on one of the final outcrops of the Livradois area above the Allier valley; the history of Franco-American relations is more important here, however, than any archaeological features.

At the age of 19, La Fayette, aware of events brewing in America, obtained a secondment contract. One month later news arrived in Paris that the American states had proclaimed their independence; La Fayette, stirred by the "rebels'" cause, decided to give it his support and he financed the cost of his expedition himself out of his own huge personal fortune. He landed in Georgetown in 1777, became friendly with Washington, and fought by the American's side.

The **castle** ⊙ itself is a vast building, flanked at the rear by a crenellated keep and at the front by two large round towers. It was bought by the La Fayette Memorial Inc. association in 1916, thanks to Mrs Astor, and contains country furniture from the 17C-18C and, more importantly, moving souvenirs of the two heroes.

The tour includes the museum (which contains memorabilia from the First World War and has a section dedicated to the defender of American independence), the guard-room, the room in which La Fayette was born, the Louis XIII dining room and the grand drawing room. A waxworks museum (L'Historial) depicts a few episodes from the general's life.

The grounds are graced by a rose garden and three small lakes.

CHAZELLES-SUR-LYON

Population 4 895
Michelin map 88 fold 18 or 246 west of fold 13
Local map under LYON: Monts du Lyonnais

Chazelles-sur-Lyon lies in the foothills of the Lyonnais area and owes its fame to the production of high-quality felt hats. The industry enjoyed its heyday in the early 20C when the village boasted some thirty factories; today, the hat-making industry has gone into deep decline, with only one company left to keep traditional knowhow alive.

In the 12C, Count Guy II of Forez set up a commandery of the Knights of St John of Jerusalem in Chazelles; all that remains now is one hexagonal tower. Tradition has it that the commanders taught the villagers the art of fulling felt which they themselves had learnt from the Arabs during the Crusades.

Felt hat with feather

Musée du Chapeau ⊙ – The hat museum is housed in a former hat-making factory and comprises ten reconstructed workshops showing the various stages in the manufacture of luxury felt hats: from blowing and basoning the rabbit or hare fur, right through to brushing and napping. The visit is completed by a video made in the last working factory, a diorama, and demonstrations by hat-makers on traditional fully-operational machines. Every year, part of the exhibition is given over to contemporary hat design, featuring creations by some famous fashion names. The millinery on show incudes hats and caps worn by, among others, Grace Kelly and the great French chef Bocuse.

Château de CHOUVIGNY

Michelin map 73 fold 4 or 239 fold 7

This Bourbonnais-style fortress is built on a spur of rock in a delightful **setting**★ in a valley, its impressive crenellated silhouette towering high above the gorge of the River Sioule flowing below. This fine example of medieval architecture was built in 1250 by William I of Chouvigny on the site of a Gallo-Roman camp called Calviniacum. Some of its most famous residents include the La Fayette family (owners of the castle for three centuries) and the Duke of Morny, Napoleon III's half-brother.

TOUR ⊙

In the private chapel, note a period picture of the Duke of Morny. The great hall or main drawing room was once used as a courtroom, and the two seats from which justice was dispensed may still be seen. The coats-of-arms of the castle's various owners are displayed above the fireplace.

Cross the small hunting gallery to the terrace, from which there is a wonderful **view** over the gorge, barred on the right by the Roc Armand. Beyond this is the watchtower, with two loopholes set at an angle to each other (allowing the bowman to protect himself) and an iron cramp (making it possible to see as far down as the foot of the castle), followed by the treasure tower equipped with a safe embedded into the wall; it dates from the days of King Louis IX, better-known as St Louis (13C).

The tour ends with a visit to the prison tower, which is separate from the castle and situated beneath the parapet walkway.

CLERMONT-FERRAND ★★

Population 136 181
Michelin map 73 fold 14 or 239 fold 19 – Local map under La LIMAGNE

Clermont-Ferrand is the natural capital of the Auvergne due to its history and industrial development.

The city centre is built on a slight rise (alt 401m/1 303ft compared to 358m/1 163ft at the railway station), all that remains of a volcanic cone. The old houses built of volcanic rock in the "Black Town" huddle in the shadow of the cathedral.

Over the past twenty years or so, Clermont's urban landscape has undergone major changes. New developments include the Jaude District (a vast shopping complex), a new *préfecture*, the St-Pierre District (new covered market), the Fontgiève District (Law Courts, residential buildings), and Place du 1er-Mai (sculpture by Étienne Martin), all of which combine contemporary architecture with an older urban environment.

Notre-Dame cathedral in the old town centre of Clermont-Ferrand

HISTORICAL NOTES

From Nemessos to Clermont – The Arverni oppidum (settlement) of **Nemessos** was built on the site of the rise now occupied by the cathedral. Its name, meaning "wooded rise" or "sacred wood", is a reminder that the spot was used by the Druids as a place of worship. Gradually, over the course of the 1C AD, Druidic rites were abandoned.

A new settlement slowly grew up at the junction of several roads below the original town and, in honour of Caesar Augustus, its name was added on to that of the Roman Emperor. Augustonemetum had several major public buildings and a large number of private residences. An aqueduct brought water from the Villars valley to the summit of the rise where it was distributed to the various urban districts from a water tower.

At its height, in the 2C, the town underwent fairly large-scale expansion and its population rose to between 15 000 and 30 000 inhabitants. An ancient description indicates that it was "well-planted with vineyards, full of people, busy with traffic and trade and much given to pomp". The town's leading citizens enjoyed a perhaps surprisingly luxurious lifestyle in the latter years of the 4C.

Early on in the town's history, a baptistery and cathedral were built in one of the suburbs. After Bishop Illidius had performed a number of miracles c AD 385 and achieved sainthood under the name of Alyre, his name was given to the small town and, later, to an abbey.

In AD 475 the town was attacked by the Visigoths and, despite valiant defence on the part of **Sidonius Apollinaris**, was forced to surrender. In the 6C Gregory of Tours described the cathedral that had been standing on the hill for approximately one century as having been built in the shape of a Cross, with 42 openings, 70 pillars, 8 doors, and walls clad in marble.

During the early Middle Ages the town went into decline. It suffered a number of destructive sieges at the hands of the Franks, the Saracens and the Vikings. It was in the 8C that the name "Clermont" was first applied to the fortress destroyed by Pepin the Short in AD 761.

In the 10C the town entered a period of economic revival. Bishop Étienne II had a new cathedral built, the population increased, the town grew beyond the old town walls and there were no less than 34 churches and chapels inside and outside the walls.

Preaching of the First Crusade (1095) – When Pope Urban II arrived in Clermont, he found it to be a large town under the authority of his bishop, Durand, a former monk from La Chaise-Dieu.

The Council opened on 14 November 1095. The Pope, in an effort to spread the Gregorian Reform, decried the abuses of the clergy and the hold of the laity on the Church. His idea was to impose the "Truce of God" on the warring nobility: a ceasefire on certain days of the week and during the periods of Advent, Lent and Easter. The noblemen's energies would then be channelled into a great cause. At the last meeting, on 28 November, he made a stirring appeal for the liberation of the holy places. A throne had been set up for him on the site of the present-day Place Delille. Back came the enthusiastic reply from 13 archbishops, 315 bishops and mitred abbots, and a huge crowd of barons, knights and ordinary people, "It is God's will!". In accordance with the words of the Gospel ("Each shall renounce his own comforts and take up the Cross"), all those present fixed a red fabric Cross on their shoulder; it was to become the crusaders' insignia.

The crusade was to be led by the Bishop of Le Puy, Adhémar de Monteil, and not by King Philippe I of France whom the Pope had excommunicated for having repudiated his legitimate wife.

Blaise Pascal, man of genius (1623-62) – The episcopal town of Clermont was rivalled by Montferrand, the Count's stronghold, and later by Riom, the seat of the Court of Appeal. Clermont finally won the day and, in 1630, Montferrand merged with its neighbour to form the conurbation known as Clermont-Ferrand.

A few years earlier, the great writer and philosopher Blaise Pascal had been born in the town. His main works, *Les Provinciales* and *Pensées* (translated into English as *Mr Pascal's Thoughts, Meditations and Prayers*) are considered as masterpieces of French literature. Pascal was not only very gifted in the arts; he was also a brilliant scientist with an enormous talent for mathematics and physics. When he was 12 it became obvious that he had quite outstanding natural ability in geometry. At the age of 16, he amazed the philosopher Descartes with his essay on conic sections entitled *Traité des sections coniques*. Two years later, he invented a calculator which can be seen in Le Ranquet museum *(see below)*. The "wheelbarrow" or "vinaigrette", a two-wheeled sedan chair, was also one of his inventions. It was Pascal, too, who had the idea of the "five *sous* coach service" travelling a fixed route and leaving at regular intervals. The coaches were an immediate success and they paved the way for the Parisian omnibus service. It was Pascal again, with his brother-in-law Périer, who proved the weight of air following an experiment at Le Puy-en-Velay.

Tyre town – It is perhaps surprising that Clermont, situated in the heart of the Auvergne far from the harbours through which rubber and cotton were imported and well away from the major wire-mills, became the leading centre of tyre production in France and, indeed, one of the leading players for this industry in the world. The story behind this, however, is one of quite humble origins.

In the heyday of Romanticism, c 1830, a former solicitor named Aristide Barbier, who had lost three-quarters of his personal fortune as a result of the difficult financial climate, set up in partnership with his cousin, Edouard Daubrée, a captain in the King's Light Cavalry who had resigned his commission in order to open a small farm machinery factory on the banks of the Tiretaine River. In order to amuse her children, Madame Daubrée, niece of the Scottish chemist **Charles Macintosh** (1766-1843) who had discovered that rubber dissolves in petroleum, made a few rubber balls as she had seen her uncle do. The balls proved so popular that Barbier and Daubrée began mass-producing them. Soon, the factory diversified its output to include other items made of rubber – hoses, belts etc – however, after a period of prosperity, it fell into decline.

PARIS-BORDEAUX
1895

1ERE VOITURE sur
PNEUS MICHELIN

MICHELIN

In 1886 Barbier's grandsons, the **Michelin brothers** (André and, later, Édouard), took over the works. These two creative genii were the first people to apply scientific methods to industrial production. By meeting clients' real needs, carefully observing reality and constantly revising the knowledge and experience they had already acquired, they were able to create the first detachable bicycle tyre (1891). This development was followed by tyres for automobiles in 1895 and the low-pressure "Confort" tyre in 1923. In 1937 the "Métalic" tyre was introduced, with a steel carcass that made lorries a viable proposition as a method of transport, and in 1946 the radial-ply tyre (marketed under the name "X" in 1949) which combined a radial carcass which overcame the problem of overheating and a triangular steel belt to ensure good road-holding. This tyre has been constantly upgraded and improved ever since and the technique has most recently been applied to the motorcycle and aviation sectors where it has been put to good use in an expanding market.

★★**Site** – For visitors arriving from the Pontgibaud direction, there is a good general **view**★★ of the town from a **bend** (**AY**) on the D 941^A. From left to right, the nearby heights of the Côtes de Clermont and Chanturgue plateau give an indication of the original level of the Limagne plain prior to the major period of erosion. Opposite the platform lies the city itself, dominated by its black cathedral. In the distance, beyond the Allier river valley, are the mountains of the Livradois area. To the right are the Comté volcanoes, Gergovie plateau and Montrognon rock.

Avenue Thermale (**AY**) (D 941^C) runs along a hilltop north of Royat. From it there are more superb **views**★ over the town of Clermont and the surrounding area.

★★VIEUX CLERMONT (OLD CLERMONT)

Place de Jaude (**EX**) – The ancient origins of the name of this square remain a subject of controversy. Two Renaissance documents use the name *platea galli*– "rooster square", since in local dialect the word for cockerel is *jô* or *jau*. The square is therefore thought to have been a poultry market.

Another explanation links the origin of the word *Jaude* to the name of a suburb of Clermont, known in the Gallic language as *Vasso Galate*. While *wasso* or *vasso* is said to be the name of a Gallic divinity, *Galate* is merely a local name which has evolved over the years into *galde* or *gialde* (10C), *jalde* (12C) and, finally, *Jaude*.

Place de Jaude is the centre of life in Clermont. It is bordered by paulownias, the only trees that manage to grow on soil infiltrated by petrifying springs *(see Additional sights: Fontaines pétrifiantes de St-Aylre below)* and surrounded by department stores, cinemas and, on the south side, by the Centre Jaude, a vast modern shopping complex. At one end of the square are a statue of General Desaix (1768-1800), the hero of the Battle of Marengo who was born in Ayat-sur-Sioule, at the other a statue of Vercingétorix the Gaul, a lively piece of work by Bartholdi mounted on a base surrounded by columns.

St Pierre-les-Minimes (**EX**) – This vast domed church building in the Classical style has some fine wood panelling in the chancel.

Walk down Avenue des États-Unis then turn right into Rue des Gras.

Rue des Gras (**EV**) – A flight of steps used to lead from here right up to the cathedral. The west front of the cathedral is majestically integrated into the line of fine lavastone house fronts. At no 28, note the straight flight of steps, gallery and balcony dating from the 17C. No 22 has two entrances opening onto small inner courtyards. One of them, dating from the 15C, is carved with a man's head; the other is topped by a lintel on which angel musicians are shown surrounding a young woman. At the corner of Place des Gras, a Romanesque bas-relief set in the house front represents Christ washing the disciples' feet.

Marché Saint-Pierre (EV) – This market is situated at the heart of an old urban district that has been renovated, and stands on the site of a Romanesque church that no longer exists. It is a bustling centre on which narrow, picturesque shopping streets such as Rue de la Boucherie converge.

Return to Rue des Gras then, at Place de la Bourse, turn left into Rue Ph.-Marcombes (north of the cathedral) which leads to Place de la Poterne.

★**Fontaine d'Amboise** (EFV) – This fountain erected in 1515 by Jacques d'Amboise, Bishop of Clermont, is a very fine piece of Renaissance architecture, carved in lavastone from Volvic. The basin is decorated with charming foliage in the Italian style. The central pyramid is adorned with small, naked figures with water pouring from their mouths, or from the part of the anatomy for which their cousin in Brussels is famous. A hirsute Hercules at the top carries the coat-of-arms of the House of Amboise.

There is a fine view over the Puy de Dôme, along the whole length of the hillfort on the Côtes and over Chanturgue plateau.

Insider's guide to Clermont-Ferrand

Shopping – The area between Place de Jaude and Place Delille, around the cathedral district, has numerous pedestrian streets lined with shops catering for those in search of pretty knick-knacks or antiques. The Centre Jaude comprises a wide variety of stores grouped around the FNAC (CDs, videos, books etc.).

Photographs – If you can't wait to see those holiday snaps, you can get them developed at: Espace Photo (18, rue Fontgiève EV); Master Lab (place Gaillard); Rapid Lab (opposite Grand Pavois).

Local specialities – Chocoholics should head for Trianon (26, rue du 11-Novembre EV), where they can sample such hand-made delights as the Pascaline (raspberry-flavoured dark chocolate) or the Volcania (truffle).

The numerous little bistrots of Old Clermont and the city's gastronomic restaurants *(see Michelin Red Guide France)* offer culinary specialities featuring locally grown produce.

Sport – Clermont's excellent leisure facilities include a swimming pool (place P. de Coubertin EX), skating rink (boulevard G. Flaubert CZ), bowling alley (88, avenue du Brézet CY) and 9-hole golf course (at Royat).

Shows and festivals – Clermont hosts a short-film festival (early February) and a rock music festival, Rock au Maximum (early July).

Variety shows are performed at the Maison des Sports (place Bughes FV), and classical music concerts generally at the Maison des Congrès (boulevard Gergovial EX) where music-lovers can listen to the Orchestre d'Auvergne. Churches, auditoriums (Conservatory) and lecture halls (Law faculty) host concerts of chamber music. Plays are put on regularly at the Opéra municipal (boulevard Desaix) or the Maison des Congrès. Film buffs should check out VO... Le Rio (rue Sous-les-Vignes BY).

Entertainment – There is a huge variety of bars, brasseries, cinemas, crêperies, pubs, restaurants and tea-rooms in various parts of the city centre:

Place de Jaude (EX): Le Rabelais, Le Suffren and Le Thorens (piano-bar) attract an eager crowd of merry-makers. Set back from the square, Le Lutécia (21, avenue Julien DX) is a welcoming pub-style bar reflecting the cheery personality of the captain of the French rugby team who runs it.

Cathedral district: 1513 crêperie (rue des Chaussetiers EV); Chardonnay (place Philippe-Marcombes) and Relais Pascal (Rue Pascal FV) wine bars; La Perdrix and Whist (rue terrasse EV) bars (cocktails, beers).

Place Sugny (FX): the Winston pub organises musical entertainment every week, while jazz fans should seek out the 15e Avenue cellar (rue des Petits gras).

Rue Fontgiève (EV): this district has recently been renovated and has plenty to offer night-owls, from café-théâtre (Le Petit Vélo) to disco (Le George V).

Place Gaillard (EV): pale or dark, full-bodied or light, beer to suit all tastes is on offer at Palais de la Bière (rue de la Michodière). The Captain's Cabin (18, avenue des États-Unis) and the Blue Sport Café with its saloon decor (place de l'Étoile) organise a variety of events at the end of each week.

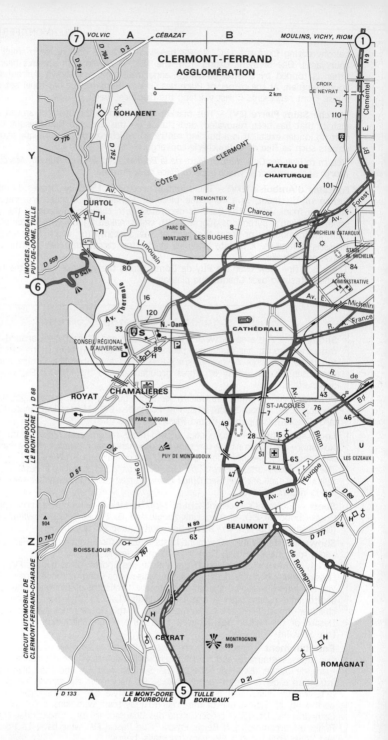

*Every year
the Michelin Red Guide France
revises its selection of hotels and restaurants which*

- *are pleasant, quiet, secluded;*
- *offer an exceptional, interesting or extensive view;*
- *have a tennis court, swimming pool or private beach;*
- *have a private garden...*

It is worth buying the current edition.

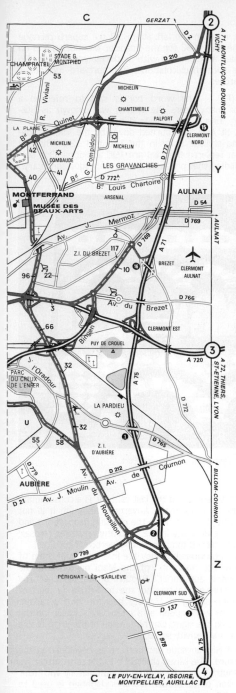

CLERMONT-FERRAND

*The current edition of the annual Michelin Red Guide France
offers a selection of pleasant and quiet hotels in convenient locations.
Their amenities are included (swimming pools, tennis courts,
private beaches and gardens...)
as well as their dates of annual closure.
The selection also includes establishments which offer excellent cuisine:
carefully prepared meals at reasonable prices, Michelin stars for good cooking.
The current annual Michelin Camping Caravaning France lists the facilities offered
by many campsites (shops, bars, restaurants, laundries, games rooms,
tennis courts, miniature golf courses, playgrounds, swimming pools...)*

Rue du Port (FV) – In this street, note on the left at no 38 the superb carriage entrance of the residence built in the early 18C for the financier Montlosier, and on the right at the corner of Rue Barnier, a 16C house with machicolated barbican. No 21 *(right)* is a narrow old house with machicolations; its courtyard includes a double gallery over basket-handle arches.

★★Basilique Notre-Dame-du-Port (FV) – The word *por* is said to refer to a marshy dip in the ground but for many years the church was known as Ste-Marie-Principale, from *princeps* or "first", the title held by the Count.

Founded in the 6C by the Bishop, St Avit, and burned down by the Vikings, the church was rebuilt with outstanding stylistic unity in the 11C and 12C. The bell towers and lavastone roof slabs that replaced the tiles are 19C additions. One section of the narthex belongs to a building that preceded the Romanesque sanctuary.

Detail of the façade of Notre-Dame-du-Port

Exterior – The east end, which was restored during the last century, is a consummate example of Romanesque architecture as used in the Auvergne. Although it is not possible to stand very far back from the building, note the pleasing proportions and the purity of the lines unaffected by the diversity in the decorative features (mosaic of coloured stonework, rose windows, carved modillions, chequerboard cornices).

A Romanesque door is decorated with carvings but they are in a very poor state of repair. Scenes on the lintel represent the Adoration of the Magi on the left, the Presentation in the Temple in the centre, and Christ's Baptism on the right. On the tympanum, surrounded by an arch projecting beyond the half-circle (a sign of oriental influence), the Lord is shown sitting in Majesty between two seraphim (six-winged angels). The other carvings were added at a later date – Isaiah on the left of the door, and John the Baptist on the right. On the outside of the arch, to the left, is the Annunciation; to the right is a Nativity scene.

Interior – The plain, robust design of Romanesque architecture as developed in the Auvergne is apparent from the entrance. The raised **chancel★★★**, the most attractive part of the building, is strikingly beautiful. It is flanked by an ambulatory with four radiating chapels. There is a profusion of decorative features. Lighting is used to emphasise the details on the **capitals★★**, which are among the most famous in the Auvergne. The feelings of the characters are expressed in a lively, energetic manner. Note the second capital on the left of the ambulatory: on the side facing the altar there is an angel holding the Book of Life and guiding the hand of a benefactor towards it. In his other hand, the benefactor has a capital. The other sides show the struggle between Virtues and Vices. Charity, dressed in chain mail, is fighting, shield to shield, with a hirsute man representing Avarice. Wrath is stabbing his own chest with the point of his lance; his arm is being restrained by a winged demon dressed in armour who is advancing, masked, across the corner of the capital from where he is directing the battle. Generosity and Charity are facing each other, stabbing the shoulders of defeated demons with their crossed lances.

Crypt – This dates from the 11C. Beneath the chancel, the "Underground" dear to the hearts of the local people has the same layout as the east end. In front of the altar is the carved edge of a well (16C) that existed before the church was built, probably during the days of the Celts and Gauls. On the altar is a small black statue of the Virgin Mary; it is a reproduction of a Byzantine icon, known to exist here since the 13C. Every year, a pilgrimage in honour of the statue attracts huge crowds.

Leave the church through the narthex and the steps down to Place Notre-Dame-du-Port.

The bare, heavy west front forms a contrast with the remainder of the building; it is preceded by a 16C porch. The austerity and bareness of the old wall are tempered by a row of triple arching beneath the gable, itself consisting of a mosaic of multi-coloured stonework. The unhappy square bell tower above it was added in the 19C. It is built of lavastone from Volvic.

Rue Pascal (FV) – *"The streets climb up between careworn façades where gateways open, yawning, onto damp courtyards. In the depths of the iron-coloured shadow is the turret of a spiral staircase, a decorated gallery, a doorway with a lintel shaped like the point of a shield"* (Henri Pourrat).

The old house at no 22 has bosses on the ground floor and a wrought-iron balcony. The entrance hall has sturdy pillars and the floor is decorated with a lavastone rose.

No 4 is M de Chazerat's residence; he was the last Intendant of the Auvergne and his mansion is a fine late 18C building. The **oval courtyard**, broken up by Ionic pilasters designed in accordance with the principles of the Colossal Order, gives an impression of majesty. Further down Rue de l'Oratoire that runs along the left of the mansion is the Fonds Régional d'Art Contemporain d'Auvergne *(metal doorway on the left)*, a modern art centre housed in the stables; it specialises in temporary exhibitions.

Cross the tiny Place du Terrail with its fountain (1664) and go down Rue du Terrail. Turn right into Rue Fléchier to Rue des Grands-Jours which skirts the east end of the cathedral. The wall of the Fléchier wing of the Hôtel de Ville is covered with decorative paintwork. At no 2, in an angled section of wall, there is a wooden doorway that opens onto a courtyard containing the superb early 17C Lambs' Door.

★★Cathédrale Notre-Dame-de-l'Assomption (EFV) ⊘ – The cathedral is strikingly different from Notre-Dame-du-Port basilica. The revolution in building techniques which occurred in the 13C is obvious here *(see Introduction: Architecture, p 36)*.

This is a lovely Gothic church with a design based on the cathedrals in Île de France (the region around Paris, where Gothic architecture first developed). Its black colour is due to the Volvic lavastone used in its construction; it is the only major cathedral built of this particular type of stone. The church standing today was begun in 1248, under the direction of Jean Deschamps; a Romanesque church previously stood here, itself replacing one or two earlier churches. Deschamps worked on it until his death c 1295, by which time the east end, transept and first span in the nave had been completed. The work continued during the first half of

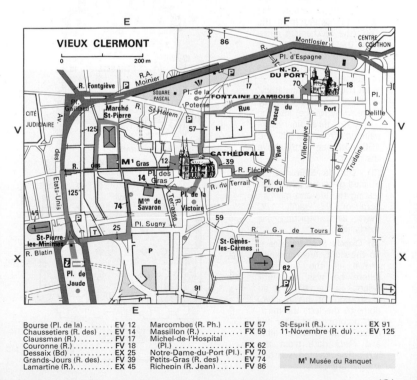

M¹ Musée du Ranquet

131

the 14C under Pierre de Cébazat, one of the master builders involved in building the monastery in La Chaise-Dieu. From 1866 onwards, the military architect Viollet-le-Duc built the narthex, two additional spans in the nave and the fine lavastone spires that can be seen from some distance away on the approach to Clermont; all the additions were built in the 13C style. Enter by the north door into the transept, beneath the Bayette tower. Adjacent to the tower is the Guette turret, once topped by a lookout post. The impression of ethereal lightness in the nave and, in particular, around the chancel shows the technical skills inherent

South rose window in the cathedral

in the Rayonnant Gothic style. The use of lavastone made it possible to reduce the width of the pillars, the arches of the vaulting, and the various sections of the openings. Note the **stained-glass windows★★** dating from the 12C to the 15C; the dominant colours are red and blue. The scattering of the French fleur-de-lys motif and the towers of Castile visible on some of the windows would seem to suggest that they date from the days of St Louis; the King may have given them to the cathedral on the occasion of the marriage of his son (the future Philippe III) in the cathedral in 1262. The transept is illuminated by two magnificent rose windows: the one in the south arm is deep red; the one in the north arm is deep violet. The lancets are set within a square.

Set in the gallery of the north transept arm is a clock with a jack o' the clock which strikes the hours (**1**) dating from the 16C (the mechanism dates from the 17C and 18C); it was taken from the town of Issoire during the Wars of Religion.

Walk round the ambulatory. Note, above the doorway (flanked by foliage) into the vestry (**2**), three fine votive paintings from the 13C and 15C, each one partly above the other.

(**3**) **Chapelle St-Georges** – Stained-glass window illustrating the life and martyrdom of the saint. 13C **fresco** also depicting his martyrdom.

(**4**) **Chapelle St-Austremoine** – To the right, Austremoine's arrival in the Auvergne where he was the first bishop. In the centre is an illustration of his martyrdom; to the left, the miracles accomplished after his death. The Baroque altar and *Pietà* date from the 17C. The painted wooden statues are 19C.

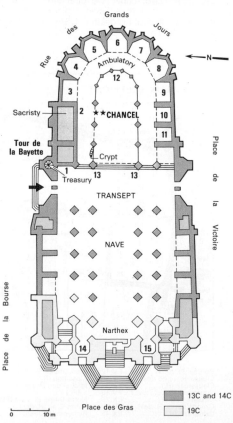

NOTRE-DAME-DE-L'ASSOMPTION

(**5**) **Mary Magdalene windows** illustrating the end of her life. 17C and 18C altar and *Pietà*. Statues of the Bishops of Clermont, St Arthème and St Alyre. Painting representing the martyrdom of St Sebastian.

(**6**) **Apsidal chapel** — To the left is the life of John the Baptist; in the centre, the childhood of Christ and to the right the miracle worked by Theophilus. Modern altar made of *repoussé* gilded lead by the sculptor, Kaeppelin, representing the Coronation of the Virgin Mary. The Romanesque statue of the Blessed Virgin Mary in Majesty, once known as Our Lady of Good Death, is remarkable for the draping of the clothes (in a "V" at the neck and in a reverse "V" on the arms and shoulders).

The statue dates from the same period as the ones in Marsat and Orcival and was probably a copy of the golden Madonna belonging to Étienne II, the prototype statue that was destroyed during the French Revolution *(see Introduction, p 26)*. Originally the statue was painted but the ebony paint that has covered the face and hands since 1833 led to its being considered, wrongly, as a Black Virgin.

(**7**) **St Bonnet windows** — St Bonnet was Bishop of Clermont in the 7C. To the left is a funerary painting of Canon Thomas Besson (d 1495) being presented to the Virgin Mary by his patron saint. A 16C painting shows the canons, laity and members of the Jeu family being welcomed to Heaven by an angel.

(**8**) **Funeral chapel of the bishops** — In the centre are 12C stained-glass windows from the former cathedral which illustrate the Life of Christ.

(**9**) **Chapelle Ste-Marguerite** — Lancet windows on the left illustrating the life of St Privat, Bishop of Mende in the 3C, and to the right the life of St Margaret. Altarpiece and Adoration of the Shepherds (17C).

(**10**) **St Agatha windows**.

(**11**) **Chapelle St-Arthème** has an altarpiece which was rebuilt in 1840 using 17C statues. The **chancel**★★ is closed off by large but light arches. Above the triforium, the long 13C and 14C stained-glass windows (**12**) have a *grisaille* background and have only one large figure per lancet. Recognisable among the illustrations is the Assumption of the Virgin Mary. In the chancel, note the gilded copper High Altar designed by Viollet-le-Duc, a fine paschal candlestick of gilded bronze made by Caffieri in 1771, and furnishings (1977-79) by Kaeppelin. There is also a monumental Crucifix, an altar and an ambo decorated with the figures of the Evangelists. Set against the pillars in the transept (**13**) are two statues of the Virgin Mary and St John; they were originally part of the rood screen which was demolished during the Revolution. They date from the 15C and were made in an archaic style.

Crypt ⊙ — The crypt was built in the 10C with an ambulatory and radiating chapels, and was altered when the Gothic cathedral was built. It contains a very fine 4C white marble **sarcophagus**★ decorated with scenes from the Life of Christ, including the Resurrection of Lazarus and Christ's Entry into Jerusalem on Palm Sunday. The ambulatory contains 12C-13C murals illustrating, among other scenes, the Multiplication of the Loaves and the Sermon on the Mount. At the west end of the inner north aisle (**14**), note the 14C statue of Christ of the Last Judgement, which was once set against the tympanum of the north doorway.

At the west end of the inner south aisle (**15**) is a stained-glass window (1982) by Makaraviez illustrating the Apocalypse of St John.

★**Treasury** ⊙ — *Enter via the Bayette tower.* Situated above the canons' sacristy, on a level with the clock (this is an opportunity to admire from close up Tempus flanked by Mars and Faunus), the treasure includes items dating from the 12C to the 19C. There is gold, silver and enamelware including pyxis, reliquaries, burettes, chalices, ciboria, monstrances and bishops' crosiers, as well as sacerdotal and liturgical vestments dating from the 17C, 18C and 19C: copes, chasubles, gremials and a superb frontal. Note the Romanesque sculptures (Virgin Mary in Majesty, large Crucifix and a head of Christ) and the 16C statues (the twelve Apostles).

Tour de la Bayette ⊙ — *250 steps.* From the top of the tower there is a fine panoramic view of Clermont and the surrounding countryside. Leave the cathedral by the doorway in the south transept which was designed to be flanked by two towers. The one on the right was demolished during the Revolution; the other one was apparently never finished.

The statues in the doorways, like the carvings on the tympanum and arching, were destroyed in 1793.

Place de la Victoire (**EVX**) — In the centre is a monument commemorating the Crusades, and a fountain with a statue of Pope Urban II. From here there is a general view of the cathedral.

Rue des Chaussetiers (**EV 14**) — Furniture and carpet shops fill the vaulted ground floors of old houses, and there is an abundance of doors and arches. At no 3, at the corner of Rue Terrasse, is the **Maison de Savaron**, a mansion built in 1513. The **courtyard**★ contains a staircase turret linked to the main building by three floors of overhanging landings. The turret includes a superb carved doorway known as the

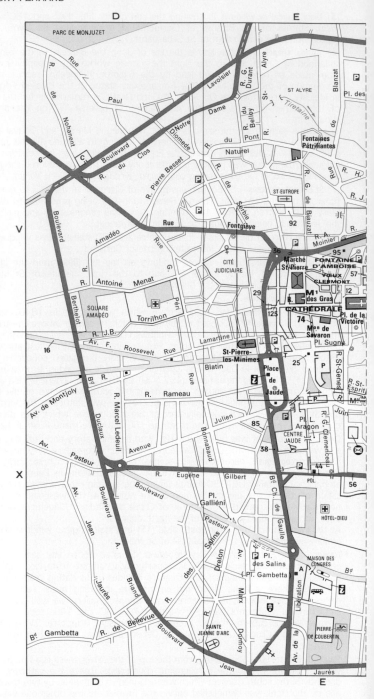

"Door of the Wild Men". At no 10 there is a Gothic doorway and wrought-iron grilles at the windows. At the corner of Rue des Petits-Gras are Romanesque arches (12C, the oldest examples of this style to be seen in vernacular buildings in Clermont).

Rue des Petits-Gras (**EVX 74**) – At nos 4-6 (windows with grotesque masks), in the second of the two buildings beyond the courtyard, there is a monumental three-storey **staircase★** supported by corbels and oblique basket-handled arches. The straight flights of steps and landings are a particularly successful example of 18C architecture. Note the wrought-iron balustrade and its lantern with hanging keystone.

Opposite the house is an unusual fountain.

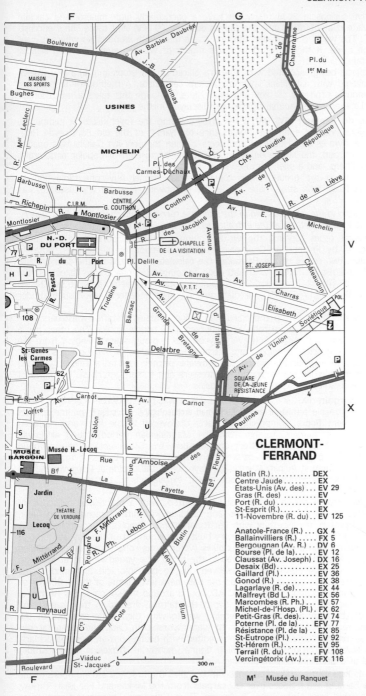

CLERMONT-FERRAND

M¹   Musée du Ranquet

ADDITIONAL SIGHTS

Fontaines pétrifiantes de St-Alyre (EV) – Clermont has twenty-two **mineral springs** with temperatures ranging from 6°C to 18°C/42°F to 64°F. Most of them rise from a fault running from Place des Salins to the St-Alyre District. This break in the ground is obvious in the sharp change in level at the end of the hill on which the old town is built, to the west, and is most clearly seen on Boulevard Desaix, beside the *préfecture* (County Buildings). On Place des Salins, the water has a high carbon dioxide content; it was used to produce soda water and lemonade. Other springs rich in bicarbonate of soda produce table waters.

The five springs in St-Alyre, which have a particularly high mineral and calcium carbonate content, flow into the **Grottes du Pérou** ⊘ (**EV**) and cause "lime encrustment". The water is channelled through ducts filled with wood chips where it loses its iron oxide. It then flows down over flights of wooden steps, forming slender waterfalls.

The objects being encrusted with lime are placed on the steps and, in a few weeks, are covered with a brilliant layer of calcium carbonate. A method of incrustation over moulds produces cameos and low-reliefs, although this takes a much longer time. Lime-encrusted animal figures are displayed in the park.

Musée du Ranquet (**EV**) (**M¹**) ⊘ – After crossing the foyer used for temporary exhibitions, visitors enter the Renaissance **courtyard★** of the old Fontfreyde Residence, known as the "House of Architects". When the new Art Gallery was opened in Montferrand, the Musée du Ranquet became a museum of popular arts, crafts and traditions, and a science museum.

The room on the ground floor contains a traditional Auvergne table and an enamelled cast iron stove (late 19C). The winnowing machine was used to sort grain.

After admiring the motifs carved in the staircase turret, go up to the first-floor gallery. There is a penny-farthing at the entrance to the Pascal room.

The Pascal room contains the writer's funeral mask, a portrait of his sister, Jacqueline, by Philippe de Champaigne and a selection of mementoes. Note, in particular, two copies of the *Pascaline*, the calculator invented by the young Blaise Pascal to assist his father, who had been appointed Intendant "for Taxes and the Raising of Tithes" in Rouen. An adjoining room commemorates Louis Charles Antoine Desaix (1768-1800), a distinguished French general who fought under Napoleon.

There are two rooms on the third floor. One contains distaffs, waistcoats, lace bonnets with their fluting irons and nineteen 19C heddle hooks. The other has a fine collection of furniture and everyday objects – ploughshares hanging from the walls, hurdy-gurdies, bagpipes, and pitchers in the shape of owls' or pigs' heads. There is also a *mélard*, a glazed earthenware pitcher used as a vinegar jar, two traditional Auvergne box beds, clocks, dressers and a marriage chest. Examples of toys include small chests and magic lanterns.

★Musée Bargoin (**FX**) ⊘ – This museum, which was built between 1899 and 1903, houses a sizeable **prehistoric and Gallo-Roman archaeological collection★** on the ground and basement floors, comprising artefacts discovered in the local area: chipped flints and deer-hunters' tombs from the Magdalenian period, found at Enval, Blanzat and St-Diéry; axes, pottery and jewellery from the Neolithic period, found at the Cébazat dig; a magnificent set of bronzes at Manson; traces of Ancient Celtic civilizations found at Aulnat, Martres-de-Veyre or in the oppida at Gergovie and the Côtes de Clermont; discoveries from recent excavations in the city of Clermont itself.

The Gallo-Roman period is the best represented, with a marvellous collection of statuettes of animals, men, women and children in white terracotta from Allier, sigillated pottery from Lezoux with particularly fine examples dating from the 2C, vestiges of the great temple of Mercury built on the summit of the Puy-de-Dôme at the beginning of the Imperial era; **clothes** (voluminous robe with sleeves, woollen stockings, kidskin slippers) discovered in the tomb of a young woman at Martres-de-Veyre are exceptionally well-preserved due to carbonic acid contained in the waters of a nearby spring. Finally, on the basement level, some of the 3 000 or so **wooden ex-votos★** dating from the 1C AD, found around the spring at Les Roches in Chamalières, are on display. These depict the faithful dressed in their capes, and parts of the body which had something wrong with them. The presence of the Romans reinforced the existing cult of water-worship in Gaul, and the numerous thermal springs, some of which were credited with healing power, were particularly highly revered. The group of standing figures, subtly lit, frozen in rigid attitudes devoid of expression, is most striking.

Musée du Tapis d'Art – This carpet museum occupies the first and second floors of the Musée Bargoin and includes over 80 carpets from the Middle and Far East: Turkey, the Caucasus, Iran, Afghanistan, Turkestan, Tibet, China etc. These rare pieces, some of which date from the 18C, are the expression of civilizations marked by their nomadic way of life and are at the same time devotional objects rich in spiritual symbolism, invaluable items for everyday domestic use and dazzlingly colourful works of art. Persia (modern Iran), traditionally the land of carpets, which have been hand-crafted here since the 6C BC, occupies a major place in this chronological exhibition.

The second floor is reserved for temporary exhibitions on particular themes.

Jardin Lecoq (**FX**) – This attractive park stretches over an area of 3ha/7 acres. Near the lake is a 14C entrance brought here from the Château de Bien-Assis, built for the Duc de Berry and owned, in the 17C, by Florin Périer, Blaise Pascal's brother-in-law.

Musée H-Lecoq (FX) ⊘ – This museum is named after the naturalist Henri Lecoq (1802-71) whose wide-ranging collections of stuffed animals, local rocks and local plants make this a natural history museum very much centred on the Auvergne.

Rue Fontgiève (DEV) – Note, at no 46, the fragment of 15C rood screen from the cathedral.

St Genès-les-Carmes (FX) – This church, built in the Southern French Gothic style, has a wide nave and a fine apse.

★★ VIEUX MONTFERRAND (OLD MONTFERRAND) (BCY)

Montferrand was founded by the Counts of Auvergne who built a fortress on a rise that is now the site of Place Marcel-Sembat, in order to counter the authority of the Bishop, who was also Lord of Clermont. In the early 13C the town was rebuilt on the orders of a powerful woman named Countess Brayère and was turned into a *bastide*, a fortified hilltop town laid out to a strictly symmetrical geometric pattern. Two main roads cut across each other at right angles; they led to the four gates in the town walls. Narrow alleyways acting as firebreaks were built between the houses. Montferrand was a commercial centre, for it lay at the junction of several roads and, in the 15C, the wealthy middle classes began to commission town houses. The narrowness of the plots of land made available by Countess Brayère's town plan, however, forced the architects to design houses that were deep rather than wide: on the street, there was a narrow shop flanked by an entrance porch; beyond, stood an inner courtyard with two or three storeys of galleries and a staircase turret leading to the apartments; on the other side of the courtyard were warehouses for goods. Most of the houses were built of lavastone. Montferrand was so commercially successful that, in the 16C, the king set up law courts – known as the Cour des Aides – there to try fiscal and criminal cases. This brought new work for local architects, who had to design mansions for the *noblesse de robe* (new aristocracy whose rank was derived from holding high state office).

The proximity of Clermont caused rivalry and jealousy between the two towns. Montferrand eventually went into a decline; in 1630 Richelieu transferred the Cour des Aides to Clermont and set plans in motion for the annexation of the town to its neighbour. In 1731, the conurbation came into official existence and the dual origin of the town was no longer evident other than in its double name.

In 1962 work was undertaken to renovate Montferrand old town, a project which covered some 80 old townhouses. Over the past few years, numerous mansions have recovered their original façades, decorated with carved heads, balustrades, staircase turrets, cornerstones and lavastone arches contrasting with the honey-coloured "Montferrand roughcast". There are three types of houses, all clearly distinguishable. They range from the modest houses of the farmers, wine-growers and vegetable producers, which have a flight of steps on the exterior (southeast side of the town) to the half-timbered houses of the shopkeepers in which the stone ground floor includes the arches for the shopfronts, and finally the superb mansions of the wealthy merchants and officials, built of Volvic stone and decorated with carvings.

Park in Place de la Rodade.

Place de la Rodade – This square was once known as Place de Belregard because of the view over the Puys range. The metal barriers are used during the annual livestock fair. In the centre stands the Four Seasons Fountain made of lavastone from Volvic.

Enter Montferrand old town via Rue de la Rodade.

Hôtel Regin (W) – At no 36. This 15C and 16C townhouse belonged to a family of magistrates and is typical of the mansions built in Montferrand. In the **courtyard★** there is a fine statue of St Christopher. To the right, the gallery above is carved with an Annunciation scene (which has led to the mansion's also being known as the Maison de l'Annonciation).

Hôtel Doyac (B) – At no 29. Late 15C mansion built for Jean de Doyac, Royal Bailiff of Montferrand and minister to Louis XI. Huge, imposing Gothic doorway.

Hôtel du Bailliage (E) – At no 20. Bailiwick House is the former Consuls' Residence. Its gargoyles and vaulted rooms are of particular interest.

After Rue de la Rodade widens, a fine set of timbered houses with corbelling comes into view on the left in the renovated district. Their rounded doorways and shop-fronts are set out on high landings that reveal the original level of the roadway. At no 6 there is a fine inner courtyard and a balustered staircase.

Turn back; at the corner marked by the Maison de l'Échauguette (Watchtower House), turn right into Rue Marmillat.

Hôtel de la Porte (D) – At no 5 Rue Marmillat. In the courtyard of this mansion, also known as the Architect's House, there is a staircase turret decorated with an interesting Renaissance sculpture dating from 1577.

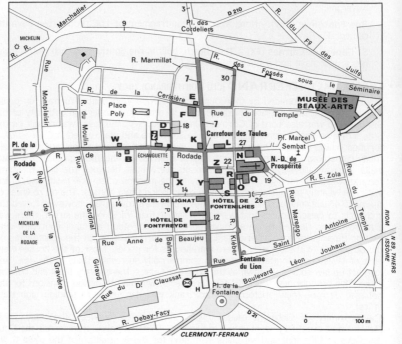

VIEUX MONTFERRAND

Clémentel (R. Étienne) 3

B Hôtel Doyac
D Hôtel de la Porte
E Hôtel de la Faye des Forges
F Maison à double galerie
    de bois
K Maison de l'Apothicaire

L Halle aux Toiles
N Hôtel d'Étienne Pradal
O Chanterie
Q Maison d'Adam et Ève
R Maison de l'Éléphant
S Maison de l'Ange

V Hôtel Gaschier
W Hôtel Regin
X Hôtel d'Albiat
Y Hôtel d'Albiat
    (Maison des Centaures)
Z Hôtel Mallet-de-Vandègre

Turn right into Rue de la Cerisière.

Hôtel de la Faye des Forges (**E**) – *At no 2 Rue de la Cerisière.* A glass door protects a delightful inner door with a carved tympanum decorated with lions holding a phylactery. The house opposite (**F**) has a double timber gallery, an unusual feature in Montferrand.

Turn left along Rue des Cordeliers to Rue Waldeck-Rousseau.

Rue Waldeck-Rousseau runs along the inside of the old town walls, high above the road laid out along the moat which was once liable to flooding from the River Tiretaine.

Turn right into Rue du Temple, back to Rue des Cordeliers.

Rue des Cordeliers – At nos 6 and 16, there are delightful little inner courtyards. At no 11, note the Renaissance ground floor flanked by pilasters. No 5 has Renaissance arches on the façade.

Carrefour des Taules – This is the central junction in the old town. Its name is a reminder that this was traditionally where butchers had their stalls. Here the street used to consist of a flight of steps but it was lowered in the 18C to facilitate the passage of carts so that it is now the cellars which are on ground floor level. Further down, on Rue des Cordeliers and Rue Jules-Guesde, the former ground floors lie below the level of the road, which was raised by the addition of infill.

Maison de l'Apothicaire (**K**) – *At no 1 Rue des Cordeliers.* The old Apothecary's House dates from the 15C and has two timbered upper storeys. At the top of the house, the brackets on either side of the gable are decorated with an apothecary carrying his clyster and the patient awaiting his operation.

Turn left into Rue du Séminaire.

Halle aux Toiles (**L**) – At no 3, the old cloth market, there is a long balcony supporting a fine row of four basket-handled arches and corresponding side doors.

Hôtel d'Étienne Pradel (**N**) – *At no 22.* The ground floor of this mansion has superb semicircular and basket-handled arches. On the upper storeys are mullioned Renaissance windows. Its "Montferrand roughcast" and cornerstones made of lavastone are typical of the town's architecture.

Notre-Dame-de-Prospérité – The church, built from 1304 onwards, stands on the site of the chapel that was part of the Counts of Auvergne's castle. Note the gargoyles around the exterior of the building. Their elongated outlines form a stark contrast to the regular lavastone bonding. The west front still has its north tower (the south tower was destroyed in 1793) which was used as a watchtower. It is topped by a lantern called "L'Olivière" (16C).

The wide nave (18m/59ft in height and width) is built in the Southern French Gothic style. The side chapels contain carved 17C altar screens rebuilt after the Revolution with pieces brought from the convents and monasteries that had been destroyed in Clermont. A fine Flamboyant Gothic rose window lights up the front. Beneath the left bell tower is the vaulted chapel of St Catherine containing a Romanesque statue of the Virgin Mary in Majesty, part of a tympanum that was destroyed, and on the wall a 16C fresco.

Return to Rue Montorcier.

Maison d'Adam et d'Eve (**Q**) – *At no 4.* In the courtyard on a balustrade is a 15C **bas-relief★** representing Adam and Eve. The staircase turret supports an Italianate loggia.

Chanterie (**O**) – *At no 2.* The 13C choir school.

Turn left into Rue Kléber.

★Maison de l'Éléphant (**R**) – *At no 12.* A 13C Romanesque house. The great arches on the ground floor support the twin bay windows on the first floor. On the tympanum above the central bay is a fresco that once depicted an elephant, hence the name given to the house (another interpretation has it that "elephant" is a phonetic deformation of "oliphant", the horn used to announce the arrival of an important visitor). Crowned heads decorate the brackets.

Maison de l'Ange (**S**) – *At no 14.* In the courtyard is a small, triangular tympanum above a doorway representing an angel carrying a coat-of-arms.

In Rue Ste-Marie *(left)*, at the foot of the passageway that spans the road, there is the old doorway of the Visitation Convent (note the shield flanked by scallop shells).

Fontaine du Lion – The fountain comes from a square to which it had given its name. On the gable is a lion carrying the blazoned coat-of-arms of Montferrand.

Hôtel de Fontfreyde – *At no 28.* In the courtyard of this mansion, also known as Lucretia's House, there is a delightful Madonna and Child on the Gothic doorway into the staircase turret, carved in the Renaissance style from the same block of lavastone as the tympanum. The balustrade on the gallery bears three fine Italianate medallions depicting Lucretia stabbing herself, between her husband and the man who raped her.

Hôtel Gaschier (**V**) – *At no 20.* Three rows of galleries, one above the other, open onto the courtyard (15C-16C). The first floor is supported by superb pillars. There is a tympanum decorated with a coat-of-arms on the polygonal staircase turret.

★Hôtel de Lignat – *At no 18.* This, the Lawyer's House, dates from the 16C. Gracious mullioned windows open onto the street. It opens onto Grande-Rue-du-Languedoc through a very elegant door decorated with a garland of roses in the Italian Renaissance style. The courtyard includes an attractive staircase turret rising to three levels of galleries. One of them is decorated with fleurs-de-lys and with the remainder of an Annunciation scene, although it has now worn almost completely away

★Hôtel de Fontenilhes – *At no 13.* The house, a fine residence dating from the late 16C, was built of lavastone from Volvic. The courtyard, with its three levels of galleries, has a spiral staircase turret. Note the carvings of lions, griffins, unicorns, and the succession of the three Classical Orders (Doric, Ionic and Corinthian).

Hôtel d'Albiat (**Y**) – *At no 11.* The "Centaurs' House", built for a family of bankers, owes its name to the sculpture decorating a **door★** in its courtyard, which depicts a male and a female centaur fighting an angel brandishing a sword.

Walk down Rue Notre-Dame.

Hôtel Mallet-de-Vandègre (**Z**) – This building, with its austere courtyard, is said to have been the women's prison. From the steps on Rue Notre-Dame note the fine masonry and the lavastone arches which stand out from the roughcast of the houses at nos 8 and 4 of Rue Jules-Guesde. They are indicative of several different periods of construction.

Cross Carrefour des Taules, walk along Rue de la Rodade and turn left into Rue du Dr-Balme.

At no 5 is a Romanesque house with colonnettes and capitals on the front. At no 11 there is a second **Hôtel d'Albiat** (**X**) dating from the 16C. In the courtyard, a scene (the legend of the unicorn) is visible on the tympanum above a door but it is in a poor state of repair. On the gallery there is a scene representing the risen Christ's appearance to the holy women. The corbels are carved in the shape of heads. See also the well and oven *(to the left and opposite)*.

★★ MUSÉE DES BEAUX-ARTS ⊙

A change of use – The history of these premises reflects the history of the two rival towns, Montferrand and Clermont, each in turn the seat of various official bodies. The museum stands on the site of the Palais Vieux above the town walls. It was the seat of the royal bailiwick then of the Cour des Aides of the Auvergne, the Limousin and the Marches; the monumental gateway built in the early 17C in front of the courtyard that precedes the chapel is all that remains of this building. When Montferrand and Clermont were combined, the Cour des Aides moved to Clermont and the Ursuline Order of nuns took over and reconstructed the buildings. The site was turned into a seminary after the Revolution, then into a military hospital from 1914 to 1918, and into barracks for the riot police and gendarmerie, before being transformed from 1986 to 1992 into a museum. The buildings and their surroundings are a reflection of Montferrand. They constitute the old "Gateway of the Rising Sun" and open the historic centre of the town to its suburbs.

An exemplary history – The idea of walking around a central open space, as illustrated in the Guggenheim Museum in New York, inspired the architects Adrien Fainsilber (designer of the Cité des Sciences and the Géode at La Villette in Paris) and Claude Gaillard.
The glass roof shaped like a palm-tree, made by Peter Rice, gives unity to a courtyard with a complex shape. The curves of the concrete staircase, emphasised by metal hand-rails, elegantly unfold from one floor to the next.
Visitors walk through the various rooms around the courtyard. A sculpture, painting, piece of stairway or section of glass can be seen from a distance, from an unexpected angle, through a framework of Volvic stone. In each room, the light source is concealed, creating an impression of well-being and an atmosphere of meditation.

The collections – These used to be housed in the Bargouin and Le Ranquet museums.

The collections are exhibited in chronological order, combining various art forms in the same display, with paintings hung next to sculptures, items of furniture and objets d'art.

Ground Floor *(follow the blue arrows)*:

★The **Middle Ages** – A fine display of enamelwork greets visitors to the room on the left. Note, in another display cabinet, a number of **carved ivories**. At the end of the room is a fine capital from the church in Ménat. The *Meeting of Priests* brought here from the church in Ennezat is a rare example, in France, of a late 13C painting on wood. The rigidity of the Romanesque art work is softened by the expression in the faces and hands, and the use of subtle hues of pinks and beiges. The room on the right, which deals with 14C and 15C art, includes **Guillaume Savaron's travelling chest**, a valuable item made of embossed and gilded leather, representing bathing scenes, hunts, games and dancing. All the figures are dressed in elegant 15C costume.

The **Renaissance** – Fine furnishings, columns from Clermont Hospital and carved wooden panels from Cantal are set out next to a number of outstanding paintings which include a *Portrait of a Young Man* by Bronzino and the dreamlike *Belshazzar's Feast* by Gillis van Valkenborsch.

First Floor:

17C – The first room contains the **decor★** from a grand gallery in the Château d'Effiat, unfurled like a screen. The illustrations of nature (lushly fertile valleys, streams, dense forests) create a mysterious presence in which the hero Roland is seen as described in the poem by Ariosto, *Orlando Furioso*. In the same room is *The Imprunete Fair* in Florence and *The Miseries of War* inspired by Jacques Callot but painted by his nephew. There is also a magnificent **Portrait of Vincent Voiture★** by Philippe de Champaigne and *The Conversion of St Paul* by Jean Daret.
The last 17C room includes some interesting Dutch interiors (the paintings are accompanied by a cabinet of the same origin, decorated with marble and lapis lazuli), seascapes (display cabinets) and an extraordinary *Elves Dancing* by David Ryckaert III.
The **18C** begins with the artistry of the portrait-painter. There is a formal portrait notable for the rigidity of the composition (*The Duchess de Maine Picking a Piece of Orange Blossom* from Rigaud's studio), a more intimate and sensual portrait of Christine Van Loo, and a fine study by Duplessis: **Portrait of Antoine Léonard Thomas★**. It

shows a refined treatment of very ordinary clothing, gives nobility of expression to facial features of a commoner, and indicates attentive, uncompromising observation of the model.

A corridor running along the atrium leads to a vast room in which the *Portrait of Louis XVI* by Antoine Callet differs from the usual paintings of sovereigns. The 25-year-old King has a robust physique, a full face, a quizzical expression and an air of haughtiness. *Les Lavandières*, a rural landscape by Boucher, is a very free piece of interpretation: a twisted tree mirrors the bend in the path; the light, airy foliage rises up to a cloudy sky where it disappears.

The **chapel** is used for exhibitions and concerts, and with its black lavastone bonding it is reminiscent of the austere harmony of Renaissance buildings in Florence. The last two rooms are devoted to 18C landscapes (*Seascape* by Joseph Vernet) and to Neo-Classical painting.

Second Floor:

The **19C** – History, archaeology, tropical landscapes, the Auvergne has inspired artists who shook off the constraints of Classicism and overturned the hierarchy of genres. The great **19C gallery★** reflects this eclecticism and, through sculptures and paintings, gives an insight into the profusion of artistic creativity during this period. The rediscovery of Vercingétorix as a national hero and emblematic figure representing patriotism may be seen in the vast work by Théodore Chassériau, *The Defence of the Gauls*, which was first hung at the World Fair in 1855, and in the plaster equestrian statue by Bartholdi (the original can be seen on Place de Jaude). Behind the painting are five sketches and statuettes of Gauls.

Other artists chose landscapes as a medium in which to express their search for somewhere different. There is the *Egyptian Landscape at Sunset* by Prosper Merilhat and *Midnight Sun on the Island of Hestman in Norway* by Knut Baade. In the other rooms, a collection of objects and costumes from China, Saigon and the Middle East accompany Oriental-style paintings, or works dealing with subjects specific to the Auvergne such as the delightful **Little Reaper★** by Thomas Degeorge, hung opposite the *Harvester and the Young Girl* (1836). In one of the small rooms is a striking painting by Gustave Doré, *The Tumblers*.

The **20C** is represented by busts (*Madame de Massary* by Camille Claudel), the paintings from the Maurice Combe Bequest – *In the Forest, The Kept Woman* by Edouard Goerg (1893-1969), and *The Moulin Rouge* by Gen Paul – and a tapestry by Jean Lurçat, *The Shadow Eater*.

CHAMALIÈRES (AYZ)

Chamalières (population 17 305) is an important residential and business centre and the headquarters for some of the tourist and spa amenities in **Royat** *(see alphabetical entry)*. The bank notes for the Banque de France are printed here.

Notre-Dame (AY) – Of the five churches that once stood in Chamalières, only one is still extant. Its nave consists of the remains of an early building, dating back to a time before the year AD 1000. In the 12C the chancel was extended and rebuilt. In the 17C the barrel vaulting was partly turned into ogival vaulting. The belltower dates from the 19C. The east end includes a number of carved capitals.

At the end of the nave are two Carolingian capitals above two green marble columns, probably originally part of a Roman monument.

Moulin de la Saigne (AY S) – *Beyond the church take Rue de la Coifferie and Rue du Languedoc*. The fast currents of the River Tiretaine have always favoured the installation of water-wheels: there have been flour mills along the river since the 10C and papermills from the 15C. This old mill, once the property of the Jesuits, operated until 1939. Note the *trompe-l'oeil* mural on the walls giving onto the square.

Galerie d'Art contemporain (AY D) ⊘ – Cross Place de Geretsried to no 3 Avenue de Fontmaure, within the Carrefour-Europe residential and shopping complex.

Space is fairly limited in this Modern Art Gallery but the exhibitions are interesting and they attract all the latest names in modern painting and sculpture. The works donated by artists to the Gallery form its permanent stock.

EXCURSIONS

The Battle of Gergovia – In the year 52 BC Caesar was carrying out his 7th military campaign in Gaul; he had just defeated the Gallic army in Bourges and the Gauls had retreated to the mountains of the Massif Central, pursued by six Roman legions. **Vercingetorix**, the leader of the Gallic coalition, had retreated to the Arverni's hillfort in Gergovia, which was defended by a dry stone wall 6m/almost 20ft high. From the ramparts of the Arverni hillfort in **Nemessos**, which might be the "Gergovia" mentioned by Caesar where Vercingetorix came to seek refuge, the Gauls had an extensive view down over the main Roman encampment in Montferrand. One night,

Caesar captured their advanced position in Chanturgue, by surprise, and set up a lesser encampment there, linking it to the main camp by a ditch along which he could move his troops.

Caesar then ordered his troops to implement a diversionary movement by night, along the Bédat valley that skirted the Arverni's hill-fort, to give Vercingetorix the idea that his army might be attacked from the rear. The next day, three Roman legions moved from the main camp up to the lesser camp and, shortly after midday, launched an attack. Vercingetorix, however, was a good strategist and had concealed troops behind the Puy de la Mouchette who put up fierce resistance against the Romans. Further-more, the Gauls on the plateau – alerted by the shouts of the womenfolk – ran quickly back to the scene of the real battle and routed the Roman legions. At the same time the Aedui, allies of the Romans, arrived from the plain and appeared to the right of the Roman army, and promptly changed allegiance.

46 centurions and 700 legionaries were killed beneath the walls of Gergovia.

Vercingetorix wisely brought his troops to a halt on the plain. Caesar lifted the siege for a few days. The Gauls' success was short-lived, however: their chieftain was besieged in Alésia and finally surrendered to Caesar at the end of the summer.

The site of this historic battle is said by some to be Chanturgue plateau, by others to be Gergovie plateau.

★Plateau de Chanturgue – *2km/1mi north of Clermont-Ferrand.*

The Chanturgue plateau (alt 553m/1797ft) constitutes the remains of a vast volcanic table which erosion has worn down into several sections. To the north, looking from left to right, the horizon is barred by the Côtes de Clermont that rise to 40m/130ft above the plateau and are separated from it by the tiny Puy de la Mouchette, and by the Puy de Var. The hillsides still bear a few traces of what was once a famous wine-growing area but the vineyards are gradually being replaced by housing.

In the bases of drystone walls, covered with stubble or concealed by the under-growth, archaeologists have found the remains of what may have been Caesar's lesser encampment; they included the remains of ramparts with their walkway, the base of a tower, redans, a trap for a small detachment of attackers, a watchtower, the main road, and the usual geographically-oriented barracks. Chanturgue, then, is perhaps a Roman encampment dating back to the days of Caesar's Gallic wars.

★Plateau de Gergovie – *7km/4mi south of Clermont-Ferrand. Local map under Lac d'AYDAT.*

The Gergovie plateau stands almost 400m/1 300ft above the Allier valley and the current level of the Limagne plain. It is 1 500m/4 875ft long and 500m/1 625ft wide and its sides form scarp slopes. The basalt table above it, which is 20 to 30m/65 to 98ft thick, was formed by a lava flow. The table rises to an altitude of 745m/2 421ft and protects the lower levels of marl and limestone from erosion, thereby producing "inversion relief".

The archaeological remains found here are displayed in an exhibition centre (Maison de Gergovie) which recounts the famous battle.

Maison de Gergovie ⊙ – *Access from the terrace or down the hill.* The information centre on the plateau has a threefold exhibition – one on geology and local flora illustrated by photographs and models, one on archaeology (grave containing the skeleton of a young woman, day-to-day life of the Gauls in the hillfort) and a third on the history of this important site, Napoleon III's visit and the archaeological digs that have been carried out here. A diorama retraces the various stages in the battle between the Romans and the Gauls. The last room gives visitors information on the controversy between scholars who favour Chanturgue as the site of the battlefield and those who believe that the battle was fought here on Gergovie plateau.

Plateau du COIRON

Michelin map 76 folds 19, 20 and 80 folds 9, 10 or 246 folds 20, 21

The deeply-eroded volcanic bar that forms the Coiron plateau marks, to the north, the limit of the Lower Vivarais area. Its black basalt rocks cut across the line of hills from the Escrinet pass to the River Rhône, creating the starkly contrasting Rochemaure dikes.

The upper part of the Coiron plateau takes the form of a vast, bare *planèze* with an average altitude of 800m/2 600ft rising from the banks of the Rhône in a northwest-erly direction.

The edge of the plateau consists of a series of indentations like deeply-veined oak leaves. Above the sediment, the upper layer of basalt is clearly visible. The basalt crowns are far and away the most characteristic feature of the Coiron plateau around Villeneuve-de-Berg and Privas, where they form a row of regular bars high above the limestone lowlands.

1 VILLAGES AND VIEWPOINTS ON THE COIRON PLATEAU

Round trip of 45km/28mi from Villeneuve-de-Berg – about 2hr

Villeneuve-de-Berg – This peaceful town with an atmosphere redolent of southern France conserves the remains of its old 14C ramparts and an attractive old town centre *(to the south)*.

Leave Villeneuve-de-Berg on the D 258 to Mirabel then turn right into the road to Le Pradel, the D 458 and D 458A.

Le Pradel – This is an area of experimental farming. Note the 17C farmhouse.

Turn right, back onto the D 258 and follow the signs to Mirabel.

★**Mirabel** – Once a stronghold guarding the main route from the Rhône to the Cévennes, Mirabel can now only boast a square keep on a base of basalt. There is a good **view**★★ from the road climbing off to the left at the entrance to the village.

Take the D 258 to Darbres; follow signs to Lussas but turn right almost immediately into the narrow D 324.

St-Laurent-sous-Coiron – This is a village of black basalt houses. From the terrace near the church there is a superb **view**★ over the Aubenas basin with the Tanargue massif in the background, the Mirabel keep to the left and the Ste-Marguerite mountain to the right.

Return to Villeneuve-de-Berg via Lussas and the D 259 and D 258.

From these roads, there are alternating views of the Tanargue and the basalt caps on the Coiron plateau.

★★ 2 COIRON TOUR

77km/48mi from Privas – allow half a day. Head south from Privas along the D 7, following the signs to Villeneuve-de-Berg.

The road crosses the Ouvèze basin, then enters the sun-baked Bayonne gorge.

6km/4mi further on, turn left into the road leading to Verdus museum.

As the road climbs the hillside, there is a succession of superb views of Privas and the surrounding area.
Suddenly, though, where the basalt has covered the base of the mountain, the scenery becomes darker and gloomier.

At the junction with the road to Freyssenet, turn left towards Taverne.

The *planèze* stretches away as undulating moorland dotted with juniper bushes, box and broom, a landscape bereft of human habitation were it not for the hamlet of Taverne.

In Taverne, take the D 213.

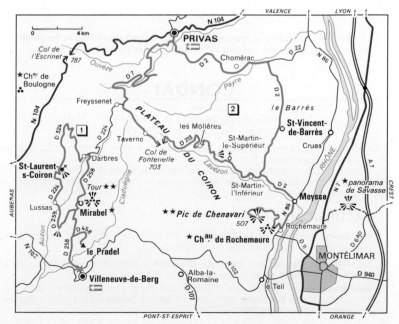

Between the Fontenelle pass (Col de Fontenelle) and the hamlet of Les Molières, a broad gap in the hills provides a view of the River Rhône in the distance. In the foreground are basalt columns down which runs a thin stream of water. On one of the hillsides to the right, erosion has worn the rock down to the underlying limestone layer. The road then runs steeply down to Les Molières along the side of the ravine where the various strata in the rock are clearly visible.

Before arriving in St-Martin-le-Supérieur, the road gives a delightful view of the charming little Romanesque church with its belfry-wall.

Beyond St-Martin-l'Inférieur turn right along the lower Lavézon valley. The river bed is covered with large, rounded, black and white boulders.

Meysse – *15min Rtn on foot.* The old village can be discerned behind its façade of more modern housing. Around the old Romanesque church, now deconsecrated and in a poor state of repair, is a network of narrow streets and vaulted passages.

Leave Meysse on the N 86 south.

To the right of the road on the outskirts of the village stands a pinnacle of basalt rock. Beyond it are the ruins of Rochemaure castle.

★**Château de Rochemaure** ⊙ – *Near Rochemaure church (follow signs to "Château") take the minor road to the right of the mairie.* The ruins of Rochemaure castle stand on an impressive **site**★★ on the southern edge of the Coiron plateau, where basalt rocks (*Rochemaure* means "black rocks") contrast with the limestone escarpment along the Rhône.

Members of the many noble families which have owned the castle – Adhémar, Anduze, Levis-Vendatour, Rohan-Soubise – are buried in the 13C Gothic chapel. The castle (12C to 14C) was besieged by the Huguenots in the 16C and 17C and abandoned in the 18C.

The imposing 12C square keep is surmounted by a pentagonal tower which enabled the archers to vary their angle of fire.

The **view**★ embraces *(below)* the 19C pseudo-medieval Rhône suspension bridge, *(north)* the cooling towers of the Cruas-Meysse power station and the Rochemaure dam, *(east)* the Montélimar plain and *(south)* the Donzère gorge.

★★**Pic de Chenavari** – *4.5km/2mi north of Rochemaure castle and 45min on foot.* From the top (507m/1 663ft) there is a view of Rochemaure castle and the Rhône, *(east)* of the Vercors and the Barronies and *(south)* of the Lower Ardèche.

Return to Meysse and follow the D 2 up the lower Lavézon valley; turn right towards St-Vincent-de-Barrès.

The road runs through the vast **Barrès** basin with its fertile farmland. It then follows a tributary valley of the River Rhône which separates the limestone uplands of Cruas to the east from the volcanic Coiron plateau to the west.

St-Vincent-de-Barrès – This is a lovely village perched on a basalt neck jutting up from the Barrès plain. It is dwarfed by the basalt towers of its old fortress. From the esplanade in front of the church there is a view over the Barrès area.

Return to Privas via Chomérac.

Use the Index to find more information about a subject mentioned in the guide – towns, places of interest, isolated sights, historical events or natural features.

CONDAT

Population 1 262
Michelin map 76 fold 3 or 239 fold 30
Local map under Le CÉZALLIER

Condat lies in the centre of a fertile basin into which flow the Rhue d'Égliseneuve, Bonjon and Santoire rivers.

Its numerous, slate-roofed villas standing on the sunlit slopes of the Rhue valley were almost all built by local people who went elsewhere to seek their fortune, many of them as linen-drapers.

EXCURSIONS

★**The alpine pastures of Le Cézallier** – *55km/34mi – about 3hr 30min. Leave Condat on the D 679 south. See Le CÉZALLIER.*

Belvédère de Veysset and Forêt de Maubert – *Round trip 18km/11mi – about 45min. Leave Condat via the steep, winding D 62 north.*

Belvédère de Veysset – Superb view of Condat and the surrounding countryside.
The road leads to **Montboudif**, birthplace of **Georges Pompidou** (1911-74), who was President of France from 1969 to 1974.

Turn left before the church onto the D 622 and, a short distance further on, left again onto the D 722.

Forêt de Maubert – The beautiful State-owned Maubert et Gaulis forest consists of landscaped woodland with a predominance of pines but also beech, lime and a few oaks. The pines and beech grow to remarkable heights and produce prime timber.

At the junction with the D 679 turn right. About 1km/0.6mi further on, turn right onto a very steep forest road. Leave the car and walk on 100m.

To the right of the path is the Pierre-et-Paul Buffault beech tree; it is 44m/143ft tall and its 28m/91ft trunk has a circumference of 2.90m/about 9ft 6in.

Return to the D 679 and turn left towards Condat.

Égliseneuve-d'Entraigues – *11km/7mi northeast on the D 678.* This delightful drive takes you through the Rhue valley to Égliseneuve-d'Entraigues, a small summer holiday resort at an altitude of 952m/3 094ft.

The **Maison des Fromages** ⊙ is of interest to those wishing to find out about the history of, and techniques used to produce, local cheeses (St-Nectaire, Cantal, Bleu d'Auvergne, Fourme d'Ambert). An audio-visual presentation ends the visit.

Abbaye de Féniers – *Round trip of 26km/16mi – about 1hr. Leave Condat south on the D 679 towards Allanche.* The road skirts a stretch of water that is a recent reconstruction of a lake originally built in the 12C by monks.

Abbaye de Féniers – *Park in the hamlet of Féniers and walk to the abbey ruins.* The Cistercian abbey founded in the late 12C was rebuilt in 1686 and closed down during the French Revolution. The buildings were partially destroyed by fire in 1872; only a few ruins of the abbey buildings, cloisters and church survived.

A small oratory chapel backing onto the ruins houses a statue of the Virgin Mary dating from the 15C.

Turn right onto the D 16.

The road to St-Bonnet-de-Condat runs down into the Santoire valley and through a picturesque wooded **gorge**.

In St-Bonnet-de-Condat turn left onto the D 36 and return to Condat via Marcenat and the D 679.

Château de CONROS

Michelin map 76 fold 12 or 239 fold 41

On a spur of rock high above a meander of the River Cère stands the massive medieval keep that once belonged to the Astorgs, Lords of Aurillac. Over the centuries it was transformed into a majestic residence. The square tower topped by a strange lantern-turret dates from the 12C as does the main part of the building, which was extended in the 15C. It is flanked on the north side by a machicolated tower with a pepperpot roof.

Château de Conros

TOUR ⊙

In the weapons room an audio-visual presentation retraces the various stages in the restoration of the castle. The lower chamber, once a wood store, contains items connected with popular arts, crafts and traditions: barrels, hemp-spinning and weaving tools, a cheese press, a clogmaker's bench.

The guardroom on the first floor has an attractive Renaissance fireplace, the upper section of which is decorated with 15C frescoes. Maxims in old French have been carved on the lintel.

On the second floor is the surprisingly large Knights' Chamber, measuring 20m by 8m/65ft by 26ft. A tour of the attic gives visitors an opportunity to admire the superb oak rafters and the roof of stone slabs, all of them pegged into place. In the north tower, the floor is covered with shingle as protection against fire.

La CÔTE-ST-ANDRÉ

Population 3 966
Michelin map 77 fold 3 or 246 fold 3

This small town, a liqueur-producing centre built in a semicircle on a hillside above the Bièvre plain, is the birthplace of **Hector Berlioz** (1803-69). Every two years the **Berlioz Festival** *(see Calendar of events)* is held simultaneously in Lyon and in the covered market and parish church of La Côte-St-André.

The artist **Jongkind** (1819-91), one of the precursors of Impressionism, spent the last years of his life here.

A local lad – Hector Berlioz, the son of a wealthy local doctor, was born in La Côte-St-André in 1803. At the age of 17 he went to Paris to study medicine. He attended lectures but, at the same time, he was a frequent visitor to the opera houses and the library in the Royal Music School where, three years later, he began learning composition with Lesueur and Reicha. In 1828 he enjoyed early success with *Huit Scènes de Faust*. In 1830 he wrote his *Symphonie Fantastique* and won the Grand Prix de Rome.

Thereafter he worked as a music critic in order to earn a living, while at the same time continuing to compose works that brought him success and failure in turn. Among his works were *Requiem, Benvenuto Cellini, Romeo and Juliet, Hungarian March, The Damnation of Faust, The Childhood of Christ* and *The Trojans*.

It was in foreign cities that he enjoyed his greatest success – in Berlin, Weimar, Vienna, Prague and St Petersburg. He seldom returned to La Côte-St-André. Having failed to win the fame he deserved during his lifetime, Berlioz died in Paris in 1869, but his genius won immense posthumous acclaim.

Musée H. Berlioz, J.-L. Bouttier, La Côte St-André

Hector Berlioz

Among European musicians, Berlioz is considered to be the creator of the "symphonic poem", a daring and innovative style of music which, by means of complex orchestration, more flexible rhythmic expression and unexpected combinations of sounds, expressed the aspirations of the Romantic ideal with its enthusiasm for the fantastic and the grandiose. He also left a number of written works, including a *Grand traité d'instrumentation et d'orchestration moderne*.

SIGHTS

Musée Hector-Berlioz ⊙ – *Rue de la République*. This museum is housed in the composer's birthplace, a townhouse built in the late 17C and restored in 1969.

In the hall are a bust, musical scores and letters from admirers such as the composers Camille Saint-Saëns and Richard Strauss, and various musical instruments including the Spanish guitar that the musician broke in a fit of temper.

On the first floor are the kitchen and the dining room which contains an 18C fresco in a naive style, and portraits of Harriet Smithson. There is also Dr Berlioz' surgery and the room in which Hector was born. The drawing room contains Louis XV woodpanelling.

On the second floor there is a collection of portraits, caricatures, autographs and musical scores, while lithographs by Fantin-Latour based on Berlioz' works adorn the bedrooms of the composer's sisters. In the auditorium, visitors have an opportunity to listen to some of the master's works.

Note, at the rear of the house, the cobbled courtyard and the wooden balcony, both typical features of houses in La Côte-St-André.

Take Passage des Halles opposite the museum.

Note the old houses with timber balconies.

Covered market – The 16C covered market *(halles)* is striking for its exceptionally large size (29m x 76m/95ft x 249ft). There are five aisles; note the rafters.

Follow Rue Laval off the market square (north) to the old castle.

Castle ⊘ – The castle, built in the 13C for Philip of Savoy on a fine defensive site, was designed as both fortress and residence; it suffered extensive damage during the wars in the 16C but was rebuilt thereafter.

Inside, the Henry Gérard room (named after the artist Gérard, 1860-1925) has a Renaissance fireplace, a set of paintings by the artist and a number of fine pieces of Provençal furniture.

The upper terrace offers an extensive **view** of the red roofs of La Côte, the Bièvre plain and the Alps.

Follow Rue des Remparts to the church.

Church – This sanctuary, built between the 11C and 15C, has an interesting belfry of rounded pebbles and brick with white limestone quoins. Its outline and rich colours often provided the artist Jongkind with inspiration.

Inside, in the Gothic left aisle, note the springers of the fan vaulting on the pillars and, in the chancel, the 18C statue of Christ on the rood screen.

Musée des Liqueurs ⊘ – *East of Rue de la République, at the junction between Avenue de Verdun and Avenue C Rocher.* The Cherry Rocher company, which was set up in 1705 by Barthélemy Rocher (1675-1747), offers tours of its plant; visitors start in the small poster museum containing advertisements for liqueurs, brandies and other cordials. The museum proper contains a collection of old machinery (fruit press, stills, rectifiers, infusers). A diorama illustrates the development of the techniques used in the production of fruit and plant-based liqueurs. During the tour of the cellars, note the vast Hungarian oak cask which holds 32 400 litres/over 7 000 gallons. At the end of the tour there is a chance to taste one of these liqueurs that have resulted from many years of traditional know-how.

COURPIÈRE

Population 4 674
Michelin map 73 fold 16 or 239 fold 21 – Local map under Monts du FOREZ

The town lies at the entrance to a gorge formed by the River Dore. In addition to its fine church, Courpière also boasts a number of picturesque houses. Over the past few years the local economy has flourished thanks to a range of different industries such as stainless steel, coachwork, timber, clothing, boxes etc.

During the summer season visitors can take the **Livradois-Forez tourist railway** ⊘ which runs between Courpière and Ambert.

★Church – This interesting Auvergne-style Romanesque building is topped by a Gothic bell tower. Walk along the left side of the church to see the east end huddling between old houses. Inside, note the unusual capitals: on the pillar to the left, at the entrance to the nave; in the transept crossing; on the stringer of the lower arch at the end of the oven vaulting in the chancel. Other interesting features include a 15C Holy Sepulchre at the end of the right-hand aisle *(the light switch is behind the arch on the right)*, a painting dating from 1585 depicting the Martyrdom of St James the Elder in the north transept and a Romanesque statue of the Virgin Mary made of painted wood in the second chapel in the left-hand aisle.

Near the church, beside the fountain, stands a Renaissance house *(restored)*.

EXCURSION

Château d'Aulteribe ⊘ – *6km/4mi northwest.* This castle was rebuilt in the 19C in the Romantic style, on the site of an austere medieval construction. It was originally the property of the **La Fayette** family, was purchased in 1775 by the Marquis de Pierre de Bernis and bequeathed to Onslow de Pierre who was an avid collector of furniture and 17C paintings.

Inside, note in particular a portrait of Henri IV by Pourbus, a portrait of Richelieu by Philippe de Champaigne and a portrait of **Mademoiselle de Fontanges** painted in the style of Mignard. There are also Louis XV and Louis XVI chairs and items of furniture, and five outstanding Flemish tapestries made to designs by Teniers.

Vallées des COUZES★★

Michelin maps 73 folds 13, 14 and 76 folds 3, 4 or 239 fold 18, 19, 20, 31

Several different rivers that rise in the Monts Dore or the Cézallier and flow into the Allier bear the name "Couze", hence there are several Couze valleys.

In mountain areas they are clear limpid torrents flowing through deep gorges between hillsides bristling with basalt rocks; in the Limagne area, the valleys widen out, and the woods that cover the sheer hillsides and the forests dotted with rocks give way to terraced vineyards and fields of crops.

EXPLORING THE COUZES VALLEYS

1 Couze de Chambon and Couze de Pavin

55km/34mi – about 3hr – local map below opposite

Champeix – This village stands between hillsides that were once covered with vineyards. The ruins of the old medieval castle, the "Marchidial", stand high above the village on a sheer-sided spur of rock. On the right bank is the church, which has a Romanesque apse; the lintel above the door on the left is decorated with a carving of the Holy Trinity.

Leave Champeix heading west towards St-Nectaire on the D 996.

Montaigut-le-Blanc – The village lies in the shadow of its ruined castle. Its somewhat Mediterranean appearance – houses with flat roofs and rounded tiles, terraced vineyards, and fruit trees at the head of the valley – heralds the Limagne plateau.

Carry on along the D 996 for another mile or so.

The granite base of the Massif Central shows through at the sides of the road.

Turn right onto the D 640.

The layers of lava which make up the cliff to the right of the road are clearly visible. Much of the pastureland has been abandoned and is now overrun by broom and hawthorn. In June and July, the fields are bright with cornflowers, making something of a comeback in rural France, having been largely wiped out by the use of herbicides.

Just after Treizanches, turn left onto the D 150.

Farges – This hamlet is home to an interesting group of **troglodytic houses** ⊘, hollowed out of the white tufa, which date from the Middle Ages. Visitors may also like to discover more about the maturing process of St-Nectaire cheese, in a cellar where this takes place. The traditional method of making St-Nectaire can be viewed at **Ferme Bellonte** ⊘, where the cheese is produced.

A little further on from Farges, a quarry comes into sight to the right of the road. The powdery white rock extracted here is pumice stone, evidence of the tremendous volcanic eruptions that shook this region millions of years ago.

Carry on along the D 150, then turn left.

★**Puy de Mazeyres** – Alt 919m/3 015ft. From the hilltop, there is a beautiful panorama of the Monts Dore *(viewing table)*.

Rejoin the D 150.

★★**St-Nectaire** – *See ST-NECTAIRE.*

From St-Nectaire-le-Bas, take the D 996 towards Champeix, as far as Saillant.

Cascade de Saillant – In this village the river tumbles over a basalt outcrop, forming a waterfall. There is a pretty view of it from the D 622.

Return to St-Nectaire and take the D 996 towards Mont-Dore.

★★**Château de Murol** – *See MUROL.*

Leave Murol on the D 996, then turn left at the junction with the D 5.

The road runs along the slopes of the Tartaret volcano. Note to the left, in a tiny quarry, the volcanic cinders which make up the cone.

★★**Lac Chambon** – *See Lac CHAMBON.*

Return to Murol and turn right onto the D 5 towards Besse-en-Chandesse. After 2km/1.2mi turn right onto the D 619, then after about 100m turn left.

★**Puy de Bessolles** – Alt 1 045m/3 428ft. This peak is one of the best lookout points in the Couzes region, giving an impressive view of the Monts Dore and Chambon lake.

Follow the footpath signposted "Plateau de Bessolles – panorama". Allow 45min there and back on foot to get to the viewpoint, and 2hr to follow the footpath right round the plateau (waymarked in yellow).

The footpath climbs gently uphill, giving pretty views of the Château de Murol. Ash and willow trees – the remnants of earlier hedges – grow around the edges of the old pastures, which are fast being overrun by broom, hawthorn, dog-roses and the occasional pine tree plantation. To the left, a magnificent **panorama**★★ opens out , with Lac Chambon in the foreground, neatly contained by the debris from the eruption of the Tartaret, the sunken crater of which is clearly visible from here. In the background, the ladnscape is dominated by the Monts Dore.

At this point, it is possible to retrace one's steps, or to carry on along the path round the plateau *(circuit découverte)*. The waymarked path leads uphill onto the plateau, between broom and hazel trees. The north slope, which is more uneven terrain, is adorned with a handsome beech grove, a vestige of the great forests which once covered the Auvergne region. The relatively low temperature and high precipitation here have resulted in the growth of a variety of flora specific to this spot, which visitors should be careful not to abuse or damage.

The footpath leads on over the moors and through copses until it unfolds a panorama of the Puys mountain chain. Buzzards and kites circle the sky above the meadows, which are still in use as pasture.

On the way downhill take a little path to the left *(waymarked in yellow)*, overlooked by a flow of basalt which has solidified in prisms, to the village of Roche Romaine (named after the unusual, "Roman"-shaped rock nearby).

Take the tarmacked road to the right towards the village, following the orange waymarkings.

At the exit to the village, take the road on the left, and after about 200yds, in a bend, turn right onto a small forest path *(1.5km/1mi)*. This eventually joins the main road *(onto which you should turn left; take care not to turn onto the little Bessolles road!)* which leads back to where you left the car.

Carry on along the D 619.

After Roche Romaine, there is a good view to the left of the columnar basalt overlooking the village. Other such rock formations can be seen in the bend in the road before Roussat. Further on downhill, the road runs along the foot of a long flow of prismatic lava which has been laid bare by erosion.

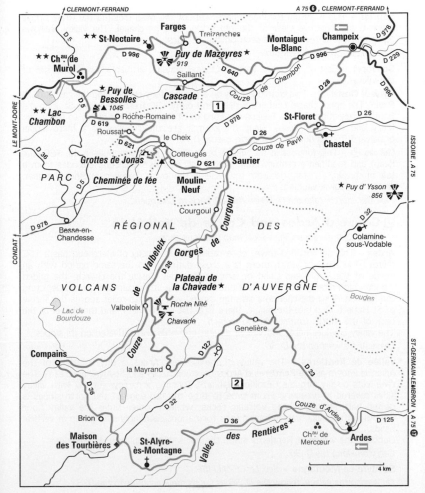

At the junction with the D 621, turn left. At Cheix, take the road on the right towards Jonas which shortly afterwards crosses the Couze de Pavin.

Grottes de Jonas ⊙ – The most rudimentary of these man-made caves carved out of the volcanic tufa in a cliff were doubtless inhabited by humans in prehistoric times. Over the centuries their descendants also made use of them: in the Middle Ages a chapel – its vaulting still bears traces of frescoes dating from 1100 – and a fortress were built in the caves. The tower of the fortress contains a spiral staircase with about 80 steps carved into the rock; it leads up to apartments on several floors. On the right, on the way up, note the sink containing a drain for waste water. Note also the Council Chamber with the place reserved for the men-at-arms, the prison and the bread oven.

Return to Cheix and turn right onto the D 978 then right again onto the D 621.

Cheminée de fée de Cotteuges – *15min on foot Rtn. Before reaching the hamlet, turn right onto the Bedeaux track.* This path leads through a wood to an **earth pillar** standing among excavations. This amazing geological formation is a clay column topped by a block of hard rock.

Beyond Cotteuges the road crosses one of the *cheires* (lava flows) that are a characteristic feature of this area. Further on, high above to the left of the road, stand a number of superb sheer-sided rocks. The river has carved a course in the granite bedrock, resulting in rugged, rocky valley sides to which pine trees cling precariously.

Continue along the D 621.

Moulin-Neuf – In a tiny farm is a small **Musée auvergnat** ⊙ recreating the atmosphere of life in the Auvergne in the late 19C – the kitchen with its box-beds, the byre, the pigsty. There is also a large collection of tools used by blacksmiths, joiners and wine growers, together with cheese presses and farm implements.

Continue along the D 621.

Saurier – This is an old fortified village. Left of the road crossing the River Couze there is an attractive view of the old bridge and its chapel. The valley narrows again and basalt rocks can be seen on the hillsides.

Take the D 26 towards Issoire.

St-Floret – First of all, take a look at Chastel plateau, probably the original site of the village.

Église de Chastel ⊙ – This church is built on a promontory overlooking the river Couze Pavin. The north chapel contains a delightful early 15C fresco depicting St John the Baptist presenting Jean de Bellenaves, Lord of St-Floret, and his family to the Virgin Mary and the Child Jesus. Near the church are the remains of a Merovingian graveyard (tombs dug into the rock, ossuary).

Château ⊙ – This fortress in the village of St-Floret itself was built in the 13C (the keep) and modified a century later. Large 14C **frescoes**★ depicting episodes from a tale of chivalry (Tristan) decorate the walls in the lower chamber; another chamber, above, has ogival vaulting.

Past the church, take the D 28 on the left back to Champeix.

② Couze d'Ardes and Couze de Valbeleix

55km/34mi – about 3hr – local map previous page

Ardes – This old fortified town, once capital of the Duchy of Mercoeur, has a 15C **church** ⊙ in front of which there is a cross dating from the same period with an image of the Virgin and Child on one of its sides. Inside the church, the gilded wooden high altar (17C) features eight remarkable little sculpture groups depicting the Passion. Near the chancel a strange carved wooden bas-relief adorns the shrine of St Hubert. Opposite the pulpit, there is a 16C stone Pietà, and the chapel at the back of the church contains a 15C lectern.

The valley is wider here, and vineyards and orchards are cultivated on its slopes.

Leave Ardes west on the D 36.

★**Vallée de Rentières** – The valley of the Couze d'Ardes, a tiny tributary of the Allier, is known as the Rentières d'Ardes between Ardes and St-Alyre upstream. The river cuts deeply into the Cézallier plateaux, forming a narrow furrow with valley sides covered in greenery. From time to time the top edge of the north slopes is dotted with strange-shaped volcanic rocks, while at other times the valley floor bristles with equally bizarre basalt rock formations seemingly stacked up in vertical heaps.

Opposite the village of Rentières stand the ruins of the Château de Mercoeur.

Carry on along the D 36.

St-Alyre-ès-Montagne – *See Le CÉZALLIER.*

On leaving the village, follow the D 36 as far as the junction with the D 32.

J. Damase/EXPLORER

Peat bogs

Maison des tourbières et du Cézallier ⓥ – This is an information centre on two little known natural habitats present in the local area: wetlands, relics of the Ice Age and home to their own specific flora including interesting species such as a type of sundew (Drosera), a tiny carnivorous plant; and peat bogs containing a wealth of fascinating evidence of the past trapped in the peat over the centuries.

Carry on along the D 36.

The road takes you through the village of **Briom**, overlooked by some very striking basalt columns.

Follow the D 36.

Compains – Not far from this village is the spot where the Couze de Valbeleix rises; the river is most probably fed by the waters of Montcineyre lake *(see BESSE-EN-CHANDESSE: Excursions).*

Take the D 26 east.

The road crosses the lava flow emitted by the Puy de Montcineyre when it erupted in this valley 6 000 years ago. The lava, which forms a particularly rocky soil, is covered by a beautiful beech grove, as the ground has remained impervious to any efforts to cultivate it.

Valbeleix – Glacial action has sculpted the countryside around this village into some particularly interesting forms.

The valley of the Couze de Valbeleix forms an almost perfect U-shaped cross-section. The round-topped hill which rises above the village and closes off the valley is a good example of a glacial threshold.

Further on, tiny hanging glacial cirques on the west bank of the Couze give an idea of the depth of the ice which filled this valley 10 000 years ago.

After several more miles, beyond La Valette, the valley seems to close off completely. The glacier was unable to penetrate the very much narrower Courgoul gorge.

Turn right, past the church in Valbeleix, onto the D 127 for just over a mile, then left onto the D 641 towards La Chavade.

★**Plateau de la Chavade** – To reach this plateau the road climbs up through the heart of a beech grove. Leave the car in the parking area cleared at the foot of a stand of pine trees twisted into strange shapes by their exposure to the elements. Walk to the two viewing tables, one of which can be seen from the car park, about 300yds off to the right.

Plateau de la Chavade *(1st viewpoint)* – This gives a magnificent **view★★** of the U-shaped valley of the Couze de Valbeleix and of the Monts Dore. There are some interesting notes on projects for the agricultural exploitation of the plateau on the viewing table.

La Roche Nité *(2nd viewpoint)* – There is a superb **view★★** of the volcanic mountain ranges of the Cézallier and Monts Dore, in which lava flows were truncated 10 000 years ago by gigantic tongues of ice whose passage left traces on the surrounding countryside which are still clearly visible.

Rejoin the D 127 towards Mayrand. Past Genelière, turn right onto the D 23 back to Ardes.

These two trips described above are linked by the Gorges de Courgoul, running for 11km/7mi.

The road follows the winding course of the River Couze de Valbeleix (which flows into the Couze de Pavin a short distance before Saurier), which cuts a magnificent, deep ravine with tall sides close to each other, bristling with sheer-sided rocks and covered with thick vegetation. In several places the road (D 26) crosses the river (unfortunately lined by a canalization) as it flows beneath the closely-entwined branches of trees.

CRÉMIEU

Population 2 855
Michelin map 88 fold 9 or 246 fold 1

Crémieu sits in a narrow valley between fairly rugged hillsides and was once a fortress standing guard over one of the gateways into the Dauphiné region; it was also a busy trading centre.

Among the local gastronomic specialities are *sabodets* (a variety of sausage) and *foyesse* (a type of cake).

OLD TOWN *1hr 30min*

Start at Porte de la Loi.

Porte de la Loi – This gateway, once part of the 14C town walls, has a helm roof and machicolations.

Go through Porte des Augustins.

Place de la Nation (15) – The name of this square dates back to the days of the French Revolution. In the northeast corner is a lever-operated well built in 1823.

Hôtel de Ville (H) ⊙ – The town hall stands on Place de la Nation and is housed in part of what was once an Augustinian friary founded in the 14C. The entrance hall has a coffered ceiling. The doorway on the left leads into the Council Chamber which also has a coffered ceiling; the doorway on the right opens on the Justice of the Peace's Court, once the monks' calefactory. Its pointed vaulting is supported by a central pillar.

Cloisters – The former cloisters *(cloître)* in the Augustinian friary are entered from Place de la Nation through a beautiful 17C wrought-iron gate. The gravestones, used as a pavement in the galleries crowned by quadripartite vaulting, were brought here from the church in the late 19C. Some have carvings of craftsmen's tools including the paring knife used by brickmakers or leather tanners. In the southwest corner of the cloisters, on a grid, is the symbol of the Augustinian Order: a heart topped by a flame and pierced by two arrows.

Church ⊙ – The church was the monastery chapel from 1318 to 1791 and has undergone a number of alterations. The wrought-iron grille from which visitors can see the interior was made by Redersdorff (1982). The furnishings are of particular interest; note the wood panelling on the choirstalls and pulpit, and the wrought-iron grilles in the side chapels. Note, too, the geometric form of the pillars, all of them different, and the narrow side aisles with their close quadripartite vaulting.

From the square in front of the church there is a wonderful **view** across to the castle and over the old houses decorated with double or triple eaves.

Take Rue Porcherie to the covered market.

Halles – The covered market was built in the 14C. The roof covered in *lauzes* is supported at each end by a thick wall comprising three arches. Beneath the splendid rafters, note the three aisles, each corresponding to a specific type of trade. At the end on the right are the stone troughs over which the corn measures were once fitted; the grain ran down chutes into sacks.

Take Rue Mulet then turn right into Rue du Four-Banal and on to Porte Neuve.

Fortified gateways – **Porte Neuve**, also known as the François I gate, was built in the 16C; **Porte de Quirieu**, which has steps and a central gutter, dates from the 14C.

Head along Rue du Marché-Vieux.

On the right, at no 14 **(N)**, note the 14C Window of the Three Hanged Men (Fenêtre des Trois Pendus).

Carry on up Montée St-Laurent.

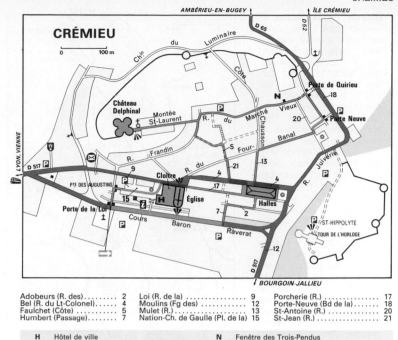

CRÉMIEU

H	Hôtel de ville	**N**	Fenêtre des Trois-Pendus

Château Delphinal – This fortress on St-Laurent hill dates back to the 12C. On the terrace is a chapel dedicated to Notre-Dame-de-la-Salette and from here there is a superb **view** over the stone-slabbed roof of the church and the old monastery. On St-Hippolyte hill to the left are the remains of a 16C fortified Benedictine priory, including the old clock tower.

Go back down Montée St-Laurent; at the bottom turn right and then left into Côte Faulchet.

At the crossroads with Rue du Four-Banal is a 16C house with mullioned windows which houses the tourist office.

Go down Rue St-Jean, Rue du Lieutenant-Colonel-Bel and, after skirting the southwest corner of the covered market, Rue des Adobeurs.

This street is lined with tiny low houses that used to contain craft workshops, including those belonging to the town's many tanners.

Passage Humbert on the left leads to Cours Baron-Ravenat.

From level with the church there is a fine **view** of its hexagonal belfry; the spire rises above one of the old towers in the town walls.

ÎLE CRÉMIEU: Land of Stone Roofs

56km/35mi round trip – about 3hr – local map overleaf

With its cliffs, lakes, roofs covered in heavy stone slabs known as *lauzes*, fields bordered by standing stones, and country houses, the Île Crémieu region is quite unlike the countryside elsewhere in this area.

Leave Crémieu on the D 52 northeast and follow the signs to Optevoz.

As the road runs up the hill there is a delightful view of Lake Ry and, further up the slope, of the large, modern **Château de St-Julien**.
As the road reaches the plateau there are a number of views of the Bugey area and the Alps.

Beyond the cool Optevoz basin, follow the D 52 as far as Surbaix then turn left into a pleasant little road (D 52⁸) which runs through a valley full of trees and meadows.

St-Baudille-de-la-Tour – This charming village contains an attractive 15C fortified house, known as the Maison des Dames, with a tower covered in *lauzes* and a porch decorated with a coat-of-arms.

Torjonas – This is a well-preserved traditional hamlet in which every house has a roof of *lauzes*.

★**Grottes de la Balme** ⊙
– *270 steps.* These caves lie at the foot of the cliff that marks the edge of the Île Crémieu plateau. They were discovered during the Middle Ages, visited by François I, described as one of the "seven wonders of Dauphiné", and are said to have been used in the 18C by the infamous brigand **Mandrin**. A huge porch 40m/130ft high covers two superimposed chapels and leads into a vast chamber, known as the Grand Dome, filled with rock falls. Several galleries lead from the chamber: the very narrow Mandrin Gallery on the left leads to the balcony of the same name, high above the entrance to the cave; the Lake Gallery skirts a series of small pools forming terraces of waterfalls before reaching the underground torrent. A climb up into the area known as the Upper Cave where the concretions are particularly numerous brings visitors to the François I Gallery, a veritable labyrinth that leads to a balcony some 30m/97ft above the river bed at the entrance to the cave.

Turn back along the D 65 then take the first on the left, to Hières-sur-Amby.

Hières-sur-Amby – This tiny village stands at the end of the Amby valley, at the foot of the Larina plateau. Below the church is the former rectory, dating from the 18C and with a stone-slabbed roof, which is now the **Maison du Patrimoine** ⊙ (Heritage Centre). It houses objects discovered during archaeological digs at Larina *(see below)* including bones, tools, coins and jewellery, and includes a model of a Merovingian farm. Models, videos and a display trace the origins of the people living in Île Crémieu, and present examples of popular arts, crafts and traditions.

Special effects reconstruct the tomb, found under a tumulus, of a Celtic prince (8C) which was discovered in July 1987 at St-Romain-de-Jalionas. Particular treasures from the tomb include gold jewellery (torque, bracelet, pin) and the oldest iron knife found in Europe.

At the entrance to Hières-sur-Amby turn left into D 52A which climbs up through Amby gorge.

Gorges d'Amby – The river twists and turns along the foot of rocks covered here and there with scrubby vegetation. There is a view of the 15C Brotel fortified house on the cliff.

A narrow road off to the right opposite an old cement works crosses the River Amby and runs up a steep hill to Chatelans. In the centre of the village, turn right into a narrow road that runs for 2.5km/1mi to the tip of the plateau, where the Larina archaeological site is located.

★**Parc archéologique de Larina** – *Signposted tours and information panels.*
The Larina site covers an area of 21ha/51 acres. To the north and west it is bordered by the cliffs overlooking the Rhône plain and Amby valley; to the south and east, by a stone rampart almost 1km/0.6mi long. The existence of human settlements on this site has been proved by objects dating from the Neolithic era (c 3000 BC). From the 5C to the 1C BC, an oppidum (settlement) stood here. Within its walls were huts made of timber or wattle and daub. The discovery of an altar and huge blocks of foundation stone confirmed the existence here in Roman times of a temple dedicated to the god Mercury. Stone quarries were also worked at this period, to provide slabs for roofing. A working face to the north of the main dwelling shows the structure of the sub-soil in Larina, consisting of gritty limestone strata that were easy to cut into flagstones.

At the end of the Roman era and in the early days of the Dark Ages, two large farms existed in succession on this spot. The earlier one (4C and 5C) had a villa at its centre and included a number of farm buildings made of earth and timber over stone foundations that are still clearly visible. From the 6C to 8C another farm developed around a large stone-built house with a stone-slabbed roof and various outbuildings. On the hillock to the north were two graveyards. In the second one, graves of children and adults have been uncovered; the dead were buried in coffins made of stone slabs.

From the northernmost tip of the cliff, where there is a statue of the Virgin Mary, there is a superb **view** of the Bugey and Dombes hills, the Beaujolais and Lyonnais mountains, the Feyzin flares and Mont Pilat. In the foreground the view includes the River Rhône and the Bugey nuclear power station.

Take the D 52 to Annoisin-Chatelans.

Annoisin-Chatelans – The modest **church** here, standing alone in the middle of a meadow, has a tiny octagonal belfry curiously placed adjacent to the east end.

Beyond the houses roofed with *lauzes* the route crosses the chalky marsh of the plateau to lead to Chatelans. At the centre of the village is the **Musée de la Lauze** ⊙ which explains the traditional techniques in this region for cutting and fitting the stone slabs.

The road to Siccieu provides a number of picturesque views of the Alps.

Return to Crémieu via the D 52 and Lake Ry.

CREST

Population 7 583
Michelin map 77 fold 12 or 246 fold 6

The town of Crest, situated at the spot where the River Drôme flows into the Valence plain, is particularly proud of its castle keep. The town has grown up around it, with a dual role as market town and a community specialising in food processing. Among the many local gastronomic specialities are *défarde*, a stew made with lamb's tripe, and *picodons*, small goat-cheeses.

SIGHTS

Steps up to the keep (Y) – *Access via steps left of St-Sauveur church, up Rue du Vieux-Gouvernement and along Rue de la Tour.*

★**Keep** (Y) ⊙ – *184 steps to the upper terrace.*

The keep in Crest, also known as the "Tower", is all that remains of a fortress which was dismantled in 1632 on the orders of Louis XIII. The keep was erected over Roman foundations on a spur of rock, in various stages between the 11C and the 15C. The north wall, the tallest of the four, reaches a height of almost 52m/169ft; the base of the tower lies at an altitude of 263m/855ft.

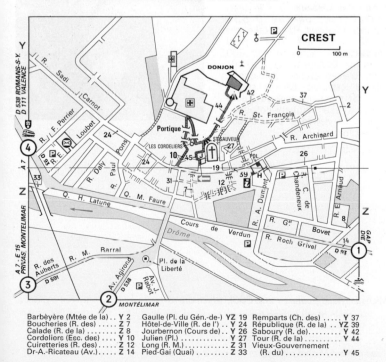

Barbèyère (Mtée de la) .. **Z** 2	Gaulle (Pl. du Gén.-de-) **YZ** 19	Remparts (Ch. des) ..... **Y** 37
Boucheries (R. des) ..... **Z** 7	Hôtel-de-Ville (R. de l') .. **Y** 24	République (R. de la) .. **YZ** 39
Calade (R. de la) .... **Z** 8	Jourbernon (Cours de) .. **Y** 26	Saboury (R. de) .... **Y** 42
Cordoliers (Esc. des) .... **Y** 10	Julien (Pl.) .... **Y** 27	Tour (R. de la) .... **Y** 44
Cuiretteries (R. des) ..... **Z** 12	Long (R. M.) .... **Z** 31	Vieux-Gouvernement
Dr-A.-Ricateau (Av.) ..... **Z** 14	Pied-Gai (Quai) .... **Z** 33	(R. du) .... **Y** 45

The various dungeons and vaulted chambers inside are all empty. In 1851 the dungeons were used to imprison 600 Republicans who opposed Louis-Napoleon's *coup d'état*.

The first terrace has a floor of huge stone slabs, all carefully bonded and all sloping down to a central gutter which took rainwater down into the reservoir. The roof, which was added in the 15C, is supported by huge arches and enormous rafters.

From the upper terrace there is a view over the rooftops of Crest and beyond, in a superb **panoramic view★** to the northeast over Glandasse mountain and the outcrops of the Vercors, and to the south over the Roche-Courbe range with the Trois-Becs, and Roche Colombe further in the distance. To the west the horizon is broken up by the long narrow ridge of the Vivarais area rising to the Gerbier de Jonc and Mézenc, both of which are visible in clear weather.

At the bottom of Rue de la Tour, on descending to the town from the keep, fork right and follow the hilltop path that runs round the east end of the old Franciscan church (Église des Cordeliers).

Further down the hill, on the left, are a few steps leading to a vaulted alleyway. This is the 5-arched **Portique des Cordeliers (Y)** which opens onto the monumental **Escalier des Cordeliers (Y 10)**. With its 124 steps, 80 of which have been carved directly into the rock, this is an impressive sight, especially when seen from below.

Old houses – Along the main thoroughfare and the picturesque neighbouring streets are some of the vast mansions built for the wealthy *bourgeoisie* in Crest in the 16C and 17C. There are entrances with bossages at no 11 Rue des Cuiretteries (**Z 12**), in Rue des Boucheries (**Z 7**) just before the vaulted alleyway leading to Rue de l'Hôtel-de-Ville, and at no 2 Place Général-de-Gaulle (**YZ 19**). At no 10 Rue de la République (**YZ 39**) the rounded entrance includes a keystone carved with foliage; at no 14 the frontage is decorated with three heads in high relief.

EXCURSION

Jardin des Oiseaux ⊙ – *In Upie. Leave Crest on the D 538 towards Chabeuil, then take the D 142 to the left.* This superb **bird sanctuary** is home to over 200 different European and exotic birds: crested grebes, flamingoes, pelicans, ostriches, parrots etc. A fascinating **Hummingbird House** allows these brightly-coloured birds to be viewed in a simulation of their natural habitat.

Crowned pigeon of New Guinea

Le Jardin aux oiseaux, Upie

Michelin Maps (scale 1 : 200 000), which are revised regularly, show at a glance:
- *main roads linking the main towns and sights*
- *regional roads*
- *side roads for a quiet drive*

Keep current Michelin Maps in the car at all times.

CRUSSOL★★★

Michelin map 76 fold 20 or 246 fold 19 – Local map under Moyenne vallée du RHÔNE

On the top of Crussol mountain (200m/650ft above the plain) stands the ruined **Château de Crussol**, one of the most grandiose **beauty spots** in the Rhône valley. The smooth grain of the white Crussol stone makes it ideal for building.

A hilltop fortress – In the 12C Bastet de Crussol chose this site for his fortress. The ambition of the "insignificant lords of Crussol" took them to the highest-ranking offices in the kingdom. One of the Crussols was Chamberlain to Louis XI, another became heir to the County of Uzès through marriage. His son, Seneschal of Beaucaire and Nîmes, took part in the Italian Campaigns with Charles VIII and Louis XII. Their official duties took the Crussols away from the uncomfortable ancestral home and it was partially demolished in the 17C. Bonaparte is supposed to have scaled the cliff at Crussol in a particularly death-defying feat of bravado with one of his brothers in 1785 while garrisoned in Valence.

TOUR

In St-Péray take the road past the Château de Beauregard (not open to the public); there is a car park at the end of the road behind the statue of the Virgin Mary, then a path to the ruins (1 hour Rtn on foot).

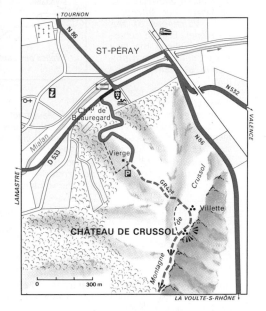

After passing the fortified north gateway in the old castle walls, follow the path on the left. It climbs up through the remains of the "**villette**", where the people who lived on the plain sought refuge in times of danger. During the climb, there is a view over the Valence plain, the Bourg-lès-Valence dam, and the confluence of the rivers Rhône and Isère. The peaks of Vercors, Roche Colombe and Trois-Becs form a magnificent backdrop.

At the tip of the spur of rock are the old apartments. In the northeast corner are the remains of a lookout tower, forming an outstanding observation platform high above a breathtakingly sheer drop. The scarp slope on the south side *(add about 30min extra)* provides a **view**★★ of the ruins jutting up from amid the rock and over the last outcrops of the Massif Central.

DAUPHINÉ D'AUVERGNE★

Michelin map 73 fold 14 or 239 folds 19 and 20

At the end of the 12C, the region to the southwest of Issoire between the Cézallier and the Allier valley, comprising rugged countryside scored by the various rivers Couze *(see Vallées des COUZES)* flowing between hilly outcrops and basalt plateaux, formed the Dauphiné d'Auvergne, a sort of local, royal fief whose lords and their entourage set up a glittering court in Champeix, Vodable and Mercoeur successively. For some years now, an association of local *communes* has been making efforts to reawaken interest in this forgotten little fief, which sank into obscurity before the end of the Middle Ages. Its efforts were rewarded in 1992, when the Dauphiné d'Auvergne was officially declared a "Pays d'Art et d'Histoire" (Region of Historic and Artistic Interest).

VOYAGE OF DISCOVERY LEAVING FROM ISSOIRE

60km/37mi – allow half a day – local map overleaf

Two distinctive volcanic features dominate the landscape of this region:

– necks or plugs (old volcanic chimneys stripped bare by erosion of the softer volcanic matter which hid them from view), such as the rocky pinnacle towering over Vodable and the Puy d'Ysson;

– tables (old lava flows which have formed a protective layer over the underlying rocks), such as the Perrier plateau.

★★Issoire – See ISSOIRE.

Leave Issoire to the west on the D 996, towards Champeix.

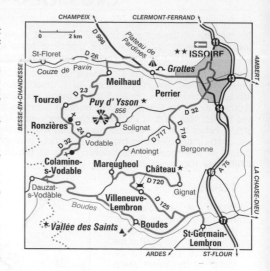

Perrier – This village is overlooked by a plateau bristling with bizarrely shaped rocks, evidence of the violent eruptions which took place millions of years ago in the Monts Dore region, which unleashed gigantic flows of mud mixed with boulders, or **lahars** *(see Introduction: Volcanoes of the Auvergne).* Erosion subsequently sculpted the fantastic rock formations known as "fairies' chimneys".

From the tip of one of these enormous outcrops, there is a view of the feudal keep of Maurifolet. The mountain on which Perrier stands is well known in geologists' circles as a site where numerous bone fragments have been discovered from animals long since disappeared from the region such as mastodons, elephants and tapirs.

Artificial caves – *1hr walk there and back. From the church in Perrier, take the footpath to the caves ("chemin des grottes").*

These caves were hollowed out of the volcanic rock and used as troglodytic dwellings.

Plateau – *From the caves, follow the route indicated as "vue panoramique".*

From the plateau there is a remarkable **view★** of the surrounding rocks, the feudal keep, the village and the river Couze Pavin. A footpath runs along the plateau's edge, amidst myriad and abundant plantlife.

On leaving Perrier, take the D 26 left for 2km/1.2mi, then turn left again into the D 23.

Meihaud – On the right as you enter the village stands an old bridge spanning the Couze Pavin. Old fortifications lend a well-protected air to the church.

Continue along the D 23.

Tourzel – Small wine-growers' houses in this village bear witness to a viticultural past, specifically during the 18C and 19C when Tourzel's main source of income was wine. One of these lava-walled houses is home to a small museum on the pork butcher's trade. Further down, another house typical of the region contains a display evoking scenes from local history, as well as a wide variety of local farm produce.

Follow the D 23 for another 1km/0.6mi, then turn left into the D 124.

Ronzières – At the entrance to the village, a narrow track *(closed to traffic)* climbs up to a basalt plateau on which a pre-Romanesque church stands. This building was modified in the late 12C, and features a 15C doorway. Inside, the chapel on the left houses a beautiful Romanesque statue of the Virgin Mary in Majesty, made of polychrome wood and protected behind an imposing 19C set of railings. The capitals supporting the arches of the cupola are Carolingian, from the previous building.

In the church graveyard, on the edge of the plateau, two viewing tables give information on the view of the surrounding countryside, which stretches over the Puy d'Ysson, the river Couze Pavin, Perrier plateau and Sembron plain. Examples of the two volcanic features so characteristic of the Dauphiné d'Auvergne region are easy to pick out.

Take the D 124 as far as Vodable and turn left into the D 32 to Solignat.

★Puy d'Ysson – Alt 856m/2 782ft. This cone is formed by the chimney of a volcano which emerged during the Tertiary era; the plug of lava was laid bare by erosion. From the summit, there is a fine **panorama** of the Monts Dore, the extinct volcanoes of the Comté region, the Limagne around Issoire, the Livradois mountains and the Cézallier.

From here, the villages through which you have already travelled can also clearly be seen: Vodable at the foot of its basalt needle, to the right Ronzières with its church perched up high, and Perrier in the shadow of its plateau.

Drive back down to Solignat and take the D 32 back to Vodable.

Colamine-sous-Vodable – The church ⊙ here still stands surrounded by its grave-yard, on the side of a coomb. It boasts a pretty Romanesque chancel (11C, but restored) and a fine group of polychrome wood statues, among them a remarkable 12C **Virgin Mary in Majesty★**. The statues were discovered in 1979 during restoration work; they had been walled up since the mid 18C behind the carved 17C altar-piece.

Rejoin the D 32 and travel for 4km/3mi towards Dauzat-sur-Vodable, then turn left into the D 48.

Boudes – Well sheltered by a range of hills to the north and by the Avoiron pinnacle to the west, this village was the only one in the entire region to escape the ravages of phylloxera. Thanks to the good soil here (a mixture of clay, limestone and basalt pebbles), local vines produce fine quality wine, including a particularly highly thought of white wine. The layout of the vineyards on a single slope well-exposed to the sun and the brightly coloured houses make a striking sight. While the villages visited so far on this journey have been characterised by the sombre tones of the lava from which they are built, the red roofs and pale walls of Boudes are a reminder of the clays and sandstones present in the surrounding sub-soil.

Leave Boudes to the south, crossing the Couzilloux, and take the track to the right which runs along the side of the graveyard.

★**Vallée des Saints** – *1hr walk there and back. leave the car at the start of the track.*
A waymarked path enables visitors to explore this area to the full, admiring the giant red and ochre pyramids with which it is populated, between 10-30m/30-100ft high and strangely sculpted by erosion. Their outlandish silhouettes, like gigantic statues, have earned the valley its name.
The red, iron oxide-bearing clay, from which these features are made, was formed by the transformation of gneiss in the hot and humid tropical climate which prevailed at the beginning of the Tertiary era.

Return to Boudes and turn right at the church to rejoin the D 48.

St-Germain-Lembron – This small, once fortified village in the midst of an agricultural region still boasts some 18C houses with double-gabled roofs.

Take the D 48 towards Boudes once again, then turn off to the right after 1km/0.6mi onto the D 125.

The road climbs towards Châlus, from where there are beautiful views of the volcanic necks and tables rising above the Limagne.

Villeneuve-Lembron – Narrow streets lined with old houses and wash-houses surround a 15C church.

★**Château de Villeneuve** – This 14C seigneurial castle was built for the Aureille family, one of whose members was the diplomat Rigault, who served under Louis XI, Charles VIII, Louis XII and François I and fought alongside Charles VIII in the Italian campaigns. It was Rigault who initiated the restoration and refitting of the family château at the end of the 15C.
The castle has a square ground plan with a round tower at each corner and is surrounded by dry moats, for ornamental purposes only. The main building stands around a central courtyard with a covered gallery.
A tour of the interior reveals many treasures, such as handsome ceilings with rafters, interesting woodwork and valuable pieces of furniture. Note in particular the two fireplaces in the kitchen, the Italian portraits in the room where the deceased were laid out, and the two Nativity scenes, one in wood and one in slate, which adorn one of the rooms.
The courtyard gallery houses some marvellous 15C paintings (restored) on sub-jects which reflect Rigault's unhappy married life. On leaving the castle, take a look at the stables, in which the vast barrel roof vault is decorated with late 16C frescoes.

Carry on along the D 125 and turn left into the D 720.

Mareugheol – This is a typical example of a fortified village built during the Middle Ages in order to protect the inhabitants from the marauding bands of robbers which plagued the region. Old stone houses stand along narrow streets within a rectangular fortified wall of which only a few stretches of wall and a stump of corner tower remain. At the bottom of the village there is a tiny village square adorned with a fountain.

Take the D 720 as far as Gignat, then turn left into the D 719, which leads back to Issoire.

Consult the Index to find an individual town or sight.

La DOMBES★

Michelin map 74 folds 1, 2 or 244 folds 3, 4, 14, 15

The Dombes plateau, situated between Lyon and Bourg-en-Bresse and bordered by the rivers Ain and Saône, owes its unusual appearance and its particular charm to the presence of over one thousand lakes dotted across its entire area. Here and there are low hills, formed by moraine, which were transformed in the Middle Ages into veritable earth fortresses surrounded by moats.

Rural housing in the Dombes region is built mainly of cob *(pisé)* while the castles and outer walls are built of rough red bricks known as *carrons* (terracotta).

The region's history, too, is somewhat out of the ordinary. Dombes was raised to the rank of a principality by François I following the confiscation of the property belonging to the Constable of Bourbon in 1523. A sovereign parliament sat in Trévoux, its main town; it continued to sit until the mid 18C.

GEOGRAPHICAL NOTES

The impermeable soil encouraged local people very early on in their history to turn their fields into lakes enclosed by mud dikes. The **Grand Étang de Birieux**, one of the most extensive of the lakes (330ha/741 acres) but now subdivided, dates from the 14C. In the Middle Ages lakes were popular with the nobility because they required little upkeep and, consequently, only a reduced work force. In the 16C Dombes boasted almost 2 000 stretches of water. The excessive number of lakes filled with stagnant water led to an unhealthy climate, however; average life expectancy in Dombes was very low in the days before the French Revolution. In the 19C, thanks to the work instigated by the monks of the Abbey of Notre-Dame-des-Dombes, the area of water was decreased by fifty percent. The land reclaimed in this way was given over to crops.

Nowadays, water still covers an area of approximately 10 000ha/over 24 000 acres. Most of the lakes are intermittent, one being emptied to fill another; they are filled with water and stocked with fish for a period of six or seven years; they are then drained – using a system of posts to facilitate rapid drainage – and for one year turned over to agriculture.

The Dombes region is a major producer of milk and beef, though stock breeding is equalled by the cultivation of cereal crops (wheat, oats, maize) and oil-producing crops (oilseed rape). Fishing produces some 2 000 tonnes of fish per year (pike, tench, and broach), making this one of the most important lake fishing centres in France; it is well worth an angling trip here in autumn. Dombes, which lies between the Bresse, Lyon and Beaujolais areas, has gained a solid reputation for good food. Waterfowl is to be found here in abundance. The breeding of cross-bred horses is a traditional activity here and it is not unusual to see horses up to their withers in the water of the lakes grazing on *brouille*, a sort of marsh clover of which they are particularly fond.

★TOUR OF THE LAKES

Round trip of 99km/61mi from Villars-les-Dombes – allow one day

Storm brewing above a lake in the Dombes

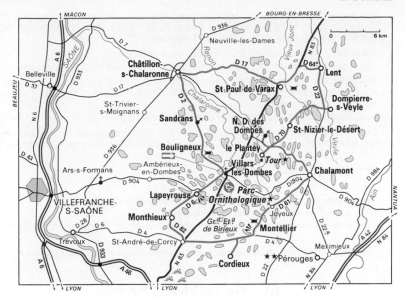

Leave Villars on the D 2 west.

Bouligneux – In a setting typical of this area stands a 14C brick-built **castle** that looks rather more like a fortress.

Sandrans – This village is known for its medieval earth fortress on which was built, in the 19C, a large house. Today a hillock remains, clearly visible and surrounded by a moat, and crowned with a round tower built of brick. The part-Romanesque **church** is, though plain, one of the most characteristic sanctuaries in the Dombes area. It has a single nave and an apse decorated with Romanesque blind arcading in which the strange shuttle-shaped pilasters bear elongated human figures. There is a rood-beam at the entrance to the chancel. Note the statuary and the Gothic font.

Châtillon-sur-Chalaronne – *See CHÂTILLON-SUR-CHALARONNE.*

St-Paul-de-Varax – The Romanesque **church** dates back to the 12C. Its west front has fine stonework and blind arcades. The tympanum above the central door shows Christ in Majesty between two angels. A frieze running above the arcading shows the life of the apostle St Paul and the Last Judgement. The transept crossing is topped by a dome.
St-Paul also boasts one of the prettiest manor-houses in the Dombes region.

Lent – The village still boasts fine 16C monuments: the church belfry (restored in the 18C) and some timber houses. The origins of the Romanesque church here date back to the 9C though its current architecture dates from the 16C.

Dompierre-sur-Veyle – This village grouped around a Romanesque church is near the largest lake in the area (100ha/247 acres): Le Grand Marais.
Take the D 70 west to St-Nizier, passing to the right of various stretches of water which are extensions of Le Grand Marais.

St-Nizier-le-Désert – This pleasant village offers facilities for fishing and gentle rambles.

Le Plantay – The village is surrounded by the waters of the Grand Châtel. The **tower**★ here, of large red bricks and decorated with white stone around the machicolations, is a symbol for the region.

Abbaye Notre-Dame-des-Dombes ⊙ – Monks from this abbey – founded by Cistercians in the 19C – helped to drain the area and cultivated those sections of land which are fertile.

Chalamont – Alt 334m/1 095ft. This is the highest point in La Dombes. Rue des Halles is lined with some old houses (15C but restored) with overhanging upper storeys, and an old wash-house.
Take the D 61 to Joyeux.

There is an attractive 19C house in Joyeux.

The castle at Le Montellier comes into view on the right.

Montellier – The brick-built **castle** *(private)*, the most impressive in Dombes, is flanked at one end by a keep rising on its earth mound. The village church, of Gothic origin, contains a fine 18C carved altarpiece.

Cordieux – A handsome red brick manor house stands here.

Rejoin the D 4 and turn left (west) to St-André-de-Corcy; take the D 82 to Monthieux.

Monthieux – The attractive red brick Romanesque church contains the tombs of the local seigneurs. Breuil manor house (16C), just north of the village, has an interesting Saracen well.

Head towards Ambérieux-en-Dombes and turn right onto the D 6.

Lapeyrouse – From the war memorial there is a delightful view of the Alps and, in the foreground, the Grand Glareins lakes and the 15C Château de Glareins *(private)*.

Take the D 904 back to Villars.

The chapter on art and architecture in Introduction of this guide gives an outline of artistic creation in the region, providing the context of the buildings and works of art described in the Sights section.

This chapter may also provide ideas for touring – why not read it while planning your trip?

Monts DÔMES★★★

Michelin map 73 folds 13, 14 or 239 folds 18, 19

The range of volcanic cones known as the Puys or Monts Dômes rises to the west of Clermont-Ferrand and stands high above the Limagne plain. The 112 extinct volcanoes, which look almost as they did when they were active, stretch in a line over a distance of some 30km/18mi *(see Introduction: Volcanoes of the Auvergne)*.

From the summit of the Puy de Dôme, the highest of the "cones" with an altitude of 1 465m/4 761ft, the view extends right across the range, over this extraordinary and magnificent landscape.

Geological formation – The Monts Dômes are the youngest volcanoes in the Auvergne. They came into being in the Quaternary era and the earliest human settlers may have witnessed their eruptions. The cones, which rise up from the plain in a long string, stand on a plateau of crystalline rocks 900m to 1 000m/2 925ft to 3 250ft high. Most of the volcanoes rise by only 200m or 300m/650ft or 975ft above this plateau, with the exception of the Puy de Dôme which rises to 500m/1 625ft above it. These extinct volcanoes do not all have the same shape. Several of them, such as the Puy de Dôme, are shaped like bells or domes; others contain a single or double crater, while a few have a breached crater. Some of the hillsides are covered only with short grass or moorland but many are wooded. Areas of forest grew naturally but much of it has been planted since the Count de Montlosier set the first example in the early 19C, showing that forests could be grown on land thought of as barren – he was initially taken for a fool. Long black lava flows known as *cheires* form heaps of rocks dotted with juniper and pines; they are scattered all across the plateau. One of these flows, created by the Puy de Lassolac and the Puy de la Vache, closed off the Veyre valley and created Lake Aydat.

★★★① LE PUY DE DÔME
11km/7mi from Royat, then 1hr Rtn on foot – see PUY DE DÔME.

★★★② THE PUYS
Round trip from Royat
120km/74mi – allow half a day – local map opposite

‡‡ **Royat** – See ROYAT.

Leave Royat on the D 941ᶜ southeast then turn right onto the D 5.

The road climbs above the plain until it reaches the granite base from which the volcanic cones rise.

Puy de Gravenoire – There are pozzolana quarries here. This old volcano, now clothed in pine forests, juts up from the great Limagne fault. Its lava flowed down through the fault towards Royat and Beaumont, then the cone was formed from the materials thrown up during the eruption: ash, scoria and volcanic bombs.

At the top of the rise is the village of **Charade** at the foot of its own extinct volcano, the **Puy de Charade**. This basalt cone has a lava flow trailing as far as the Puy de Gravenoire. From the summit there is a **view** of the Monts Dômes, the Limagne, and the mountains of Forez and Dore.

The road then runs along the southern section of the **Clermont-Ferrand-Charade Racing Circuit**. Follow the road through Thèdes and St-Genès-Champanelle and, in Theix, take the N 89 which crosses the lava flow at Aydat.

Cheire d'Aydat – This is a lava flow 6km/4mi long and 1 200m/3 900ft wide. It was thrown up by the Lassolas and La Vache volcanoes, and cooled to form a heap of blackened scoria. The desolation of this volcanic landscape is softened to some extent by juniper bushes, broom, birch trees and, on the shores of Lake Aydat for which the lava flow forms a dam, a forest of pines and spruces planted in the second half of the 19C.

Just beyond Col de la Ventouse pass, turn right onto the D 5 and right again along the D 788. At the junction turn right towards Randanne.

On the way to Randanne the road skirts the Puy de Combegrasse where the first gliding competition to be held in France was held in 1922.

From Randanne the D 5 leads to the Puy de la Vache.

Puy de la Vache – *See Puy de la VACHE.*

Return to Randanne and turn right onto the N 89.

Near the village of Recoleine, the road crosses a landscape dotted with volcanic rocks (basalt and labradorite) just breaking the surface of the ground. At the crossroads of Les Quatre-Routes, the D 941^A on the right runs up towards the Puys until it reaches the Col de la Moreno (alt 1 102m/3 582ft) between the Puy de Laschamp (south) and the Puy de Monchier (north), both of which are covered in forest. From the Col de la Moreno the route runs along the D 52 northwards to Ceyssat and Champille, providing interesting views of the numerous volcanic cones above the road. The narrow D 559 (right) crosses the lava flow from the Puy de Côme, swathed in beeches and conifers, then meets the D 941^B; turn right towards the Col des Goules and La Fontaine du Berger.

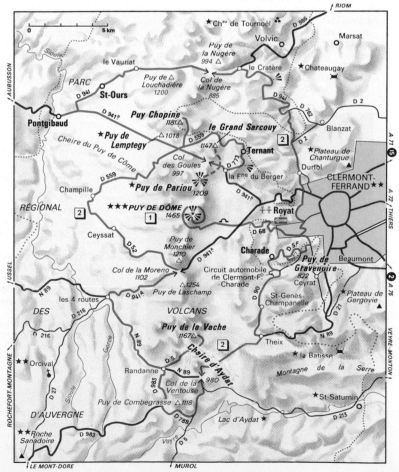

Le Grand Sarcouy – *1hr 30min Rtn on foot along a well-marked footpath leading off the D 941ᴮ just after the Col des Goules.*
The Grand Sarcouy (alt 1 147m/3 727ft) is still known as a "cauldron" because of its shape. In the south side of this gigantic mass of domite is a vast cavern.

★**Puy de Pariou** – *See Puy de PARIOU.*

Ternant – Just before reaching Ternant, when on a level with the great Cross in the village, the road (D 773) provides superb views over Clermont and the Limagne plain.
The D 559 skirts the north side of the Grand Sarcouy.
300m before the junction with the D 941ᴮ, take the path on the right.

Puy Chopine – In dry weather the path provides access to the summit of the volcanic cone *(2hr Rtn on foot).*
Carry on along the D 559 to the junction with the D 941ᴮ and turn right towards Pontgibaud.

★**Puy de Lemptégy** ⊘ – This **open-topped volcano** (alt 1 018m/3 340ft) is an old pozzolana quarry hollowed out of a volcanic cone. The site is particularly impressive, as visitors can go down into the very centre of the volcano and see evidence of three successive phases of volcanic activity from 60 000 years ago. A footpath has been laid out, along with a botanical trail, to give the best possible overview of the many and varied volcanic features which pepper this landscape and the different kinds of volcanic material which accumulated during its active period: ash, lapilli (cinders), remarkable volcanic bombs and lava.
At the end of the trail, an exhibition centre and a video complete this volcanic tour.
Carry on along the D 941ᴮ.

Pontgibaud – This large peaceful village on the river was known in Gallo-Roman times for its silver-bearing lead mines. **Château Dauphin** ⊘ is a lavastone fort which was built in the 12C; six towers of the walls remain in good condition. The main building – a large rectangle with machicolations and crenellations – incorporates a round keep. Inside, there are 18C paintings and miniatures, and 16C-18C furniture. In season, a weekly tour is organised in the evening, when the castle is illuminated, which includes a visit to a magnificent **chapel**★.
The 15C church has interesting furnishings including the font, the marble altar (18C) and some fine paintings.

S. Sauvignier/MICHELIN

One of the towers at Château Dauphin, Pontgibaud

The D 941 begins to climb the west side of the mountain range.

St-Ours – This village has a monument to the French Resistance.

Beyond St-Ours and Le Vauriat the road provides stunning views of the Puy de Louchadière, one of the main extinct volcanoes in the range, which reaches an altitude of 1 200m/3 900ft and has a breached crater 150m/488ft deep. Further on, to the left, is the easily-recognisable outline of the Puy de Nuguère (alt 994m/3 230ft).
Beyond the Col de la Nuguère and Le Cratère the road winds down to the Limagne plain. There are several magnificent views from the road as it runs through Durtol to Royat.
Near Durtol is the Château de Sarcenat, birthplace in 1881 of **Pierre Teilhard de Chardin**, a Jesuit who became known as a scientist and a philosopher.

Monts DORE ★★★

The Monts Dore range consists of a set of extinct volcanoes. It is one of the most picturesque areas in the Auvergne thanks to the dramatic power of some of the peaks, the depth of its valleys, its waterfalls and its lakes.

The highest peak in the range, the Puy de Sancy, rises to an altitude of 1 885m/6 126ft and is the highest summit in central France.

FIRE AND ICE

Three huge volcanoes – The mighty system of volcanoes, of which the last remains form the Monts Dore range, evolved at the end of the Tertiary era. At its zenith, it covered an area three times larger than that of Vesuvius and consisted of three large cones in juxtaposition (Sancy, Banne d'Ordanche and l'Aiguiller) whose craters opened at an altitude of almost 2 500m/8 125ft. Lava flowed over lava on the mountainsides, forming flows more than 1 000m/3 250ft thick, but glaciation during the Quaternary era cut radiating valleys into the slopes. The Sancy cone consists of a plug of trachyte where the exterior has been worn away by erosion. Volcanic lakes add a touch of beauty to the landscape which, at altitudes of between 1 100 and 1 400m/3 575 and 4 550ft, is covered with forests of pine, spruce and beech. Lower down the slopes are valleys with meadows and hedgerows.

Rhinoceros in the Auvergne – Between the periods when the volcanoes were active, life returned to the Dore area.

Sancy mountain massif

Footprints and bones found among the volcanic ash prove that laurel, bamboo and other plants which are now found only in hotter climes once grew on the slopes of the volcanoes, while rhinoceros, elephants and ferocious carnivores such as sabre-toothed tigers roamed the countryside.

Former glaciers – The great period of glaciation which spread across Europe at the beginning of the Quaternary era covered the Monts Dore range with an ice cap more than 100m/330ft thick. This considerable mass dug out corries and deep valleys, created the scarp slopes down which the waterfalls cascade, and threw into relief the most resistant sections of mountain, the peaks and enormous rocks that add to the picturesque beauty of the Monts Dore.

Final throes – Decapitated and dismantled by the glaciers and by the surging meltwaters that accompanied the fusion of the ice flows, the central area of the range looked very much as it does today when the first human settlers arrived. It was then that a new volcanic upthrust occurred along the edges; secondary volcanoes erupted, closing off valleys with their cones and lava flows, gouging out craters and creating a number of lakes. These were the final throes of volcanic activity in the Monts Dore.

★★★ ① PUY DE SANCY

4.5km/3mi from Mont-Dore then 1hr 45min Rtn on foot via steps up from the upper cable-car station ⊙.

★★★**Panorama** – *Viewing table.* Rising to an altitude of 1 885m/6 126ft, Puy de Sancy in the Monts Dore range is the highest peak in central France.

When the weather is exceptionally clear the **panoramic view** stretches as far as the Alps of the Dauphiné. Nearer are the Dômes range to the northeast, the Cantal range to the south and, in the foreground, the Monts Dore.

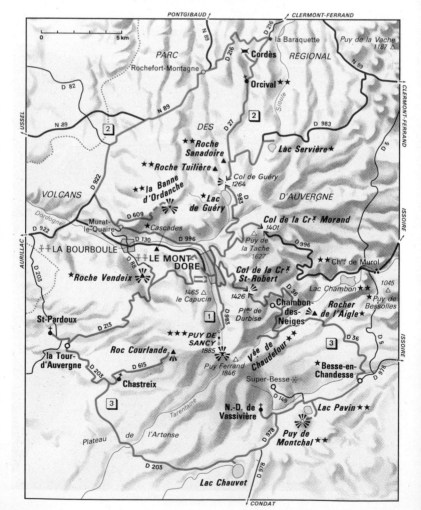

★★★② THE NORTHERN SLOPES

Round trip from Mont-Dore

85km/53mi – allow half a day – local map below

It is also possible to start this trip from La Bourboule. From December to April, the D 983 northbound, the route beyond the entrance to the corrie, may be blocked by snow.

★★Le Mont-Dore – *See Le MONT-DORE.*

Col de la Croix-Morand – The D 996 leads to this mountain pass (alt 1 404m/4 553ft) which is also known as the **Col de Diane**, although the real pass of this name is set away from the road. It used to have a bad reputation, for according to a local saying, "The Col de la Croix-Morand kills a man a year."
Return to the D 983 and turn right.

After driving through the forest then through a valley with hillsides covered with basalt rock falls, the road reaches Lake Guéry (**view** of the Sancy massif).

★Lac de Guéry – The lake (alt 1 244m/4 043ft) covers an area of 25ha/61 acres and reaches a maximum depth of 16m/52ft. It was formed by a basalt flow which arrived from a southeasterly direction, closing off the end of the valley. The pastures are studded with black rocks and the surrounding pine forests create a rather austere environment lightened in the springtime by great expanses of snow.
To the south are the outlines of the peaks in the Sancy range. The road runs high above the wooded Cirque du Chausse.

★★Roches Tuilière et Sanadoire – From the Col de Guéry there is a superb **view**★★ over the deep, wooded Chausse corrie from which jut up the rocks of Tuilière and Sanadoire.

To the left is Tuilière rock consisting of prismatic columnar trachyte in sheaves, once the chimney of a ruined volcano. Sanadoire rock to the right is all that remains of a volcanic cone. Until the 15C it was topped by an almost impregnable castle which was used as a refuge during the Hundred Years War by the mercenaries who terrorised the area. The large valley between the rocks was dug out by a glacier.

Near the junction of the D 27 and D 983, a path off the D 983 leads to a rocky promontory; from here, if facing Sanadoire rock, a surprising echo created by the phonolite can be heard.

★Lac Servière – This lake is a former crater with gently sloping sides, except to the south where it cuts into the Puy de Combe-Perret. It covers an area of 15ha/37 acres and has a depth of 26m/84ft. A round lake as unruffled as a mirror, its shores are lined with pines and firs, except on the east side where there are meadows and where its waters skim the rim of the crater. This is a beauty spot with plenty of character.

Roche Tuilière

★★Orcival – *See ORCIVAL.*

Château de Cordès – *See ORCIVAL.*

In La Baraquette turn left onto the N 89 towards Rochefort-Montagne and beyond, taking the D 922 and continuing to Murat-le-Quaire. Turn left onto the D 609.

★★La Banne d'Ordanche – *See La BOURBOULE.*

Beyond Murat-le-Quaire, return either to La Bourboule on the D 609 or to Le Mont-Dore on the D 996.

As well as the long-distance footpaths (Grande Randonnée), marked with red and white stripes, and the local paths (Pays Balisé), marked in red and yellow, there are many other interesting footpaths. Information available from the local Tourist Information Centre.

★★③ TOUR OF THE SANCY RANGE

Round trip from Le Mont-Dore
85km/53mi – allow one day – local map p 166

Some of the roads may be blocked by snow from November to April. The trip can also start from La Bourboule.

⁋⁋ Le Mont-Dore – *See Le MONT-DORE.*

Leave Le Mont-Dore on ② on the map (the D 983 south) and turn left onto the D 36 up to the Col de la Croix-St-Robert.

Col de la Croix-St-Robert – Alt 1 426m/4 635ft. From the pass there is a superb **panoramic view★★** to the west over the Millevaches plateau, to the east over Lake Chambon, Murol plateau and castle and, in the distance, the mountains in the Forez and Livradois areas.
The road runs down beyond the pass towards Besse-en-Chandesse across the **Durbise plateau** with its vast expanse of pasture where the winter sports resort of **Chambon-des-Neiges** has been built.

★★Vallée de Chaudefour – *See Vallée de CHAUDEFOUR.*

★Rocher de l'Aigle – From "Eagle's Rock" there is a striking view of the Chaudefour valley and the Monts Dore range.

★Besse-en-Chandesse – *See BESSE-EN-CHANDESSE.*

★★Lac Pavin – *See Lac PAVIN.*

Vassivière Chapel – *See BESSE-EN-CHANDESSE.*

Take the D 203 west towards La Tour d'Auvergne.

Lac Chauvet – The path to this lake crosses a meadow then heads for a house on the edge of a wood. Lake Chauvet is surrounded by woods and pastures, and was formed by a series of volcanic eruptions which caused soil subsidence.

Chastreix – *Winter sports in Chastreix-Sancy.* The **church** is a fine building with a nave but no side aisles. Note the 14C porch and, to the left of the nave, the 18C altarpiece.

Turn right onto the D 615.

Roc Courlande – The road leads to the winter sports resort of Chastreix-Sancy then to Courlande rock on the west side of the Puy de Sancy. From the car park to the right of the road there is an extensive **view★** of the Artense plateau in the foreground, overshadowed by the Cantal mountains. The Dordogne valley lies to the right.

La Tour-d'Auvergne – This is a small town in a delightful, rustic setting crisscrossed by streams forming waterfalls. It lies at an altitude of 990m/3 218ft on a basalt plateau ending in prismatic columnar basalt that can be seen near the church. The marketplace laid out on the top of these prisms seems to be made of gigantic cobblestones.

St-Pardoux – This village has an interesting Gothic **church** which still has 13C strap hinges on its doors.

★Roche Vendeix – *Access along a footpath off the D 88 by an inn. 30min Rtn on foot.* This rock of prismatic basalt carries the ruins of a castle which was re-fortified in the 14C by Aimerigot Marcheix, an infamous local brigand who was finally caught by the king's men in 1390; he was taken to Paris and subsequently beheaded and quartered. From the summit of the rock (alt 1 131m/3 710ft) there is a good panorama over the region.
Return either to La Bourboule by continuing along the D 88 beyond Vendeix rock, or to Le Mont-Dore by turning right onto the D 213. There are some wonderful views of the resort from the road as it runs downhill.

Despite having identical names, the Dore mountain torrent – which, flowing into the Dogne, creates the River Dordogne in the Monts Dore range at the foot of the Puy de Sancy – and this River Dore, which flows through a narrow gorge separating the Livradois and Forez ranges, should not be confused. This Dore is a tributary on the right bank of the Allier, rising in the mountains of the Livradois area. It flows down in a southeasterly direction into deep, granite gorges then turns northwards to cross, at a leisurely pace, the Ambert plateau, a small gully lined by the mountains of Forez.

Downstream from Ambert, the Dore crosses the granite bedrock on which Olliergues stands; it pours through picturesque gorges with moderately steep, wooded sides before entering the Limagne area, its waters now swollen by the Couzon and Durolle, and going on to flow into the River Allier south of Vichy at the bridge in Ris, after covering a distance of 140km/87mi.

Industries are strung out along the length of the valley. There is the manufacture of high quality paper, the production of electric cars and stainless steel, cardboard, ducts and electric cables, plastics, surgical equipment, lace, pharmaceuticals, and modern sawmills or simple "sawpits" in farms that work with timber from the surrounding mountainsides.

Hydroelectric plants at Olliergues and Sauviat use water from the Dore to produce electricity.

Livradois-Forez tourist railway ⊙ – In the summer, a 1959 Renault **train** travels from Pont-de-Dore *(see below)* or Courpière to Ambert or Arlanc, giving visitors an opportunity to see the typical landscapes of the Livradois-Forez regional park around Thiers, Ambert, the granite uplands of Forez, and the plateaux and pine forests in the Livradois.

FROM DORE-L'ÉGLISE TO PONT-DE-DORE

85km/53mi – about 4hr – local map overleaf

Dore-l'Église – The village, situated at the confluence of the Dore and Dorette, has a 12C church which underwent alterations in the 15C. A wide flight of steps leads up to a fine porch with triple coving, the last of which is decorated with imaginary animals. The doors still have their 14C strap hinges. To the left of the church is a Gallo-Roman memorial.

Take the D 906 north.

Arlanc – This small market town with its typical old streets occupies a delightful site tucked between the Forez and Livradois mountains; it is one of the end stations of the **Livradois-Forez tourist railway** *(see above)*.

South of the town stands the **church of St-Pierre**, a Romanesque building with particularly fine stonework; note the capital carved with long faces (2nd pillar on the right). The **Musée de la Dentelle** ⊙ (Lace Museum) is housed in the vaulted cellars of the Mairie (town hall). Throughout the Auvergne the lace-making tradition dates back to the late 16C, though its heyday in Arlanc was in the late 19C when the Chabrier company launched a type of handmade lace, named "Renaissance", which was an immediate success. The museum has several pieces *(in the drawers)*: tablecloths, handkerchiefs, veils, a few dresses, together with lace-making equipment. An audio-visual display *(in French)* explains the techniques used for making bobbin lace. In season, visitors can watch a lace-maker at work.

The valley widens out, overshadowed by the first outcrops of the Forez mountains to the right and by the wooded slopes of the Livradois to the left.

Marsac-en-Livradois – On the square to the south of the church is the old White Penitents' Chapel. It houses the **Musée des Pénitents blancs du Livradois** ⊙, a museum filled with memorabilia relating to this brotherhood. A recorded commentary *(in French)* accompanied by religious music retraces the life and rituals of the old penitent order.

Ambert – *See AMBERT.*

Continue along the D 906, then turn right onto the D 66 and right again onto a narrow road leading to Volpie rock.

★**Rocher de la Volpie** – *1hr Rtn on foot.* Park beside a group of houses and follow the footpath waymarked in red, which climbs through woodland to the left of a farm building. From the rocky Volpie peak the **view**★ stretches over the Livradois mountains with the Ambert plain in the foreground.

Those preferring not to attempt the climb can take a path to the right beyond the farm, which leads across the meadows to the foot of the rock *(20min Rtn)*. This is a particularly peaceful spot.

Rejoin the D 66 and turn right.

Job – The small town has a superb 15C church topped by a large square belfry.

Take the D 67 to rejoin the D 906.

Vertolaye – Pharmaceuticals, bellows and shoelaces are produced here.

Olliergues – Pleasantly situated on the north bank of the River Dore, over which there is a pretty 15C bridge to the south of town, Olliergues has terraces of houses rising up the hillside. At the top is a castle (restored) which once belonged to Marshal Turenne's family. 15C and 16C houses add interest to the street leading from the town hall to the church. The most interesting house, with overhanging upper storeys, is in Rue du Pavé. The former castle chapel (now the **church of Notre-Dame**) was extended in the 15C and 16C. It contains a fine 14C granite tomb and a 17C altarpiece.

Opposite the church's pretty bell tower stands the square castle keep, which houses a museum of traditional local crafts and trades, the **Musée des Vieux Métiers** ⊙. The display concentrates on four main crafts – clog-making, cartwright/blacksmithing, weaving and cheese-making – with collections of tools and machinery associated with each, as well as videos showing the craftsmen at work in the sorts of conditions which prevailed in days gone by.

2km/1mi north of Olliergues, in **La Chabasse**, is an old **parish church** ⊙ built in the purest of Gothic styles and decorated with trefoiled windows. It stands at the top of a hill overlooking the Dore valley.

In Giroux turn right onto the D 314.

Augerolles – The impressive 14C **church** still has its Romanesque chancel thought to date from AD 980.

On the altar in the right side aisle, note the 16C carved wooden panel depicting a Dance of Death.

Take the D 42, turn left onto the D 906; then turn right onto the D 316.

Sauviat – This village, attractively situated on a spur of rock, stands high above a meander of the River Dore as it flows through a narrow valley.

From the observation platform behind the old town hall, the view extends over the dam and the hydroelectric power station it supplies.

The 14C granite church has a single aisle and a massive square belfry.

Take the D 315 and D 906 to Courpière.

Courpière – See COURPIÈRE.

Follow the D 906 and turn left onto the D 223.

Château d'Aulteribe – See COURPIÈRE: Excursion.

Take the D 44 then turn left onto the D 906.

Pont-de-Dore – The town stands at a major road junction.

Use the Map of principal sights to plan a special itinerary.

ÉBREUIL

Population 1 148
Michelin map 73 fold 4 or 239 fold 7
Local map under Gorges de la SIOULE

The small town lies on the banks of the River Sioule which, having crossed the famous gorge of the same name, flows through a wide, fertile valley.

★St-Léger – The church, built in the 10C and 13C, was part of a Benedictine abbey whose buildings were replaced in the 18C by the present hospice *(to the right of the west front)* and by an abbot's palace *(behind the east end)* that is now a retirement home.

The timber-roofed nave and transept were built in the Romanesque style; the chancel and its radiating chapels are early Gothic.

The belfry-porch, remarkable for the purity of its architectural design, was added to the 11C west front in about 1125; it consists of two storeys, the first decorated with rounded bays containing loopholes and the second with traceried bays. The roof and bell turret are modern. Above the portal is a tympanum decorated with three Romanesque high-reliefs – a figure of Christ giving Benediction flanked by two of the Apostles. The strap hinges and door knockers date from the 12C.

The interior includes superb **frescoes★** dating from the 12C and 15C. The 12C paintings decorating the gallery depict St Austremoine, first Bishop of Clermont, the martyrdom of St Valery and St Pancras, and the three archangels, Michael, Gabriel and Raphael. The 15C fresco on a pillar to the right of the nave shows St George slaying the dragon. Above the transept crossing, the dome over squinches used to be topped by an octagonal belfry; it was removed in 1794.

Behind the high altar on a stone column is the superb **reliquary of St Léger★** (16C) made of wood covered with silver-gilt. In one of the apsidal chapels is a 16C statue of the Virgin Mary seated.

J.-L. Barde/SCOPE

Detail of a fresco in St-Léger church

EXCURSIONS

★★Gorges de la Sioule – *See Gorges de la SIOULE.*

Between the Rivers Sioule and Buron – *Round trip east of Ébreuil, see GANNAT: Excursions.*

Michelin Maps (scale 1 : 200 000), which are revised regularly, indicate:

– golf courses, sports stadiums, racecourses, swimming pools, beaches, airfields,
– scenic routes, public footpaths, panoramas,
– forest parks, interesting sights...

The perfect complement to the Michelin Green Guides for planning holidays.

Keep current Michelin Maps in the car at all times.

Château d'EFFIAT ★

Michelin map 73 fold 5 or 239 fold 8 – Local map under La LIMAGNE

On the Vichy-Aigueperse road, which runs through Montpensier forest, stands the Château d'Effiat, a fine Louis XIII building of great historic and architectural interest.

TOUR ⊙

At the end of a wide avenue of lime trees rises a majestic gateway built of lavastone from the Volvic area. The gateway's pediment is decorated with the coat-of-arms and marquis' crown of the Marshal of Effiat, who owned the château; these emblems are surmounted by a helmet between battle standards. Beyond lies a courtyard, bordered by the main building flanked by two pavilions. The façade of the château is decorated with twinned Doric pilasters of lavastone which add an air of great nobility.

The gateway, Château d'Effiat

Apartments – The mainly 17C furniture, works of art and historical memorabilia have been collected by the Moroges family who bought the château in 1856, at a time when it seemed doomed to be demolished. In the Louis XV boudoir, note the stained glass (from the Sèvres factory) illustrating scenes from the life of **Cinq-Mars**. Henri Coiffier de Ruzé, Marquis de Cinq-Mars (1620-42), was a favourite of Louis XIII. He conspired against Richelieu and was consequently executed; his father was a Marshal of France. Note also the Marshal's seal, and the manuscript relating the trial and execution of Cinq-Mars and his great friend De Thou. In the next room are some of the young Marquis' writings, and edicts promulgated by Louis XII and his brother, Gaston of Orléans. The guardroom contains a 17C fireplace with a mantelpiece depicting the port of La Rochelle on the west coast of France. It also has Louis XIII furniture which belonged to the Marshal of Effiat, and a number of 18C paintings. The main drawing room has a beamed ceiling which was painted by Italian artists in 1627. Note, too, the wood panelling and the monumental fireplace bearing a mythological scene on the mantelpiece, *Vulcan's Forge*, said to be the work of the painter Louis Le Nain. The house also contains reminders of the Effiat royal military academy (1593-1648).

Gardens – The gardens, laid out by André Mollet (godfather of the celebrated landscape architect Le Nôtre), are typical of the 17C with vast lakes supplied from underground springs, ancient oak trees, a terrace and a grotto.

ENNEZAT ★

Population 1 915
Michelin map 73 southeast of fold 4 or 239 north of fold 20
Local map under La LIMAGNE

Ennezat, a large farming village on the Limagne plain, lies near marshes in a landscape of vast, geometrical fields separated by drainage ditches and rows of aspen trees and willows. Digging reveals a black earth which is very fertile, as is obvious from the huge silos at the northwest exit to the village along the road to Clerlande (D 20); they help to maintain the Limagne's reputation as a "grain store". The streets are laid out in a regular pattern which, in days gone by when large bands of pillaging brigands roamed the countryside, helped the inhabitants to withstand attack.

★Church – *30min.* This former collegiate church, sometimes known as the "Cathedral of the Marshes", consists of two very different sections. The nave, side aisles and transept are built of arkose – a pale-coloured stone – in the purest of Auvergne Romanesque styles; they date from the 11C. The chancel of lavastone, surrounded by an ambulatory and radiating chapels, was rebuilt in the 13C in Gothic style to a more extensive layout, to replace the old Romanesque chancel. From the outside, the east end is tall and elegant. The nave and chancel have been restored, the narthex and south and west doorways are 19C.

Enter the church through the south doorway which was moved and rebuilt in the 19C.

The **Romanesque section★** is pleasingly pure and well-proportioned. Note among the capitals to the left of the nave at the transept crossing, that depicting a miser.
In the Gothic section, besides the keystones and corbels, there are some works of art of particular interest:

– in the 2nd span of the left side aisle in the chancel is a fresco dating from 1420, depicting the Meeting of the Three Living and the Three Dead;
– to the right of the door into the sacristy is a deeply moving and expressive, 17C wooden Pietà;
– the lectern in the Lady Chapel at the east end dates from 1773;
– the radiating chapels contain a number of old statues including a 15C polychrome statue of St Blaise *(chapel to the right of the Lady Chapel);*
– just beyond the transept in the 1st span of the south side is a wax painting dating from 1405 which represents the Last Judgement.
In the sacristy *(north of the chancel)* note the carved door dating from 1699.

Vallée de l'EYRIEUX★

Michelin map 76 folds 18 to 20 and 244 folds 34 to 36

The River Eyrieux rises to the north of St-Agrève at an altitude of 1 120m/3 640ft then tumbles down from the high plateaux of the Vivarais area and flows into the Rhône after covering a distance of 70km/44mi. The upper valley has a mountainous appearance, with steep slopes covered with chestnuts and spruce; this is the area known as Les Boutières. Downstream from Le Cheylard the torrent flows into gorges, then less rugged basins and rocky narrows alternate until the waters reach the final plain, where they enter the Rhône valley.

Fearsome spates – The Eyrieux flows swiftly, like a torrent. Because of the sloping ground on its upper course, autumn storms can suddenly swell the main river and its tributaries. From 0.8m³/s in July and August, the rate of flow can increase to a phenomenal 3 600m³/s in just a few hours. During the spate of September 1857, the waters in the Pontpierre narrow near St-Fortunat reached a height of 17.25m/56ft.

Peach trees in blossom

Sectors of activity – Old, isolated hamlets cling to the hillsides marked into strips by the low walls surrounding the terraced fields. Larger villages and small towns grew up in the small inner basins in the valley, or at the mouths of tributaries. Some of them have a degree of industrial activity; at Le Cheylard, for instance, there is leatherworking, weaving, dying, plastics manufacturing and jewellery-making. The predominant character of the valley, though, derives from the farming of peaches.

PEACH-TREE VALLEY

In the spring the peach trees turn this rugged valley into a carpet of pink-petalled blossom. Over the seasons, fields of green vegetables and strawberries complete the agricultural scene.

A model orchard – The widespread cultivation of orchards in the Eyrieux valley is due to particularly favourable natural conditions: light, warm soil which is easily drained; the valley's sheltered site from the Mistral and the winds from the south; spring frosts which are rare; and summers which begin early – all these factors help the fruit to ripen quickly.

The success story of the orchards is also largely due to the determination of the local people. The first trees were planted in 1880, on an experimental basis, at **St-Laurent-du-Pape** which has remained a pilot community ever since. Production methods, carefully improved since that time, have been copied by farmers in neighbouring regions. Gradually the orchards spread over more land in the valley although, since the introduction of mechanisation, the cultivation of peach trees up the hillsides has fallen into a sharp decline.

Production – Each orchard covers an average area of no more than 1.5ha/about 3.5 acres. This divison of the land can be explained by the demands of a type of farming which remains, for the most part, a family business. When it reaches maturity, a tree produces between 25-40kg/55-88lbs of fruit. 1ha/2.5 acres commonly produces 10-16 tonnes of peaches.

Eyrieux peaches have gained a reputation for quality both nationally and on the export market. A large cooperative in Beauchastel now undertakes most of the marketing of the fruit. The valley as a whole produces some 12 000 tonnes of peaches every year.

TOUR

In the spring, at the end of March, the D 120 is the best route to follow in order to admire the fairytale sight of the peach trees in blossom. The season lasts for some time, beginning with the orchards in the lower valley, and creates an extraordinary symphony of colours ranging from pale pink to carmine red and through to purple.

★★★**Corniche de l'Eyrieux** – *54km/34mi round trip leaving from Vernoux-en-Vivarais. See VERNOUX-EN-VIVARAIS.*

★★**Les Boutières** – *64km/40mi round trip leaving from St-Agrève – allow 2hr 30min.*
St-Agrève – This is a pleasant resort beside **Mont Chiniac**★★ (alt 1 120m/3 674ft), a pine-covered mountain offering extensive views over the Mézenc range.
Take the D 120 south. At the exit to St-Julien-Boutières, turn right onto the D 101.

Fay-sur-Lignon – This mountain-village (pronounced fa-yee) offers cross-country skiing facilities in winter. There is a good **view**★ of the surrounding mountains from the graveyard next to the church.
Take the D 262 south and turn left to St-Clément.

St-Clément – From here there are good **views**★★ over the upper valley of the River Saliouse.
Rejoin the D 262; turn left onto the D 410. Continue to Lachapelle-sous-Chanéac and, beyond, to Armanas. This is a winding and attractive route with lovely views over the basin of the upper Eyrieux and of the confluence of the Eysse and Eyrieux rivers.
In Armanas turn left and then right onto the D 478 to Le Bourget and Rochebonne.

★**Ruins of Rochebonne** – *Park by the side of the road.* The magnificent **site**★★ is the setting for the fissured, granitic ruins of the medieval castle, overlooked to the west by Mont Mézenc.
Walk down to the ruins *(30min Rtn)*. A path leads past other rocks framing a ravine, dotted with pine trees, where a torrent falls in small cascades.
Continue along the D 478 towards Beauvert and down to the D 21 which leads back to St-Agrève.

Tourists should not go sightseeing in a church during a service.

Monts du FOREZ ★★

Michelin maps 73 folds 6, 16, 17 and 88 folds 4, 16, 17 or 239 folds 22, 23

The granite mountains in the Forez area form a range some 45km/28mi long. Along the edge are parallel offshoots separating the picturesque valleys, some of which run down to the Dore while others head for the Loire. The eastern slope stands high above the Forez plain; the slope to the west, the only part of the mountain in the Auvergne, drops sharply down to the Dore basin and includes some attractive beauty spots and magnificent views.

Up to altitudes of 800-1 000m/2 600-3 250ft, the mountainsides are covered with fields (rye, potatoes) and meadows – this is the zone in which villages have been built. The pure, abundant water supply that rushes down all the slopes of the Forez mountains is used to irrigate the meadows where it is cool even in the height of the summer, and to turn the waterwheels in the mills, sawmills, and the last papermill in the Lagat valley; it also supplies the cutlery works in Thiers. Above are the pine and beech forests covering the hillsides.

At altitudes above 1 200-1 300m/3 900-4 250ft lie the summer pastures which are called the "Hautes-Chaumes" (alpine pastures) of the Forez. On the bare mountain peaks a few spurs of rock jut up from the middle of scree slopes; Pierre sur Haute is the highest of them all (alt 1 634m/5 311ft).

The Forez mountains are part of the **Parc naturel régional Livradois-Forez** ⊘ which was set up in 1984 and covers an area of almost 300 000ha/over 740 000 acres. Its aims are to revitalise a declining rural environment and to present and promote local heritage, especially crafts and industry. The park also seeks to encourage rural holidays which do not disturb the environment.

Monts du Forez

★ ⬜ ROUND TOUR STARTING FROM BOËN

Via the Col de Béal 95km/59mi – about 3hr not including the climb up to Pierre sur Haute – local map overleaf

Boën – Boën (pronounced "Bowen"), situated high above the left bank of the Lignon, specialises in metalworking and small-scale mechanical engineering. Boën was the birthplace of Father Terray (1715-78), Comptroller-General of Finances at the end of Louis XV's reign. The unpopular measures he was forced to take in order to re-establish a balanced budget following the excessive spending of the royal court brought him the nickname "Emptier of Purses".

Château de Boën ⊘ – This elegant 18C abode has richly-decorated rooms, in particular the Italian Salon. Upstairs (under the eaves) is a small **Winemaking Museum** which recalls this once-popular activity in the region.

Leave Boën on the N 89 northwest. It is possible to take a small detour straight on to the attractive fortified village of **L'Hôpital-sous-Rochefort** ★ *(two gateways remaining of 15C town wall; 12C church, fortified in 15C, with Romanesque chancel and transept,*

housing a late 15C polychrome wood **Virgin and Child★★** *). Otherwise, 2.5km/1mi on from Boën, turn left onto the D 6 to Sail-sous-Couzan; at Sail turn right onto a very steep tarmacked road.*

★Château de Couzan – *Park at the foot of the ruins; 15min Rtn on foot.* The ruins of this 13C-15C fortress, one of the most extensive in the region, stand on a rocky promontory squeezed between the narrow valleys of the Lignon and Chagon rivers. What remains of the curtain walls and towers still suggests the strength of the seigneurs of Couzan, the oldest barons of the Forez. There is a good view of the castle walls from a rocky promontory behind the fort, and panoramic **views★** over the countryside from the ruins.

The road (D 6) runs along the sheer-sided, wooded Lignon valley.

At the entrance to Chalmazel, turn right onto the D 101 (signposted "Jeansagnière").

The road runs along the crest of the hill up above the upper Lignon valley overshadowed by Pierre sur Haute before reaching Jeansagnière. Continue on to the pass, **Col de la Loge**, where a curtain of pine trees opens onto a clearing carpeted with grass. Before La Chamba, the forest gives way to more pastoral scenery and the road, skirting a succession of corries filled with fine pastures, provides several outstanding views of the Dore basin and the Livradois area.

Fork right out of La Chamba and after 2km/1mi turn left towards Le Brugeron.

La Chambonie – A village nestling in a pastoral corrie.

Immediately beyond a sawmill turn right onto the D 37.

After a long climb up through the forest, there is a magnificent view over the Monts Dômes range. Beyond another stretch of road through the forest lie alpine pastures dotted with farmsteads (*jasseries*).

★Col du Béal – From this pass there is a wide **panoramic view** over the mountains of the Auvergne and the Lyonnais area. The pass forms a threshold between the two sides of the Forez mountains.

★★Pierre sur Haute – *2hr 30min Rtn on foot, recommended in clear weather.* Climb directly up to the summit across the alpine pastures and along the crest of the mountain or take the **cable-car** ⊘. Pierre sur Haute, the highest peak in the Forez range (alt 1 634m/5 311ft) is a dome-shaped granite mountain topped by military radar installations. The windswept moorland that carpets its slopes is gashed here and there by huge rockfalls. Small farmsteads dot the hillsides.

Summer pastures

The Monts du Forez, culminating in Pierre sur Haute (alt 1 634m/5 311ft), feature a wide range of scenery, much of it covered by dark pine forests. Once above the treeline, the mountain summits, often shrouded in mist or cloud, are vast bleak stretches of moorland – the **Hautes Chaumes**. This somewhat eery landscape can look more like a moonscape in certain lights. The vast bare wastes are broken only by granite rocks, deep peat bogs or clumps of broom. Nonetheless, man – or rather, woman – has attempted to scratch a living from this unwelcoming environment. A matriarchal society evolved in the mountain farmsteads *(jasseries)* during the summer months: while the menfolk were down in the valley dealing with the harvesting, the women and children would be in charge of looking after the livestock in the summer pastures up in the mountains, where they would also make the famous local Fourme cheese and gather medicinal plants.

This harsh way of life gradually died out, and there are now no more working *jasseries*. However, some of them have been converted into open-air museums which inform visitors on the daily work and traditions of these "Amazons of the mountains".

From the summit (beacon and Cross) to the right of the military installations, the **panorama** stretches right across the Forez, the mountains in the Lyonnais area and Beaujolais, the Limagne, the Monts Dômes, the Monts Dore, Cantal and the mountains in the Velay and Vivarais areas.

Three types of scenery succeed each other during the rapid trip down from Col du Béal to Chalmazel – alpine pastures, then a superb pine forest and, finally, an area of pine trees and meadows.

7km/4mi from Col du Béal, a road cuts off to the right; it leads to the ski slopes and the Pierre sur Haute cable-car.

On the outskirts of Chalmazel there is an attractive view of the castle down below.

※**Chalmazel** – This mountain village, which clings to the hillside in the Lignon ravine, is a bustling place during the winter sports season. It is dominated by the old **Château des Talaru-Marcilly** ⊙ (13C), a huge bastion flanked by corner towers which still has its parapet walkway.

The D 6 to the right climbs up through the Lignon valley. In Sail-sous-Couzan turn right towards Trelins; turn right again onto the D 20ᴬ.

Château de Goutelas – The château stands on a terrace high above the Forez plain; it is a delightful late 16C residence which has been restored and is now used for courses and seminars. The courtyard is open to visitors and it is possible to walk round the exterior.

Turn back and take the D 8 back to Boën.

★② ROUND TRIP STARTING FROM MONTBRISON

Via Col des Supeyres

70km/44mi – half a day – local map opposite

Montbrison – The town is built around a volcanic mound and dominated by the 18C dome of the old Convent of the Visitation (today the law courts) and by the imposing belfry of its Gothic church, Notre-Dame d'Espérance, which was founded in 1226 (restored 1970). It has a 15C Flamboyant porch with a 14C Virgin and Child on the tympanum. The **interior★** has a long nave, triple lancet windows and a Rayonnant Gothic chancel. Opposite the church stands **La Diana** ⊙, built in 1296; its 14C interior has a coffered and painted wooden ceiling. The **Musée d'Allard** ⊙ contains a good collection of minerals and stuffed birds; upstairs is a doll museum.

Leave Montbrison to the west along the D 101 which climbs up the bare, rocky Vizery ravine. A short detour leads to the village of Essertines.

Essertines-en-Châtelneuf – From the village, with its small Gothic church with Flamboyant Gothic decoration, there is a view over the Forez plain from which emerges the rocky pinnacle of St-Romain-le-Puy.

Rejoin the D 101 and continue up the valley before turning left onto the D 44ᴬ. In Roche turn left onto the D 44 and continue via the D 113 to the Col de Baracuchet.

From the road there are several glimpses of the Forez plain. The road continues to climb through valleys filled with farms and fields and dominated by wooded peaks. Near the pass, the trees become gnarled and twisted until eventually they give way to a vast clearing from which there is a view of the Ance valley *(left)* and, opposite the road, the crest of the Forez mountains.

The road *(D 106)* climbs up to the Col des Supeyres through alpine pastures, carpeted with heather and dotted with farmsteads, and past the Grand Génevrier farmsteads *(left)*.

Col des Supeyres – Alt 1 366m/4 440ft. This pass on the eastern edge of the Livarois-Forez natural park is surrounded by a landscape more reminiscent of steppes: badly-drained mountain pastures, without a soul in sight. The sense of ruggedness and isolation is particularly strong at the bottom of the road leading to Pierre sur Haute (it becomes a dirt track 1km/0.6mi from the start). A viewing table on "La Montagne des Allebasses" and a thematic footpath *(2hr 30min)* shed light on the way of life in this region (farmsteads, summer pasturing etc).

The route down from the pass towards St-Anthème passes the group of farmsteads known as **Les Jasseries du Grand Genévrier**, one of which is open to the public.

Jasserie du Coq Noir – A visit to this old farmstead (Black Cock Farm) used during the seasonal moving of livestock provides an insight into life in the mountains, into the art of thatching roofs and into the production of Fourme cheeses. A snack of milk, rye bread and Fourme de St-Anthème is available.

As the road runs down to St-Anthème there are views of the volcanic cones in the Velay area – Meygal, Lizieux, Mézenc and Gerbier du Jonc.

St-Anthème – The red-roofed village nestles in the depths of the Ance valley.

Follow the D 496 from St-Anthème to return to Montbrison.

Beyond the Col de la Croix de l'Homme Mort, the road provides some very attractive views of the Forez plain, the mountains in the Lyonnais area, and Mont Pilat.

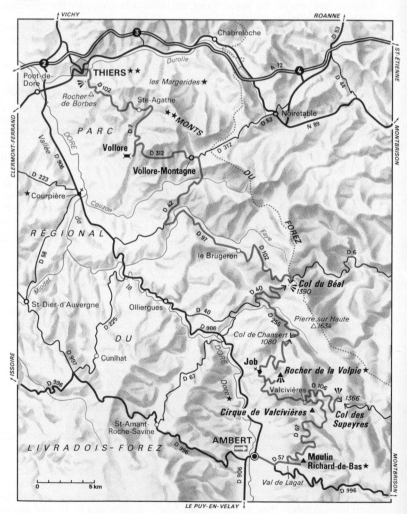

Except when otherwise stated,
all recommended town tours are intended as walks.

★★ ③ THE AUVERGNE SLOPES

Round trip from Ambert to Thiers

130km/80mi – allow half a day – local map left

Ambert – *See AMBERT.*

From Ambert take the D 966 east; turn left onto the D 57 which climbs the Lagat valley.

★**Moulin Richard-de-Bas** – *See Moulin RICHARD-DE-BAS.*

Turn around and turn right onto the D 67.

As the road climbs it offers good views over the Ambert plain, La Chaise-Dieu plateau and the Livradois. The winding road then skirts the Valcivières cirque.

Cirque de Valcivières – This attractive cirque shelters several hamlets on its stream-strewn slopes and among the fields.

Turn right onto the D 106 which climbs sinuously past fields and meadows, through a beechwood and up to the Col des Supeyres, offering a **panoramic view**★ of the cirque, the Livradois and, in the distance, of the Monts Dore and the Monts Dômes.

Col des Supeyres – *See* ② *above.*

Turn back.

After Valcivières the route follows a rock-strewn ravine to emerge above the Ambert plain and then descends the lower slopes of the Forez mountains.

★**Rocher de la Volpie** – *See Vallée de la DORE.*

Job – *See Vallée de la DORE.*

Beyond Job turn right.

The climb to Chansert pass (alt 1 080m/3 543ft), which initially offers far-reaching views, travels through beautiful pine forests. A picturesque descent into the valley of the Vertolaye then follows. The route *(turn right over the stream and right again onto the D 40)* climbs once more, through a pleasant forest and up to the higher pastures where the farmsteads are, to reach the Col du Béal.

Col du Béal – *See* ① *above.*

Leave Col du Béal on the D 102.

The road crosses vast expanses of pasture and soon provides a superb view of the mountains of the Livradois area, the Monts Dore, the Monts Dômes and the Limagne around Clermont.

Vollore-Montagne – This mountain village is an ideal centre for walkers.
The forests, the charming landscapes of woodland and meadow, and the attractive local beauty spots make this part of the journey extremely enjoyable.

Château de Vollore ⊙ – This 17C building of pale granite stands on a spur, and is flanked to the south by a large 12C keep and to the north by a 14C tower. Inside, the rooms are sumptuously furnished with paintings, tapestries, furniture and decorative objects, and mementoes of **General La Fayette** and his involvement in the American War of Independence.

7km/4mi beyond Ste-Agathe, the road begins its descent to Thiers. This is very picturesque owing to the superb view of the Borbes rock and of the town and its terraces of flat-roofed houses which are visible above the Durolle valley.

★★**Thiers** – *See THIERS.*

In the forest

OAK – The common oak is predominant in Tronçais Forest; it can easily reach 250 to 300 years of age.
GROVE – This is a stand of trees grown from seed (unlike copses, where the new shoots grow from old stumps); a grove is called regular when the trees are obviously of about the same age.
STAND – A group of trees growing on a particular piece of land.
ROUGH TIMBER – The trunk of a felled tree, stripped of its branches, which is ready to be turned into timber.
STAVE WOOD – A plank of oak for making the casks in which brandy *(cognac)* is matured.
"ROND" – This is the French name for the point where forest roads meet; it may be named after a former forest warden or a past event.

GANNAT

Population 5 919
Michelin map 73 fold 4 or 239 fold 8 – Local map under La LIMAGNE

This small, ancient town lies on the edge of the Limagne plain and the granite base below the mountains of the Auvergne, on the threshold of the "Gateway to Occitania" which stretches from Broût-Vernet on the plain to the Champs hills, the point of contact between two old forms of French language – *langue d'oc* and *langue d'oïl*.
The area is very important archaeologically, and ongoing digs have recently uncovered three well-preserved rhinoceros skeletons thought to be at least 23 million years old, together with the remains of crocodiles and fossilised birds.

World Culture Festival – Every summer Gannat is filled with the sounds of traditional folk dancers, musicians and singers who come here from all five continents to take part in an international cultural event which resounds with colour and excitement (*see Calendar of events*).

Folklore Festival, Gannat

SIGHTS

Ste-Croix – Traces of the original Romanesque church are still visible, especially the north part of the apse where, outside, there is a strange capital depicting the Nativity. The church was rebuilt in the Gothic period and underwent minor alterations on several occasions until the 17C when the east end, ambulatory and belfry were rebuilt.

Castle – The 12C fortress, dismantled in 1566, was used as a prison from 1833 to 1967. The castle has tall 14C walls flanked by corner towers.

Musée municipal ⊙ – The old warders' apartments and the prison cells now house the museum. Among the items on display (14C-18C parchments from the town's archives, 12C wrought-iron grilles, restored statues, votive images) is a beautiful **Gospel Book★** with elegant illuminations on vellum. The binding dates from the 10C but was given additional decoration in the 12C. It is covered with silver-gilt and adorned with an antique cameo surrounded by cabochons and *cloisonné* enamelwork. On the other side is an ivory plaque depicting the Crucifixion and the Holy Women at the tomb; it is carved in the Byzantine style (10C).
A typical Bourbonnais kitchen, clogmaker's workshop, saddlery and farm implements are also on display.
The section called the **Musée de la Résistance** has on display photographs, press cuttings and medals which recall the period of French Resistance in the history of the Gannat area. The **tack room**, originally from Veauce castle, contains a wide range of saddles, harnesses, bridles, stirrups, boots and whips.
At the end of the courtyard is an exhibition of horsedrawn vehicles (brougham, shooting brake, mail coach), also from Veauce castle.
Several more rooms are given over to an exhibition of palaeontology; one houses the mounted skeleton of a prehistoric rhinoceros.

St-Étienne – This Romanesque church (11C and 12C) dedicated to St Stephen is only used for services on special occasions. It still has its 17C wooden bas-reliefs.

EXCURSIONS

Veauce – *18km/11mi northwest.* From the entrance to the village there is an attractive view of the east end of the 12C **church** ⊘ built of beautiful golden stone. Inside, note the pleasing arrangement of the chancel and ambulatory (it has no radiating chapels).

Near the church, in a park of mature trees, stands the **castle** ⊘ built between the 9C and 15C on a rocky promontory overlooking the River Veauce. It was partly altered during the Renaissance and in the 19C. A tour of the interior includes the Weapons Gallery, the portrait gallery and the stained-glass gallery. The covered watchpath and the guardroom still have their original chestnut rafters (12C).

.Between the Rivers Sioule and Buron – *Round trip of 60km/37mi west of Gannat – about 4hr.*

Leave Gannat on the N 9 to the north and after 4km/3mi, take the D 42 left.

Jenzat – The late 11C **church** here is decorated with 15C paintings in tempera (right side aisle) which go by the name of frescoes by the Masters of Jenzat. These realistic, naïve works depict the Passion of Christ and the Martyrdom of St Catherine. The **Maison du luthier** ⊘ contains a museum on the craft of lute-making, of which Jenzat was European capital in the 19C (the village still has two resident lutemakers).

Leave Jenzat southwest on the D 216. Turn right in Mazerier onto the D 37.

The road to St-Bonnet-de-Rochefort provides a number of attractive views of the Rouzat and Neuvial viaducts, the first civil engineering projects completed by Gustave **Eiffel**.

In St-Bonnet, take the D 35 south.

Ébreuil – *See ÉBREUIL.*

Leave Ébreuil south on the D 207, which becomes the D 12 after crossing the A 71 motorway.

★**Château de la Roche** – *See Château de la ROCHE.*

Carry on along the D 12.

Aigueperse – *See La LIMAGNE.*

Leave Aigueperse north on the N 9 and on the outskirts of town turn right onto the D 51.

Butte de Montpensier – *See La LIMAGNE.*

Carry on along the D 51.

★**Château d'Effiat** – *Château d'EFFIAT.*

Take the D 437 left along the graveyard.

Biozat – *See La LIMAGNE.*

Take the D 119 west back to Gannat.

Viaduc de GARABIT★★

Michelin map 76 fold 14 or 239 fold 44
Local map under Gorges de la TRUYÈRE

The Garabit viaduct is an elegant, and very bold, construction designed by an engineer named Boyer and built (1882-84) by **Gustave Eiffel**. It has an overall length of 564m/1 833ft and stretches across the River Truyère at a height of 123m/400ft. Its 448m/1 456ft superstructure is supported by a bold metal arch.

Since the Grandval dam was built, the water below the viaduct has risen to the level of the supporting piles of the bridge, which still stands 95m/309ft above the maximum level of the dam's waters. It was the experience gained in Garabit that enabled Eiffel to design and build his famous 300m/975ft tower in Paris for the 1889 World Fair.

Garabit viaduct

EXCURSIONS

Boat trips ⊘ – Boats operate on the Grandval reservoir and along the river to Alleuze castle.

Château de Chassan – *See Château de CHASSAN.*

★**Écomusée de Margeride** – *See La MARGERIDE.*

La GARDE-ADHÉMAR

Population 1 108
Michelin map 81 fold 1 or 246 fold 23 – Local map under Moyenne vallée du RHÔNE

This old village is signalled from some distance away by its church, perched on a rise. It is an ideal spot for a stroll, with its picturesque limestone houses, its vaulted alleyways and its narrow, winding streets with their arches. In the Middle Ages this village was a major fortress belonging to the Adhémar family. In the 16C a Renaissance château was built for **Antoine Escalin**, Baron de la Garde, who started life as a mere shepherd, then became a soldier; he ended his career as one of François I's ambassadors and as General in charge of the French galleys.

Old town walls can be seen on the north side; to the south of the village is a fortified gate and a few ruins, not far from the huge Cross erected on a Roman base.

SIGHTS

★**Church** – This Romanesque building is remarkable for its two apses and the attractive outline of its two-storey octagonal belfry topped by a stocky pyramid. Thanks to the writer **Prosper Mérimée** (1830-70), at the time Inspector of Historic Monuments, it underwent major restoration in the mid 19C. A finely carved frieze runs round the western apse and the apsidal chapels. The very plain interior has a high, short nave flanked by narrow side aisles. On 24 December, a Provençal Midnight Mass is celebrated here, which includes a Nativity play with live animals.

Chapelle des Pénitents ⊙ – This chapel has 12C twinned windows on the west side; they can be seen from the church square. From the 17C to the 19C the chapel was the meeting-place of the members of a brotherhood of White Penitents, as shown on the fresco decorating the south wall; today it houses an exhibition about La Garde-Adhémar and an audio-visual presentation, "Le Tricastin en Images", which gives a historical view of the region.

★**View** – From the terrace there is a panoramic **view** of the Pierrelatte plain below the outcrops of the Vivarais area, with the Dent de Rez jutting up from the rocks. Immediately below the terrace is a garden filled with aromatic and medicinal herbs and plants.

Chapelle du Val-des-Nymphes – *2km/1mi east on the D 472.* In a valley kept cool by many little waterfalls and which, as its name suggests, was once a place of pagan worship, stand the ruins of a 12C chapel. For a long while a ruin, this Romanesque chapel was restored from 1991 and an elegant timber ceiling now covers the nave. The fine semicircular apse still has its two rows of arcading. The upper section of the west front is decorated with three blind arches topped by a pediment.

GERBIER DE JONC★★

Michelin map 76 fold 18 or 244 fold 34 – Local map under Gorges de la LOIRE

The Gerbier de Jonc, rising at an altitude of 1 551m/5 041ft on the crest of the range separating the Loire and Rhône basins, looks like a giant haystack or a huge heap of sheaves when seen from a distance.

Etymological notes – The word "Gerbier" is a Latinisation of the Indo-European root "gar" meaning "rock". Similar names are found in other regions of France, in particular in the Pyrenees (pic du Gar, pic du Ger, pic du Jer). The word "Jonc" is derived from the Latin "jugum" meaning "mountain". Gerbier de Jonc therefore literally means "rocky mountain", despite the gentle image the name evokes of a sheaf of rushes. The Gerbier de Jonc, which is part of the Mézenc range, consists of phonolithic rocks that have a tendency to flake, forming unstable scree slopes and clothing the mountainside in a scaly shell. At the foot of the southwestern slope are several small streams; they constitute the sources of the Loire.

Access – The most striking view of the Gerbier de Jonc is from the road from St-Martial *(to the northeast)* or from Ste-Eulalie *(to the south).*

The climb – It is a hard climb to the summit *(45min Rtn on foot).* From the top, though, there is an impressive **panoramic view★★**. On the northeast side the view extends over the dip formed by the Eysse, a tributary of the River Eyrieux. From the depths of the ravines comes the rumble of the mountain torrent. The view is particularly fine to the southeast where there is a seemingly endless horizon beyond ridges and peaks along the entire length of the range from Eyrieux to Ardèche. Mont Alambre, the Mézenc and the volcanic Sara close off the horizon to the north; Montfol obstructs the view to the west; the conical La Barre, easily recognisable for its tabular outline, lies in the foreground on the south side.
A stretch of the Alps can also be seen in clear weather.

Le Gerbier de Jonc

B. et J. Dupont/EXPLORER

HAUTERIVES

Population 1 202
Michelin map 88 fold 20 or 246 fold 4

The village of Hauterives, situated at the foot of a hillock bearing the ruins of the medieval castle which once belonged to the lords of Clermont, has an unusual tourist attraction – the "Ideal Palace".

A postman with a vision – In the late 19C the postman in Hauterives, **Ferdinand Cheval**, began bringing home strangely-shaped stones every day which he had picked up during his round. In the evenings he would add them to an unusual construction he was building in his garden, based on books he had read and dreams he had had, and possibly also inspired by the remains of petrified springs that were commonplace in this area of the Drôme. When he retired, Cheval continued his work despite the mockery of the local people, tirelessly bringing sand and stones back to his home in a wheelbarrow. After thirty-three years of relentless labour, he finished his weird and wonderful "Palace". Cheval then spent the last ten years of his life building his own grave in the cemetery, in the same style. He died in 1924.

The Postman's Ideal Palace

★**Palais Idéal** ⊘ – Postman Cheval's Ideal Palace (300m²/358yds² and some 10m/32ft high) stands in the middle of his garden. It is his dream building, bristling with strange ornamentation and incorporating every conceivable architectural style.
The east side, the strangest and most intricate of them all, is decorated with huge female idols made of reddish pebbles; the entrance to the palace is on the other side. Imitation plants stand side by side with reminders of oriental or medieval palaces. The interior is full of galleries and grottoes. Narrow flights of steps lead to an upper platform in the centre of the postman's fantasy world. The building is dotted with captions and sayings revealing Cheval's general world view and state of mind, and comments indicating his patient determination to complete the fantastic project he had set himself.

HÉRISSON

Population 801
Michelin map 69 fold 12 or 238 folds 43, 44

The artist **Henri Harpignies** (1819-1916) often stayed in Hérisson and this region provided him with the inspiration for some of his finest paintings. Two 15C fortified gateways and old houses including the "Mousse" house (15-18C) are to be seen in the village.

Castle – The impressive mass of beautiful russet-coloured ruins stands high above the village. The castle was built in the 13C, with fortifications added to it under Louis de Bourbon in the 14C.

★**View** – *South bank of the River Aumance; access via Rue du Calvaire.* From the Calvary chapel on the hillside, the **view** extends over the entire village with its porch-belfry, all that remains of the former collegiate church of St-Sauveur (12C-17C), over the castle and the Aumance valley.

VALLÉE DE L'AUMANCE *Round tour of 35km/22mi – allow 1hr*

This pretty valley is drained by a gently-flowing river which rises near Le Montet, eventually flowing into the Cher not far from Tronçais forest.

Leave Hérisson on the D 157 northwest.

Châteloy – The 12C **church** stands firmly and proudly on the rocks above the valley. Frescoes dating from the 13C to 17C (with later restoration) decorate the chancel and nave. A music festival is held here in season.
The graveyard provides a **view**★ of the elegant bell tower and over the Aumance valley.

Château du Creux – The Classical architecture of this large château comes as a surprise in an area that is dotted with fortresses. The 18C building flanked by two projecting wings is set back from extensive outbuildings with mansard roofs.

Meaulne – This town is situated at the confluence of the Aumance and Cher rivers. **Alain-Fournier** (1886-1914) gave its name to the hero in his great novel *Le Grand Meaulnes*, which was set in and around Épineuil-le-Fleuriel (the fictional Ste-Agathe), on the opposite bank of the Cher *(5.5km/3.5mi southwest on the D 4; see Michelin Green Guide Berry-Limousin in French).*

Leave Meaulne south on the N 144 towards Montluçon.

Vallon-en-Sully – This village on the banks of the Berry canal is home to some charming buildings in the local pink sandstone, such as the 12C church. **Vallon Arts et Traditions** ⊙ houses animated tableaux illustrating scenes of daily life and labour in the region in days of yore.

Take the D 11 back to Hérisson.

The main through routes are clearly indicated on all town plans.

ISSOIRE★★

Population 13 559
Michelin map 73 folds 14, 15 or 239 fold 20
Local map under DAUPHINÉ D'AUVERGNE and Le LIVRADOIS

Issoire, which lies on the banks of the River Couze in the middle of rich fertile countryside, has one of the largest Romanesque churches in the Auvergne. Since the last war the town has become a major industrial centre.

Little Geneva – In 1540 a former Dominican monk arrived in Issoire from Germany and converted the Consuls to the Lutheran faith. Among the newly-converted was Jean Brugière, a rent-collector. The bailiff, wishing to set an example, sentenced Brugière to be burnt alive but the latter's unwavering faith in the face of death led, in fact, to numerous additional conversions. Issoire became a "Little Geneva", washed in the blood of the many martyrs to the new faith.

Captain Merle (1548-90) – Merle was descended from a family from Uzès who were noble but poor, and Merle began an army career early on in life. He was noted for his extraordinary bravery: "With him", said one of his leaders, "I would attack Hell itself, even if it had 50 000 devils in it." The intrepid soldier was a fanatical Protestant, but also cruel and greedy. After the St Bartholomew's Day Massacre he launched a pitiless campaign against Roman Catholics with only a handful of men. On 15 October 1575 he captured Issoire at night, by surprise, then demolished the towers on the church. Priests and monks were subjected to horrible torture. The Catholic Army, led by the King's brother, the Duke of Anjou, recaptured the town in 1577, ransacking and pillaging it to an extent seldom seen, and setting fire to it.

A leader in the aeronautics industry – In addition to the modern Technical Training Establishment for Army NCO's, the town has a number of large factories, specialising mainly in metalworking; they are situated on its industrial estate to the northeast. Two of them supply stamped and forged metal parts. One is Airforge which has a 20 000 tonne press and which specialises in the production of aluminium and titanium parts for the aeronautics industry; the other is Interforge whose gigantic 65 000 tonne press (imported from Russia) is the most powerful of its kind in the West. Again in the aeronautics sector, Issoire-Aviation manufactures parts in composite materials and sheet metal. Above all, Issoire is the Western European centre of aluminium and light alloy transformation for use in semi-finished products for the aeronautics industry.

High flyers – The gliding club at Issoire-le-Broc aerodrome to the southeast of the town attracts numerous French and foreign glider pilots who come to enjoy the strong thermal currents in the locality. These currents can lift gliders released at 800m/2 600ft up to an altitude of more than 10 000m/32 500ft.

★★ANCIENNE ABBATIALE ST-AUSTREMOINE

St-Austremoine, once the church of a Benedictine abbey, was built in the 12C; it is now the parish church, replacing the neighbouring St-Paul which was destroyed shortly after the French Revolution. The belfry, west front and many of the capitals were altered in the 19C.

Exterior – The **east end**★★ stands on a wide esplanade. This is the most perfect section of the building, a consummate example of Romanesque architecture as it developed in the Auvergne. No other church has such harmonious proportions, such purity of line and such restraint in its decoration. Its powerful, well-balanced design consists of various different elements; note the mosaics and sculptures representing the signs of the Zodiac.

Interior ⊙ – The two-storey nave is especially striking for its magnificent proportions; the painted decoration was added in the mid 19C. Walk up the nave as far as the pulpit to see the ensemble including the transept supported by four huge quadripartite arches lightened by bays, the dome rising to a height of 23m/75ft, and the chancel flanked by its ambulatory. In the right arm of the transept are two outstanding capitals, one illustrating lewdness (**1**) and the other the Annunciation (**2**).

At the southern entrance to the ambulatory there is one of the finest, and most complete, views of the building as a whole. Walk round the chancel; it is particularly interesting for its superb narrative **capitals**★ depicting the Last Supper (**3**) and the Visit of the Holy Women to the Tomb (**4**). From the back of the Lady Chapel there is a good view down the nave. In the northern arm of the transept note two more capitals: one depicting a man carrying a sheep illustrates the parable of the Good Shepherd (**5**); on the other is a demon dragging away two condemned souls (**6**).

Crypt – This is one of the finest crypts in the Auvergne. The stocky columns supporting the vaulted roof give an impression of strength that is further emphasised by the total lack of decoration. In the centre is a graceful statue of the Virgin Mary.

★**The Last Judgement** (**7**) – *South of the narthex.* This 15C fresco depicts in a very lively manner a theme that was dear to many artists of the day. Here it is treated with character and great verve.

ST-AUSTREMOINE

Pl. Altaroche

0   10 m

★★ EAST END

←—N—

Ambulatory
4
3

CHANCEL

6 5   2 1
Crypt   Crypt

TRANSEPT

Sacristy

NAVE

7

Narthex

Rue Gambetta

ADDITIONAL SIGHT

Historial ⊙ – *Rue des Fours.* Housed in the Maison des Échevins (16-18C aldermen's house) are a dozen waxwork tableaux depicting the main events in the town's history.

EXCURSIONS

Parentignat – *4km/2.5mi southeast on the D 996.*
The **château**★ ⊙ here was built towards the end of Louis XIV's reign (early 18C) and has remained in the same family since. The main courtyard has formal grass parterres, contrasting with the English-style landscape gardens bordered by orange trees and roses. Among the ancestral treasures are paintings and furniture by Nicolas de Largillière, Mme Vigée Lebrun, Rigaud and Van Loo. The main stairway and the floor of the dining room are made of marble from Nonette.

Nonette – *9km/5.5mi southeast on the D 996, D 34 and D 722.*
The village is built on a promontory overlooking the Allier. The part-Romanesque, part-Gothic **church**, once part of a priory, has a carved Romanesque doorway and, inside, a superb late 14C bust of Christ *(north chapel)*. The ruins of the 14C castle *(45min Rtn on foot via a steep path)* stand on a height offering a good **panorama** over the valley and the mountains.

★**Dauphiné d'Auvergne** – *Round tour southwest of Issoire.*
See DAUPHINÉ D'AUVERGNE.

LAMASTRE

Population 2 717
Michelin map 76 north of fold 19 or 246 fold 19

The economy of Lamastre, standing at an altitude of 373m/1 212ft on the banks of the River Doux, relies on small-scale industry (safety shoes, camping gear, aluminium processing, cabinetmaking, general mechanical engineering) and crafts such as the manufacture of regional products.

Church – The church is situated at the top end of the town, in the old Marcheville district, and is built of attractive pink stone in the Romanesque style. Only the apse, which is decorated on the outside with a multi-lobed opening, dates from the 12C; the remainder is modern. From the terrace in front of the church there is a view down over the town, which lies in the shadow of the remains of its medieval castle.

★DOUX BASIN

Round trip of 60km/37mi – about 1hr 30min

The plateaux in the Upper Vivarais area slope down to the River Rhône; they consist of ancient rocks (granite and gneiss). The altitude, which exceeds 1 200m/3 900ft near Le Velay, climbs to 700-900m/2 275-2 925ft around Lamastre. To the north, the Lalouvesc mountains are the only area of high land in this vast sloping plain which escapes monotony thanks to the Doux, Ay and Cance basins and to the tributaries of the Eyrieux. The dips in the plateau form vast areas of farmland (crops and animal farming) surrounded by the chestnut woods that give the Upper Vivarais area its beauty.

Head northwest from Lamastre along the D 236.

At the start of the rise there is a view over the ruins of Retourtour castle. As far as Nozières, the road runs along the crest of the rise, providing extensive **views**★ over the hills between the Doux and Eyrieux rivers then, to the right, over the mound on which stands Boucieu-le-Roi. 2.5km/1.5mi beyond Nozières, a track branches off from the left of the road; the path beyond it leads to the ruins of Rochebloine.

★★**View from Rochebloine** – Off a sharp righthand bend, there is a track leading to the tip of the promontory *(15min Rtn on foot)* where there are still a few remains of an ancient fortress. There is a striking **view** of the Upper Doux basin.

Col du Buisson – Alt 920m/3 018ft. *Park in the car park.* On a clear day there are far-reaching views to the northeast beyond Pailharès, over to Mont Blanc, les Grandes Rousses and La Meije. South lies the Doux basin and to the west the peaks of Mont Mézenc and the Gerbier de Jonc. At the intersection of the D 273 and D 236 is the **Village ardéchois en miniature** ⊙, a model of a typical local village made from granite.

Turn right onto the D 273.

As the road descends, the red roofs of Pailharès come into view.

Pailharès – The village, which stands out from the surrounding countryside on a platform, still has the rectangular layout dating from the days when its old town walls were built.

St-Félicien – The church is interesting for its Romanesque sections – the arcading in the north aisle where the pilasters are topped by engaged columns.

In St-Félicien take the D 234 south; turn right onto the D 578 and take the D 209 (left).

Boucieu-le-Roi – This village was once the seat of the old royal bailiwick in the Upper Vivarais area. The church (13C-16C) has an attractive silhouette.

Le Crestet – In front of the village church is a fine carved stone Cross.

Return to Lamastre via the D 534.

★FROM DOUX TO EYRIEUX

Round trip of 64km/40mi – about 3hr. Leave Lamastre on the D 2 south and turn right onto the D 283 to Cluac.

From the road there are delightful views *(right)* of the Sumène valley and the upper Doux basin.

In Cluac, turn right onto the D 21.

The descent to Nonières provides a view over a landscape bristling with volcanic domes; then, as the D 241 rises to St-Julien-Labrousse, there is an extensive **view**★ over the cones in the Mézenc range from a bend in the road.

Chemin de fer touristique de montagne

Vivarais Steam Railway along the Doux Gorge

Chalencon – This old village, once a fortified town, was the seat of a major barony. From the esplanade bearing the war memorial, in the oldest part of the village, there is a view down over the Eyrieux gorge.

Vernoux-en-Vivarais – *See VERNOUX-EN-VIVARAIS.*

Château de la Tourette – *Access and description under VERNOUX-EN-VIVARAIS.*

Leave Vernoux on the D 14 northeast and return to Lamastre on the D 105 (left) and D 2 (Col de Montreynaud).

The route in the shade of the chestnut trees provides a pleasant drive. Note the low cottages on the Châteauneuf-de-Vernoux plateau. From the pass there is a view of the Lamastre basin and the upper Doux valley, dominated to the north by the Lalouvesc mountains.

★**Doux Gorge by the Vivarais railway** ⊙ – *A steam train ride from Lamastre to Tournon.*
An original turn-of-the-century train (steam engine, wooden carriages, viewing platforms) descends the mountain and snakes along the valley, passing orchards and vineyards, ferns, pines and chestnut trees.

Château de LAPALISSE★★

Michelin map 73 fold 6 or 239 fold 9
Local map under Vallée de la BESBRE and VICHY

Lapalisse lies on the banks of the River Besbre and is dominated by the outline of its castle.

Monsieur de La Palice (15-16C) – Jacques II de Chabannes, Lord of La Palice, Marshal of France, won renown for his valour during the campaign to capture the Milan region. He was finally taken prisoner at the Battle of Pavia, but his capture provoked a dispute between an Italian and a Spaniard. The latter, having run out of arguments, chose to resolve matters by simply shooting the old warrior in the chest.

Little remains of the original medieval castle; the building standing today dates from 1527 and was designed by Florentines whom Jacques II is said to have brought back with him from Italy. It is, as a result, an example of early Renaissance architecture.

The façade overlooking the courtyard is made less austere owing to the diamond shapes and a chequerboard pattern in multi-coloured bricks. Sandstone detailing emphasises the ridges of the towers and the window surrounds, in accordance with the fashion of the day. There are also ogee lintels, mullioned windows, medallions on the doorway to the central tower, scrolls of foliage, pilasters and Corinthian capitals.

TOUR ⊙

Ground floor – The hall, which contains an early Flemish painting, leads to the dining room furnished in the Italian Renaissance style.
The drawing room once had walls covered with leather from Cordoba; it contains the Chabannes family portraits.

Château de Lapalisse

First floor – In the library hangs a large painting from the school of Veronese, *The Republic of Venice Receiving Gifts from the Four Provinces*.

The **Golden Salon**★★ is decorated with a magnificent gilded coffered ceiling and two tapestries of knights, representing Godefroy de Bouillon and Hector. The tapestries, of 15C Flemish manufacture, come from a series of hangings 3.80m/12ft high and 4m/13ft wide, with a 30cm/12in border.

The chapel was rebuilt in the mid 15C but was pillaged during the Revolution. Its crypt contains the Chabannes family vaults. In the **outbuildings** (fine timber ceiling) there is a collection of standards and flags gathered by a priest from Doyet.

LAVAUDIEU ★

Population 238
Michelin map 76 fold 5 or 239 folds 32, 33

The hamlet still has the remains of an abbey founded in the 11C by St Robert, the first abbot of La Chaise-Dieu. The Benedictines continued to live here until the French Revolution.

Church – The octagonal belfry has two storeys of semicircular bays. Inside, the nave is decorated with fine 14C **frescoes**★ in the Italianate style: they represent scenes and people from the Bible including the Scourging of Christ, Christ carrying the Cross, the Crucifixion, Christ being taken down from the Cross, nine Apostles watching the Virgin Mary asleep, the four Evangelists, and the crucifixion of St Andrew. In the north transept an early 16C fresco, which has been removed from the wall, illustrates the martyrdom of St Ursula.

★**Cloisters** ⊙ – Little remains of the abbey buildings but there are particularly fine cloisters (restored), the only ones in the Auvergne to have escaped destruction. They include charming single or double colonettes, some of them twisted, some cylindrical or polygonal, with capitals decorated with carvings of foliage and animals. The projecting upper storey is supported by oak posts. In the refectory is a 12C **mural** (restored) which covers the entire end wall; it shows the Virgin Mary sitting in Majesty flanked by two angels and the Apostles. Above is an image of Christ surrounded by the symbols of the four Evangelists. From the vaulted cell beneath the refectory, there was once an underground passage to Lugeac castle to the southwest.

Maison des Arts et Traditions populaires ⊙ – This traditional arts and crafts museum is housed in an old peasant baker's house dating from the late 19C. The oven, well, bread trough and counter are still visible. On the ground floor, the living room contains a collection of everyday domestic items. The byre houses tools from old crafts (clogmaking, carpentry). Beside it is the *veillade*, the room where people gathered of an evening to chat, sing and tell stories. The cupboard contains an interesting collection of headdresses and nightcaps. On the first floor are three bedrooms. The so-called Lacemaker's Room contains superb samples of pillow, crochet and bobbin lace and a few lengths of trimmings.

LEZOUX

In the 2C Lezoux was a major centre of the ceramics industry, which was based on the plastic clay quarried in the Limagne. Within a radius of 3km/2mi, the remains of more than 200 potters' kilns have been uncovered, and pottery made in Lezoux has been found as far away as England and Prussia.

The town, in which there is now a large oil-making plant, still has a 15C belfry topped by a tower. It stands adjacent to one of the old town gates.

Musée archéologique ⊘ – *Rue Pasteur*. The museum contains collections of sigillated pottery (marked with a seal) dating from the 1C to 4C AD – vases, cups, dishes, goblets, bowls etc. It is everyday crockery, brick-red in colour, with rough but varied decorations in relief (animals, figures, floral motifs...). Stamps indicate the names of the potters. The museum also contains moulds and various items used in the building trade, as well as funereal objects, coins etc. Some of the fragments dating from the 4C bear the influence of Christian iconography.

EXCURSION

Moissat – *5km/3mi south*. The Romanesque **church at Moissat-Bas** is awaiting the return of the magnificent **St Lomer's reliquary★★** which has been temporarily removed to Clermont-Ferrand cathedral. This work of art dates from the 13C and is made of chased copper over a wooden shell, with figures picked out in relief.

Note inside the church the very early dome on squinches, the modest triumphal arch, the paintings and the old giltwood statues. The restoration work being undertaken in the chancel has revealed Romanesque arcading with columns and capitals, and paintings dating from the 14C and 15C.

La LIMAGNE

Limagne is a common noun designating any low-lying fertile area. The Limagne de Brioude and the Limagne d'Issoire are fairly narrow basins separated by rocky gorges. The Grande Limagne or Limagne de Clermont, usually and more simply referred to as "La Limagne", spreads out at the threshold of granite rocks below Coudes and is crossed by the River Allier. It is 90km/56mi long and ranges in width from 15-40km/9-25mi.

To the south, the plain bristles with spurs of rock and volcanic hills – there were seven phases of eruption and more than one hundred craters. To the north, the landscape would be monotonous were it not for the lines of poplars and willows and the wicker-work fences. Seen from the hills, the Limagne looks like a vast patchwork. In the east the "Varennes", or gravel terraces created by shingle from the River Allier, are covered with forests (Marcenat, Randan, Montpensier).

J. Damase

Limagne plain

Formation of the Limagne – During the Tertiary era, as a consequence of alpine folding, the granite of the Auvergne hills broke away after being worn down by erosion. The Limagne slowly subsided by more than 2 000m/6 500ft compared to the neighbouring areas and was boxed in between a high plateau to the west and the Forez mountains to the east. At the same time, erosion began to wear down the highest peaks. In the lake that covered the Limagne at that time, sediment (sand, sandstone, clay, limestone, marl) began to build up to a thickness of more than 1 500m/4 875ft, filling in most of the dip. Once the lake had silted up, the River Allier and its tributaries began digging down into the sedimentary soil. Between 300-400m/975-1 300ft of sediment was removed by the action of the water. The Allier then covered the plain with alluvium that combined with the volcanic dust carried in the water and the wind.

Fertile land – The silica-rich alluvium and the volcanic dust full of potash and lime made the Limagne exceptionally fertile. The layer of heavy, black earth is very thick, sometimes attaining a depth of 3m/10ft. This is crop-growing country (corn, barley, maize) and certain areas also grow sugar beet and tobacco, or oil-producing plants such as oilseed rape and sunflowers. The production of maize seed (Limagrain) is of vital importance here. Cattle farming, on the other hand, has almost completely died out, causing the disappearance of meadows and fodder crops. Trees, too, are fewer in number than in the past with the exception of apple trees (although they are in constant decline). Only angelica has remained as a speciality of Clermont. On the hillsides, the vineyards now cover an area of only 2 000ha/4 942 acres and stock other than the Gamay grape (850ha/2 100 acres) is gradually being replaced by new crops. In some places the land is being left to lie fallow.

The population has decreased much less sharply here than in mountain areas; most people live in large villages with narrow streets. Some of the white houses have southern French-style flat roofs of interlocking curved tiles, while others have the sloping roofs of flat tiles more common in northern climes. Livestock farmers traditionally live in long, low houses – the home, barn and byre are all under the same roof. Winegrower's houses are built upwards, with an outside staircase – the wine-cellar is on the ground floor. The industries in the valley have, along with the rich crops, encouraged the population to stay in this area.

A few of the villages in the Limagne still have their **dovecotes**. Some stand alone in the middle of fields; others stand adjacent to, or near, farm buildings. Most of them are square with tiled roofs and central turrets with the niches that enable the pigeons to fly away and come home to roost. They are half-timbered and mounted on posts to protect the young birds from predators. Until the last century, pigeon droppings were a precious source of fertiliser for the soil.

Compared to the picturesque mountainous areas, the Limagne might be said to have less to offer the tourist, yet it has unusual churches, interesting castles, and offers some superb views. One of the finest sights in the Auvergne, for those arriving on the edge of the plateaux, is the sudden, swooping view down over the Limagne.

TOWNS AND SIGHTS
listed alphabetically

Aigueperse – Treasures inside the **church of Notre-Dame** (rebuilt in the 19C in Gothic style), with its 13C east end and transept, include a 15C wooden Descent from the Cross, fine family tombs, *The Nativity* by Ghirlandaio, a 13C fresco and 18C panelling. The **Sainte-Chapelle** ⊘ is the 15C chapel from the old castle (disappeared) and has a Flamboyant doorway and a gargoyled and pinnacled west front. The **hôtel de ville** ⊘ (town hall) is housed in a 17C convent building; note the three jack o' the clocks who chime the hours.

Dovecote

Archives MICHELIN

Artonne – The village has numerous sections of medieval town wall. St Martin of Tours came here to pray at the tomb of St Vitaline. The **church** ⊘, formerly a collegiate church founded in 1048 and built over a pre-Romanesque building that included Gallo-Roman features, is strangely set in the middle of the village. It is a huge building and has undergone extensive alteration but it still has a 10C and 11C nave with ribbed barrel vaulting and a vast east end. Fine wrought-iron grilles close off the chancel rebuilt in the 12C. The former chapter-house is situated in the north aisle. Around the ambulatory are three chapels built to a square design.

★**Billom** – See BILLOM.

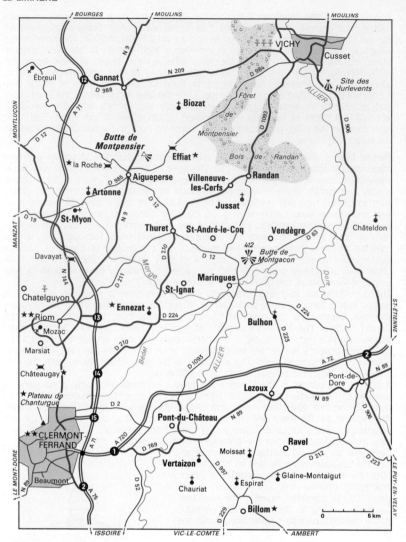

Biozat – The village has a beautiful, vast Romanesque **church** typical of the Limagne area with its barrel-vaulted nave, quarter-circle vaulting in the side aisles, dome over squinches and a number of interesting capitals.

Bulhon – The **church** ⊙ dedicated to St Vital and St Agricol became a priory church in the 11C when the Lord of Bulhon gave it to La Chaise-Dieu abbey. It has some interesting capitals with stylised foliage and narrative carvings.

★**Effiat** – *See EFFIAT.*

★**Ennezat** – *See ENNEZAT.*

Gannat – *See GANNAT.*

Jussat – There is a very plain Romanesque country church here.

Lezoux – *See LEZOUX.*

Maringues – This large village of Gallo-Roman origin, a busy agricultural trading centre, stands along the recently-canalised Morge. Until the mid 19C, wool and leather working were the traditional local activities; in around 1850 there were 60 tanneries operating along the river. The **Grandval Tannery** ⊙ explains the processes involved. The 12C Romanesque **church** has interesting carved capitals and keystones, and a 15C Entombment. There are some interesting old houses near the old corn exchange.

Montpensier (Butte de) – Montpensier "Hill" (alt 441m/1 433ft) is a typical volcanic neck. From it, there is a fine view over the Limagne plain.

A fortress once stood on the hilltop and it was here that King Louis VIII, the father of St Louis, died in 1226 on his return from the Albigensian Crusade. The castle was razed to the ground on the orders of Richelieu in the 17C. The village has a small Romanesque church.

Pont-du-Château – For a long time the strategically important town was fortified; it was the location of the only bridge across the River Allier between Moulins and Brioude. Until the 19C it was a very busy port loading up goods for Paris; this history is recalled in the **Musée Pierre-Mondanel** ⊙, housed in the kitchens of an old château. It uses models of boats among the exhibits to tell of river fishing, life for the mariners etc.

Randan – This is a small town on the edge of the woods of the same name.

Ravel – *See RAVEL.*

St-Ignat – A picturesque dovecote stands on the north side of the church.

St-Myon – There is here a charming little Romanesque church with a fine stone-slabbed roof and a west front overlooking a tiny square with trees.

Thuret – A 13C keep dominates the village. The **church** is largely 11C; it comprises a handsome ensemble of east end and bell tower, with a fine south doorway. Inside, there is a Black Virgin and some interesting carved and painted capitals (Adam and Eve, Eucharistic symbols etc).

Vendègre – A fine dovecote is to be seen here.

Vertaizon – On a terrace overlooking the old town are the ruins of the east end and transept of the old parish church. There is a panoramic view of the Limagne plain.

Villeneuve-les-Cerfs – In a meadow on the Jussat road is a picturesque **dovecote**★.

Le LIORAN★

Michelin map 76 fold 3 or 239 fold 30 – Local map under Monts du CANTAL

The winter and summer holiday resort of Le Lioran (alt 1 153m/3 747ft) is encircled by the magnificent pine forests that cover the slopes of the Alagnon valley above meadows dotted with old shepherds' huts (*burons*, used for cheese making).

The tunnels – The **road tunnel** (alt 1 172m/3 809ft) dug in 1839 to avoid the mountain pass which was blocked by snow in the winter months was, for many years, the longest in France (1 412m/4 589ft). A new road, the D 67, leads across the Col de Cère *(see Monts du CANTAL)* in the summer. The **railway tunnel** up the line from the picturesque station in Le Lioran is 1 960m/6 370ft long. It was dug in 1868 at a depth of 30m/97ft below the road tunnel.

★**Gorges de l'Alagnon** – *3.5km/2mi northeast towards Murat, then turn right (signpost) and follow a path 500m long down to the upper reaches of the river. When the water level is low, it is possible to follow the river bed to the left over a distance of almost 200m. At the head of this very attractive ravine are piles of huge boulders. (The lower reaches of the river are described under BRIOUDE: Excursions).*

Maison du Buronnier ⊙ **at Laveissière** – *1.5km/1mi north of the railway station in Le Lioran, downstream from the standpipe, turn right; beyond the bridge over the Alagnon, bear left. Turn right onto the D 439.* This shepherd's house within the Regional Park is a former cheese-making hut. The exhibits have been laid out to give some insight into the everyday life of the cowherd, the bottler and the herdsman who used to produce the real mountain Cantal cheese.

✳SUPER-LIORAN

Situated opposite the high grassy Font-d'Alagnon corrie and closed off by pine-woods, this modern **winter sports resort** stands in very attractive surroundings.

WALKS TO THE PEAKS

★★**Plomb du Cantal** – *45min Rtn by cable-car and on foot from Super Lioran. Viewing table.* At 1 855m/6 029ft, this is the highest peak in the Cantal range. From the summit there is a vast **panoramic view**★★. To the west, beyond the Cère valley, there are Cantal's great volcanic cones – Griou, Peyre-Arse, Mary, Violent and Chavaroche; to the north are the Monts Dore sloping down to the right towards the undulating countryside of the Cézallier; to the east and southeast is the *planèze* with the Margeride range above it; to the south and southwest the Carladez plateau, the Châtaigneraie and, in the distance, the Rouergue. A number of footpaths lead from the summit to the **Puy Gros** (view of the Cère valley at Thiézac) or to the Prat de Bouc via the Tombe du Père pass.

***Puy Griou** – *4hr Rtn on foot from Super-Lioran. Head for the pastures in La Font d'Alagnon then turn left through the woods to the buildings of a children's holiday camp; there, bear right.* The path rises towards the alpine pastures of the Col de Rombière (superb **view**★ over the Jordanne valley and the great volcanic cones in Cantal) then turns left. A short distance further on, the clear, sharp outline of the Griou comes into view. To get to the summit, there is a strenuous climb over the andesite and phonolithic basalt rocks. From the top, at an altitude of 1694m-5506ft, there is an exceptional **panoramic view**★★★ of the Puy Mary, the Puy de Peyre-Arse, and the Plomb du Cantal barring the horizon to the north. To the south, to each side of the Elancèze ridge are the Cère and Jordanne (Mandailles) valleys.

Storm clouds looming over Puy Griou

Le LIVRADOIS

Michelin map 73 fold 15, 16 or 239 folds 20, 27, 32, 33

Le Livradois is an area lying between Comté and the Dore valley. It consists of a succession of plateaux and rounded granite hills interspersed with dips that gradually rise from the level of the Limagne to an altitude of 1 200m/3 900ft (Notre-Dame-de-Mons stands at an altitude of 1 210m/3 932ft) then slopes rapidly down to the Ambert plain. Farmland covers the lower area; in the upper slopes there are forests and clearings, meadows and moorlands. The Livradois is part of the **Parc natural régional Livradois-Forez** *(see Monts du FOREZ).*

TOWNS AND SIGHTS *listed alphabetically*

Garde (Pic de la) – *From the D 253, a tarmacked track leads to a water tower where vehicles can be parked. Viewing table.* From the summit of La Garde peak *(30min Rtn on foot)* at an altitude of 780m/2 535ft where there is a statue of the Virgin Mary, there is a fine view over the volcanoes in the Comté, the gully gouged out by the River Allier and the Monts Dore.

Mailhat – There is a small Romanesque church here, with a square belfry with double openings, and a five-sided apse decorated with blind arcading and modillions. There are interesting carved capitals: on the doorway is a representation of Lust (a woman breast-feeding two serpents) and Avarice (a long-armed man clutching his purse to his chest). In the chancel, the capitals are decorated with figures and foliage.

Manglieu – The village, once the site of a Benedictine abbey, lies in the Ailloux Valley, at a short distance from D 225 between Vic-le-Comte and Cunlhat. The **abbey church**★, which has undergone extensive external restoration, is particularly interesting for its interior. Enter the church by the attractive Romanesque doorway.

Beneath the porch topped by a gallery is a sarcophagus to the left and two gravestones, the one on the left dating from the Carolingian period and the other Merovingian in origin. The nave was rebuilt in the 16C. The narrow 10C chancel is spoilt by distemper and a modern ceiling; it opens out from a triumphal arch supported on two ancient columns that were re-used for this purpose.

Martinanches (Château des) ⓥ – Nestling at the bottom of a valley and surrounded by a moat is a **castle**, built originally in the 11C but altered in the 15C and the 19C. Inside there are beamed ceilings, fine porcelain and earthenwares, and period furniture.

★Mauzun (Château de) – *30min Rtn on foot. In the village of Mauzun, follow the path that runs up to the ruins.* The mighty **fortress** standing on a spur of basalt rock, once the property of the Bishops of Clermont-Ferrand, originally had two outer walls and twenty or more towers. Eleven of them are still standing along the outer wall; there are four in the castle. The famous preacher, Bishop Massillon of Clermont, had the fortress demolished because he did not have enough money for its upkeep. He retained only a few rooms for priests who were being detained for disciplinary reasons.

From the ruins there is a magnificent **panorama★** to the west over the Monts Dore, the volcanoes of the Comté area, and the Monts Dôme; to the north is the Limagne and to the east, the mountains of the Forez and Livradois areas.

Montmorin (Château de) – *See BILLOM: Excursions.*

St-Dier-d'Auvergne – The 12C **church** here was fortified in the 15C; it has a buttressed west front with arcading. Three aisles, a large chancel and three radiating chapels make up the inside. Note the interesting carved capitals (figures, foliage, sirens etc).

St-Germain l'Herm – Summer holiday resort.

Sauxillanges – The 12C church with 15C alterations contains a 17C painting depicting the lives of St Crépin and St Crépinien and a 15C statue of Our Lady of the Woods. The Prior's Chapel, now a heritage centre, **Maison du Patrimoine** ⓥ, is part of the remains of a 14C and 15C priory attached to the Cluniac Order. The Gothic vaulting is decorated with interesting hanging keystones bearing the coats-of-arms of the various priors.

★Usson – *See USSON.*

Gorges de la LOIRE★

Michelin map 73 folds 7, 8, 17, 18 or 239 folds 10, 11, 23, 34, 35, 46, 47

From the Gerbier de Jonc to Roanne, the Loire valley develops from a high, pastoral vale to a series of narrow channels and gorges, and wide basins; the result of a lively geological history.

The course of the River Loire follows an ancient marine ditch which felt the effects of the alpine uplift at the end of the Tertiary era. The Puy, Forez and Roanne basins – veritable rift valleys – forced the river to carve a route for itself through the plateaux separating these basins.

In the Velay region the river had to battle against the volcanic outpourings at the end of the Tertiary era and at the beginning of the Quaternary. At Arlempdes the river managed to find a way through the basalt flows; in the Puy basin, however, the course of the river was forced to shift eastwards.

In Forez the Loire gorges, carved through the crystalline base, present a particularly wild appearance at Grangent lake and around the meanders of St-Victor-sur-Loire.

195

Artificial lakes – In addition to the spectacular works of nature, there are also attractive manmade landscapes: dams have flooded the former valley to produce La Palisse, Grangent and Villerest lakes; another dam is planned upriver from Le Puy-en-Velay.

Ancient castles and sanctuaries – Overlooking the river stand some fine ruined fortresses and a few old châteaux, perched on rocky spurs or on the side of the wider banks: Arlempdes, Bouzols, Lavoûte-Polignac, Rochebaron...
Romanesque churches, originally often linked to a priory, dot the route along the gorges; the most impressive of these is at Chamalières-sur-Loire.

★THE UPPER VALLEY (THROUGH THE VELAY)

☐ From Gerbier de Jonc to Le Puy-en-Velay
115km/71mi – allow a day – local map overleaf below

★★**Gerbier de Jonc** – *See GERBIER DE JONC.*
The route descends along the pastoral valley; houses with thatched roofs may still be seen at Ste-Eulalie and near Usclades-et-Rieutord. The road then runs beside La Palisse lake and, a little further, beside an attractive basalt flow *(left)*. The narrow, banked up valley of the Gage is crossed.

Lac d'Issarlès

★**Lac d'Issarlès** – The waters of this round and intensely blue-looking lake, with a surface area of some 90ha/222 acres, occupy an old volcanic crater, 138m/452ft deep. The waters are used to run the hydroelectric power plant at Montpezat, which can therefore affect the water level, though between 15 June and 15 September the lake is kept full to provide an attractive place for bathing.
The winding road then loses the Loire a few times as the waters flow through deep gorges.

★**Arlempdes** – *See ARLEMPDES.*

Goudet – This small hamlet is dominated by the ruins of Beaufort château.

St-Martin-de-Fugères – From the D 49 above the village there is a good panoramic **view**★.

★★★**Le Puy-en-Velay** – *See Le PUY-EN-VELAY.*

☐ From Le Puy-en-Velay to Retournac
58km/36mi – allow a day – local map overleaf below

Leave Le Puy-en-Velay to the north on the D 103.
Leaving the Puy basin the River Loire enters into a wild granite channel: Peyredeyre gorge.
At Peyredeyre turn right onto the D 71.

Chaspinhac – The small Romanesque **church**, attractively built of red volcanic stone, contains interesting carved capitals. Beside the church, there are extensive views of the Velay countryside.

Château de Lavoûte-Polignac ⊙ – The fortress was owned by the Polignac family as early as the 13C, but was later transformed into a comfortable manor house as the castle at Polignac itself remained a powerful stronghold. The building, which stands impressively above a *"voulte"* (loop) in the river, was restored after the Revolution. Inside there are family **memorabilia★**: paintings, fine furniture, tapestries, letters etc.

Lavoûte-sur-Loire – Above the high altar in the small Romanesque **church** ⊙ there is a remarkable 13C wooden **statue of Christ★**.

Vorey – This is a small summer resort.

2km/1mi from Vorey turn left onto the D 89.

Roche-en-Régnier – This is an old village hanging above the west bank of the river which is overlooked by a volcanic stump crowned by an old defensive tower. From the foot of this tower there is a fine **panorama★** over the mountains of Velay and Forez, and the volcanic cones of Yssingeaux.

Chamalières-sur-Loire – The village stands at the foot of Mont Gerbizon (1 064m/3 490ft high); it is noted for its Romanesque **church★** ⊙. This early 12C sanctuary has attractive blind arcading along the exterior (south side and around the apse). Inside, the oven-vaulted apse is of a spectacular size. Note the three rows of small orifices which each correspond to an acoustic vessel buried in the stonework; blind arcading in the apse links the four apsidal chapels. Note also the monolithic carved pier from the old cloisters which was later used as a font; the four figures represent David, Solomon, Isaiah and Jeremiah. On the left pier of the transept, on the side of the high altar, there is a 13C mural of the Virgin in Majesty between two angels; the original 12C panelled door of the church stands in the south aisle.

Retournac – The part-Romanesque church is of handsome ochre stone and has a sturdy belfry and a stone-slabbed roof; the two apsidal chapels are decorated with a large pearl motif. Inside, note the dome on squinches, the elegant chancel, a 16C Italian Madonna and Child, the modern altar and stained-glass windows. Two twisted columns in the right aisle flank the original entrance.

★BETWEEN FOREZ AND VIVARAIS

③ From Retournac to Aurec

35km/22mi – about 2hr – local map overleaf

North of Retournac take the D 46 which runs along the plateau west of the Loire.

Beauzac – The small 12C-17C **church** here has a Flamboyant portal and an elegant three-storey belfry; a Romanesque crypt lies under the apse. A few houses in the village, built within the old ramparts pierced by two gates, have unusual wooden galleries under the roof which rest on huge corbels.

Château de Rochebaron – *45min Rtn on foot.* The ruins of this medieval castle (11C-13C), perched on a spur overlooking the Loire, are preceded by three rows of protective walls. Only one round tower, with vaulted rooms linked by a spiral staircase, remains intact. From the end of the spur, there is a good **view★** of the Loire valley.

Monistrol-sur-Loire – The town has a surprisingly Mediterranean feel about it, both in its appearance and its climate. An avenue of lime trees leads to the large round towers of the old bishop's palace (15C-17C), which now houses the tourist office as well as hosting temporary exhibitions. The church has unequal-sized aisles which are larger than the nave, a Romanesque dome over the crossing, and a 17C bell tower. A network of narrow, medieval-looking alleys runs between the church and the old palace.

④ From Aurec to St-Just-St-Rambert

30km/19mi – about 3hr – local map overleaf

Aurec-sur-Loire stands at the beginning of the dammed **Lac de Grangent★★**. The **road★★** *(D 108 and D 32)* from Semène to Grangent dam follows a scarp ledge offering lovely views over the wild, sometimes submerged meanders of the river.

Cornillon – The **château** *(private)* rising on a spur overlooking the gorges was once the seat of one of the most powerful baronies in Forez.

Chambles – The setting here is one of the loveliest along the Loire gorges: beside a squat church stands the tower of the old castle, on the edge of a high escarpment overlooking the meanders of the Grangent. This tower is a typical example of medieval fortifications with its entrance halfway up, accessible only up a collapsible ladder. Modern visitors can make the climb *(quite taxing)* through a more recent doorway. From the top of the tower there is a vast **panorama★** of the Forez and Lyon regions, with the outlines of Vassalieux and Essalois castles to the left.

2km/1mi beyond Chambles turn right onto a small road to the ruins of the Château d'Essalois.

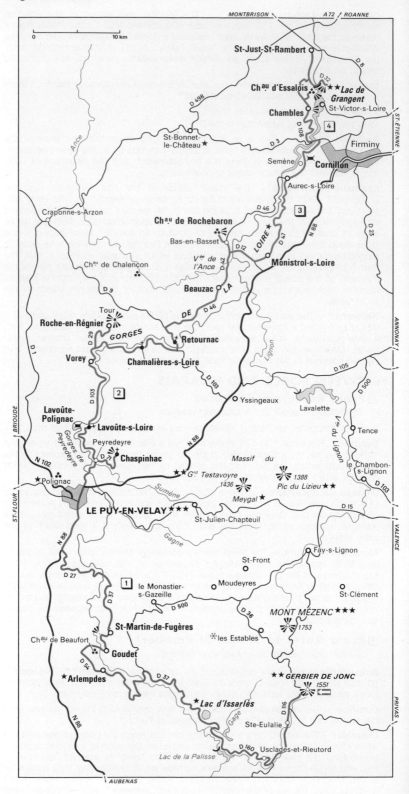

The towns and sights described in this guide
are indicated in black lettering on the local maps and town plans.

Château d'Essalois – The sturdy outline of this ruined castle *(restored)* overlooks a sheer gorge and commands a superb **view★★** over Grangent reservoir and island. Near the castle a Celtic oppidum bears witness to the strategic importance of this site. History has endowed this part of the world with a sense of mystery and magic still tangible today.

On the opposite bank further good views of the Loire can be had from sites such as **Danse plateau** (prehistoric remains) or **St-Victor-sur-Loire** (sailing base). **River cruises** ⊙ are available from here.

Grangent reservoir

Île de Grangent – This island was created when the manmade lake isolated the tongue of a rocky spine on which sit the ruins of Grangent castle (12C tower) and a small chapel with a red-tiled roof.

St-Just-St-Rambert – This town was once a Gallo-Roman village, clinging to the flank of a mound. The **church of St-André★** is a sturdy 11C and 12C building crowned by an 11C fortified bell tower (west front) and the 12C main **bell tower★**; it consists of a square lower level decorated with blind arcading and an upper level with twinned openings topped by mitre shapes, between which are small arched openings.

Inside, the arches between the nave and the aisles increase in size towards the chancel which gives a deceptive appearance to the perspective. At the transept crossing a dome on squinches supports the central bell tower. Note the small statue of a Black Virgin in the south apsidal chapel and the Gothic arcade around the font decorated with small angels.

To the north of the church stands the 11C chapel of St-Jean, once used as the baptistery. To the south of the church is a local museum, the **Musée Le Prieuré** ⊙, containing a variety of objets d'art linked with the town's past, and also more internationally flavoured collections including works of art from the South Pacific and Africa, most notably some fine **bronzes★** from Benin.

South of St-Rambert, at the mouth of the Forez basin, the volume of the Loire is increased by the waters of the Furan at the level of Andrézieux, and the river spreads out to flow across the plain between low-lying banks.

★GORGES ROANNAISES DE LA LOIRE

See ROANNE: Excursions

Michelin Maps (scale 1 : 200 000), which are revised regularly, provide a wealth of useful motoring information.

Keep current Michelin Maps in the car at all times.

General view of Lyon from Fourvière, with the Cathédrale St-Jean in the foreground

Twenty centuries of history and a superb geographical situation at the confluence of the Saône and Rhône rivers give Lyon an appearance quite unlike any other city.

The Greater Lyon District (Communauté Urbaine de Lyon) covers an area of 50 000ha/over 123 000 acres with a population in excess of one million two hundred thousand, and includes 55 outlying towns and villages which, through a delegate council, provide a range of communal services and draw up major town planning and road projects. This is the second largest urban district in France. In addition, ADERLY (The Association for the Development of the Lyon Region) seeks to promote the district on an international level and to attract foreign companies to invest in the area. Lyon's current dynamism serves as a reminder of the fact that the city's finest hours, during the Roman Empire and the Renaissance, were times when trade was of major importance and the city succeeded in taking full advantage of its outstanding geographical situation. It is, after all, on the road to Italy, between central and eastern France, and midway between northern France and the southern provinces.

Lyon is not only an industrial city specialising in metalworking, chemistry and building trades, and famous for its silk and synthetic fabrics; it is also a university town and a world-famous centre in the field of medicine. It has a Court of Appeal and an archbishopric (the Archbishop of Lyon bears the title "Primate of the Gauls"). The city is a popular tourist venue, famous for its cuisine; it is one of the best-known gastronomic centres in France.

TWENTY CENTURIES OF HISTORY

Capital of the Gauls – According to a Celtic legend two princes, Momoros and Atepomaros, stopped here one day at the confluence of the rivers and decided to build a town. While they were digging the foundations, a flock of crows flew down around them. Recognising the event as evidence of divine intervention, they decided to call their city Lugdunum ("Crows' Hill").

Julius Caesar set up his base camp here during his determined campaign to conquer Gaul. After his death one of his lieutenants, Munatius Plancus, brought Roman settlers here (43 BC). Shortly afterwards Agrippa, who had been ordered by Caesar Augustus to organise Gaul, chose Lugdunum as his capital. The network of imperial roads began in Lyon and five major routes radiated out from the city towards Aquitaine, the Ocean, the Rhine, Arles and Italy. Caesar Augustus stayed in the town; Emperor Claudius was born here. In the 2C, aqueducts brought water to Fourvière from the surrounding mountains.

GALLO-ROMAN LYON

LUGDUNUM

The city, governed by its council, held a monopoly in the trade of wine throughout Gaul. The mariners in its harbour were powerful shipowners; its potters were veritable industrialists. The wealthiest of the city's traders lived in a separate district, on the Île des Canabae, around where St-Martin-d'Ainay *(see La Presqu'Île, below)* stands today. On the slopes of La Croix Rousse was the Gallic town, Condate. The Amphitheatre of the Three Gauls (the votive inscription was uncovered in 1958) and the Temple of Rome and Caesar Augustus were the setting for the noisy Assembly of Gauls once a year.

Christianity in Lyon – Lyon became the meeting-place for businessmen from all over the country. Soldiers, merchants and missionaries arrived from Asia Minor and began spreading the new Gospel. Soon, a small Christian community developed in the town. In AD 177 a popular revolt broke out and led to the famous martyrdom of St Pothin, St Blandine and their companions. Twenty years later when **Septimus Severus**, having defeated his competitor Albin (who enjoyed popular support from the locals), decided to set fire to the town, he found that there were still 18 000 Christians in Lyon. He had them massacred; among their number was St Irénée, St Pothin's successor.

This faith has continued through the ages. On **8 December** each year, the Feast of the Immaculate Conception is celebrated in Lyon with a great deal of pomp and enthusiasm. In the evening, thousands of multi-coloured lanterns can be seen in the windows of the

Fabish, who was not able to deliver the statue by the deadline of 8 September. Accordingly the ceremony was postponed until 8 December, the Feast of the Immaculate Conception. On the day itself, heavy rainfall resulted in cancellation of the evening festival; however, contrary to all expectations, the rain stopped at precisely the time the festivities had been scheduled to start. All over the city, thousands of balconies were lit up by tiny lights placed there in a spontaneous gesture by Lyon residents. This religious custom has become a traditional festival on which, among other things, the city councillors and store owners inaugurate their Christmas displays.

Lyon in the Middle Ages – After Charlemagne's reign, Lyon passed from one family to another through legacies and dowries. Finally, the city was placed under the temporal authority of its archbishops.

During this period a large number of major building projects were completed. Churches and abbeys sprang up in Lyon and the surrounding area. Pont du Change (Exchange Bridge) was built over the River Saône; Pont de la Guillotière, designed by the Pontiff Brothers, provided access to the other bank of the Rhône.

In the early 14C Lyon was directly annexed to royal authority and it obtained the right to elect twelve consuls. A municipal charter was proclaimed at Île Barbe in 1312. The consuls, all of them members of the rich *bourgeoisie*, raised taxes and ensured that there was law and order. The people of the working classes, who were quick to rebel and who had had no hesitation in besieging the archbishop in his palace, discovered to their cost that the consuls were even more heavy-handed than the clergy had been.

A Cultural Centre – At the end of the 15C the setting up of fairs and the development of banking attracted traders from all over Europe. Social, intellectual and artistic life blossomed, stimulated by a visit from François I and his sister, Marguerite, who held the most dazzling court.

Famous "booksellers" took the fame of Lyon's printers far and wide. There were 100 printer workshops in the town in 1515, and more than 400 by 1548.

Painters, sculptors and potters, all of them steeped in Italian culture, prepared the way for the French Renaissance.

Lyon boasted brilliant poets and storytellers such as François **Rabelais** (1494-1553). He was a doctor at the local hospital and, for the fairs in 1532 and 1534, published his works *Gargantua* and *Pantagruel*.

It was, though, a woman, **Louise Labé**, who embodied the spirit of the day, not only for her grace and beauty but also for her skill in poetry. At the age of twenty, Louise had developed comprehensive linguistic (Greek, Latin, Spanish and Italian) and musical talents. After a stint at the siege of Perpignan (not for the faint-hearted!), she eventually married a gentleman-ropemaker (Fr.: *cordier*) from Lyon and opened a salon for poets, artists and men of learning, just as Madame de Sévigné was to do a century later. The "Belle Cordière", as she was known, penned some pleasing verse herself, as well as encouraging others.

Scientific advances – The arts reigned in the Lyon of the 16C. Science became all the rage in the 18C, with the **Jussieu brothers**, famous botanists, and Bourgelat, who founded the first veterinary school in Europe in Lyon in 1762. In 1783 **Jouffroy d'Abbans** tested steam navigation on the Saône with his *Pyroscaphe*, the first really viable steamboat; however, it brought him nothing but the ironic nickname of "Jouffroy the Pump".

In 1784 Joseph **Montgolfier** and Pilâtre de **Rozier** succeeded, at Les Brotteaux, in rising into the air on board a hot-air balloon. This was one of the first flights. A few years later, **Ampère**, the great physicist, and **Jacquard**, who invented a weaving loom, showed their own form of inventive genius.

"Lyon is no more" – During the French Revolution, the residents of Lyon resisted the Convention. Retribution was harsh: on 12 October 1793 the Committee of Public Safety declared that "Lyon waged war on liberty. Lyon is no more". Houses were destroyed, countless local people died, and Lyon was renamed "Free Commune".

Lyon's "Mr Punch" – **Guignol**, the popular wooden puppet who is well-known throughout France, his wife Madelon and his usual sparring partner, Gnafron, whose fine bass voice has coarsened somewhat through excessive consumption of Beaujolais, all embody the popular spirit of the local people in a way that provokes laughter without giving offence. **Laurent Mourguet** (1769-1844), who created Guignol, was a local weaver. The few neighbours for whom he first performed his comedy shows were enthusiastic. Soon, as his success grew, so did his public; he staged performances all over Lyon, in the Petit Tivoli, and in the main avenue in Les Brotteaux where, on Sundays, three rows of chairs were set out. After Mourguet's death his 16 children, all of whom had been trained by him, perpetuated his art form. Nowadays, comedies based on current affairs are played out on the stage of the Guignol de Lyon theatre *(see Old Town, below)*.

The silk industry – It was silk which, in the 16C, made Lyon a major industrial city; until then most of the silk fabrics in France had been imported from Italy. Two main figures dominate the history of this new industry. In 1536 **Étienne Turquet**, a man from Piedmont in Italy, offered to bring to Lyon silk and velvet weavers from Genoa and set up a factory in Lyon. François I, who was anxious to stem the flow of money out of the country as a result of purchases of foreign silks, accepted his offer. In 1804 Joseph-Marie **Jacquard** invented a loom which, by using a system of punched cards, enabled a single worker to do the work of six. The Croix Rousse district was filled with its characteristic house-workshops – the upper storeys contained the looms on which the workers wove the silk provided by the manufacturer.

In 1875 a revolution occurred in the silk industry; the introduction of mechanical looms and the change in fashion away from figured fabrics and brocades quickly reduced the silk-workers to abject poverty. Only a few looms continued to exist in Lyon, capable of producing special fabrics at exorbitant prices. Ordinary silks were made by workers in rural areas where labour was less expensive.

Today natural silk imported from Italy or Japan now represents only a minute proportion of the quantities of fabric processed here. It is subject to extremely meticulous care and attention in the silk-workers centre (Maison des Canuts, *see below*).

The so-called "silk-style" weaving, though, using all sorts of fibres (glass, carbon, borum, and aramide) remains one of Lyon's specialities. The traditional know-how of the silk weavers has found direct applications in the production of highly sophisticated parts for the aeronautics, space and electronics industries. These activities are closely linked to chemistry (in research and the combining of new molecules).

Other industries – Metalworking and mechanical engineering, which employ more than 54 000 people, are the most important industries in the Lyon district. A large number of specialist companies are involved – foundries, metalworking, consumer durables but, most important of all, car manufacture and the production of transport equipment. Car manufacturing began very early on thanks to the pioneers from Lyon. Nowadays Lyon is one of France's major production centres of Heavy Goods Vehicles (the Berliet plant here is part of Renault's Industrial Vehicles Division).

Electrical goods remain one of the district's specialist sectors, including heavy consumer durables, engines, wires and cables.

In the chemical sector, the colouring agent and dye activity, which was based on silk dyeing techniques, enjoyed an initial period of expansion in the 19C. Other fields include para-chemical activities, for example Lumière/Ilford photographic products. The pharmaceuticals sector is also present here, with a number of world-famous laboratories.

Heavy chemistry and petro-chemicals are concentrated in a small number of very large factories, while the building and civil engineering industries have some twenty or more large companies here.

Lyon has also become a major centre of tertiary and service industries (banks, insurance companies). In the scientific and medical field, the city enjoys international renown. There are highly-efficient specialist units such as the Severe Burns Unit in the Édouard-Herriot hospital, laboratories in the CNRS (National Scientific Research Centre) specialising in all the major fields including nuclear physics and biochemistry, the International Cancer Research Centre which has been in Lyon since 1965, and research centres belonging to the Institut Pasteur and the Institut Mérieux.

Lyon Fair – In the Middle Ages, Lyon was "one of the keys to the kingdom", situated as it was on the frontiers of Savoy, Dauphiné, Italy and Germany on one side, and Beaujolais, Burgundy, Languedoc, Forez and the Auvergne on the other. In 1419 the heir to the French throne, the future Charles VII, having realised the value of this geographical situation in commercial terms, ordered two fairs to be held here every year; he made Lyon one of the largest warehouses in the world. Traders and merchants flocked here from every direction.

From 1463 onwards, thanks to Louis XI, the fairs were held four times a year.

Re-established in 1916 after a long break, the **Lyon International Fair** maintains the city's tradition as a major centre of international business. Running concurrently with the main fair are a number of specialist exhibitions.

Lyon puts on a new face – There has been much development in Lyon since the "daring" tower blocks of the 1930s – including both new projects and restoration schemes in the old parts of the city.

In order to ensure its success in the future, Lyon is developing a number of science parks in suburban areas, which bring together scientific research, higher education and industry. The recently completed Cité Internationale, between the Rhône and the Tête d'Or park, is the site of an International Conference Centre (capacity 2 000), the head offices of Interpol (the International Criminal Investigation Organisation), a hotel complex and a museum of contemporary art, all housed in a boldly innovative building. To the east, around the university campus, there are major technical research offices and, further out of town, the new Lyon-Satolas TGV station, designed by Spanish architect **Calatrava** to resemble a bird taking flight, which provides a TGV link to the local airport.

The Gerland district (**BR**) is undergoing continued major development *(see below)*. The west of Lyon has a large complex of higher education establishments set amid computing companies, scientific and technical research centres and tertiary sector businesses (banks, insurance companies).

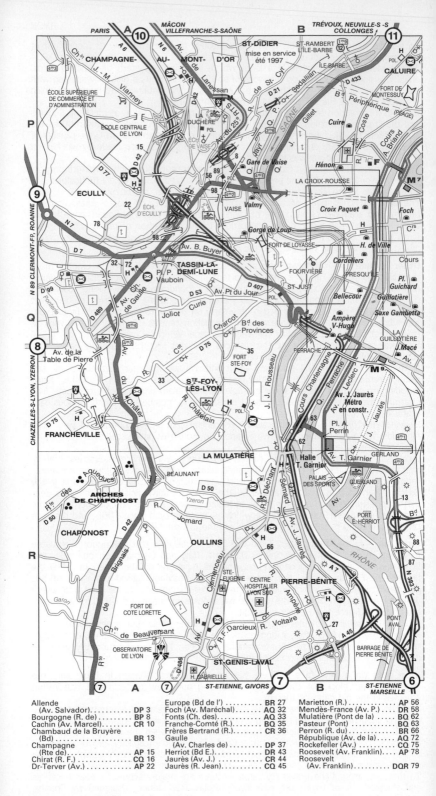

*Admission times and charges for the sights described
are listed at the end of the guide.
Every sight for which there are times and charges
is identified by the symbol ⊙
in the Sights section of the guide.*

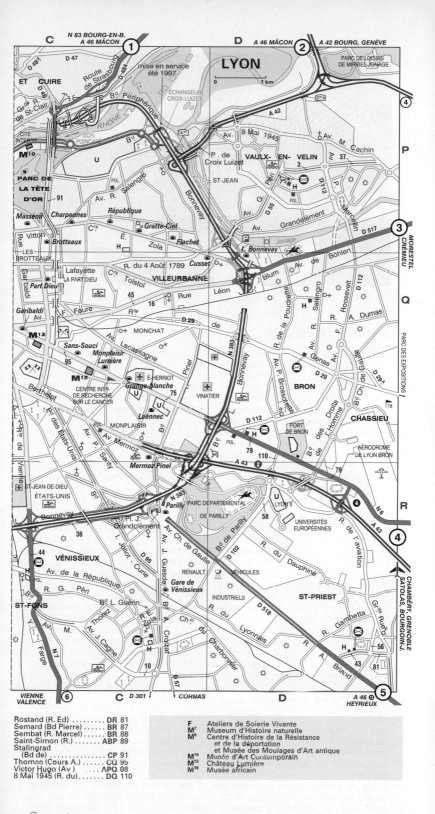

Gourmets...
The introductory chapter of this guide describes the region's
gastronomic specialities and best local wines.
The annual Michelin Red Guide France
offers an up-to-date selection of good restaurants.

Lyon-Satolas TGV station

A PRIVILEGED SITE

★★★**Setting** – The rivers Rhône and Saône provide the magnificent sight of their very differing courses as they flow past the foot of the two famous hills, Fourvière and La Croix Rousse, facing the low plain of Dauphiné. Flowing down from the north, the Saône skirts the small Mont-d'Or range and enters the Pierre-Scize gorge gouged out between Fourvière and La Croix Rousse. The Rhône arrives from the Alps, a wide river that washes the lower slopes of La Croix Rousse. During Roman times, the confluence lay at the foot of the hill *(see plan above)*. The alluvium built up by the Rhône gradually pushed the confluence further south and the resulting peninsula became the main centre of the city. The Fourvière and Croix Rousse hills have numerous terraces from which to admire the town; the views from some of these is famous, including the Fourvière basilica viewing table, Place Rouville and Rue des Fantasques in La Croix Rousse. Further away but no less outstanding are the panoramic views from Esplanade de Ste-Foy and Mont Thou.

A European crossroads – Lyon lies at the centre of a motorway network that links the city to northern and southern Europe in the north-south direction and to the Massif Central, Switzerland and Italy in the east-west direction, via St-Étienne, Clermont-Ferrand, Geneva, Annecy, Chambéry and Grenoble.

Since 1981, in addition to the many fast rail links with the rest of France, Lyon has enjoyed even more rapid communications due to the high-speed train (TGV) service which brings the city to within two hours' travelling of Paris. There is a busy international airport, Lyon-Satolas, to the east of the town and, despite the fact that the wide-gauge river link joining the Mediterranean to the North Sea *(see Vallée du RHÔNE)* has not yet been completed, the Édouard-Herriot harbour to the south of the Gerland district is already full of heavy barges waiting to sail up to Auxonne on the Saône (32km/20mi southeast of Dijon). A direct river-sea route with no need to offload cargo nor make intermediate stops was opened with Piraeus in 1984, with Algiers in 1986 and with Haïfa in 1991.

FOURVIÈRE *1 day – local plan p 212*

The Fourvière district of Lyon stands on a hill of the same name; "Fourvière" is said to come from the Latin "Forum vetus", relating to the forum which was situated in the heart of the Roman colony established in 43 BC; its theatre, odeon and aqueducts have survived to this day. The forum, which stood on the site now occupied by the esplanade in front of the basilica, is said to have collapsed in AD 840.

In the 3C people moved from the side of the hill and the stones were re-used to rebuild the town at the bottom of the slope. In the Middle Ages the hill was largely given over to farming (in particular vineyards). In the 17C numerous religious orders set up monasteries and convents here, which inspired the historian, Michelet, to make his famous comment about Fourvière, "the hill that prays", opposite La Croix-Rousse, "the hill that works".

Nowadays Fourvière with its basilica, Roman monuments and museum is, with the old town some 100m/325ft below, one of the most popular tourist venues in Lyon.

Les montées

The *montées* or rises consist of winding flights of steps or steeply-sloping streets that climb the Fourvière hill, providing superb views down over the old town. Each of them has its own particular charm.

Montée des Carmes-Déchaussés and Montée de Nicolas-de-Lange (HJV) – The former derives its name (Rise of the Barefoot-Carmelites) from the monastery founded in the early 17C which now houses the departmental Archives; it has 238 steps. The second has 560 steps which means that there is a total of 798 steps down to Place St-Paul from the metal tower *(tour métallique)* on Fourvière.

Montée du Change (JV) – This links the Rue de la Loge and the Montée St-Barthélémy. On the way down, there are interesting views of the spires on St-Nizier church which rises from the buildings on the banks of the Saône.

★**Montée du Garillan (JV)** – This is a remarkable series of zigzag flights of steps *(224 steps)*.

Montée des Chazeaux (JV) – With its 228 very steep steps, this leads into the Montée St-Barthélémy.

Montée du Chemin-Neuf and Montée St-Barthélémy (HJX) – From these steps there is an extensive view over the rooftops of the old town and the archbishop's palace.

Montée du Gourguillon (HJX) – Set on the hillside in the Fourvière district, this was the usual route taken by carriages heading for the Auvergne in the Middle Ages. It is difficult to imagine the heavy loads climbing such a steep slope. It was also the direct route between the cloisters of St-Jean belonging to the Canon-Counts, and St-Just, the fortified town of the Canon-Barons. At no 2 stands a Renaissance house. Slightly further up the hill is the **Impasse Turquet (JX)**, a picturesque passageway with old timber galleries.

Montée des Épies (HX) – This rise climbs up above the St-Georges district, high above the church dedicated to St George, a Neo-Gothic building designed by Bossan, the architect also responsible for Fourvière basilica.

Illuminations on Fourvière hill

OUT AND ABOUT IN LYON

Travelling round town – The underground train/subway *(métro)* is the most convenient mode of public transport, and is especially well-adapted to the needs of tourists. The best-value ticket to buy is the **ticket-liberté**, valid for a day for unlimited travel on the Lyon urban transport network (métro, bus, funicular railway, trolley-bus). Details from TCL (Transports en Commun Lyonnais) kiosks or call ☎ 04 78 71 70 00.

Organised tours – The Lyon tourist office offers tours of the city on foot, or by bus, boat, taxi or even helicopter. **Lecture tours** ⊙ are available around Old Lyon and the Croix Rousse district.

Bateaux-mouches river trips ⊙ – These enable visitors to discover a different face of Lyon, seen from its four river banks: one trip explores the confluence of the Saône and Rhône; the other follows the Saône up to and round Île-Barbe islet.

Exploring Lyon by bateau-mouche

Recommended programmes for visiting Lyon – For those with only **one day** to explore Lyon, we recommend spending the morning discovering the delights of the Old Town (on foot) and its famous, picturesque old passages *(traboules)*, then taking the funicular up to the Fourvière terrace and the Roman theatre ruins (you will not have time for the museums here); in the afternoon, visit the peninsula with its historic textiles museum and either go on to the fine art museum or follow the Gros-Caillou footpath on the Croix-Rousse hillside.

Two days in Lyon will enable you to explore the Fourvière hill and its museums in more depth, and to take a stroll along the banks of the Saône on day one. Then day two can be devoted to the peninsula and its museums (Tissus, Imprimerie, Hospices civils), followed by one of the walks recommended round the Croix-Rousse district.

In **three days** visitors may like to include such sights as the natural history museum and Tête d'Or park, the French Resistance museum, the motor museum at Rochetaillée or the collection of dolls in the château at Lacroix-Laval park.

Last but not least, it goes without saying that the longer you allow for your visit to Lyon, the longer you will also have to savour the delights of the excellent local cuisine!

Life in Lyon – As the "Gateway to the South of France", where much of what is good about the north of France can be found in a more Mediterranean context embodied not least by the red pantile roofs, Lyon enjoys not only the reputation of being a hard-working, major city, but also of having an outstanding standard of life in which good food plays a leading role. Life in Lyon is characterised above all by its lack of stress or complication. The Lyonnais are creatures of habit, and some of their favourite pastimes can be appreciated by visitors to the city as well, such as watching (perhaps even playing?!) the odd game of boules, especially during the boules tournament at Whitsun, taking a quiet stroll along the banks of the Saône or Rhône, or a gentle

Place des Cordeliers. The Part-Dieu shopping centre, one of Europe's largest, comprises 260 shops and restaurants. Antiques are to be found in the Cité des Antiquitaires (150 boutiques), 117, boulevard Stalingrad in the suburb of Villeurbanne.

Cultural entertainment – For dance, Maison de la Danse, 8, avenue Jean-Mermoz. For music, the Opéra, Place de la Comédie; or the Halle Tony Garnier, 20, place Antonin-Perrin; or the Auditorium-Orchestre National, 149, rue Garibaldi. For theatre, the Théâtre des Célestins, Place des Célestins, which puts on a varied programme in a luxurious setting; or the Théâtre National Populaire, which moved to the suburb of Villeurbanne in 1973 and which aims to put on high quality productions accessible to a maximum number of people; or the Théâtre "Guignol de Lyon", rue Louis-Garrand, with its famous local satire.

Lyon also hosts an international puppet festival and a cinema library festival *(see Calendar of events)*, organised by the Institut Lumière.

Contemporary art is well represented here, with large exhibitions held at the Perrache Centre d'Échanges, the upper level of which is designated the Espace Lyonnais d'Art Contemporain, at Villeurbanne in the Nouveau Musée, and at the Cité Internationale in the Musée d'Art Contemporain *(during the Biennale d'Art Contemporain)*. Villeurbanne also boasts an ultra-modern multi-media reference library, the Maison du Livre, de l'Image et du Son, which was designed by architect Mario Botta.

Eating out – The "World Capital of Gastronomy" is home to numerous eating establishments, including the *bouchons*, small restaurants typical of Lyon, for example: Chez Brunet at 23, rue Claudia; La Voûte at 11, place Antonin Gourju; La Machonnerie at 36, rue Tramassac. Rue Mercière, lined with restaurants, brasseries and cafés, is well worth a visit or two. Brasserie Georges at 30, Cours Verdun, has become an institution. Great French chefs such as Paul Bocuse (at Collonges-au-Mont-d'Or) continue to build Lyon's reputation as a great gastronomic centre. *See the Michelin Red Guide France.*

Night-life – The city itself puts on evening dress every night, enhanced by the subtle illuminations of the **Plan Lumière**★★ *(see box overleaf).*

Cinémascope Opéra restaurant, 22, rue J. Serlin, organises evening entertainment on various themes for cinephiles; Eden Rock Café, 68, rue Mercière, is somewhere to relax to the rhythm of 1960s rock music; other interesting atmospheres can be found in pubs such as Le Monocle at 15, rue Mercière, or Le Pub at 4, rue de la Baleine, or in the café-théâtre La Mi-Graine at 11, place St-Paul; the bars of La Tour-Rose and La Cour-des-Loges in rue du Bœuf, offer entertainment in lavish surroundings.

Sport – Lyon is well-equipped with sports facilities: Palais des Sports at 360, avenue Jean-Jaurès; Stade Gerland, in allée de Coubertin; Tête d'Or cycle track at the park of this name; Charlemagne skating rink, cours Charlemagne; Lyon-Chassieux golf course, road from Lyon to Chassieux; a dozen or so swimming pools, gymnasia and sports fields, and the parks of Miribel-Jonage, Bron-Parilly and Lacroix-Laval.

Lyon Old Town, which stretches for over 1km/0.6mi between Fourvière and the Saône, includes the **St-Jean district** (**JVX**) in the the centre, the **St-Paul district** (**JV**) to the north and the **St-Georges district** (**HJX**) to the south. This was once the town centre and the seat of all the corporations, in particular those representing silk workers. There were 18 000 looms here at the end of the reign of François I (mid 16C). Traders, bankers, clerks and royal dignitaries lived here, in magnificent town houses.

Almost 300 of these mansions still stand, forming a quite exceptional example of Renaissance housing. In this area, which is covered by a conservation order and has undergone extensive restoration, it is worth noting the variety of decorative features on the houses, the craftsmanship involved in the construction of the mansions, and their substantial height as a result of lack of space. Many of these four-hundred-year-old houses originally had four floors; additional storeys were added in the 16C in order to provide more light for the looms.

One of the main features of the Old Town is the numerous passages or alleyways known as "**traboules**" (from the Latin *trans ambulare* meaning "walking through") especially between Rue St-Jean, Rue des Trois-Maries and Quai Romain-Rolland, Rue St-Georges and Rue Fulchiron. Because there was not enough space to build an extensive network of streets, these passageways, all perpendicular to the Saône, were built to link the buildings. They consist of corridors with vaulted or coffered ceilings leading to inner courtyards with Renaissance galleries.

The houses reflect their period of construction (15C to 17C) and there are several architectural styles.

The **Late Gothic houses** are distinguishable by the elegant decoration on the Flamboyant façades – multi-foiled or ogee arches, flowerets, carved gables decorated with crockets. The windows are often set asymetrically into the walls. A vaulted corridor leads to an inner courtyard where a corner turret contains a spiral staircase.

Most of the old houses, among them the most beautiful of all the mansions, are built in the **Renaissance style**. The basic structure remains unchanged but the buildings are bigger and include new decorative features of Italian inspiration. The polygonal staircase turrets are beautifully designed and built; each courtyard has its succession of galleries, one above the other, each with surbased arches.

The **French Renaissance houses** are fewer in number. There is a noticeable return to Antiquity with the inclusion of architectural orders. The famous architect **Philibert Delorme** (1515-70), a native of Lyon, launched the new fashion with the gallery on squinches at 8 Rue Juiverie *(see below)*. The main staircase, which was often rectangular, was set in the centre of the façade.

The **late 16C and pre-Classical houses** are distinguished by severe architectural lines. The decoration on the façade appears above the ground floor and includes triangular pediments with a central arch-stone in relief, and rusticated bonding. The galleries overlooking the courtyard show Florentine influence with rounded arches supported by round columns.

While walking around the courtyards and passages, besides appreciating the *traboules* themselves, keep an eye open for statues of the Virgin Mary in courtyards or corner niches, attractive carved shop signs, wrought-iron imposts and railings, old wells, and amusing corbels supporting the spring ends of the diagonal ribs of the vaulted passageways.

Start from Place du Change and follow the route marked on the map below.

Place du Change (**JV**) – This square, originally called Place de la Draperie, was frequented by moneylenders in the 15C and 16C. The **Loge du Change** was designed mainly by Soufflot, the architect who altered the original design between 1747 and 1750. On the upper storey are engaged columns topped by Ionic capitals and carved entablatures. Since 1803 the building has been used as a Protestant church.

Opposite, at no 2, is the **Maison Thomassin** (**B**) which has a 15C façade built in the 14C style. On the second floor the mullioned ogee bays rising to trefoiled arches are set into Gothic arches decorated with coats-of-arms.

Turn into Rue de la Loge. Opposite is Montée du Change.

Rue Juiverie (**JV 17**) – The Jews were expelled from this street in the late 14C and the Italian bankers who replaced them had luxurious mansions built. At no 23, at the corner of Rue de la Loge, is the **Maison Dugas** (**D**) whose long façade is decorated with bosses and lions' heads. Opposite, at no 22, is the **Maison Baronat** (**E**) which has a corbelled corner turret overlooking Montée du Change. The mansion at no 20 was built by a wealthy 15C gentleman, E Grolier. The façade is decorated with mullioned windows flanked by colonnettes. Note in the courtyard a tower with a spiral staircase inside and the rib-vaulted galleries. The house at no 21 has ogee windows with rounded frontons. There is a Gallo-Roman cellar in its basement.

The **Maison de Paris** (**Z**) at no 18 dates from the 15C and has a courtyard decorated with six-branched Jewish stars set in the quadripartite vaulting of the balconies.

Between nos 16 and 18 is the picturesque, hilly **Ruelle Punaise** (**JV 32**), which leads into Montée St-Barthélémy. In the Middle Ages it served as an open sewer.

The Renaissance façade on the **Maison Antoine Groslier de Servières** (**F**) (no 10) has five arches on the ground floor topped by triangular or broken pediments of black marble. In the courtyard is a round tower with mullioned windows containing a spiral staircase. The corbels on the balcony on the first floor are carved with human figures.

At no 8, the second courtyard in the **Hôtel Bullioud** (**K**) contains the famous **gallery**★★ designed by Philibert **Delorme**, a gem of French Renaissance architecture in Lyon. Delorme built it in 1536 on his return from Rome. Note the squinches supporting the corner pavilions decorated in the Antique style: a Doric frieze with an entablature on the lower level including metopes and triglyphs *(see Introduction. Art and Architectural Terms),* and pilasters with Ionic volutes on the upper level.

The **Hôtel Paterin** (**L**) also known as "Henri IV's house" at no 4 is an outstanding example of Renaissance architecture. The **staircase** in the courtyard, with its three tiers of arches, one above the other, supported on massive columns, is particularly impressive. To the right is a niche containing a statue of Henri IV.

Palais de la Miniature ⊘ (**Y**) – This small museum has collections of dolls' houses, scenes of daily life, architectural models and miniature cradles in all shapes and sizes. Note also the egg sculptures and the items of origami (folded paper).

For the best view of the courtyard and west wall of the Hôtel Paterin, climb Montée St-Barthélémy to the church of St-Paul.

Église St-Paul ⊘ (**JV**) – St-Paul church was built between the 12C and the 16C, and is now composed of a mixture of Romanesque, Flamboyant Gothic and Renaissance styles. The north wall is supported on the outside by piers topped by pinnacles.

At the transept crossing is a 12C **lantern-tower** consisting of two octagonal domes set one above the other.

Inside, the ogival vaulted nave has semicircular arches opening onto side aisles. In the third chapel on the right, the keystone of the pointed arch has a piece of delightful Flamboyant Gothic decoration, a frieze of angels playing musical instruments. In the south arm of the transept is a chapel with ribbed vaulting connecting five hanging keystones; the one in the centre is shaped like a crown.

Take Rue François Vernay. To the left is Rue Garrand. The main building in this street is the Palais du Conservatoire where the Guignol de Lyon theatre stages its shows.

Exploring the *traboules*

The *traboules* are private property and some are therefore kept closed by their owners. Many of the most interesting are nonetheless open to visitors, under the terms of an agreement drawn up between the city of Lyon, the owners and the urban community. They can be accessed by pressing the entry button usually to be found above the interphone or entry code number pads by each main street door. Other *traboules* not usually open to the public can be visited as part of a guided tour organised by the Lyon tourist office. Before beginning a visit, it is advisable to ask at the tourist office for the list of passages that are open to visitors.

The best time to explore many of the interior courtyards described in this section is in the morning.

FOURVIÈRE
VIEUX LYON

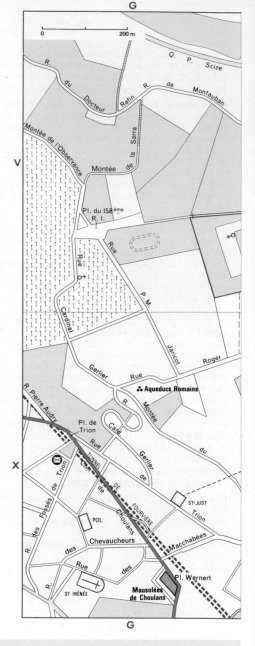

B Maison Thomassin	**L** Hôtel Paterin
D Maison Dugas	**M¹** Hôtel de Gadagne
E Maison Baronat	**M²** Musée de Fourvière
F Maison d'Antoine Groslier de Servières	**M³** Musée de la Civilisation gallo-romaine
K Hôtel Bullioud	**N** Maison des Avocats

Théâtre "Le Guignol de Lyon" (**JV T**) ⊘ – Guignol, the satirical puppet, is characterised by his black cap under which he has a short plait which he calls his "sarsifis". His naivety and waggish banter make him a perfect example of the "urchins" of Lyon.

His wife, Madelon, with whom he has frequent arguments, is a model wife, if somewhat fond of grumbling.

His friend, from whom he is inseparable, is Gnafron whose most notable features are his tall stature and his ruddy nose, an indication of his marked liking for Beaujolais. If anybody asks him what he does for a living, he answers, "Educated people call us cobblers or botchers; the uneducated call us gowks" *(gnafres)*.

In this theatre Guignol shows today are a blend of tradition and modern innovation, influenced by contemporary authors and even films.

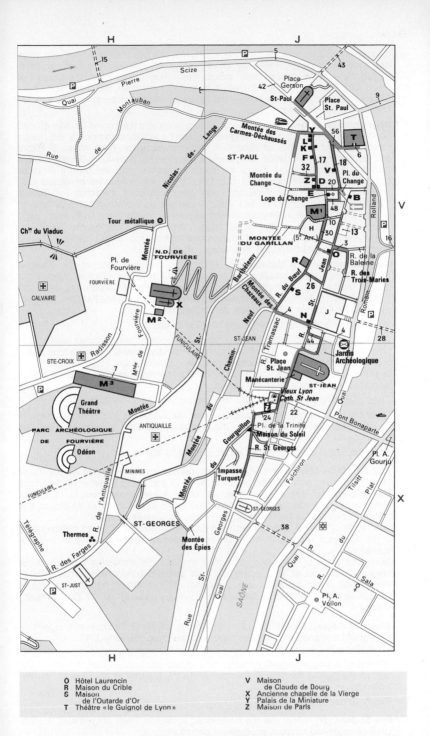

Rue Lainerie (JV 18) – In the courtyard of no 10, note the striking cantilevered staircase. The **Maison de Claude de Bourg (V)** at no 14 has a 15C flower-decked façade which is typical of Lyon, with ornately-carved accolades. On the second floor is a shell-shaped corner niche containing a statue of the Virgin Mary.

Cross Place du Change and go down Rue Soufflot to Rue de Gadagne.

★Hôtel de Gadagne (JV M¹) ⊘ – This mansion stretches from no 10 to no 14 of Rue de Gadagne and is the largest Renaissance building in the Old Town. In 1545 it was purchased by the Gadagne Brothers, bankers of Italian origin who had amassed a colossal fortune. Indeed, the expression "as rich as Gadagne" became a local figure of speech. On the façade set slightly back from the street, note the cant-walled tower and, to the left, the wrought-iron grid of the cellar window, a masterpiece of ironwork. In the inner courtyard, the two main buildings with large mullioned windows are linked by three storeys of galleries. The well, which is topped by a dome covered with scales, was brought here from the Chamarier House (37 Rue St-Jean, *see below*); it is said to have been designed by Philibert Delorme. The residence now houses the Lyon local history museum and the international museum of puppetry.

★**Musée historique de Lyon** – In the local history museum the rooms on the ground floor have been laid out with **religious sculpture★**, including bas-reliefs and sculptures from old churches or abbeys in Lyon, in particular from Ainay, St-Pierre and Île Barbe (Annunciation bas-relief, a mantlepiece known as "Charlemagne's Crown"). The other three floors are partly concerned with the history of Lyon, from the Renaissance period to the 19C. There are collections of glazed earthenware, pewter, local furniture, and an outstanding collection of Nevers faïence dating from the 17C and 18C. Numerous documents relating to Lyon in the days of the French Revolution and Napoleonic mementoes (18C town keys) are also on display. In two other rooms the exhibits describe the history of journeymen, including some of their masterpieces and a few guild emblems. There are also paintings and engravings of the town.

★**Musée International de la Marionnette** – Housed on the first floor of the Gadagne Residence, its exhibits include not only Guignol and a number of glove puppets but also an outstanding collection of string and rod puppets and shadow figures from France, England, Belgium, Holland, Venice, Turkey, Russia and the Far East. South of the Hôtel de Gadagne is the Montée de Garillan.

Walk across Place du Petit-Collège and into Rue du Bœuf.

At no 6, "La Cour des Loges" hotel occupies a fine set of four restored houses. It is possible, with discretion or perhaps stopping for refreshment, to have a look at the beautiful courtyard with its U-shaped galleries on three floors.

In the courtyard at no 3, the handrail on the staircase has been replaced with a wooden banister made to an old design.

Cross over to no 24 Rue St-Jean via the traboule *from no 1 Rue du Bœuf.*

Cross the vast courtyard of the **Hôtel Laurencin** (**O**) which has a crenellated octagonal tower containing a spiral staircase. The loggias on the superimposed galleries have ribbed vaults.

Cross Place de la Baleine and turn into Rue des Trois-Maries.

Rue des Trois-Maries (**JV**) – The street derives its name (Street of the Three Marys) from the niche on the pediment of no 7 containing a statue of the Virgin Mary flanked by two holy women. At no 3 a handsome example of French Renaissance has a staircase surmounted by a tower in the centre of its façade; this feature is repeated in the house at no 5 Place du Gouvernement.

The façade of no 4 is adorned with a regular arrangement of fluted pilasters and, in the courtyard, a tower in which the spiral staircase is clearly visible through the openwork.

Next door, at no 5, there is another shell-shaped niche containing a statue of the Madonna and Child. At no 6, a *traboule* leads across two restored courtyards to 27 Rue St-Jean. From the other side, numerous other *traboules* lead off downhill to the Saône; that from no 9, for example, gives a view of no 17 Quai Romain-Rolland.

Place du Gouvernement (**JV 13**) – The façade of no 5, its doorways topped by wrought-iron imposts and a stone balcony, dates from the early 17C.

The Hôtel du Gouvernement (16C) stands at no 2. The upper courtyard stands at the end of a long passageway roofed with ribbed vaulting. All that remains of the well to the right is the shell-shaped top (note the *traboule* at no 10 quai Romain-Rolland).

Return to Rue St-Jean.

★**Rue St-Jean** (**JV**) – This was the main street in the Old Town of Lyon and, as such, royal corteges and religious processions passed along it.

No 7 has a Flamboyant Gothic façade.

Turn back.

The façade at no 27 has mullioned windows framed by fluted pilasters.

No 28 conceals a magnificent **courtyard★★** with an imposing tower with a spiral staircase inside it. Note the ceiling of one of the galleries which is decorated with an unusual pattern of ribs *(see photograph under Lyon in the Admission times and charges section)*. At no 36, a house dating from the late 15C, there is a polygonal tower containing a spiral staircase. The keystones in the galleries are decorated with coats-of-arms on the first two floors and the well is protected by a shell-shaped canopy decorated with pearls. The niche at the corner of Rue St-Jean and Place-Neuve-St-Jean contains a statue of John the Baptist.

The old Hôtel de la Chamarerie at no 37 was built in the 16C for the cleric responsible for overseeing the cathedral cloisters, who was known as the *chamarier*. The façade, which was modified in the 19C, is in the Flamboyant Gothic style.

At no 54, the longest *traboule* in Old Lyon crosses five courtyards before getting to 27 Rue du Bœuf *(see below)*.

No 58 has an unusual feature in the shape of a well with tripartite roof so that it is accessible from the courtyard, the staircase and the workshop.

Place-Neuve-St-Jean (JV 26) – This old street was transformed into a square under the Consulat. At one end is the sign signalling the beginning of Rue du Bœuf, and at the other a niche housing a statue of John the Baptist. At no 4 is a vast building set slightly back from the others which features a superb staircase over arches corresponding to galleries with flattened arches.

Rue du Bœuf (JV) – This street owes its name to the statue of an ox (or more precisely a bull!) at the corner of

Tour Rose, Rue du Bœuf

the Place Neuve St-Jean, a work attributed to M. Hendricy. The street contains some lovely examples of Renaissance architecture, some of which are occupied by luxury hotels.

No 14 leads into a pretty courtyard with a polygonal tower and galleries supported on ogee arches surmounted by a frieze of Greek motifs.

The **Maison du Crible★ (R)** at no 16 dates from the 17C. It has an ornate doorway with bosses and ringed columns topped by a pediment decorated with a small carving of the Adoration of the Magi said to have been the work of Giambologna. An alleyway with ogival vaulting supported on carved corbels leads to an inner courtyard in which the elegant round tower, with staggered openings, owes its name, Tour Rose or the "Pink Tower", to the colour of its famous roughcast. *Do not go up to the terraced gardens.*

The "Tour Rose" is also the name of the famous hotel complex which has moved to no 22. It is possible, with permission from the hotel, to have a look at its two terraced courtyards. A drink in the hotel bar will enable to you see one of the two remaining real tennis courts in Old Lyon.

The **Maison de l'Outarde d'Or** (House of the Golden Bustard) **(S)** stands out at no 19 because of its carved stone sign. The courtyard is particularly interesting for its two turrets. One of them is round and built over a squinch; the other, corbelled, turret is a rectangle built on an upturned pyramid. Other buildings of interest can be seen at no 23 (moulding on the mullioned windows and the spiral staircase with openings supported on arches), no 27 (the longest *traboule* in Lyon, leading to no 54 Rue St-Jean) with an elegant 16C spiral staircase preceding a succession of three courtyards, and no 29 (wrought-iron balconies decorating the galleries in the courtyard).

No 36 opens onto a pretty courtyard decorated with restored galleries. It is interesting to compare these *(turn round)* with those of no 38, which are largely sealed up by additional structures. Most of the galleries were closed off when the district's fortunes sank, to make more space and to keep in some heat.

Go down Rue de la Bombarde.

Maison des Avocats (JV N) – The arcading in the galleries of the Barristers' House is supported on massive columns and the outbuildings have pink roughcast. Seen from Rue de la Bombarde, the house presents a fine example of 16C architecture in the Italian style.

Walk past the Palais de Justice to no 52 Rue St Jean.

The house of printer Guillaume Leroy (late 15C) has a spiral staircase in a round tower. The bays are supported on arches.

Turn back as far as no 37 Rue St-Jean.

The house at no 37, built for the member of the cathedral chapter responsible for finance and procurements, has a strange spiral staircase with shell-shaped squinches set into the corners.

Take Rue Ste-Croix.

Jardin archéologique (JX) – In this archaeological garden visitors can see the remains of the four buildings which have occupied the former site of the church of St-Étienne to the north of the present cathedral, since the 4C. They include Gallo-Roman baths, a Palaeo-Christian baptistery, and an arch from the 15C church of Ste-Croix.

Place St-Jean (JX) – In the centre of the square is a fountain with four basins topped by a small open-work pavilion containing a sculpture of the Baptism of Christ. To the east of the square is the cathedral of St-Jean and the choir school.

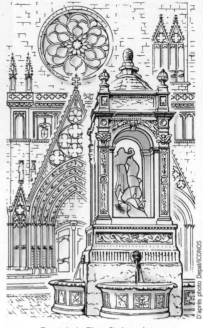

Fountain in Place St-Jean, Lyon

★**Primatiale St-Jean (JX)** ⊘ – Dating originally from the 11C, St-Jean cathedral is a Gothic building erected to complete a Romanesque apse. On the exterior the most notable features are the four towers, two on the west front and two over the arms of the transept. They are only slightly higher than the nave.

In 1245 and 1274 the cathedral was the setting for the two Councils of Lyon. In the following century it was chosen for the consecration of Pope John XXII. In 1600 Henri IV married Marie de' Medici here. More recently, in 1943, the Sixth Grand Pardon was celebrated here. The event is celebrated approximately once every century, when Corpus Christi coincides, on 24 June, with the Feast Day of St John the Baptist, to whom the church is dedicated. On 5 October 1986, Pope John Paul II came here to pray.

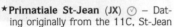

West front – Its horizontal lines are emphasised by the pointed gables on the doorways and the point of the central gable topped by a statue of the Eternal Father. The west front was built in the 15C and constituted the last stage of the building project.

The three portals, with their gables and quatrefoils, were originally decorated with statues but the ornamentation was destroyed during the Wars of Religion by the troops of Baron des Adrats.

The jambs, however, have retained their remarkable early 14C **decoration★**. More than 300 medallions form a sequence of narrative scenes.

On the central portal are illustrations of the labours of the months, the signs of the Zodiac, the story of John the Baptist and the story of the Creation. Those on the left-hand portal depict the stories of Samson, St Peter and the Apocalypse. The portal to the right includes a depiction of the legend of St Theophilus.

Interior – Note the absence of an ambulatory, a characteristic feature of churches in Lyon. The nave, in which the sexpartite arches are supported by slender engaged columns, is a splendid example of Gothic architecture.

13C stained-glass window (detail)

R. Lanaud/EXPLORER

The **chancel★★** is the oldest part of the church, with the apse; the foundations date from the 12C. The decoration in the apse is typical of Romanesque architecture as seen in the Rhône valley. Round the apse is a series of fluted pilasters supporting a blind storey topped by a frieze of palmettes with russet-red cement incrustations *(see Cathédrale St-Maurice, VIENNE).* Another two similar friezes run above and below the triforium which, with its pilasters and semicircular arcading, contrasts with the Gothic arcading in the nave. The Bishop's Throne **(1)** is set against the wall of the apse. Above the simple pillar that forms the back of the throne, note the tiny Romanesque capital representing Christ. The lower windows in the chancel have early 13C **stained glass**. The most outstanding sections are the medallions in the central window, depicting the Redemption. The stained glass in the clerestory (13C) has undergone extensive restoration; the windows are decorated with figures of the prophets.

The rose windows in the transept and the great rose window in the west front have Gothic stained glass. In the north transept is an **astronomical clock★ (2)** ⊙ dating from the 14C. It has a strange chime called the Hymn to St John and includes the sound of a cock crowing, and a set of automata representing the Annunciation. The late 15C **Bourbons' Chapel★** has remarkably elegant Flamboyant Gothic decoration.

Revaud/PIX

Ivory casket (9-10C), St-Jean cathedral treasury

★Treasury ⊙ – *Access from the western end of the south aisle.*

The cathedral treasure, housed on the first floor of the choir school, includes pieces of church plate including a beautiful processional Cross decorated with Limoges enamelwork and a cover from a Rhenish psalter, both dating from the 13C. There is also a bishop's crozier (late 16C) made of silver inlaid with niello, objects and liturgical ornaments that belonged to Cardinal Fesch, and 17C Flemish and Aubusson tapestries. Note the beautiful Byzantine ivory casket (9C) decorated with scenes from circus games.

Manécanterie (Choir School) (JX) – To the right of the west front on Place St-Jean is the 12C choir school. The front of the building, which lost 0.80m/2ft7ins of its overall height when the ground level was raised, is decorated with a blind storey topped by red brick incrustations, colonettes and niches containing statues of human figures. Despite alterations, it has retained its Romanesque appearance.

From the railway station (Gare St-Jean) it is possible to take the funicular railway up to the top of Fourvière hill and come back down the same way after visiting the basilica, Gallo-Roman museum, and Roman theatres (see below). Take Rue Mourguet as far as Place de la Trinité.

Maison du Soleil (JX) – The "Sun House", which became famous after inspiring the backcloth for the Guignol puppet-theatre, bestows an air of old-fashioned charm upon the square. The corner recesses in the façade contain statues – St Peter on the right and the Virgin Mary on the left. The sun emblem is set above a mullioned window on the first floor.

The courtyard within *(access via no 2 Rue St-Georges)* has elliptical balconies.

Rue St-Georges (**HJX**) – The ground floor of no 3 has basket-handled arches and the springer of the door is decorated with two wrought-iron lions rampant. At no 3a the springer is decorated with a phoenix rising from the flames. At no 6, the 16C house has a fine interior courtyard *(art gallery)*. The spiral staircase is set in a round tower with sloping windows. At no 7 the twinned windows are topped with trefoiled arches.

Fourvière Sanctuary *local map Vieux Lyon pp 212-3* (**HV**)

The history of the religious buildings erected in honour of the Virgin Mary on the site of the Roman forum spans almost eight centuries. The massive basilica standing today at the top of Fourvière hill is an integral part of the Lyon landscape.

Notre-Dame de Fourvière (**HV**) ⊘ – The basilica is a famous place of pilgrimage built to designs by an architect named Bossan after the Franco-Prussian war (1870) in fulfillment of a vow taken by Monsignor de Genouilhac, the Archbishop of Lyon, who undertook to build a church if the enemy did not approach the city. Crenellated walls with machicolations, flanked by octagonal towers, form an odd blend of Byzantine and medieval features. The abundance of decoration inside (nave and crypt) is no less unusual. The triple-domed nave has mosaics telling the story of the Virgin Mary and her place in the history of France on the right; on the left is a representation of her place in the history of the Church. By the doorway of the west front is a commemorative stone slab embedded in the pavement recalling the visit of Pope John Paul II in 1986.

Ancienne chapelle de la Vierge (**HV X**) – To the right of the basilica stands the real pilgrimage chapel dating from the 18C: the former Lady Chapel containing a miraculous statue of the Virgin Mary (16C).

Musée de Fourvière (**HV M²**) ⊘ – This museum, housed in the chapel and buildings once belonging to the Jesuit Order, contains a collection of polychrome wooden statues (12C-19C), various projects designed for the basilica in the 19C, and numerous votive offerings.

Viewpoints – From the **esplanade** left of the basilica there is a famous **view**★ over the peninsula and the west bank of the Rhône overlooked by the tower of the Crédit Lyonnais bank *(see below)*. In the distance, to the east, the mountains silhouetted against the skyline are Bugey, Grandris, the Alps, Chartreuse and Vercors.

For a 360° **panoramic view**★★, climb to the foot of the basilica's **observatory** ⊘ *(287 steps, viewing table)*; from there the hillsides of the Lyonnais area, Mont Pilat and Mont-d'Or are visible and, in good weather, also the Alps and Mont Blanc to the west and the Puy de Dôme to the east.

Parc des Hauteurs – This ambitious project was set up to enhance visitors' appreciation of Fourvière hill by laying out panoramic walks. The most original construction is that of the Chemin du Viaduc, a 72m/236ft-long footbridge which gives a breathtaking **view**★ down onto Lyon and Croix-Rousse.

Tour métallique (**HV**) – This metal tower was built in 1893 to the same design as the Eiffel Tower but on a smaller scale (85m/279ft high); it is now used as a television transmitter.

★Parc Archéologique de Fourvière ⊘
local map Vieux Lyon pp 212-3 (**GHX**)

Fourvière archaeological site was opened in 1933 and has brought to light ancient and medieval public buildings in the district. Further work is underway in Rue des Farges (Roman remains) and Rue des Macchabées (medieval village of St-Just).

★★**Musée de la Civilisation gallo-romaine** (**HX M³**) ⊘ – This museum stands on the hill at Fourvière, at the heart of the district that was once the plateau of the ancient town of Lugdunum. The building designed by the architect Zehrfuss is an unusual spiral concrete structure sunk into the hillside. The museum displays thematic exhibitions showing the very high level of civilization enjoyed in the Lyon region from the Neolithic Era to the 7C AD, with particular emphasis on the capital of the Gauls *(see above)*. There is a particularly rich collection of epigraphs.

The prehistory section displays a processional chariot from La Côte St-André, dating from the Hallstatt period (8C BC). Following sections illustrate the founding of Lugdunum, its town planning, municipal and provincial authorities, the army, religions, theatre and circus shows, economic and domestic life, worship of the dead and the early days of Christianity in Gaul. There are a number of particularly outstanding items including a **Claudian tablet**★★★, a fine inscription on bronze of the speech made by the Emperor Claudius to the Roman Senate in AD 48, and a **Gallic calendar** from Coligny, also engraved in bronze during the Roman era. Other items worthy of note are the dedicatory inscription of the Three Gauls amphitheatre, a bust of the Emperor Caracalla, a silver goblet decorated with Gallic gods, some larvae or funeral masks, and a mosaic depicting circus games (wrestling, lion-taming).

Treasures from the temple of Cybele built in AD 160 include the altar and the statue head of an oriental god. The work of potters, glass-makers, ironmongers and goldsmiths is represented in the collection of ceramics, vases, tools and jewellery. Treasure from a Gallo-Roman villa uncovered in 1992 in the Vaise district has been added to the museum's collection.

The room displaying scale models of the Roman theatres contains a large window from which visitors can admire the actual remains.

Théâtres romains (HX) – The group of buildings uncovered near Rue de l'Anti-quaille includes a theatre built during the reign of Caesar Augustus (1C BC) and extended during the reign of Hadrian (2C AD) and an odeum dating from the 2C AD.

Grand théâtre – *See diagram in Introduction.* This is the oldest theatre in France. It is similar in size to those in Arles and Orange (108m/354ft in diameter) but smaller than that in Vienne.

The initial construction dates from the pre-Christian era. The number of tiers of seats was later increased by building on top of the promenades. The paving in the orchestra pit has been reconstructed. The outer circular wall of the theatre shows substructures in which archaeologists have noted the particular attention paid by the builders to exits via underground corridors and to ground drainage through a system of pipes and sewers.

The stage curtain machinery, housed in the orchestra pit, is some of the best preserved of its kind in the Roman world. A model of how it worked is on display in the museum.

Climb the staircase leading to the top of the tiers of seats.

From here, the full size of the theatre can be appreciated. It is possible to walk round the upper section by following the Roman road of large granite slabs.

Walk down the Roman road to the odeum.

Odéon – Odeums were an elegant venue reserved for music and conferences, and were frequented by the élite. The layout is identical to the theatre but the building was on a much smaller scale.

The thickness of the outer wall suggests that the tiers of seats were protected from the elements by a large overhanging roof. Note the delightful geometrical decor of the pavement in the orchestra pit, which has been reconstructed using fragments found on site, including pink breccia, grey granite and green cipolin.

Behind the odeum, excavations have uncovered traces of a portico running alongside a row of shops.

Area overlooking the theatre (HX) – Beyond the paved road behind the theatre, recent excavations have revealed the existence of an impressive residence and not, as was thought at one time, a temple dedicated to Cybele. From the late 1C BC there stood on this huge rectangular esplanade a vast and magnificent house, bordered on one side by shops sheltered by a portico. Early in the 1C AD it was replaced by a large public building. To the east, above the theatre, lie the powerful foundations of an extended platform. At an indeterminate date an enormous cistern was installed here which was no doubt linked to Gier aquaduct.

Aqueducs romains (GX) – On either side of the start of Rue Roger-Radisson (once the road west to Aquitaine) are the interesting remains of one of the four aqueducts which once provided the town's water supply. Note the fine reticulated and diamond-shaped masonry work on the pillars and the alternating stone and brick voussoirs at the base of what were once the arches.

Mausolées de Choulans (GX) – In the centre of Place Wernert are three mauso-leums that serve as reminders of the Gallo-Roman burial ground situated outside the town walls. That in the centre, the oldest of the three (1C BC), bears an inscription on one of the sides indicating that the monument was built by emanci-pated slaves once belonging to Calvius Turpion.

LA PRESQU'ÎLE

One day (2 hr without museums) – local map p 221

Lyon's main city centre districts lie around Place Bellecour. "La presqu'île" – the peninsula – has long been the setting of the Lyon trading centre, and until the 19C commerce centred on Rue Mercière (FT). Two main pedestrian precincts run across it linking Place des Terreaux and Perrache railway station. They are Rue de la République to the north (FST) and Rue Victor-Hugo to the south (EFU).

Rue de la République is bustling with department stores, shops, cinemas and bistros, and the street is lined with buildings typical of 19C Lyon. Their façades incorporate tall windows and lintels decorated with cut sheet-metal signs. Two other shopping streets run from north to south, Rue du Président-Herriot (FST) and Rue Paul-Chenavard (FT).

The districts to the south of Place Bellecour skirt the former Île des Canabae district, the site of Ainay abbey.

Place Bellecour (FT) – This famous Lyon square, overlooked by the distinctive outline of Fourvière basilica on its hill to the west, is one of the largest in France (310 × 200m/1 017 × 656ft). The huge symmetrical Louis XVI façades lining the west and east sides of the square date from 1800.

The equestrian statue of Louis XIV is known to the locals as the "bronze horse". The pedestal is decorated with two bronzes by the Coustou brothers (17C-18C) representing the Rhône and the Saône, each facing in the direction of its respective river. On either side of the pedestal is the inscription: "Masterpiece by Lemot, sculptor from Lyon". An earlier equestrian statue of the great King by Desjardins (1691) was erected on this spot in 1713. The symbol of royalty was overturned, smashed and melted down during the French Revolution. The present statue (1828) was itself threatened in 1848: it was about to be pulled down when the Commissary Extraordinary of the Republic saved it by suggesting that, if the pompous inscription in honour of Ludovicus Magnus were replaced by a homage to the talent of Lemot, this would constitute just as much of an attack on royalty.

To the southeast of the square, the bell tower of the 17C former almshouse, the **Hôpital de la Charité**, stands on its own in front of the main post office.

To the northeast of the square, the Banque Nationale de Paris stands on the site of the cinema in which the first films by the cinematographer **Lumière** were shown.

North of Place Bellecour

Musée des Hospices civils (FT M⁴) ⊙ – This Hospice Museum is housed in the 17C part of the Hospital, whose long façade on the banks of the Rhône was extended in the 18C by the architect Soufflot. It has a fine collection of old apothecaries' jars, pewterware and *objets d'art*, notably a bust by Coustou and a statue of the Virgin Mary by the Lyon-born sculptor Coysevox (Coustou's uncle). Three rooms contain the wooden panelling from the almshouse, which no longer exists. The most outstanding panelling, dating from the reign of Louis XIII, is that from the **Apothecary's Shop★**, which is decorated with carved motifs (the Tooth-puller), and that from the old Archives Room (18C).

Exhibits also include an old hospital bed for four patients and other unusual reminders of medical and hospital techniques in bygone days.

Place des Jacobins (FT) – The main feature of the square is the majestic Dominicans' fountain, erected in 1886 in memory of four local artists, Philibert Delorme (architect), Hippolyte Flandrin (painter), Guillaume Coustou (sculptor) and Gérard Audran (engraver), each dressed in the costume of their day.

St-Bonaventure (FT) – St Bonaventura's church, which the people of Lyon hold dear, has retained its original Franciscan layout.

The generously-sized nave was required for the purposes of preaching. The bareness and simplicity of the architecture, on the other hand, are a reminder of the Franciscans' respect for all forms of poverty. St Bonaventura, one of the most famous of all Franciscans, died during the second Council of Lyon in 1274.

St-Nizier (FT) ⊙ – Tradition has it that the present St-Nizier's church, much of which dates from the 15C, was built on the site of Lyon's very first church. On the outside, the nave is supported by double flying buttresses which can be seen clearly from Rue de la Fromagerie.

The spires on St-Nizier's bell towers are one of the outstanding features of Lyon's urban landscape. The Gothic north spire, built of warm-coloured brick, contrasts with the traceried spire on the south bell tower (19C).

The Renaissance portal is set between four Doric columns and is surmounted by a coffered oven vault; it is topped by a neo-Gothic gable.

The main characteristic of the interior (restored) is its 15C Flamboyant Gothic decoration: the ribbed vaulting includes keystones embellished with coats-of-arms; the keystone in the second bay is covered by a clock; an intricately carved triforium runs round the entire church.

Note the charming **Madonna and Child★** by Coysevox in a chapel in the south transept.

★★Musée de l'Imprimerie et de la Banque (Printing and Banking Museum) (FT M⁵) ⊙ – The first sections show the importance of banking in Lyon and its contribution to the town's industrial and commercial expansion from the 16C onwards.

The following rooms retrace the glorious history of printing, from the first engravings on wood to the discovery of typography, developments in the art of page layout, and modern photocomposition techniques.

At the same time, posters, notices and a large number of old and valuable editions give an insight into the aesthetics of print and books, the development of printing techniques, cutting procedures (prints, carved woodblocks, engraved copperplates, etchings) and pay homage to Lyon's great book publishers, humanists, illustrators and engravers.

Owing to refurbishment work in the museum due to be carried out until 1998, certain rooms may be closed and their works moved elsewhere. Details given below are therefore subject to modification.

The fine arts gallery presents an exceptional overview of art through the centuries, throughout the world. Its collections are organised into five separate departments: painting, sculpture, *objets d'art*, antiquities and graphic arts.

★**Paintings** – The rooms contain a selection of works from the great periods in European painting. Canvases from the Italian Renaissance include *The Ascension* by Perugino, a gift from Pope Pius VII to the city of Lyon, a tender *Nativity* by Lorenzo Costa and a set of Venetian paintings including *Bathsheba* by Veronese, *Danaë* by Tintoretto and two battle scenes by Bassano. There are also works from the Bolognese School *(Moses in the Bulrushes* and *Adoration of the Magi)*, Neapolitan School *(Woman Playing the Clavichord* by Bernardo Cavallino), Florentine School *(St John the Evangelist* by Francesco Furini) and Roman School *(Anthony and Cleopatra* by Pietro da Cortona). The Venetian landscapes of Bellotto and Guardi represent the 18C. Spanish works include the *Legend of St Michael* by Miguel Alcañiz (15C), *The Sharing of the Tunic* by El Greco and a striking *St Francis* by Zurbarán. Among the German paintings are *Christ Carrying the Cross* from the Cologne School and a portrait of a woman by Cranach the Elder. The Flemish and

Ascension of Christ by Perugino

Musée des Beaux-Arts, Lyon/Basset, Calluire

Dutch schools are represented by the *Lineage of St Anne* by Gerard David, *Madonna and Child Surrounded by Angels* by Metsys, and *The Adoration of the Magi* and *St Dominic and St Francis Protecting the World from God's Wrath* by Rubens.

The section on French painting has a large collection of works by 17C masters, including Simon Vouet *(Crucifixion)*, Jacques Stella *(Solomon Sacrificing to Idols)*, Jacques Blanchard *(Danaë)*, Philippe de Champaigne *(Adoration of the Shepherds)* and Charles Le Brun *(Resurrection of Christ)*. The 18C is represented by J.-B. Greuze *(The Lady of Charity)*, Boucher *(Light of the World)* and A.-F. Desporte *(Still Life with Peacock)*. The "Salon des fleurs" heralds the 19C with a graceful statue of Juliette Récamier by J. Chinard, a delightful bust of a young girl by Houdon, colourful floral compositions by Antoine Berjon *(Fruit and Flowers in a Wicker Basket)* and J.-F. Bony *(Spring)*. A large section is devoted to the native artists of Lyon from the 19C including J.-M. Grobon *(Lyon's Old Fishery District)*, Fleury Richard *(Vert-Vert*, the parrot from a convent in Nevers who is the subject of a poem by J.-B. Gresset–see the Michelin Green Guide Burgundy Jura), Pierre Révoil *(14C Tournament)* and A.-J. Duclaux *(Lyon Artists at Île-Barbe)*. Other 19C artists from Lyon with work on display here include Bonnefond *(Portrait of Jacquard)*, Hippolyte Flandrin *(Pietà)* and Louis Janmot whose *Poem of the Soul* – a series of 18 mystic paintings – brings this part of the collection to a close.

Other 19C French masters are represented by an oil painting from David's studio *(The Market Gardener)*, works by Delacroix *(Woman Stroking a Parrot)*, Géricault *(La Monomane de l'Envie)*, Daumier, Corot *(Wheatfield in the Morvan* and *The Workshop)*, Monticelli, Courbet *(The Wave)*, N.-T. Charlet *(Scene from the Russian Campaign)* and Fantin-Latour *(Reading)*. Striking works by Degas, the Impressionists Monet *(Stormy Sea at Etretat)*, Sisley *(The Seine at Marly)*, Renoir *(Woman Playing the Guitar)* – Gauguin *(Nave Nave Mahana)* and members of the Nabi movement,

The Painted Walls of Lyon

The group of artists who painted the Silk-workers' Wall has painted other surprising murals showing aspects of life in Lyon. The majority of these paintings make up the **Musée Urbain Tony Garnier**.

Other interesting murals include:
− *Journey through Time in Lyon*, 98 Avenue Lacassagne (3ᵉ)
− *Lyon, Health, Life*, 115 Avenue Lacassagne (3ᵉ)
− *Introducing Famous Lyon Faces*, 49 Quai St-Vincent (1ᵉʳ)
− *La cour des Loges*, 3 Place Fousseret (5ᵉ)

Bonnard and Vuillard lead into a general overview of 20C painting beginning with compositions by Dufy, Villon, Gleizes, Braque, Jawlensky, Chagall, Severini and Foujita. Contemporary artists include names such as Masson, Atlan, Max Ernst, Dubuffet and de Staël.

Sculpture − From the Romanesque period, there is a fragment from an archivolt depicting a juggler (Bourges), a statue of the Virgin Mary Enthroned from the Auvergne, and capitals from the Rhône valley. European works from the Gothic and Renaissance periods include an alabaster Madonna and Child from Île-de-France (the region around Paris), a Florentine work by Mino da Fiesole representing John the Baptist, a graceful group statue of the Annunciation, a female bust in a medallion from Vienne (Isère), a striking Swabian polychrome woodcarving of the Last Judgement and a Dormition of the Virgin Mary from the Burgos School.

Among the 17C to early 20C works, the most outstanding are two busts (*Colbert* by Coysevox and *Fontenelle* by Lemoyne), the Three Graces by Canova, a series of small busts by Daumier, marble and bronze statues by Etex, Pradier, Bourdelle, Maillol, J. Bernard and Rodin *(Helmeted Minerva)*.

Classical Art − This department consists of three sections organised by theme. The **Egyptian section** contains the most extensive collections covering art from all the Ancient Egyptian periods. The theme of "life after death" is well-illustrated by some magnificent sarcophagi in polychrome wood, amulets and ushabtis (funerary figurines). The Ptolemaic period is represented by the monumental temple doors from Mehamoud. As well as religious practices, everyday life is evoked through steles and funerary masks, instruments and common objects such as a harp, sandals and jewellery. Models in painted wood reproduce scenes showing the main occupations of the Ancient Egyptians. In the **Near and Middle East section**, note the "priest's head" from Assyria, heads of statues from Cyprus and lead sarcophagi from Roman Syria (3-6C). The final section covers art from **Ancient Greece and Rome**, and includes an exceptional Korah (statue of a young girl) from the Acropolis illustrating the degree of skill attained by the sculptors of Ancient Greece. The famous black figure ceramic ware, rivalling the later red figure style in beauty and technique, makes up part of a vast collection of amphorae, kraters, hydria and other vases. A huge variety of artefacts from Etruria, Campania and Lucania bear witness to the creativity which flowed from workshops on the peninsula; note a beautful Etruscan funerary urn in polychrome terracotta and the striking fluted pythos, which are displayed alongside more practical or everyday objects such as rings, bracelets, cooking pots, bottles and jars for toilettries, oil lamps etc.

Objets d'art − This section of the museum comprises a huge variety of exhibits from all ages and all continents. From the Middle Ages there are intricate ivories such as the triptych attributed to the Master of the Soissons Diptych; this outstanding degree of workmanship is also evident in the Romanesque and Gothic enamels, many of which are from Limoges, or in the gold- and silverware (late 15C reliquary arm). Islamic art is well represented with ceramic and bronze ware, and a Persian basin from 1347, with particularly finely worked decoration (silver and gold). There is a set of armour for a horse from the French Renaissance with painstakingly precise ornamentation. This period also encompasses the development of Hispano-Moorish faïence, Italian majolica, some of which is decorated with narrative scenes (1533 plate depicting *Hercules and Cacus*, Urbino) and painted enamels such as the altarpiece with 27 plaques attributed to Jean 1ᵉʳ Limousin (late 16C). Subsequent periods are also featured, with 18C French faïence, the "La Norenchal" drawing room with its characteristically neo-Classical *trompe-l'oeil* decor and Art Nouveau furniture by Hector Guimard.

Note also the Raphaël Collin collection which includes numerous ceramics from China, Korea and Japan (6C to 19C). The collection of over 40 000 medals, dating from Ancient Greek times to the present, is housed in a room with a splendid coffered ceiling.

Place Louis-Pradel (**FS**) − The square is decorated with a fountain and sculptures by Ipoustéguy, and is an aesthetic combination of old and modern forms.

Lyon opera house seen from the Hôtel de Ville

Opéra de Lyon (FS) – On the south side of the square, opposite the Hôtel de ville, stands the new Lyon opera house, the result of a successful modernisation scheme. The façade of the old building has been preserved and the eight muses of the pediment appear to hold up the enormous glass semi-cylindrical roof, the design of the architect Jean Nouvel. Inside, beyond the original Rococo foyer is the concert hall itself, an Italianate chamber with a seating capacity of 1 300, and a restaurant under the glass roof. The building takes on a particularly impressive appearance during the evening illuminations, which floodlight it in predominantly red tones, throwing its architectural contours into sharp relief.

The successful restoration of the building was rewarded by Lyon Opera being promoted to the rank of a national opera company.

South of Place Bellecour

Basilique St-Martin-d'Ainay (EU) – This church, which was consecrated by Pope Pascal II in 1107, has undergone major alteration. The porch-belfry is topped by a pyramid roof, surrounded by unusual corner acroteria which give it its characteristic outline. Note the animal frieze beneath the cornice between the 2nd and 3rd levels, and the decoration of inlaid bricks.

Inside, the nave is separated from the side aisles by large columns dating from Roman times which support semicircular arches. To the right of the chancel, the Romanesque **capitals★** depict Adam and Eve with the serpent, the Annunciation, Christ Enthroned, and to the left, Cain killing Abel, Cain and Abel's offering, St Michael slaying the dragon and John the Baptist showing Christ to his followers.

The south arm of the transept contains St Blandine's chapel, which was originally separate from the main building. Its short crypt is believed to have contained the remains of the martyrs of the year AD 177.

From the corner of Rue Bourgelat and Rue Adélaïde-Perrin there is a good view of the church including the bell tower on the west front and the square transept tower.

★★★**Musée historique des Tissus (FU)** ⊘ – The textile museum, founded by Lyon Chamber of Commerce over a century ago and housed in the Hôtel de Villeroy (1730), former residence of the governor of the province, is the pride of the Lyon people, and a veritable "repository" of decorative fabrics. The prestigious collections come from the most influential countries as regards fabric design and production, and are displayed in large showcases protected from daylight. The museum also houses the International Ancient Textiles Research Centre (Centre International d'Études des Textiles Anciens).

The first room introduces visitors to the various techniques used in the working of silk, to make satin, silk serge, taffeta, velvet etc. After a video on silk working, the exhibition presents examples of **French textiles** with magnificent material manufactured mainly in Lyon since the beginning of the 17C, the period when the Lyon "factory" was renowned for its excellence. Place of honour is dedicated to one of Lyon's most skilled textile craftsmen, **Philippe de Lassalle**, who during the reign of Louis XVI created innovative woven portraits (one of Louis XV, in profile and in cameo, framed by multi-coloured flowers). Note also the **Meuble Gaudin★**, a famous hanging made for Empress Josephine's bedchamber at Fontainebleau.

At the beginning of the 19C, textile artists turned to Classical Antiquity for inspiration, as seen in the "Pompeian motif" panel modelled on the dancers of the Herculanum. In the old theatre decorated with *grisailles* of Psyche, small **portraits on velvet★** illustrate the high degree of precision it was possible to achieve using Gaspard Grégoire's technique (painting on silk thread). The 19C was also marked by the production of printed textiles on a large scale and the fad for "Indian shawls", such as the magnificent **Nou-Rouz★** with decorative motifs inspired by Persia. The French collection finishes with exhibits from the 20C including an Art Deco dress by Mariano Fortuny, a contemporary carpet after Nathalie du Pasquier and *Bucolique* by R. Matta.

The section devoted to the **Far East** exhibits items dating from the 16C to 19C. Japan is represented by embroidered and painted panels, kimonos, and a superb satin collar known as the "cloud collar". From China, there are Imperial robes in K'o-ssu (cut silk tapestry).

The museum possesses a large collection of **liturgical ornaments★** and robes spanning European production from the 12C to 18C. From Italy there are some extremely rare fabrics from Palermo (the fragment known as "St Merry's chasuble", 12C), also fabrics from Venice (13C cope with symbols of the Four Evangelists embroidered in silk and gold thread), sumptuous Genoese and Florentine velvets from the Renaissance period with a stylised thistle and pomegranate motif, and 17C-18C brocaded lampas. There are textiles from northwest Europe, besides priceless examples of the art of embroidery, also typical examples of 15C Franco-Flemish art such as some medallions illustrating the life of St Martin of Tours. Spain is represented by Hispano-Moorish fabrics with motifs strongly influenced by Arabian art, and more from the Mudejar period, and by some remarkable 16C silk velvets. Note the cope given to the first archbishop of Grenada by Isabella the Catholic in 1494. Civil costumes are also on display, with the outstanding 14C **doublet★**, made of 32 sections, belonging to Charles de Blois, as well as various robes and costumes from the 18C.

The museum also houses, in its **Oriental section**, numerous items typically produced by Ancient Eastern civilizations: woollen and linen Coptic tapestries found during archaeological digs at Antinoöpolis, such as the Greek "fish" hanging dating from the 2C-3C; Sassanian fabrics decorated with hunting scenes or animals fighting; delicate embroideries from the Egypt of the Fatimid Dynasty; Byzantine fabrics including a fragment said to be of St Austremoine's shroud (late 8C); or the unusual "long-sleeved knight's coat" (Iran, c 6C). The visit ends with a magnificent collection of **carpets★** – Persian, Turkish, Chinese and Spanish – from the 15C-19C.

★★Musée des Arts décoratifs (FU) ⊘ – This museum is housed in a mansion built in 1739 and is mainly devoted to 18C furnishings. The collection includes pieces of furniture, most of them bearing the stamp of great cabinetmakers (Oeben chest of drawers, Riesener writing desk), *objets d'art*, tapestries (Gobelins, Beauvais, Flanders, Aubusson), priceless pieces of gold- and silverware, porcelain (St-Cloud, Sèvres, Meissen) and faïence (glazed earthenwares). Note in particular the faïence from Lyon, Moustiers, Marseilles and Paris (Pont aux Choux).

Among the sections devoted to Medieval and Renaissance art, the gallery containing over 200 examples of 16C Italian faïence is of special interest.

LA CROIX ROUSSE *about 3 hours – local map p 230*

La Croix Rousse (literally "the russet cross") owes its name to a coloured stone Cross which stood at one of the district's crossroads in the days before the French Revolution. The district still has all the character and flavour of a small village community and today remains the last bastion of true Lyon traditionalism. The most fiercely proud inhabitants of La Croix Rousse are deeply attached to the "plateau" and look down from a distance on the hustle and bustle below. They might even spend months on end without going down the hill. Each autumn, the air is filled with the smell of roast chestnuts and the local crêpes *(matefaim)* as the main boulevard of La Croix Rousse plays host to the "**Vogue**" funfair, an annual event since 1865.

The invention of new looms by **Joseph-Marie Jacquard** (1752-1834) led the *canuts* or silk workers to abandon the low cottages in the St-Jean district and move to large, austere buildings with wide windows that let in the light. In the 19C the streets echoed with the rattle of the hand looms operated by some 30 000 silk workers.

The *traboules* in La Croix Rousse follow the lie of the land and include a large number of steps. They were used to move bolts of silk about the district without any risk of damage from inclement weather. In 1831, and again in 1834, they were the scene of bloody uprisings when the silk workers waved black flags symbolising poverty and bearing the famous motto: "Life through work or death through conflict".

Below are two suggested walks on the hillsides and plateau of La Croix Rousse.

The rooftops of Lyon

Take Montée des Carmélites and Rue Pierre-Dupont to Impasse des Chartreux.

St-Bruno (**KZ**) – This church, built on a terrace, is crowned by a fine octagonal dome with bull's-eye windows and a lantern. The interior is an example of Baroque style. Note the layout of the transept: its arms are concealed by mock apses containing large paintings by Trémolières (18C) – their ornate frames were designed by Soufflot. Beneath the central dome is a monumental canopy by Servandoni covering the High Altar.

Turn back and take Rue Ornano to Place Rouville.

Place Rouville (**KZ**) – From the square there is a fine **view★** over Lyon. Jutting up from the seemingly endless sea of red rooftops on the peninsula is the belfry of the hôtel de ville and the Part-Dieu district overlooked by the tower of the Crédit Lyonnais bank on the left, and on the right, the spires of St-Nizier church. The final meander of the Saône flows past the hill at Fourvière; the belfry of St-Paul church can be seen at the foot of the hill. On the north side of the square, nos 5 and 6 house the **Maison Brunet** (**KZ**) with its 365 windows, a typical silk worker's dwelling.

Head down toward the quaysides of the Saône via Passage Gonin.

To the west, the shady terraces of the Chartreux gardens overlook the river. Note the games areas reserved for playing boules.

Quai St-Vincent (**KZ**) – From the quay there are views over the meander in the Saône overlooked by a row of buildings with Art Nouveau façades (caryatids, floral patterns).

Follow Rue de la Martinière as far as no 35.

École la Martinière des Jeunes Filles (school for young ladies), built at the turn of the century, is a fine example of the architecture of this period, with its polychrome mosaics and wrought-iron entrance. Note the *trompe l'oeil* wall painting at the junction with Rue Terme.

Rue Terme and Rue d'Algérie lead back to Place des Terreaux.

ADDITIONAL SIGHTS

Unless otherwise indicated, consult the plan of Lyon and its conurbation near the beginning of this chapter.

Quaysides along the Rhône – The Quai Augagneur, by the Hôtel-Dieu, is lined with imposing *bourgeois* houses built in the late 19C. This wonderful esplanade beneath the plane trees is enhanced by the lively atmosphere of an open-air market *(except Mondays)*, and is particularly attractive in misty weather, when the river is turbulent and fast-flowing. The district of Les Brotteaux (**BP**), with its geometrically laid out streets, stretches to the east; it lies on the site of sandbanks (or *brotteaux*) once deposited by the Rhône, hence its name. From Wilson bridge (**FT**) – *see the plan of La Presqu'île* – the **view★** extends to the heights of La Croix Rousse on the other bank, where the tall houses of the former silk workers rise one above the other.

To the south of Wilson bridge is La Guillotière bridge, built in 1958 to replace the one built in the 13C by the Pontiffs. It offers a fine **view** over Fourvière hill.

LA CROIX-ROUSSE

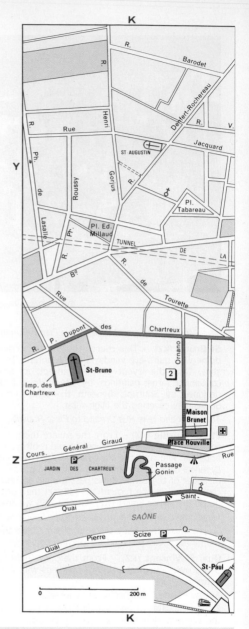

B « Condition publique des Soies »   **D** Statue de J.-M. Jacquard

★**Parc de la Tête d'Or** (**BCP**) ⊙ – The English-style gardens surrounding the Conference Centres cover an area of 105ha/259 acres. The park's name derives from local folklore, which claims that a golden head of Christ is buried here. The entrance is marked by huge wrought-iron gates. The park is an ideal place for city dwellers to go walking and cycling and there is also a narrow-gauge railway. A subway leads to Île du Souvenir, a small island rising from the lake.

Jardin botanique ⊙ – The **botanical gardens** are laid out to the southeast end of the park and consist of 6ha/15 acres of outdoor plants, great glasshouses containing $7000m^2/75\ 320ft^2$ of lush tropical vegetation including numerous palm trees, and an alpine garden where visitors are taken on a miniature tour of the world's mountainous areas and their plantlife.

★**Grande Roseraie** ⊙ – The **great rose gardens** are laid out between the lake and the Quai Achille-Lignon, and boast some 70 000 plants representing 350 varieties which are a stunning sight between June and October.

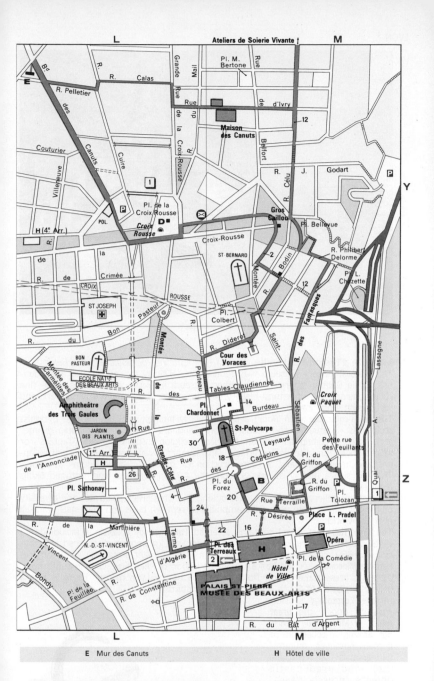

Ateliers de Soierie Vivante

E Mur des Canuts   **H** Hôtel de ville

Jardin zoologique ⊙ – The **zoological park** situated to the north of the botanical gardens is one of the oldest in Europe (1858). It has 1 100 animals including numerous wild animals from outside Europe. East of the zoo lies the deer park.

Cité Internationale (**BCP**) – This vast complex, comprising an imposing conference centre (Palais des Congrès) of 15 000m²/161 500ft², cinemas (14 screens), hotels and a museum of contemporary art, was installed between Tête d'Or park and the Rhône. A new park is planned to bridge the gap between the Tête d'Or and the banks of the river.

Musée d'Art contemporain (**PC M¹⁰**) ⊙ – This new cultural focus in the Cité Internationale complex is built around the atrium of the old market hall. Its modern structure allows for great flexibility of display and for works of art to be exhibited to best advantage. The museum collection is presented as a permanent exhibition juxtaposed with display "areas" which are rotated regularly. The collection is very varied, as since its first acquisition (*Ambiente Spaziale* by Fontana) the museum has been a "production centre" with works by Baldessari, Brecht, Filliou, Kosuth, Yvonnet and numerous other artists.

Tête d'Or park

★★Museum d'Histoire naturelle (BP M⁷) ⊘ – *Entrance on Boulevard des Belges.*
This Natural History Museum was founded in 1879 by the industrialist and scientist, Émile Guimet (founder of another museum in Paris), and houses some fine collections not only of natural history but also of Far Eastern and Egyptian art, and sections on ethnography.

The **Asian collections** *(5th floor)* are particularly interesting. They include Buddhist sculptures – statuettes and heads – from Gandhara (India) and Cambodia (Khmer art), objects relating to Tibetan tantrism (religion inspired by the "Tantras" or sacred books) and Chinese ceramics. Japanese art is represented by ancient weapons and, more especially, a reconstruction of the 17C "Stork Room" in Kyoto. There is also a display of masks from the African continent and tattooed skulls from New Guinea.

The wildlife gallery *(4th floor)*, overlooking the Great Hall, illustrates the diversity of the animal kingdom with fish, amphibians, reptiles, birds and mammals from all over the world.

The **Great Hall** *(1st floor)* contains splendid **Palaeontology** collections including the vertebrates that were Early Man's contemporaries (mammoth discovered in Choulans in 1859, cave bears, great hart from Ireland, giant armadillo). The comprehensive **Mineralogy** section has a unique collection of **chessylites**. On the same floor, dioramas present the typical flora and fauna of the Lyon region. There is also a delightful display of South American hummingbirds.

In the **Egyptology** section *(ground floor)*, the **great sphinx of Medamoud** stands out among a collection of human mummies, mummified animals (cat, crocodile etc), and predynastic objects (breccia vases, schist plates). On the same floor, the life of prehistoric man is illustrated in housing, tools and small craft objects. Note the mummies of Peruvian women. Wildlife from the tropics and the Rhône can be seen in the aquariums.

Part-Dieu district (CPQ) – The name of the district ("God's Area"), would suggest that it was once placed under divine protection by a landowner during the Middle Ages.

Choulans mammoth, Musée Guimet

A vast complex, built on 22ha/54 acres of what was once Army land, incorporates government offices, shops, banks and cultural venues.

It is built around a pedestrian precinct (raised 6m/20ft above ground level) and consists of a large number of buildings and towers, including government offices, a hotel, the shopping centre (three floors of shopping arcades covering 110 000m²/1 183 600ft²), the Radio Studios and the Library. To the northeast stands the striking **Maurice Ravel auditorium**, built in the shape of a shell and with a vault spanning 70m/230ft.

The **Crédit Lyonnais tower**, affectionately known as the "pencil" by the locals, rises to a height of 140m/460ft above the town below. It has now become the second most famous landmark in the city after the towers of Fourvière, and its brick-red colour blends well with the rooftops of the old urban districts.

To the east is the new Part-Dieu station built to accommodate the TGV high-speed train. Hotel facilities and residential apartments complete this new development. Modern sculptures and gardens enhance the esplanades.

Level 0 corresponds to the city road network and is reserved for traffic only.

★**Centre d'Histoire de la Résistance et de la Déportation** (BQ M⁹) ⊙ – *12 Avenue Berthelot.*

The museum is housed in part of the buildings which from 1882 to the early 1970s were the Military Medical School and which, from 1942 to 1944, held the headquarters of the Gestapo in this region. The aim of the museum is to keep alive the memory of the events relating to the Resistance and the Deportation of the Jews, in France and in Lyon in particular. It is also a study centre and serves as an archive.

An audio-guided tour begins on the first floor with documents, posters, film clips and recorded discussions with major figures of the time. It shows the important part Lyon played in the formation and development of the Resistance Movement. The events of July 1941, the arrest of the Resistance hero Jean Moulin in June 1943, and the large-scale public executions held here in August 1944 are all recounted.

Another section looks at the Deportation of the Jews and a chronology of their genocide. The importance of propaganda and information in times of war is reaffirmed in the mock-up of a small square pasted with contemporary propaganda posters. An interior has a radio replaying the "personal messages" broadcast from London. Other rooms have clandestine printing equipment and secret radio transmitters.

Musée des Moulages d'Art antique (BQ M⁹) ⊙ – *In the right wing at the entrance to the museum buildings at 12 Avenue Berthelot.* The museum houses a very comprehensive collection of moulds of major masterpieces of Greek and Roman sculpture, preserved in museums in France and abroad. Exhibits of particular interest include moulds of the sculptures on the pediment and frieze of the Parthenon in Athens.

Musée africain (CQ M¹³) ⊙ – *150 Cours Gambetta.* This museum belongs to the African Missionary Society and has three floors exhibiting over one thousand objects from West Africa, particularly Benin and the Côte d'Ivoire.

Among the collections illustrating the everyday life and the social and religious aspects of these countries, note *(first floor)*, the bronze statuettes from Benin, Touareg weaponry and braiding and above all *(second floor)* a set of geometric and figurative weights (Ashanti from Ghana and Baule from the Côte d'Ivoire) used for weighing gold dust. The third floor contains examples of statuettes, masks and other ritual objects from an art steeped in symbolism.

Musée Urbain Tony-Garnier – *Here and there along Boulevard des États-Unis, P14 and P15 of Michelin map no 30.* This group of buildings was built in the 1930s by the urban architect Tony Garnier, a native of Lyon whose most famous landmark in Lyon is the great covered market. Since 1991 many of the blind walls of these large buildings have been decorated with murals painted by a group of artists calling themselves "The City of Creation".

Having chosen to make an open-air museum, this group produced a series of enormous wall paintings on the theme of Garnier's works: Gerland stadium, the clocktower, the covered market... To the south, six more murals are in progress.

Gerland district (BQ) – This district sits opposite the confluence of the Rhône and the Saône and has Tony Garnier's great covered meat market at its centre. The area is one large "science park" and incorporates a high school, the Institut Pasteur, the Institut Mérieux and a sports centre. The International School, built to designs by the architects Jourda and Perraudin, is a glass construction overlooking the **Parc du Confluent** (10ha/24 acres), which offers good sporting facilities.

Halle Tony-Garnier – *R9 on Michelin map no 30.* Garnier created this huge meat market or abattoir in 1914. Its restored gigantic metal framework rises to a height of 24m/111ft and is now the setting for various cultural and commercial events. Its original architectural style is well set off by nocturnal illuminations.

S. Weiss/RAPHO

Île Barbe

Château Lumière (CQ M¹²) ⊙ – *25 rue du Premier-Film, Lyon-Monplaisir.* Antoine Lumière, the father of Auguste and Louis who invented the cinema and the autochrome plate had this residence built between 1889 and 1901 in the majestic style favoured by the wealthy bourgeoisie during the transitional period between the Second Empire and Art Nouveau. The interior is strikingly decorated with lavish wood panelling, sophisticated chandeliers, marquetry floors and floral designs. It houses the **Institut Lumière** and hosts events based on still and moving pictures.
Old cameras are displayed in a number of exhibition halls.

Île Barbe (BP) – From the mass of greenery on the Île Barbe peeks the tip of a Romanesque bell tower. The island was once the site of one of the region's most influential abbeys, founded in the 5C, but is now a quiet area of private housing.

WEST OF LYON

Leave Lyon on ⑨ and follow the D 7 towards Charbonnières.

The road heads towards the vast **Lacroix-Laval park** (119ha/284 acres), one of the "lungs" of Lyon. A small tourist train, **le Furet** ⊙, takes visitors on a tour of the château and park.

★**Château de la poupée** ⊙ – At the eastern end of Lacroix-Laval park stands an elegant 18C château which houses an exceptional private collection of dolls dating from the 18C to the present.
The upper level looks at the manufacture and decoration of dolls, and on the lower level there is a display on the history of dolls as art objects; in each room there are explanatory videos. In a setting mimicking a theatre set, the old ways of making dolls are shown, especially of making their heads: made of papier-mâché until the early 19C, they were then made of wax, porcelain and finally biscuit ware. Both porcelain and biscuit are kaolin-based but porcelain turns white during firing whereas biscuit retains its coloured appearance and is therefore nearer to the colour of the human complexion, allowing a more realistic look on a doll. Biscuit heads are entirely painted.
Further rooms display beautiful dolls' houses and clothes from the 19C. A reconstruction of a contemporary doll-moulding workshop shows the complex techniques involved in making a doll; note the machine for attaching hair to the dolls' heads.
The end of the tour presents, thematically, the extensive **collection of dolls**, including historical, religious and sorcerers' dolls.

⚓ **Charbonnières-les-Bains** – *10km/6mi on ⑨ then the N 7.* Set in woodland formerly worked by the charcoal burners, the Vale of Charbonnières is a traditional holiday resort popular with the people of Lyon.
The ferruginous spring here was officially discovered by a priest in 1778. Pump rooms and a casino were soon opened. In 1900, people flocked to the spa, which quickly gained a reputation for excellence. At present, it provides treatment for the after-effects of burns, rheumatic complaints and poor circulation.

★BANKS OF THE SAÔNE

38km/24mi – allow 3hr – leave Lyon on ⑪

The D 433 follows the east bank of the river, bordered by thick vegetation, as far La Rochetaillée. The river banks are a favourite weekend destination with Lyon residents, who come to stroll along the towpath, or to indulge in a light lunch of fried fish washed down with a bottle of Beaujolais in one of the many riverside restaurants.

★★Musée Henri-Malartre ⊘ – *At the entrance to Rochetaillée-sur-Saône; 2km/1mi after Fontaines-sur-Saône, follow the signposts to the right.* This restored 15C castle purchased by Lyon City Council, and its terraced grounds overlooking the Saône, contain some remarkable collections of motor cars (1890 to 1986), cycles (1818 to 1960), motorcycles (1904 to 1964) and public transport vehicles (1886 to 1935), all in full working order.

In 1929 M Malartre was the manager of a breaker's yard. He began his collection in 1931 with a 1898 Rochet-Schneider with a still-working engine, then two years later bought a unique Gobron-Brillié double phaeton, also from 1898.

Of the 150 **cars** on show, 50 date from before 1914 and 18 were built in Lyon, which serves as a reminder of the fact that there were over one hundred manufacturers in the region in the adventurous early days of the motor car.

Some of the exhibits are unique, such as the Rochet-Schneider (1895), the Gobron-Brillié (1898), the Luc Court (1901) and the Thieulin (1908). Others marked an era in technological developments such as the Model 'T' Ford (1910), the Peugeot B.B. (1913) and the Voisin four-door saloon (1932). The Scotte steam-powered omnibus (1892), the Mildé electric-powered car (1900), and the prototype of the Citroën 2 CV (1936), transformed into a van during the Occupation, were both unique and technologically in advance of their time.

Lorraine-Dietrich (1925), Musée Henri-Malartre

Worth noting also are a De Dion Bouton coupé-docteur (1900); a Marne taxi; a set of three Sizaire cars (1908, 1924, 1927); a Bugatti convertible (1930), Hitler's armoured Mercedes (1942), the Hispano-Suiza (1936) used by General de Gaulle after the Liberation of Paris, and the "Pope-mobile", a Renault Espace used by Pope John Paul II during his visit to Lyon in 1986.

The Gordini Hall displays a collection of **racing cars**, driven by some of the great champions. They include a Rolland Pilain (1923), Talbot Lago (1949) and Gordini (1952).

The collection of **cycles** ranges from the hobby horse to Anquetil's bicycle, not forgetting the amazing "penny-farthings".

Over 50 **motorcycles** are on show, including a Herdtlé-Bruneau (1904), the Koehler-Escoffier (1935) ridden by Georges Monneret, side-cars and a Zundapp (1937) used by the German Army in Africa.

There is also a hall devoted to **public transport**. Exhibits include a double-decker two-way open-top horse-drawn tram (1880; the two horses could be harnessed at both the front or the rear in order to avoid having to turn the vehicle round), the "saloon motor carriage" (1900), the first Lyon trolleybus (1935) and the engine of the "Blue Train", which until 1957, passed by the foot of Rochetaillée on its way to the bathing areas and open-air cafés in Neuville-sur-Saône.

Neuville-sur-Saône – The town lies in a picturesque setting on a bend of the Saône. The **church** ⊘, topped by twin bell towers dating from the 17C, contains a set of wood panelling by Perrache, a well-known sculptor from Lyon (18C).

Trévoux – See TRÉVOUX.

Take the D 933 and turn left onto the D 504 towards Villefranche.

Villefranche-sur-Saône – *See VILLEFRANCHE SUR-SAÔNE.*

★MONTS DU LYONNAIS

The attractive mountains to the southwest of Lyon have a pastoral appearance with chestnut groves and oakwoods.

★Arches de Chaponost (**AQR**) – At the bottom of the Yzeron valley there stand the impressive remains – about 40 arches – of one of four Gallo-Roman aqueducts which together daily brought 77 000m³ of water to Lyon. The sophisticated engineering of this syphon-bridge incorporated an overflow reservoir downstream, where the openings for the pipes are still visible.

Chaponost Arches

★★Signal de St-André – *West of Lyon on* ⑧, *the D 489 to Yzeron. Take the D 122 south to St-Martin-en-Haut and the D 113 southeast for 2km/1mi. 45min Rtn on foot.*
A path off the D 113 leads up to this beacon (alt 934m/3 064ft) from which there is a lovely panoramic **view** *over to the Alps (southeast) and the attractive hanging villages (northwest).*

★MONT-D'OR LYONNAIS

Round tour of 55km/34mi – allow 2hr 30min – see MONT-D'OR LYONNAIS.

La MARGERIDE

Michelin map 76 folds 5, 6, 15, 16 and 80 folds 5, 6 or 239 folds 44, 45

La Margeride is a granite range lying parallel to the volcanic mountains of Velay. It stretches from the River Allier in the east to the high volcanic plateaux of the Aubrac area in the west; its highest point is the Signal de Randon beacon (alt 1 551m/5 041ft).

The highest section, known as the **"Montagne"**, lies at an average altitude of 1 400m/4 550ft. It consists of rounded plateaux covered with vast, monotonous pastures interspersed with forests of pines, fir and birches. North of Mende, the Palais

du Roi and Boulaine plateaux bristle with granite boulders, which have been worn down by erosion and now resemble colonnades or obelisks, and rounded blocks teetering one on top of the other. Below the Montagne are the undulating **"Plaines"** broken up by numerous spurs of rock. The population is denser here, living in large, isolated farmhouses or grouped in small hamlets.

The main resources in La Margeride are timber and cattle, and also uranium. The Music Festival at Saugues *(see Calendar of events)* is a major event.

Since 1975 the **Écomusée de Margeride** has specialised in a study of rural society in this region. The museum helps to preserve the natural and cultural heritage and gives visitors an insight into traditional lifestyles through the restoration of typical buildings, exhibitions, walks and regional discovery holidays.

To the west of the range is the **Gévaudan**, a lower-lying plateau (alt 1 000-1 200m/3 250-3 900ft) that forms a sort of corridor dominated by the Aubrac which has the same physical features as La Margeride.

The southern stretch of La Margeride and the town of Marvejols are described in the Michelin Green Guide Pyrenees – Languedoc – Tarn Gorges.

★ÉCOMUSÉE DE MARGERIDE

This local information centre has its headquarters at **Ruynes-en-Margeride** *(east of the Garabit viaduct)*, and is divided into four main sites:

Tour de Ruynes ⊙ – In the building adjoining this medieval tower, an exhibition entitled "Voyage en Margeride, une aventure de Pierre Plantade" presents the region in an instructive and entertaining manner: soil structure, flora, aspects of rural life, landscapes.

Outside, a botanical garden – **Jardin de St-Martin** – surrounding the tower contains various plants found in the natural environment of the Margeride, mainly heath and peat bog. The inner courtyard evokes the culture of yesteryear by hosting various events in the local tradition.

Domaine de Longevialle ⊙ – *11km/7mi south of Ruynes-en-Margeride, via the D 4 and D 48.* This old squire's house on the south bank of the River Truyère now houses an exhibition on the human and technical achievement that went into the building of Garabit viaduct.

★**Ferme de Pierre Allègre** ⊙ – *17km/11mi south of Ruynes, via the D 4, the D 48 and the N 9.*

This country farmstead, situated in the centre of **Loubaresse** village, evokes the way of life of a typical Margeride peasant family in the late 19C. The restoration is so faithful to detail, including the various domestic appliances and farming implements which would have been in use at the time, that visitors find themselves expecting the Allègre family themselves to materialise and carry on the running of the farm as if they had never left off.

Écomusée de la Margeride, Ruynes-en-Margeride

On the ground floor is the living room which was also used as a kitchen, dining room and bedroom (box beds); the chimney-stove *(tchantou)* made this a cosy place to spend winter evenings with family and friends. At the back of the room is the scullery for work that involved using water. On the first floor are the communal bedroom and a tiny bedroom destined for the eldest son and his wife. Adjoining the main buildings are the byre (ground floor) and the barn (upper floor).

The tour then takes in the rest of the complex, enclosed by hedges of elder and hawthorn, including the woodshed, the bread oven and the bee-hives (in front of the house), the pigsty and the shed (in front of the byre) and the vegetable patch and orchard (to the east). Caravaning enthusiasts should take a look at the hut mounted on a cart (in the shed) used by the shepherd during the summer up in the mountain pastures.

École de Clémence Fontille ⊙ – *5km/3mi southwest of Ruynes on the D 13, or 9km/6mi northwest of Loubaresse on the N 9 and D 13.* This old class-room illustrates what rural primary school education was like at the beginning of the 20C: school benches and desks with inkwells, slates, teacher's desk on a dais, blackboard with a "morally uplifting" sentence written on it, old wood stove. Exhibitions are held on the first floor on themes related to school life.

ADDITIONAL SIGHTS

★★Viaduc de Garabit – *See Viaduc de GARABIT.*

Mont Mouchet – Mont Mouchet (alt 1 495m/4 859ft) is one of the peaks in the Margeride range and, in May 1944, it became one of the main centres of the Resistance in the Massif Central. On 2 June, 3 000 men from the French Maquis pushed enemy forces back beyond Paulhac. On 10 June, after occupying Ruynes-en-Margeride where twenty-seven civilians were massacred, a large German detachment pillaged and set fire to Clavières but were halted by the Resistance Movement and had to turn back to St-Flour. The following day the Germans again attacked Clavières but the Maquis had had time to organise its defences. Until nightfall, the Resistance withstood attack by the enemy; it then retreated.

A national monument to the French Resistance Movement was erected in memory of these battles, facing the Mont Mouchet Forestry Commission Centre that had been used by the Resistance in the Auvergne as its headquarters.

A **museum** ⊙ contains documents and photographs from the war describing the Resistance Movement in the Auvergne and the risks taken by those who fought in the shadows.

Saugues – *See SAUGUES.*

MAURIAC★

Population 4 224
Michelin map 76 fold 1 or 239 fold 29

This small town, which is an important agricultural trading centre, consists of black lavastone houses on the edge of a vast basalt plateau.

★Basilique Notre-Dame-des-Miracles – *30min.* This is the most important Romanesque building in Upper Auvergne. The building itself dates from the 12C but the west door and four spans are early 13C. The belfry has been demolished and rebuilt several times since the 14C.

Exterior – The elegant east end, the first part of the church to come into view, has three apsidal chapels. To the right of the door, on the right side of the building, is a late 14C Lantern of the Dead which once stood in the graveyard. The vast main doorway at the west front is the best piece of Romanesque carving in Upper Auvergne; the tympanum depicts the Ascension of Christ and has the signs of the Zodiac on the archivolt.

Interior – The interior is plain and simple, and the nave is dimly lit from the clerestory directly above the great arches (there is no gallery). There are some interesting furnishings, including two fine 17C and 18C altarpieces in the north and south arm of the transept and, at the back of the chancel, the statue of Our Lady of Miracles carved from walnut wood *(Pilgrimage in early May)*. To the right in the transept is a 16C statue of the Virgin Mary with a bird.

In the south aisle stands the superb multi-coloured Romanesque **font★** carved out of trachyte (a volcanic rock). It is decorated with fourteen arches, each containing a different motif. The artist even depicted himself, next to the tools of his trade. Nearby, on the wall, are the famous "Saracen's irons" which are steeped in legend; in the 11C two men from the Auvergne, who had just been taken prisoner by the

Arabs, prayed to the Virgin Mary of Miracles with such fervour that, the next morning, they were found asleep, with their legs still in irons, in front of the church in Mauriac which stood on the site of the basilica standing today.

Around Place Georges-Pompidou are a few old houses including one with double Romanesque bays.

ADDITIONAL SIGHTS

Monastère St-Pierre ⊙ – This monastery was once a daughter-house of St-Pierre-le-Vif in Sens. It is possible to see a few Gallo-Roman remains, some of the foundations of the Carolingian church (early 9C), the 11C **chapter-house** (columns made of local marble) and part of the **cloisters** (14C-15C) separated from the chapter-house by an arch with double columns.

Hôtel d'Orcet – Now the *sous-préfecture*. This 16C-18C building incorporates the 12C tympanum that decorated the doorway into the monastery refectory; the carving depicts Samson slaying the lion. On the other side of the street is the monumental gateway to the former Jesuit college.

Musée ⊙ – The museum, housed in a former prison, has a range of collections: Gallo-Roman ceramics, religious artefacts etc. There are temporary exhibitions of regional arts and crafts (leather-working, cheesemaking etc).

Puy St-Mary – *Follow the road that branches off the D 678 on the northwest outskirts of the town. 500m further on turn into the hamlet of Les Vaysses; park. Climb up (30min Rtn on foot) to the chapel at the top of the grassy hill known as the Puy St-Mary.* From here there is a panoramic view of Mauriac and the mountains of Cantal on one side and the plateaux on the borders of the Auvergne and the Limousin on the other.

EXCURSIONS

Château de la Vigne ⊙ – *11km/7mi south.* This 15C castle is flanked by two round towers topped by pepperpot roofs, and a square tower that served as a keep and to which, in the 18C, a second building was attached; a watchpath runs around the top. Inside, there are 16C frescoes on the walls and ceiling of the Salle de Justice; other rooms are also well furnished (fine panelling; canopied bed with barleytwist columns; coffered ceiling). The 18C dining room has lovely tapestries, items of Delftware and a huge sideboard.

Salon de l'automobile miniature ⊙ – This collection of model vehicles (Dinky Toys, Solido etc) includes examples of touring cars, utility vehicles, sports cars, heavy goods lorries, public service vehicles...

Vallée du Falgoux★, Gorge de St Vincent★, Château de Chanterelle – *16km/10mi east. See Monts du CANTAL, itinerary* ②.

Northwest Cantal Mountains

Round trip of 40km/25mi – about 2hr. Head northeast from Mauriac on the D 922 and turn right onto the D 678.

Le Vigean – In the small church with its unusual belfry there is a delightful **reliquary★** made of 13C Limousin enamelwork. On the back there is an illustration of the murder of Thomas à Becket, Archbishop of Canterbury.

Follow the D 678 to Pons and turn right onto the D 22.

Anglards-de-Salers – The Auvergne-style church with its octagonal belfry is built in a fairly pure style. It has a ribbed barrel vault and a dome over pendentives. Below it stands the **Château de la Trémolière** ⊙ (15C) which houses a collection of 16C Aubusson tapestries.

Rejoin the D 678.

Moussages – Overlooking a square decorated with an old fountain and surrounded by old houses is the **church** whose Romanesque east end includes carved modillions. Inside is a Romanesque statue of the **Virgin Mary★** in Majesty and a carved wooden figure of Christ.

Trizac – This large farming village has a Romanesque church with a belfry-porch dating from the 13C. Inside, note the capitals in the chancel, the statue of the Virgin Mary seated (12C-13C) and the Baroque altarpieces. The stained-glass windows in the transept and chancel have been largely restored by two master glass artists using recently discovered stained glass dating from the late 15C. The windows depict two scenes from the life of St Nicholas; one of them, an original composition, features a wild duck.

Southeast of the village, in the upper valley of the Marthiou on the sites of Preydefont and Cotteughes, there are a hundred or so **dry-stone huts**, vestiges of dwellings dating from the Middle Ages which are dotted amidst predominantly beech woods.

From the pass, Col de la Bessaye (alt 1 048m/3 046ft), there is a superb view over the Bort-les-Orgues area and the Limousin plateaux to the west, and over the Monts Dore to the north.

The road crosses the alpine pastures and skirts the foot of the columnar basalt rocks in Peyre-Grosse before reaching Valette.

800m from the junction with the D 3 stands the 19C Château de St-Angeau.

★ **Riom-ès-Montagnes** – *See RIOM-ÈS-MONTAGNES.*

MAURS

Population 2 350
Michelin map 76 fold 11 or 239 fold 40

Maurs is situated to the southwest of the mountains in Cantal on a hill beside the River Rance, and is the main town in the **Châtaigneraie** ("chestnut grove") area. The granite plateau is almost entirely covered with undulating moorland and gashed by green valleys where most of the local population lives. Sweet chestnut trees cover the hillsides and, with stock breeding and crop farming (rye and potatoes), provide the area with most of its income.

There is in Maurs, which still has the circular layout dating back to the days when it was a fortress, a definite air of the South of France; this is the start of the "Cantal Riviera" with its flowers and vineyards, and Maurs is the "Nice of Cantal". The Benedictine abbey in Maurs, founded in the 10C, no doubt gave rise to the development of the village. By the late Middle Ages, Maurs had become one of the six "good towns" of Upper Auvergne and the seat of a provostship. It suffered during the Wars of Religion: captured and recaptured by the Huguenots in 1568 and 1583, it was pillaged and ransacked; in 1643 peasant rebels from the Rouergue sought refuge here and the King's troops were forced to intervene. The French Revolution brought serious disorder in its wake, in particular the destruction of the monastery.

Bust reliquary of St Césaire

Church – This former Benedictine minster dating from the 14C is preceded by a carved doorway (15C-16C); inside there is a nave but no side aisles like most of the churches in southern France. In the chancel is a set of fifteen 16C choir stalls topped by eleven 15C wooden **statues★** surrounding the altar. The statue of St John, to the right of the Cross, is particularly expressive – note the way in which he is looking towards Christ. To the left of the Cross is St Benedict, holding a crozier in his right hand and the Rule of the Order in his left.

The chapel on the right contains one of the most remarkable pieces of gold- and silverware in Cantal. It is a **bust-reliquary★** of St Césaire made of wood but covered with silver and gilded copper (13C); it contains the head of the Archbishop of Arles who is shown wearing his liturgical vestments. The statue is especially striking for the strangeness of the wide-open eyes and the symbolic lengthening of the fingers.

J.-D. Sudres/SCOPE

Don't leave anything to chance!
Consult the French videotex service Minitel 3615 MICHELIN
to choose your route, the sights to see, a hotel or a restaurant.

Massif du MÉZENC

The volcanic Mézenc range (the final "c" is not pronounced) forms a natural barrier that divides the rivers flowing to the Atlantic from those flowing to the Mediterranean. It rises to an altitude of 1 753m/5 679ft at Mont Mézenc, which gave its name to the range as a whole.

Extending northwards into the Meygal, southeastwards into the Coiron, the Mézenc forms the centre of a volcanic trail that cuts across the axis of the Cévennes. It is flanked to the west by the granite mountains at La Margeride and to the east by the crystalline plateaux of the Upper Vivarais. A vast tract of land called the **Zone nordique du Mézenc** is popular in the winter months for the **cross-country skiing** it offers; more than 100km/62mi of pistes are maintained around the towns and villages of Fay-sur-Lignon, Chaudeyrolles, Freycenet-la-Cuche, Les Estables and St-Front.

All types of volcanoes – During the Tertiary era, alpine folding broke up the old central plateau in places, causing a series of volcanic eruptions. Where the Mézenc lies today, there were the first craters, though they are no longer recognisable. Later, further eruptions led to the formation of great *planèzes* on the eastern slopes of the Mézenc, followed by huge phonolithic cones. The Quaternary era brought with it the extension of the glaciers, then the last eruptions which filled the valleys with thick flows of basalt.

Despite the erosion, which was particularly marked on the hillside overlooking the Rhône valley because of the lie of the land, geologists can still see, in the rugged terrain of the range, almost every possible type of volcano: Hawaiian where the lava flows were very fluid (planezes on the slopes overlooking the Velay area, and Ray-Pic); Strombolian where the scoria is rough and rugged (Coupe d'Aizac, Bauzon); Vulcanian where the lava has been pulverised into ash and fine scoria (Gravenne de Montpezat); Pelean with thick domes and lava peaks (phonolithic cones such as the Gerbier de Jonc). Throughout the range there are numerous different types of lava: black labradorite; basalt that, in some places, has a bluish tinge but is more commonly purplish-black; and phonoliths, light ringing rocks (hence their name) which are pale grey in colour.

Hillsides with contrasting appeal – On the Velay side of the Mézenc the range looks like a vast, bare plateau. In the summer months it resembles a windswept steppe dotted with low farmhouses crowned with thatched or stone-slabbed roofs. The Vivarais side of the range is rugged terrain, suddenly sweeping down towards the Rhône. The streams have worn the ground down to the granite rocks underneath. On the crest, all that remains of the ridges are the volcanic peaks.

Splendid basalt flows – On the hillsides flanking the valleys, erosion has revealed extensive basalt lava flows that are particularly impressive in the upper reaches of the River Ardèche and its tributaries (the Volane, Bourges, Fontaulière and Lignon). These flows, which now take the form of prismatic columnar basalt, have created famous beauty spots such as the Ray-Pic waterfall, the Thueyts causeway, Pourcheyrolles rock, Jaujac and Antraigues.

Mont Mézenc

A majestic procession – The phonolithic cones that appeared at the end of the Tertiary era form a majestic procession to each side of Mont Mézenc. To the north is Mont Signon (1 454m/4 753ft), to the east Roche Borée and Touron (1 290m/4 193ft), to the southeast Sara (1 520m/4 940ft), Gerbier de Jonc (1 551m/5 041ft), the cones of Montivernoux (1 441m/4 683ft) and Areilladou (1 448m/4 706ft), to the south the dome-shaped Pal and Bauzon, to the southwest Montfol (1 601m/5 203ft), and to the west Rocher-Tourte (1 535m/4 989ft) and Mont d'Alambre (1 691m/4 596ft).

Flora in the peaks – The upper Mézenc has flora which will delight botanists, including a certain variety of groundsel which, in all the Massif Central, can only be found at the summit of the Mézenc: the famous "Mézenc grass" with silvery leaves and beautiful bright yellow flower-heads. The great mountain violet, alpine anemone, all sorts of gentians, globe flowers, arnica, willow-herb and saxifrages are the commonest of the plants but it is when the narcissi flower in June that the mountain acquires its finest appearance. A traditional market of medicinal herbs, known as the "Violet Fair", is held in **Ste-Eulalie** every year *(see Calendar of events).*

★★★ MONT MÉZENC

Access via the Peccata Cross – *3km/2mi northeast from Les Estables. Park at the Peccata Cross (alt 1 570m/5 103ft) then follow the path on the right (1hr Rtn on foot).*

This route climbs up through the woods then twists and turns amid the heather and juniper bushes.

Bear left towards the north summit (1 749m/5 684ft) topped by a cross.

Access via the Boutières Cross – *2.5km/almost 2mi from Les Estables via the D 631 east. Park at the Boutières Cross (alt 1 580m/5 135ft).*

From the rock above the pass at the Boutières Cross, to the right, there is a superb **view★★** over Sara, the Roche Borée and Les Boutières.

Follow the footpath numbered GR7 (1hr 15min Rtn) which climbs up to the left towards the summit.

Head for the south summit via the flat ground in between the two peaks.

★★★**Panoramic view** – From the summit there is a vast **panoramic view.** To the north are the Meygal and Forez mountains; to the west, the Puy basin, the Velay area and the mountains of the Auvergne. To the south lie Issarlès lake and a string of volcanic cones, and to the east the Saliouse and Eysse gorges, both of which cut into the Boutières area towards the Upper Eyrieux, where deep ravines are interspersed with ridges and peaks. Various planes intermingle, forming the fore-ground, middle distance and background, stretching down to the Rhône valley. Beyond it are the Alps, the highest peaks of which can be seen in clear weather.

Weather permitting, the sunrise behind the Alps is an unforgettable sight but those attempting this must leave Les Estables very early in the morning and should be warmly dressed.

Le MONASTIER-SUR-GAZEILLE

Population 1 828
Michelin map 76 fold 17 or 239 folds 46, 47

This large village in Haute-Loire derives its name from the largest Benedictine monas-tery in the Velay area, founded in the late 7C. St Calmin, Count of Auvergne, founded the monastery and became its first abbot. In AD 728 St Théofrède, his successor, was murdered during a Saracen raid. The monastery was raised from the ruins and for several centuries enjoyed an extraordinarily wide-ranging influence. In the late 12C the abbey boasted 235 daughter-houses or priories. The monastery went into a rapid decline in the 16C when commendatory abbots replaced the regular abbots. The abbey buildings standing today, which now house the town hall, were built in the 18C.

Stevenson's Travels – In front of the post office is a memorial commemorating the travels undertaken across the Cévennes, in the autumn of 1878, by the Scottish writer **Robert Louis Stevenson**, author of *Treasure Island*. As much to satisfy his wish to travel as to try and retrace the spirit that once fired the *Camisards*, or Protestant rebels, Stevenson, then aged 28, decided to cross the Cévennes on foot from Le Monastier to Alès, accompanied only by a somewhat capricious donkey. Sleeping outdoors or in any inns he happened to come across (with one menu for all, and all visitors sleeping in the one room), he took twelve days to reach Alès, via Goudet, Pradelles, Langogne, la Bastide, le Bleymard, Pont-de-Montvert, Florac and St-Jean-du-Gard. His travel note-book is a mine of humorous and penetrating observations on the wonderful countryside he discovered and the many different people he met on his way. In the heart of the Cévennes, the nobility of spirit in the local people left a deep impression on him.

His travels were full of comic incidents, which he recounts with glee. To carry the strange sleeping bag that he had had made for himself, Stevenson acquired the donkey which he immediately christened Modestine. The conflict between the obstinacy of the Scottish novelist and the strong will of the donkey from the Velay lasted for the entire trip: "Modestine's pace is quite beyond description. It was something much slower than a stroll, when a stroll is much slower than a walk. She held back each hoof for an incredibly long time..." Finally, a wily peasant supplied Stevenson with a goad, which did wonders for Modestine's enthusiasm.

★ABBEY CHURCH *30min*

The Romanesque church built in the 11C underwent extensive alterations in the 15C.

★**West front** – The façade was built in the 11C. Its volcanic stones of different colours illustrate the decorative technique of Romanesque architects working in the Velay area. The play of colours is most noticeable on the upper storey above the hollow porch, especially around the main window, the corner colonnettes with red twisted bases, and the alternating dark and light keystones topped by mosaic stonework. The cornice along the main triangular pediment is decorated with a frieze of animals, grotesque figures and foliage.

Interior – The mighty grey granite pillars in the nave form a stark contrast to the Flamboyant chancel of light-coloured arkose. Alterations to the church during the Gothic era are obvious in the bays in the nave which, between the original ribbed arches, support quadripartite vaulting; transept and side aisles have retained their Romanesque vaulting. Note the capitals decorating the consoles for the ribbed arches in the nave.

The 15C chancel is surrounded by a small ambulatory opening into five radiating chapels. The second on the right, the last one to be built, is an example of Renaissance style at its purest with its coffered ceiling decorated with coats-of-arms and medallions.

In the north aisle is a fine **organ**★ dating from 1518 (restored) with delicately-painted decoration and fine tracery adorning the loft. It is supported by a carved gallery in which the load-bearing beam bears a hexameter in Gothic script. In the upper section are the arms of the abbot, Gaspard de Tournon, in a shield.

Treasury ⊙ – *In the sacristy off the north aisle.* The abbey's treasures includes a multi-coloured stone *Pietà* dating from the 15C, two lengths of Byzantine silk that were used to shroud the bodies of the founding saints, and a painted wooden statue of the Virgin Mary dating from the 17C. The main exhibit is St Théofrède's **bust-reliquary**★ made of oak covered with silver sheets studded with precious stones.

ADDITIONAL SIGHTS

Musée municipal ⊙ – The local museum is housed in the beautiful vaulted chambers of the **abbey castle** (basement and ground floor). The building which stands today, flanked by four large round towers, was built in 1525 over the foundations of a 14C castle by Charles de Sennecterre (or Saint-Nectaire) whose family provided ecclesiastical dignitaries for the Velay area for more than a century and a half (coat-of-arms with 5 tapers topped by a crozier).

The collections illustrate the history of regional life (lace, traditional costumes), and the prehistoric period in the Upper Loire valley. One of the rooms deals solely with Robert Louis Stevenson; another has an archaeological collection (remains of the abbey). On the first floor in the south tower is the abbot's chapel where there are traces of 17C frescoes.

St-Jean – At the southernmost end of the village stands the old parish church of St-Jean, built in the 9C and altered in the 15C; it has a certain austere elegance.

EXCURSIONS

La Recoumène Viaduct – *2km/1mi. Leave Le Monastier on the D 500 east towards Fay, and turn right onto the D 535 towards Aubenas.* This fine piece of engineering crossing the Gazeille rises to a height of almost 66m/215ft. It was built between 1921 and 1925. Its eight basalt arches were designed to provide a link between the Le Puy-Niègles (Ardèche) railway line but the line was never brought into service.

Château de Vachères – *7.5km/5mi southeast of Le Monastier on the D 38. Private.* A massive keep flanked by towers with pepperpot roofs gives this 13C castle with its blocks of black basalt outlined in white mortar a typically Velay-style appearance.

Le MONT-DORE ✚✚

Population 1 975
Michelin map 73 fold 13 or 239 fold 18 – Local map under Monts DORE

Le Mont-Dore stretches out along the banks of the upper reaches of the River Dordogne at an altitude of 1 050m/3 413ft, in a magnificent corrie in the shadow of the Puy de Sancy; it is a spa town (the season lasts from mid-May to early October) and a remarkably well-equipped winter sports resort. The slopes (30km/19mi of pistes) cover the north face of the Puy de Sancy and the slopes of Le Capucin. Paths that are waymarked in winter provide an opportunity to discover the unexpected beauty of the volcanic landscape under snow.

In summer the resort offers a wide range of leisure facilities and is an ideal base for ramblers or those touring by car.

THE SPA TOWN

The waters were used by the Gauls in swimming pools, the remains of which have been discovered beneath the Roman baths. The latter were a splendid sight and much larger than the present establishment in which it is possible to see the surviving sections. It was not until Louis XIV's reign that the "Mont d'Or", as Mme de Sévigné wrote, regained its clientele – in spite of the fact that there was no road to the resort. The road was not built until the 18C, and the fashion for "taking the waters" arrived in the 19C thanks to the works of Dr Michel Bertrand and the visit here by the turbulent Duchesse de Berry in 1821.

The water has the highest silica content in France and is heavily-charged with carbon dioxide. It flows out from lava seams inside the pump rooms at temperatures of between 38°C and 44°C/100°F and 111°F. The best-known springs are Madeleine, César, les Chanteurs and Ramond. The water is used in drinks, inhalations, sprays, baths and showers, to treat asthma, respiratory disorders and rheumatism (in this latter case, thermal gases are also injected sub-cutaneously).

MONT-DORE

Favart (R.)	**Y** 12
Panthéon (Pl. du)	**Z** 22
République (Pl. de la)	**Z** 26
Rigny (R.)	**Z** 28
Apollinaire (R. S.)	**Y** 2
Artistes (Promenade des)	**Z**
Belges (Av. des)	**Y**
Bertrand (Av. M.)	**Y**
Chazotte (R. Capitaine)	**Y** 4
Clemenceau (Av.)	**Z** 5
Clermont (Av. de)	**Y** 8
Crouzets (Av. des)	**Y**
Dr-Claude (R.)	**Y**
Duchâtel (R.)	**Z** 9
Ferry (Av. J.)	**YZ**
Gaulle (Pl. Ch.-de)	**Y** 14
Guyot-Dessaigne (Av.)	**Y** 15
Leclerc (Av. du Gén.)	**Y**
Libération (Av. de la)	**YZ**
Melchi-Roze (Promenade)	**Y**
Meynadier (R.)	**YZ**
Mirabeau (Bd)	**Y** 18
Montlosier (R.)	**Y** 19
Ramond (R.)	**Z** 24
Sand (Allée G.)	**YZ** 29
Vernier (R. P.)	**Y**
Wilson (Av.)	**Y** 30
19-Mars 1962 (R. du)	**Y** 32

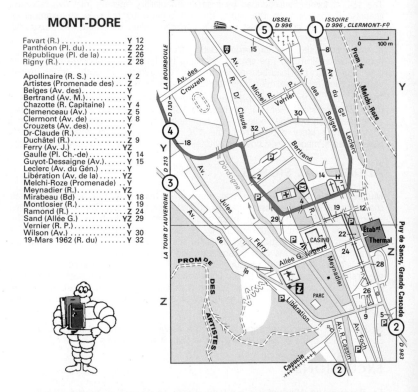

Établissement Thermal (Pump Rooms) **(YZ)** ⊘ – These were built between 1817 and 1823, rebuilt between 1890 and 1893, and later extended and modernised. The interior decoration is impressively ornate, drawing on Byzantine, Roman and Auvergne Romanesque art for inspiration. The most remarkable rooms are the **Hall des Sources** and the **Salle des Gaz Thermaux** on the ground floor, and the **Galerie César★** and the main foyer (**Salle des Pas Perdus★**), with rib-vaulted ceilings painted with frescoes, on the first floor.

Note the height of the rooms, designed to let the "healthy mountain air" infiltrate as much as possible, and the shallowness of the steps, a concession to sufferers of asthma.

Salle des Gaz Thermaux, Établissement Thermal

Promenade Melchi-Roze (Y) – *About 1hr on foot.* This flat path overlooking the town is a delightful place for a stroll in the late afternoon or in cool weather.

Salon du Capucin ⊙ – *8min by funicular then 5min on foot.*
This pleasant clearing, which is a very popular destination during the peak season, lies at an altitude of 1 286m/4 180ft. It is reached by a picturesque funicular railway dating from the Edwardian era.

★**Le Capucin** – *1hr walk from Salon du Capucin.* The path runs for some distance through the woods. From the summit of Le Capucin (alt 1 465m/4 761ft) there is a particularly fine view of Le Mont-Dore and the Sancy valley.

★**Grande Cascade** – *1hr 30min on foot.* This wonderful waterfall drops down a height of 30m/97ft.

EXCURSIONS

★★★**Puy de Sancy** – *4.5km/3mi then 1hr Rtn by cable-car and on foot. See Les Monts DORE.*

Puy de la Tache – *5km/3mi east then 1hr 30min Rtn on foot.*
The road rises in a series of hairpin bends up to the Col de la Croix-Morand (alt 1 401m/4 553ft) where the landscape becomes increasingly rugged and bare.
From here it is possible to walk up to the summit of the Puy de la Tache (alt 1 627m/5 288ft) by following the route of the old ski lift. At the top there is a vast **panorama★★** over the ridge dominated by the Puy de Sancy to the south, and over

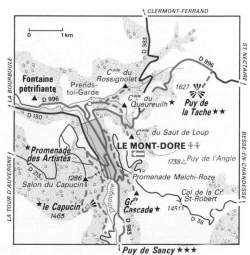

the Puy de Dôme to the north, easily recognisable for its television transmitter. In the valley, note Lake Chambon to the southeast and Lake Guéry to the northwest.

★**Promenade des Artistes** – *About 2hr on foot, 1hr if following the path running down to the tennis courts – see map.* This walk leads through the woods and offers attractive views of the resort.

Waterfalls – *3hr on foot. Leave on ① on the map, the D 996 north, and return via the hamlets of Prends-toi-Garde and Le Queureuilh and ⑤ on the map.*
The most outstanding of the three cascades (Saut du Loup, Queureuilh and Rossignolet) is the **Queureuilh★** which drops down a basalt cliff (30m/97ft) in a very attractive natural setting.

Fontaine pétrifiante (Petrifying spring) ⊙ – *3km/2mi via ③ on the map. For details of petrification see CLERMONT-FERRAND: Additional Sights.*

Le MONT-D'OR LYONNAIS ★

Michelin map 246 folds E, F

High above the Saône upstream from Lyon is the small Mont-d'Or range, an area full of rustic charm. From the peaks there are a number of attractive views.

An island of limestone – From the north, the Mont-d'Or looks like a reef emerging from the ample Saône valley, because of its modest proportions (6km/4mi long and 12km/8mi wide) and the altitude of its peaks (Verdun 625m/2 031ft, Thou 609m/1 979ft, Cindre 469m/1 524ft). The limestone outcrops bring a rich yellow-ochre colour to the landscape. The quarries were first worked in the 15C.

Vegetation and housing – The south-facing slopes are fairly arid and are dotted with wild box and shrubs; the north-facing slopes are more wooded. Orchards, vineyards, flower-filled gardens, meadows and small fields of crops make up the delightful landscape of the inner valleys. Here and there, particularly near Lyon and on the hillside overlooking the Saône, there are modern houses and bungalows; a number of old houses, however, built in traditional southern French style, and fields of crops contained within dry stone walls, can still be seen, especially around Poleymieux.

TOUR OF THE PEAKS

55km/34mi – about 2hr 30min – local map below

Leave Lyon on ⑪ on the town plan under LYON, the N 6 northwest, and turn right onto the D 42 to Limonest. In the centre of the village turn right onto the D 73 then, at the exit to the village, left onto the D 92 towards Col du Mont Verdun.

The road skirts **Château de la Barollière** (18C), flanked by square towers, and provides a number of good **views**★ of the mountains in the Lyon area.

At the pass, **Col du Mont Verdun**, stands a fort built in 1875 *(private)*.

At the pass, turn left.

During the descent there are attractive views of the Saône valley.

Beyond the first few houses in Poleymieux, turn left then right and drive along a dirt track for 200m. Walk up to Croix Rampau (the path climbs up to the left).

★**Croix Rampau** – *Viewing table.* The **panoramic view** extends, in good weather, from the Puy de Dôme to Mont Blanc.

Return to Poleymieux, head for the church, then drive up the valley to Ampère's house.

Maison d'Ampère ⊘ – The scientist **André-Marie Ampère** (1775-1836) from Lyon spent his childhood and early manhood here. His discoveries in mathematics, physics and chemistry placed him among the foremost pioneers in the scientific field in the 19C, though his absent-mindedness is also legendary. In the chapel on the right an audio-visual presentation *(in French)* recounts Ampère's life and work. The "drawing room" gives an indication of the family's lifestyle. The "Three Ampères" chamber recalls the scientist's life, his father's death on the guillotine in 1793, and the life of his son, Jean-Jacques, a historian and literary figure. In the **Musée de l'Électricité**★ is a range of equipment that can be used to carry out basic experiments on electrical currents, magnets etc. A large collection of electronic devices and electric generators help to give a better understanding of the history of electricity.

Follow the signs to St-Didier then, at the first junction, bear left towards Mont Thou.

★**View from Mont Thou** – 50m from the summit *(private: army property)* there is an esplanade commanding a view of the Saône valley, Mont Cindre and the Greater Lyon district.

On the way down from Mont Thou, head for Mont Cindre. Pass to the right of the transmitter and turn onto the D 92 to St-Cyr. In St-Cyr, dominated by its old keep, turn right onto the D 65 towards Limonest then right again onto the road leading to St-Fortunat.

St-Fortunat – The village stretches along its narrow main street on top of a steep rocky ridge. Halfway up the hill is a chapel with a Flamboyant Gothic doorway.

At the top end of St-Fortunat turn left and drive back down towards St-Didier then immediately turn right onto the D 73.

There are views of the mountains in the Lyon areas, with Fourvière in the background.

Return to Lyon via Limonest, on the N 6 and ⑪ on the town plan under LYON.

MONTÉLIMAR

Population 29 982
Michelin map 81 fold 1 or 246 folds 21, 22 –
Local map under Moyenne vallée du RHÔNE

The name Montélimar derives from a feudal fortress, "Mont-Adhémar" built in the 12C by the powerful Adhémar family. The last member of the family was the Comte de Grignan who lived in the 17C and was the son-in-law of **Mme de Sévigné**, the lady of letters. Of the nine gates that were once part of the town walls, only the **Porte St-Martin** (Y) to the north of the town, still stands.
The diversion of the Rhône towards Montélimar feeds the **Châteauneuf power plant**.

Nougat – The nougat industry is fairly recent; originally the confection was made by artisans. In the 16C almond trees were brought to France from Asia; Olivier de Serres had some planted in his estate at Le Pradel (west of Montélimar). The popularity of almond-growing across the entire Gras plateau, and the easy supply of honey from Provence and the Alps, were behind the growth of the nougat industry in Montélimar. In the first half of the 20C factories were opened and production underwent massive expansion.
Most of the nougat shops are on Allées du Champ-de-Mars *(to the north)* and the Marseilles road *(south)*.

SIGHTS

Château (Y) ⊘ – The original fortress (12C) to the east of the town was extended in the 14C by order of the Pope. It was used as a prison from 1790 to 1929. Only the seigneur's lodgings (main apartments) and the watchpath are open to the public.

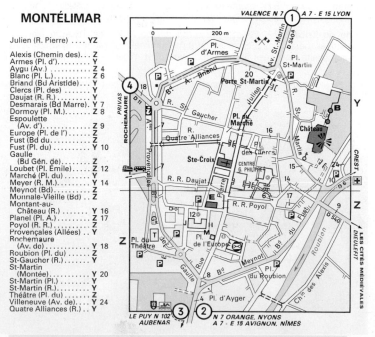

MONTÉLIMAR

Julien (R. Pierre) .... **YZ**

Alexis (Chemin des)... Z
Armes (Pl. d') .... Y
Aygu (Av.) .... Z 4
Blanc (Pl. L.) .... Z 6
Briand (Bd Aristide) .. Y
Clercs (Pl. des) .... Y
Daujat (R. R.) .... Y
Desmarais (Bd Marre). Y 7
Dormoy (Pl. M.) .... Z 8
Espoulette
   (Av. d') .... Z 9
Europe (Pl. de l') ...... Z
Fust (Bd du .... Z
Fust (Pl. du) .... Y 10
Gaulle
   (Bd Gén. de) .... Z 12
Loubet (Pl. Émile) ..... Z
Marché (Pl. du) .... Y
Meyer (R. M.) .... Y 14
Meynot (Bd) .... Z
Monnaie-Vieille (Bd) .. Z
Montant-au-
   Château (R.) .... Y 16
Planel (Pl. A.) .... Z 17
Poyol (R. R.) .... Z
Provençales (Allées) .. Y
Rochemaure
   (Av. de) .... Y 18
Roubion (Pl. du) ...... Y
St-Gaucher (R.) .... Y
St-Martin
   (Montée) .... Y 20
St-Martin (Pl.) .... Y
St-Martin (R.) .... Y
Théâtre (Pl. du) ...... Z
Villeneuve (Av. de) ... Y 24
Quatre Alliances (R.) .. Y

B Tour de Narbonne   **E** Maison de Diane de Poitiers

On the north side is the massive **Narbonne tower** (**Y B**). From the ground floor in the keep, a spiral staircase leads up to the parapet walkway from which there is a vast **panoramic view** westwards over the town and eastwards over the pre-Alps in Drôme. The west front of the main apartments has nine beautiful **Romanesque windows** on the 1st floor.

Old Town – In the centre, around the 15C **Collégiale Ste-Croix** (**Y**), rebuilt after the Wars of Religion, most of the streets have overhanging eaves.

Place Émile-Loubet boasts **Diane de Poitiers' house** (**Z E**) on the north side; it has a beautiful façade with mullioned windows.

EXCURSIONS

Savasse – *Leave Montélimar on the N 7 towards Valence. At L'Homme-d'Armes take the D 165 to Savasse. After about 2km/1mi take the second road on the left up to the television tower, signposted "Table d'orientation".*
From the summit of the mountain (alt 388m/1 273ft), on whose southern slopes is the old village of Savasse with its crumbling town wall and 12C church, there is a sweeping **panorama**★: to the west, the Vivarois slopes with Cruas-Meysse nuclear power station in the foreground; to the north and east, the pre-alps of Drôme, including the Trois-Becs peak; and to the south, Donzère gorge and the Tricastin mountains with Mont Ventoux summit visible in the background.

★**Château de Rochemaure** – *7km/4.5mi via the D 11 northwest – about 45min.* See Plateau du COIRON.

★★**Pic de Chenavari** – *4.5km/2mi from Château de Rochemaure and then 45min Rtn on foot.* See Plateau du COIRON.

★**Défilé de Donzère** – *14km/9mi south on the D 73 and D 144 to Donzère and then the D 486 to the river.* This is a very picturesque canyon through which the River Rhône flows. The vertical wall of the west bank contrasts with the isolated peaks lining the east bank. The sharpest of these is crowned by a statue of St Michael, the guardian of this passage which was once feared by boatmen. This point is traditionally considered to be the gateway into Provence. The bridges upstream and downstream of the canyon offer attractive views of it.

★**La Bégude-de-Mazenc** – *15km/9mi east on the D 540; turn left in the modern village and take the small road to the fortified gateway.* This attractive medieval hanging village, partly-ruined, is a particularly good example of the pretty old villages of this type in the area around Montélimar.

Alba-la-Romaine – *17km/10mi west on the N 102.* Remains of a Gallo-Roman town and a **medieval village**★ surrounding a castle.

★**Grignan** – *24km/15mi southeast on the D 4.* Impressive **château**★★ with fine furnishings where **Mme de Sévigné** stayed with her daughter.

★**Plaine du Tricastin** – *23km/14mi south on the N 7.* The Tricastin plain, with **Pierrelatte** at the centre, is encircled by three mountainous ranges, in which veins of iron and lignite have been found, which were first mined as long ago as the 4C BC

Rock and castle at Alba-la-Romaine

by the Celts. The capital of this region under the Romans was St-Paul-Trois-Châteaux. The area is a transitional one between the north and the south of France, with a climate and vegetation not unlike those of Provence. There is major industry here, most of it linked to the production of nuclear energy, though a zone has been set aside for agricultural use.

Bollène is an agricultural marketing centre and was once one of the richest possessions of the Popes of Avignon. Shaded boulevards mark the line of the old ramparts, and a web of narrow streets lie at the centre. A few old houses and fine doorways, and the attractive former collegiate church, serve as reminders of the town's former importance. Upstream of the town is a hydro-electric power station, which harnesses the energy from the river water trapped by the dam (12m/7ft thick and 195m/640ft long) at this point, producing 2 thousand million kWh per year. Slightly further upstream of this power station is the vast **Tricastin nuclear power plant** ⓥ

MONTLUÇON

Population 44 248
Michelin map 69 folds 11, 12 or 239 fold 6

The economic capital of the Bourbonnais area, situated in front of the first outcrops of the Combraille hills, huddles round the castle that once belonged to the Dukes of Bourbon but its industrial suburbs stretch over a long distance northwards, up the Cher valley.

Successful rebirth – The completion of the Berry Canal in 1841 linked the iron seams of Berry and the coalfields of Commentry. Because of this, throughout the Second Empire when the steel industry began to develop, Montluçon enjoyed rapid expansion. It became the centre of a major railway network and its functions as a trading and administrative centre spilled over into the surrounding countryside.
By the turn of the century, the iron seams and coal faces had been exhausted and the death knell sounded for the smelting works. A serious crisis, with vast social repercussions, hit the town and its surrounding area.
The current industrial activity is fairly diverse and includes electro-mechanics, tyre making, mechanical engineering, chemistry, furniture etc.

Musical Son – **André Messager** (1853-1929), the composer, first became known as a conductor in Covent Garden in London, then in the opera house in Paris. However, he quickly gained a reputation as a brilliant composer of operettas containing a large number of popular and elegant airs, refrains and ballets. One of his most famous performances was in 1902 when he directed and conducted Claude Debussy's opera *Pelléas and Mélisande.*

★OLD TOWN

Start from Avenue Marx-Dormoy and head for the castle.

Château des Ducs de Bourbon (CZ) ⓥ – The castle was built during the Hundred Years War (14C-15C) by Louis II de Bourbon and his successors, Jean I and Charles I.
Banks of flowers climb the old walls, and the castle itself consists of a vast rectangular building flanked, on the town side, by a turret and a large rectangular tower with crenellations.

Turn right into Rue des Serruriers and continue into Grand-Rue.

This old street is lined with 15C houses (nos 42, 39 and 27).
Continue to Place Notre-Dame with its 18C buildings. Stroll through **Passage du Doyenné** which leads to Place de la Comédie. On Saturday mornings this part of the old town is filled with colour and bustle thanks to its flower market.

Notre-Dame (CZ) – The church, never completed, was built on the orders of Louis II de Bourbon in the 15C; it stands on the site of a Romanesque sanctuary of which one apsidal chapel still remains. The south aisle is very plain and is topped by an attractive traceried balustrade. Inside, only the nave and south aisle were rebuilt. On the north side, the Romanesque wall has pointed arches opening onto three side chapels. The church contains a number of works of art: a stone statue of Christ awaiting His torturers (late 15C) at the end of the nave, a 15C *Pietà*, a statue of John the Baptist in the first chapel on the left, and a statue of Our Lady of Montluçon (17C) to the right of the chancel.
The polyptych attributed to Jéhan and Jacques de Montluçon has been temporarily transferred to the municipal museum *(see below).*

Turn left along Rue du Château.

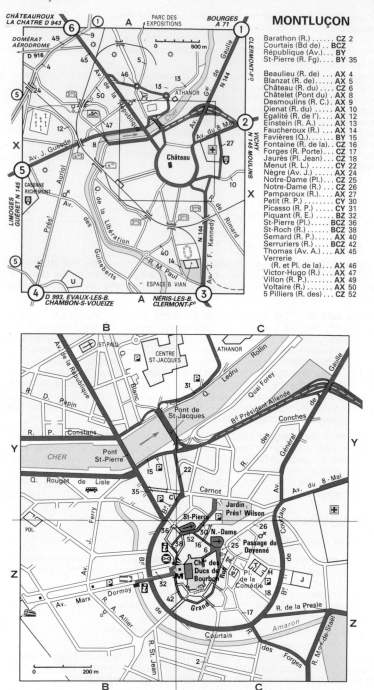

MONTLUÇON

Castle esplanade (**CZ**) – This is a pleasant spot for a stroll. From here there is a **view★** over the entire town, the industrial estates beyond and, in the distance, the first outcrops of the Massif Central, the peaceful Cher valley and the Berry region. On this side, the castle stands in the shadow of the clock tower and its first floor is decorated with a timbered gallery including red and black surbedded brick hoardings.

Musée des Musiques Populaires (**CZ M**) ⊘ – During restoration of this museum (scheduled 1996-99), the majority of the collection of musical instruments is housed in the Château de la Louvière *(see below)*.

Return to Place Notre-Dame and turn left into Rue de la Fontaine.

Rue Pierre-Petit leads to the **Président-Wilson gardens**; Rue des Cinq-Piliers on the left leads to the picturesque Place St-Pierre.

St-Pierre (CYZ) – The church of St-Pierre, built in the 12C and 13C, is hidden by houses, some of which date from the 15C. The impressive cylindrical pillars at the transept crossing give the **interior★** a simplicity and nobility that are totally unexpected.

Narrow passages known as *berrichons* lead from the nave to the transept crossings. There are several notable works of art including the font and a 15C statue of Christ (left of the nave), a 16C *Pietà* in a chapel to the right, a 16C stone Cross (behind the high altar) and, in the apsidal chapels, another *Pietà* and a magnificent statue of **Mary Magdalene★★** dating from the late 15C, "a very young girl with a slender waist, almost still a child" (Émile Mâle).

Auvergne bagpipes (detail)

Musée des Musiques populaires, Montluçon/Th. Charley, Studion Image

Rue St-Roch and Rue des Serruriers lead back to the foot of the castle opposite the statue of Marx-Dormoy, former Mayor of Montluçon.

EXCURSIONS

Château de la Louvière ⊘ – *Leave Montluçon on ② on the town plan, taking the N 145 towards Montmarault. 500m past the hospital, turn right onto the Avenue du Cimetière de l'Est.*
In 1926, François Joseph Troubat, an art enthusiast, had this château built, based on the design of the façades of the Petit Trianon in Versailles. The castle grounds combine French and English style gardens.

⚓ **Néris-les-Bains** – *8km/5mi southeast on the N 144.* This peaceful spa town was once a Gallo-Roman city.

Huriel – *12km/7mi west on the D 916.* 12C **keep** ⊘ and church.

MORESTEL

Population 2 972
Michelin map 88 south of fold 10 or 244 fold 16

The D 517 from Crémieu gives a delightful **view** of the village of Morestel, dominated by its Gothic church and the remains of a 12C square tower. The lovely setting and the special quality of the light here have attracted countless artists since the mid 19C, among them Corot, Daubigny and Turner; this has won Morestel the nickname "Painters' Town".

EXCURSIONS

Round trip north – *25km/16mi – half a day. From Morestel take the D 16 to Creys then turn right towards the plateau.*
Château de Mérieu – The mainly 17C château lies in a magnificent **setting★** on the west bank of the River Rhône, amid meadows and woodlands that stand out on the scarp slopes of the southern end of the Bugey area.
From the terrace there is a view of the Rhône and the St-Alban gorge.
Return to Creys and turn right towards the nuclear power station.
Centrale nucléaire de Creys-Malville ⊘ – From the observation platform at the end of the car park there is view right across the site.
Built on the alluvium of the Rhône facing the mountains in the Lower Bugey area, "Superphénix" is a nuclear power station with a sodium-cooled fast breeder reactor. It was built by the NERSA company and produces 1200MW of electricity. It was an industrially-sized prototype for super reactors and it produces more fissile (energy-producing) material than it uses, thereby ensuring large stocks for the future. This is

the meaning of the stylised phoenix (a mythical bird which rose from its own ashes) painted on the east side of the machine room. The tour *(in French)* takes in two documentaries *(each lasts 20min)* and a short talk, the reactor itself (protected within a cylinder 85m/276ft high and flanked by four steam generators), and the machine room where two 620MW turbo-alternators produce the electricity that is finally fed into the Electricité de France (EDF) grid system.

Return to Morestel on the D 14 and N 75.

Parc d'attractions Walibi Rhône-Alpes ⊙ – *15km/9mi. Leave Morestel on the N 75 south towards Grenoble and in Veyrins turn left towards Les Avenières; the D 40 on the right leads to the park (signposted).*
The park surrounded by lakes has much to offer those who enjoy thrills and spills. In an atmosphere styled on the Wild West, visitors can ride the Big Dipper, the Big Wheel and the water toboggan, and enjoy the "Canadian river" and the "Fairytale Waters" show.
Small merry-go-rounds, clowns and a ranch with ponies provide amusement for younger visitors.
The park can also be visited in a miniature train and the lake crossed by paddle steamer.

MOULINS ★

Population 22 799
Michelin map 69 fold 14 or 238 fold 46

Moulins lies on the banks of the River Allier and is the quietly charming main town of the Bourbonnais area. It boasts a range of economic and industrial activities linked to the rich farmland of the Moulins region, with food industries, shoe factories and machine tool production.
The wide avenues and streets of the old town are an ideal place for a stroll.

HISTORICAL NOTES

The Duchy of Bourbonnais – Bourbon lands first appear in the history books in the early 10C but it took more than three centuries for the Lords and, later, the Counts of Bourbon to create a State capable of competing with its powerful neighbours, Berry and Burgundy. The Bourbons achieved their aim by taking advantage of their geographical location between the kingdom of France and the Duchies of Auvergne and Aquitaine, placing their troops at the service of the crown. In the name of Philip Augustus, Guy de Dampierre led the conquest of the Auvergne and was then entrusted with its protection. Archambaud VIII was a leading figure in the Albigensian Crusade, and Archambaud IX accompanied St Louis to the Holy Land.
This alliance with royal authority, combined with a skilful policy of marriage (Béatrice de Bourbon married Robert Count of Clermont, St Louis' sixth child, in 1265), facilitated the building of a vast state and led to eight Bourbons becoming King of France. In 1327 the Barony of Bourbon became a duchy and, in the following year, it was raised to the peerage by Philip VI.

Arts at the Court of Moulins – The duchy enjoyed its golden age during the 15C and, at the same time, the court in Moulins entered a period of splendour and brilliance, with artists summoned here by Charles I, Jean II, Pierre II and Anne of France. Pierre de Nesson recounted the misfortunes of Jean I; the Flemish musician Jean Ockeghem sang for Charles I before moving on to the king's chapel. Sculpture flourished under Jean II, firstly with Jacques Morel, then with Michel Colombe and his followers, Jean de Rouen and Jean de Chartres. It is, however, the painters who produced the finest works, with Jean Perréal, Jean Richer and above all the **Master of Moulins** who created the famous "Triptych". The court also attracted poets such as Jean Lemaire de Belges and Jean Marot.

Rebellion and Death of the Constable of Bourbon – After his marriage to Suzanne, the daughter of Pierre II and Anne de Beaujeu, Charles III, the ninth Duke of Bourbon, found himself at the head of a state comprising the Bourbonnais, Marche, Beaujolais and part of the Auvergne. His energy and courage during the Siege of Genoa in 1507 earned him his investiture as Constable.
However, hostility suddenly flared between the king, Francois I, and Charles III. Both jealousy by the monarch of the luxury and opulence enjoyed by the Court of Moulins, and advances (in vain) made by Louise of Savoy towards Charles III have been suggested as reasons, though the most likely explanation is that the monarchy, having won over Burgundy and Brittany, had had its fill of the last great principality in France. After being unfairly condemned and losing his lands to the queen mother, the Duke of Bourbon turned to Henry VIII of England and the Holy Roman Emperor Charles V for support in his fight against Francois I. Bourbon was appointed lieutenant general by the Emperor and placed in charge of the enemy armies in Robecco,

Pavia, Milan and finally Rome. Dressed in a white surtout in which he stood out from all around him, Charles III launched the attack on the Eternal City on 6 May 1527. He was killed during the early stages of the battle. His death caused feelings to run high among his soldiers, and they turned to pillaging. In that same year, his lands were confiscated. The Bourbonnais was annexed to the Crown in 1531.

CATHEDRAL DISTRICT

★Cathédrale Notre-Dame (DY) ⊘ – A good overall view of the cathedral may be had from the old covered market, a 17C arcaded building. The towers and the nave (both 19C) are an extension of the former collegiate church built in Flamboyant Gothic style between 1474 and 1507, which includes the chancel and ambulatory with flat east end.

A pomegranate by the lintel serves as a reminder of Charles I of Bourbon. The tripartite vaulting at the east end is supported on engaged pillars that are staggered compared to the pillars in the chancel.

The cathedral is particularly interesting for its works of art and **stained-glass windows★★**, which depict famous figures from the Bourbons' Court.

1) St Catherine's or the Dukes' Window – Late 15C. The window shows the Cardinal of Bourbon on the right and Pierre II and Anne of France on the left, worshipping St Catherine; at the top is an illustration of the life of St Catherine of Alexandria. On the right is a statue (16C) of St Appollonia.

2) Crucifixion Window – Late 15C. The blood of Christ is being collected by angels. The bottom of the window shows **The Entombment of Christ★** (16C).

3) Window of the Virgin Mary Enthroned – Late 15C.

4) Tree of Jesse Window – 16C. On the left, beside the Virgin Mary's family tree, is King David on horseback. The top of the window depicts the Virgin Mary's parents.

5) Elegant spiral staircase.

6) Window of the Suffering and Triumphant Church – Early 16C.

7) Window of the Church Militant – 16C. The Crown of Thorns is given to the King.

8) Chapel of the Black Virgin – The Black Virgin, a replica of the one in Le Puy-en-Velay, serves as a reminder that Moulins was one of the stopovers used by pilgrims on their way to Le Puy-en-Velay and Santiago de Compostela. A wooden polychrome low-relief depicts the death of the Virgin Mary.

9) Chapter Chapel – The centre of the stained-glass window depicts the martyrdom of St Barbara. Note the Holy Trinity above the altar and the Cross of the Cardinal of Bourbon.

10) Classical Painting – Two Carthusian monks.

11) The Annunciation – 18C painting on each side of the doorway.

12) Window depicting the life of the Virgin Mary.

13) St Mary Magdalene Window – 16C.

14) Window of Christ on the Cross – Late 15C.

15) St Elizabeth of Hungary's Window – Early 16C.

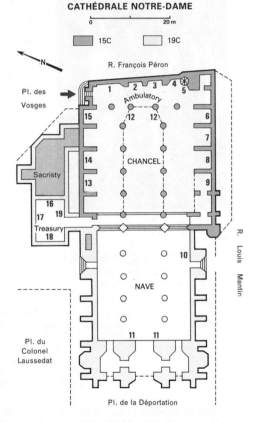

CATHÉDRALE NOTRE-DAME

15C | 19C

★★★Triptych by the Master of Moulins (16) – This splendid painting on wood, probably completed in 1498, is considered to be one of the last masterpieces of Gothic painting in France. There is still some doubt as to the identity of the artist, the names of Jean Bourdichon, Jean Perréal and Jean Prévost have been mooted in the past but the current opinion of art critics tends to favour Jean Hey. There are

TELARC/GIRAUDON

Right panel of the Triptych
by the Master of Moulins

affinities with the Flemish School in the attitudes of the figures, while the drawing of the faces and foreheads suggests the Florentine School. The very human realism in the depiction of the Donors contrasts with the composition of the centre panel which is almost insubstantial and highly stylised. The vivid colours and graceful attitudes of the figures give the work a wonderful freshness. The triptych was commissioned by Pierre II, Duke of Bourbon, and his wife Anne of France (Anne de Beaujeu, 1462-1522).

The outer panels are decorated with a painting of the Annunciation in *grisaille*. On the inside, the Donors are being brought before Christ and the Virgin Mary. On the left, Pierre II kneels in his ducal robes and is being presented by St Peter wearing a richly embroidered cloak. On the right, Anne de Beaujeu is shown in a state of meditation. She is dressed in a gold embroidered surcoat decorated with precious stones, and has a crimson cape round her shoulders. She and her daughter, Suzanne, are being led by St Anne. On the centre panel the Virgin Mary, her eyes lowered towards the Infant Jesus, stands out against a background filled with the sun and a rainbow, which gives great perspective to the picture as a whole. The light emanating from Christ and His mother brings a luminous quality to the entire composition.

The room also contains a 17C ivory crucifix reliquary (**17**) mounted on an ebony stand, the Aubery Triptych (**18**) and the Bethlehem Triptych (**19**) attributed to the 16C Flemish painter Joos van Cleve; the subject matter is taken from the Life of Christ.

Leave by the north door, walk round the east end of the church and go down Rue Grenier, then Rue des Orfèvres.

★**Jacquemart (DY)** – The belfry, topped by a timber-framed roof and a campanile housing the bells and automata, was once the symbol of the town's privileges as a borough. Today, the Jacquemart family announce the time of day for those working in, or visiting, the city. The clock tower was burnt down in 1655 and was again ravaged by fire in 1946. The following year it was rebuilt by public subscription.

Father Jacquemart, in his grenadier's uniform, and his wife Jacquette sound the hours, while their children Jacquelin and Jacqueline strike the half and quarter hours.

Musée de Folklore et du Vieux Moulins (DY M¹) ⊘ – The museum is housed in a 15C building (the 3rd floor balconies over the courtyard are original) with 17C restorations.

The ground floor includes a cooper's shop, cartwright's and carpenter's tools and farm implements. A fine 17C wooden staircase leads to the first floor. There is a reconstruction of a late 19C Bourbonnais interior. Two rooms house a splendid collection of old dolls and costume dolls brought back from travels, and some 160 household irons (box irons, hot presses, irons heated by methylated spirits), the oldest of which dates from the 16C.

The other floors contain exhibitions on life in the home (oil lamps, jugs), mills in France and abroad, the construction of the Moulins bridge, popular crafts and traditions (head dresses, hats, costumes) and religious art (statues, decoration, 17C wood panelling from St-Joseph hospital).

Take Rue de l'Ancien-Palais.

Vieux Château (DY) – All that remains of the Old Castle is a massive keep restored in the 15C and named the "Dishevelled" because of its roof; this was originally the angle tower in the northwest corner of the old ducal palace.

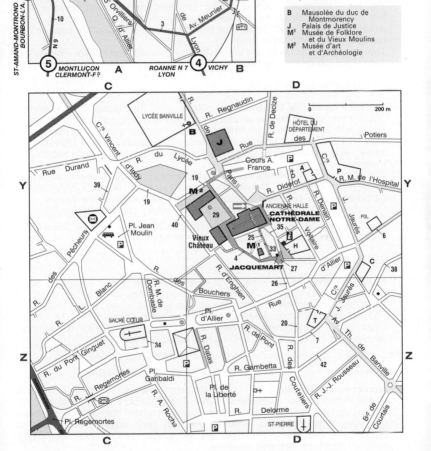

MOULINS

Allier (Pl. d')	**CDZ**
Allier (R. d')	**DYZ**
Flèche (R. de la)	**DZ** 20
Horloge (R. de l')	**DZ** 26

Alsace-Lorraine (Av. d')	**BX** 3
Ancien-Palais (R.)	**DY** 4
Bourgogne (R. de)	**DY** 6
Brechimbault (R.)	**DZ** 7
Cerf-Volant (R.)	**BV** 8
Clermont-Ferrand (Rte de)	**BX** 16
Desboutins (R.)	**DY** 19
Fausses-Braies (R. des)	**DY** 19
Grenier (R.)	**DY** 25
Hôtel de Ville (Pl. de l')	**DY** 27
Jeu de Paume (R. du)	**BV** 28
Laussédat (Pl. du Col.)	**DY** 29
Leclerc (Av. Gén.)	**BX** 30
Libération (Av. de la)	**AX** 31
Montilly (Route de)	**AX** 32
Orfèvres (R. des)	**DY** 33
Pascal (R. Blaise-)	**CZ** 34
Péron (R. F.)	**DY** 35
République (Av.)	**BX** 36
Tanneries (R. des)	**DY** 38
Tinland (R. M.)	**CY** 39
Vert-Galant (R. du)	**CDY** 40
4-Septembre (R.)	**DZ** 42

B	Mausolée du duc de Montmorency
J	Palais de Justice
M¹	Musée de Folklore et du Vieux Moulins
M²	Musée d'art et d'Archéologie

★★**Musée d'Art et d'Archéologie** (**DY M²**) ☉ – This museum occupies the so-called Anne de Beaujeu pavilion, the only remaining part of the extension to the ducal palace commissioned by the princess around 1495.

This elegant construction is one of the very first examples of Renaissance architecture in France and was used in later years by King Charles VIII.

A porch-tower stands in front of the Italianate façade, which has six arcades decorated with the initials of Peter and Anne of Beaujeu and the emblems of the Bourbons (the belt of hope, thistle and stag beetle).

The ground floor is devoted to archaeology, sculpture and medieval painting. In Room I (*gallery to the left of the entrance*), exhibits include a comprehensive collection of prehistoric and protohistoric artefacts (stone tools, rare objects from the late Bronze Age) and numerous items from the Gallo-Roman civilization (smooth and sigillated ceramic vases marked with seals, white clay figurines, bronzeware).

255

Rooms 2, 3 and 4 exhibit **medieval works** from the 12C-16C. The most notable of all the statues from the Romanesque period is a female figure, a poignant sculpture originating from Souvigny. The rich Gothic statuary results from the munificence of the Bourbon Court and includes a portrait assumed to be of the Cardinal of Bourbon, and the *Head of a Young Man* attributed to Jean de Chartres. Note also a striking late-15C varnished terracotta statue of St Louis, pieces of frescoes and various fragments (notably a "weeping mourner" in carboniferous limestone). There are also some superb altarpiece panels from the Austrian School and Flemish School, in addition to a Madonna with Child known as the "Beautiful Madonna", a work by an early 15C artist from Salzburg.

The first floor (Rooms 5 to 10) contains a range of collections. Room 5 has rare 12C Meuse enamel, Limoges enamelware, processional Crosses, pewterware, furniture, tapestries and Moulins cutlery. Room 6 has a fine collection of 16C-18C **faïence** (French and Italian). Room 7 contains swords and fire-arms.

Rooms 8, 9 and 10 house a fine selection of **paintings from the second half of the 19C** including works by Gérome, Bouguereau and Harpignies *(Landscape around Hérisson)*.

Among the canvases Ernest Meissonier painted on the subject of the Napoleonic era, one of the most interesting is *Matin de Castiglione* which was begun in 1890 and remained unfinished on his death the following year. Also on display is the model made by his pupil Detaille for the composition *Vers la Gloire* produced for the apse of the Panthéon in Paris.

The preparatory study of a painting by J P Laurens entitled *Les Hommes du Saint-Office* can be compared with the final work.

ADDITIONAL SIGHTS

★**Mausolée du duc de Montmorency (CDY B)** ⊘ – The mausoleum, completed in 1653, is the work of Parisian artists, the Anguier Brothers, and was commissioned by the wife of Henri II of Montmorency after she was widowed by Richelieu in 1632 and sent to the Convent of the Visitation in Moulins (now a *lycée*, or high school). It was transported in pieces by road from Paris to Montargis and then by waterway.

The Duke, dressed in a finely worked suit of armour, and the Duchess, surrounded by Strength, Generosity, Bravery in Battle, and Faith, lie on a heavy marble sarcophagus. The pediment is decorated with the collars of the Orders of St Michael and the Holy Ghost flanking the Montmorency coat-of-arms.

Palais de Justice (Law Courts) (DY J) – This fine building is a former Royal Jesuit College and is typical of 17C Bourbonnais architecture.

EXCURSIONS

Église St-Pierre ⊘ – *In* **Yzeure**, *1km/0.6mi east via the Rue de Bourgogne,* ③ *on the plan* (**BV**). The village of Yzeure is older than Moulins, and was the seat of the parish until the Hundred Years War. At the back of a vast square stands the 12C-15C **church**, which is dedicated to St Peter and is unusual for its 18C square tower topped by a balustrade. Note the Burgundy style capitals on the main doorway and in the nave. The 11C crypt is particularly interesting.

★★**Souvigny** – *13km/8mi west on* ⑥ *then the D 945. See SOUVIGNY.*

★**St-Menoux** – *14km/9mi west on* ⑥ *then the D 953. See ST-MENOUX.*

★**Arboretum de Balaine** ⊘ – *16km/10mi northwest on* ①, *the N 7, then the D 433 right just past Villeneuve-sur-Allier.* This 20ha/50 acre botanical gardens, founded in 1804, is landscaped English-style and includes numerous species: various types of fir (Caucasian, Spanish, Douglas), giant sequoias, oaks, cedar of Lebanon and local trees. The trees are set amidst beautiful shrubs of rhododendron, azalea, bamboo and dogwood.

★**Château de Fourchaud** – *17km/10mi south on the N 9 to Chemilly, the D 65 and the D 292.* Huge, imposing castle dating from the 14C, with two sturdy towers with pepper-pot roofs and a solid-looking keep.

The **Michelin Green Guide France**.
A selection of the most unusual and the most typical sights along the main tourist routes.

MOZAC ★★

Population 3 496
Michelin map 73 fold 4 or 239 fold 19

Mozac lies at the gateway to Riom and is famous for the capitals and treasure in its church. An abbey was founded here by St Calmin in the 7C.

★ Church ⊘ – It is still possible to see sections of the pre-Romanesque building: the lower storeys of the belfry-porch and the crypt with re-used Gallo-Roman masonry. The church was built in the 12C to a design inspired by the great churches of the Auvergne but underwent major reconstruction in the 15C following an earthquake. During the French Revolution the cloisters and part of the abbey buildings were demolished.

Remains from the Romanesque period include a series of fine **capitals**★★ in the nave and north side aisle which are renowned for their importance in the history of Romanesque sculpture. At the end of the nave are two of these very beautiful 12C capitals; they were originally part of the ambulatory, which no longer exists. One depicts four kneeling telamones and the second, the more famous of the two, depicts the female saints around Christ's tomb, holding jars of perfume in their hands. On another side of the capital is a carving of three soldiers asleep in front of Christ's tomb. Their coats of chain-mail, conical helmets with nasal protector, and almond-shaped shields are valuable illustrations of 12C military armour.

On the approach to the chancel there is a rich Romanesque bestiary visible, with griffins, men astride goats, dragons, a corded monkey (3rd pillar on the left), centaurs, birds of paradise, masks etc.

On the floor of the chancel is a third capital depicting four angels closing the mouths of four other characters; this is an illustration of a passage from St John's Book of Revelations. The chancel also contains 15C stalls. The stained-glass windows date from the same period but have undergone major restoration. In the left arm of the transept, note an unusual 14C wooden Crucifix. Christ is dressed in a skirt and skull-cap, and the Cross is covered in painted cloth. A 15C wood carving of the Madonna with a Bird stands near the baptistery.

The right aisle leads off to the former cloisters where the old tympanum (12C) may be seen.

★★ Treasury – The most priceless object is the enamel **reliquary of St Calmin**★★, which is said to date from 1168. It is displayed in a glass case in the right arm of the transept. The chapel protected by railings in the right aisle contains the reliquary of St Austremoine (17C), one of only a very few painted reliquaries in France.

The sacristy also contains the seal of Pepin the Short – used to seal the relics of St Austremoine when they were brought here by Pepin in the 9C – an 11C Byzantine Crucifix, reliquaries, 17C-19C copes and chasubles and 18C wood panelling.

MURAT ★

Population 2 409
Michelin map 76 fold 3 or 239 folds 30, 31
Local map under Monts du CANTAL

Murat lies in the pleasant Alagnon valley, in a scenic **setting**★★. Its grey houses with stone-slabbed roofs rise picturesquely on terraces up the slopes of the basaltic Bonnevie hill. Two other steep peaks overlook the small town: Chastel rock to the northwest and Bredons rock to the southeast topped by an interesting Romanesque church. Murat stands at the crossroads of Upper Auvergne and is also an ideal centre from which to tour the volcanoes of Cantal and enjoy rambling in the surrounding state-owned forest. Murat thrives on food-processing and chemical industries *(see below)* and skilled trades (masonry, cabinetmaking, stone-slab roofing).

In July there is a large influx of cartoon enthusiasts who come to participate in the annual Strip Cartoon Fair (Fête de la Bande dessinée et du dessin d'humour).

Diatom processing – At the bottom of the valley, powerful chimneys expel water vapour in an often spectacular way. They belong to the factories of the Celite company which treats 200 tonnes of diatomite every day. Diatom is a silica-rich earth extracted from a seam at Foufouilloux (4km/3mi away), containing thousands of fossilised microscopic algae. It is known for its isolating properties and is used in the filtering of foodstuffs and in certain industrial situations but is indispensible to the chemical and pharmaceutical industries. Crushing and drying processes (the earth contains 60% humidity) precedes the final calcination. Over half of the 60 tonnes produced goes to the beer-producing regions in Northern Europe.

Nothing is impregnable to the French – The **Count of Anterroches**, who was born near Murat, is remembered for his reply to the proposal by the English, at Fontenoy, to fire first: "Gentlemen, we never fire first. Fire yourselves." This was not simply a gesture of courtesy but rather an application of the tactic by which troops would come under fire first and then march on the enemy while the latter were reloading their muskets. Anterroches is also credited with another famous saying: as he stood before Maastricht, someone declared that the town was impregnable; "Nothing", replied Anterroches, "is impregnable to the French."

SIGHTS

Notre-Dame-des-Oliviers – The church dates from the late Gothic period but has a modern west front. The central chapel in the left aisle contains a picture by the Spanish School depicting an episode from the life of St Dominic: his pilgrimage to Santiago de Compostela. Another chapel situated in the left side aisle has a Black Virgin which is the subject of an annual ceremony.

Covered market – This is a fine example of 19C ironwork architecture.

Former Bailiff's Court – *Opposite the southwestern corner of the church.* The building dates from the 16C and opens into Rue de l'Argenterie through a doorway decorated with moulding.

Walk down Place Marchande to the junction with Rue du Bon-Secours.

Maison Rodier – This elegant Renaissance style building has some attractive bonding in trachyte (a type of volcanic rock) and a corbelled watchtower.

Continue along Rue du Bon-Secours.

Maison de la Faune ⊘ – The building has a late 15C turret. Inside, a large collection of beetles and butterflies, stuffed birds and animals are displayed in reconstructions of their natural environment.

Turn left.

Tribunal – *Top of Faubourg Notre-Dame.* This small Louis XV building once belonged to a convent of Dominican nuns; it was rebuilt after a fire in 1771.

Consul's Residence – *Faubourg Notre-Dame.* The late 15C stone façade has two storeys with narrow windows topped by an ornament. Note the two carved angels above the door, part of which consists of linenfold panels.

Rocher de Bonnevie – The sides of this hill feature strange basalt columns which are remarkable for the uniformity and length of their prisms. A castle once stood on the hill but it was razed to the ground on the orders of Richelieu; it did, however, take six months and six hundredweight of gunpowder to complete the task...

A statue of Our Lady of Upper Auvergne, clad in white, now stands on the site of the former castle. There is a fine view over Murat, the Alagnon valley, the mountains of Cantal and the Chevade valley.

EXCURSION

★**Albepierre-Bredons** – *2km/1.2mi southeast.*

This tiny village built on a volcanic hill overlooks the Alagnon valley. Underground houses were once built into the caves in the rock.

The small fortified 11C **church**★ ⊘ is all that remains of the Benedictine priory. The doorway on the south side has billet moulding. Inside, note the monumental gilt-wood altarpiece completed in 1710 for the high altar; the intricate detail and abundance of gold and polychrome make this a grandiose piece of decoration. The Resurrection is depicted in the centre. Other giltwood altar screens decorate the chapels.

From the esplanade there is an interesting **view** down over the town and, in the distance, of Bonnevie rock.

MUROL★

Population 624
Michelin map 73 folds 13, 14 or 239 fold 19
Local maps under Vallées des COUZES and Monts DORE

Murol (alt 833m/2 732ft) is set in charming surroundings on the banks of the Couze de Chambon, at the foot of the wooded slopes of Tartaret volcano near beautiful Lake Chambon; it is a pleasant place to stay in summer and an excellent base for sightseeing.

HISTORICAL NOTES

It was a descendant of the lords of Murol, Guillaume de Sam, an erudite baron and patron of the arts, who completed the original, inner fortress by building the keep, the second chapel and the eastern buildings. The castle, after passing into the hands of the powerful d'Estaing family in the 15C, was richly decorated and, at the beginning of the following century, encircled by a huge curtain wall flanked with towers.

Murol emerged victorious from a siege during the time of the Catholic League. Peril having been averted, Jean d'Estaing forsook his vast abode and built the charming pavilion at the foot of the inner castle. Abandoned some time afterwards, Murol was spared by Richelieu because of the d'Estaing family's influence at court. After being used as a prison for some time, it became a robbers' hideout during the Revolution. During the 19C it fell into ruin and the inhabitants of the region came here looking for building stone. Its classification as an historical monument put an end to the pillaging.

★★CASTLE ⊘

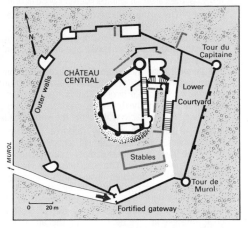

Over the last few years, extensive alterations have been made to the castle. Guided tours and colourful evening shows are organized by the *Compagnons de Gabriel* to provide an authentic medieval atmosphere. Visitors pass through the outer curtain wall through a fortified gatehouse on the southside, passing the Murol tower on the right. The Renaissance pavilion (**1**) stands in the outer courtyard, its dilapidated façade decorated with fine mouldings and pilasters in the antique manner. The windows provide an attractive view of the Capitaine tower.

To the north is the inner castle (*château central*), its 10m/33ft walls rising above a 15m/49ft thick basalt base. Next to the keep, connected to a tower of smaller dimensions by a curtain wall, are the chapels. The first (**2**) was built in the 13C; the second (**3**) in the 15C, and though of greater proportions is less graceful. A stepped ramp leads up to an elegant door (**4**) decorated with the Murol and Gaspard d'Estaing coats-of-arms. In the inner courtyard, note the gallery once surmounted by the Knights' Hall, a 16C door (**5**), the kitchen, the bakery and its outbuildings (**6**). The actual living quarters were to the northwest

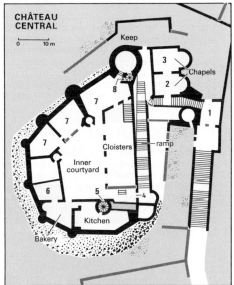

(**7**). A spiral stairway (**8**) leads up to the top of the curtain walls, which can be followed right round the inner castle (several vertiginous passages), and visitors may also climb to the top of the keep from which there is a very beautiful **panorama★** of Murol, the Couze valley, Lake Chambon, the Monts Dore and Tartaret volcano.

EXCURSIONS

★★**Lac Chambon** – *2km/1mi west. See Lac CHAMBON.*

★**Puy de Bessolles** – *See Vallées des COUZES* ①.

Michelin Maps which cover the area described in this guide are nos 69, 73, 74, 76, 77, 80, 81 and 88.

ORCIVAL★★

Population 381
Michelin map 73 fold 13 or 239 east of fold 18
Local map under Monts DORE

Orcival, a small town in a cool valley watered by the River Siolet, has a superb Romanesque church founded by monks from La Chaise-Dieu.

★★**Basilique Notre-Dame** – *30min*. This grey mass of volcanic andesite was probably erected during the first half of the 12C and, to judge by its remarkable stylistic unity, is the result of uninterrupted construction.

Exterior – The many tiers of the rear part of the building rise attractively up to the spire (truncated during the Revolution) of the octagonal two-storeyed bell tower with its twin openings. The very beautiful, although sparsely decorated, east end has four radiating apsidal chapels; one of these, on the south side, encompasses the crypt level.

The panels of the three doors still have their Romanesque hinges and ironwork; the most elaborate, with ornamental foliage and human heads, are on the south door (known as St John's door). Chains have been hung from the blind arcades in the southern part of the transept, next to the entrance, in thanksgiving for released prisoners. A high gable wall forms the west façade.

Interior – The most striking features are the slender pillars and the way the light disperses through the church, through an increasing number of windows from the nave to the transept, culminating in the chancel where most of the light is concentrated. The vaulting is varied – semicircular barrel in the nave; groined in the side-aisles divided into compartments by transverse arches resting on engaged columns; domed in the crossing of the transept supported by powerful arches with triple bays; half-domed in the chancel, which is bordered by eight slender columns topped by elegant foliate capitals. Other capitals of particular interest are to be found in the ambulatory (carved with fabulous animals, birds, fish and demons) and in the nave where most have foliate designs. Only one is historiated, that decorating the 1st pillar to the south, surmounted by the words "Fol dives" and depicting the chastisement of the Miser or Money-Lender. The granite high altar rests on a serpentine marble base. Behind it, on a column, is a famous **Virgin Enthroned**★ with silver and gilt ornamentation. This venerated statue attracts numerous pilgrims, particularly on Ascension Thursday *(see Calendar of events)*.

Under the chancel a vast, well-lit crypt follows the same plan. Note the gilt-lead altar (a modern work by the sculptor Kaeppelin) and a charming wooden 14C Virgin with Child.

EXCURSION

Château de Cordès ⊘ – *2.5km/2mi north*. An avenue lined with hedgerows enclosing two beautiful formal flowerbeds designed by André Le Nôtre (17C) leads up to this charming 13C-15C manor house, restored in the 17C. Inside, the tour includes the drawing room with its plasterwork decoration, the dining room, and the basement rooms including a guardroom with an old well which still has its winch and wheel. The chapel contains the magnificent tombstone of Yves II of Allègre, who died in Ravenna in 1512, and a beautiful Carrara marble altarpiece.

*Travel with **Michelin Maps (scale 1 : 200 000)** which are revised regularly.*

Aven d'ORGNAC★★★

Michelin map 80 fold 9 or 245 fold 14 or 246 fold 23
Local map under Gorges de l'ARDÈCHE

Until 19 August 1935 the people of Orgnac-l'Aven had paid little attention to the swallow-hole known to them as "Le Bertras". **Robert de Joly** (1887-1968), President of the Speleology Society of France, who explored it at that time, then described its wealth of interesting features to them. He was an engineer with the College of Electricity in Paris and an enthusiastic pot-holer. He was also a daring explorer of this area of the Cévennes, where he lived, and he played a vital role in the development of equipment and techniques used in underground explorations. The huge chambers in the swallow-hole were formed by the action of underground water from infiltrations in the cracked limestone rocks. The first concretions, some of which were 10m/33ft in diameter, were broken by an earthquake at the end of the Tertiary era. These truncated or overturned columns then became the base for more recent stalagmites.

Upper chamber, Aven d'Orgnac

TOUR ⊘ *About 1hr*

Temperature underground 13°C/55°F. 788 steps up or down.

The upper chamber, in which there is an enormous, conical rockfall, is amazing for its sheer size and the views in and around it. The dim light from the natural mouth of the swallow-hole gives it a bluish tinge that appears somewhat unreal. The overall height of the underground gallery beneath this opening is 40m/130ft high. It contains a number of magnificent stalagmites, in an incredible variety of shapes. The resemblance of the largest to palm trees is due to their having been formed by a relatively rapid dripping of water infiltrating the cavern. Some have the appearance of pine cones, characterised by a narrowing of their shaft, caused by climactic changes. Other, more slender stalagmites look like piles of plates, as a result of the slow oozing of water through the high, thin roof. Beneath the lower sections of cave roof are slim candle-like formations, with straight or tapering sides. For the most part, the height of the gallery roof has prevented stalagmites from joining up with the stalactites overhead to form columns; instead they have thickened at their base until some reach quite impressive dimensions.

In the niche of a huge formation of draperies and stalagmites like organ-pipes is an urn containing the heart of Robert de Joly.

In the Rockfall Chamber (Salle du Chaos), filled with concretions from the upper chamber, there are magnificent "drapes" of various colours – white, red and brown – hanging from a crack in the cave roof. The varied lighting picks out the stalagmites and stalactites in succession. Here the cave roof is thicker than that of the upper chamber, so stalactites have formed more densely.

The first Red Chamber (Salle Rouge) has fantastic-looking décor centred around colossal pillars of calcite. The red chambers owe their name to the layer of clay, the residue of the dissolving calcite, which covers floor, walls and concretions alike. Here is also where the deepest interior well in the swallow-hole (34m/110ft) leads down to another chamber deep below the surface.

Rando' souterraine ⊘ – Cave enthusiasts may like to take part in this underground ramble, available to groups of restricted size only, through the red chambers, a magnificent part of the cavern which has been left as it was when discovered apart from the installation of electric lighting. This walk is an ideal compromise between standard guided tours of caves and full-blown pot-holing "in the raw", and is not unduly problematic or taxing physically.

Musée de Préhistoire ⊘ – The rooms, laid out around a terrace, contain the finds from archaeological digs in Ardèche and the north of Gard. They date from the Lower Palaeolithic to the Iron Age (from 350 000 to 750 years BC). Reconstructions – Acheulian hut from Orgnac 3, flint workshop, decorated Lion's Head cave – provide an insight into the everyday life of prehistoric man.

Lac de PALADRU ★

Michelin map 88 fold 22 or 244 fold 27

Lake Paladru (390ha/964 acres) lies at the bottom of a depression originally formed by a glacier, surrounded by the green hills of Lower Dauphiné. The lake, mainly supplied by rain and snow, has a tributary at its southern end, the Fure, which flows down to the River Isère. Its beautiful emerald-coloured waters form a lovely stretch 6km/4mi long which, during summer months, attracts many watersports enthusiasts and ramblers from Lyon and the Dauphiné region. Anglers will find a wide variety of fish to test their skill, including char and freshwater crayfish.

The hillside farms overlooking the lake and upper Bourbre valley will appeal to those interested in traditional rural architecture; these houses are remarkable for their enormous eaves, sometimes reaching over the barn almost right down to the ground. The walls are made of mud, sometimes combined with shingle.

WOOD CIVILIZATION

The southern part of Lake Paladru harbours two extremely interesting submerged archaeological sites. Far from reinforcing the existence of lake dwelling communities (houses built on stilts), the discovery of a large number of piles and planks which emerge at low water level proves the existence of houses built directly on lacustrian chalk shoals which were affected on several occasions by variations in the level of the lake.

The variety and abundance of the remains discovered as well as an analysis of pollen contained in the sediment have helped define the nature of the surrounding forest mantle and the daily activities of the inhabitants, who were mostly woodlanders. Wood, which was abundant in the region, was used for numerous purposes, including building and for domestic items.

Summer resort of Baigneurs – This is a neolithic farming village which underwent two phases of successive occupation around the year 2700 BC, both connected with the Saône-Rhône civilization. The presence of axe handles, wooden spoons, flint stones, spindle-whorls and calcinated debris indicate the practice of several different crafts as well as burn-beating after deforestation – fertilisation of the soil by burning felled trees – in preparation for cropping (wheat, poppies, flax).

Village of Colletière – This site to the south, currently under 6m/20ft of water, reveals a fortified village set up towards the end of the 10C, following a considerable drop in the level of the lake as a result the climate warming up. The inhabitants were forced to abandon their belongings and flee the village in early 1000, however, after a sudden rise in the water level. Colletière is of great archaeological interest because the total immersion of the site has protected it from pillage or decay.

The inhabitants were farmers, stock-breeders and fishermen. The good state of preservation of the dwellings has enabled specialists to reconstruct the original with a good degree of accuracy, using a model to represent the three buildings identified. At the centre is the main residence with a square-pitched thatched roof and mud walls. The two other dwellings are similar in design, but smaller. The complex was protected by a 4-5m/13-16ft high fence. Archaeologists estimate that the village accommodated about 100 people. The lakeside environment has preserved numerous everyday objects, usually too fragile to survive to modern times: such as intact leather shoes, textiles, rare wooden musical instruments (tambourine, oboe, mouthpiece of some bagpipes), games (a complete chess set) and even toy weapons (crossbow). The study of the remains of food and of other debris suggests that tasks were equally shared by members of the community and that there was little or no hierarchy.

The discovery of riding equipment, lances and heavier weapons would indicate that there were knights with regular military duties who protected the community. The peasant-fisherfolk of Colletière were thus also warriors. This pre-feudal society was governed by egalitarian laws concerning work and seems to have been more than able to provide for all its needs.

Towards 1040, and the abandonment of the lakeside villages, the colonisation of the lake shores continued with earth castles *(mottes castrales)* being built on the neighbouring hills or slopes. Many were replaced by stone constructions in the 12C and became the strongholds of the great Dauphiné families – the Tour de Clermont *(see below)*, Les Trois Croix (in Paladru), Château de Virieu, La Louvatière and Château de Montclar.

Musée du Lac de Paladru – This museum displays the finds of underwater archaeological excavations of the drowned Neolithic and medieval villages. Superb models and audio-visual presentations help to evoke the way of life for local people during these two periods of transition in the lake's history.

EXCURSIONS

Leaving from **Charavines**, a number of easy walks are possible, giving good views of the lake and surrounding countryside. It is possible to walk all round the lake, for details ask at the tourist office in Paladru. The Maison du pays d'art et d'histoire de Paladru organises heritage trails (**Visites-découvertes du patrimoine** ⊘).

Tour de Clermont – *45min. From Charavines, take the footpath along the Fure as far as the D 50 bridge, then take the trail waymarked in yellow off to the left which goes uphill through fields. After going through the hamlet of La Grangière, take the path on the left up to the Tour de Clermont.*
This proud 13C pentagonal keep with three storeys is all that remains of the powerful stronghold of Clermont, destroyed at the beginning of the 17C. The top of the tower has disappeared, and the doorway was knocked out after the original date of construction (before this, a footbridge was lowered from the first floor). This was the residence of one of the oldest families of the Dauphiné, which would marry into Burgundy to give rise to the Clermont-Tonnerre branch of the family.

La Croix des Cochettes – *45min. This is a steeper walk than that described above, but it is better signposted. From the car park in Colletière, take the footpath uphill, waymarked in orange, towards Louisias. Where the land levels out, turn east along the hillside to join a footpath waymarked in blue which leads to the Cochettes cross. Panoramic view of the lake.*

★**Tour of the lake** – Two scenic roads – the D 50 and D 50^D (which becomes the D 90) – encircle the lake (15km/10mi). They connect the lively resort of Charavines on the southern point of the lake to the more peaceful village of Paladru at the other end. Along the walk, it is possible to see swans and other birdlife which make their home amng the reeds on the lake shore.
Taking the A 48 motorway towards Chambéry *(signposted route)*, note the purety of line of the 16C **Silve bénite** ⊘ tithe barn which houses temporary exhibitions in season.

★**Château de Virieu** ⊘ – *7.5km/5mi northwest on the D 17.*
The castle overlooking the upper Bourbre valley dates from the 11C to 18C, and was restored at the beginning of the 20C; it still looks like a fortress.
Note, in particular, the ancient 15C kitchen with its huge flattened arch, and a plaque bearing the original coats-of-arms of the Carthusian Order, the Great Hall, the bedroom of Louis XIII where he slept in 1622 on his way back from Montpellier after signing the peace treaty. During his stay in Virieu he donated several cannon which have been preserved, together with their *fleur-de-lys* mounts, under the arcades of the inner courtyard.

Puy de PARIOU ★

Michelin map 73 fold 14 or 239 fold 19 – Local map under Monts DÔMES

Puy de Pariou is one of the most beautiful crater volcanoes in the Puys chain. It consists of two volcanoes one inside the other *(see Illustration in Introduction: Volcanoes of the Auvergne)*.

Access ⊘ – *Take the D 941^B west of Clermont; beyond Orcines, 500m after the Shepherd's Fountain (Fontaine du Berger), park beside the road. Take a path off to the left (1hr 30min Rtn on foot).*

The volcano – Step over the side wall of the first crater which produced the still-visible lava which stretches across the road near Orcines. From here it is possible to climb to the second and more impressive crater, a regular funnel with a circumference of 950m/3 116ft and a depth of 96m/315ft. From the edge of this crater (alt 1 209m/3 966ft) there are outstanding views of the Monts Dômes, in particular, to the west, beyond the Clierzou and the Puy de Côme with its two craters fitted perfectly inside one another; to the north, over the Puy Chopine, the Puy de Chaumont and, behind the Puy des Goules, the Sarcouy; to the south, over the Puy de Dôme.

Lac PAVIN★★

Access – *Via the D 149, which is a one-way road, joining up with the D 978 from Besse to Condat, or via the "Fraux road" south of Besse which connects Besse to Pavin via a pasture-covered mountain. There is no time-limit in the parking area at the intersection of the D 978 and the by-road; the lakeside car park is restricted to one hour.*

The Fraux parking area offers a lovely **view★** of the lake.

Lac Pavin

★★**Lac Pavin** – This 44ha/109 acre lake (alt 1 197m/3 926ft) surrounded by forests and superb rocks, is one of the most beautiful in the Auvergne. Its glittering waters are populated by char and trout which sometimes reach an enormous size. The lake is ideal for boating and fishing. It is almost circular in shape and has a maximum depth of 92m/302ft.

The lake bed was formed by a formidable volcanic explosion which hollowed out a crater on the northern flank of the Puy de Montchal.

In the past, it was said that the old town of Besse was swallowed up by the lake as a divine punishment, and that throwing a stone into it would unleash terrific storms; this is why it is called Pavin, from the Latin *pavens* meaning dreadful.

A gentle path offers a very pleasant promenade around the lake *(about 45min on foot)*. It is possible to climb to Puy de Montchal from here.

★★**Puy de Montchal** – *Access: from either the south end of Lake Pavin or the end of Fraux Road – 1hr 30min Rtn on foot.*

The summit (alt 1 411m/4 628ft) offers a magnificent **panorama★★**: to the northwest, the Monts Dore massif; to the north, the Monts Dômes, clustered around the Puy de Dôme; further to the east, the Couzes and Comté valleys; to the northeast and east, the Livradois and Forez mountains and to the southeast, in the far distance, the Chaise-Dieu plateau and Velay mountains. In the foreground, Anglard falls, Montcineyre puy and lake, and the Cézallier mountains; to the southwest, the Cantal mountains. To the west, the view is masked by the edge of the crater.

Every year
*the **Michelin Red Guide France***
revises the town plans:
  – through routes, by-passes, new streets, one-way systems, car parks
  – the exact location of hotels, restaurants, public buildings...
Up-to-date information for easier driving in towns.

PÉROUGES★★

Population 851
Michelin map 88 folds 8,9 or 246 fold A – Local map under La DOMBES

Pérouges is perched on a hilltop and surrounded by ramparts; it remains a model of medieval architecture, with narrow winding streets and ancient houses, making it very popular with visitors.

Pérouges has such an authentic historical flavour that it is often used as the setting for period films by French directors.

Grandeur and decadence – Pérouges is said to have been founded before the Roman occupation by an Italic colony from Perugia (*Pérouse* in French). During the Middle Ages and up until the French annexation (1601) the town was disputed many times by the sovereigns of Dauphiné and Savoy; the siege of 1468 remains famous as one such episode. Claude Fabre de **Vaugelas** (1585-1650), the famous Academician and arbiter of French grammar, was one of the barons of Pérouges.

In the rich and active town centre, hundreds of craftsmen wove fabric from hemp grown in the surrounding fields.

In the 19C the town's prosperity waned considerably: Pérouges was too far from the railway line and local craftsmen could no longer compete with industry. From the 1 500 people who lived here during its days of glory, the population fell to 90.

In 1909-10 the town nearly disappeared altogether; many of the owners turned to mass destruction and entire blocks of old houses were torn down. Fortunately, an historical society from Lyon and a few artists from Pérouges stepped in, helped by the School of Arts. The most interesting houses were bought, sensitively restored, and classified as historical monuments. The main part of the town was saved.

This effort to safeguard the town's history continues under the auspices of the Historical Pérouges Committee and the inhabitants.

Old streets, old houses – Most of the houses in Pérouges, rebuilt after the 1468 siege, are in a transitional style. Many feature basket-handle arches and rectangular windows with stone latticework, often joined in twos or threes. The houses of the gentry and richer townsfolk can be recognised by their large dimensions and luxurious interiors: spacious rooms with high ceilings, carved beams, monumental fireplaces, frescoes both inside and out. The houses of the artisans and merchants were more modest, with semicircular openings to light the workshop or serve as counters to display their goods. The oldest houses are half-timbered, with projecting upper storeys. The streets have barely changed since the Middle Ages. Narrow and winding, they had double-sloping paving with a drainage channel in the middle. The roofs, with their large eaves, protected the inner side of the pavement, reserved for people of quality; the commoners had to give way to them and walk in the middle of the street.

★★OLD TOWN *2hr*

Park outside the town wall to the left of the church or in the car park downhill.

★**Porte d'En Haut** – This Upper Gateway, the main entrance to Pérouges, was also the most exposed, due to the gentle slope of the land. Its defence was reinforced by the fortress-church and a barbican. A house, Maison Vernay, can be seen through the Gothic doorway.

From the forecourt, there is an attractive view of the countryside on the other side of the moat.

★**Rue du Prince** – This was the main road. Butchers, basket-makers, drapers, the armourer and apothecary held shop here. The stone tables of the street stalls can still be seen. At one end stands the **Maison des Princes de Savoie** ⊙, now a museum *(see below)*.

★★★**Place de la Halle** – This market square is one of the prettiest market places in France. It derives its name from the covered markets or *halles* which stood here and were burnt to the ground in 1839. The splendid lime tree in the middle is a Liberty Tree planted in 1792 in commemoration of the Revolution. The houses around the square are almost without exception utterly charming.

Ostellerie (B) – This inn has a sign bearing the town's coat-of-arms. The half-timbered east façade is 13C while the south front is Renaissance. The main room on the ground floor has a 15C monumental fireplace as well as furniture and ceramics from Bresse.

Musée du Vieux-Pérouges (M) ⊙ – This museum is installed partly in the Maison des Princes de Savoie *(see above)* and in the Maison Heer which opens onto Place de la Halle through an arcade with Gothic pillars. The museum collections illustrate the history and archaeology of Dombes and Bresse and include engravings, utensils, furniture and fine pottery; a weaver's workshop with a loom has been recreated on the ground floor.

From the watchtower there is a **panoramic view** of the town's red roofs and chimneys, with Bugey mountains In the distance and, below, the hortulus (medieval garden) of the Maison des Princes de Savoie.

Maison du Vieux St-Georges (D) – A shell-shaped niche on the façade houses an unusual wooden 15C statue of St George, patron saint of Pérouges, mounted on a horse.

Take the narrow street which goes downhill from the corner of the square.

Place de la Halle

Maison Herriot – This is a very sumptuous-looking house with large windows (semi-circular on the ground floor, mullioned on the first floor).

Return to the square and take Rue de la Place, to the north.

Maison Cazin (**E**) – This, one of the loveliest houses in Pérouges, has projecting upper floors and half-timbering. The semicircular windows on the ground floor are latticed.

Turn right into Rue des Rondes.

Opposite Maison Cazin, with its back to the northern ramparts, stands the **Manoir de l'Ostellerie**, once known as Maison Messimy.

★**Rue des Rondes** – This street still has most of its ancient paving and central drainage channel. The old houses on either side, including the **Grenier à sel** (Salt Store) and **Maison Thibaut**, are protected by wide eaves.

Porte d'En-Bas – The Lower Gateway is older than the Upper Gateway, and is semicircular. On the outside there is an inscription referring to the siege of 1468, in rather approximate Latin, which can be translated as follows: "Pérouges of the Pérougians! Impregnable town! Those rascally Dauphinois wanted to take it but they could not. So they went off with the doors, the hinges and the locks instead. May the devil take them!" Next to the gateway there is an attractive **view★** of the surrounding countryside, Bugey Mountains and, in fine weather, the Alps.

Rue des Rondes leads round to Place de l'Église.

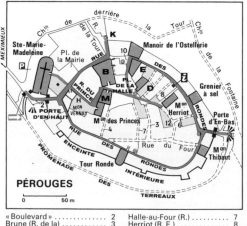

PÉROUGES

0   50 m

«Boulevard»	2	Halle-au-Four (R.)	7
Brune (R. de la)	3	Herriot (R. E.)	8
Contreforts (R. des)	4	Place (R. de la)	10
Filaterie (R. de la)	6	Tambour (R. du)	12

B	Ostellerie	**E**	Maison Cazin
D	Maison du Vieux-St-Georges	**K**	Puits de la Tour
		M	Musée du Vieux-Pérouges

Ste-Marie-Madeleine ⓞ – This 15C church looks like a fortress with its north-western wall incorporating crenellations, arrow slits and very high, narrow openings. The belfry, destroyed during the Revolution, was rebuilt under the Empire and given the four-webbed vault typical of the Franche-Comté. The watchpath, which went right round the curtain wall, continues through the church above the side vaults and along the galleries on the façade. Inside, note the set of emblazoned keystones; the central vault, in particular, has the blazon of the House of Savoy and the symbols of the four Evangelists. On the right of the chancel stands a 17C polychrome wooden statue of St George.

Rejoin Rue des Rondes and turn left to Rue de la Tour.

Puits de la Tour (**K**) – For a long time this well supplied water to the entire town. The tower built by the Romans was destroyed in 1749 (the presbytery occupies part of the site).
A lantern in the upper part of the tower was used to send light signals to similar towers forming a relay right to Lyon.

The two curtain walls – The path uphill from the Upper Gateway leads to **Promenade des Terreaux★** in the moat of the outer curtain wall of which there are now only vestigial remains; the inner curtain wall *(enceinte intérieure)* is almost complete; it serves as a foundation for the houses along Rue des Rondes.
The **round tower**, against which the house of the Sergeant of Justice is built, was used as a prison.

Château de PESTEILS

Michelin map 76 fold 12 or 239 fold 41

This beautiful medieval castle, built on a rocky promontory on the north bank of the River Cère overlooking the town of Polminhac, east of Aurillac, was one of the strongholds designed to defend the valley; it took the name Pesteils in the 16C. Some of the scenes in Jean Cocteau's film *Love Eternal* (*L'Éternel Retour*, 1943) were filmed here.

TOUR ⓞ *45min*

The imposing 13C square keep, 35m/115ft high, is crowned with a machicolated watchpath. It overlooks terraces which closely follow the line of the old ramparts.
The tour begins with the guard room followed by the main drawing room, lavishly decorated with tapestries, paintings and fine furniture. Two bedrooms on the first floor have ceilings which were painted in the 17C.
One of the rooms in the keep, which is connected to the second floor of the main building by a small stone bridge, has two 15C frescoes, one depicting a master and his pupil, and the other four heroes from antiquity.
On a clear day, the summit of Plomb du Cantal can be seen from the watchpath.

Mont PILAT★★

Michelin map 88 folds 18, 19 or 246 folds 16, 17

Mont Pilat lies to the east of St-Étienne, between the Loire basin and the Rhône valley. The influence of the Mediterranean to the east and the Atlantic to the west makes it something of a watershed, particularly at Chaubouret pass (alt 1 363m/4 471ft); it also acts as a water tower, particularly for the St-Étienne region. The coolness of its fir plantations, swift streams and high pastures contrasts with the industrial aspect of the Ondaine, Janon and Gier valleys.
Formation of the massif goes back to the Hercynian fold; it was then a high mountain with its folds lying in a southwest-northeast direction. During the Secondary era, erosion reduced it to a plateau, sloping down towards the present-day Rhône valley; the plateau was then covered with water leaving several layers of sediment. During the Tertiary era, the water withdrew. The Alpine fold then caused subsidence of the Rhône valley and tilting of the massif. Mont Pilat, having been "rejuvenated", rose to an altitude of 1 500m/5 000ft while the rivers – the Gier in the north and the Limony in the south – slid to the foot of the faults. During the Quaternary era, erosion took its toll once again.
The grass-covered summits of Mont Pilat – Crêt de la Perdrix culminating at 1 432m/4 697ft and Crêt de l'Œillon (alt 1 370m/4 494ft) bristle with strange piles of granite blocks called *chirats* which are the result of complete erosion of the summits.
Many rivers rise near the summits and flow rapidly down towards the Gier, the Rhône or the Loire along steep-sided valleys. The Gier itself, close to its source, crosses a chirat at Saut du Gier falls.

Parc naturel régional du Pilat ⓥ – Created in 1974, the park covers 65 000ha/160 000 acres and contains about fifty towns and villages in the Rhône and Loire *départements*. The countryside is extremely diverse – forests of beech and fir at high altitude, pastureland on the plateaux, orchards and vineyards on the banks of the Rhône. Committed to conserving nature and the environment, Pilat park promotes rural, craft, tourist and cultural activities.

To facilitate an introduction to flora and fauna within the regional park there are 350km/217mi of nature trails, including sections of GR7 and GR42 (Grande Randonnée long-distance footpaths, marked with red and white stripes) and eight special trails (brown and white stripes) each identified by a number.

The **Jean-Jacques Rousseau trail**, from Condrieu to La Jasserie – *see ① on map below* – is a reminder that the philosopher and writer came to Mont Pilat in 1769 for botanical reasons; the **flora trail** ⑨ takes the rambler quickly (22km/14mi) from the almost Mediterranean vegetation of the Malleval region to the subalpine formation of Perdrix ridge, from prickly pear to mountain tobacco.

The **ornithological trail**, between St-Pierre-de-Bœuf and the chapel of St-Sabin features up to 90 registered species of birds (particularly from mid-May to mid-June), including mallard on St-Pierre lake, diving cingle near the torrents, crossbill in the fir forests and the rock bunting on the gorse heath.

Tourist and sporting facilities include the St-Pierre-de-Bœuf leisure park which has an artificial river for canoeing and kayaking; the canoe base at Terrasse-sur-Dorlay; downhill ski resorts at La Jasserie and Graix, and cross-country ski clubs at Le Bessat, Burignes, St-Régis-du-Coin and St-Genest-Malifaux. Other sites are suitable for climbing, hang-gliding, cycling and orienteering. Cross-country cycling facilities are being developed, with numerous waymarked tracks categorised by degree of difficulty. To promote traditional activities and revive near-forgotten crafts, the park has opened the **Maison-de-l'Eau** ⓥ (Water House) and the **Maison des Arts et Traditions La Béate** ⓥ in Marlhes, the **Maison de la Passementerie** ⓥ (Trimmings) in Jonzieux and the **Maison des Tresses et Lacets** ⓥ (Braids and Ribbons) in La Terrasse-sur-Dorlay.

Festivals such as Apple Day on 11 November at Pélussin (the headquarters of the park), the Farm Produce Fair in Bourg-Argental in June and the Wine Fair in Chavanay (2nd weekend in December), and the Cheese and Wine Fair in Condrieu (1 May) provide an introduction to local produce. Information on all aspects of Pilat park is available from the **Maison du Parc**.

FROM ST-ÉTIENNE TO CONDRIEU

89km/56mi – about 6hr, St-Étienne not included – Local map right

St-Étienne – *2hr. See ST-ÉTIENNE.*

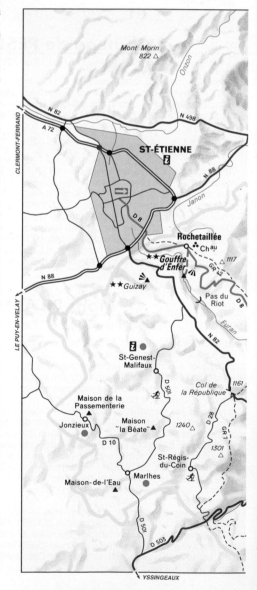

Leave St-Étienne on the D 8 southeast.

During the climb, the strategic site of Rochetaillée can be seen.

Rochetaillée – This is a small village perched on a narrow rocky channel between two ravines, below the ruins of a feudal castle.

★★**Gouffre d'Enfer** – *1hr Rtn on foot.* To the right of Auberge de la Cascade inn, a path follows the bed of the old torrent to the foot of the dam. The site is impressive: the heavily gouged walls of rock come together to form a dark, narrow gully, dramatically named "Chasm of Hell". The dam was built in 1866 to supply water to St-Étienne; steps lead up to the top of it. The reservoir laps the edges of fir-covered slopes. 50m on the left, steps lead to the **viewpoint** opposite Rochetaillée.

Rejoin the D 8 towards Le Bessat.

There are attractive views *(right)* over the dams of Gouffre d'Enfer and Pas-du-Riot.

Le Bessat – Small summer and winter resort.

Beyond Le Bessat, take the D 63 towards La Croix-de-Chaubouret.

★**Crêt de la Perdrix** – *Just after La Croix-de-Chaubouret turn left onto the D 8A towards La Jasserie.*

The road winds past spruce, mountain pastures and heathland.

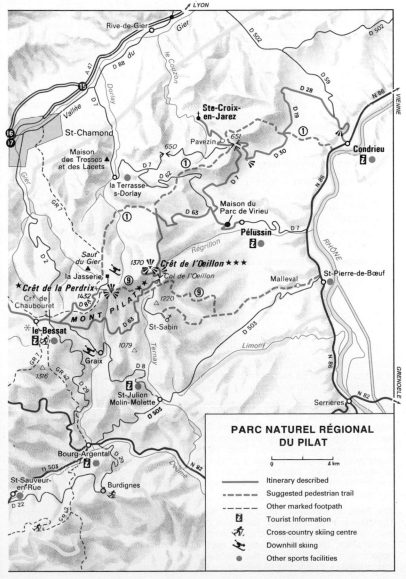

PARC NATUREL RÉGIONAL DU PILAT

0   4 km

——— Itinerary described
----- Suggested pedestrian trail
- - - Other marked footpath
🛈 Tourist Information
🎿 Cross-country skiing centre
🎿 Downhill skiing
● Other sports facilities

After about 5km/3mi, at the top of the climb, park near the path leading to Perdrix ridge (15min Rtn on foot) which is crowned with a chirat (granite rock).

The **panorama** from the viewing table takes in the peaks of Mézenc, Lizieux, Meygal and Gerbier de Jonc.

Rejoin the D 63 to Crêt de l'Œillon.

The road meanders alternately through fir trees and moorland covered in broom.

★★★**Crêt de l'Œillon** – *15min Rtn on foot. At the Croix de l'Œillon pass, take the road on the left leading to the turn-off to the private road up to the television relay station. Park in the car park. At the top, walk to the left around the fence; the viewing table is on the eastern end of the promontory, at the foot of a monumental cross.*

Regional parks are different from national parks in their concept and purpose. They are inhabited areas selected for development of the local economy through specific activities (the creation of co-operatives, promotion of crafts), the preservation of the natural and cultural heritage (museums, architecture) and the appreciation of the distinctive character of the region.

The **panorama** is one of the most spectacular in the Rhône valley. In the foreground, beyond the rocks of Pic des Trois Dents (Three Teeth Peak), there is a bird's eye view of the Rhône valley, from Vienne to Serrières. In the distance to the east, the view stretches right to the Alps; southeast to Mont Ventoux; west to the Puy de Sancy and the Forez mountains; north to the Lyonnais mountains and northeast to the Jura.

Continue to Pélussin.

From Faucharat viewpoint, there are lovely views of the Régrillon valley, the Rhône valley and Pélussin.

Pélussin – *Park on Place Abbé-Vincent in front of the hospital. Walk down Rue Dr-Soubeyran and take Rue de la Halle on the left.*

The old covered market provides a view of the Rhône plain and the town of Pélussin. Go through a fortified gatehouse and turn left. Note the ancient chapel and castle.

Turn back the way you came and take the D 7 right to Pavezin pass.

Ste-Croix-en-Jarez – *See STE-CROIX-EN-JAREZ.*

At Pavezin pass and turn left onto the D 30 which, as it begins its descent, offers a beautiful view of the Rhône valley. Turn left and continue along the D 19 and D 28 to Condrieu.

Just before arriving, in a bend with a Calvary overlooking the town, there is a panoramic **view**★ of the Condrieu basin and the bend in the Rhône below.

Condrieu – *See Moyenne vallée du RHÔNE.*

POLIGNAC ★

Population 2 384
Michelin map 76 fold 7 or 239 fold 34
6km/4mi northwest of Le PUY-EN-VELAY

Rising proudly on its basalt hillock, the fortress of Polignac still has imposing remains of its powerful martial past from both Antiquity and the Middle Ages. The view of the site, from the N 102, is superb.

The oracle of Apollo – The rock has been famous since Roman times when it was the site of a temple dedicated to Apollo famous for its oracles. The Emperor Claudius visited it in the year 47. The oracles were pronounced by an enormous mask of Apollo. The pilgrim, arriving at the foot of the rock, placed his offerings in a room where he said his wishes out loud. He was unaware that his words were heard distinctly in the temple through a funnel-shaped well hollowed out in the rock. While he laboured up the hillside, the priests prepared their answer; using a megaphone, they made the words come out of the god's stone mouth, before the admiring yet terrified pilgrim.

The Polignac family – The troubled times of the early Middle Ages then followed. The hill was in such a strong defensive position that the lords of Polignac, protected inside their fortress, became the masters of the region, the "Kings of the Mountain". One of them, the Viscount Heracles, participated in the First Crusade and fell before Antioch in 1098. Some of the Viscounts of Polignac were, however, somewhat unprincipled; a church council held in Le Puy in 1181 condemned another Heracles to go barefoot with a candle in his hand to the porch of St-Julien church in Brioude to be scourged on his knees by a monk as a punishment for the wanton acts of which he was guilty.

In the 17C Melchior de Polignac, an extremely well-read and skilful diplomat and high dignitary of the Church, negotiated the Treaty of Utrecht; he became cardinal in 1713 and entered the French Academy. Pope Alexander VIII said to him, "I don't understand how you do it – you always seem to be of my opinion yet it is always I who end up being of yours".

The family's brief and heady period of good fortune was above all due to Yolande de Polastron, the wife of Jules de Polignac. Her friendship with Marie-Antoinette brought her large amounts of money and jewels, the title of duke for her husband and a county which the king pretended to sell to them. This abundance of favours incited the anger of the people; during the Revolution, the couple hastily emigrated.

Their second son, made prince by the pope, was to become Charles X's prime minister. He was to contribute indirectly to the conquest of Algeria; and his orders provoked the 1830 revolution.

SIGHTS

To reach the castle from Place de l'Église, take the path between the mairie (town hall) and Auberge du Donjon. Shortly afterwards, take the flight of steps on the right, then follow a steep asphalt path; go under the 13C Gothic arch gateway with its wooden door; a little further on is the house in which the keeper lives during the summer months.

E. Baret

Polignac

★**Château de Polignac** ⊙ – The building, which could house 800 soldiers as well as the family and servants, is perched on an enormous basalt platform, the remaining fragment of a lava flow; the platform sits on a softer strata of rock which has been protected from erosion as a consequence. The rock is nearly 100m/330ft higher than the alluvial plain levelled by the Loire and the Borne below. Furthermore, the plateau has sheer sides, which dispensed with the need to build high curtain walls.

First visit the 15C and 17C remains of the owners' dwellings, south of the keep, in the middle of which there is a large well 83m/272ft deep. On the ground floor of the three-storey keep, constructed between 1385 and 1421, there are some Antique fragments, including the mask of Apollo *(see above).* The top of the **keep** offers a beautiful **panorama★** of Le Puy basin, the Velay mountains, and Meygal and Mézenc massifs.

Return to the keeper's house via the watchpath which begins on the left, leaving the keep.

Note, on the way past, the spy-holes in the wall to enable the sentries to keep a watch on the surroundings.

Church – This is a beautiful Romanesque building with a Gothic porch; the interior has been restored. Note the 12C Romanesque-Byzantine dome; there are 15C frescoes in both the chancel and the chapel on the right of the chancel. Above the door of the southern side-aisle is a modern stained-glass window representing three of the most famous members of the Polignac family: on the right, Viscount Heracles who died in the battle of Antioch; in the centre, Cardinal Melchior de Polignac; on the left, Prince Jules de Polignac.

In the apse there are two alcoves, one with a 13C polychrome wood statue group of St Anne, the Virgin and Child; the other contains a reliquary said to be of the True Cross and two silver candelabra (18C).

PRIVAS

Population 10 600
Michelin map 76 folds 19, 20 or 246 fold 20
Local map under Plateau du COIRON
Town plan in the current Michelin Red Guide France

Privas occupies an unusual **site★** in the Ouvèze basin, at the foot of Mont Toulon; a good example of relief inversion, the lava flow on which it stands was once at the bottom of the valley and is now in relief since the ancient unprotected calcareous heights have been eroded.

Business in the town concentrates on small industry (milling, sprung bed bases) and the manufacture of *marrons glacés* (candied sweet chestnuts), of which it is the capital.

SIEGE OF PRIVAS

The "Rampart of the Reformation" – Privas played a key role in the Wars of Religion which earned it the title of "Boulevard de la Réforme". It was a priest from Privas, Jacques Valery (or Vallier), who first introduced the Reformation to Privas in 1534.

Right in the thick of the religious wars, the town was one of the strongholds conceded to the Protestants by Henri IV under the Edict of Nantes in 1598.

The taking of Privas – Richelieu's unification policy and the undying hatred of the people revived the religious conflict which was fanned in the Vivarais by a question of marriage: Paule de Chambaud, widow of the Huguenot leader, Jacques de Chambaud, heir to the barony of Privas, had the choice of two suitors, one Roman Catholic and the other Protestant. She chose the youngest, Claude de Hautefort-Lestrange, a Roman Catholic, to the outrage of the people of Privas, most of whom were Protestants and opposed to having a follower of the pope as their lord.

Fighting resumed. In 1629 the Royal Army, under the command of Schomberg and Biron, set up camp near Privas. Cardinal Richelieu took up lodgings in Entrevaux castle while Louis XIII was housed in the southern part of the town, in a dwelling now known as the Logis du Roi (King's Abode).

The townspeople, who counted only 1 600 defenders, were no match for the 20 000 strong Royal Army. After 16 days of siege, the town was taken by storm, pillaged and burnt, and the inhabitants were massacred. The booty was declared "very rich", the Protestants of Boutières having brought their most precious possessions into the town square for safety.

Some of the defenders took refuge on Mont Toulon; one of the leaders, preferring to "be burned rather than hung", set fire to the gunpowder. His companions, panic-stricken, ran outside where they were killed by the king's soldiers.

Revenge of Privas – The inhabitants who managed to escape later obtained the right to return although they were pursued from court to court by their lord, the Viscount of Lestrange, who claimed the price of his destroyed castle – at least until 1632. He was implicated in one of Gaston d'Orléans' plots against the king, was taken prisoner and whipped publicly in Privas, then executed in Pont-St-Esprit.

Shortly afterwards, the construction of a bridge over the Ouvèze sealed the reconciliation between Royal power and the people of Privas, who gradually rebuilt the ruins of their city.

SIGHTS

Musée de la Terre ardéchoise ⊙ – *Place des Récollets*. This museum is housed in the buildings of a former convent of Recollect Nuns, and hosts temporary exhibitions on local archaeology, history and geology.

Boulevard du Mont-Toulon – *Southwest off Place des Récollets*. This hillside road offers good views over the town, the Ouvèze valley, the Rhône and the Alps.

Pont Louis-XIII – *South of town centre*. The bridge over the River Ouvèze has preserved its coping of rough stone corbels and offers a good view of Privas.

LA JAUBERNIE CAVES

3km/2mi. Leave Privas on the N 104 east.

Coux – This is a picturesque old village built round a hillock in the middle of the Ouvèze valley.

Turn left towards La Jaubernie (via a narrow road opposite the bridge). Park at the entrance to the hamlet. A rocky path leads to the foot of the caves (30min Rtn on foot).

Grottes de La Jaubernie – These caves were fitted out in the 15C and 16C to provide refuge for Protestants during the Wars of Religion.
Morning is the best time for this excursion. A good view of the Privas basin and the Ouvèze valley is to be had from here.

LE COIRON

Round trip of 77km/48mi – allow half a day. See Plateau du COIRON.

★BETWEEN OUVÈZE AND EYRIEUX

Round trip of 88km/55mi – allow half a day. Leave Privas on the D 2 north.

The D 2 goes up a hillside crisscrossed with the stone walls of terrace cultivation and offers a good **view**★ of the town. Beyond Le Moulin-à-Vent, the descent towards Ollières-sur-Eyrieux winds through shaded hillsides planted with chestnut trees.

Follow the Eyrieux upstream from Ollières to St-Sauveur-de-Montagut and take the D 211 on the left.

At Tauzuc turn left onto the D 8 and at St-Étienne-de-Serre turn right onto the D 244 to Foulix and la Pervenche. The **crest road**★ overlooking the Orsanne and Auzène valleys offers lovely views of isolated hamlets.

Turn left onto the D 344 and continue to Le Bouschet de Pranles, passing through Pranles.

Le Bouschet de Pranles – A small **Protestant museum** ⊙ has been set up in the birthplace of **Pierre Durand**, one of the Desert Fathers in the 18C, and his sister **Marie Durand**. This 18C Huguenot heroine was locked up in the tower of Constance d'Aigues-Mortes for 38 years (1730-68). Pranles has become the Mecca of Viviers Protestantism; a Protestant gathering is held on Whit Monday every year.

The D 2 leads back to Privas.

PUY DE DÔME★★★

Michelin map 72 folds 13, 14 or 239 fold 19 – Local map under Monts DÔMES

The ascent of the Puy de Dôme and the extraordinary panorama visible from the summit, best seen at sunset, are quite unforgettable.
This former volcano is the oldest, the highest (alt 1 465m/4 614ft) and the most famous of the Monts Dômes chain, of which it is the centre.
Although more than 1 000m/3 280ft above Clermont, it is barely 500m/1 640ft above the plateau on which it stands. It was only in 1751 that the volcanic origin of these mountains was recognised; until then, it was believed that they were part of gigantic fortifications built by the Romans.

Atmospheric phenomena – During the cold season, a "temperature inversion" often occurs: while the weather in Clermont might be bitterly cold, it might be almost mild on the Dôme. On the 26 December 1879, at 6am, a temperature of -16°C (+3°F) was recorded at Clermont and +4°C (+39°F) at the top of the Puy de Dôme. This phenomenon, which only occurs during calm weather, is caused by the heavier layers of cold air gradually sinking down into the depression below.
It is for a similar reason that a magnificent "sea of clouds" can sometimes be seen from the Puy de Dôme. While the Limagne plain disappears under a thick carpet of fog, the surrounding mountains emerge like sparkling islands in the sun. This phenomenon mainly occurs in autumn (particularly in November).

Sacred Mountain – From the earliest times the solitude of this Puy, which is so difficult to get to, has been awe inspiring. The Gauls made it a sanctuary for their god Lug. The Romans replaced it with the cult of "Mercury of the Dome". They built a magnificent temple to him, the foundations of which were discovered in 1872 during construction of a look-out post. This temple and all its treasures were destroyed by the barbarian invasions. A Christian sanctuary replaced it.
In the 12C a small chapel, a site of pilgrimage, was dedicated to St Barnabas, one of St Paul's companions. It was very popular for many centuries, then fervour began to wane; in 1631, visiting pilgrims only donated 7 francs during the whole year. The chapel disappeared in the 18C.
According to popular superstition, all the sorcerers of the Auvergne meet on the deserted mountain top for bloodcurdling midnight revels.

J. Damase

Puy de Dôme

The weight of air — It is on the Puy de Dôme that **Blaise Pascal** carried out the experiment in 1648 which proved the theory about the weight of air. It had already been noted that mercury rises to about 76cm/25in in a tube in which a vacuum has been created. To explain this phenomenon, it was said that "nature hates vacuums". This axiom however did not satisfy Torricelli; he put forward the hypothesis that it is the weight of the air that pushes the mercury up.

Captivated by this idea, Pascal thought that, if this were the case, the weight of the air should be less at the top of a mountain. As Pascal was in Paris, he asked his brother-in-law to help. The latter chose a fine day, left a mercury barometer in Clermont and went with the Minimes Fathers to the top of the Puy de Dôme. He was overjoyed to see that the mercury rose 8.4cm/3.25in less than it did in Clermont. The theory about the weight of the air had been proven.

Puy-de-Dôme rather than Mont-Dore — In 1790, following the Revolution, administrative *départements* replaced the former provinces in France. There was talk of giving the name Mont-d'Or (Golden Mountain) — as Mont-Dore was then spelled — to the Lower Auvergne constituency, but the deputy for Clermont, Gaultier de Beauzat, was alarmed that such a wealthy-sounding name would attract the attention of the tax department. He asked for the less compromising name of Puy-de-Dôme, and it was accepted.

The Dôme ablaze — In 1862 Napoleon III and Eugénie visited Clermont; the emperor wanted to know what progress was being made with the excavations he had ordered on Gergovie plateau in order to reconstruct the battle between Caesar and Vercingétorix.

As entertainment for the royal couple, it was decided to set fire at night to the mountain tops surrounding the town, especially the Puy de Dôme. 6 000 faggots and 20 wagons of wood were to create an immense, flame-belching blaze; two vats, containing 8 000kg/17 600lb (over 3/4 ton) of resin and oil, were to send fire flowing over the sides of the extinct volcano. Unfortunately, it all went up in a dismal puff of smoke which, in the dark of night, could not even be seen.

The Michelin Grand Prix — In 1908, when Henri Farman was making the first circular flight (1km/0.6mi) in the world, the Michelin brothers offered a Grand Prix of 100 000 francs to any aviator who could fly from Paris, with a 75kg/165lb passenger on board, to the top of the Puy de Dôme in less than six hours, skirting the cathedral of Clermont by 1 500m/5 000ft on their right. Only three years later, on 7 March 1911, despite predictions that this feat could not possibly be achieved within less than a half a century, the aviator **Eugène Renaux**, with his passenger Senouque, successfully met the prescribed conditions in just 5 hours and 11 minutes.

ASCENT

Grotte du Puy de Dôme ⊙ – A subterranean gallery in a lava flow from the Petit Puy de Dôme has been opened up for visitors. Glass cases attractively present a rock collection from both the Auvergne and throughout the world. A working stonecutter's workshop completes the visit.

Ascent via the toll road ⊙ – In 1926 this road replaced the tracks used by the miniature steam train which had operated for about twenty years. The road, which is well designed, has a constant slope of 12% for about 4km/2.5mi. As it spirals around the Dôme it offers a wonderful variety of views, becoming more extensive higher up. As the road comes out of the woods on the lower part of the mountain it cuts through domite, a white porous volcanic rock, which can be seen wherever the surface layer has been weathered away.

The first ascent on bicycle took place in 1891 in 28 minutes; in 1913 a high-powered car reached the summit for the first time, in just 11 minutes.

Ascent on foot via the Roman road – *Allow 2hr Rtn*. Park at Ceyssat pass (alt 1 078m/3 536ft) in a forest of fir trees. It was up this winding path (35-40% slopes) that chariots pulled by five to eight tandem-driven horses transported the materials needed to build the Roman temple and subsequently, in the 19C, the look-out post.

THE SUMMIT *1hr Rtn on foot*

A shuttle service operates during July and August (buses every 10min).

Reception and information centre ⊙ – This houses a display on volcanoes and exhibitions specifically on Puy de Dôme and the various other sites of interest to discover in the locality.

A pedestrian road and a footpath lead around the television transmitter to two viewing tables.

Note the stone commemorating Pascal's experiment set into the main façade of the television building.

★★★**Panorama** – To the north and south, over a distance of about 30km/19mi, can be seen the hundred or so extinct volcanoes forming the Monts Dômes, a marvellous museum of volcanic shapes, a lunar landscape unique in France and perhaps in the world.

To the north can be clearly distinguished volcanoes of the same origin as the Puy de Dôme which resemble enormous craterless molehills: Petit Suchet, Clierzou and Sarcouy. The others are all cones of debris topped with craters: Petit Puy de Dôme or Nid de la Poule ("Hen's Nest"), Grand Suchet, Puy de Côme, Pariou, Loucha-dière.

All the volcanoes to the south have craters: Monchier, Barme, Laschamp, Mercœur etc. On the horizon rise the Monts Dore. The east overlooks the Limagne with its myriad of towns, villages, fields, hillsides and isolated peaks. In the distance, the heights of Livradois and Forez border the plain. To the west lie the soft contours of the hills of the Limousin plateau.

Renaux landing on Puy de Dôme summit

275

The view extends over eleven *départements*, one eighth of the total surface area of France. Visibility varies almost from one minute to the next, depending on the clouds and fog. The *puys* may be covered with grass or heath, with fir-groves or hazel copses. The chain itself is uninhabited as any rain which falls soaks into the volcanic rocks. In summer, flocks from the plateau graze on the *puys* but since there is no water, they all return to the stable at night.

It is at sunset that the view is most spectacular. Fiery trails weave through the volcanic cones. The mountain throws its shadow to the east, covering first the Orcines plateau then suddenly reaching Clermont before gradually invading the plain: the extreme tip of its shadow goes right to Thiers.

Temple of Mercury – *No access*. This beautiful Temple to the God Mercury (now a ruin) was built by the Romans. Originally it was twice the size of the famous Maison Carrée (1C AD) in Nîmes; fifty sorts of marble were used to decorate it. The television transmitter stands on the original site of a monumental bronze statue of Mercury by the Greek sculptor Zenodorus. It was, according to Pliny the Elder, one of the marvels of the ancient world. On the upper terrace of the ruins can be seen the square base of the sanctuary or *cella*.

The path winds around the ruins and passes in front of the monument recalling Renaux's exploit. It is just below this monument that daring adepts of hang-gliding and para-gliding sometimes hurl themselves into empty space.

Many camp sites have shops, bars, restaurants and laundries;
they may also have games rooms, tennis courts, miniature golf courses, play-grounds, swimming pools...
Consult the current edition of the **Michelin Camping Caravaning France.**

Le PUY-EN-VELAY ★★★

Population 21 743
Michelin map 76 fold 7 or 239 fold 34 – Local map under Gorges de la LOIRE

The **site★★★** of Le Puy-en-Velay, one of the most extraordinary in France, is unforget-table. Out of a rich plain set in a depression rise enormous peaks of volcanic origin: the steepest, the St-Michel rock (or Mont d'Aiguilhe) is surmounted by a Romanesque chapel making it even higher; the largest, Corneille rock (or Mont d'Anis), looks almost as though it is being scaled by the town houses and the cathedral. This strange and splendid vision is complemented by a visit to the church of Notre-Dame du Puy, no less strange, almost oriental, which houses the Black Virgin still venerated by numerous pilgrims.

In autumn, the **Festival of the Bird King** (Fêtes du roi de l'Oiseau) is held, in commemo-ration of an age-old local custom: it is a competition to determine the town's best archer, celebrated in a Renaissance atmosphere which pervades the upper end of the town during these festivities *(see Calendar of events)*.

The region's resources come from food processing (liqueurs, canning), mechanical engineering (production of TGV (high-speed train) parts), the manufacture of hand-made and machine-made lace, and tourism. Since 1977 a Michelin production unit in a nearby industrial estate has been making giant tyres for earthmoving machines.

In the town itself the Pierre-Cardinal Centre (**BY**), set up in a former convent, hosts various cultural events.

On Saturday, market day, the town makes a striking sight; Place du Breuil and the old streets between the square and the market become incredibly busy.

The Puy basin – The Puy basin owes its initial formation to the collapse of the Vellave plateau, an after-effect of the alpine folding which occurred during the Tertiary period. Sediment stripped from the surrounding hills then partly filled the basin in which a gorge was cut by the River Loire. At the end of the Tertiary era a series of volcanic eruptions convulsed the region; the bed of the Loire was shifted east.

During the Quaternary era the erosion began again, forming spurs from the most resistant of the volcanic reefs, of various origins; these include basalt tables, the remains of lava flows (Polignac rock), volcanic chimneys (St-Michel rock, Espaly and Arbousset peaks), parts of eruptive cones (Corneille and Ceyssac rocks, Denise vol-cano). As the lava flow cooled, combinations of prismatic columns were formed, such as those at Espaly. It is to these volcanic phenomena that the basin owes its highly original physiognomy.

The basin is closed on all sides apart from two openings formed by the Loire; that to the south, cut into clay and marl, is the larger; that to the north, forged through granite, is narrow.

From the rim of the surrounding plateaux there are lovely views of the Puy basin, particularly when the golden tones of its large thatched roofs are caught by the rays of the setting sun.

HISTORICAL NOTES

City of the Virgin – The Velay capital of the Roman era, Ruessium, has been identified at St-Paulien nearby, to the northwest.

The site of Le Puy seems to have been an ancient place of pagan worship (remains of a 1C sanctuary among the cathedral foundations), evangelised in the 3C. Apparitions of the Virgin and miraculous cures near a dolmen capstone (since known as the "Fever Stone") encouraged the first bishops to come and settle here, probably at the end of the 5C. A basilica was erected, then a cathedral, around which a town soon developed, the old Ruessium having been deposed.

In the Middle Ages pilgrimages to Le Puy were particularly popular since it was also a point of departure for the pilgrimage to Santiago de Compostela in Spain. With Chartres, Le Puy is the oldest site of Marian worship in France. Kings, princes and crowds of humble origin flocked here to invoke the mother of God, and the bishop here consequently gained great prestige. In 990 the bishop imposed a highly innovative Truce of God (whereby fighting was suspended on certain days of the week or seasons of the year) on the turbulent feudal lords of Velay. In 1095 he welcomed Urban II and, as Papal Legate, he was put in charge of the Crusade; in 1163 the king made him a count.

The Black Virgin brought even greater fame to Le Puy. She was brought from the east by Louis VII or by St Louis. When she was mutilated and burnt during the French Revolution, it was discovered that the statue was in fact a representation of the goddess Isis. Le Puy-en-Velay (in the Middle Ages, Le Puy-Notre-Dame or Puy-Ste-Marie) has remained the city of the Virgin; the tall statue of Notre-Dame-de-France, at the top of Corneille rock, evokes both a past and a destiny.

Les Cotereaux – In the 12C the havoc wrought by a group of privateers, known as Les Cotereaux, posed a serious threat to the pilgrimages and all they contributed to the town in terms of prosperity and renown.

Merchants from Poitou, Provence and Spain no longer came to display their weapons, their fabrics and jewels. Troubadours no longer held their court here.

The Virgin, in an apparition to a carpenter named Durand, ordered a holy war against the Cotereaux. The new crusaders, with their white cotton hoods, attacked the brigands and hung them 500 at a time. Unfortunately, however, the crusaders acquired a taste for these expeditions and rose up in rebellion. The royal troops had to massacre them in turn.

City of lace – In Le Puy and the Velay, as well as in the region of Arlanc, hand-made lace was once an important part of the local economy. It probably originated in the 15C but it was in the 17C that it really began to develop and a special organisation was established. In all the villages, women worked at home for merchants in the neighbouring towns. "Collectors" who provided the lace-makers with thread and cartoons (patterns), served as intermediaries. This extra income was vital to the poor peasants in the region.

Originally reserved for the gentry, lace became so popular that, in 1640, the Toulouse Parliament outlawed its use as clothing. A Jesuit father, Jean-François Régis (1597-1640), moved by the distress of the lace-makers who suddenly found themselves out of work, managed to have the ban lifted. Moreover, he invited his fellow missionaries to make Le Puy lace known throughout the world. This benefactor from Le Puy, canonised under the name of **St François Régis**, later became the patron saint of lace-makers. The chapel of the Jesuit college, where he spent five years of his ministry, is now the St-Georges-St-Régis church (**BY**). The lace trade retained its religious overtones for a long time; the art was passed on not only from mother to daughter but also by religious women known as "the beatified" who also taught catechism and cared for the sick.

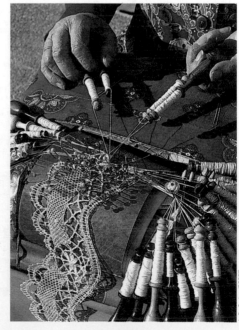

Lace-making

Le PUY-EN-VELAY

At the **Centre d'enseignement de la dentelle au fuseau et à l'Atelier Conservatoire National de la Dentelle du Puy** ⊙ (*2, rue Du-Guesclin, west of Boulevard Carnot*, (**AY**)), it is possible to see lace-makers at work and an exhibition on needlepoint and bobbin lace since the 17C.

In the summer, a small **tourist train** ⊙ takes visitors round the town's main sights.

***CATHEDRAL CITY* 2hr

The cathedral dominates the upper part of the town, which is one large conservation area and is currently undergoing extensive restoration.

Start from Place des Tables with its graceful Chorister Fountain (15C) and walk up to the cathedral via the picturesque **Rue des Tables** (**AY 52**) lined with stone steps bordered by several old houses.

***Cathédrale Notre-Dame** (**BY**) ⊙ – This marvellous Romanesque building owes its unusual appearance to the influence of the Orient; Byzantine influence, a result of the Crusades, can also be seen in the octagonal domes over the nave.

The original church corresponds to the present east end. When work was begun to extend it in the 12C, shortage of space quickly became a problem. The last bays of the nave (built two by two, in two stages), together with the west porch, were built virtually above a sheer drop, with the tall arcades serving as open piling. At the end of the 12C, the For porch and St-Jean porch were added. Extensive restoration was carried out on the cathedral in the 19C.

West front – A wide staircase leads to the unusual west front with its polychrome floor slabs and mosaics where Hispano-Moorish influence is evident. The fourth level, with small stonework, is lit through three windows, and the top level is crowned by three gables. The ensemble is supported by the arches around the three doorways.

Route under the cathedral – Steps lead to the "Golden Door" under the four bays built in the 12C. At the level of the 2nd bay, two 12C **panelled doors★** close off two side chapels; their faint decoration in relief recounts the life of Christ. In the following bay, two restored **frescoes** can be seen: the Virgin Mother (13C) on the left and the

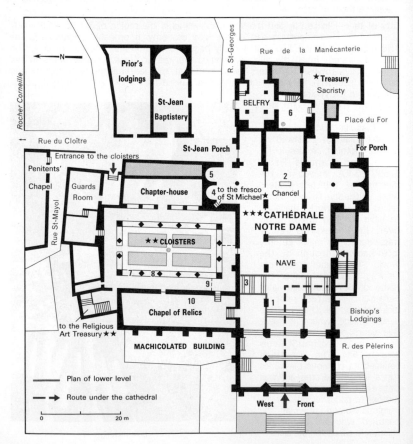

Transfiguration of Our Lord on the right. Go through the "Golden Door", framed by two red porphyry columns. The 4th bay contains the "Fever Stone" *(see above)* next to which a sick person is said to have been cured by the Virgin, though this myth dates back perhaps to the time of the druids. This marks the turn-off for the staircase which used to lead right into the cathedral, opposite the high altar, and which led to the saying that "one enters Notre-Dame du Puy through the navel and leaves through the ears".

Take the right fork which leads to a door in the side aisle.

Interior – The most unusual feature of the church is the series of domes which cover the nave (that over the transept crossing is modern). Note the pulpit (**1**) and the beautiful high altar (**2**), built by the chapter in 1723, which supports the wooden statue replacing the original Black Virgin burnt during the Revolution.

In the north aisle hangs a large painting by Jean Solvain known as the "Vow of the Plague" (1630) (**3**) illustrating a thanksgiving procession in Place du For.

In the north arm of the transept are beautiful Romanesque frescoes, recently restored: the Holy Women at the tomb (**4**) and the Martyrdom of St Catherine of Alexandria (**5**).

A small staircase on the left leads to a gallery where there is a **fresco of St Michael★** ⊘ (late 11C-early 12C), the largest known painting in France depicting the Archangel Michael.

The finest pieces of the **treasury★** ⊘ displayed in the sacristy are, from the 15C, a *Pietà* oil on panel of the Burgundian School, a gold-plated copper head of Christ; from the 17C, an ivory Christ, a Rhône boat crew's cross and walnut panelling.

For Porch – This porch with highly elaborate capitals dates back to the late 12C. The smallest door is known as the "Papal Door" because of the inscription above it. In the inside corner, the ribs rest on a pilaster which supports an open hand coming out of the wall.

From the small Place du For there is an attractive view of the modern part of the town, and a good view of the belfry, a pyramid-shaped construction with seven levels standing out slightly from the highly-restored east end.

Walk around the east end via Rue de la Manécanterie.

St-Jean Porch – This porch preceded by a large flattened arcade was designed for sovereigns to pass through. The leather-covered doors have beautiful 12C strap hinges (wrought-iron brackets). The porch connects the cathedral to the 10C-11C baptistery, its entrance flanked by two stone lions.

Pass under the belfry to the small courtyard adjoining the east end of the cathedral.

Note, on the way past, the tombs of abbots and canons, and in the courtyard (**6**), behind the Romanesque well, the Gallo-Roman low-reliefs incorporated into the base of the east end and the frieze above: they depict hunting scenes.

Machicolated Building – This massive structure sheltering behind the Chapel is the old Velay State Room. The building was part of the fortifications of the cathedral and bishop's palace in the 13C.

It comprises four levels, two of them accessible to the public: the third floor houses the Chapel of Relics, access to which is via the north aisle of the cathedral, and the fourth floor contains the Religious Art Treasury which is part of the Cloisters Museum.

Chapel of Relics ⊘ – The Chapel of Relics or winter chapel (it opens off the north aisle of the cathedral), located on the third floor of the Machicolated Building, derives its name from the beautiful gold altarpiece which, until the Revolution, housed relics brought to Notre-Dame du Puy. The room, the former library of St-Mayol University, was decorated on its eastern wall in the 15C with the now famous painting depicting the **Liberal Arts★** (**10**). Each of the liberal arts (Grammar, Logic, Rhetoric, Music) is represented by a seated woman and an allegorical character. The detail of the fabrics and jewellery provides a good insight into the tastes of the period.

St-Jean Baptistery – This building, dating back to the 10C and 11C, and connected to the cathedral by the porch of the same name, served as a baptistery for all the parishes in the town during the Revolution. The southern entrance is flanked with eroded stone lions. Inside is a pyramid-shaped font.

Prior's Lodgings ⊘ – Adjoining St-Jean Baptistery, the vaulted rooms of the former residence of the administrator of baptisms house an historical exhibition on Velay, and a remarkable collection of rural and craftsmen's tools.

★★**Cloisters** (**BY**) ⊘ – The beautiful cloisters abut the north face of the cathedral; each gallery is from a different period; the oldest, to the south, is Romanesque. The whole building was restored in the 19C. These galleries open onto a cloister garth through semicircular arcades supported by square pillars flanked by monolithic columns. The **historiated capitals** include one (**7**) depicting a dispute about an abbot's crook, and another (**8**) showing a centaur.

A remarkable **Romanesque railing**★ (**9**) closes the west gallery. From the southwest corner of the cloisters, a Romanesque chimney can be seen rising above the altar-boys' house.

Around the cloisters, above the arcades, is a delicately decorated **cornice** illustrating a medieval bestiary. The polychrome archstones and the quoins with their black, white, red and ochre lozenges form a decor reminiscent of Islamic art.

A door in the east gallery leads to the **chapter-house**, which in the 14C was a funeral chapel, with its entrance framed by ribbed pilasters with double fluting (a rare design). It is decorated on the south wall with a 13C fresco representing the Crucifixion *(light switch by the entrance)*.

★★**Religious Art Treasury** ⊘ – The Treasury, displayed in the former Velay State Room above the Chapel of Relics, contains a large number of works of art, including an 11C silk cope, a 13C engraved enamel reliquary, a polychrome stone 15C nursing Virgin, Bishop John of Bourbon's *fleur-de-lys* tapestry (late 15C), a magnificent 16C embroidered cloak for the Black Virgin, and a remarkable piece of 15C parchment showing the Genesis of the World to the Resurrection.

The paintings include the *Adoration of the Magi* by Claude Vignon (1640) and *The Holy Family* attributed to the Master of Flémalle (late 15C). The art of the Montpellier sculptor, Pierre Vaneau (1653-94), who worked extensively for the Bishop of Le Puy, is represented by panels illustrating mythological subjects and by two statues of slaves carved in walnut.

Penitents' Chapel (**BY B**) – The entrance is through a panelled wooden door carved in the Renaissance style and flanked by two groups of wreathed columns.

Inside, the paintings decorating the gallery, the panelled walls of the nave and, in particular, the beautiful coffered ceiling, recount the life of the Virgin Mary. They were produced in the 17C and 18C.

The numerous staffs of the Brotherhood of the White Penitents, founded in 1584, are still carried during processions *(see Calendar of events)*.

Rocher Corneille (**BY**) ⊘ – This is the remainder of a cone, no doubt belonging to the volcano of which St-Michel rock is the chimney.

From the platform there is a panoramic **view**★ of the red rooftops of the town and Le Puy basin, and of St-Michel rock (northwest), behind which can be seen Polignac castle.

The rock is surmounted by a monumental **statue of Notre-Dame de France** erected in 1860 by national subscription. This cast iron statue is 16m/52ft high and weighs 110 tonnes. 213 cannon from among the trophies from the capture of Sebastopol given to contractors by Napoleon III were melted down to cast it. It is possible to go up inside the statue to neck level.

Return to Place des Tables.

★OLD TOWN

The tall, red-roofed houses of the Old Town cluster around the foot of Corneille rock, while the circular boulevards mark the beginning of the lower-lying, more modern town.

From Places des Tables in front of the cathedral (**AY 49**), there is interesting view over the city. At no 56 Rue Raphaël, on the left, stands a handsome 16C building on five levels, known as the **Logis des Alix Selliers**.

At the end of this street turn left into Rue Roche-Taillade.

On the corner with Rue Cardinal de Pol is the 15C **Hôtel du Lac de Fugères** (**L**) and, further to the right at no 8, the **Hôtel de Polignac** (**D**), the Polignac family mansion with its 15C polygonal tower.

Back beyond Rue Roche-Taillade, at no 3 Rue Vaneau, rises the **Hôtel des Laval d'Arlempdes** (**F**). Walk back down Rue Roche-Taillade which becomes Rue Chênebouterie; note, at no 8, the courtyard with a 15C turret, and opposite at no 9, the birthplace (16C) of Marshal Payolle. The road leads to **Place du Plot** (**AZ 38**) which, at the end of the week, bustles with a colourful market around **La Bidoire fountain**, dated 1246. Nearby, at no 8 **Rue Courrerie** (**AZ 20**) there remains an interesting 16C façade next to the Hôtel de Marminhac with arched windows bearing keystones carved with masks. Continue to Place du Martouret – the site of many executions during the Revolution – where the hôtel de ville stands.

Return to Place du Plot and follow Rue Pannessac.

This part-pedestrianised street is bordered by elegant 16C and 17C Renaissance houses with overhanging fronts, sometimes flanked by a tower or watch-turret (nos 16, 18, 23). To the right, some of the alleys – **Rue Philibert** (**AY 36**), **Rue du Chamarlenc** (**AY 10**) – retain a medieval character. The façade of no 16 Rue Chamarlenc, known as the **Demeure des Cornards** (the Cornards were companions whose prerogative it was to poke fun at the town's burghers) is adorned with two horned heads, one laughing, the other sticking out its tongue, surmounted by satirical inscriptions.

LE PUY-EN-VELAY

Aiguières (R. Porte)... **AZ** 2
Chaussade (R.) .... **BZ**
Fayolle (Bd Mar.) ..... **BZ**
Foch (Av. Mar.).......... **BZ**
Pannessac (R.) .... **AY**
Raphaël (R.) .... **AY** 39
St-Gilles (R.) .... **AZ**
St-Louis (Bd) .... **AZ**

Becdelièvre (R.) ...... **AY** 3
Bouillon (R. du) ...... **BY** 5

Card. de Polignac (R.).. **BY** 8
Chamarlenc (R. du)... **AY** 10
Chênebouterie (R.) ... **AY** 13
Collège (R. du) .... **BZ** 17
Consulat (R. du) ...... **AY** 19
Courrerie (R.) .... **AZ** 20
Crozatier (R.)......... **BZ** 23
Dr. Chantemesse (Bd) **AY** 24
For (Pl. du)........... **BY** 27
Gambetta (Bd) .... **AY** 30
Gouteyron (R.)........ **AY** 31
Grangevieille (R.) .... **AY** 32
Martouret (Pl. du) ... **ABZ** 34
Monteil (R. A. de) .... **AY** 35
Philibert (R.) .... **AY** 36

Pierret (R.) .... **BZ** 37
Plot (Pl. du) .... **AZ** 38
République (Bd de la) **BY** 40
Roche-Taillade (R.) ... **AY** 42
St-François
  Régis (R.) .... **BY** 43
St-Georges (R.)....... **AY** 45
St-Jean (R. du Fg) ... **BY** 46
St-Maurice (Pl.) ...... **AY** 47
Séguret (R.)........... **AY** 48
Tables (Pl. des)...... **AY** 49
Tables (R. des) ...... **AY** 52
Vallès (R. J.) .... **BY** 54
Vaneau (R.) .... **AY** 55
Verdun (R.) .... **BY** 58

B	Chapelle des Pénitents	**K**	Tour Pannessac
D	Hôtel de Polignac	**L**	Hôtel du Lac de Fugères
E	Atelier Chaleyé	**S**	Portail du prieuré
Γ	Hôtel des Laval d'Arlempdes		de Vorey

At no 42 Rue Pannessac, the **Logis des André**, and at no 46 the 17C **Logis des Frères Michel** decorated on the ground floor with masks and carved quoins, and on the upper storeys with masks, garlands and scrolls, both reveal the opulence of the wealthy merchant who lived in this district. At the end of the street, the 13C **Pannessac tower (K)** retains a level of trefoiled machicolations. It is the last remaining trace of the original 18 fortified gateways, with twinned towers which allowed access through the town walls.

The writer Jules Vallès, a native of Le Puy, described the tough childhood he endured in the Old Town in the first volume of his trilogy *L'Enfant, Le Bachelier* and *L'Insurgé*.

★★CHAPELLE ST MICHEL D'AIGUILHE (AY) ⊘ *45min*

St-Michel chapel crowns St-Michel rock, a gigantic needle of lava which rises up in a single shaft to a height of 80m/262ft above ground level. Its slender belfry, in the form of a minaret, looks like a pointed finger of rock. 268 steps lead up to it.

D. Faure/SCOPE

St-Michel chapel

This chapel probably replaced a temple dedicated to Mercury. The building standing today, which dates from the late 11C, shows Oriental inspiration in its tre-foil portal, its decoration of arabesques and its black, white and grey stone mosaics. Inside, the highly irregular ground plan follows the contours of the rock. The complexity of the vaulting testifies to the architects' ability to make the most of the site. The small columns, which form a sort of ambulatory around a short nave, are surmounted by carved capitals.

The vaulting above the small apse is decorated with 10C paintings. On the right, *objets d'art* found under the altar in 1955 are on display; note in particular a small 11C wooden reliquary Christ and a 13C Byzantine ivory cask.

A covered watchpath goes around the chapel, overlooking **Vieux Pont** (**BY**), the old cusp bridge across the River Borne.

Chapelle St-Clair (**AY**) – This 12C building at the foot of St-Michel rock was perhaps a baptistery or the chapel of a former hospital. The exterior is decorated with blind arcades and lozenges, which is characteristic of the Velay region.

ADDITIONAL SIGHTS

Musée Crozatier (**AZ**) ⊘ – The Henri Vinay garden, in which this vast museum stands, includes, among other monuments, the beautiful portal from Vorey Priory (**BZ S**).

The basement houses a beautiful 18C "French berline" coach.

On the ground floor, opposite the section on regional palaeontology and prehistory, is a **lapidary collection★** (Romanesque and Gothic art) containing chancel panels and historiated capitals from the cathedral. On the mezzanine level, two rooms contain works by the sculptor Pierre Julien (1731-1804) as well as working models of machines.

In the section on local arts *(first floor)* there is a 16C tapestry with the Polignac and Pompadour arms, a gilded polychrome stone Annunciation from the late 15C and, in particular, a rich collection of hand-made **lace★** from the 16C to the present day, including magnificent bobbin and needlepoint work. On the same floor, tribute is paid to Emile Reynaud, inventor of the praxinoscope, an ancestor of the cine projector.

The second floor, reached by a 17C revolving door brought from the Convent of the Visitation, is given over to the fine arts. Among the paintings and sculptures covering the period from the 14C to the 20C are the 15C **Virgin in a Cloak**, with its surprising composition and colours, works by local artists such as Guy François (1578-1650), and landscapes by the pointillist painter Dubois-Pillet *(St-Michel Chapel in the Snow)*.

The top floor houses the natural history section with an ornithological collection containing nearly 400 species.

St-Laurent (**AY**) – The church of St-Laurent is a rare example of Gothic art in Velay; it dates from the 14C and was part of a Dominican convent. The doorway of the west front was built in the 19C in the Flamboyant style; note the three canopied alcoves in the tympanum.

Inside, the nave, shouldered by two side aisles and covered with ribbed vaulting, is surprisingly large. In the chancel, on the right, lies the tomb of **Bertrand du Guesclin** which contains the entrails of the Commander in Chief of the French armies, a national hero who died in 1380 during a siege. Work carried out in the chancel led to the discovery of the tomb of Bishop Bernard de Montaigu (13C).

On the left of the church a former 14C chapel, known as the chapter-house, has been uncovered.

Atelier Chaleyé (BY E) ⊙ – The studio of the post-Impressionist painter **Chaleyé** (1878-1960) is located on the 1st floor of the dwelling in which he spent the last years of his life.

Numerous paintings, many of flowers and landscapes, are exhibited. He also created lace patterns, some of the cartoons of which are kept in the Musée Crozatier *(see above)*.

EXCURSIONS

Vallée de la Borne

Round trip of 25km/16mi – allow 2hr

Leave Le Puy northwest, on ③ on the map, the N 102 towards Brioude. 1km/0.6mi after crossing the Borne, turn right onto the D 13, which gives good views of Le Puy.

★**Polignac** – *See POLIGNAC.*

Leave Polignac west on the D 136, then at the junction take the N 102 for 3km/2mi before turning left onto the D 112.

Château de St Vidal

Château de St-Vidal ⊙ – This castle, its massive towers dominating the village which clusters below around a rise in the Borne valley, was the fief of Baron Antoine de la Tour, governor of Velay in the 16C. The castle has retained from its feudal days the vaulted cellars and Gothic kitchen with its immense fireplaces. Gothic and Renaissance decorative elements from the alterations carried out in the 15C and 16C still remain, including the galleries with ribbed vaulting lining three sides of the inner courtyard, the beamed ceiling and carved stone doorway of the State Room, and the southern façade. A spiral staircase leads to the top floor of the church tower (14C) which was reserved for the artillery.

Carry on along the D 113, which crosses the Borne, then at the second junction turn left onto the D 590 towards Le Puy.

Espaly-St-Marcel – *Leave the D 590 just after passing underneath the railway, to turn left onto the street signposted "St-Joseph" to the car park.*

Piton d'Espaly – This peak was formerly crowned with a castle which, after serving as a residence for the bishops of Le Puy (Charles VII, while Dauphin then subsequently King of France, was given hospitality here during his frequent pilgrimages), was ruined during battles involving the Catholic League.

Rocher St-Joseph ⊙ – The upper terrace, built at the foot of the statue, offers a **view★** of the Old Town of Le Puy-en-Velay, with its cathedral, Corneille rock and St-Michel chapel.

Round trip to Bouchet lake

Round tour of 49km/30mi – about 2hr. Leave Le Puy south by ③ on the map.

The N 88 winds up through the plateaux overlooking Le Puy basin.

At Montagnac turn right onto the D 33 to Cayres, then take the D 31 towards Le Bouchet-St-Nicolas; after 1.5km/1mi, take the D 312 on the right to the lake.

★**Lac du Bouchet** – *A path through the woods encircles the lake (45min).* The lake lies at the bottom of an old crater at an altitude of 1 205m/3 953ft; it has a surface area of 43ha/106 acres and is 28m/91ft deep. Its almost circular form is surrounded by fir, spruce and pine woods which were planted between 1860 and 1900; much of this forest was replanted after a devastating storm in 1982. There is no known river or stream feeding the lake, nor any overflow outlet, yet the clearness and freshness of the lake's waters show that they are being constantly renewed.

Turn around. 500m from the lake turn left onto the road through the forest, then right onto the D 33.

There are good views of the slopes of the Devès and the Velay mountains.

At Cayres turn left onto the D 31 and continue along the D 621 which winds across a plateau at an altitude of more than 1 000m/3 200ft.

On the left, the crest line of the Devès can be seen.

At Bains turn right; the D 589 leads to Le Puy-en-Velay.

There are additional impressive views of the town and its surroundings.

★Massif du Meygal

Leave Le Puy on ① and take the D 88 towards St-Étienne. After 7km/5mi, at the roundabout, turn right to St-Julien-Chapteuil. Continue east along the D 15 towards Valence. Just beyond Boussoulet turn left into the forest.

The range is made up of phonolithic rocks dotted with boulders. The grey rock is used to provide roofing tiles.

Take the right fork to the parking area.

★★**Grand Testavoyre** – Alt 1 436m/4 711ft. A path through ferns and bilberry bushes leads to the summit from which there are splendid **panoramic views** over the volcanic landscape.

Continue through the forest. At the crossroads take the D 18 left which joins the N 88 returning to Le Puy.

RAVEL

Population 486
Michelin map 73 fold 15 or 239 fold 20
6km/4mi miles south of Lezoux – Local map under La LIMAGNE

This village, set among the pasture and woodland of the Limagne, is easily identified by the château which overlooks it and its church.

★**Château** ⊙ – *Access is either from Ravel by a street, with several very steep sections, which leads off a small square opposite the church, or by a route through the undergrowth off the D 223 southeast of Lezoux.*
The castle was given by Philip the Fair (1268-1314) to his chancellor Pierre Flotte and passed by inheritance and marriage to the d'Estaing family which had it renovated in the 17C.
The most beautiful and best preserved part of its decoration dates from the 18C.
The terrace designed by the landscape architect **Le Nôtre** (17C) looks over a beautiful **panorama**★ of the Limagne countryside and Monts Dômes chain.
The walls and towers of the eastern façade of this vast construction date back to feudal times, the main courtyard was built in the 17C and the western wing in the 18C.

Interior – Some of the original furniture still remains. A tour of the wings leads to the genealogy room (family portraits), the coats-of-arms room with its terracotta paved floor (emblems from the former states of the Auvergne), the great gallery (mementoes of Admiral d'Estaing including a scale model of his ship, paintings depicting naval battles, navigation instruments), the music room (panelling decorated with musical instruments), the richly-decorated gold room (beamed ceiling, four-poster bed, Aubusson tapestries).

Church – The building in very pure Gothic style has two 14C stained-glass windows in the nave and another (late 13C) in the sacristy. A strange Romanesque capital acts as a support for a 12C stone stoup. A 14C carved wooden staircase-door is protected by a second door.

Moyenne vallée du RHÔNE ★★★

Michelin map 246

The Rhône is the most powerful and fastest-flowing of the major French rivers. It is also the most majestic; downstream of Lyon, as it flows southwards between the slopes of the Massif Central and the Alpine foreland, it offers a luminous vista of magnificent grandeur.

At every turn, the valley takes on a new beauty – lofty hills, at times forbidding and at others inviting; broad valleys opening out as the river approaches Provence; narrow gorges closing in suddenly. The 200km/125mi or so of the river's course, to where it spills into the Mediterranean sea, are set amidst magnificent scenery such as this.

Roman remains; precariously perched ruins conjuring up times of pillage and violence; churches and castles clinging to promontories, opposite villages tumbling down the valley slopes to the river's edge and linked to each other by suspension bridges; imposing technological developments and industrial complexes alongside terraced vineyards and orchards stretching across the valley floor – these features form an incomparable landscape continually shaped by generations of Rhône valley inhabitants.

THE RHÔNE VALLEY

Profile of the valley – South of Lyon, the middle valley of the Rhône is an immense furrow, an old oceanic trough, boxed in by the Massif Central and the pre Alps. It widens suddenly in places – basins formed by erosion of the soft soil on the west bank, banks of small rounded pebbles or sandstone from the Dauphiné, the limestone plateaux of Tricastin alternating with gorges formed by the river's gradual carving a course into the old igneous rock base or sometimes, as in Donzère, into a limestone dike. Further south, as the river flows through the Vivarais region, the basins become larger spreading out towards the east.

The contrast between the Rhône's banks is emphasised by the different profile of its tributaries; on the west bank, they emerge suddenly from gorges cut into the steep side of the embankment; on the east bank, they flow towards the Rhône across low-lying alluvial plains.

A powerful, fast-flowing river – Throughout the year, the Rhône carries a large volume of water at high speed. Its swift flow is due to the relatively steep gradient – 0.5m per km/2ft 8in per mi between Lyon and Valence, reaching 0.77m per km/4ft 1in per mi between Valence and the Ardèche confluent, before dropping to 0.49m per km/2ft 7in per mi between the confluence of the Ardèche and the Gardon. Further downstream, the gradient levels off considerably.

The hydraulic power of the Rhône is remarkable: 1 350m^3/s (47 675ft^3/s) at average water levels in Valence. To generate such power, the river's speed is about 2.5m/s (8ft 2in/s). As it flows through France, the Rhône is joined by various types of tributaries – alpine rivers in spate in the spring and summer, torrents from the Vivarais in autumn and winter, with the result that, even in summer, the Rhône maintains a relatively high water level. Its spates are linked to those of its tributaries. The greatest of these occur in autumn (see Vallée de l'ARDÈCHE). The Rhône then becomes Chateaubriand's "great wild river" and Michelet's "raging bull down from the Alps".

The mistral – There are times when this wind dominates the whole valley. It may begin weak in the north, but it gathers force south of Valence and fairly sweeps across the plain. The difference in temperature between the increasingly hot valleys nearer the Mediterranean explains the violence of the mistral's blast and its sudden gusts.

From boatmen to self-propelled barges – The Greeks who setted in Marseille in about 600 BC used the Rhône to bring back tin from Cornwall in Britain. During Roman times, commercial boating became even more important; the river was the main artery for the wine trade. The Rhône boatmen formed the most powerful of all the corporations in the Roman towns.

Under the Ancien Régime (before the French Revolution) passenger barges connected the riverside towns, which all had their own port, leading to an intensely active life on the river. This beautiful waterway is, however, very dangerous when in spate or when the mistral blows. **Madame de Sévigné** suffered hours of anguish knowing that her daughter was travelling along "that devil of a Rhône".

In 1829 steam boats appeared on the Rhône and traffic became even more dense. The advent of the railway nearly ruined river transport, but the discovery and exploitation of water's potential as a source of energy, and engineering work on the river rejuvenated the Rhône. After work carried out by the Compagnie nationale du Rhône, the tugboats of the past were replaced by 1 500-tonne self-propelled barges and push tows of 5 000 tonnes and more. The annual traffic (4 100 000t) includes hydrocarbons, metallurgical and agricultural products and building materials.

Bridges – While the Romans built only two bridges over the Rhône, one of wood between Arles and Trinquetaille, and the other of stone in Vienne, architects in the Middle Ages overcame the difficulties involved and erected three more bridges. St-Bénézet bridge in Avignon was built in 11 years, from 1177 to 1188, by the Pontiff Brothers, who also built in the following century the Guillotière bridge in Lyon and the bridge at Pont-St-Esprit.

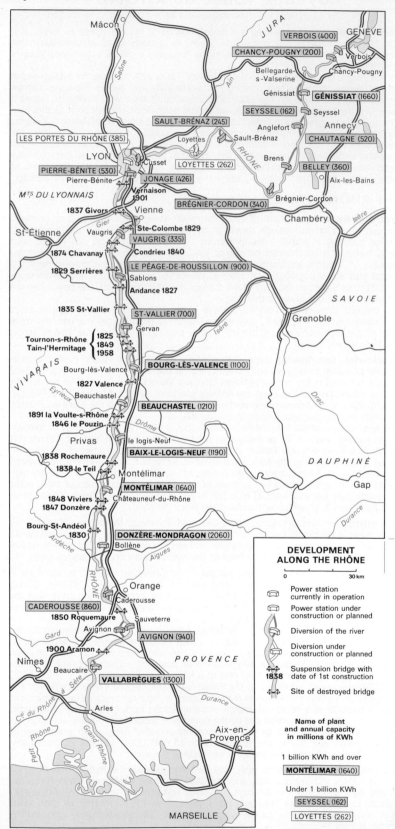

DEVELOPMENT
ALONG THE RHÔNE

0 — 30 km

Power station currently in operation

Power station under construction or planned

Diversion of the river

Diversion under construction or planned

Suspension bridge with date of 1st construction 1838

Site of destroyed bridge

Name of plant and annual capacity in millions of KWh

1 billion KWh and over

MONTÉLIMAR (1640)

Under 1 billion KWh

SEYSSEL (162)

LOYETTES (262)

In the 19C the **Seguin brothers** invented the technique of building iron-cable suspension bridges and provided an economical solution to the problem of crossing the Rhône. The first suspension bridge built across the river was that at Tournon in 1825; it was demolished in 1965 (the bridge that can be seen today dates back to 1846).

The Second World War brought about an almost total destruction of the Rhône's suspension bridges. They have been reconstructed using state-of-the-art technology (Vernaison, Tournon, Teil, Viviers). The main suspension arch is frequently more than 200m/650ft long (Teil: 235m/770ft, Vernaison: 231m/758ft).

Pre-stressed concrete was used to build the non-suspension bridges; the most remarkable is the railway bridge at La Voulte (1955). The latest bridges opened to road traffic are those of the Vienne by-pass (A 7 motorway) in 1973, that of Chavanay upstream of the Roussillon toll gate, at the end of 1977, and the Tricastin bridge on the feeder canal from the Donzère-Mondragon falls, in 1978.

Cruas-Meysse nuclear power station

Development along the Rhône – The development of the Rhône's industrial potential has been in the hands of the Compagnie Nationale du Rhône since 1934 and comprises three main activities: boating, irrigation and electricity. No less than 23 construction projects along the river's course between Lake Geneva and the Mediterranean have transformed it into a huge aquatic step-ladder capable of generating about 16 thousand million kWh per year.

Downstream from Lyon, the valley is wide and given over to agricultural concerns. Its low-lying banks are not suitable for the installation of hydro-electric dams, so in places the river itself has been diverted by a dam into a feeder canal which supplies a power station, before the river is fed back into its original course along another canal. Locks have been built so that river traffic can pass along the canals.

Irrigation projects covering 200 000ha/494 000 acres of the river plain have increased the yields of this fertile land, on which orchards thrive particularly well.

Technological adaptations of the river's course with their inherent benefits have attracted industry, significantly altering the character of the valley. Factories and other industrial plants line the river from Lyon to Avignon, their products including oil refining, mechanical construction, glass, fertilisers, paper, cardboard, chemicals, textiles and cement. **Nuclear energy plants** such as those at St-Alban-St-Maurice, Cruas-Meysse, Tricastin and Pierrelatte add to the Rhône's already significant role as energy generator for the French nation.

★THE INDUSTRIAL CORRIDOR

① From Lyon to Vienne

30km/18mi – about 5hr, not including Lyon – local map p 290

★★★**Lyon** – *2 days. See LYON.*

Leave Lyon on ⑦, the A 7 motorway.

At the exit to Lyon, the section of road which runs along the riverside is lined by the rows of tall industrial buildings of **Pierre-Bénite** and **Feyzin**. Sun and sky are reflected in the metal-clad buildings of this large industrial complex which includes a refinery. The A 7 motorway crosses the river just upstream from the Pierre-Bénite dam.

At the foot of the hillsides, the slopes of which are covered in greenery with the odd tenaciously clinging church belfry peeking out here and there, more industrial plants come into view: Givors, Loire-sur-Rhône nuclear power station.

Vienne appears in a sweeping bend in the river, and the valley opens out into a small basin.

★★**Vienne** – *Allow half a day. See VIENNE.*

The Rhône valley at Tain-l'Hermitage

★★★ORCHARDS AND VINEYARDS

② From Vienne to Valence

147km/91mi – allow one day, not including a tour of Vienne and Valence local map p 290

Leave Vienne via the main bridge over the Rhône (⑦ on the town plan).

St-Romain-en-Gal et Ste-Colombe – *See VIENNE.*

Immediately after the bridge under the railway, turn left onto the D 502.

As the road climbs up the first foothills of Mont Pilat, it gives extensive **views**★ over the Rhône valley and then over that of the Gier.

At Croix-Régis turn left onto the D 59 to Condrieu.

After running beside the last escarpments of the Pilat region (Mont Monnet: 789m/2 588ft) the road descends, offering a far-reaching **view**★ from the bend with a calvary in it, just north of Condrieu. Between the river and the line of the hills, the land is covered with orchards (apricot, pear, cherry and peach trees).

Condrieu – One of the largest markets in the region is held here, specialising in fruit and early vegetables. The **church** has a Gothic doorway with a tympanum bearing fragments of a Romanesque bas-relief. Next to it stands a house with an attractive 16C façade. The port – the town was once renowned for its sailors – is a pleasant place for a stroll, with its slightly Mediterranean feel.

Follow the N 86 and beyond Vérin take the narrow, twisting road (D 34) up to St-Michel.

St-Michel-sur-Rhône – There are strange corner acroteria (plinths for statues) on the church belfry. From the east end of the church the view stretches over the sinuous curves of the river; to the right, in the foreground, rise the chimneys of the factories at St-Clair-du-Rhône.

The road snakes along the crest of the hills, dominated to the right by Mont Pilat; the descent to Chavanay goes through old terraced gardens. To the left stand the installations of St-Alban-St-Maurice nuclear power station.

Turn right onto the D 503 to Malleval.

Malleval – *See SERRIÈRES: Excursion.*

Rejoin the N 86.

Serrières – *See SERRIÈRES.*

Champagne – The **church** here is largely 12C and is the only one in the Rhône valley to have a nave vaulted with a series of domes on squinches; three domes cover the nave and a fourth hangs over the transept crossing. The vaulted aisles are surmounted by a gallery which opens on to the nave by twinned, trefoil-arched openings. There are beautiful 15C choir stalls and, on the tympanum above the central door, scenes of the Last Supper and the Passion.

Pratta/ICONOS-EXPLORER

At the entrance to Andance, at the foot of some granite needles, it is possible to see, in the distance on the east bank, the silhouette of the tall Albon tower.

Andance – The church here houses a remarkable **Crew's Cross**★ in the right chapel; there are also fine Romanesque pilasters.

Cross the Rhône via the suspension bridge (1827) and take the D 122A under the motorway to Albon tower.

Tour d'Albon and Château de Mantaille – The ruined Albon tower commands a view to the horizon. It was the counts of Albon who, by increasing their territories, from the 11C onwards, created the Dauphiné region. The various graffiti adorning the tower include one commemorating the centenary of the fall of the Bastille. From the foot of the tower the vast **panorama**★ takes in the Rhône valley, from St-Vallier gorge to St-Rambert plain, the mouth of the Valloire, and the Cévennes to the west.

4km/2.5mi east stand the ruins of Mantaille castle; it was here that Boson was crowned king of Burgundy in the year 879.

Return to Albon and turn left (D 122) to Beausemblant. Turn left by the church onto the D 312 towards St-Uze. After 2km/1mi, just after a sharp left-hand bend, turn right onto a small road; 400m further on, by a pylon, turn left onto a narrow road (very few passing places) which winds down to St-Vallier.

The road overlooks to mouth of the gorge, opposite Sarras. The lines of the hillsides close in, seeming to choke the valley.

St-Vallier – The Poitiers family, counts of St-Vallier, occupied the **château** *(private)* here; **Diane de Poitiers** spent part of her childhood in it.

Cross the river to Sarras; take the D 6 southwest towards St-Jeure-d'Ay and then after 5km/3mi turn left onto the D 506.

The steep descent to Ozon offers spectacular **views**★★ from two sharp bends over **St-Vallier gorge**★, and over the orchards and vineyards occupying the terraces along the river.

Return to Sarras and St-Vallier, then take the N 7 to Tain-l'Hermitage along the east bank of the Rhône.

This section of the valley, which narrows into a corridor again, is the most evocative of the Rhône in medieval times; ruins of feudal strongholds and old defensive towers and watchtowers line the escarpments. The entrance to **Serves-sur-Rhône** is preceded by a superb **view**, ahead, of the impressive remains of its castle. On the west bank stands the rival tower of **Arras-sur-Rhône**.

Beyond the turning to Crozes-Hermitage a wild-looking hill known as Pierre-Aiguille, into which the railway line disappears, forces the road back towards the river. Note the small, table-shaped rock with a sign on it; when the river is in spate, it disappears beneath the water level. To the left, the hillsides fall back, revealing the Hermitage slopes adorned with the characteristic stripes of its vineyard.

Moyenne vallée du RHÔNE

★Belvédère de Pierre-Aiguille – Alt 344m/ 1 128ft. The far-reaching views from here encompass Tain-l'Hermitage and its famous vineyard; the town of Tournon across the river; the foothills of Vercors with the Alps in the background to the east; the Doux valley, the Mézenc and the Gerbier de Jonc peaks to the west.

Take the suspension bridge across the Rhône.

★Tournon-sur-Rhône – *See VALENCE: Excursions.*
From Tournon to Valence the **panoramic road★★★** along the hillside offers magnificent views.

Leave Tournon to the south-west via Rue du Dr-Cadet and Rue Greffieux towards St-Romain-de-Lerps.

The road out of town climbs steeply in a series of hairpin bends, giving breathtaking views.

In Plats turn left by the War Memorial onto the GR42.

★★★View from St-Romain-de-Lerps – On a platform bearing a television transmitter, near a small chapel not far from the tower, are two viewpoints. The **panorama** from here is immense, covering 13 *départements*. This is one of the most impressive views to be had along the Rhône: to the east, above the Valence plain, rises the Vercors bar, dominated by the Moucherolle needle and the dome of the Grand Veymont; beyond sparkle the distant, snow-capped peaks of the Alps and the mass of Mont Blanc. To the north, along the axis of the Rhône and slightly to the left, stands Mont Pilat; to the south looms Mont Ventoux. Westwards lie the plateaux and the green-houses of the Vivarais. The summit of Mont Mézenc overlooks this jumble of ridges from a distance.

From St-Romain-de-Lerps the D 287 down to St-Péray offers wonderful views over the Valence basin.

Ahead stands Crussol mountain with the jagged outline of its ruined castle.

★★★Crussol – *See CRUSSOL.*
The N 532 leads to Valence.

★Valence – *2hr 30min. See VALENCE.*

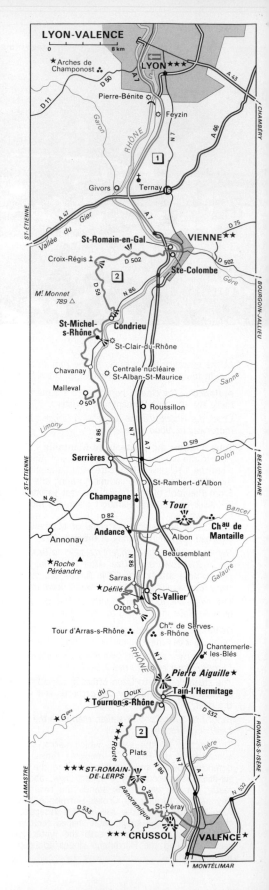

Les RHUES★★

Michelin map 76 folds 2, 3 or 239 fold 29, 30

A number of streams and rivers on the north side of Cantal bear the name Rhue. The largest of them, the Grande Rhue, flows into the Dordogne below Bort-les-Orgues after crossing a bar of rock known as the Saut de la Saule *(see BORT-LES-ORGUES)* but an underground drainage channel takes some of its water into the Bort reservoir. The Grande Rhue rises in the south of the Monts Dore near the Biche corrie. Once its waters have been swollen by the Rhue de Cheylade that flows down from the mountains of Cantal, the Grande Rhue flows through very picturesque wooded gorges.

★★VALLÉE DE LA RHUE

From Bort-les-Orgues to Condat

30km/19mi – about 1hr 15min – local map below

Bort-les-Orgues – *See BORT-LES-ORGUES.*
From Bort-les-Orgues drive southwards along the D 979.

East of Bort, the road begins to climb, offering an attractive view of the columnar basalt for which Bort is famous. It then reaches the Artense glacial plateau.

Champs-sur-Tarentaine – *See l'ARTENSE.*

Between Champs and Sarran the road follows a wide, dry valley through which the Rhue once flowed. The valley then rejoins the river and runs up the north bank below huge boulders.

Barrage de Vaussaire – *Near Embort.* Thanks to the work on the Upper Tarentaine (its waters power the turbines in the plant at Auzurette further upstream, producing 100 000 000kWh annually), this dam can drain off 757 000 000m^3 of water on average every year, which a 13.5km/8mi tunnel then carries through the wall of the Bort dam.

★★**Gorges de la Rhue** – Upstream from Embort, the river flows through a magnificent gorge with sides covered in greenery. The ravine widens out at the confluence of the two Rhues, near the Coindre hydro-electric power station (annual output: 100 000 000kWh).

Cascade de Cornillou – *30min Rtn on foot. 50m before the exit from the hamlet of Cornillou, park and turn left into a cart track. Just before reaching a deserted barn, turn right onto an uphill track that soon runs along the shores of a small lake-cum-reservoir. Turn left across a small bridge; 200m further on, an overgrown path (brambles) leads to the top of the waterfall. A steeply sloping path runs down to its foot.* The Gabacut, set in superb natural **surroundings**★ in the middle of the forest, has dug numerous cauldrons into the rock and drops down the hill in two successive small waterfalls.
The road enters a lovely pine forest from which there are some fine views of the Les Essarts lake-reservoir. After leaving the forest, the delightful countryside around Condat comes into view.

Condat – *See CONDAT.*

★★VALLÉE DE CHEYLADE

From Condat to the Pas de Peyrol

50km/31mi – about 2hr 30min

Head west from Condat along the D 678.

This narrow hillside road through the woods on the south bank of the Rhue provides a number of beautiful views of the gorge, with Les Essarts lake in the background.
After crossing the dry Sapchat valley, once the bed of the Rhue, and the Rhue de Cheylade valley, the road overlooks the wooded Véronne valley and runs along its hillside. Riom-ès-Montagne appears in the midst of a fresh pastoral setting.

Riom-ès-Montagnes – *See RIOM-ÈS-MONTAGNES.*

4km/3mi from Riom-ès-Montagne, there is a superb **panoramic view** to the left over the Monts Dore and the upper plateaux of the Cézallier area. Beyond lie the ruins of the Château d'Apchon and the mountains of Cantal.

Apchon – This is a characteristic Cantal village with its sturdy houses in volcanic stone. On the village square stands a **church** with a belfry-porch and a huge 17C gilded wood altarpiece inside. A footpath leads off from Rue de la Porte-du-Barre to the **castle ruins** *(30min on foot Rtn)*. There is a good **view**★ of the surrounding countryside from the top of the rocky pinnacle where the ruins stand.
South of the village *(4km/3mi on the D 249)* the 19C pilgrimage chapel of **La Font-Sainte** ⊙ can be seen in the middle of the fields.

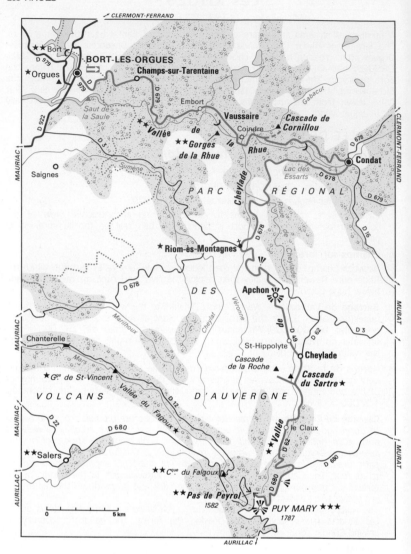

The D 49 runs through St-Hippolyte and down to the Rhue de Cheylade. After crossing the river, the Puy Mary is visible to the right of a long ridge starting at the Puy de Peyre-Arse.

Cheylade – This resort above the Rhue is popular with anglers. The interior of its church has undergone alteration on several occasions; the chancel, which still has a few carved capitals (mermaids, acanthus leaves, interlacing), and the apse are the oldest parts of the church. The nave and side aisles were roofed in the 17C with a remarkable **coffered ceiling**★ made of oak and painted with angels, flowers and animals in a naive style. Note the 15C stoup. At the end of the church, behind a wooden door decorated with a carving of the Baptism of Christ, is the 15C font. In the chancel stands a stone roadside Cross. Behind the high altar there is a 14C wooden Crucifix and, to the left of the chancel at the entrance to the Sacred Heart Chapel, a shield bearing the arms of the d'Estaing family, one of whose members found glory on the battlefield at Bouvines in 1214. There is also a wooden statue of St Leger (15C).

2.5km/2mi south of Cheylade, turn right onto the D 262. Park near a bridge and walk a further 100m to the right.

★**Cascade du Sartre** – The waterfall is formed by the Rhue which flows down a drop of 30m/97ft. Continue along the D 262 and, beyond another bridge, turn right into a path from which there is an attractive view of **Cascade de la Roche**, a waterfall formed by a tributary of the Rhue which drops down over the rocks in a series of mini-cascades.

Turn back.

Beyond Le Claux, the view of the Puy Mary and the Cheylade valley with its forested floor becomes increasingly impressive. The road rises in a series of hairpin bends and continues through woods until it reaches the alpine pastures. It then crosses the Col de Serres and arrives at the Impradine valley, hollowed into a bowl shape by ancient glaciers. During the final climb up to the Pas de Peyrol, the road crosses the Eylac pass, clings to the sheer sides of the Puy Mary and provides a number of splendid **views**★ over the Impradine and Rhue de Cheylade valleys, the Monts Dore, and the Cézallier area. Few roads in the Auvergne provide such breathtaking views.

★★ **Pas de Peyrol** – *See Monts du CANTAL.*

Château du RIAU

Michelin map 69 fold 14 or 238 north of folds 45, 46

The Riau estate comprises several buildings dating from the 15C to the 18C which lie in a lovely green setting; the most remarkable of these is the **tithe barn**★ ⊘ built in 1584, with its stables on the lower ground floor and grain storage on the three upper floors; the top floor, with its beautiful timber roof, provides an attractive view of the castle, moat, fortified gatehouse and dovecote.

The fortified gatehouse contains the chapel (prayer stool inlaid with mother-of-pearl) and the guard room. The castle itself consists of a 15C central building and two symmetrical wings built at right angles in the 17C. The outbuildings date from the 16C and 17C. Inside, the decoration and furnishings are mainly 18C. In the square tower, a 15C staircase with a wooden balustrade leads to bedrooms decorated in Louis XV, Louis XVI and Empire styles.

Moulin RICHARD-DE-BAS ★

Michelin map 73 fold 16 or 239 fold 22 – 5.5km/3mi east of Ambert

Old houses and paper mills, still surmounted by pine stretchers on which paper or printed sheets were hung to dry, are evidence of the industrial importance of the Lagat valley which, for several centuries, was one of the main papermaking centres in France. Today, Richard-de-Bas is the only remaining mill in activity.

TOUR ⊘

The mill was put back into operation in 1943 following efforts by La Feuille Blanche ("The White Sheet"), an association of Friends of Paper and the Graphic Arts. A paper museum is housed within the mill, where visitors may participate in the different stages of papermaking, using materials and techniques which have barely changed during the last 500 years. The museum is also interesting for the insight it brings on the way of life of the Masters and Fellows of Papermaking.

The **main room** served as a kitchen and eating room; seven or eight people gathered around the table to eat: the governor, his family, his worker and his apprentice; the women ate standing up. The furniture on view today belonged to the last inhabitant here, who died in 1937. There are also frying pans in which the *pandale* – grated potato pancake – was cooked, and a salt-mill shaped like a curled-up fox. The **bedroom** has three built-in beds, one of which is almost entirely enclosed: this was reserved for the apprentice, who began his training at the age of 7 or 8. The lacemaker's frame on the table was illuminated by a *doulie*, a glass ball filled with water which magnified the light from the candle.

Making a sheet of paper the traditional way

J. D. Sudres/SCOPE

293

The **Tsaï-Loun Room** follows the history of paper since its invention by the Chinese, who were inspired by wasps' nests, to the year 1326 when three men from the Auvergne who had been taken prisoner in Damascus returned and introduced the technique to the Ambert region, using the acidic spring waters of the Forez mountains. Other rooms look at the production of the 20-25kg/44-55lb of paper made here each day. A paper worker used to work from midnight to midday, as the waters needed to run the mill were diverted to irrigate fields during the day. Old fragments of white fabric (linen, cotton) are cut into small pieces; pine mallets with steel teeth are then used to crush the pieces of fabric. The paper paste, rinsed through with water to which glue has been added (to stop the paper absorbing too much ink) is poured into a vat; at this stage the petals and ferns which are used to make Flower Paper (one of this mill's specialities) are added. After it has been drained through a brass wire strainer (the "forme" or mould on which the watermark of the mill is sewn in relief), the still damp sheet of paper is placed between two sheets of felt; a press then exerts a pressure of 40 tonnes down on lots of 100 sheets, which are then hung up to dry in the drying rooms.

RIOM★★

Population 18 793
Michelin map 73 fold 4 or 239 fold 19 – Local map under La LIMAGNE

The old town of Riom perched on a small hill on the western edge of the Limagne region, still reflects the splendour of bygone days within the ring of boulevards laid out on its now demolished walls.

HISTORICAL NOTES

St Amable – St Amable, the first parish priest of Riom in the 5C, subsequently became an object of veneration and this has continued to modern times; each year, on the Sunday following 11th June, *brayauds* (peasants in traditional costume) carry his reliquary in procession through the town. It is the anniversary of the day in 1125 when Riom, under siege, was saved from being razed to the ground thanks to the relics of St Amable being exhibited on the ramparts.
In the 18C the relics were the object of such a jealous cult that when the illustrious Bishop of Clermont, Massillon, came to Riom, the inhabitants, afraid that he would take them away, refused to show them to him.

Riom capital city – At the beginning of the 13C Philippe Auguste's campaign was instrumental in making Riom's fortune as the monarchy decided to base the officers of its administration here. Under **Alphonse de Poitiers** the town was given a charter of immunity called the "Alfonsine". Riom, which until then had been confined to the area around St Amable Church, was built to a regular plan. The original 13C houses, gutted by fire, were replaced by sumptuous mansions at the end of the 15C.
In 1360 Duc **Jean de Berry**, the son of Jean le Bon (the Good), was given the Land of Auvergne, elevated to a duchy, as an apanage. The Duke, ostentatious and extravagant, was surrounded by a brilliant court of artists *(see Michelin Green Guide Berry Limousin in French)* and chose Riom as one of his favourite places of residence. He ordered extensive work to be carried out on the old castle which he had converted by the architect Gui de Dammartin. In one of the towers, cages were built for the wild beasts which accompanied the Duke wherever he went. Today, only the Holy Chapel remains from this old castle, which was destroyed in the 19C to build the Law Courts. It was in the chapel that in 1389, at the age of 60, he married his second wife, a 12-year-old countess of Auvergne. The marriage provoked much ridicule as the Duke was not a popular man; his rapacity knew no bounds and he had no hesitation in throwing into prison any of the Riom consuls who refused to provide money for his public relations operations.
After the Duke's death, Riom and the Duchy of Auvergne passed to the Bourbon family. The town remained very much attached to the king; when **Joan of Arc** needed powder and arrows for the siege of La Charité-sur-Loire, she appealed to the people of Riom, who were reputed for their wealth. They pledged 60 gold écus but were slow to send them. In 1430 the townspeople received a letter of reminder; the priceless letter has been preserved at the town hall, though the saint's hair, caught in the wax seal on the letter, has now disappeared.

TOWN CENTRE

Start from Place des Martyrs-de-la-Résistance.

★**Sainte-Chapelle** (L) ⊙ – *In the Palais de Justice.*
The chapel (14C), the only remainder of the Duke of Berry's castle, has some remarkable late 15C **stained-glass windows**★ in the chancel.
On leaving the Palais de Justice, take Rue Delille.

★**Musée régional d'Auvergne (M¹)** ⊙ – This regional museum of arts, crafts and traditions, on three floors, houses a remarkable collection of farming implements, rural and craft tools, furniture, games, domestic items and costumes which, with the reconstruction of typical Auvergne interiors, reflect the physiognomy of the province prior to the Industrial Revolution. The collection of head dresses and the room of religious statuary (13C-18C) are particularly interesting.

Rejoin Rue de l'Hôtel-de-Ville.

★**Musée Mandet (M²)** ⊙ – This museum is arranged in two private mansions: one, Hôtel Dufraisse (built 1740), houses the painting collections; the other, Hôtel Desaix, houses the Richard Bequest.

The first rooms display the painting collection. On the first floor, rooms decorated with delicate woodwork present a series of paintings from the 17C Flemish and Dutch schools and the 17C and 18C French schools. The second floor is given over to 19C painting, particularly the works of Alphonse Cornet, an artist from Riom.

The Richard Bequest includes interesting collections of decorative *objets d'art*. From Antiquity, there is a wax-on-linen portrait of a woman from the 2C AD which was discovered in the Fayyum region of Egypt *(room 2)*. From the Middle Ages and the Renaissance period, a Romanesque Virgin in Majesty from near Clermont-Ferrand *(room 4)*, a late 15C stone pilgrim's head *(room 5)* and a set of wooden statuettes from Flanders and northern France *(room 7)*. Next to the German and Italian primitives is a Virgin and Child from the school of Rogier Van der Weyden and a Crucifixion by Engelbrechtsz *(rooms 6 and 7)*.

The visit ends in richly furnished rooms devoted to the 16C, 17C and 18C, with a remarkable collection of household silver and gold plate, a beautiful set of French ceramics and a showcase of weapons.

Walk along Rue de l'Hôtel de Ville to the town hall.

Hôtel de Ville (H) ⊙ – In the vestibule is an enamelled stone plaque reproducing the letter from Joan of Arc to the people of Riom *(see above)*. The lovely 16C courtyard★ is decorated with vaulted arcades, a staircase turret with a carved door, and a war memorial by Rivoire.

★**Maison des Consuls (B)** – 16C. The ground floor of the Consuls' House has five archways. The first-floor windows support an elegant frieze above which are placed two busts of women and two busts of Roman emperors.

Carrefour des Taules (36) – Near this crossroads (*taule* is an old word for stall), which forms the intersection of the main streets of old Riom, stand some of the town's most interesting old houses.

There are houses with carved windows at the corner of Rue de l'Hôtel-de-Ville and Rue de l'Horloge. Rue de l'Horloge: at no 5, Renaissance clock tower on a Gothic base and, at no 7, the Hôtel Arnoux-de-Maison-Rouge with its corridor, lit with oval windows, leading to a delightful early 17C courtyard; on the other side of the street, notice the windows at no 4 and especially at no 12 (Hôtel Guimoneau).

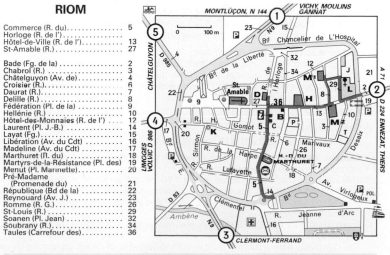

RIOM

B	Maison des Consuls	K	Fontaine d'Adam et Ève	M¹	Musée régional d'Auvergne
D	Hôtel Guimoneau			M²	Musée Mandet
H	Hôtel de ville	L	Sainte-Chapelle		

★**Hôtel Guimoneau** (**D**) – 16C door. *Go through the corridor into an attractive courtyard.*

The staircase is decorated with delicate carvings including an Annunciation. On the left, the gallery incorporates four statuettes representing, from left to right, Fortitude, Justice, Prudence and Temperance.

Note the medallions on the courtyard walls; two of them, at the back, depict the master and mistress of the house looking through small windows.

Return to the crossroads and take Rue du Commerce.

Rue du Commerce (**5**) – The modern sculptures of lavastone contrast with older works of the same material (at no 6, the caryatids at the Hôtel Robert-Duval).

★**Notre-Dame-du-Marthuret** – This church was built in the Languedoc style; it dates from the 14C and 15C. The west front was extensively damaged during the French Revolution; a copy of the Virgin with a Bird *(see below)* stands against the pier.

The interior was altered in the 17C and 19C by the addition of chapels (chancel and south side) and false side aisles. There are several interesting 15C and 16C stained-glass windows, and, in particular, in the first chapel on the right, the splendid **Virgin with a Bird★★★**. This famous 14C work came from the sculpture studios established by Jean de Berry; their reputation equalled those of the court of the Dukes of Dijon. It was saved during the Revolution by the butchers' corporation, who hid it in a cellar. The comparison is striking between this Gothic Virgin and the Romanesque Virgin in the church at **Marsat** *(3km/2mi south)*.

On Place J-B-Laurent, the Fountain recalls the Hero of the Battle of Marengo, General Desaix (1768-1800), who was born in Ayat-sur-Sioule.

ADDITIONAL SIGHTS

Basilique de St-Amable ⊙ – Only the nave and part of the transept remain from the original 12C church. The chancel, from the early 13C, is a mixture of Romanesque and Gothic (capitals with full-face figures and large crockets). The northern side chapels, with their fine ribbing on carved figure bases, date from the 15C; the southern side chapels and the west front are 18C.

The sacristy features fine wood panelling (1687) around the chapter's chancel, and an interesting collection of silks.

Fountains – The numerous fountains that were erected in Riom in the 17C and 18C make strolling through the town very pleasant. One of the most famous is the 17C **Adam and Eve Fountain** (**K**), decorated with caryatids, by the Riom sculptor Languille; opposite stands a Renaissance house with arcades.

EXCURSION

Round trip of 60km/37mi – allow half a day

Leave Riom west on ④ on the town plan, the D 986 towards Pontgibaud.

Volvic – *See VOLVIC.*

North of Volvic, before the D 15-D 83 junction, turn left.

★**Château de Tournoël** – *See Château de TOURNOËL.*

Return to Volvic and take the D 15 left alongside the graveyard. At the D 15 exit to Enval, leave the car just before the bridge over the Ambène.

★**Gorges d'Enval** – *30min Rtn on foot.*

Having crossed the bridge, take a path uphill to the left along the shady banks of the river. After a few minutes of at times quite strenuous walking, cross the ford over the mountain stream, which forms a waterfall here that drops down into a picturesque gorge.

Follow the D 15 to St-Hippolyte.

Châtelguyon – *See CHÂTELGUYON.*

Leave Châtelguyon on the D 415 towards Manzat.

Château de Chazeron ⊙ – To the east of this castle is a rest area in a pleasant setting with a good view of Châtelguyon.

This medieval castle was altered in the 17C by the architect Mansart. A staircase was built on the site of the former east tower, three of the outer walls were also demolished and the moat filled in, then two wings were built, one of them containing the servants' kitchen (south wing).

From the top of the 25m/82ft high west tower there is a good view of the Allier, the Limagne and the Sardon valley.

The château is now a cultural centre, with exhibitions of drawings and avant-garde furniture.

Follow the D 415 to the junction with the D 227. Turn right at Pont de la Ganne onto the D 19 towards Combronde.

★**Gour de Tazenat** – *Allow an hour on foot Rtn.*
A footpath leads around the lake; leave from the refreshment stand in an anti-clockwise direction. The first part of the footpath is flat but becomes steep in places along the second part. *It is possible to reach the viewpoint over the lake by car along a small track 200m on from the start of the footpath.* The green waters of Tazenat lake lie in a volcanic crater, or maar. The lake has an area of 32ha/79 acres and a maximum depth of 70m/228ft, and marks the northern boundary of the Puys range. The lakesides are over 50m/164ft high and are wooded, except for the north and northeast sides which are carpeted with stubbly grass.
Take the D 19 to Combronde, then south of the village take the D 412.

Sources pétrifiantes de Gimeaux ⊙ – These natural thermal mineral springs are a geological phenomenon known locally as the "volcano". The industry of encrusting objects with lime dates back to the early 19C and uses tried and trusted techniques *(see CLERMONT-FERRAND: Sources pétrifiantes de St-Alyre).*
Carry on along the D 17 on the banks of the Danade.

Château de Davayat ⊙ – A fine avenue of chestnut trees leads to this Louis XIII manor-house built by Blaise Roze, a wealthy merchant from Riom. The ambitious plans for the house and formal gardens were curtailed at Roze's death.
Inside, the rooms contain paintings, fine furniture and decorative items. In the dining room, covered with an unusual ceiling which helps to reflect light around the room, there is a collection of Greek terracotta figurines dating from the 4C BC. A collection of fans is on display in the games room, and various costumes (18C ballgown, gentlemen's outfits, court robes) and miscellaneous objects of interest in the billiard room. The main courtyard offers a good view of the façade and its two sundials, one showing the hours, the other the seasons.
Return to Riom via St-Bonnet along the N 144.

RIOM-ÈS-MONTAGNES ★

Population 3 225
Michelin map 76 fold 2 or 239 fold 30
Local map under Les RHUES

The cheese industry and cattle fairs here make this small town an important commercial centre.

★**St-Georges** – The only remaining parts of the original 11C church are the chancel, the apse, the dome and the transept. The nave is 12C, the belfry Gothic. Inside, the capitals in the chancel are interesting: on the left is a scene from local history showing the battle between the knights of the Auvergne and the Saracens (carrying round shields); opposite, the judgement of Solomon.

Maison de la Gentiane ⊙ – On the ground floor of this centre dedicated to the gentian plant is an exhibition of medicinal plants from the region. Outside, a botanic garden includes several species of high-altitude, meadow, wayside and peat-bog plants, including *gentiana lutea*, used to make the famous yellow aperitif, gentian bitters.
In the basement, an audio-visual projection explains how the plant is grown on the Auvergne mountain slopes and the manufacture of gentian bitters. It is not the leafy part of the plant which is used to make the drink or used in pharmaceuticals but the root or rhizome. It takes about 30 years for a seed to become a rhizome.

ROANNE

Conurbation 77 160
Michelin map 88 fold 5 or 239 fold 11

Rodumna, as the town was called in ancient times, dates back to more than a century before the birth of Christ. In the 11C the lords of Roanne built a fortress. The Seigniory of Roanne belonged in turn to the counts of Forez, Jacques Cœur, the Dukes of Bourbon and the Dukes of Roanne.
The inauguration of the Roanne-Digoin canal in 1838 brought intense activity to the port of Roanne, thereby determining the town's industrial vocation.

Cabins and St-Rambertes – Until the end of the 17C, traffic on the River Loire was only possible downstream of Roanne. Oak boats called cabins, after the shelter they offered, carried passengers and goods between Roanne and Paris, on the Briare canal (opened in 1538), or between Roanne and Nantes.
In the 18C work was carried out on the Loire to make it navigable upstream of Roanne. New fir boats, built in St Rambert – from which they derived their name, "St-Rambertes" – transported coal and wine from St-Étienne to Roanne and Nantes. On

arriving at their destination, they were either sold or dismantled because they could not sail upstream. Every year, the bargemen would visit their corporation's chapel, St-Nicolas-du-Port, near the wharf.

Port activity – Traffic on the canal from Roanne to Digoin and in the port of Roanne, which decreased regularly until 1976 (19 541 tonnes), has started to increase. Since 1981 the total tonnage of goods transported on the waterway is between 40 000 and 50 000 tonnes, consisting of 75% coal, 10% crude ore and 15% foodstuffs.

Originally the canal was used almost exclusively in the direction Roanne-Digoin to transport coal from St-Étienne. Today, coal from Montceau-les-Mines is taken up to Roanne. There has been an increase in pleasure boating with the opening of locks on Sundays during the summer months. **Barge trips** ⊙ are also organised on the canal.

Modern Roanne – Roanne is one of the best-known French textile centres for ready-made garments, hosiery and knitted goods (2nd in France) and towelling. Its other economic activities are highly diversified: food processing, metallurgy, armoured tanks, tools, boilermaking, tanning, dyes, paper mills, plastics and tyres. A Michelin tyre production unit has been operating in the northeast of the town since 1974. Appreciation of the local gastronomy has led to the development of a new industry here: vacuum-packed pre-cooked foods.

SIGHTS

Musée Joseph-Déchelette (**CY M**[1]) ⊙ – This eclectic museum is housed in an early 18C mansion, the former home of the archaeologist Joseph Déchelette, a native of the town and author of an archaeological text book. To the right of the entrance hall is a room dedicated to the works of the Fauvist painter **Jean Puy** (1876-1960), who was born in Roanne. The house itself is reached via an inner courtyard. The ground floor is partly devoted to prehistoric and Gallo-Roman antiquities, found during archaeological digs in the region.

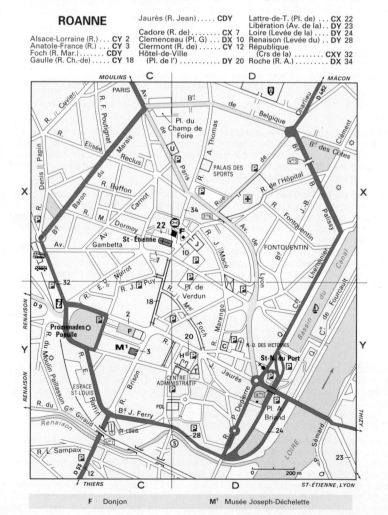

F : Donjon   M¹ : Musée Joseph-Déchelette

Revolutionary faïence (Nevers, 1793)

There are some fine collections of faïence including, among the 300 pieces ranging from the 16C to the 20C, items of 16C and 17C Italian *maiolica*, tin-glazed earthenware from Delft and Nevers.

Display cabinets present 18C faïence, boxes and hand-painted buttons. Roanne production is represented by pieces from the workshops of the Nicolas brothers and Jacques-Maurice Gay.

On the first floor, the room on the right is devoted to a display of faïence decorated with **motifs on the theme of the Revolution★**, which includes some highly original works (bottles shapes like books and decorated with historical scenes).

Other rooms show paintings from the French, Scandinavian and Italian schools of the 17C to the 19C. There are more works by Jean Puy among several paintings representing the main artistic movements during the first quarter of the 20C.

Place de Lattre-de-Tassigny (CX 22) – The site of the old castle (part of its keep still stands) is flanked by the **church of St-Étienne** with its 15C stained-glass window depicting the martyrdom of St Sebastian *(on the right, 2nd bay of the nave)*.

Gallo-Roman potters' kilns (2C AD) are visible beyond the chancel. North of the church is the "Caveau de Roanne", a small half-timbered house.

Promenades Populle (CY) – Pleasant public gardens.

Chapelle St-Nicolas-du-Port (DY) – The small chapel can be seen near the wharfs of the port. The date on the pediment – 1630 – marks the year the bargemen made a vow to erect a chapel to their patron saint if they escaped from the plague.

Écomusée du Roannais ⊘ – *Passage du Général Giraud (leave the car in Rue du Général Giraud)* Located in the heart of a long standing textile region, the aim of this museum, installed in an old towelling-material factory, is to highlight the area's industrial heritage and promote traditional arts and crafts. It offers an interesting retrospective of the textile business around Roanne over the span of a century.

An audio-guided tour explains the different manufacturing stages, the expansion in various types of material and the development of the industry in the region until its decline in the 1970s.

The textile industry took off around Roanne in 1880, when 6 000 textile workers were employed. By the end of the 19C its impact stretched from the Monts de la Madeleine in the west to the hills of Beaujolais in the east. From the 16C cloth-making, a cottage industry without any specific framework, began to be organised by merchants from Lyon who provided the raw materials and established conditions for the manufacturing system.

Home weavers worked in a separate building or annexe to their home and continued to work the land to increase their income. Various looms are on show, including an imposing steam version dating from 1905, together with the reconstruction of an early 20C peasant-weaver's "boutique" or workroom, a room half dug out of the ground and illuminated by a window at floor level.

Musée de la Maille ⊙ – *At **Riorges** 3km/2mi west on the D 31.*
On the second floor of a 19C mansion, the Château de Beaulieu set in parkland, is a museum tracing the history of knitted goods. At the peak of the textile industry Riorges was the second most important centre for knitted goods after Troyes. The processing of wool and cotton from its raw state to a product which can be worked on a machine is shown. Various 20C knitting machines are on display, together with a strange, 19C "grazeuse", a machine to raise the pile of woollen garments through the use of rollers made of natural thistles.

EXCURSIONS

*Gorges roannaises de la Loire
Round tour of 139km/87mi – allow half a day

Leave Roanne to the southeast over the Loire; immediately beyond the bridge fork right into Avenue de la Libération. Turn right by the station onto the D 43 and then right again onto the D 56 to Commelle-Vernay viewpoint (signposted).
Construction of the Villerest dam upstream of Roanne created a new "Loire lake", 33km/20mi long, which attracts numerous sailing enthusiasts in the summer.

* **Belvédère de Commelle-Vernay** – The **view** encompasses Roanne and its outskirts and the Vernay bridge to the north, the town and dam of Villerest and the modern installations of the Villerest paper mills to the west with, in the background, the Monts de la Madeleine.

Barrage de Villerest – Designed to combat low water levels and floods on the Loire, this is a solid concrete arch gravity dam with a crown length of 469m/1 538ft. Its curved shape reinforces its stability. The variable level barrage is 30km/19mi long and has an average width of 250m/820ft; its normal operating capacity is 128 million m^3/4 520 million ft^3. The hydrostatic pressure is designed to produce 167 million kWh per year.

Tache and Rouchain dams in the Côte roannaise

A recreational area with water sports facilities, a golf course etc has been developed around the storage reservoir. **Boat trips** ⊘ are organised from Villerest to St-Maurice or to Château de la Roche from the landing-stage at the foot of the dam, on the west bank of the Loire.

Cross over the dam to Villerest.

Villerest – The old **medieval town**★ is a pleasant place to visit; there are many houses with corbelled construction or timber-framed walls, and the remains of ramparts. The 13C **Porte de Bise** is the starting point for a tour on foot; points of particular interest are highlighted on information boards. During the summer, crafts are sold from the traditional street stalls.

Musée de l'Heure et du Feu ⊘ – This unusual museum is in two parts, the **Section on Fire**★ traces the history of the creation and the upkeep of the domestic fire since Antiquity and across different countries. A display on *amadou*, a mushroom which grows on trees and ignites very easily, and on its treatment to produce tinder recall the importance of this fungus, together with a flint and a piece of metal, in the creation of fire. Various displays show an assortment of lighters, for instance a Japanese miniature lighter from the 18C, a knife-cum-lighter with pincers dating from the Revolution and the famous hydropneumatic lighter by Gay Lussac, which was however dangerous to operate as it ran on hydrogen. Another interesting piece is the electrochemical lighter by Lorenz, which was used in the European courts of the 19C.

The other section houses an eclectic mix of unusual watches and clocks from the 18C to the 20C, more lighters, amusing caricatures, and numerous items fashioned from bits of munitions by soldiers in the trenches. A collection of ship-to-shore radios occupies the first floor.

Leave to the west and head for St-Jean-St-Maurice.

★**St-Maurice-sur-Loire** –
This town occupies a picturesque **site**★ overlooking the river. The old houses cling to a spur crowned by the ruins of a medieval castle. La Mure-Chantois manor house has an ornate doorway featuring statues of Adam and Eve, and a staircase tower with a fine sculpted fronton. The church has a Romanesque apse decorated with 13C murals depicting the Annunciation, the Visitation, the Nativity and the Flight into Egypt *(left)*, the Massacre of the Innocents and the Garden of Eden *(right)*.

Drive towards Bully, down the hill towards the Loire and over the bridge at Presle. Turn right onto the D 56 and continue along the east bank of the river.

The route goes through an attractive rocky passage past **Château de la Roche** *(private)*. Upstream the valley has a more pastoral appearance.

Shortly after the Chessieux viaduct the road meets the

Romanesque murals in the church at St-Maurice-sur-Loire

F. Da Costa

N 82 near Balbigny; turn left towards Neulise. After 6km/4mi turn right onto the D 5.

St-Marcel-de-Félines – This peaceful village facing the Forez mountains has a 12C fortified house which was altered in the 16C into a **château** ⊘; it has attractive rooflines, low towers and golden stonework. A bridge over the old moat leads to an inner courtyard of Italian inspiration. Inside, the decoration of the reception rooms is unified by the 17C wall and ceiling **paintings**★. In the Jeanne d'Arc Salon, note the rare portrait of the saint dressed in women's clothes.

Rejoin the N 82 and continue to Neulise; turn right onto the D 38. At Croizet turn right, cross the River Gand and take the path to the right.

Château de l'Aubépin ⊙ – This lovely old château (16-18C), flanked by corner pavilions topped with a watch-turret set back from an avant-corps decorated with masks, is set on a terraced hillside framed in greenery.

Return to Roanne on the N 82.

The road offers views of the Roanne vineyards and the Loire valley downstream.

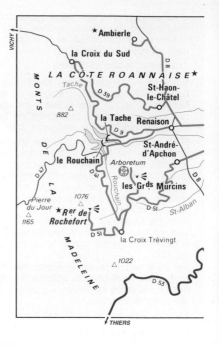

*★Côte roannaise

Round tour of 114km/71mi – allow half a day

A line of vineyard-covered slopes running north-south, known as the "Côte", dominates the Roanne basin to the west. Beyond the Côte and separated from it by the Rouchin and Tache valleys, rise the **Monts de la Madeleine** granite hills culminating in Pierre du Jour (1 165m/3 821ft), and forming an extension of the Monts du Forez and Bois Noirs (Black Woods).

In contrast with the harshness of the Madeleine mountains, the Côte is gentle and colourful, with rectangular houses, often roughcast with green shutters and red-tiled double pitched roofs, reddish soil, and vineyards which produce reputed AOC *(Appellation d'origine contrôlée)* red wines, and also rosés and whites.

Leave Roanne on the D 9 west and turn left onto the D 51 to St-André-d'Apchon.

There is an pretty view of the hills up ahead.

St-André-d'Apchon – At the centre of the town, in a secluded setting, stands a 16C château built for the Marshal of St-André which has preserved its original façade decorated with Renaissance medallions.

From the War Memorial, walk up the street on the corner with the Lion d'Or hotel, then along the covered passageway 30m on the right, next to a butcher's shop.

The **church** ⊙, in Flamboyant Gothic style, is decorated with 16C stained-glass windows. Note the Renaissance portal to the right of the bell tower; on the tympanum is a beautiful stone statue of St Andrew (16C), surmounted by a small effigy of the Eternal Father. Note also the glazed tile roof.

Continue along the D 51 to Arcon.

The road twisting uphill above St-André offers a series of vistas of the Roanne plain.

Leave Arcon to the north, to Les Grands-Murcins and its arboretum.

Les Grands-Murcins – *15min Rtn on foot.* The arboretum, created in 1936-37 at the heart of a 150ha/370 acre national forest (average altitude 770m/2 526ft) is particularly rich in coniferous trees, including Himalayan weeping pines, *Abies alba* fir trees, *Tsuga canadensis* with their curtain-like branches and Douglas firs which prosper in the region at an altitude of less than 900m/2 952ft.

From the viewing table, there is a good **view** of the Roanne plain and Lyonnais hills.

Return to Arcon and head south to La Croix Trévingt. Turn right onto the D 51 towards St-Priest.

★Rocher de Rochefort – The Rochefort rock is surmounted by a viewing table; **views** of the Roanne plain, the Beaujolais and Lyonnais hills.

Return to La Croix Trévingt. Turn left onto the D 51 and left again onto the D 41 along the Rouchain valley to the dam.

Barrage du Rouchain – Duplicating the Tache dam to supply Roanne with drinking water, this dam (1977), made of rockfill, is 230m/754ft long, 9m/30ft wide at the crown and 190m/623ft at the base. Equipped with a spillway on the River Rouchain, the barrage has a capacity of 6 500 000m³/230 000 000ft³ and occupies three valleys. The D 47 linking Noës (west) with Renaison (east) follows the banks of the reservoir. A car park and a pedestrian zone lead to the dam. The foot of the dam is accessible from the road to Tache dam.

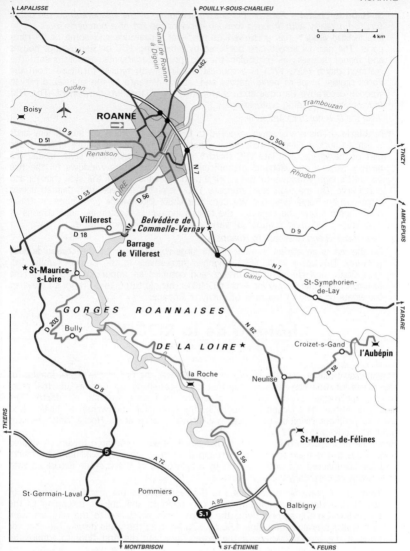

Barrage de la Tache – This dam (221m/725ft long and 51m/167ft high) was built from 1888 to 1892. Its width, which is only 4m/13ft at the top, increases to 47.5m/156ft at the base. It is a gravity dam, that is, the sheer mass of the dam resists the pressure of the water. It has a capacity of 3 326 000m³/117 458 000ft³. Paths from the car park at the foot of the dam lead up to the crown. From the far right of the crown *(30min Rtn on foot)*, near the D 41, there is an attractive view of the reservoir behind the dam.
The road down towards Renalson, lined with attractive groves of blue Atlas cedars, offers views of the vineyards of the Côte roannaise.

Renaison – This is the economic heart of the Côte roannaise. Its neo-Gothic church houses a Romantic organ by organ-builder John Abbey.
At the junction with the D 9 turn left to La Croix du Sud.
On the way, a lookout rock ↖ on the left offers an attractive view of Tache reservoir. The road up to the pass looks out over the Monts de la Madeleine.

La Croix du Sud – This pass is a major intersection on the rise separating the Monts de la Madeleine from the Côte, and the valley of the Teyssonne from that of the Tache.
During the **descent**★ along the D 39 *(sharp right)*, notice the different bands of vegetation depending on the altitude: on the crest, heathland or woodland; below, pastureland and small crops; further down there are vineyards and, in the distance, the plain with its meadows and vast estates. Before arriving just above the red soil of the vineyards, the road offers views of the villages of St-Haon-le-Vieux and St-Haon-le-Châtel.

St-Haon-le-Châtel – *Park on the square at the top of the village and go through a fortified gateway with studded wooden doors to the left of a butcher's shop.*
The **fortified village**★ has preserved its medieval appearance and some of its ramparts. The narrow streets are bordered by interesting 15C or Renaissance houses and manor houses, in particular the old provost marshal's establishment. The restored **church** (12C-17C) is a modest building, with typical furniture from the Forez region: a set of naïve statues and, at the entrance to the chancel, a carved wooden decorative Baroque arch, surmounted by a large wooden Christ. The 16C murals are undergoing restoration.
Take the D 8 north to Ambierle.

★**Ambierle** – This pretty town, exposed to the morning sun, is set amidst vineyards which produce a pleasant rosé wine. There is an old Cluniac priory in the upper part of the village. The late-15C **church**★ is in Flamboyant Gothic style. Inside, the nave is narrow and elegant; magnificent 15C stained-glass windows fill the five 13m/42ft high windows of the chancel, and the windows of the side chapels and north aisle. On the high altar stands a 15C Flemish altarpiece with painted panels attributed to Rogier van der Weyden. The **Musée Alice-Taverne** ⊙ focuses on traditional home life in the region – the fascinating games, costumes, superstitions of local life – and has recreations of various interiors (workshop, inn etc).
Take the D 8 and D 9 back to Roanne.

On the left is an attractive view of the large round tower of the **Château de Boisy** *(private)*. This castle (14C-16C) belonged successively to the Couzan family, Jacques Cœur, and the Gouffier family, and occupies an important position in the history of Roanne: it was for Arthur Gouffier, his old tutor, that François I elevated the estate of Boisy to the rank of duchy of Roanne.

Château de la ROCHE★

Michelin map 73 fold 4 or 239 folds 7, 8
2km/1mi northwest of Aigueperse

This medieval manor, slightly altered in the 16C, was the fief of the vassal families of the dukes of Bourbon. It was elevated to a castellany by Charles III, the rebel commander-in-chief of the French armies, for Jean de L'Hospital, his doctor. The illustrious Michel de L'Hospital (1506-73), the chancellor and writer on justice who tried to promote religious tolerance, was probably born at La Roche which he was given as a dowry in 1537.
Enter the first courtyard through a door framed by two crenellated towers. A vaulted porch leads to the main courtyard surrounded on three sides by buildings. The fourth side has been closed off since the 16C by a balustrade of Volvic stone decorated with four fawns representing the four seasons.

Tour ⊙ – A staircase tower joined to the keep leads to the first-floor bedroom of Michel de L'Hospital containing historical souvenirs and objects belonging to the Chancellor. On the second floor, the guard room which led to the rampart walk (cob walls) contains some fine 15C to 17C armour; the walls display the coats of arms of the various owners of the castle. Return to the first floor to admire the 17C drawing room decorated with a beamed ceiling and a wooden fireplace; the walls are hung with an Aubusson tapestry depicting Solomon and the Queen of Sheba; there is a also a beautiful marquetry cabinet and a 15C carved wedding chest. The only light in the tiny oratory enters via the stained-glass window. The visit ends with an 18C room (collection of monogrammed plates) and the old kitchen (14C fireplace, copper pans and a *cantou*, a sort of bench which also served to hide the salt, in order to pay less tax).

ROMANS-SUR-ISÈRE

Population 32 734
Michelin map 77 fold 2 or 246 fold 5
Town plan in the current Michelin Red Guide France

The town is built on a hillside opposite Bourg-de-Péage, whose name is a reminder of the toll once collected by the Chapter of St Barnard to cross the bridge linking the two towns. Romans, a flourishing trade centre in the Middle Ages, is now the site of both traditional industries such as footwear and tanning, and new businesses: metallurgy, nuclear fuel, precision mechanics and foodstuffs. Lovers of good food will appreciate the local *pogne*, which is a type of *brioche* or sweet bread flavoured with orange blossom, St-Genix *(praline pogne)* and goat's cheese *tomme* (which is also used to make the local dish, *ravioles*).

Dauphiné joins France – It was in St-Barnard collegiate church that the treaty unifying the Dauphiné region, until that time part of the Holy Roman Empire, to France, was solemnly signed on 30 March 1349.

From the 11C on, the counts of Albon, natives of Vienne, gradually took over the region – stretching from the Rhône valley to the Alps – which was eventually to form Dauphiné. The origin of the name "Dauphin", given to members of the dynasty which then reigned over Dauphiné, remains uncertain.

The last of the Vienne dauphins, Humbert II, lived mostly at Beauvoir castle, opposite St-Marcellin *(25km/15mi northeast)*. After the death of his son, which left him without an heir, he sold Dauphiné to the French crown (30 March 1349). This province was to become the attribute of the oldest sons of the kings of France, who subsequently bore the title of Dauphin.

OLD TOWN *2hr*

Start from Place du Pont.

A maze of picturesque streets surrounds St-Barnard collegiate church and, half-way down the hill from the church, Place de la Presle and Place Jacquemart.

Collégiale St-Barnard ⊙ – *Quai U. Chevalier.* In the 9C St Barnard, archbishop of Vienne, founded a monastery here. It was destroyed in the 12C and replaced by a Romanesque church of which the western porch, the northern portal and lower parts of the nave still remain. Towards the middle of the 13C the chancel and transept were rebuilt in Gothic style. Largely destroyed by the Protestants in the 16C, the church was completely restored in the 18C.

Exterior – Seen from the bridge (Pont Vieux), the massive silhouette of the church is reflected in the Isère. To the west, on the piers of the Romanesque portal, are statues of apostles, grouped in pairs and resting on lions, one of which is devouring a human and the other a sheep. Although damaged, they are nevertheless very interesting.

Interior – The interior is unusual for its Romanesque arcade reinforcing the walls of the nave; the arches rest on columns with capitals decorated with foliate designs or narrative scenes. Above is a Gothic triforium comprising 160 arches which go right round the building. In the chancel there are 14C frescoes.

On the right of the nave, the **Chapel of the Holy Sacrament** ⊙ contains a 16C **hanging**★★ consisting of nine panels and believed to be of Flemish inspiration. These remarkable pieces embroidered in wool and highlighted with silk thread depict scenes from the Passion, from the Garden of Gethsemane on the Mount of Olives to the Resurrection. The figures, in reddish-brown tones, form compact groups against a dark blue background; notice, on the altar side, the Crucifixion, Golgotha and Deposition from the Cross. On the central vault, a 15C fresco retraces two episodes evoking the departure of the Dauphin Humbert III for the crusade. There is beautiful 17C woodwork in the sacristy.

Take Rue Pêcherie, opposite the west end of the church, for 200m.

Escalier Josaphat – These **steps** go down from Rue Pêcherie towards the houses with their wooden balconies in Place de la Presle.

It is part of the "Great Journey" or Way of the Cross which attracts a large crowd of people on Good Friday.

Turn back up the steps to Rue Pêcherie, and turn left into Rue du Fuseau, which runs straight on into Rue de l'Armillerie.

At no 15 Rue du Mouton, off to the right, the Gothic windows on the first floor are now mullioned windows; above, the outline of a sheep's head carved in a projecting stone can just be made out.

At no 17, the semicircular door features nail-head ornamentation.

Continue along Rue de l'Armillerie and take the next turning on the right.

Walk down to the square with the modern fountain of a flautist and follow round to the left to reach Côte Jacquemart.

Côte Jacquemart – The hill is lined with 13C and 14C houses.

Le Jacquemart – This is an old square tower from the outer curtain wall of Romans, converted into a belfry in the 15C and given a Jack-o'-the-clock, which since 1830 has worn a costume of a 1792 volunteer.

Facing towards the river, turn left to Côte des Cordeliers which runs along part of the moat of the inner curtain wall; walk down to Rue Fontaine-des-Cordeliers and the junction with Rue St-Nicolas.

Hôtel Thomé – This fine town house has a Renaissance façade with beautiful mullioned windows on the upper floors. On the right, a Virgin and Child stands in a niche.

Continue towards the river via Rue Sabaton and turn right into Rue des Clercs.

Rue des Clercs – The street is very picturesque with rounded cobblestones. Notice, opposite the library, the portal decorated with fine chiselling.

The house at the junction with Rue Merlin has a corner turret.

Rue des Trois-Carreaux – This is an extension of Rue des Clercs. At its intersection with **Place aux Herbes** there is a monumental door, surmounted by an unusual corbelled construction with machicolations.

Place Maurice-Faure – Beside St-Barnard, to the right of St-Jean door on the north side of the church, is a beautiful house with a corner tower.
On the northwest corner of the square is **Rue de l'Écosserie**, in which the first houses are joined by an arch.

ADDITIONAL SIGHTS

Musée International de la Chaussure ⊙ – The shoe museum is located to the east of town in a vast building – the old Visitation Convent – which was constructed between the 17C and 19C. The museum entrance is reached through the gateway in Rue Bistour, across terraced gardens in front of the building which is adorned with an elegant colonnade.

★ **Shoe Collection** – The museum aims to present the technical, ethnographic and aesthetic aspects of footwear. Numerous documents and other material trace the evolution of the shoe-maker's craft and associated activities in the town of Romans (dressing and tanning leather etc.).

Lady's shoe
(late 17C, Guillen Collection)

Collection Guillen/Musée de la Chaussure et d'Ethnologie régionale

In the old nuns' cells, the collections of footwear are displayed in chronological and thematic order from Antiquity to 1900. Some of them are extremely comprehensive, such as that of Paris designer Victor Guillen which comes from five continents and covers four millenia. The Jacquemart collection and Harms' original collection of buckles are also interesting. Exhibits include the mummified feet of ancient Egypt to the original designs of André Pérugia (20C). These sumptuous, amusing and enigmatic shoes reveal the ingenuity of their creators and evoke the customs of their country of origin and fashion throughout the ages: Roman sandals, cracowes whose length varied with social rank, pattens inlaid with tortoiseshell and pearl from Mauritania, Indian moccasins from North America, shoes from Ardèche used to open chestnuts, ankle boots from the Belle Époque... The collections, which are constantly being enriched by numerous donations, are displayed in rotation in temporary exhibitions.
18C and 19C paintings on the theme of shoes and shoemaking add another angle of interest to the museum visit.

Musée de la Résistance and Déportation – Three rooms in the right wing retrace the secret life of the members of the Resistance in this *département* during the Second Word War, with the aid of documents and an audio-visual projection *(20min)*.

Viewpoints – From Esplanade Bellevue, to the west of Côte des Chapeliers, there is an attractive view of Romans and Bourg-de-Péage with Vercors in the background.
From Place Aristide-Briand, on the south bank next to Bourg-de-Péage town hall, the houses of Romans can be see in terraces up the hillside.

EXCURSION

Mours-St-Eusèbe – *4km/3mi north. Leave Romans on the D 538.* The village church has kept only its bell tower, at the west end, and the south wall of the nave from the 11C. It houses an interesting **Musée diocésain d'Art sacré** ★ ⊙ with rich collections of sacred art (from 15C to 20C) arranged according to a new theme each year. Among the liturgical objects used in various Drôme churches there are a beautiful set of vestments (copes, embroidered and woven chasubles, often highlighted with gold or silver thread), altar cloths in fine lace from Le Puy, Bruges and Chantilly, poignant polychrome wooden statues representing St Roc, St John and the Virgin, a magnificent monstrance designed by Viollet-le-Duc and made by Armand Calliat, a goldsmith from Lyon. Popular piety is represented by procession banners, Isère boatmen's crosses, gonfalons (standards used by ecclesiastics and corporations) and small objects made from paper rolls. At the back of the church, the old sacristy houses a collection of religious plate of Dauphiné origin.

The main shopping streets are printed in red
at the top of the street lists accompanying town plans.

Rocher de RONESQUE★★

Michelin map 76 fold 12 or 239 fold 42 – 30km/19mi southeast of Aurillac

This basalt rock forms a plateau 280m/918ft long and 180m/590ft wide, dominating the entire countryside. It was formed in the same way as Carlat rock during different geological eras on an old plain first covered by volcano activity then deeply gashed by large valleys. The picturesque **hamlet** at the foot of the rock is typical of the Cantal where the houses often have roofs of stone slabs called *lauzes*. There used to be a fortified castle in Ronesque, given by Hugues, Count of Rodez, to Alphonse II, King of Aragon, in 1167. Alphonse wanted to establish a kingdom from Catalonia to Aquitaine for which Ronesque and Carlat would have been the outlying posts. Subsequently, the castle became the property of the Rastinhac de Messillac family.

Ascent of the rock – *The little chapel can be reached by car. Viewing table (on the north side, opposite the chapel).* From here the immense plateau and a magnificent **panorama**★★ can be seen: Carlat rock lies to the northwest *(move slightly to the right)*, the Cantal mountains to the north and the Aubrac mountains to the south. To the north, below, stands Messillac castle in the Goul valley.

ROYAT‡‡

Population 3 950
Michelin map 73 fold 14 or 239 fold 19

Royat, on the heights overlooking Clermont-Ferrand from the west, is a large, elegant thermal spa terraced on the slopes of the cool Tiretaine valley. It lies on the western fault of the Limagne and it is to this location that it owes its springs. The Tiretaine flows down from the granite plateau at the base of the Monts Dômes; until it leaves Royat, it is a torrent. The bottom of its bed was filled with a lava flow from the Petit Puy du Dôme, the waters then cut gorges in it; as a result, many sills are crossed by waterfalls, making the spa very picturesque. Old Royat, with its fortified church, dominates the spa town which is built on the side of the Tiretaine ravine and spreads out around the opening of the river into the Limagne.

The waters – The waters of Royat were known to the Arverni, whose capital Gergovie was close by, and were subsequently exploited by the Romans who built magnificent public baths here. Although the baths met with mixed success until the mid 19C, they have had unfailing popularity and fame ever since. A hydropathic establishment was built and the visit here by Empress Eugénie in 1862 launched Royat as a spa. Until 1914 it was the stopping place of kings and princes.

Five springs are used. The most abundant is the Eugénie spring whose Gallo-Roman water catchment was rediscovered. It has a flow rate of 1 000l/220gal per minute at a temperature of 31.5°C/88.7°F and releases a large amount of radioactive thermal gas at the same time. The temperature of the other springs goes down to 14°C/57°F. St-Mart, which has a Celtic water catchment, bears the name of the saint who, in the 6C, founded a monastery on the site of the present Spa Gardens.

St Victor's spring, which is currently out of operation, was tapped by the Romans. The other springs are César, with a Gallo-Roman water catchment, and Velleda. The waters are used for drinking, carbo-gas baths and thermal gas injections, for the treatment of heart and artery complaints, cellulitis and osteo-arthritis. A new spring, the Auraline spring, captured and put into service in 1989, ensures that most of the needs for thermal water are met. Royat also offers the usual distractions of a watering place: parks, casino, concerts, theatre, cinema, tennis, 9-hole golf course in Charade *(6km/4mi)*.

SIGHTS

★St-Léger (A) – This very interesting fortified building, which varies considerably from the classical type of Auvergne Romanesque church, resembles the churches in Provence. It was built at the end of the 11C on the site of a former sanctuary and belonged to Mozac Abbey which enlarged it by rebuilding the chancel, and fortified it at the beginning of the 13C to withstand the assaults of the Count of Auvergne. The belfry is 19C. The old priory, joined to the left arm of the transept, was also fortified. There are two beautiful Gothic rose windows, one in the wall of the south transept, the other at the east end. It is possible to visit the crypt where 10C capitals have been re-used.

Nearby, on Place Cohendy, is a calvary, sculpted in lavastone, dated 1486.

Parc Thermal (Spa Gardens) (B) – This garden, completed by the new park through which flows the River Tiretaine, contains the hydropathic establishment and the casino. The remains of the Gallo-Roman public baths, which included several pools, can be seen. One of the pools, uncovered and restored, had mosaic-covered arches and marble-covered walls. Terracotta pipes brought the water which then flowed into the pool in small, semicircular cascades. The other rooms, used as sweating-rooms, and the underground heating system, have not been excavated.

Monument aux Morts (A) – *Leave the town to the south.* The War Memorial consists of a moving sculpture by Mabru, erected on a wooded knoll.

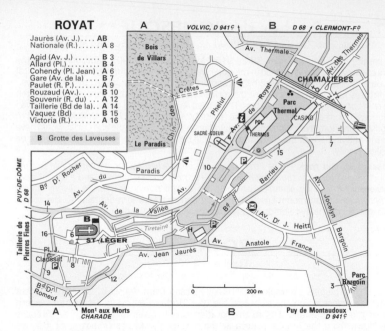

ROYAT

Jaurès (Av. J.).... **AB**
Nationale (R.)...... **A 8**

Agid (Av. J.) .... **B 3**
Allard (Pl.)......... **B 4**
Cohendy (Pl. Jean) . **A 6**
Gare (Av. de la) .... **B 7**
Paulet (R. P.)....... **A 9**
Rouzaud (Av.)....... **B 10**
Souvenir (R. du) ... **A 12**
Taillerie (Bd de la).. **A 14**
Vaquez (Bd) .... **B 15**
Victoria (R.)........ **A 16**

B Grotte des Laveuses

Parc Bargoin (**B**) – This is a well laid-out park on hilly land, and a botanical garden. It is home to some magnificent trees, including the largest maple in France (250 years old, diameter of 7.5m/25ft). From the top of a little tower there is a lovely view of Clermont-Ferrand.

Grottes des Laveuses (**A B**) – The "Washerwomen's Cave" is on the banks of the Tiretaine. Several springs gush forth from the volcanic walls and gather in a pool before flowing into the Tiretaine.

Taillerie de Pierres Fines (Stone cutting workshop) (**A**) ⊘ – *Leave the town to the west.* Semi-precious stones – rock crystal, agate, tourmaline, amethyst etc – are cut and made into jewellery.

Le Paradis (**A**) – This pleasant site is reached by taking Avenue A-Phelut; it offers lovely views of the Spa Gardens and Clermont-Ferrand. Avenue du Paradis overlooks the old part of Royat clustered around the church.

Bois de Villars (**A**) – *1hr on foot.* These woods contain superb undergrowth and offer lovely views of the Limagne and the Livradois mountains. Well-preserved remains of the Roman way between Clermont-Ferrand and Limoges may be seen.

Puy de Montaudoux – *1hr walk. Leave Royat on the D 941ᶜ to the southeast.* At the junction with the D 5, take the track on the left which leads up to the *puy.* From the summit (alt 592m/1 942ft) there is a lovely view of the Limagne.

ST-ANTOINE ★

Population 873
Michelin map 77 fold 3 or 246 fold 4

Nestling in an undulation of the Chambaran plateau north of the river Isère is the old village of St-Antoine-l'Abbaye, which is dominated by an imposing Gothic abbey church.

St Anthony's fire – In the 11C a noble from Vienne, Jocelyn de Châteauneuf, made a pilgrimage to the Holy Land. On his return he brought back from Constantinople the bones of **Anthony the Great**, the original "desert father", who lived in the Upper Nile Valley. In the Middle Ages this saint owed his popularity as much to the pig who was the daily companion of his hermitic life as to his battles with the devil.

The relics in the church of Motte-St-Didier, which took the name of St-Antoine, were entrusted by the Bishop of Vienne to Benedictines from Montmajour abbey. A first monastery was built. Not long after, in 1089, a dreadful epidemic broke out in Dauphiné – erysipelas, or St Anthony's fire. It was a sort of gangrene which burnt away the limbs. The saint's relics drew a large crowd of sick and poor people; to help and care for them, a group of young nobles created the Brotherhood of Charity.

A powerful order – In the 13C the brothers managed to supplant the Benedictines. In 1297 the brotherhood became the Hospital Brothers of St Anthony; the Antonine monks founded hospices all over Europe.

The great abbey church of St-Antoine, which took from the 13C to the 15C to build, was visited by popes, emperors from Germany, and kings of France who came to kneel before the relics.

★ABBEY CHURCH (ABBATIALE) *1hr*

Leave the car in the car park below, then take Chemin des Buttes (5) and Grande Rue to Place F-Gilbert (6).

The entrance to the abbey church is at the top of the village, through the 17C **main entrance gate** (entrée d'honneur), now the hôtel de ville (**H**), with its glazed mosaic tiles. Three portals with broken pediments decorate the façade. The frame around the central portal, which has preserved its wooden doors, has two Ionic columns. The side portals have nail-head ornamentation.

Walk through the portal which leads to an esplanade surrounded by the old hospital buildings now occupied by craftsmen, artists and antique dealers. Continue up to the church.

The square in front of the church provides an attractive view of the façade and the two monumental doors. One of the doors leads to the old gardens and the other overlooks a set of steps going down to the village.

Façade – Flamboyant Gothic portals are extended on each side by the low windows of the first side chapels, and an immense Flamboyant opening punctuates the middle of the façade. The **centre portal★**, decorated with arching adorned with statuettes, is the work of Antoine le Moiturier, who stayed at St-Antoine from 1461 to 1464 before going to Dijon to execute the tomb of the Duke of Burgundy, John the Fearless. In the centre of the portal is the Eternal Father surrounded by cherubs. The lower row depicts, seated, Moses with the Tablets of the Law, on the right, and above, the Sibyl.

Interior ⊙ – The interior is quite large: 62m/203ft long, 22m/72ft high and 36m/118ft wide. The nave has seven bays and a false transept marked with galleries at mid-height. Chapels lead off the side aisles; the 2nd and 6th chapels on the left and the 2nd, 4th and 7th on the right have restored 15C and 16C frescoes.

The three bays of the chancel end in a polygonal apse with a circular base (13C) which is the oldest part of the building. The triforium reveals the progression of the construction: in the apse there are twinned pointed arches, in the nave, later trefoil arches.

97 stalls by the master carpenter François Hanard furnish the chancel. Ten Aubusson tapestries (17C) depicting the story of Joseph decorate the chancel, the transept and chapels along the right side-aisle; they bear the coat of arms of the Antonine monks, recognisable from the T or *tau* representing the Cross of St Anthony.

The high altar, designed as a marble mausoleum covered with chiselled bronzes, houses the shrine of St Anthony, covered with embossed silver plate (17C). The organ case is 17C (restored); concerts are regularly held.

★**Treasury** ⊙ – It houses a 16C ivory **Crucifix★** famous for its expression of agony, various reliquaries and reliquary busts, and surgical instruments donated by the last patient to be cared for by the Antonines and recalling the hospital vocation of the Order.

In the second room hangs a painting by Ribera, *St Mary the Egyptian* (17C); the third room is decorated with delightful woodwork of the Rococo style; it contains a cope chest.

Walk down the steps at the corner of the church square. The descent offers an attractive view of the old houses in the village. Grande-Rue, then Chemin des Buttes, lead back to the car park.

ADDITIONAL SIGHT

Musée Jean Vinay (M) ⊙ – This museum, located in the monastery's old novitiate, contains works by Jean Vinay (1907-78), a landscape artist from Dauphiné, and thematic exhibitions by his friends from the École de Paris, and exhibitions on the Middle Ages or the Antonine Order.

ST-ANTOINE

Abbaye (Pl. de l') 2
Anges (Montée des) . 3
Buttes (Ch. des) 5
Gilbert (Pl. F.)........ 6
Hôpital (R. de l') 8

H Hôtel de ville
M Musée départemental Jean-Vinay

Population 329
Michelin map 88 fold 19 or 246 fold 17 – Local map under Mont PILAT

The Carthusian monastery of Ste-Croix (Holy Cross) was founded in 1280 by Béatrix de Roussillon. During the Revolution the Carthusian fathers, who spent their time praying, studying and performing manual tasks, were forced to leave Ste-Croix; the monastery was then divided up, the cloisters demolished in 1840 and, in 1888, Ste-Croix became a municipality.

The village which occupies the buildings of the former Carthusian monastery, in the upper Couzon valley, is therefore somewhat unusual.

FORMER CARTHUSIAN MONASTERY *1hr*

Façade – On the façade of the former convent buildings, a **monumental granite doorway** was opened up in the 17C, flanked by round towers made of schist quarry stone. In the centre are the armorial bearings of the Carthusian monks: a globe bearing a cross, surrounded by seven stars symbolising St Bruno, founder of the order, and his six companions. Below, a broken-pediment surmounts an empty shell-shaped niche.

On each side of the main portal can be seen the ancient curtain wall, incorporated into houses and defended, at each end, by two angle towers.

Pass through the doorway into the first courtyard.

Cour des Frères – This vast rectangular courtyard is bordered by buildings which, in the past, housed the activities of the lay and oblate brothers (linked to the order not by vows but by civil contracts) who were needed to maintain the material life of the community: presses, cellars, bakery, workshops, forges, stables etc. The church bell tower, visible from the courtyard, dates from the 19C. On the left, a sloping covered passageway (**1**) leads to the entrance to the vegetable garden, which runs along the River Couzon; notice the beautiful wrought-iron transom (18C) (**2**) above the old wooden door.

The end of the courtyard, on the left, gives onto a cobbled street, which, in the past, was completely covered – the "**corridor**" leading to the common rooms (refectory for Sunday meals and certain feast days, library etc).

Walk along the corridor.

Church ⊙ – The portal is marked by two stone holy-water stoups on each side. The 17C building has 16C and 17C woodwork and 14C stalls, with misericords and arm-rests decorated with carvings: grimacing mask, local peasant woman's head dress, animals etc. The back wall, above the portal, is decorated with three paintings depicting the Martyrdom of St Sebastian (a copy of a painting by Mantegna) in the centre, St Charles Borromeo, kneeling, on the left, and St Bruno, refusing the episcopate, dressed in the white scapular of the Carthusian habit, on the right.

The chancel leads to the remains of the original church: the **former chapter-house** (**3**) and **former sacristy** ⊙ (**4**) from the 13C, containing restored 14C **frescoes** which illustrate, with a certain degree of realism, the Coronation of the Virgin Mary, the Crucifixion (inspired by Giotto) and the funeral of Thibaud de Vassalieu who, in 1312, negotiated with Philip the Fair to attach the Lyonnais region to the French crown.

Above the Crucifixion can be seen a group of Carthusian monks from Ste-Croix.

On leaving the church, the old vaulted kitchen with its monumental fireplace is visible, opposite (exhibitions). At the end of the corridor there is a second courtyard. To the left of the monumental entrance is the reception, in the old monastery bakery.

Cour des Pères – This courtyard used to have cloisters around it, leading into the monks' cells. The cloisters are no longer extant and the cells have been turned into flats, the town hall, a school etc. Each cell had an oratory, a bedroom, a terrace and promenade at courtyard level; on the lower level was the wood-house, the workshop and garden; on weekdays, the monks received their food through a hatch next to their cell door.

Over one of the cells, on the western side of the courtyard, is a low-relief depicting St Bruno meditating on death (**5**).

In the southeast corner is the so-called **Clock Tower**, which lost its dial during the Revolution.

ST-ÉTIENNE

Conurbation 313 338
Michelin map 88 fold 18 or 246 fold 17
Local map under Mont PILAT
Map of conurbation in the current Michelin Red Guide France

St-Étienne lies at the bottom of the Furan depression, close to the green massif of Mont Pilat, Grangent lake and the Forez plain. Including the suburban estates of the Ondaine valley and the Gier depression, St-Étienne has a total population of 450 000 people.

The town is located at the centre of a coal basin which supplied over 500 million tonnes of coal until the mines were closed in the 1980s; since then St-Étienne has adopted a new image: the façades of its buildings have been cleaned, its gardens and parks renovated in the city centre. The busiest area lies along a north-south axis: Place Jean-Jaurès, Place de l'Hôtel de Ville. The 15C-16C main church of St-Étienne, popularly known as the "**Grand'Eglise**", remains dear to the hearts of the native *gagas*, the nickname still used by the inhabitants of St-Étienne when speaking of themselves.

St-Étienne, the home of the composer Jules Émile Frédéric **Massenet** (1842-1912), has an intellectual and artistic life which extends over the whole of Forez. The town has a Cultural and Communication Centre, a sports stadium and, thanks to the "Comédie de St-Étienne" theatre company, the city is also an active centre of dramatic art. The presentation of modern art collections in the new museum to the north of the city has sparked off new interest in cultural activities.

On the site of the old Manufrance factory, famous for its mail-order catalogue and which remains a symbol for the people of St-Étienne, a conference centre is to be built, together with offices, apartments and a shopping arcade.

HISTORICAL NOTES

In the 12C St-Étienne was nothing more than a village on the banks of the Furan, by-passed by the major communication routes. Owing to the presence of coal, however, and the enterprising spirit of the inhabitants, it was later to undergo extraordinary development, the population of the town climbing from 3 700 people in 1515 to 45 000 in 1826, and to 146 000 in 1901, while the industrial estate spread to the west, the east and the north.

Armeville – In 1296 the people of St-Étienne started working coal quarries for domestic needs, then to feed the forges which produced the first knives, followed by cutting and thrusting weapons, cross-bows and finally, firearms – St-Étienne was quick to make this change in direction in the manufacture of arms.

In 1570 the Arms Manufacturers' Lodge consisted of 40 trades. Mass production was already being practised. In 1746 the Royal Arms Factory was founded. During the Revolution this activity was to earn the town the name of Armeville. Today its activities are focused on nuclear and chemical detection equipment.

From St-Étienne to Andrézieux – In May 1827 the first French railway, built to plans by Beaunier, was inaugurated; it ran between St-Étienne and Andrézieux over a distance of 21km/13mi and was used to transport coal; the wagons were pulled by horses. This ancestor of modern means of transport, perfected in 1829 thanks to the tube boiler developed by **Marc Seguin**, led to a revolution in transport and a prodigious boom in industry.

The town that made everything – To the ribbon industry, imported from Italy, was added shirred fabric at the end of the 19C. In metallurgy, the ore dephosphorisation process discovered by **Thomas** in 1878 was responsible for development of the iron and steel industry in Lorraine.

To escape the Depression, the region of St-Étienne had already specialised in quality steels, tools, hunting guns, bicycles and automobile parts.

Out and About in St-Étienne

Travelling around town – The famous St-Étienne tramway is the most convenient mode of transport.

Shopping – Nouvelles Galeries (department store), rue Gambetta; Fnac (cds, books etc.) and Galerie Dorian (shopping centre), rue Blanquil; numerous off-the-peg clothes boutiques in the busy Rue du Général Foy.

Entertainment – National drama centre at the Comédie de St-Étienne, avenue E.-Loubet; theatre, dance and music at Maison de la Culture et de la Communication (Point-Virgule) in the botanical gardens; comedy and music hall shows at Théâtre de la Poche, rue de la Mulatière; music at Palais des Spectacles, boulevard J.-Janin.

Nightlife – The vast Place Jean-Jaurès has numerous possibilities, including cafés (Café des Artistes, Le Bistrot de Paris, Les Jardins), brasseries (Le Commerce, La Brasserie Pauläner), cinemas (Gaumont, near the cathedral) and bars (Midi-Minuit, Le London Pub). Another good area to go in the evenings is Rue Dormoy, which has restaurants and discos (Rock-City, Vera-Cruz-Café). A bowling alley, billiards and ice-rink are to be found in Boulevard J.-Janin.

Local gastronomy – St-Étienne's speciality is the *rapée*, a savoury potato pancake.

Dates for your diary – Bric-à-brac fair in May (Place Villebœuf); Forez rally in June; book fair in October (Place de l'Hôtel-de-ville).

Industrial redeployment – The mines, which were the basis of industrial development in the past, saw their coal production decrease regularly between 1960 and 1980.

This gradual closing was planned, allowing the metallurgical and textile industries time to restructure themselves; they now operate in conjunction with diversified activities such as precision mechanics, electronics, food processing, plastics and cardboard manufacturing.

The town has a National School of Mining Engineering, a Technical Centre for the Mechanical Industries, and to develop new technologies, the Industrial Automation Pole for the Rhône-Alps Region has been set up.

★★MUSÉE D'ART MODERNE ⊙ *2hr*

*4.5km/3mi from the city centre. Leave St-Étienne northwards via Rue Bergson (**X 9**) towards La Terrasse and follow signs to the Musée d'Art Moderne.*

This vast art gallery located in the town of St-Priest-en-Jarez was designed by the architect D Guichard; it is devoted to 20C art, of which it provides an interesting retrospective owing to its policy of continual acquisition. The sober, functional building looks like an industrial structure from the outside. Its walls, covered with black ceramic panels, are a reminder of the important role played by coal in this region in the past. The exhibition area, arranged to encourage contemplation, covers nearly $4\,000m^2/43\,000ft^2$.

The museum is a lively meeting place with a specialised library, conference rooms, a children's workshop, a museum shop and a restaurant.

Contemporary art since 1945 – The paintings, generally large, are displayed in the central part of the museum, just behind "Espace Zéro", a vast composition in white ceramic tiles by Jean-Pierre Raynaud, which contrasts with the exterior of the building.

The 1950s saw an abundance of new types of **abstract art**: the Geometric Abstraction incarnated by Sonia Delaunay, Hélion, Herbin, or Bram van Velde and Atlan contrasted with the Lyrical Abstraction leaning towards Graphism of Hartung and Soulages.

The 1960s marked the peak in consumer consumption; the **New Realists** rediscovered everyday objects. They are assembled by Arman, compressed by César, "trapped" by Spoerri or torn by Hains. Space itself is materialised by Klein *(Monochrome)*. Adepts of Narrative Figuration, such as Monory, Rancillac, and Adami, used photographic or advertising media, sometimes even comic strips.

In the United States it was the era of **Pop Art** with Dine, Warhol *(Self-Portrait)* and Lichtenstein. The formalist abstraction of Noland and Stella *(Agbatana II)* resulted in stark canvases with perfect contours while Judd and Lewitt produced modular geometric structures (wood, painted metal).

The Italians – Merz, Zorio and Penone – of Arte Povera, seeing Art as an active force, sought to portray the energy of the simplest objects.

Preceded by Hantaï who, in 1960, set colour free by the use of crushed or folded fabrics, the Supports/Surfaces group is well-represented here with Viallat (paint on tarpaulin), Dezeuze (strips of wood stapled together and stained), Grand, Saytour.

Musée d'Art Moderne

Agbatana II by Frank Stella

The German **neo-Expressionist** movement, first recognised in 1980, was followed by Baselitz *(Elke VI)*, Gerhard Richter *(Glenn)*, Penck *(Meeting)* while new realist movements asserted themselves with artists such as Denis Laget.

A large space is given over to **Dubuffet**, the initiator of l'**Art brut** ("raw art") in 1942, with a dozen or so works including *Le Site illusoire*, *Le Déchiffreur* and works executed after 1980.

Modern Art (1900-45) – The small- and medium- sized works which form a collection showing clearly the development of abstract art are exhibited in the rooms to the left of the main entrance.

Next to a **Monet** *(Water Lilies)* and a Kupka *(The Blue Ribbon)*, hangs Chabaud's *Red Nude*, its pure colours characteristic of Fauvism. *Lyrical Explosion* by Magnelli and *Still Life with a Newspaper* by Severini are later examples of the **Cubism** defined by Braque and Picasso. Note the *Portrait of Madame Heim* by Robert Delaunay and *Four Elements* by Gleizes. Russian avant-garde is expressed by Alexandra Hexter and Koudriachov.

Picasso is represented by two still lifes from the 30s and Léger by the masterful *Composition with Three Women* and *Country Outing* in which both objects and people are geometrised, devoid of all expression.

In reaction to the First World War, the **Dada** movement produced derisive, even absurd works: *The Fiancé* by Picabia, *Assemblage* by Schwitters, *Ventre de Carosse* by R Hausmann.

Following in their wake, the Surrealists, with Brauner, Ernst, Miró and Masson, sought to introduce the dream world into their works. During the 1930s, abstract art developed another vision of the world with Hélion, Freundlich, M Cahn and Magnelli. Interesting sculptures accompany the paintings: *Cubist Head* by Czaky, works by **Rodin**, Laurents, Arp, Béothy and Calder (mobile).

Graphic Art – A room on the first floor holds temporary exhibitions of drawings, lithographs and photographs.

The **Bibliothèque Jean-Laude** is a library open to the public offering one of the most comprehensive information centres on modern and contemporary art.

★OLD TOWN *about 2hr on foot*

Start from **Place Boivin (Y 12)**, which marks the site of the former 15C north rampart, and walk down Rue Émile-Loubet; there is a fine façade adorned with five caryatids at no 12, the 16C **Maison de "Marcellin-Allard" (B)**. Return to the square, one corner of which is occupied by the church known as the Grand'Église.

Grand'Église ⊘ – The church of St-Étienne is the only remaining example of Gothic architecture in St-Étienne, and its parish is the oldest in the city. The church was built in local Forez sandstone in the 15C; the bell tower was added in the 17C. In the first chapel on the left there is a fine 16C polychrome Entombment. The chancel in Flamboyant Gothic style dates from the mid 15C and the stained-glass windows visible today date from the 19C.

On the left, on leaving the church, there are two handsome façades (15C and 16C). No 5, known as the **Maison François I (D)** is decorated with five Renaissance medallions. On the right, Rue du Théâtre is bordered by houses with overhanging upper floors.

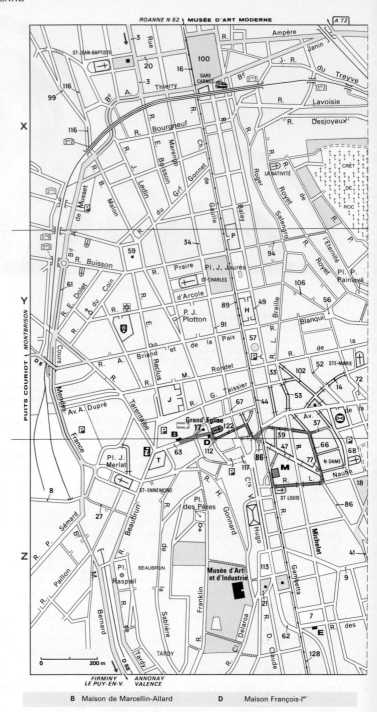

B Maison de Marcellin-Allard   **D**   Maison François-Iᵉʳ

Go down Rue de la Ville.

The first house on the left has mullioned windows and five medallions representing figures. No 22 housed, in the 17C, the town hall.

Place du Peuple (**Z 60**) was the market square in the Middle Ages. On the corner of Rue Mercière a 16C tower rises above an arcade; a timber-framed house stands opposite.

Cross the avenue used by the trams to reach Rue Denis-Escoffier, which marks the entrance to the old Outre-Furan district. At the junction of Rue des Martyrs-de-Vingré is an unusual mid-18C house, adorned with a statue, which is typical, with its

ST-ÉTIENNE

E   Château Étienne-Mimard   M   Musée du vieux St-Étienne

caves with four rows of tiles and its large, visible beams, of the urban architecture to be found in Forez. On the left at no 3 Rue Georges-Dupré a massive façade includes imposing lintels in one piece. Turn back and into Rue des Martyrs-de-Vingré; nos 19 and 39 are examples of 18C houses incorporating weaving lofts or workshops. Note also the arcades with bosses on the second floor.

Beyond Place Neuve turn right into Rue Nautin and right again into Rue Gambetta.

Musée du vieux St-Étienne (Z M) ⊘ – *Entrance in the 2nd courtyard on the left.* An 18C toll marker, from the old Outre-Furan district, signals the entrance to the Hôtel de Villeneuve (18C). The city museum inside is arranged on the first floor, in a series of rooms with fine moulded and coffered ceilings. The first charter mentioning St-Étienne (1258) is on display, together with various maps and engravings showing the expansion of the city. A carved Baroque altarpiece and various statues from local churches are among the other exhibits. The opening of the first industrial railway line in St-Étienne in 1828 is commemorated through various documents including the first ticket sold on the line.

ADDITIONAL SIGHTS

Musée d'Art et d'Industrie (Z) ⊘ – *Scheduled to be reopened at the end of 1997, following extensive restoration work.*
The museum is located in the former Palais des Arts. It is now a real repository of local and regional know-how relating to toolmaking and to the evolution of tools, equipment and machinery from the 16C to the present.
The different levels of the museum are organised around a well-defined theme.

Ribbonmaking, weaving – The textile machine room illustrates the weaving of ribbons and braiding of laces, from the 16C to modern times. The "Ribbon Room" contains a beautiful collection of ribbons, trimmings, weaving looms, old fabrics and embroidery. There is a reconstruction of a furnishing trimmings workshop.

★**Weapons** – There is an interesting and varied collection including cutting and thrusting weapons and firearms – some of which are very finely worked – exotic weapons, helmets and armour. Display cases trace the history of the manufacture of firearms, particularly shotguns, from their origin to bored guns. The armour and helmets include some very rare specimens such as a basinet forged from a single piece of metal, a 16C German horse's nose band of intricately-wrought iron and a set of 16C helmets. Note the collection of African, South Pacific and Oriental arms.

Cycles – On the top floor fifty or so cycles, from the hobby-horse to the monocoque frame cycle, follow the history of the bicycle.

Some of the finest buildings from the 19C and the first half of the 20C, the age of the town's industrial apogee, have survived in good condition; many of these were the work of the **Lamaizière brothers**. These architects designed the headquarters of the armourers Colcombet (8 Place de l'Hôtel de Ville), the Manufacture des Armes et Cycles (Arms Factory), and the **Château Étienne-Mimard (E)**, a neo-Renaissance mansion for the founder of the Arms Factory.

Site of the old Manufacture des Armes et Cycles de St-Étienne – *Cours Fauriel.*
This site established under the Second Empire to be, together with Avenue de la Libération, one of the showcases of the industrial expansion in St-Étienne, was occupied by the buildings of the Arms Factory which were built by Léon Lamaizière in 1893, and which were in use until 1985. One part of the site has been restored and adapted since April 1993 into a conference centre, with offices, shops and a planetarium.

Rue Michelet (Z) – This artery, pierced along the north-south axis parallel to Rue Gambetta, contains some examples of innovative architecture from the 1930s (nos 34, 36, 42 and in particular no 44, an imposing building in reinforced concrete).

Rue Daguerre – This is where some of the architectural curiosities of the town may be found: at nos 54 and 56 stand the **houses without staircases★** which were built by the architect Bossu in 1933; the buildings were designed around an inner court giving onto the various rooms of each apartment. Enter the hall to admire the spiral access ramp.

View – From the paths of the botanical gardens, and in particular from the terrace in front of the **Maison de la Culture (Z)** (1969), there are typical **views** of the town which lies in the hollow of the Furan basin and is dominated, on the opposite slope, by Ste-Barbe hill and, further away, by two coaltips, gradually being covered with vegetation.

"Up the Greens!"

St-Étienne boasts a football team in a distinctive green strip whose performance is keenly followed by local townspeople. The St-Étienne team was founded in 1931, when the Geoffroy-Guichard stadium was built with funds from Casino supermarket chain. It was not long (1938) before the team reached the first division, and it continued to excel on the field, culminating in its participation in the European Cup Championships in 1976. Many St-Étienne players have played at international level and been nominated football champions in France.

Unfortunately, in 1982 the team was involved a fraud scandal and its performance has since slumped. The St-Étienne townspeople, however, refuse to lose faith in "Les Verts" and continue to hope for a repeat of their former triumphs.

*Puits Couriot, Musée de la Mine ⊘ – Puits Couriot was exploited from 1913 to 1973 by the Houillères du Bassin de la Loire (Loire Basin Coal-Mining Company). During its peak the seam here produced 3 000 tonnes of coal per day and employed 1 500 miners. The inner courtyard is adorned with a monument to the miners and with modern extracting machines.

The visit begins in the **Salle des Pendus**★, a vast locker room where, as space was limited, their clothes were hung from the ceiling to dry, creating an interesting effect. The adjoining shower is evidence of the collective life they led. Visitors are taken down to the lower galleries in the cages used to take miners down at the start of their shift and then to bring up the coal during the rest of the day, and sometimes for bringing up the wounded. By the lift is the reception area, the departure point

Puits Couriot

Musée de la Mine, St-Étienne

for the wagon trains which travel through the part of the complex which has been adapted for tours. Each stop on the journey sets off an explanatory video-commentary and shows one stage in the evolution of extracting techniques. The tour goes back in time from the 1960s, when the highly automated and electrified methods of extraction used a technique involving placing supports as the cutting edge advanced, then removing them to provoke a collapsing of the gallery roof.

The 1950s saw the introduction of metal supports which replaced the former wooden posts, and these arches constitute the framework of the modern gallery. The coal is hewn by the pick-man with a pneumatic pick, which produced a daily average of 10 tonnes. This was just the beginning of mechanisation.

The 1930s were marked by the installation of extracting equipment which worked on compressed air, which led to a vigorous rationalisation of work, and the use of portable lighting.

The tour continues with the faithful reconstruction of a coal face in 1900, when everything was done by hand: mining with a pick-axe (producing an average of 3 tonnes per day) and the transportation in tubs pushed by children as far as the widening of the tunnel. The reconstruction of a stable recalls the importance of the horses which spent their lifetime down the mine and which were the only pulling power available to bring the tubs up to what is now the reception area. The hard life underground for these animals, one of the characteristics of the old mining ways, is described in Zola's epic novel, *Germinal*.

Before returning to the surface, a representation of St Barbara, the patron saint of miners, may be seen in a niche, bringing to mind the religious and lay festivals in which all mining towns participate on 4 December each year.

EXCURSION

★★View from Guizay – *Leave St-Étienne on the N 82 south. At Planfoy turn right to Guizay.*

From the foot of the Sacré-Coeur statue there is a fine extensive view over the town. The village of Rochetaillée can be seen, to the far right, perched on its crest. To the left unfolds the Ondaine corridor: le Chambon-Feugerolles, Firminy and the hills of Forez. The road back down to St-Étienne continues to offer attractive views over the city and its surroundings.

*Book well in advance
as vacant hotel rooms are often scarce in high season.*

ST-FLOUR ★★

Population 7 417
Michelin map 76 folds 4, 14 or 239 south of fold 31

St-Flour is perched on the end of the *planèze* which bears its name, at an altitude of 881m/2 890ft on a basaltic table 100m/330ft above the River Ander. The beauty of its **site★★** can be best appreciated from an eastern approach which reveals a line of houses dominated by the massive towers of the cathedral, looming above rocky escarpments.

The town developed around the tomb of St Flour, one of the evangelists preaching in the Auvergne in the 4C. During the Middle Ages, under the administration of three elected consuls, it had a population of 7 000 people. In 1317 the pope made it a cathedral town.

Revolt of the Tuchins – During the Hundred Years War St-Flour was close to the battlefield. The Treaty of Brétigny (1360) made St-Flour a frontier town, "France's key to Guienne" (Aquitaine). Fear of the English grew but it was the mercenaries, more than the English, who controlled the country between the fortresses of Saillant and Alleuze. The town was often attacked, its outlying districts burnt and pillaged. The consuls made pacts with the enemy who, in return for a fee, agreed to leave the people of St-Flour in peace. However, the truce was endangered by some of the inhabitants, nicknamed the "Tuchins", who saw it as tantamount to capitulation, and who were seen as patriots by the lower classes. Formed secretly into a band, they waged implacable guerilla warfare on the occupant. After 1384 the Tuchins also attacked the rich and privileged orders, and became outright robbers. Having become dangerous and unnecessary, they were overcome by the troops of the Duc de Berry. At the beginning of the 15C St-Flour had difficulty recovering; it had lost a good part of its inhabitants and suffered from epidemics. It was governed by an oligarchy of merchants and men of law. In 1419, conflict between the Burgundians and Armagnacs was rife; the bishop and the lower classes supported the Burgundians. The monarchy made St-Flour one of the six "good towns" of Upper Auvergne. Charles VII came twice, particularly in 1437, to foil a conspiracy against himself.

Consul Brisson saves the town (1578) – On one occasion during the Wars of Religion, St-Flour was about to be captured. During the night of the 9th August 1578 the Protestant captain **Merle** crept up to the walls of the town; some of his men had already scaled the ramparts when Consul Brisson, woken by the noise, sounded the alarm bell, rounded up the townspeople and turned back their assailants. Once again, it could be said of St-Flour, "No one ever took you by force except the wind".

SIGHTS

★**Cathédrale (B)** – The cathedral, built in late Gothic style, stands on the vast Place des Armes and is a reminder of the town's vocation as a stronghold. Its construction, begun after the collapse in 1396 of the Romanesque basilica which preceded it, was not completed until the end of the 15C. The architect had previously worked for the Duc de Berry, which explains why the construction is not in the usual style of the region. On the west front, the right-hand tower is pierced with square mullioned windows letting daylight into two rooms once used as a prison.

Inside, the lines of the five aisles are strikingly sober. Under the organ loft, a 15C mural depicts Purgatory and Hell. Note, against the left pillar at the entrance to the chancel, the large wooden **Crucifix★** (13C or 15C) known as the "Beautiful Black God"; the 15C *Pietà* in the chapel of the Holy Sacrament and, in the Tomb Chapel, a gilded bronze shrine containing the relics of St Flour.

Terrasse des Roches (B D) – From this square on the old ramparts there is a lovely view of the lower part of the town, the Ander valley and the Margeride mountains.

Musée de la Haute-Auvergne (B H) ⊘ – This museum is located in the former bishop's palace rebuilt in the 17C. Displays in the low 15C vaulted rooms explain how blue-veined *fourme* cheese is made ("Cantal", "Salers") and the different facets of pastoral life, particularly the shepherd's huts or *burons* where the cheese is made.

On the ground floor, in the former chapel, note a 12C polychrome wooden statue of St Peter from the church at Albepierre-Bredons, a 14C statue of St Flour, nine 16C carved-wood panels and a lovely set of Marian statues from the 12C to the 18C. The next room leads to the chapter-house, the only vestige of the Cluniac priory, where the treasure of the cathedral of St-Pierre and portraits of bishops are displayed.

The exhibits on the first floor concentrate on Auvergne folklore: popular music and its traditional instruments, hats and headdresses, a collection of regional carved-wood pieces, Cantal furniture (chests, cupboards, dressers, wooden bed panelling). The contents of the archaeological section mainly come from the digs at Mons and also from Laurie, near Massiac. A beautiful bronze **brassard★** consisting of six rings attached with a bar, and bracelets and swords are the main items displayed.

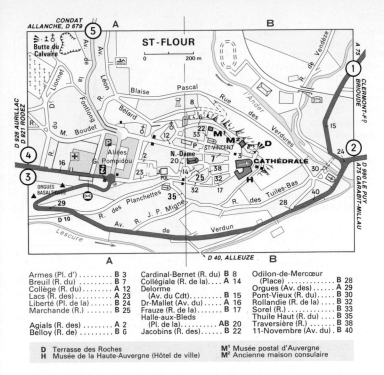

Armes (Pl. d') . . . . B 3	Cardinal-Bernet (R. du) B 8	Odilon-de-Mercœur
Breuil (R. du) . . . . B 7	Collégiale (R. de la) . . . . A 14	(Place) . . . . B 28
Collège (R. du) . . . . A 12	Delorme	Orgues (Av. des) . . . . . . A 29
Lacs (R. des) . . . . A 23	(Av. du Cdt) . . . . B 15	Pont-Vieux (R. du) . . . . . B 30
Liberté (Pl. de la) . . . . . B 24	Dr-Mallet (Av. du) . . . . . A 16	Rollandie (R. de la) . . . . B 32
Marchande (R.) . . . . B 25	Frauze (R. de la) . . . . . . B 17	Sorel (R.) . . . . B 33
	Halle-aux-Bleds	Thuile Haut (R. du) . . . . B 35
Agials (R. des) . . . . A 2	(Pl. de la) . . . . AB 20	Traversière (R.) . . . . B 38
Belloy (R. de) . . . . B 6	Jacobins (R. des) . . . . . . B 22	11-Novembre (Av. du) . . B 40

D Terrasse des Roches	**M¹** Musée postal d'Auvergne
H Musée de la Haute-Auvergne (Hôtel de ville)	**M²** Ancienne maison consulaire

Ancienne maison consulaire (Former consul's house) (**B M²**) – Consul Brisson, who once saved the town *(see above)*, lived here. The façade dates from the 16C. The courtyard *(enter through no 17 bis)*, from which can be seen three houses successively bought by consuls in the 14C and 15C to serve as their consular establishment, has an old well, a 15C staircase turret and various painted inscriptions.

Musée A-Douët ⊘ – Beyond the entrance hall with its collection of ancient weapons are the library, the guard room with its monumental fireplace, the bedrooms with painted ceilings and the Consul Room which contains a display of fine Limousin enamels. Flemish, Spanish and other furniture, Aubusson tapestries, earthenwares, and paintings of the 17C and 18C French and Dutch schools decorate the various rooms. In a small oratory, note a *Pietà* and a 15C Christ with His hands bound.

Musée postal d'Auvergne (**B M¹**) ⊘ – This postal museum, occupying an old monastery, contains a collection of 6 000 items retracing the history of the postal service since the 17C. The local postal service is given special emphasis, with the reconstruction of Ytrac post office (1900), and a horse-drawn sledge used until 1950 to enable the post to be delivered in the Margeride mountain region even when it was under a thick covering of snow.

Old streets – From Place d'Armes, lined with arcades and old façades (particularly at the corner of Rue de Belloy), walk to Rue Sorel and the church of St-Vincent, a former Dominican convent.

Follow Rue des Jacobins on the left, then Rue de la Collégiale named after a disused 14C church: **Notre-Dame collegiate church** (**AB**) whose apse has Flamboyant windows. **Rue Marchande** (**B 25**) has a few interesting old houses, including no 31, the governor's house, a 15C mansion whose façade and courtyard can be seen, and at no 15, Hôtel Brisson with a 16C courtyard, its original windows separated by columns with rope moulding.

Other interesting streets include **Rue du Breuil** (**B 7**) (15C house at no 8), and **Rue du Thuile-Haut** (**B 35**) (old houses).

Butte du Calvaire (**A**) – This hill offers a sweeping view.

EXCURSION

★**Plateau de la Chaumette** – *Round tour of 20km/12mi southeast – about 1hr – see map overleaf.*

Leave St-Flour south on the D 40. After 2km/1mi turn left up a slope. Park 1km/0.6mi further on, off a wide bend to the right, 20m/65ft after a high voltage line.

Take a path to the left *(30min Rtn on foot)* along the edge of a field and then around it. Continue along the edge of the field towards the plateau in the direction of the calvary which affords an attractive **view** of St-Flour.

Turn around, bear left on the D 40, then, in the village, take a small road on the left towards Les Grisols across the River Ander. Turn left to visit the gorge.

319

Gorges de l'Ander – Continue along the edge of the river which runs between both rocky and wooded slopes. The path ends in a very picturesque meander, at the hamlet of Le Bout du Monde ("World's End").

Turn around and return to St-Flour via Bellegarde and the N 9.

Villedieu – *8km/5mi. Leave St-Flour southwest on the D 10.*

The **church**, half-Romanesque, half-Gothic, has an attractive door with a wrought-iron knocker. In the chancel, notice the beautiful high altar, the staffs and finely carved lectern.

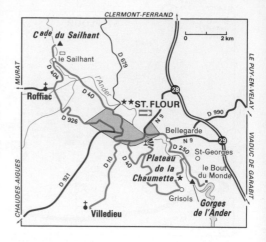

Cascade du Sailhant – *Round trip of 20km/12mi northwest. Leave St-Flour on ⑤ on the map. After 1.5km/1mi turn left onto the D 40. Park in the hamlet of Sailhant.*

The path *(15min Rtn on foot)* to the Sailhant (or Le Babory) waterfall weaves among the houses bordering the beautiful volcanic rocks on which the Château de Sailhant is built.

The tiny cascade falls into a semicircle of tall cliffs; in the hollow lies a small lake. It is also possible to park at the entrance to the château and walk the short distance to the edge of the cliff, which offers a bird's eye view of the cascade and the lake in its rocky surrounds.

Take the D 404 to Roffiac.

Roffiac – The church is a little Romanesque building from the beginning of the 12C; it belonged to the castle (14C) whose only remains are a tower.

The D 926 returns to St-Flour.

ST-MENOUX★

Population 936
Michelin map 69 fold 13 or 238 fold 45

This peaceful village has one of the loveliest places of worship in the Bourbonnais.

★**Church** – *30min.* Half a century was needed to construct the current 12C building which rises on the site of a 10C sanctuary built in honour of Menulphus, a Breton bishop, who died in the village in the 7C.

Exterior – The east end is organised elegantly beneath the high silhouette of the belfry, flanked by its staircase tower. A large semicircular portal leads into the 11C **narthex**. It is decorated with primitive capitals, and houses a lapidary museum which has a bas-relief depicting, in a mandorla, Christ giving Benediction, surrounded by the symbols of the four Evangelists and a Paschal Lamb.

Interior – The 13C nave, altered in the 15C, and the bas-reliefs display numerous works of art, including a 16C Compassionate Virgin in the right side-aisle and a carved oak **altar** in the left side-aisle.

Chancel, St-Menoux Church

J.-L. Barde/SCOPE

The **chancel**★★, with its pleasing proportions, is closed by pillars with capitals surmounted by plain arches separated from the upper windows by a Greek key pattern.

In the **ambulatory** the alternate use of pillars and fluted pilasters shows Burgundian influences. The sarcophagus behind the high altar houses the remains of St Menoux who, in centuries past, had the reputation of healing the simple-minded (*berdins* or *bredins* in the language of the Bourbonnais). The people to be cured put their heads into a cavity in the side of the sarcophagus, whence comes the name *débredinoire*, given to this odd monument.

ST-NECTAIRE

Population 664
Michelin map 73 fold 14 or 239 fold 19
Local map under Vallées des COUZES

Two villages are grouped together under this name: the thermal spa of St-Nectaire-le-Bas (Lower St-Nectaire), which spreads out over 2km/1mi in a green valley, and the old village of St-Nectaire-le-Haut (Upper St-Nectaire) dominated by its magnificent **church**.

Mont Cornadore, on which St-Nectaire is built and which means "water reservoir", was inhabited in Celtic times. The Romans built public baths here. In the Middle Ages a Benedictine Priory was established as an offshoot of La Chaise-Dieu Abbey; a castle, no trace of which remains, was also built on the hill. It was inhabited by the glorious St-Nectaire family whose most famous member was **Madeleine de St-Nectaire** – young, beautiful and virtuous, widowed early, always followed by sixty men on horseback; she sided with the Protestants in the Wars of Religion, defeated the king's lieutenant in Upper Auvergne and ended up killing him by her own hand.

The name "St-Nectaire" is also given to a well-known cheese, made with pasteurized or unpasteurized milk *(see Introduction: Food and drink)* which has been produced for centuries in a well-defined area within the Cantal and Puy-de-Dôme *départements*.

ST-NECTAIRE-LE-HAUT *(photograph p 50)*

★★**St-Nectaire** ⊘ – This building constructed around 1160 is typical of Romanesque architecture in the Auvergne; it occupies a very beautiful site near the Monts Dore. The church was built in honour of St Nectaire, the companion of St Austremoine and monks from La Chaise-Dieu were the first priests in charge of it. The damage which occurred during the Revolution required extensive renovation work in 1875 (belfry, towers, west front).

A good **view** of the church may be had from Chemin de la Parre, east of the church, beyond the tributary.

Exterior – The west front, crude, almost sparse, has a simple rounded doorway. The east end, on the other hand, with its magnificent ground plan, is crowned with a belfry rebuilt in the 19C. The restrained decoration of the east end includes a delicate mosaic frieze incorporating rose windows; blind arcades with fine colonnettes; small gable walls supporting the chapel roofs.

Interior – The inside is remarkable for the unity of its style. A narthex with a robust three-bay arcade decorating its upper storey precedes the nave, which is barrel-vaulted without transverse ribbing and flanked by narrow side-aisles with groined vaulting surmounted by galleries. The attractive chancel, not as high as the nave, has six elegant columns topped by interesting capitals, and an ambulatory opening onto three radiating chapels.

103 magnificent **capitals**★★, carved by an artist with a lively imagination and a strong sense of composition, decorate the nave and chancel. Although the figures are somewhat heavy, the verve with which they have been treated gives them enormous vitality. The Life of Christ, the Old and New Testaments, scenes from Revelations and the miracles of St Nectaire provide most of the themes, together with those of the bestiary (Donkey playing a Lyre, Monkey Trainer etc).

Despite having been pillaged during the Revolution, the **Treasury**★★ still contains some beautiful works: the gilded copper bust of **St Baudime**★★ (12C); the polychrome Virgin of Mount Cornadore (12C); a 15C embossed silver reliquary arm of St Nectaire; two gold binding plates decorated with Limoges enamelwork (12C).

Marchidial – *Follow the street north of the church, beyond the Tourist Office.* This is a beautiful 15C stone Cross. From the esplanade there is a lovely view of the Puy de Châteauneuf, Murol castle, the Monts Dore chain and Puy d'Éraigne.

Grottes du Cornadore ⊘ – *Just west of the church.* The Romans built public baths here, where today visitors can discover the source of the spa water, its medical uses and petrifying properties.

Maison du St-Nectaire ⊘ – In a cellar, a video show explains *(in French)* the origin of St-Nectaire cheese, how it is made and matured. There is sampling at the end of the visit.

Puy de Châteauneuf – *30min Rtn on foot. Fairly steep climb. Follow the street climbing up from the northeast end of the church, then take a rocky path on the left.*

The path leads to the top of the *puy* (alt 934m/3 063ft) from where there is an attractive view of the Monts Dore. The side of the mountain is hollowed out by nine caves which, like the Jonas caves *(see Vallées des COUZES)*, were probably inhabited in prehistoric times, then used again in the Middle Ages.

ST-NECTAIRE-LE-BAS

The thermal spa, with smart shops lining the D 996, has more than forty springs. Their waters gush forth at temperatures ranging from 8° to 56°C/46° to 133°F. Its treatment installations are grouped together in the modern Gravières spa establishment; the waters are used to treat kidney and metabolic complaints.

Fontaines pétrifiantes ⊙ – The water gushes forth at more than 50°C/122°F from volcanic faults *(see CLERMONT-FERRAND).*

Dolmen – There are standing stones in the upper part of the park, east of the river.

Puy d'Éraigne – *30min Rtn on foot. Follow a rocky and very difficult path branching off to the left from the road to Sapchat, the D 150.* From the summit (alt 895m.2 936ft) there is a beautiful view of the Monts Dore.

Some hotels have their own tennis court, swimming pool, private beach or garden. Consult the current edition of the annual **Michelin Red Guide France.**

ST-PAUL-TROIS-CHÂTEAUX

Population 6 455

Michelin map 81 folds 1 or 246 fold 23 – Local map under Moyenne vallée du RHÔNE

The old town is surrounded by the remains of ramparts but has never had the three castles its name – St-Paul-Three-Castles – would suggest. It was appointed capital of the region during Roman times, under the name "Augusta Tricastinorum". During the second half of the 4C, the first part of its Roman name was replaced by the name Paul, commemorating one of the town's first bishops. The name of the old capital of "Tricastini" may possibly have been Frenchified by a clerk in the 16C to "Trois Châteaux", though there is no evidence for this theory.

The town was a bishopric until the Revolution.

Modern St-Paul sits at the heart of the main truffle region of France.

SIGHTS

★**Cathedral** – This imposing building, begun in the 11C and completed in the 12C, is a remarkable example of Provençal Romanesque architecture.

Exterior – Most striking is the exceptional height of the transept walls and the powerful aspect of the nave. A few decorative details contrast with the austerity of the walls, particularly the portal on the west front: finely carved arching frames the 17C wooden doors.

Interior – *Enter through the south door.* The nave with its three bays, barrel-vaulted on transverse arches and supported by side-aisles, has a magnificent elevation (24m/79ft). The bay preceding the transept has a blind triforium on the 1st floor; the alcoves, framed by pilasters and colonettes, surmount a frieze of finely carved drapery. A dome on pendentives covers the transept crossing. The apse, with its oven vault, has flat ribbing; access to the crossing is via a triumphal arch with a double offset.

Other features of interest include the organ case built in 1704 by the Avignon sculptor Boisselin; the bas-relief on the second pillar on the left, depicting the Last Judgement; the 14C and 15C frescoes; a 12C mosaic behind the high altar. The 17C giltwood former high altar stands in the north side-aisle.

Numerous jobbers' marks can be seen on the stonework both inside and outside the church.

Maison de la Truffe et du Tricastin ⊙ – The Truffle Centre, located inside the tourist centre *(eastern end of the cathedral)*, houses an exhibition with posters, show-cases and a video projection on the cultivation and marketing of what is known as the "black diamond" of the Tricastin region, and an ingredient in many tasty local dishes.

In the vaulted cellars below, wines from the Tricastin hills are on display, together with several old wine-making implements.

EXCURSIONS

St-Restitut – *4km/2.5mi southeast*. The village **church**★ in Provençal Romanesque style has wonderful **carved decoration**★ (polygonal east end with finely carved cornice; south door; elegant cornice around the nave; arcading in the apse). A tall, square tower is joined by an arch bearing a carved frieze. The **funerary tower** to the side of the church is said to

Truffle-hunting

be the tomb of St Restitut. It has an 11C base with a frieze and a carved cornice; the frieze consists of a chequered border around carved panels depicting Biblical themes, a medieval bestiary or contemporary trades. The upper part was restored when the church was built. The **Chapelle du St-Sépulcre** nearby is a small hexagonal chapel built in 1504 by a bishop on his return from a pilgrimage to the Holy Land.

★ **Barry** – *5km/3mi south via St-Restitut*. Backing onto a cliff into which several of its houses are carved, this troglodytic village has been inhabited by humankind from prehistoric times to the Second World War; though now abandoned, it is undergoing restoration. The chapel (17C) and various houses may be discerned. Fine **views**★★ over the valley.

★ **Clansayes** – *5km/3mi northeast. Park the car and head for the far end of the promontory, with its monumental statue of the Virgin.* From here there is an extensive **view**★★ over the Tricastin area and its peaks carved by erosion.

ST-POURÇAIN-SUR-SIOULE ★

Population 5 159
Michelin map 69 fold 14 or 238 fold 46
Town plan in the current Michelin Red Guide France

This small market town, which is an important crossroads on the River Sioule, is popular with trout fishermen and those enamoured of country walks.
It owes its name to St Pourçain (died c 532), a former slave, turned monk, who defended the Auvergne from the ravages of Thierry, son of Clovis, the king of the Franks.

One of the oldest vineyards in France – Tradition has it that the grapevine first appeared on the sunny hillsides of the Bouble and the Sioule valleys a little before the Christian era. The stony ground of this region is particularly suitable to vine growing, which developed rapidly during Roman times, and later at the demand of the monasteries and local squires. At the end of the 18C, 8 000ha/19 760 acres were under cultivation. Owing to a concern for quality rather than quantity, however, the vineyards were reduced to cover only 890ha/2 200 acres.

SIGHTS

From Place Maréchal-Foch, with its attractive fountain dominated by the **belfry** of the ancient monastery, walk through the covered passageway to the carefully restored courtyard, the Cour des Bénédictins, which offers a beautiful view of the bell tower and imposing roof of the church of Ste-Croix.

★ **Musée de la Vigne et du Vin** ⊙ – Great care has been taken in presenting the history of the region's main agricultural activity. A spiral staircase in the clock tower (15C) leads to rooms with attractive beams and stonework. Here a large number of items show the different aspects of vine-growing and wine-making: cooper's tools, weights and measures, a show-case on phylloxera, wine-making instruments etc. Room VI contains the museum's two most important exhibits: a four-chambered horse-drawn still dating back to 1889 and a huge 17C press with a vertical wheel which, turned by three or four men, could press up to 300kg/660lb of grapes. Popular arts and traditions are displayed in the last room: clothing from 1900, the banner of the wine-growers' brotherhood (18C), a late 19C accounts book belonging to a wine merchant from St-Pourçain and hand-embroidered head dresses from the Bourbonnais region.

Enter the church, flanked by houses on each side, through the door leading into the Cour des Bénédictins.

323

★**Ste-Croix** – This vast, former abbey church was constructed in several stages from the 11C to the 15C. The chancel, built fairly late, is not in the axis of the nave, which has Gothic arches surmounted by a false triforium. Whimsical, humourous carvings decorate the misericords of the 15C stalls. The north arm of the transept houses a 16C **Ecce Homo**; this polychrome sculpture cut from a single block of stone depicts Christ at the hands of Pontius Pilate. In the apse, the two northern semicircular chapels with arched windows are Romanesque; those facing south, from the 14C, are three-sided with a pointed window. On the right of the chancel, in the Chapel of the Holy Sacrament, is a dazzling sun dating from the days of Napoleon's Empire; the altar is decorated by a coat of arms dedicated to the glory of God borne up by angels.

The sacristy, in the five remaining bays of the cloisters, has carved capitals and a 15C stone *Pietà* (damaged). For a good view of the east end, leave by the main portal and turn right towards Place Clemenceau.

ST-ROMAIN-LE-PUY

Population 2 616
Michelin map 88 fold 17 or 239 fold 23 – 7km/4mi south of Montbrison

The church of the former priory of St-Romain-le-Puy which, at the end of the 10C, belonged to the Abbey of St-Martin-d'Ainay in Lyon, rises on a volcanic peak emerging from the Forez plain, dominating a St-Gobain glassworks at the foot of the peak. Water is bottled from a mineral spring (Source Parot) northeast of the village near the D 8.

★**Église du Prieuré** ⊘ – *Access by car from Place Michalon to a car park halfway up the slope.*

From the plateau in front of the church, the panorama encompasses a vast circle of mountains: those of Forez to the west, the Monts d'Uzore to the north, the Tarare mountains and those of the Lyonnais from the northeast to the southeast.

The combination of the church's location, its age, its unusual construction and its carved decoration all make it a very curious building. Traces of several successive construction periods can be seen. The oldest remains are pre-10C (the part near the door and, on the right-hand side, two walled-up doors with bands of brick-work). In the 11C the monks, who wanted to extend the church, demolished the original apse and built a crypt to provide a foundation for the chancel and new apse. Further alterations were made in the 15C and 16C. The walls are made of pink and grey granite quarry stone, mixed with blocks of basalt. The east end is the most interesting part of the church, with its semicircular arch, its partially reticulated masonry work and, in particular, the unusual carved frieze recessed into the underside of the arch, consisting of square and rectangular slabs and decorated with very sober relief motifs.

Interior – The archaic appearance and the asymmetry of the ground plan are particularly striking. The floor of the apse and chancel is higher than the level of the earlier nave. The capitals have geometric decoration.

Remains of murals (restored) painted in several stages from the 12C to the 15C are visible in various places. The capitals on the crypt columns depict for the most part animals fighting.

ST-SATURNIN ★

Population 778
Michelin map 73 fold 14 or 239 fold 19

This village in the Monne valley was the home of the barons of La Tour d'Auvergne who later became the Counts of Auvergne. This is the family which produced Catherine de' Medici – daughter of Lorenzo de' Medici and Madeleine de La Tour d'Auvergne – who became Queen of France after marrying Henri II.

St-Saturnin attracted a colony of painters and several writers, including novelist and critic **Paul Bourget** (1852-1935).

The location of St-Saturnin near the Monts Dômes and the Couzes and Comté valleys, its picturesque streets, its castle and its little square with a charming 16C fountain, make this an attractive tourist destination.

SIGHTS

Parking recommended at Place du 8-Mai (shaded square beside the D 8).

★★**Church** – *30min.* The church was built in the 12C and is very simple. Despite the lack of apsidal chapels, the **east end** is nevertheless attractive. The radiating transept chapels, the wide ambulatory around the semicircular chancel, and the powerful mass of the transept, which has the best-preserved octagonal bell tower in the

Auvergne, form a remarkable architectural whole. The external decoration is elaborate, with its strings of billet-moulding, its wood chip modillions and its capitals supporting a set of arches, some of them remarkable just for the alternate colouring of their basalt and arkose archstones. In contrast to this wealth of decoration, the side buttresses and simple end-wall of the west front are striking in their lack of ornamentation.

Inside, note the high barrel-vault of the nave, the galleries above the side aisles with their groined vaulting, the elevation of the transept crossing with its supporting diaphragm arches and the crypt resting on powerful pillars.

In the chancel is a giltwood high altar from the castle chapel, bearing the monogram of Henri IV and Marguerite de Valois, Queen Margot *(see USSON)*, the lady of St-Saturnin. Next to the church is the small 11C **chapel of Ste-Madeleine** ⊙, fortified in the 14C.

Castle ⊙ – This imposing fortress, which has undergone extensive restoration, is typical of the military architecture of the Middle Ages: triple curtain wall, ramparts, towers with machicolations and crenellations. The main part of the building, with a massive, late-15C roof, is flanked by two wings (14C and 15C). The keep, the watch-path (views of the village and its surroundings) and formal gardens are open to visitors.

EXCURSION

Abbaye Notre-Dame-de-Randol – *2km/1mi southwest on the D 28 and D 28ᴬ*. The road to Randol provides an attractive view of this modern church overlooking the Monne valley.

The church is noteworthy for its pleasing proportions and the height of its nave. Inside, the most striking element is the soaring aspect of the **chancel**★ brought on by the slope of the nave and the height of the slender pillars, which rise right up to the vault. The oval chancel, flooded with light diffused through modern *grisaille* windows, is extremely elegant.

The righthand chapel is devoted to St Benedict. In the chapel on the left, dedicated to the Holy Family, note the stained-glass windows depicting the Mysteries of the Rosary.

SALERS★★

Population 470
Michelin map 76 fold 2 or 239 fold 29
Local map under Monts du CANTAL

Salers is one of the prettiest little towns in Upper Auvergne and has a very distinctive character. It stands at an altitude of 951m/3 120ft on its *planèze* and has retained, from its military and judicial past, a rare set of ramparts and old houses, grouped together on a pinnacle giving a magnificent view of the confluence of the Aspre and the Maronne rivers. Just outside Salers, on the road to Pas de Peyrol, is Notre-Dame-de-Lorette chapel.

HISTORICAL NOTES

Arms and the gown (15C and 16C) – The twofold character of the buildings in Salers can be explained by the town's history. Initially unwalled, it suffered cruelly at the hands of the English and the mercenaries "free companions" who roamed the highways; as a result the ramparts were built, and still stand today. At the end of the 15C Salers became the seat of the bailiwick of the Upper Mountains of the Auvergne and the established *bourgeois* families, from which the judges were selected, started building their impressive turreted houses.

Religious orgies (18C) – The main feast day in Salers was traditionally the anniversary of the Birth of the Virgin Mary. On one occasion, the coveted title of King of the Festival was auctioned off, and the recipient, a vainglorious burgher, had the idea of running wine through the public fountains – a much appreciated act of generosity which then became customary. During the ensuing pilgrimages, however, the free-flowing wine led to countless brawls and beatings, leaving people wounded or even dead. In the end, such excesses had to be forbidden, the taverns closed and the brawlers fined; subsequently, the number of pilgrims decreased considerably.

VISIT *Park near the church*

★**St-Matthieu** – A 12C porch still remains from the Romanesque church which predated the present church, begun in the 15C. The bell tower, which was struck by lightning, was rebuilt during the last century.

Note, on the portal, the billet-moulding and sculptures on the upper covings. Inside, on the right, is an **Entombment**★ given to the church in 1495; it is made of polychrome stone and was inspired by Burgundian art. On each side of the chancel are paintings attributed to Ribera (17C). In the chancel there is a lectern from the end of Louis XIII's reign (mid 17C); above hang four 17C Aubusson tapestries. At the back of the church, a fifth tapestry depicts the Descent from the Cross.

SALERS

On leaving the church, pass a fountain on the left and follow Rue du Beffroi uphill.

Go under the Tour de l'Horloge (Clock Tower also known as Belfry Gate, **B**), flanked by a round tower with machicolations. Just beyond the gate, on the right, is the house of Pierre Lizet with its Gothic window and Renaissance portal.

★★**Grande-Place** (Place Tyssandier-d'Escous) – The old houses of dark lavastone with their clean, sober lines, flanked by corbelled round or polygonal turrets, and their pepperpot or many-sided roofs, look like a stage-set; the scene is completed by a fountain in the centre.

In Grande-Place itself, a monument has been raised to Tyssandier d'Escous who improved the region's breed of cattle in the 19C and made it famous under the name of the "Salers breed".

Ancien Bailliage (**E**) ⊘ – This Renaissance building, the old bailiff's court, stands at the corner of Rue du Beffroi. It is a vast residence of fine architectural design, flanked by two corner towers. Inside are several rooms open to view, one of which has a beautiful Renaissance fireplace.

In the inner court, adjoining the main building, rises a massive octagonal tower with a watchtower.

Maison de Flojeac (**F**) – The house has a turret with canted corners.

Hôtel de la Ronade – This building has a tower rising five storeys high.

Hôtel de ville (**H**) – The town hall is a pastiche of a previous 15C building.

At the entrance to Rue du Couvent, on the right, a wooden door leads to a large courtyard.

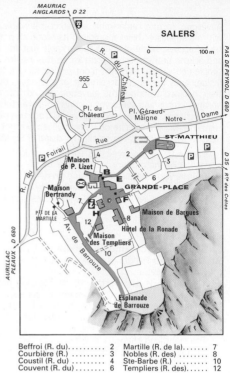

Beffroi (R. du)	2	Martille (R. de la)	7
Courbière (R.)	3	Nobles (R. des)	8
Coustil (R. du)	4	Ste-Barbe (R.)	10
Couvent (R. du)	6	Templiers (R. des)	12

B	Tour de l'Horloge	**F**	Maison de Flojeac
E	Ancien bailliage	**H**	Hôtel de ville

Grand-Place, Salers

Maison de Bargues ⊘ – *At the far end on the right.* An attractive passage with pointed vaulting leads to the main courtyard (late 15C) dominated by a carved balcony.
Inside the house there are two beautiful 17C wood-panelled bedrooms with four-poster beds.

Maison des Templiers ⊘ – The 15C building houses an exhibition on the town's folklore and past: reconstruction of Auvergne interiors, cheesemaking, hunting room etc.

Turn left up to Avenue de Barrouze and turn left again.

Esplanade de Barrouze – The small, shaded park here offers an impressive **view**★ of the Maronne, Rat and Aspre valleys and the Puy Violet massif.

Turn back up Avenue de Barrouze.

Maison Bertrandy – The house has a round tower and an attractive door.

Return to Grande-Place, then take Rue du Beffroi back to the church.

SAUGUES

Population 2 089 ·
Michelin map 76 fold 16 or 239 fold 45

Saugues is a small town favoured by anglers, and the site of a number of large markets. It is dominated by an ancient keep known as the "Englishmen's tower".
On Maundy Thursday, at nightfall, a longstanding traditional Procession of the Penitents is held *(see Calendar of events);* among the White Penitents with their lanterns and the staff of their brotherhood are other penitents, dressed in red, barefoot, with a cowl over their heads, carrying the Cross and Instruments of the Passion (crown of thorns, nails, spear etc).

SIGHTS

Tour des Anglais ⊘ – The name of this tower dates back to the Hundred Years War. The Treaty of Brétigny (8 May 1360) put an end to the contracts of the "mercenaries" enlisted in the English army. They became **free companions**, dubbed "The Englishmen", living on pillage and robbery, and soon took over this town. The royal troops did not succeed in ousting them and it was only once they had been paid off in gold that they finally left.
The square tower, with its machicolations and arrow slits, is an example of 12C military architecture. Inside, there is an exhibition on the forest and a large painting of fields and the crafts and trades of the past. A panorama of the region can be enjoyed from the top of the tower.

Church – The church, surmounted by an octagonal bell tower, houses a 12C Auvergne Virgin and a 15C *Pietà* as well as the shrine of St Bénilde. Three beautiful gold processional crosses are displayed in the treasury chapel.

Diorama de St Bénilde ⊘ – Thirteen set-pieces retrace the life of **Pierre Romançon** (1805-62), Brother Bénilde of the Christian Schools, the first state primary school teacher in Saugues, who was canonised in 1967. The exhibition is held in the actual school where he taught and was the principal.

SERRIÈRES

Population 1 154
Michelin map 88 fold 19 or 246 fold 17
Local maps under Mont PILAT and Vallée du RHÔNE

This old bargemen's town on the banks of the Rhône contains an interesting museum – housed in the chapel of St-Sornin (12C-14C) in the southern part of the town – recalling the old way of life along the river.

Musée des Mariniers du Rhône ⊘ – Under the church's wooden roof are displayed the humble souvenirs of the famous *culs-de-piau* ("leather bottoms" because of their leather-lined trousers): megaphones, rudder bars used to fix the towing horses' chains, a crew's table from a riverside inn, journeymen's staffs, embroidered ceremonial waistcoats, horsehair rings decorated with glass beads, several specimens of **crew's crosses**. The crosses, fixed to the prow of the boat, were to protect the crew from the ever-present perils of the river. They were decorated with emblems of the Passion, naively carved and painted: nails and studs, Judas purses, legionnaires' dice, whips, droplets of Christ's blood, the hand of Justice etc. At the top was a cock, symbol of virility and, in particular, of the captain's constant vigilance.

EXCURSION

Malleval – *10km/6mi on the N 86 north and the D 503 left just after St-Pierre-de-Bœuf*. The road climbs the deep Malleval gorge with its sinister/sounding name ("valley of evil"). Just after the pretty Saut de Laurette waterfall on the right, turn right onto a narrow road which leads up to Malleval.

The 16C houses of the village, once fortified, are built on a rocky spur crowned by the church and the ruins of the old castle. Malleval is the departure point for the flora trail through the Parc naturel régional du Pilat.

There is a lovely view of Malleval and the gorge from the road towards Pélussin–pull over and park shortly after a very sharp lefthand bend.

Gorges de la SIOULE★★

Michelin map 73 fold 3, 4 or 239 fold 7

The upper course of the River Sioule has a winding, undulating character as it flows down the Monts Dômes, contrasting with the lower course which is flat with numerous islands in the Limagne basin. As erosion brought down the level of this calcareous basin, the Sioule, flowing at an increasing speed, cut into the granitic plateau upstream thereby hollowing out an extremely picturesque gorge between the outlying areas of Ébreuil and Châteauneuf-les-Bains. A large network of footpaths and bridlepaths enable visitors to discover the attractions of the area, which is also ideal for fishing and canoeing.

Gorges de la Sioule

J. Damase

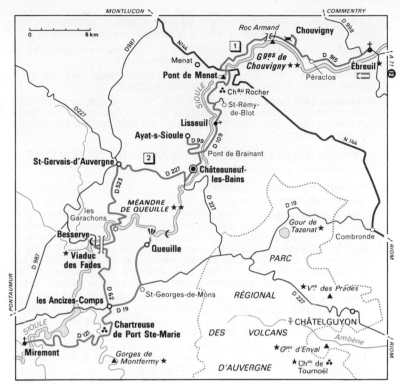

① FROM ÉBREUIL TO CHÂTEAUNEUF-LES-BAINS

35km/22mi – about 3hr – local map above

Ébreuil – *See ÉBREUIL.*

Leave Ébreuil on the D 915 west.

4km/2.5mi from Ébreuil, the corniche road overlooks the Sioule. On the steeper and more rugged slope on the right, bare granite alternates with heather. Beyond Péraclos, the road descends down to the river's edge.

Château de Chouvigny – *See Château de CHOUVIGNY.*

★★Gorges de Chouvigny – At the entrance to the gorge the road cuts through a rocky headland, the left part of which, detached from the rest, is called **Roc Armand**. The summit can be reached by a staircase cut out of the rock. Upstream, there is a beautiful view of the gorge – wooded slopes spiked with granite tips – while downstream, Chouvigny castle can be seen.

On the other side of the road, opposite Armand rock, are some beautiful granite pyramids, the result of the effects of erosion. These needles of rock have been dissociated, carved by the continuous action of the elements and, it is said, by the hand of prehistoric man. Beyond Armand rock, the gorge becomes very picturesque.

At the entrance to a tunnel there is a **viewpoint** on the left, over a bend in the Sioule dominated by high cliffs. Once again, the effects of erosion are visible in the appearance of granite tips and the mass of fallen rocks. This is how the slopes of a valley gradually come to form a V-shape. The bed of the Sioule is being hollowed out continually, almost as one looks.

Further upstream, the Sioule flows silently and smoothly down. Below the viewpoint, however, it flows quickly and noisily through a mass of pebbles; it is gradually wearing down a shelf which interrupts the natural slope. The valley, in turn wider, or strangled into wild-looking gorges and short narrow channels, continues on its way, very green and picturesque.

Pont-de-Menat – This is an ideal point of departure for canoeing and kayaking. Crossing the river, there is an attractive view *(right)* of the old humpback bridge. Soon, on the edge of a cliff ahead, the romantic ruins of **Château-Rocher** (13C) come into view. Immediately below the ruins is an attractive view of a bend in the Sioule, a typical example of an incised meander: the concave bank *(this side)*, excavated by the direct attack of the current, is steep: the convex bank *(opposite)*, which receives the alluvial deposits, is low and cultivated.

The road then rises, providing greater views of the river; it reaches its culmination just before the intersection with the D 99 from St-Rémy-de-Blot. Forming a ledge above a small, still-active mill, it offers a remarkable view of the entire valley.

Lisseuil – Here the road reaches the bottom of the valley. The village church has a beautiful Romanesque Virgin (13C) in its restored chancel.

Ayat-sur-Sioule – An attractive road leads to this village, once the home of General Desaix (1768-1800), one of Napoleon's officers.

Châteauneuf-les-Bains – This thermal spa (alt 390m/1 279ft) actually consists of several hamlets. 22 springs are tapped here, providing cold water for bottling and hot water (ranging from 28-36°C/82-96°F) for the baths treating rheumatism and nervous complaints.

② FROM CHÂTEAUNEUF-LES-BAINS TO MIREMONT
60km/38mi – about 3hr 30min – local map previous page

Châteauneuf-les-Bains – *See above.*

Take the D 227 west.

St-Gervais-d'Auvergne – The village is built on a knoll. Its Gothic church still has some Romanesque features: a portal in the transept and, on the left, a watchtower with a curious gargoyle. Beautiful lime trees shade the terrace by the church.
South of St-Gervais the road winds through the middle of a wood, offering some lovely views of the Sioule before crossing the river at the foot of Les Garachons hydro-electric power station. It then runs along the east bank which follows numerous meanders and circumvents the seams of porphyry which lie in its path.

*★**Viaduc des Fades** – This structure, built by the engineer Vidard at the beginning of the 20C, has a total length of more than 440m/1 440ft and is the highest rail viaduct in Europe. Its metal deck is supported by two granite piers 144m/472ft apart and 92m/302ft high. It stands 133m/436ft above the Sioule.

Barrage de Besserve – The **dam**, located upstream of the viaduct, is a gravity dam – its strength is provided by its sheer mass. It has a summit width of 8m/26ft, a height of 68m/223ft and a crown 235m/771ft long.

Les Ancizes-Comps – This is a tourist centre and small industrial town concentrating on the manufacture of steels and special alloys.

*★★**Méandre de Queuille** – *Park by Queuille church.* Walk behind the east end of the church (past the superb limetrees) and continue through the undergrowth to a viewpoint at the end of the promontory overlooking the Queuille meander, formed by the Sioule after it was widened by a dam. This side, the concave bank of the loop, is high and spiked with rocks; opposite, on the convex side, the river forms a tight circle around the Murat "peninsula", a long wooded headland.

Barrage de Queuille – Downstream from the meander is another gravity **dam** *(see above)*, with a summit length of 116m/380ft. It is 5m/16ft wide at the top and 24.30m/80ft at the base, where there is a power plant.

Return to Les Ancizes-Comps and turn left onto the D 61.

The road provides a magnificent descent through the Sioule valley.

Chartreuse de Port-Ste-Marie – At the bottom of the valley, perched on the edge of a rock, are the ruins of a **Carthusian monastery** founded in the 13C. The site remains unspoilt.

The road climbs back up to the plateau, offering views of the River Sioulet.

Miremont – The Romanesque church here with its massive square bell tower rises up on a peak dominating a loop in the River Sioulet.

SOUVIGNY★★

Population 2 024
Michelin map 69 fold 14 or 238 fold 45

Souvigny, which lies in the middle of a rich farming area, retains the most beautiful sanctuary in the Bourbonnais region, a reminder of the town's past splendour.

Resting place of the Dukes of Bourbon – In 916 Aymard, lieutenant of the Duke of Aquitaine, sold his land at Souvigny to the monks of Cluny; in doing so he bestowed an uncommon destiny upon the former Carolingian villa here.
Two famous abbots from the powerful Burgundian abbey died in the monastery founded here: St Mayeul in 994 and St Odilon in 1049. The saintliness of the two men, soon united in the same tomb, drew numerous pilgrims to Souvigny, and the oldest of the Cluny priories, showered with gifts, developed dramatically.
The lords of Bourbon, descendants of Aymard, created a state around Souvigny which was to become the Duchy of the Bourbonnais *(see MOULINS)*. In the 14C and 15C the monastery underwent further alterations when Duke Louis II and Duke Charles I decided to make the sanctuary their necropolis.

★★ÉGLISE PRIEURALE ST-PIERRE-ET-ST-PAUL ⊙

The west front of the original Romanesque edifice, of which only the left door remains, was preceded in the 15C by an avant-corps with a portal and a wide Flamboyant opening. Two Romanesque bell towers, connected since the 15C by a gable with a rose window, dominate the priory. The third floor of the left bell tower was altered in the 14C. The three Romanesque bays in the centre of the façade belonged to the original building consecrated in 1064. The northern flank shows the church's different stages of construction: the towers, the second side aisle and the ambulatory are 12C while the upper part of the nave and the transept are 15C.

Nave and aisles – The interior has surprisingly large dimensions: 87m/285ft by 28m/92ft. The double side aisles flanking the nave, and the double transept are evidence of Cluniac influence.

The inner aisles, built in the 11C, are very narrow with barrel vaulting while the outer aisles, which are later, have groined or pointed vaulting.

1) Finely carved tomb of St Mayeul.

2) Capital depicting monks minting money, a reminder of the priory's ancient privilege.

3) Fragment of a 13C bishop's tomb.

4) Bas-relief of the Immaculate Conception.

5) Stone **reliquary-cupboard**★ (15C), with four wooden shutters painted with scenes from the lives of St Mayeul and St Odilon.

★**Chapelle vieille** – The old chapel has a beautiful stone screen in Flamboyant Gothic style.

6) Tomb of Louis II of Bourbon, known as Louis the Good, and his wife, Anne of Auvergne. The two marble recumbent figures are still extremely realistic, despite the defacements.

7) 15C Entombment.

★★**Chapelle neuve** – The new chapel is larger than the old chapel and has a very fine enclosure.

8) Tomb of Charles I and his wife, Agnes of Burgundy. The recumbent figures, clothed in flowing cloaks, rest on a black marble slab.

9) A graceful Mary Magdalene from the late 15C.

10) The Virgin, Child and St John (16C).

11) Small 15C *Pietà*.

The left apsidal chapel, off the ambulatory, houses a 13C polychrome statue of Our Lady of Joy (**12**).

The sacristy, built in the 18C, has some fine wood panelling and an ivory Christ.

Cloisters and chapter-house – *Access via the south aisle of the church or via the monastery buildings erected in the 17C, to the right of the church.*

Only one side of these 15C cloisters remains, with groined vaulting because of the arrangement of the pillars. The chapter-house dates from the late 12C.

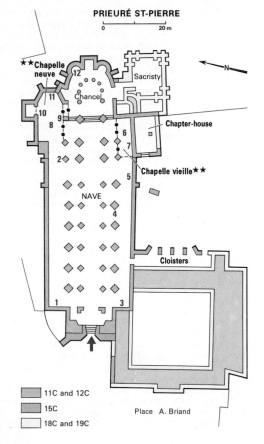

PRIEURÉ ST-PIERRE

ADDITIONAL SIGHTS

St-Marc – This church, now disused, stands opposite the northern side of the priory church and is built in the Burgundian Romanesque style. The interior is currently being converted into an auditorium.

Musée de la Grange Nord ⊙ – This museum to the right of the priory church houses lapidary and local history collections, as well as a glassworking exhibition.

Next to the sarcophagi, recumbent figures and capitals stands a 12C **calendar**★★, the most striking piece in the collection. This 1.80m/5ft 11in octagonal pillar, weighing 840kg/1 848lb (over 0.75 tonne), is carved on two sides with scenes showing the labours of the months and the corresponding signs of the Zodiac; symbols of strange peoples and fabulous animals adorn the other faces. Other exhibits include a collection of silver coins minted by the Souvigny monks during the Middle Ages.

Local history is recalled in the Souvigny glassworks founded in 1755: master glassmakers' tools, examples of glassware (carafe stoppers, pharmacy bottles, champagne glasses) on show are reminiscent of this ancient craft.

A 3-tonne dug-out canoe, hollowed out of a tree trunk, which was discovered in the River Alliers in 1980 is also on display; it dates from around the year 1000.

J.-L. Barde/SCOPE

12C calendar, Musée de la Grange Nord, Souvigny

Massif du TANARGUE★★

Michelin map 76 south of fold 17, 18 and 80 north of fold 8 or 239 fold 47, 48 and 240 folds 3, 4

At the southern end of the high volcanic lands of the Velay and Vivarais rises the Tanargue, a crystalline range made up of granite, gneiss and micaschist. Its shredded appearance is due to the upheavals of the Tertiary and Quaternary eras. This is one of the wildest regions of the Vivarais.

Until the end of the Secondary era this part of the old Hercynian range, levelled by erosion, was a large plateau. In the Tertiary era the repercussions from the Alpine folding resulted in a vertical uplift of the micaschist which erosion then sliced into jagged ridges.

The Quaternary era was marked by intense volcanic activity which affected the edge of the massif and during which the Jaujac lava flow formed, which, after it had filled the Lignon valley, was largely swept away by the river.

The storms in Tanargue are famous, especially for their violence in autumn. Sudden spates, given added power by the steepness of the terrain, transform local mountain rivers into raging torrents, which nonetheless subside as quickly as they swell.

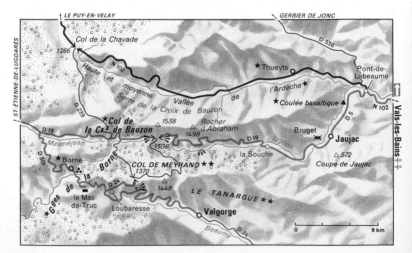

FROM VALS-LES-BAINS TO VALGORGE

80km/50mi – about 3hr – local map below left

‡‡ **Vals-les-Bains** – *See VALS-LES-BAINS.*

Leave Vals-les-Bains on the N 102 south towards Le Puy-en-Velay. At Pont-de-Labeaume take the D 5 to Jaujac.

The route passes the basalt flows of the Lignon valley; 2km/1mi beyond Pont-de-Labeaume, at a signpost, park and approach on foot the edge of the volcanic platform on which the road runs; here and there the **basalt flow★** takes on a striking appearance of perfectly vertical tube-like sections, some of a blue-grey colour.

Jaujac – This village has attractive 15C and 16C houses, especially in the Chastelas district on the west bank, and the ruins of its old fortified castle. To the southeast rises the Jaujac "dish", an ancient volcano from which the flows of the Lignon emerged, and where mineral springs emanate.

Leaving Jaujac, the small 15C **Château de Bruget** comes into sight on the right.

From La Souche the road becomes more mountainous; the tip of Abraham's Rock stands ahead to the right, dark slopes covered in pines lie to the left.

10km/6mi from La Souche there is a good **view★** along the axis of the Lignon valley; the Coiron bar rises on the horizon.

Basalt flow, Jaujac

M. Claye/EXPLORER

★Col de la Croix de Bauzon – From this pass (alt 1 308m/4 291ft) the view extends over the valleys of the Borne and the Masméjean to the mountains of the Margeride; to the east, the Lignon basin continues into the Aubenas depression. A small ski station has been created at the foot of the Tanargue slopes.

Follow the D 19 towards St-Étienne-de-Lugdarès and turn left onto the D 301 (narrow road).

★Gorges de la Borne – Beyond a stretch of route across broom-covered moorland, the descent to Borne offers plunging views over the gorge.

To the west is the profile of Le Goulet mountain. **Borne★** itself is a village in a secluded site, on a ledge above the deeply embanked torrent. Within a rocky corrie on a spur lie the ruins of a castle, overlooking the waters.

A small road leads to the tiny hamlet of **Mas-de-Truc**, seemingly lost in the mountains.

Continue to Col de Meyrand, via Loubaresse. As far as the village the road is narrow and sometimes impassable due to rockfalls.

★★Col de Meyrand – Alt 1 371m/4 479ft. From this pass a splendid ledge is suddenly revealed: there is a viewing table below the pass, to the left on an isolated rock. An extensive panorama is visible, from left to right, over the summit of the Tanargue, the Valgorge valley, the Ardèche depression overlooked by the Dent de Rez, the Valgorge ridge opposite and, to the right, the back of Mont Lozère.

Turn back.

Beyond Loubaresse there are views along the channel down to Valgorge, then of stretches shaded by chestnut trees. The road drops downhill, twisting along the upper valley of the Beaume.

Valgorge – This small village is situated within a lush setting of vineyards and orchards.

THIERS ★★

Population 14 832
Michelin map 73 fold 16 or 239 fold 21
Local maps under Vallée de la DORE and Monts du FOREZ

The **site**★★ on which the town is built – on the side of a ravine through which the River Durolle flows – the magnificent view it offers over the Limagne and the Monts Dômes, and the town's historical district make Thiers an attractive destination for tourists.

It is the waters of the Durolle which made Thiers' fortune; paper and knives have been made here since the 15C and although papermaking has nearly disappeared, cutlery making continues to contribute to the town's renown.

The town was first founded on the south bank of the Durolle, around the original Le Moutier church. Thiers was pillaged and razed to the ground by the Franks in 532 but rose from its ruins when the Bishop of Clermont, Avitus, built a sanctuary on the opposite bank, around the tomb of the martyr St Genès.

Later, a fortified castle was built near the new church and the town started to develop on the north bank. Thiers subsequently became the seat of a barony.

The Thiers cutlery trade – For many centuries Thiers has been the largest French cutlery-making centre.

The origin of the town's specialisation dates back to the Middle Ages: legend has it that the Auvergne Crusaders from the 1st Crusade brought back the secret of cutlery manufacture from the East; in fact, the Thiers metallurgical industry dates back to the 14C. By the 16C the town's cutlery trade had developed sufficiently for it to start exporting its products to Spain, the Netherlands and Lombardy. Blades of all types were sharpened on grinding wheels powered by the waters of the Durolle. Cutlery production has subsequently been modernised, however, so that the figure from popular myth – of the knife-grinder lying face down over his grinding-wheel, his dog lying on his legs to keep him warm – is no longer seen. Developments in technology and electricity have led to enormous factories. Today Thiers still has nearly 300 manufacturers or craftsmen. Up until the 19C, Thiers was also an important papermaking centre specialising in the production of playing cards.

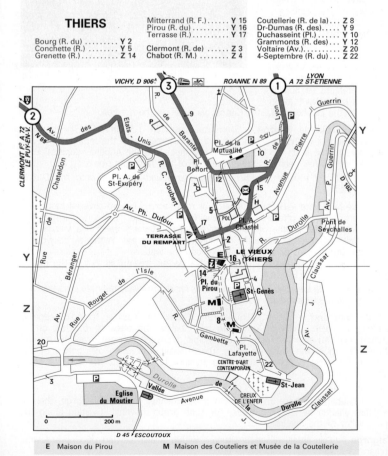

E Maison du Pirou   **M** Maison des Couteliers et Musée de la Coutellerie

Today, apart from traditional cutlery manufacture, industry in the town also includes producing surgical instruments, plastic items, utensils, kitchenware and stainless steel platters, and spare parts for cars. With its metal industry, Thiers is a natural home for contemporary metal sculpture, particularly in Rue de la Coutellerie and Rue Lasteyras.

★OLD TOWN (YZ)

A number of 15C, 16C and 17C half-timbered houses have been restored in the centre of the old town (Vieux Thiers). These picturesque houses line narrow, winding streets, many of them reserved for pedestrians.

Rue Conchette (Y 5) – In the courtyard at no 4 there is a 16C staircase; at no 10, a beautiful inner façade on pillars. At no 18, in the small courtyard with its turret, two 16C medallions.

Rue du Bourg (Y 2) – At nos 10 and 14 note the 15C doors; no 20 is a 16C house.

Place du Pirou (YZ) – This attractive square is dominated by the early-15C **Maison du Pirou★** (**E**). The house, with its pointed gables and timbered façade, is a handsome example of civil architecture of the Middle Ages.

Rue du Pirou (Y 16) – At no 11 stands the Maison des Sept Péchés Capitaux, named after the decoration (Seven Deadly Sins) on the seven beams supporting the first floor; at no 9, note a corbelled construction.

Further along rises one of the ancient towers from the Thiers feudal castle, and beyond is the "Coin des Hasards", an intersection dominated by the tower of Maître Raymond (15C).

Rue Grenette (Z 14) – No 8 is a 16C and 17C house (Maison dite de Lauzun).

Rue de la Coutellerie (Z 8) – Note the unusual houses at nos 12 and 14, the latter with wooden corbels carved in a somewhat free and vigorous style. No 21, the **Maison de l'Homme des Bois** (15C), is decorated with an enigmatic ape-like figure. This house and the ancient alderman's house at no 58 contain the Cutlers' Centre and the Cutlery Museum.

Maison des Couteliers and Musée de la Coutellerie (Z M) ⊙ – The craft workshops at the Cutlers' Centre are based at both no 21 and no 58 Rue de la Coutellerie. The craftsmen may be watched working on the different phases of the manufacture of a knife: forging, hardening, sharpening, forming and mounting of handles, carving, engraving, polishing.

Carved ivory knife handle

The Cutlery Museum retraces the history of the Thiers cutlery trade and presents various examples of cutlery production from the 15C to the present: amazing hinged knives for all sorts of purposes, prestigious table knives with horn, ivory, mother-of-pearl, tortoiseshell or ebony handles, special tradesmen's knives, scissors, razors etc.

In the basement an audio-visual show evokes the deafening world of the forge (power-hammer, furnace etc). On the ground floor, a room is devoted to contemporary creations.

On the 1st floor, a hallmark chart made in 1591 presents one thousand or so cutlery hallmarks.

The 2nd floor displays have been enriched by the Frédéric-Albert Peter Bequest (Peter was a cutler and goldsmith in Paris). The collection contains some very beautiful pieces: knives, pocket knives, cigar-cutters, quill-cutters etc.

St-Genès (Z) – This Romanesque church has undergone many alterations. The west front and the bell tower have been rebuilt but the south transept retains the interesting polychrome decoration on its gable and its graceful windows; to see it, go into Impasse Jean-Brugère which runs along the church on the right.

The north door, which gives on to Place du Palais, is preceded by an 18C porch, in the wall of which an elegantly carved 14C recess has been incorporated.

Inside, the dome over the transept crossing is the largest in the Auvergne.

ADDITIONAL SIGHTS

★**Terrasse du Rempart (Y)** – The terrace offers a beautiful **panorama★** of the Limagne, the Monts Dore and the Monts Dômes. The view of the sunset can be magnificent from here. The viewing table is made of enamelled lavastone.

Église du Moutier (Z) ⊙ – The church was part of the powerful Benedictine abbey founded in the 7C. In 1883 it was reduced in height and badly disfigured. Inside, note the capitals in the narthex and the low-reliefs in the east end wall.

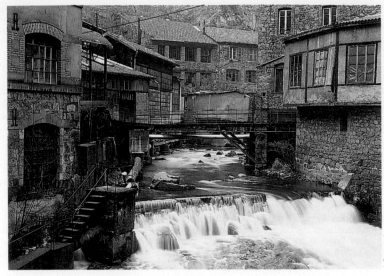

Creux de l'Enfer, Vallée de la Durolle

At the corner of Avenue Joseph-Claussat stands the "castle", the last remains of the abbey: two very damaged 15C towers.

Vallée de la Durolle – Just north of Le Moutier church is Avenue Joseph-Claussat or "Route de la Vallée" which follows the Durolle. The river's many waterfalls once operated numerous cutlery works. There were at least 140 falls over a distance of 3km/2mi. The most picturesque are those known as the Creux de l'Enfer (Hell-Hole) falls, just before St-Jean bridge, and the Creux du Salien falls, just after Seychalles bridge (15C).

Legend has it that St Genès, tracked by soldiers, made his mule jump across the valley near the Creux de l'Enfer falls. The spot where the saint came down with his mule is called Saut du Moine ("Monk's Jump").

The route is lined with many old, disused factories. The old Creux de l'Enfer works are now used to house **contemporary art exhibitions** ⊙.

St-Jean (**Z**) – St-Jean church (15C but restored) occupies a picturesque site overlooking the Durolle. From the neighbouring cemetery there is a lovely view of the plain and the Auvergne mountains.

EXCURSIONS

★**Les Margerides** – *Round tour of 15km/9mi on the N 89 northeast – about 45min.*
From the lookout point by the turn-off to St-Rémy, there is an attractive view over to the right of the Durolle gorge, Thiers and the Limagne. The opposite bank is dominated by the Margerides rocks.

Beyond Bellevue turn right onto the D 320 which crosses the river and winds through green and fertile countryside.

On leaving Vernières there is a beautiful view of the Durolle valley, the village of St-Rémy – built on the side of the mountain – and, in the background, the Bois Noirs massif.

Turn right onto the D 102. The route descends towards Thiers and makes a sharp right-hand bend, just near Borbes rock (on the left).

Rocher de Borbes – From the rock there is an extensive **view**★ of the Limagne, the Monts Dômes and the Monts Dore, the Livradois and, in clear weather, the Cantal mountains.

From the viewpoint 2km/1mi further on, there is a superb view of Thiers and the Durolle valley.

St-Rémy-sur-Durolle – *9km/6mi north on the N 89 and D 201.*
The road winds scenically through woodland before reaching St-Rémy. This cutlery-making centre is built on the southern flank of "Thiers mountain", an extension of the Bois Noirs massif.

In St-Rémy, take a road uphill on the left to the wayside cross. Leave the car near the sports ground and walk to the top of the cliff (15min Rtn on foot).

From the wayside cross, the **panorama**★ *(viewing table)* includes the Forez mountains, the Margerides, the Plomb du Cantal and the Monts Dômes.

Northeast of St-Rémy, on the right of the D 201, a one-way toll road leads to an enormous lake which offers various watersports, swimming, sailing, rowing.

Château de TOURNOËL★

Tournoël castle, rising on the crest of a rocky spur overlooking the whole of the Limagne, is one of the most interesting castles in the Auvergne. The castle was owned by the counts of Auvergne when Philippe Auguste, king of France, captured and almost entirely destroyed it in 1213. In the 14C, however, it was rebuilt by Hugues de la Roche, who widened the bases of the towers.

Two eccentric owners – Around 1500 Tournoël castle was owned by a 21-year-old widow, **Françoise de Talaru**, who used all her charms to attract the high society of Riom to the castle, with a never-ending succession of hunts, feasts, games and balls. However, a covetous rival in the shape of her brother-in-law, joint-guardian of her daughter, on whom he also appeared to have designs, gave her some cause for concern. She managed to drive him from the castle but the judge of Montferrand, to whom the matter was referred, severely reprimanded the widow calling her "Circe, Melusine, magician and witch" and stripped her of her guardianship. The artful Françoise, however, promised her seven-year-old daughter to the judge's son in marriage and even managed to bewitch the old judge himself, who married her and died soon afterwards.
Charles de Montvallet was one of the members of the Auvergne nobility to be condemned in 1665 in the wake of the Fronde uprising against the French monarchy. In his time, he had fathered so many illegitimate children, that he had had them brought up at Tournoël castle so that he could employ them as domestic servants. One was even given the job title "Chef des Bâtards". However, the noble lord was not allowed to get away with such behaviour scot-free – his wife used to beat him.

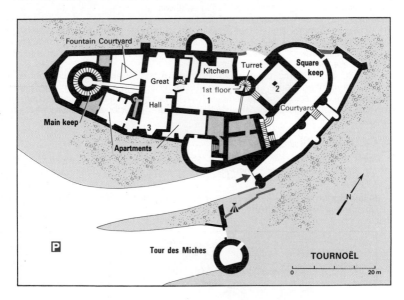

TOURNOËL

TOUR ⊙

Near the entrance to the castle is a viewing table from which there is a beautiful view of the Limagne plain, the Forez mountains and the Livradois.
Pass the 16C Tour des Miches (Loaf Tower), which used to defend the entrance, on the right. Its name derives from the lumps in its walls of lava, which looked like large loaves of bread. The castle consists of three sections: a massive square keep protected by a double curtain wall, a high circular keep enclosed within a triangular curtain wall, and, between the two, the main buildings built around a courtyard.

Ground floor   A steep climb leads up to the entrance to the first courtyard. It contains a square keep with foundations that date back to the 10C. Enter into the main courtyard (**1**); to the right of a highly ornate turret (15C) is the "Vat Room" (**2**) with its wine-press and, standing behind a large pillar, an enormous stone tun which could contain 13 000l/2 860gal of wine. On the left of the turret are the kitchen, with its impressive fireplace, and the offices and outhouses. Opposite are some of the apartments.
The Great Hall, which is now roofless, contains a beautiful fireplace. In front of the window is a stone (**3**) with two unequal cavities which was used to collect one tenth of the grain harvested on the estate, by way of taxes. The adjoining courtyard, known as the Fountain Courtyard, leads to an imposing 14C keep,

(32m/105ft high) encircled, half way up, by a series of machicolations added in the 15C. Between the keep and the Great Hall are the owner's apartments, where Lucrèce de Gadagne died in 1615.

First floor – Climb the staircase inside the turret in the main courtyard. On the first floor, above the offices, is a bedroom which was once painted. A ceilingless room in the square keep gives a view of the upper room and two beautiful fireplaces, one above the other. The gallery opening onto the courtyard is that of the chapel: an Annunciation has been carved on the back of the entrance door. In the chapel, note the wooden statue of St Anne.

Main keep – On the right, in the gallery, a staircase leads to the watch-path. A footbridge gives access to the entrance of the circular keep; its three floors are linked by a staircase hewn from the 4m/13ft thick wall. The **panorama★** from the platform encompasses the Limagne, Forez, Comté and Livradois regions. The three basaltic plateaux which form long promontories projecting from the Dômes plateau can be seen clearly: the closest is that of Châteaugay, the next is Côte de Clermont and the furthest away is the Gergovie plateau.

TRÉVOUX

Population 6 092
Michelin map 88 fold 7 or 246 fold E – Local map under La DOMBES

This town is built on different levels along the steep bank of the Saône, its colourful façades and flower-filled gardens all facing southwards.

Trévoux stands at the intersection of three Roman roads; it was once the capital of the Principality of Dombes, the seat of a sovereign parliament, and was independent until 1762. After the Duke of Maine decreed that the town's magistrates and members of parliament must also be residents here, a number of mansions were built in the 18C, along the alleyways of the old districts.

In the 17C and 18C the town was one of the most brilliant intellectual centres in France. Its printing house, founded in 1603, was famous. In 1704 the Jesuits published the first edition of the famous Trévoux Dictionary; under their direction, the Trévoux Journal campaigned against Voltaire and the "Encyclopædic" philosophers for 30 years.

OLD TOWN *1hr 30min*

Park off Boulevard des Combattants. Walk to Place de la Terrace which overlooks the Saône (viewing table). The Palais du Parlement is on the other side of Rue du Palais.

Palais du Parlement ⊙ – Parliament House was built at the end of the 17C; the Dombes Parliament sat from 1697 to 1771.

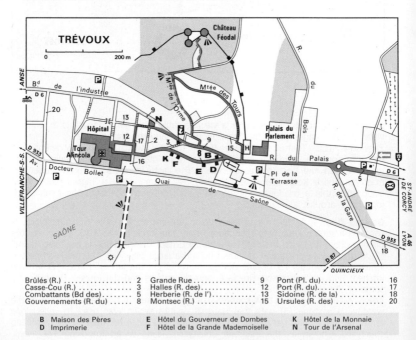

Brûlés (R.)	2	Grande Rue	9	Pont (Pl. du)	16
Casse-Cou (R.)	3	Halles (R. des)	12	Port (R. du)	17
Combattants (Bd des)	5	Herberie (R. de l')	13	Sidoine (R. de la)	18
Gouvernements (R. du)	8	Montsec (R.)	15	Ursules (R. des)	20

B	Maison des Pères	**E**	Hôtel du Gouverneur de Dombes	**K**	Hôtel de la Monnaie
D	Imprimerie	**F**	Hôtel de la Grande Mademoiselle	**N**	Tour de l'Arsenal

The hall leads into the courtroom with its beautiful beamed ceiling with painted decoration; note, on the extreme right of the second beam from the back, the pompous initials SPQD: *Senatus Populusque Dumbensis* (meaning the Senate and people of Dombes, a parody of the initials SPQR). At the back of the room is a portrait of the Duke of Maine by Rigaud.

Rue du Gouvernement (**8**) – On either side of the street, just below the church, the Trévoux Dictionary and Journal were written and printed. The Jesuits who lived on the right, in the tall, spacious Maison des Pères (**B**) – main entrance is at nos 3 and 9 Grande-Rue – had only to cross the street to take their manuscripts to the printers (**D**) opposite.

Further down are a number of old houses: the house of the Governor of Dombes (**E**), that of the Grande Mademoiselle (**F**) and the Mint (**K**), their austere façades concealing terraces overlooking the Saône. The intersection with Rue Casse-Cou (Break-Neck Street), so named because of its steep slope, offers an interesting view.

Take Rue des Halles to the hospital.

Hôpital ⊙ – The hospital was founded in 1686 by La Grande Mademoiselle; it still has the original wood-panelled pharmacy and a beautiful collection of pottery from Gien and Nevers. Alincola tower (13C-17C), surmounted by a lantern dome, can be seen on the embankment.

Return to Rue des Halles and turn left into Rue du Port. Turn right into Rue de l'Herberie.

This street was once reserved for Jews. The intersection of Rue de l'Herberie and Grande-Rue forms a triangle dominated by the square-shaped Arsenal tower (**N**) of 1405 which was later converted into a belfry.

Walk up Montée de l'Orme to the castle.

Château féodal – Remains of the medieval castle (14C); from the top of the octagonal tower there is a view of the Saône.

Walk down Montée des Tours, then return along Rue du Palais back to Boulevard des Combattants.

Forêt de TRONÇAIS ★★★

Michelin map 69 fold 12 or 238 folds 32, 43, 44

Tronçais forest is located at the junction of the Berry and Bourbonnais regions; it has a total surface area of 10 594ha/26 167 acres and contains a remarkable plantation of trees. Its many pools and beauty spots make it a popular recreational area.

Trials and tribulations – Tronçais forest, after being administered by the dukes of Bourbon, was confiscated in 1527 together with the other lands owned by the High Constable *(see MOULINS)*. Poorly managed and neglected in the 16C and 17C, it slowly deteriorated. The devastation wrought by livestock, the improper use of certain parts of the forest by neighbouring parishes or lords, and the uncontrolled felling of trees meant that by 1670 nearly three quarters of the forest had been ruined.

To meet the country's present and future requirements for ship timber, Colbert undertook to protect and replant the royal forest. The new plantations were not to be used until the trees were 200 years old. In 1788 the opening of the Tronçais Iron Foundry led to fresh destruction of the forest; two-thirds of its surface area was converted to coppice with standards, to produce the charcoal needed for the manufacture of cast iron. In 1832 conservation measures were fortunately taken and the forest was replanted on the basis of a cutting cycle of 160 years. This was extended to 180, then to 225 years in 1928.

Cultivating the forest – Tronçais forest is divided into series, which in turn are divided into blocks. Oak trees account for 70% of its plantations, with beech and Scotch fir the second most densely planted species.

The main aim of the forest remains the production of high quality timber. The most sought-after trees are therefore of exceptional dimensions, their trunks sometimes more than 20m/65ft high and 1m/3ft in diameter at a man's standing height.

To achieve this, the area around the most promising oaks must be surrounded by other trees during the oaks' growth period, then gradually cleared by successive felling.

Logs with a diameter of 50cm/20in and more are sliced in specialised industrial yards far from the forest. Some are exported to other EU countries (particularly Germany). The veneers produced supply the cabinetmaking industries and are eventually sent abroad – to Sweden, the USA, Belgium. Oaks that are 40 to 50cm/16 to 20in in diameter provide wood for cooperage – split or made into staves – to make barrels; Tronçais oak is particularly prized for the maturing of cognac and claret. Oak trees of small diameter or lesser quality are converted into building timber or firewood.

The equilibrium of the forest requires selective felling so that mature trees can be replaced by entire blocks.

"Seeing the wood for the trees" – The forest offers walkers additional attractions besides the contemplation of its oak trees. Mushroom pickers will find *boletus, hydnum, russula* and *chanterelles*. There is also quite a large population of red deer, roe deer and wild boar. On Pirot lake, great crested grebes are to be seen.

In season, **guided tours** ⊘ of the forest are organised.

✱✱✱ DISTRICTS TO THE EAST OF THE RIVER SOLOGNE

From Cérilly to St-Bonnet-Tronçais

20km/12mi – about 2hr – local map right

Cérilly – This was the home of the writer **Charles-Louis Philippe** (1874-1909), the author of semi-autobiographical novels based on his memories. The **house where he was born** ⊘, at no 5 in the street which bears his name, is open to the public.

On alternate years in autumn, a festival called the "Forestiales du Tronçais" is held here; it is devoted to forest trades and wood.

Leave Cérilly to the north on the D 111 which leads through the eastern part of the forest. Cross over Rond de Brot roundabout and the D 978A, then take the first tarred road on the left, Ligne de Cros-Chaud.

✱Étang de Pirot – Rond des Pêcheurs offers a lovely overall **view** of the vast Lake Pirot.

Take Ligne des Pêcheurs, then turn right onto the D 978ᴬ.

Fontaine Viljot – *On the right-hand side of the road (170m/500ft). Park on the left verge.* Oaks and conifers form a charming decor around the crystal-clear water of this spring. Legend has it that, if a maiden wishes to marry, she must throw a pin into the spring; if the pin pricks the bottom, the maiden has "pricked a heart". Nowadays, small change appears to have replaced pins...

South of the Rond Viljot, walk to the **Square Oak** *(chêne carré)* (**A**). This three hundred-year-old tree has a total height of 26m/85ft and, at a height of 1.30m/4ft 3in from the ground, a circumference of 5.96m/19ft 6in.

Émile-Guillaumin (**B**) **and Charles-Louis-Philippe** (**C**) **Oak Trees** – These two trees close to the roadside to the north commemorate two novelists from the region.

At Rond Gardien, turn sharp right into the Planchegross forest road (one-way) up to the car park.

Rond de la Cave – *30min Rtn on foot.* This large, sheltered picnic area lies at the very heart of the forest.

Return to **Rond Gardien** *(viewing table)* and continue to Tronçais. The factory here was built on the edge of Tronçais lake.

Take the D 250 on the right.

✱Étang de St-Bonnet – The lake, to the left of the road, sits in a very attractive setting. The bathing area and path around it are popular destinations for a walk.

St-Bonnet-Tronçais – A pleasant place to stay on the edge of the forest .

✱Futaie Colbert (**Colbert Plantation**) – Promenade *(30min on foot)* from Rond du Vieux-Morat. Beautiful plantation of 300-year-old oaks in a cool, undulating setting (protected area).

FORÊT DE TRONÇAIS

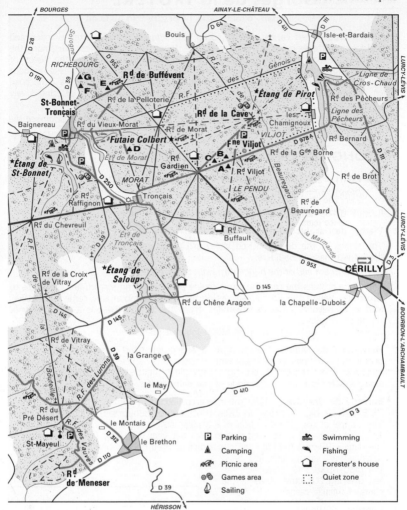

Stebbing Oak (**D**) – *1.5km/1mi from Rond du Vieux-Morat.* Isolated in the middle of a plantation of young trees is a typical three-hundred-year-old oak (37m/121ft high and 3.95m/13ft in circumference).

Rond de Buffévent – *2km/1mi from Rond du Vieux-Morat.* Short walks southwest along the forest road lead to magnificent three hundred-year-old oaks–**Jacques-Chevalier** (**E**), **Jumeaux** (the Twins) (**F**) and **Sentinelle** (the Sentry) (**G**).

★DISTRICTS TO THE WEST OF THE RIVER SOLOGNE

From St-Bonnet-Tronçais to Meaulne
30km/19mi – about 1hr – local map above

St-Bonnet-Tronçais – *See above.*
From St-Bonnet-Tronçais take the D 250 south; beyond Tronçais factory turn right; at Rond du Chêne Aragon turn right onto the D 145.

★**Étang de Saloup** – The road bisects the lake.
Turn left onto the D 39, right into Route Forestière des Lurons; turn right and then left. From the car park, take the footpath (past a no-entry sign).
The path ends at **St-Mayeul** chapel overlooking a ravine.
From the car park turn right into the narrow Route Forestière des Vauves winding through the ravine and right to Rond de Meneser.

Rond de Meneser – Various paths provide pleasant walks *(minimum 30min Rtn on foot).*
Continue on forest road; turn left onto the D 110; in Le Breton turn left onto the D 312.
The road passes through the forest to **Meaulne** in the Aumance valley.

Gorges de la TRUYÈRE ★★

Michelin map 76 folds 12 to 14 or 239 fold 42 to 44

The River Truyère has carved narrow, deep and sinuous gorges, often wooded and rugged-looking, through the granite plateaux of Upper Auvergne. These are among the most attractive natural sites in central France. Dams, built to serve the needs of hydroelectric power stations, have transformed them into one long lake without affecting their picturesque aspect, except when the waters are low. There is no road which closely follows the river for very far, though many cross it, offering lovely views.

The northern part of the gorge is described here; for the southwestern section see the Michelin Green Guide Pyrenees–Languedoc–Tarn Gorges.

★★ALONG THE GRANDVAL RESERVOIR

1 From Pont de Garabit to Chaudes-Aigues

60km/37mi – about 2hr – local map below

From the 165m/541ft long Garabit bridge there is a view of the viaduct.

★★Viaduc de Garabit – *See Viaduc de GARABIT.*

The slopes of the deeply incised valley are alternately covered with woodland or dotted with jagged boulders.

At the southern end of the bridge turn right to Faverolles.

The route crosses the rocky Arcomie ravine and the Arling stream and continues to Faverolles where the Cantal, Margeride and Aubrac mountains come successively into view. Beyond Auriac-de-Faverolles, from the D 13, there is a lovely view of the flooded valleys.
Cross the Bès and continue up to Mallet lookout point.

★★Belvédère de Mallet – Park after a sharp left-hand bend and walk to the promontory *(10min Rtn)* from where there is a splendid view over Grandval reservoir. From the D 13 turn right onto the D 40 through Fridefont, and down along a twisting route to the ridge of the dam itself.

★Barrage de Grandval – This "multiple-arch" concrete dam is 376m/1 233ft long, 78.8m/256ft high and has six 50m/164ft arches supported by thick buttresses. The central arch of the dam houses a circular power station beneath a metal dome which produces 144 thousand million kWh per year. The lake formed upstream of the dam is 28km/17mi long and has a surface area of 1 100ha/2 718 acres.

After a very sharp left-hand bend the road drops into a wooded valley, offering attractive views of the ruins of Alleuze castle.

★★Château d'Alleuze – *See Château d'ALLEUZE.*

In Alleuze turn back and take the D 48 towards Lavastrie, then the D 921 left to Chaudes-Aigues.

Chaudes-Aigues – *See CHAUDES-AIGUES.*

★THE PLANÈZE

2 From Chaudes-Aigues to Laussac

40km/25mi – about 2hr – local map right

At the foot of the Plomb du Cantal, the St-Flour *planèze* unfolds to the east and southeast at an average of 1 000m/3 281ft above sea level; a vast plateau on which few trees thrive, but where fields of crops stretch as far as the eye can see, earning the region its reputation as the agricultural heart of Upper Auvergne.

Chaudes-Aigues – *See CHAUDES-AIGUES.*

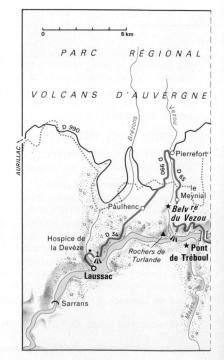

The route briefly follows the west bank of the Remontalou valley then turns right onto the planèze which offers extensive views of St-Flour plateau, and the Cantal and Margeride mountain ranges.

The narrow valley cut by the Truyère into solid granite is an ideal location for the building of hydroelectric dams. Minimal human settlement and communications routes in the valley meant that it could be flooded to create huge reservoirs without difficulty. Hydroelectric construction here spans 30 or so years, from the Brommat and Sarrans projects in the early 1930s, to Grandval and Lanau in the early 1960s.

Espinasse – From this small village there are plunging views down over the River Truyère.

From Auzolles on, the road lcings to the steep sides of the Lévandes valley, overlooking it from a fair height. A long, vertiginous descent into the valley follows, with breathtaking views of the wooded valley floor and southern slopes. After crossing the Lévandes, the road runs along the upper end of Sarrans reservoir, a particularly beautiful lake when water levels are high.

★**Pont de Tréboul** – This suspension bridge is 159m/521ft long between its piers and is a stunning piece of modern engineering. It replaced a Gothic bridge, built by the English in the 14C, which was submerged, together with the village of Tréboul, when the valley was flooded. When the water levels are low, the old bridge is still visible.

Cross the bridge and turn left to Pierrefort. 600m after the overhead bridge, beyond a bend to the right, park the car.

★**Belvédère du Vézou** – *15min Rtn on foot.* A path leads through broom and ferns up to a rocky height overlooking the confluence of the Vézou and Truyère rivers. The **view** of the lake and the jagged **Turlande rocks** is very attractive.

The D 65 climbs the initially deep and wooded Vézou valley which is covered with moorland and pastures higher up. Beyond Le Meynial volcanic rocks can be seen on either side of the road.

After Pierrefort the road runs across a plateau and then returns to the Truyère valley, dropping almost to the level of the water and offering splendid views over the lakes – especially from the Calvary in front of the Hospice de la Devèze – before crossing the Brézons via a modern suspension bridge (121m/396ft long).

Laussac – The village is built on a promontory that the flooding of the valley has turned into a peninsula.

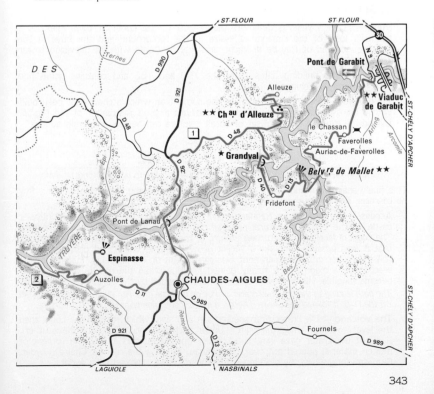

USSON ★

Population 188
Michelin map 73 fold 15 or 289 fold 20 – 4km/3mi southwest of Sauxillanges
Local map under Le LIVRADOIS

The basaltic rock of Usson was once the site of a formidable castle, of which nothing remains but the memory of Marguerite de Valois.

HISTORICAL NOTES

The Usson tiara – "Usson is a town situated on a plain where there is a rock, and three towns one on top of the other in the shape of a pope's mitre", says an ancient text. The castle was built by the Duc de Berry, and believed to be impregnable. On the door was written "Mind the traitor and the tooth!" meaning that only treason or famine could get the better of it.

Queen Margot (16C-17C) – This princess, popularised by the author Alexandre Dumas, was the sister of Charles IX who gave her in marriage to the King of Navarre (the future Henri IV), saying that, in doing so, he "had given her to all the Huguenots in the kingdom" – a somewhat indiscreet allusion to the young queen's many love affairs. Her conduct was such that she was forced to seek asylum in Carlat (east of Aurillac), where her favourite was the young Lord of Aubiac. Fleeing Carlat when the king ordered her arrest, Marguerite took refuge in Ybois castle, near Orbeil (northeast of Issoire). Henri III sent the Marquis of Canillac to lay siege to the fortress. Canillac seized the queen and Aubiac; instructed by the court, he had her favourite executed. Marguerite was locked up in Usson under the guard of the marquis.

The duped jailer – The prisoner had her revenge: she decided to give Canillac a mansion in Paris with an annuity of 2 000 livres, and covered his wife with jewels. The marquis, thrilled with the presents, rushed to the capital to take possession of his new abode; but a letter from Queen Margot to his notary preceded him, cancelling the gift. The duped legatee was the laughing-stock of the court, including the King of Navarre; Canillac's wife was stripped of her jewels and sent back to the court in shame, while all the ladies of the Auvergne sniggered at her behind their fans.

Passionate, learned and devoted – For twenty years Queen Margot led a life of passion, study and devotion – she found nothing strange in the combination. She had small chapels built in all the avenues around the castle where she would go to pray. Eventually her fortune dwindled and she had to pawn her jewels in Venice, and melt down her silverware, leaving "nothing unpledged but the air". Using the financial straits in which he held her, her husband the king wanted her to agree to having the marriage dissolved. She would only agree, however, after the death of Gabrielle d'Estrées, the king's mistress, not wanting to be replaced (so she wrote to Sully), by "such an ill-esteemed piece of trash". After that, she was able to return to Paris. Usson came to an end shortly afterwards – Richelieu had it demolished in 1633, along with most of the other fortified castles in the Auvergne.

SIGHTS

View – From a viewing table off the D 709 to the north of town there is a beautiful view of the Limagne d'Issoire in the foreground and the Puys in the background, and of Puy de la Vache and Puy de Dôme with its television tower *(right)*.

Church – The building dates from the 15C and 16C and contains some fine furniture and furnishings.

Pic d'Usson – A gentle path leads to the summit on which a chapel has been built with a colossal statue of the Virgin; it provides a good **panorama**★ of the region. During the climb, a beautiful set of basalt columns can be seen in an old quarry.

Puy de la VACHE

Michelin map 73 folds 13, 14 or 239 fold 19 – Local map under Monts DÔMES

This finely shaped volcano (alt 1 167m/3 828ft) offers, along with its neighbour, Puy de Lassolas, one of the most characteristic views of the Dômes chain.

Access – *3km/2mi from Randanne (on the N 89) on the D 5.* Pass Montlosier castle on the left *(Parc naturel régional des Volcans offices and exhibition centre)*. The **Count of Monlosier**, a returned emigré in the early 19C, wanted to demonstrate that it was possible to make a forest grow in places which had previously been considered barren; the experiment was carried out on his property. Initially considered to be a madman, he finally gained prestige when the results of his efforts became tangible. His work was taken up and extended by the Forestry Department.

The path leading to the breached crater of Puy de la Vache (1hr Rtn on foot) runs to the left off the D 5. It follows the Cheire d'Aydat, a mass of solidified lava with a rough surface.

The volcano – The crater first spewed ash and slag, which formed the cone, then the lava mounted, filling the crater. Under such enormous pressure the southern flank of the crater gave way, the volcano opened up and a veritable torrent of molten material poured out over the plateau, forming the current Cheire d'Aydat, 6km/4mi long which, by blocking off the Veyre valley, formed Lake Aydat.

VALENCE ★

Conurbation 107 965
Michelin map 77 fold 12 or 246 folds 5, 19
Local map under Vallée du RHÔNE

The name Valence derives from the Latin "colonia valentia", the name given to the town by the Romans at the beginning of the 2C BC. Its development is due to its location on the Rhône, near the meeting of the tributary valleys of the Doux, Eyrieux, Isère and Drôme which mark out a vast internal basin and where the flora and fauna of Mediterranean France begin.

The city, dominated by the cathedral of St-Apollinaire, is built on a series of terraces going down to the river. Old Valence, surrounded by boulevards built in the 19C on the site of the old ramparts, has a network of shopping streets and picturesque sloping lanes, animated in season by the "Summer Festivals" *(see Calendar of events)*.

A centre of attraction – The city, which is served by a large network of communications (A 7 motorway, RN 7 national highway, River Rhône, TGV high-speed train station, airport), forms a relay between northern and central Europe and the Mediterranean, and between the Massif Central and the Alps. It is the true centre of the middle Rhône valley and a focal point for entertainment and other attractions within the Drôme and Ardèche *départements*.

The food processing, textile and furniture manufacturing industries were responsible for the town's economic boom in the 19C. Today, business in Valence, a huge food and vegetable market, is highly diversified – electronics, precision mechanics, jewellery, chemicals, cardboard, hosiery, clothing etc.

The population of Greater Valence, including the outlying suburbs spread out on either side of the Rhône – Bourg-lès-Valence, St-Péray, Portes-lès-Valence, Granges – rose from 39 000 in 1921 to 96 000 in 1968. Today, there are more than 100 000 inhabitants, including numerous students enrolled at the law faculty and engineering schools.

HISTORICAL NOTES

Rabelaisian studies – In 1452 the Dauphin Louis, who was to begin his reign a few years later under the name of Louis IX and who, at the time, was preparing for his kingly role in his princedom of Dauphiné, founded a university in Valence consisting of five faculties, including an arts faculty. Among the students was **François Rabelais**. He was to recall his student days here in his tales of the adventures of his hero Pantagruel. Courses were given by reputed masters, including the lawyer Cujas. Besides studying under this strict academic taskmaster, Rabelais is said to have had a love affair with his daughter.

Bonaparte in Valence – In 1785 Napoleon Bonaparte, a 16-year-old military cadet, arrived in Valence to improve his knowledge of warfare at the School of Artillery. Every morning, he went to the Polygon to direct his bombardiers' tactical exercises.

He lived almost directly opposite the Maison des Têtes *(see below)* which was occupied by a bookseller named Pierre Aurel. Bonaparte soon befriended him, and in less than a year had read his entire stock. The future emperor had already embarked on a voyage of self-discovery. In a letter to a friend, he used a striking image to describe himself: "the southern blood which runs through my veins flows with the rapidity of the Rhône...".

Aurel's son was to publish the famous *"Souper de Beaucaire"*, in which Bonaparte set forth his ideas about the Revolution, a few years later in Avignon.

Scene from Pantagruel's adventures

OLD TOWN *2hr 30min*

Leave from Peynet kiosk.

Kiosque Peynet (**BZ**) – This structure, built in 1880, owes its name to the artist Raymond Peynet (born 1908) who once drew a sketch of a pair of lovers seated beside it.

Champ-de-Mars (**BZ**) – This vast esplanade, built on a hillside opposite the Rhône, overlooks Jouvet park. From the belvedere there is a beautiful **view**★ of Crussol mountains. The sunsets visible from here, which throw the mountain range into relief, are famous, although it is at sunrise that the view of Crussol is the most striking.

Take the staircase below the belvedere and turn right up Avenue Maurice-Faure towards the Old Town.

The narrow Rue des Repenties and Côte St-Estève lead round the cathedral and on to Place du Pendentif.

Pendentif (**BYZ D**) – This small funerary monument was built in 1548, in Antique style. The structure is completely open with a semicircular arch on each side, and has lovely proportions. It draws its name from the shape of its vault, reminiscent of the pendentives of a dome; note the curious lance-shaped pattern above the interior corner pillars.

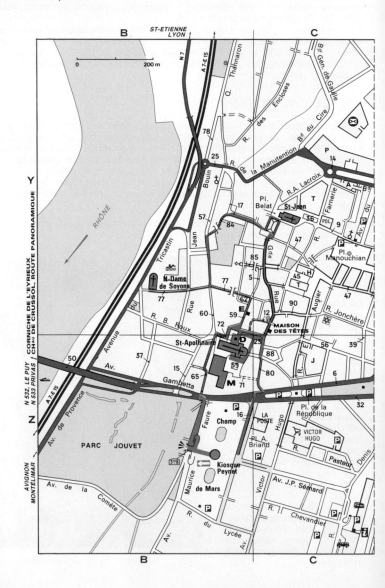

Cathédrale St-Apollinaire (**BZ**) – This vast Romanesque construction was largely rebuilt during the 17C in the primitive style.

The neo-Romanesque belfry (19C) has a white Crussol marble base; the two upper floors are made of yellow sandstone from Châteauneuf-d'Isère.

Enter the cathedral through the north door.

Under the porch, on the left, notice the lintel from the original portal; its carved compartments represent the Annunciation, the Nativity, the Adoration of the Magi and the Magi before Herod.

★**Interior** – The influence of Auvergne Romanesque architecture is evident; the nave, with its barrel vaulting and transverse arches, is lit by the aisle windows. An arcade separates the chancel from the ambulatory. Note the depth of the transept arms, unusual in Rhône buildings. Behind the chancel stalls is a cenotaph-bust of Pope Pius VI, who died in Valence in 1799.

Leave through the south door.

Under the porch *(left)*, on the carved tympanum of the original portal, is Christ giving Benediction, on the lintel Christ Multiplying the Loaves.

Walk around the east end.

Note the elegant billet-moulding above the arcades of the apse and the transept arms.

Musée des Beaux-Arts (**BZ M**) ⊘ – The Fine Arts Museum is located in the former bishop's palace and its main feature is a collection of 97 **red chalk sketches**★★, drawings and paintings by the landscape artist **Hubert Robert** (1733-1808), on the 1st floor. Most are views of Rome and the Roman countryside.

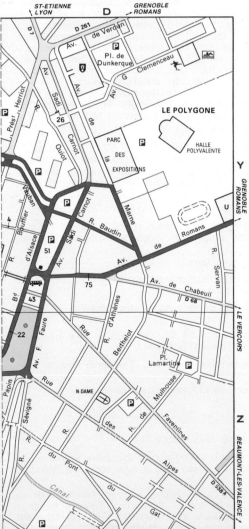

VALENCE

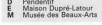

D   Pendentif
E   Maison Dupré-Latour
M   Musée des Beaux-Arts

347

The Sheltered Statue by H. Robert

After starting his career in Paris in the sculpture studio of Michel-Ange Slodtz, who was responsible for the archbishops' mausoleum in Vienne, Hubert Robert lived in Rome from 1754 to 1765, following in the wake of the painters Claude Lorrain and Joseph Vernet.

Ruins were a very fashionable subject at that time, and during his eleven years in Rome Robert filled his books with sketches and drawings in which the architecture of ancient and papal Rome served as a backdrop for scenes from everyday life.

When he returned to Paris, the painter used his sketch books as raw material for his paintings and new drawings, which show an astonishing grasp of perspective combined with an extremely light touch. The museum also has works by **Fragonard** and Ango, two of Robert's companions in Rome.

The museum has in addition an archaeological collection, including two Gallo-Roman mosaics depicting the Labours of Hercules and Orpheus charming the animals. The lapidary collection contains a Renaissance garden door from the Maison des Têtes *(see below)*.

The painting section has extensive works from the French, Flemish, Dutch and Italian schools of the 16C to the 19C, with a fine collection of naturalistic landscapes from the Barbizon school and other pre-Impressionists.

The contemporary art section, with works by the painters Bram van Velde, Michaux, Hantaï and Bryen and the sculptors B. Pagès, M. Gérard and Toni Grand, illustrates the abstract movement during the second half of the 20C.

From Place des Clercs turn into Grande-Rue.

★**Maison des Têtes** (**CYZ**) – The house "of heads" at no 57 is recognisable by the abundance and originality of the sculptures on its façade. Note two standing figures (Eve is on the left) and, under the roof, the four enormous haut-relief heads – symbolising the winds – after which this Renaissance house (1532) was named.

Follow Rue du Lieutenant-Bonaparte and Rue Pérollaire to Maison Dupré-Latour.

Maison Dupré-Latour (**BY E**) ⊘ – The interior courtyard of no 7 has a Renaissance staircase turret with a door surrounded by a remarkable carved frame.

From Place de la Pierre, walk up Côte St-Martin.

This steep little street, with its small cobblestones and short flights of steps, is one of the best preserved in the lower town.

Notre-Dame-de-Soyons (**BY**) – This church building, partly restored, has a 17C façade.

Turn around; take Rue Ambroise-Paré on the left, then walk up Côte Sylvante, a picturesque stepped street, and into Côte des Chapeliers.

St-Jean (**CY**) – This church was rebuilt in the 19C. The porch features some interesting original Romanesque capitals.

Grand-Rue, then Rue Saunière, lead back to Place du Champ-de-Mars.

EXCURSIONS

★★★**Crussol** – *5km/3mi west via St-Péray. See CRUSSOL.*

★★★**Panoramic road** – *Round tour of 49km/30mi – about 2hr. Leave Valence on the N 532 west and take the N 86, which runs along a ledge above the Rhône, to Tournon.*

★**Tournon-sur-Rhône** – This busy town on the Rhône overlooks **Tain-l'Hermitage** on the opposite bank, which is famed for its fine wines. Tournon boasts a 15C-16C **château** ⊘, containing a museum about working life on the Rhône and set in a charming **terraced garden★**, and the 14C **St-Julien** collegiate church with some fine murals and paintings beneath a coffered ceiling. The **Lycée Gabriel-Faure**

Tain-l'Hermitage and its vineyards

Meyssonnier/CAMPAGNE CAMPAGNE

has an attractive Renaissance doorway, a collection of busts and tapestries inside, and a chapel with a handsome 18C façade and a Jesuit-style interior with interesting 17C decor.

From Tournon to St-Péray, the panoramic road via St-Romain-de-Lerps is described under Moyenne vallée du RHÔNE.

★★★**Corniche de l'Eyrieux** – *Round tour of 97km/60mi – about 4 hours. Leave Valence to the west.*

From St-Péray, the D 533 west then the D 14 southwest lead along a picturesque crest road to Vernoux-en-Vivarais; from there, follow the itinerary described under VERNOUX-EN-VIVARAIS to St-Laurent-du-Pape. Return to Valence on the D 21 southeast and the N 86.

River boat trips (**BZ**) ⊘ – It is possible, in season, to cruise down the Rhône to Avignon and back up the river to Lyon.

VALS-LES-BAINS ♯♯

Population 3 748
Michelin map 76 fold 19 or 246 fold 21 – Local map under Massif du TANARGUE

This spa resort lies in a surprising setting at the bottom of the deeply-encased Volane valley. The town has developed along the valley, resulting in a narrow urban corridor of about 2km/1mi long but on average only 300m wide.

145 springs rise here and many of these have been exploited since 1600 though the town became popular as a spa resort only from the mid 19C (the Intermittent Spring was discovered in 1865). The waters here are cold (13°C/55°F) and rich in sodium bicarbonate; the difference between the springs lies in their degree of mineralisation.

The waters, which are mainly used for drinking water – several million bottles are exported from Vals each year – have a settling effect on the stomach and at the same time a stimulating effect on the liver. They are recommended for treating diabetes and nutrient deficiencies, in which case the waters may be taken in showers, baths and massages as well as taken orally.

Intermittent Spring – *East bank.* This spring gushes forth from the middle of the park at the southern end of town.It rises to a height of 8m/26ft every six hours (11.30am and 5.30pm in summer, 10.30am and 4.30pm during winter time).

Rocher des Combes – *2km/1mi east via a road alongside the hospital – 15min Rtn on foot.* From the viewing table (alt 480m/1 574ft) there is a good view over the surrounding mountains.

EXCURSIONS

★Château de Boulogne – *21km/13mi northeast on the D 578[B] southeast towards Privas. At St-Privat turn left onto the D 259. Turn right and drive through St-Michel. Private.* This was originally a fortress, built by the Poitiers family on a spur between two ravines. The castle was transformed over the centuries into a sumptuous residence which escaped the ravages of the Revolution, but was partly demolished in 1820. The magnificent **gateway★★**, which René de Hautefort had built in the late 16C, incorporates twisted columns into the Renaissance-inspired design. This elegant and extraordinary structure, lost in a rural setting and opening onto medieval ruins, is a striking sight.

The gateway of the Château de Boulogne

*★**Vallée de la Volane*** *Round trip north of 69km/42mi – about 4hr – Leave town on the D 578 north to Mézilhac.*

The valley is lined with terraced hamlets, dotted with boulders and darkened by ancient basalt flows.

Mézilhac – The village stands on the sill between the Eyrieux and Ardèche valleys. From a basalt peak crowned by a Cross there is a splendid **view★★** northwest to the Gerbier de Jonc peak and the Mézenc range, northeast to the Boutières cirque and south down the Volane valley.

Take the D 122 along the crest to Lachamp-Raphaël then take the D 215 down to Burzet.

★★**Cascade du Ray-Pic** – *See BURZET.*

Burzet – *See BURZET.*

Return to Vals via St-Pierre-de-Colombier, Juvinas and the D 243, a pretty little road through the Bézorges valley.

Les VANS

Population 2 668
Michelin map 80 fold 8 or 240 folds 3, 7 – Local map opposite

At the heart of the Lower Vivarais, in the middle of a fertile basin watered by the River Chassezac and dominated to the west by the jagged spire of the Barre ridge lies the town of Les Vans.

The setting, for those arriving from the Cévennes, is a magnificent Mediterranean scene, with an austere landscape of schist ridges to the north giving way to the dazzling white limestone of the south.

Like many other parts of France, Les Vans was caught up in the religious strife which accompanied the Reformation and Counter-Reformation, as its two churches – one Roman Catholic (15C, restored) and one Protestant (Classical façade) – indicate.

EXCURSIONS

1️⃣**Naves** – *2.5km/1.5mi west.* This is an attractive medieval village, which draws many an artist to capture its charms on canvas.

2️⃣ **Brahic** – *8km/5mi southwest.* At the entrance to this village of dark houses built of schist, a vaulted passage leads to a path up to a Cross from where there are extensive views.

★3️⃣ **Villages of the Cévennes Vivarais**

Round tour of 34km/21mi – about 2hr 30min.

Leave Les Vans on the D 10 north; turn right onto the D 250.

Chambonas – This is a village with a part-Romanesque church (carved frieze at the east end) and an old château (12C-17C) with towers covered in glazed tiles, and formal gardens said to have been laid out by Le Nôtre.

Follow the D 250.

The road runs alongside the Chassezac, crosses the Sûre and climbs a sandstone slope between vineyards and stands of evergreens.

Payzac – There is a charming rural church (12C-15C) here.

Take the D 207.

The sandstone landscape modulates from grey to red tones. After the village of Brès, with its red stone houses, the surrounding rock becomes schist and the road twists its way among chestnut groves.

St-Jean-de-Pourcharesse – A typical local church, built of schist with a roof covered in stone slabs *(lauzes)* stands in this village.

Take the road to Lauriol hamlet.

From here, the road passes more chestnut groves in a landscape slashed by ravines, to the edges of which cling tiny hamlets. Note the interesting stone-slabbed roofs.

St-Pierre-le-Déchausselat – This village is built on terraces. From the vineyards of the farm below the church there is an attractive view over the surrounding countryside.

Return to Les Vans via Chambonas.

★ 4 Vallée du Chassezac

Round tour of 77km/47 mi – about 3hr.

Leave Les Vans on the D 901 towards Villefort and take the D 113 right.

Gravières – The church ⊙ here (12C-15C) has a sturdy belfry. Inside, in the wall of the chancel (left), there is a 14C Tree of Jesse of carved stone (damaged). The gilded altarpiece and Gothic chapels are also interesting.

Les Salelles – This village overlooks a meander in the Chassezac. The church of St-Sauveur is a Gothic edifice built of warm red sandstone. The fortified belfry, destroyed by lightning, was rebuilt in the early 20C.

Follow the valley along the D 113 (note the number of hydroelectric dams and power plants along the river) and turn right to Thines.

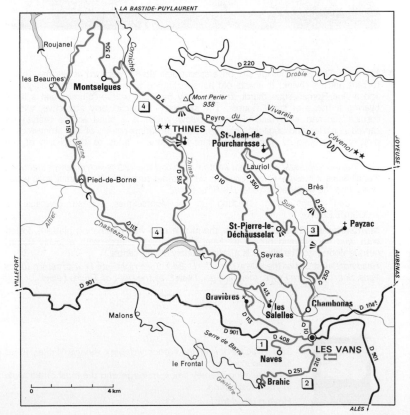

Thines

★★Thines – This small village sits on a spectacular **site★★** perched above the Thines torrent and its ravine. It boasts old houses clinging to the rock, narrow alleyways and a fine Romanesque **church**; the doorway has four statue-columns and a lintel bearing a frieze of small figures. The **east end★** is particularly attractive, with a cornice adorned with fanciful motifs below which is a blind arcade resting on carved consoles and engaged columns. The alternating colour of the stonework – pink sandstone, grey granite and white limestone – adds to the charm of the building.

Continue up Chassezac valley, past another dam and the hydroelectric power station at **Pied-de-Borne**. *Cross the River Borne. At Les Beaumes turn right into a small road which drops into the valley and crosses the River Borne.*

The road climbs again, twisting up to Montselgues plateau (average alt 1 000m/3 280ft).

Montselgues – This tiny village in the middle of a vast undulating plateau, dotted with wild narcissi and broom in June, has a sturdy church with a lovely Romanesque doorway. The village is a cross-country skiing centre.

Head northeast out of the village onto the D 340. Turn right into D 4 to return to Les Vans. Shortly before Peyre, there is a good **view★** *to the right of Thines below.*

3615 MICHELIN, on the French videotex service Minitel, saves time and trouble by calculating journey times, mileage and the most direct route to your destination.
Have a good trip!

VERNOUX-EN-VIVARAIS

Population 2 056
Michelin map 76 fold 20 or 246 folds 19, 20
Local map under Moyenne vallée du RHÔNE

Vernoux stands on the Vivarais plateau, between the Eyrieux and the Doux rivers, in the centre of a large hollow. The pleasant scene of this large village clustered around the tall steeple of its church (19C) can be seen from some way off.

EXCURSIONS

Château de la Tourette

3km/2mi. Park in the car park at Pailler farm and continue on foot: 30min Rtn. Direct access to the castle by car is possible by taking a small tarmacked road from Vernoux, following the signs to "La Tourette".

The ruins of this stronghold, which once marked the gateway to the States of Languedoc, lie in an unspoilt **setting**★ and are amongst the most evocative in the Vivarais. The main building was an enormous keep which still has some of its machicolations and corbelling. The ruins command a plunging view of the Dunière ravine which consists of a series of deeply encased meanders.

Boffres

8.5km/5mi northeast on the D 14 and D 219.

The village of Boffres is built on a projection in a semi-circle at the foot of its simple pink granite church and the remains of the old fortified castle, and overlooks a peaceful rural setting surrounded by cool chestnut groves.

Just outside the village, a bronze bust by the Ardèche sculptor Gimond has been erected at the edge of the road to the memory of **Vincent d'Indy**, the famous French composer and teacher (1851-1931), born in Paris but descended from a family in the region.

It was at **Château des Faugs** ⊙, west of Boffres, that d'Indy came to seek inspiration for his musical works (*Symphonie Cévenole* based on a French mountaineer's song, 1886; *Jour d'été à la montagne*, arrangements of Vivarais folk songs), noting themes which came to him during his walks. He composed his third melody without words from a shepherd's song heard near Les Estables, and his opera *Fervaal* one misty morning on the peaks of Mont Mézenc.

★★★Corniche de l'Eyrieux

Round tour of 51km/32mi – about 2hr 30min – map above

Leave Vernoux on the D 14 north and take the D 232 on the right.

The road winds through the hills, offering beautiful views of Vernoux-en-Vivarais in the middle of the hollow; in the background, on the left, is the Duzon valley. After Croix-de-Nodon there is an broad view of the Rhône valley; the road, lined with copses and thin woodland, overlooks the deep wooded valley of the Embroye in the foreground.

At Le Moulin-à-Vent turn right onto the D 266.

After a long wooded section, the road runs along a spectacular stretch of ledge, opposite Pierre-Gourde peak, in front of the mountain ridges enclosing the Eyrieux valley.

A track, off the D 286 to the right, leads to the Château de Pierre-Gourde. Park at a pass, in sight of the ruins.

★★**Panorama from the Château de Pierre-Gourde** – This medieval castle, now in ruins, occupies a magnificent **site**★. At the foot of the peak on which the keep was built lie the ruins of the main building, parts of the fortified curtain wall and the feudal village.

Walk left around the ruins to reach a rocky terrace.

The **panorama** encompasses the Rhône (seen through the Bas-Eyrieux gap) and Trois-Becs (along a straight axis), between the Vercors bar, the Baronnies and Mont Ventoux. Opposite, the jagged backbone of Croix de Bauzon overlooks the Haut-Eyrieux gap; on the horizon, the summit of Mont Mézenc marks the boundary of the complicated network of long, narrow Vivarois ridges.

During the descent, two panoramic bends offer a spectacular view first of the Eyrieux valley, with its clearly delineated ridges, endlessly repeated, and then of the Rhône valley, on the left.

About 5km/3mi from Pierre-Gourde, a sign on the right indicates the Serre de Pepeyrier ridge. Park about 250m along the road towards the television relay station, and climb up to the edge of the ridge.

★**View from Serre de Pepeyrier** – *15min Rtn on foot.* There is a beautiful **view** from the ridge of the mouth of the Eyrieux valley with its vast peach orchards, the town of Beauchastel and the Rhône plain; in the background, Mont Ventoux stands out clearly.

At St-Laurent-du-Pape turn right onto the D 120 then the D 21, back towards Vernoux.

As it winds up to Serre Mure pass (alt 765m/2 509ft), this spectacular crest road offers views of the Vivarois ridges, the upper basin of the Eyrieux and the Boutières region, as well as a fine view of the western slopes of Pierre-Gourde peak. As the road approaches Vernoux, during a rapid descent towards the Dunière gorge, the Château de la Tourette comes into view.

Turn left onto the D 231, then the D 331.

St-Julien-le-Roux – From the cemetery around the church, mountains can be seen right along the **horizon**★, above the ruins of Château de la Tourette.

The D 331, 231 and D 21 lead back to Vernoux.

Le VEURDRE

Population 595
Michelin map 69 fold 3 or 238 fold 33

This village, built on the west bank of the River Allier, lies at the heart of mixed woodland and pasture land.

Château de St-Augustin ⊙ – *5km/3mi northwest.* An enormous zoo-park (80ha/198 acres) contains numerous animal species from the region itself (deer, wild boar, birds etc) and from further afield (bears, lions, monkeys, zebras, llamas etc). Visitors may walk in the deer park and drive into the main courtyard of the château. The 18C hall is decorated with hunting trophies; the kitchen still has its original copper pans.

VICHY ✝✝✝

Population 27 714
Michelin map 73 fold 5 or 239 fold 8
Local map under La LIMAGNE

Vichy, a world famous spa resort and holiday town, attracts numerous visitors because of its high quality shopping facilities and the very wide range of cultural and sporting activities it has to offer – casino-theatre, cabarets, festivals, concerts, exhibitions, lectures, horse races. The parks along the banks of the River Allier add to the pleasure of staying here.

The multi-purpose sports centre (Centre Omnisports), which is situated northwest of the town, is one of the best designed sports complexes in Europe.

Lake Allier (nearly 100ha/250 acres), which was created after the construction of a dam bridge on the river downstream from the town, is used for international competitions (rowing, regattas, water-skiing etc).

The Sporting Club completes the complex with its 18-hole golf course, tennis courts and swimming pool.

THE VICHY GOVERNMENT

From early July 1940 until 20 August 1944, Vichy was the capital of the French state during Nazi German occupation of the north of France. Vichy, with a direct railway line to Paris (the "Thermal-Express"), relatively modern telephone links, and 500 hotels which could be requisitioned for government offices, was chosen in preference to cities such as Clermont-Ferrand, Marseille or Toulouse. It had the added advantage of being quite close to the line of demarcation (level with Moulins) between occupied and unoccupied France. Maréchal Pétain, hero of Verdun during the First World War, was granted full executive powers by the French parliament. He and his Cabinet had their headquarters in the Pavillon Sévigné, while most of the other government members and senior administrators were housed at the Hôtel du Parc, the War Ministry at the Thermal (now the Aletti Palace), and foreign diplomats at – appropriately enough – the Ambassadeurs. The disproportionate centralisation of government power in this city (the only government department installed elsewhere was the commission for youth projects at Châtel-guyon) was accompanied by a strictly monitored exercise of power and the laying aside of the fundamental principles of democracy. During the dark days of the Vichy regime, the city was subject to a permanent police presence, with the oppressive atmosphere further heightened by furtive and unexplained comings and goings, cowed public apathy and an overriding austerity totally at odds with the city's previous role as a health and leisure resort. On 20 August 1944, the representatives of the toppled regime who had remained in place were taken back to Germany by the Nazis as they retreated. Six days later the Free French Forces entered the city.

THE SPA

The curative properties of Vichy water were appreciated by the Romans, who built a small spa town here – Aquis Calidis. After a long period of relative obscurity, Vichy's vocation as a spa was resurrected in the 17C.

A day in the life of a 17C bather – This is an account by **Madame de Sévigné**, who came here to cure her rheumatism:

"I took the waters this morning, my dear. Oh! How awful they are! At 6am we go to the spring; everyone is there; we drink and pull the most awful faces – just imagine, the water is boiling hot, with a most unpleasant taste of saltpetre.

We walk back and forth, we come and go, we stroll about. Finally, we have luncheon. After eating, we go visiting. At 5pm we go walking in the most delightful places. At 7pm we have a light supper. We go to bed at 10pm. Today, I began taking showers. What an excellent preparation for purgatory! ... Then we get into a warm bed – and that is what makes you better."

Famous bathers – During the 18C the daughters of Louis XV, Mesdames Adelaide and Victoire, came to spend the season here. One of the springs now bears their name (Source Mesdames). In 1799 Maria-Letizia Bonaparte, Napoleon's mother, came here. In 1810 the Emperor himself created the Parc des Sources. In 1821 the Duchess of Angoulême laid the first stone of the thermal establishment. Napoleon III came on several occasions to take the waters at Vichy and the spa became extremely fashionable. A series of chalets was built alongside the new Allier park, with their façades all facing the gardens, at the emperor's request, in order to avoid the

R. Soubie/Musée de la Publicité

=VICHY=
LA GRANDE STATION THERMALE

Early advertising

obsessive ovations. Since the Second Empire, countless celebrities have come to spend a pleasant holiday here while tending their health. The local facilities are of the highest quality and the town is constantly improving them.

The Vichy springs

Vichy's mineral and thermal springs contain mainly bicarbonate of soda and carbonic acid. The main springs *(see below)* belong to the State and are operated by a contracting company founded in 1853. The waters here are used to treat conditions of the liver, gall-bladder and stomach, diabetes, migraines, nutritional and digestive disorders, and also rheumatological complaints.

Waters from the Grande Grille, Hôpital and, in particular, Célestins springs, are bottled and exported the world over.

Hot springs – These are the basis of the Vichy drinking cures.

– The **Grande Grille** is named after the grille which used to protect it from thirsty animals. The bubbling water (temperature 40°C/104°F) comes up from a depth of 1 000-1 200m/3 300-4 000ft.

– The **Chomel** (temperature 41°C/106°F) is named after the doctor who captured the spring in 1750 and managed the waters.

A third hot spring, the **Hôpital** (temperature 33°C/91.4°F), rises in a rotunda-shaped pavilion behind the Casino.

VICHY

Cold springs – Their waters are also used for drinking cures. The **Parc** (temperature 24°C/75°F) gushes forth in the Parc des Sources. The **Lucas** (temperature 24°C/75°F) is named after the doctor and inspector who bought the spring at the beginning of the 19C on behalf of the State. The **Célestins** has a temperature of 21.5°C/71°F.

Thermal establishments – The Centre Thermal des Dômes can provide up to 2 500 people with thermal and related treatment each morning. The Callou pump room (**BY**), like that of the Célestins, boasts the latest technical innovations.

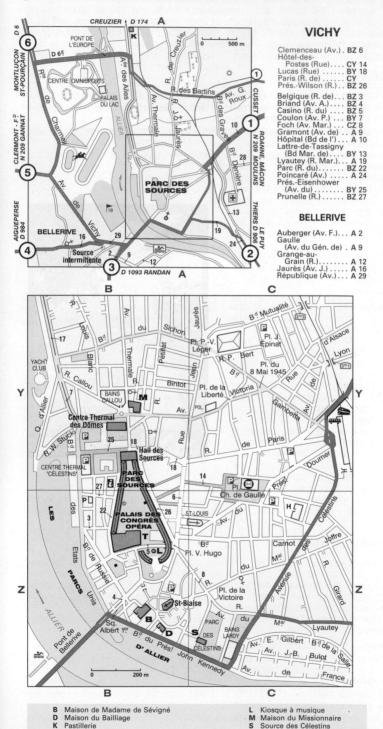

VICHY

Clemenceau (Av.) . **BZ** 6
Hôtel-des-
  Postes (Rue). . . . **CY** 14
Lucas (Rue) . . . . . . **BY** 18
Paris (R. de) . . . . . . **CY**
Prés.-Wilson (R.) . . **BZ** 26

Belgique (R. de) . . . **BZ** 3
Briand (Av. A.). . . . **BZ** 4
Casino (R. du) . . . . **BZ** 5
Coulon (Av. P.) . . . **BY** 7
Foch (Av. Mar.) . . . **CZ** 8
Gramont (Av. de) . . **A** 9
Hôpital (Bd de l') . . . **A** 10
Lattre-de-Tassigny
  (Bd Mar. de). . . . **BY** 13
Lyautey (R. Mar.). . . **A** 19
Parc (R. du) . . . . . . **BZ** 22
Poincaré (Av.) . . . . **A** 24
Prés.-Eisenhower
  (Av. du) . . . . **BY** 25
Prunelle (R.) . . . . . . **BZ** 27

BELLERIVE

Auberger (Av. F.) . . . **A** 2
Gaulle
  (Av. du Gén. de) . **A** 9
Grange-au-
  Grain (R.) . . . . **A** 12
Jaurès (Av. J.) . . . . **A** 16
République (Av.) . . . **A** 29

B   Maison de Madame de Sévigné
D   Maison du Bailliage
K   Pastillerie
L   Kiosque à musique
M   Maison du Missionnaire
S   Source des Célestins

356

★SPA DISTRICT

The "spa resort" architecture of the late 19C and early 20C, the period when Vichy – the "Queen of Spa Towns" – was at its most popular, is well worth a closer look. The buildings of the Vichy spa complex have been carefully restored and listed as protected for some years now, and make up a rich and unique part of France's architectural heritage.

Vichy architects were spurred on in their quest for originality and the unexpected by the resort's air of worldliness and sophistication; this was a place where monotony was not permitted and where extravagant gestures ruled the day. The various artistic influences at work here include Byzantine, Auvergne Romanesque and Florentine Quattrocento, with the style of English cottages and Alpine chalets also being emulated. The result is a delightfully anarchic "Baroque eclecticism" in which architecture of every style and every period can be seen.

★**Parc des Sources** (BYZ) – This beautiful park planted with chestnut and plane trees was laid out on the orders of Napoleon I and links a number of springs. The spa district effectively grew up around it, and it has remained the centre of the town's spa industry and leisure facilities.

In the morning the district is permeated with the peculiar atmosphere of the spa, punctuated by the comings and goings of people taking the waters, gathering in clusters around the springs as they await their "glass of water".

In the afternoon and on gala evenings, fashionable society comes to life, going for an evening stroll, having a drink on the terrace of the Grand Café or attending some glittering function.

★**Palais des Congrès-Opéra** (BZ) – The old Grand Casino, which opened in 1865, represents the important influence of general good spirits on people's health. The first of its kind in France, it housed various assembly rooms and gaming halls beneath a single roof. From 1900 to 1903, it was renovated and extended with the addition of a theatre and opera house under the direction of architect Charles Lecoeur. Inside, the superb Art Nouveau decor is the work of wrought-iron worker Émile Robert and master glass-artist François Chigot. The main façade, in "Belle Époque" (turn of the century) style, overlooks the park, to which it is linked by a beautiful flight of steps.

A comprehensive renovation project combined with the conversion of the gaming hall into a conference centre has restored this building to its former splendour.

Covered arcades – These are beautifully delicate Art Nouveau creations in wrought-iron, made by Émile Robert for the 1889 World Exhibition in Paris and transferred to Vichy in 1900.

The balustrade of the **band stand** (L), also the work of Robert, forms a garland of musical motifs; two concerts a week are given here in season.

Hall des sources (BY) – Fed by the waters of Vichy's six thermal springs, the **pump room** is built of glass and metal, and its very transparency and the fluidity of its design bring to mind the element which is dispensed within.

Centre thermal des Dômes, Vichy

Centre thermal des Dômes – The new luxury assembly rooms in a neo-Moorish style were designed by Charles Lecoeur, architect of the old Grand Casino, and inaugurated in 1903. The central dome and corner cupolas are covered in gold enamelled roof tiles. Frescoes *(The Bath, The Spring)* by the Symbolist painter Alphonse Osbert adorn the hall inside.

Hotels (**BZ**) – Despite the demolition of the prestigious Queen's Hotel, most of the grand hotels on which Vichy's reputation is based have survived intact. The Palais des Parcs (the old Ruhl, 15, boulevard de Russie), the Aletti Palace (old Thermal, rue Aletti) and the Hôtel du Parc (21-23, rue du Parc) are among the most impressive neo-Baroque buildings in town, while the façade of the Hôtel des Ambassadeurs (rue du Casino) exemplifies neo-Louis XIII style, and that of the Ermitage du Pont-Neuf (square Albert-Ier) Art Deco.

Chalets and villas (**BZ**) – The row of **chalets★** which lines Avenue des États-Unis (nos 101 to 109bis) was built from 1862 to house Napoleon III and his entourage, who used to come regularly to take the waters at Vichy. The "half-Swiss, half-Colonial" look lent to these frivolous buildings by their balconies or elaborate roof trims and their brick façades is typical of the fashion of their day.
However, it was after the fall of the Empire that architects unleashed the full power of their imagination to create truly eccentric buildings. There are some remarkable examples of florid design along the boulevard de Russie (Neo-classical at nos 17, 19 and **21★**, Art Deco at no 29), the rue de Belgique (Venitian inspired villa with St Mark's lions at no 7, **Castel Flamand★** at nos 2-2bis) and rue Prunelle (the mansion at no 8, which is a pastiche of an English cottage).

Source des Célestins (**CZ S**) – The water from this spring now flows as far as the pump room, but it is worth taking the short walk to have a look at the elegant Louis XV pavillion which houses the spring itself.
The Célestins park contains some magnificent evergreen trees, as well as traces of the old convent after which the spring and the park are named.

★Parc d'Allier (**BYZ**) – These beautiful landscape gardens created at the request of Emperor Napoleon III are built on land reclaimed from the river. They are graced with trees of various species, lakes with swans and ducks, rock gardens, rose gardens and flowerbeds, and are ideal for long, peaceful strolls.
The Parc du Soleil provides all sorts of attractions for children.

ADDITIONAL SIGHTS

Maison de Madame de Sévigné (**BZ B**) – The house, constructed during the time of Louis XIII, has been highly restored and converted into a hotel (Pavillon Sévigny). The Marquise of Sévigné would stay here when she came to spend the season at Vichy.

Maison du Bailliage (**BZ D**) – The Bailiwick's House was built at the beginning of the 16C.

St-Blaise (**BZ**) – The old church, altered many times over, has a highly venerated Black Virgin, known as Our Lady of the Sick and Suffering; only the statue's head is original (12C).
The new church has some beautiful modern stained-glass windows and mosaics. There is a lovely view from the belfry.

Maison du Missionnaire (**BY M**) ⊘ – This building houses a missionary museum with an exotic collection of exhibits.

VIC-LE-COMTE★

Population 4 155
Michelin map 73 fold 15 or 239 fold 20 – Local map under La LIMAGNE

Vic-le-Comte lies in the middle of **Comté**, a region made up of a series of volcanoes which appeared in the Limagne at the end of the Tertiary era, forming a transition between the plain and the Livradois mountains. The highest reaches an altitude of 807m/2 647ft, rising 400m/1 312ft above the Limagne. Most of the volcanoes have been eroded and only their chimneys remain, sometimes combined with outliers of lava flow. They are often crowned with ruined fortresses. There are more than fifty eruptive pinnacles, now covered in woodland; in the past, grape vines grew on the more exposed slopes.
In the 8C a priory was established in the village (*vicus* in Latin) – which was probably of Gallo-Roman origin – by the Benedictine Monks of Manglieu.

At the beginning of the 13C the Count of Auvergne, Gui II, after being defeated by King Philippe Auguste, saw his estate reduced to the Vic-le-Comte region, which was well protected by a ring of fortresses (Buron, Busséol etc). During the same period, the Cistercian Abbey of Bouschet, near Yronde, became the necropolis of the regional lords.

Through his marriage to an Auvergne heiress, a descendant of the kings of Scotland, **John Stuart**, Count of La Marche, took possession of the earldom and embellished the castle built by his predecessors at Vic-le-Comte. All that remains now is the door from the Sainte-Chapelle. From 1651 up to the time of the French Revolution, the earldom of Auvergne belonged to the Dukes of Bouillon.

Today, Vic-le-Comte has a papermill owned by the Bank of France which makes the watermarked paper used for bank notes printed in Chamalières.

SIGHTS

★**Sainte-Chapelle** – This, the Holy Chapel, is a beautiful Gothic building heralding the Renaissance. The cornice is decorated with sculptures of mythical beasts, crockets, thistles and human figures.

In the chancel, the statues of the apostles, sheltered by canopies along the springing line of the vault ribs, date from the Renaissance; several have been restored. Catherine de' Medici, who owned Vic-le-Comte at one time, had the gallery and balustrade added.

The richly coloured **stained-glass windows★**, depicting scenes from the Old and New Testaments, have been restored. The very fine stone **altarpiece★** (1520) is the work of the Florentine artists who made the balustrade: at the bottom, the three Cardinal Virtues and a wooden statue of St Anthony; at the top, the Three Theological Virtues. Note the 17C wrought-iron lectern and the interesting 15C painted wood polyptych, illustrating the Passion and Entombment.

St-Jean – This Romanesque church near the river was refurbished during the Gothic period. Note the fine 14C door. Inside, on either side of the chancel, are 13C and 14C frescoes depicting the lives of John the Baptist and St Blaise; in the nave, on the left, is a beautiful 15C wooden Crucifixion; the lefthand chapel contains a 16C statue of Our Lady of Compassion.

Old houses – Rue Porte-Robin (northeast of the Sainte-Chapelle) has several buildings with 15C and 16C façades. From the northwestern end of the chapel go round to the right as far as the old town gate, **Porte Robin**, the only remains of the fortified curtain wall. Place du Vieux-Marché beyond it has a 16C fountain.

Continue straight ahead towards Rue du Palais, at the entrance to which are two corbelled houses. Take the covered passage on the left, Rue des Farges, then Rue de Coulogne beyond; turn back.

EXCURSIONS

★**Puy de St-Romain** – *7km/5mi north then 45min Rtn on foot.*
The setting of the *puy* is striking : the summit, an ancient place of worship nearly 450m/1 500ft above the River Allier (alt 779m/2 555ft), offers a breathtaking **panorama★** encompassing the Comté *puys*, the Forez mountains, the Livradois mountains, the Vic-le-Comte basin, the Allier valley, the Cézallier and Cantal mountains, the Monts Dore and Monts Dômes, Clermont-Ferrand and the Limagne.

VIC-SUR-CÈRE ★

Population 1 968
Michelin map 76 fold 12 or 239 fold 42
Local map under Monts du CANTAL

The old town of Vic in the Cère valley, with its picturesque houses clustered around the church, is a spa town at an altitude of 681m/2 234ft with a mineral spring (pump-room).

HISTORICAL NOTES

The "mad monk" – In the 12C **Pierre de Vic**, the youngest son of one of the local families, who had been forced to enter the church despite not having a religious vocation, was put in charge of a rich priory when he was still very young; he turned it into a pleasure-dome, composing drinking songs and love ballads there.

He gradually wearied of his sedentary life, however, and began to travel and sing his ballads at the courts of Philippe Auguste, Richard the Lionheart and the King of Aragon. The "mad monk", as he called himself, carried off first prize at the Courts of Love Literary Tournament and won the Golden Hawk at a contest at Le Puy.

Winning barrels (16C) – During the Wars of Religion an episode occurred near Vic which exemplifies the cunning of Captain **Merle**. He was escorting a convoy of supplies for the Huguenots when the Roman Catholics ambushed him in a gorge. Merle ordered the men to cut the mules' traces and flee. After they had gone some distance, he stopped the stampeding men, having calculated that the Catholics would fall upon the casks of wine instead of pursuing Merle's men. He proved to be right; after rallying his men, he counter-attacked, wiping out his drunken adversaries.

It was about this time that the bailiff's court was set up in Vic and the magistrates began to build their stately homes in the old part of the town.

Mademoiselle de Fontanges (17C) – Marie-Angélique d'Escorailles, a favourite of Louis XIV, was born at Cropières castle (southeast of Vic). Her royal favour, however, was short-lived: she was said to be "as pretty as a picture, and as thick as a brick".

She was awarded the title Duchess of Fontanges on giving birth in 1681 to a son, but she died of complications shortly afterwards, aged barely 20 years–"killed in the line of duty", as the Marquise of Sévigné somewhat cattily put it. It can hardly be said that the king missed her – Madame de Maintenon arrived just in time to console him.

SIGHTS

Church – This partly Romanesque building has undergone many alterations. Note the graceful apse and the curious modillions on the south façade.

Maison des Princes de Monaco – *South of the church, off Rue Coffinhal.* This 15C house served as a residence on several occasions for the Princes of Monaco, to whom Louis XIII had given the Carladez region in 1642, the capital of which was Vic, and which remained in their possession until the Revolution.

The house has a turret with a mullioned window and a door surmounted by a badly damaged bas-relief depicting the Annunciation.

Cascade du Trou de la Conche and Rocher de Maisonne – *1hr 45min Rtn on foot.* Behind the church, take the street leading to a footbridge over the Iraliot. On the other side of the torrent, walk up a very steep path.

At the top of the rise the road divides: *(left)* to Trou de la Conche cascade, a very pretty setting; *(right)* to the top of Maisonne rock, surmounted by a Cross and giving a fine view of Vic and the valley below.

Rocher des Pendus – *7km/5mi southeast on the D 54; 45min Rtn on foot from Col de Curebourse.* Extensive **panorama**★★.

VIENNE★★

Population 29 449
Michelin map 88 folds 19, 20 or 246 fold 16
Local map under Moyenne vallée du RHÔNE

Vienne, "perched like an altar on the buttresses of the noble Dauphiné" (Mistral), on a bend in the Rhône, is a town of exceptional interest. In a delightful **setting**★ bathed in light reflected from the Rhône, a Gothic cathedral stands next to a Roman temple, while Romanesque cloisters and several ancient churches rub shoulders with an Antique theatre. The charm of "Vienne the Beautiful" of Roman times is enhanced by the charm of "Vienne the Holy", the Christian city.

The flower-filled pedestrian precinct, along Cours Brillier and around the hôtel de ville, is a popular place for a gentle stroll.

A large market is held in the town centre every Saturday morning.

HISTORICAL NOTES

Vienne the Beautiful – More than fifty years before Julius Caesar conquered Gaul, the stamping ground of the Allobroges tribe – of which Vienne became the capital in the 1C BC – was subjugated by the Roman legions. In the absence of a more open site, the town was chosen for its geographical location which was easier to manage than that of Lyon as there was only one river to cross.

Public monuments were erected at the foot of Mont Pipet, with private residences and trade and craft establishments on both banks. Vienne soon extended its suburbs beyond the Rhône to the present-day villages of Ste-Colombe and St-Romain-en-Gal *(see below).* Drapers, leather workers and potters had flourishing businesses and the poet Martial described the town as "Vienne the Beautiful".

Under the Late Empire, Vienne became the metropolis for a vast province called Viennoise, stretching from Lake Geneva to the mouth of the Rhône. By AD 177, the Christian community of Vienne was already very much alive: the name of its deacon, Sanctus, figures among the martyrs of the amphitheatre in Lyon. Since the Church's territorial organisation was based on that of the Roman Empire, the bishops of Vienne were soon at the head of an immense metropolitan province encompassing Valence, Die, Grenoble, Geneva, Viviers and Maurienne.

Joys and sorrows of "Greater Burgundy" – After the Western Roman Empire was dissolved in 476, Vienne was chosen as the seat of the Burgundian kings whose subjects spilled into the Rhône basin. They tried to set up a police state in the southeast of Gaul but were driven out by the Franks in 532. Despite the political confusion, Vienne remained a centre of artistic achievement: the construction of the church and necropolis of St-Pierre was continued; the foundations were laid for the abbey of St-André-le-Bas. The decoration of St Léonien's sarcophagus is a precious example of "barbaric" art. The incessant in-fighting between the Carolingians for Charlemagne's heritage enabled Boson, Count of Vienne, Arles and Provence to proclaim himself "King of Burgundy" at Mantaille castle in 879. His palace was in Vienne.

Vienne, the Holy City – As the distant Holy Roman Emperor only exercised nominal suzerainty, the temporal authority of the bishops, who were also the counts of Viennois, held sway over the city and over an area of land on the east bank of the Rhône. Around the abbey of St-André-le-Bas, which was at the height of its power, a large Jewish community plied a thriving trade. Two famous prelates sat on the throne of the "primate of the primates of the Gauls": **Gui de Bourgogne** (1088-1119), crowned pope in his own cathedral under the name of Calixtus II, and **Jean de Bernin** (1218-66), who directed the extensions to the cathedral of St-Maurice based on Gothic principles, ordered restoration of the Roman bridge over the Rhône, and built a hospital and the Château de la Bâtie.

Numerous ecclesiastical councils were held in the town, notably that which suppressed the Order of the Templars in 1312.

An unequal combat – The presence of Church land within the confines of the Kingdom and Empire did not leave the French monarchy indifferent. In 1335 Philippe de Valois annexed Ste-Colombe and had a tower built to mark the takeover. In 1349 the eldest sons of the House of France were endowed with the Dauphiné region as an apanage; they were to vie with the archbishop for temporal jurisdiction of the town itself. The Dauphin Louis, the future Louis XI, had himself appointed joint sovereign lord of the city, concurrently with the archbishop. French annexation was completed in the 15C, when Dauphiné was finally united with France.

Modern times – During the centuries of the Renaissance and the absolute monarchy, Vienne's decline offers a painful contrast with the prosperity of Lyon: commercial activity collapsed and the population dropped by one-fifth between 1650 and the beginning of the 18C. Even the bridge over the Rhône, swept away by flooding in 1651, was not rebuilt until the 19C. A certain industrial rebirth occurred once the Revolution swept away the Ancien Régime, however, with the establishment of clothing manufacturers along the Gère. Leather work, the fruit trade and numerous processing industries have reactivated local business today.

★★ROMAN AND CHRISTIAN VIENNE *Half a day*

Leave from Place St-Maurice.

★★**Cathédrale St-Maurice** (BY) – Built from the 12C to 16C, the cathedral combines both Romanesque and Gothic elements. The patronage of St Maurice is a reminder of the veneration given to martyrs of the Theban Legion in the Burgundian kingdoms.

Cathedral doorways – The west front with its three doorways is adorned with fine Flamboyant ornamentation. Although the Wars of Religion deprived it of the statues decorating the niches of the engaged piers and tympana, the delightful decoration of the covings has fortunately remained intact.

The late 14C **south doorway** (right) has two covings: the inner row depicts the prophets seated under canopies; the outer row has pairs of musician angels. The gestures and attitudes of the figures produce a very lively whole.

The **central portal**, with its cut-off gable, dates from the late 15C. It has three covings with sculptures which are to be read horizontally. The inside niche shows an episode from the life of Christ; the central niche, the scene from the Old Testament which prefigured it; the outside niche, the prophet who foretold the event.

In the niches on the 3rd level on the right can be seen:
- inner niche, Christ descending into Hell and opening the mouth of Leviathan as he snaps up a small figure (Abel), in the presence of Adam and Eve;
- in the centre, Lot leaving Sodom in flames, as his wife is turned into a pillar of salt, having turned her head in spite of the divine warning;
- in the outer niche, the prophet Hosea foretelling the victory of Christ over death.
The three niches below depict the Resurrection of Christ (soldiers asleep), Jonas coming out of the whale and the prophet Zephaniah.

In the tympanum of the portal, above the twisted columns, there are two statues personifying the Church on the left and the Synagogue on the right.

The **north doorway** (left), from the second half of the 15C, is devoted to the Virgin. At the top of the central niche two angels with folded wings are carrying the Virgin's crown. The inside coving depicts six-winged cherubim; on the outside coving, musician angels are involved in various liturgical functions.

Interior – The vast (97m/318ft long), luminous tripartite nave, with no transept, reflects a surprising harmony despite its construction over a period of four centuries.

The far seven bays enclosing the Gothic nave are Romanesque; reminiscent of Roman times, the piers are flanked with antique-style pilasters and fluted half-columns; this stage of construction, from the early 12C, is contemporary with or slightly later than the pontificate of Gui de Bourgogne.

The four bays of the nave nearest the west front were built in the 15C in pure Gothic style, their engaged columns rising in an unbroken line to the base of the ribbing.

A marble bench runs around the circumference of the apse; the bishop's throne (cathedra) sits in the axis of the nave. Above the bench, small columns support

Angels on the north doorway
of the Cathedral

A. Froissardey/EXPLORER

a cornice above a marble frieze inlaid with brown cement; a second frieze, in the same style, runs above the triforium.

This decorative technique is of oriental inspiration – the first example is to be found in the church of Hagia Sophia in Istanbul (Constantinople) – and reached the Rhône valley via Italy (San Marco in Venice); it is characteristic of Viennois-Lyonnais art: the apse of St-Jean cathedral in Lyon is a typical example. The Romanesque capitals form a decorative whole, closely inspired by Antiquity. They feature narrative scenes (right aisle) or whimsical subjects; some are in a transitional style, with the figures concealed by foliate designs.

In the apse, on the right of the high altar, stands the mausoleum of Archbishops Arnaud de Montmorin and Henri-Oswald de La Tour d'Auvergne (1747), by **Michel-Ange Slodtz**; it is one of the finest 18C works in Dauphiné.

Around the chancel 16C Flemish tapestries depict scenes from the life of St Maurice. A splendid Renaissance stained-glass window, the Adoration of the Magi, throws light from the east into the chancel from the right aisle. The stained-glass clerestory windows in the chancel date from the 16C; the central window depicts St Maurice, in armour, with St Peter.

The north aisle has interesting sculptures: between the 6th and 7th chapel a large 13C bas-relief depicting the meeting of Herod and the Magi is striking for the very noble poses; an amusing detail is the two grotesque heads on either side of Herod, symbolizing his two-facedness – one, turned towards the kings, appears to listen to them attentively while the other, unseen by them, is laughing maliciously.

A covered passageway (north aisle) once connected the cathedral to the ancient cloisters, which no longer exist. Notice, by the entrance, the capitals with their very fine foliate decorations. Above the arch is a white marble frieze reproducing the signs of the Zodiac; in the 16C these were changed around to correspond to the new order of the year fixed by the Edict of Roussillon (with 1 January as the start of the year, instead of the previous regional variations), which explains why the monogram of Christ with the alpha and omega which was originally in the centre of the frieze is now out of place.

In the passageway, a Gothic arcade frames three Romanesque statues in the archaic manner; on the left, St Peter; on the right, St John the Evangelist and St Paul. The long flowing drapery and the feet inclined on an oblique support evoke Languedoc art – note the ascetic head of St Paul, looking meditatively from under heavy eyelids.

Leave the cathedral along the covered passageway (north aisle).

Outside, the decoration on the door of the north wall combines Romanesque and Gothic elements with Roman fragments. Beneath the pointed arch, delicate griffons and leaves decorate the lintel.

Place St-Paul was once the site of the cloisters; note that the blind arcade of the ancient Romanesque side aisle was moved to the top of the wall enclosing the Gothic chapels; the ornamentation of the arches becomes increasingly rich towards the west front.

Walk to Place du Palais.

★★Temple of Augustus and Livia (BY B) – This is a rectangular building of pleasing proportions. Its dimensions (24m/79ft long, 14.5m/47ft wide and 17m/56ft high) are approximately the same as those of the Maison Carrée, the well-known Roman temple in Nîmes. A row of six Corinthian columns supports the entablature on the façade and the sides; the carved ornamentation is better preserved on the north side. The rear part, which is the oldest, probably dates from the end of the 1C BC. The façade, facing east, overlooked the forum. It was rebuilt under the reign of Augustus, perhaps after a fire. Its triangular pediment bore a bronze inscription to the glory of Augustus and Livia, his wife. Inside was the statue of the deified emperor.

The temple has undergone numerous alterations. During the Middle Ages it was turned into a church and all the columns were linked together by a wall. The seat of the Jacobite Club during the Revolution, it was used to celebrate the cult of the goddess Reason; it was subsequently used as a court, a museum and a library and it was not until the mid 19C that the walls were removed from the columns and the building restored.

Rue des Clercs leads to the church of St-André-le-Bas.

Temple of Augustus and Livia

★St-André-le-Bas (BY) ⊘ – Apart from the lower parts of the east end, the apse (except the central bay), a large part of the southern wall and a few later additions, the church is mainly 12C. The large freestone gable wall provides an unusual decorative effect. The first three levels of the bell tower (restored) were built in the 12C on an older foundation; the top level dates from the 13C. The whole of the decoration is remarkable: piers and colonnettes on the twin openings, small festooned arches ending in consoles bearing expressive masks.

Walk into the southern courtyard flanked by the base of the bell tower.

The first mask to be seen is poking out an enormous tongue.

The nave was originally covered with timber framing; the restoration in 1152 consisted of raising and vaulting it, which required the construction of outside flying buttresses and reinforcement of the walls by arches and piers.

The decoration of the fluted pilasters is attributed to Guillaume Martin who signed and dated his work (1152) on the base of the 2nd pier from the right; the most beautiful capitals depict Samson overwhelming the Lion (2nd pier from the left) and Job scratching his ulcers, next to his wife, who is showing her disgust (3rd pier). The two superb Corinthian columns at the entrance to the apse are from a Roman monument. The north wall has a recess with a large wooden statue of St Andrew (17C) with a magnificent face and, against a wall, a painted wood panel depicting the Adoration of the Magi, 1543 *(temporarily in the Museum of Fine Arts, see below)*.

Leave the church through the north door.

★Cloître St-André-le-Bas (BY) ⊘ – These small, trapezoidal cloisters date from the 12C. They have a series of blind arcades, resting alternatively on twinned colonnettes and the piers marking the bays of the nave. The capitals are carved with narrative scenes or with animals and human masks among foliage.

The capitals of the colonnettes in the south gallery show an element of fantasy: spiral or zigzag fluting, strings of beads or palm leaves with knotted stems.

The cloisters house a large collection of Christian epitaphs – that of Fœdula, a townswoman of Vienne baptised by St Martin, dates back to the beginning of the 5C – and medieval inscriptions from funerary monuments. In the southeast corner are fragments of the chancel (stone screen separating the clergy from the faithful) decorated with strapwork, rope-moulding and interlacing (9C), together with a white marble altar (11C) from the church of St-Pierre *(see below)*.

The terrace provides a view of the Rhône and Ste-Colombe.

Take Rue de la Table-Ronde to Rue Marchande.

At no 32, there is a beautiful portal with coving and a carved archstone.

Continue to Rue des Orfèvres.

No 11 has a 15C inner courtyard while no 9 has a beautiful Renaissance façade.

Turn around and take Rue du Collège on the right.

St-André-le-Haut (**CY**) – This church was once a Jesuit College chapel but was consecrated to St Louis in 1725; it has a beautiful classical façade.

Porte de l'Ambulance (**CY D**) – This monumental gateway was the entrance to the former Benedictine abbey of St-André-le-Haut.

★**Théâtre Romain** (**CY**) ⊙ – *See plan in Introduction under Roman Architecture in the Rhône valley.* The Roman theatre had been abandoned since the time of Emperor Constantine, in the early 4C, and was buried under $80\,000\text{m}^3/3$ million ft^3 of earth when excavations began in 1922; it has now been completely uncovered.

This was one of the largest theatres in Roman Gaul; its diameter (131m/430ft) is greater than that of the Roman theatre at Orange in Provence and is only 1m/3ft less than that of the great theatre of Marcellus in Rome.

Built against Mont Pipet, it had 46 tiers over a series of well-preserved vaulted passageways; the dressed masonry stone of the tiers was entirely faced with white stone slabs. It could seat nearly 13 500 spectators. The four tiers closest to the orchestra pit, reserved for officials, were separated from the others by a green marble balustrade. Some of the marble slabs on the floor of the stalls can still be seen and the front panel on the stage floor has a copy of a fine animal frieze, the original of which, made of white marble, is in the Lapidary Museum. Unusually, a temple rose above the top row of tiers.

VIENNE

STE-COLOMBE (RHÔNE)

B Temple d'Auguste et de Livie
D Porte de l'Ambulance
E Vestige d'un portique
M¹ Musée des Beaux-Arts et d'Archéologie

As in Lyon, the main theatre was coupled with a small theatre (odeum). In summer, the main theatre is used during the annual jazz festival *(see Calendar of events).*

Take Rue des Célestes, then walk down Montée St-Marcel to Rue Victor-Hugo and the archaeological gardens.

Jardin archéologique (**BY**) – A white stone double archway is the only remaining part of a **portico** (**E**), thought in the past to be part of some Roman baths; note the fine decorative frieze on the inside.

On the right of the portico is a wall which formed the northern side of a **theatre** said to have been reserved for performances of the Mysteries of Cybele. The set-backs in the wall correspond to passageways providing access to the tiered seats.

Musée des Beaux Arts et Archéologie (**BY M¹**) ⊙ – The Fine Arts and Archaeology Museum is housed in a 19C covered market and comprises several collections: prehistoric and Gallo-Roman antiquities; 18C French earthenware (Moustiers, Lyon, Roanne, Marseille, Rouen, Nevers); paintings from the 17C and 18C European schools and the Lyon, Vienne and Dauphiné schools; works by the Vienne sculptor, J. Bernard (1866-1931).

Note the large bronze statue of Pacatianus, a Vienne dignitary from Roman times, the fragments found in the Rhône of a bronze frieze of dolphins, which was part of the decoration of a Roman bridge, and, in particular, the 3C Roman silverware (goblets, platter finely engraved with pastoral and hunting scenes), discovered by accident on the current site of Place C-Jouffray (**AZ**) in 1984.

Cours Romestang, then Boulevard de la République, lead to Place St-Pierre.

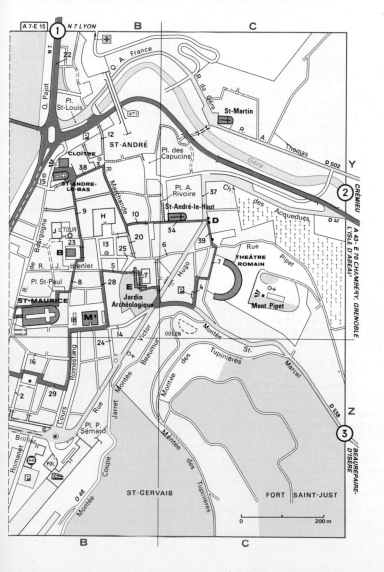

★Ancienne Église St-Pierre (**AZ**) ⊘ – The church of St-Pierre, now converted into a Lapidary Museum, is the oldest building of Christian Vienne, dating back to the 5C. The north, west and south walls are made of small neatly-cut quarry stone. Inside, notice the blind arcades on the lower part of the side walls; between the columns is a series of 5C and 6C niches. The church, mainly used as a funerary basilica, was the burial place of the bishops of Vienne. St-Pierre, built "outside the walls", was to suffer from the devastations of the Saracens in about 725, followed by those of the Carolingian princes in 882.

In the 12C the abbey of St-Pierre was at the height of its prosperity. It was at that time that the beautiful Romanesque bell tower, forming a porch at ground level, was built to a rectangular plan. The openings at the intermediate level are surmounted by trefoil arches, reminiscent of Velay art. It was at this time that the nave was divided into three by a number of large archways (restored in the 19C).

The **south door** (12C) used to lead to the abbey cloisters. Two small octagonal columns are topped by capitals symbolising Humility and Pride on the left and Charity on the right. The inscription on the tympanum frames a magnificent statue of St Peter which could be compared with the statues on the north porch of St-Maurice church, particularly with regard to the technique of the garments, with their long, almost concentric folds.

★Musée lapidaire – The Lapidary Museum began as the collection of **Pierre Schneyder** (1733-1814), a student of architecture and painting from Alsace. He had previously undertaken a Grand Tour of Rome and was so overcome by the beauty of the monuments in Vienne that he decided to stay here.

On the right and opposite the entrance are two Roman works: a monumental head of Juno and a beautiful marble statue, the "Tutela" or protective goddess of the town. The mosaics are rich and varied, illustrating themes from mythology (Orpheus charming the animals with his lyre–*undergoing restoration*) and sporting activities (athletes winning stadium games) or incorporating geometrical patterns (mosaic with canthari and fleurons).

In the apse, on the left, lies the beautiful marble sarcophagus of St Léonien, a 6C Vienne monk, with a symbolic decor of peacocks pecking grapes.

Note, in the chapel to the right of the apse, a crouching Venus, a collection of amphorae, busts of emperors and a marble low-relief depicting a sacrificial ceremony.

ADDITIONAL SIGHTS

Mont Pipet (**CY**) – *30min Rtn on foot from the bottom of Rue Pipet.*
On the top of the hill stands a chapel and a 19C statue of Notre-Dame de la Salette. The esplanade in front of the chapel offers a remarkable **view★** of the town and the magnificent bulk of the cathedral of St-Maurice. On the left, the remains of the odeum can be seen on the side of Mont St-Just; on the right, above the Gère gap, on Mont Salomon, are the ruins of the episcopal castle of La Bâtie and the new hospital buildings. The panorama encompasses some attractive bends in the Rhône.

Vienne Bridges (**ABY**) – Two bridges connect Vienne to the west bank of the Rhône. The old suspension bridge *(pont suspendu)* is now used as a footbridge; the modern bridge (1949) has a remarkable central arch with a span of 108m/354ft. A 15C humpbacked bridge spans the Gère.

Nearby, the **church of St-Martin** ⊘ (**CY**), decorated with frescoes by the Nabi painter Maurice Denis (1870-1943), has a very fine ancient carved wood crucifix.

Roman Road (**AZ**) – This fragment of paved road *(voie romaine)* was left uncovered when the public gardens were laid out. Note the tracks gouged out by the chariot wheels, the pavement along one side of the roadway and a military boundary-stone from the 4C.

Pyramid – *Leave on ④ on the map and turn right onto Boulevard F-Point.*
The monument (about 20m/65ft high) rests on a small square portico and used to adorn the central forecourt of the vast Vienne amphitheatre in the 4C.

During the Middle Ages it was thought to be the tomb of Pontius Pilate; according to legend, after leaving Jerusalem for Vienne, the Roman procurator, struck with remorse, threw himself into the Rhône. Pilat mountain range is said to be named after this event (there is a similar legend attached to Mount Pilate near Lucerne in Switzerland).

Notre-Dame de l'Île – *Access via Quai Riondet* (**AZ**).
The bell tower of this simple church (Our Lady of the Island), whose oldest parts date back to the 12C and 13C, is situated at the southern entrance to Vienne, next to the motorway.

ST-ROMAIN-EN-GAL AND STE-COLOMBE (AY) *about 2hr*

St-Romain-en-Gal and Ste-Colombe, on the west bank of the Rhône, are located in the Rhône administrative *département* while Vienne, opposite, is in the Isère *département*. In Ancient times, these three towns formed a single urban centre.

★**Gallo-Roman city of St-Romain-en-Gal** ⊙ – Excavations of the site since 1967 have unearthed an urban district including not only sumptuous villas but also businesses, workshops and thermae (hot baths). The remains found in the area of over 2ha/5 acres which has been excavated so far indicate occupation from the end of the 1C BC to the 3C AD, though the structure of the area does not correspond to the grid layout usually adopted by the Romans; three roads and two streets mark out five irregular plots, which have not been completely cleared. A portico runs along the side of **Road I**, from east to west. **Roads II** and **III**, which run approximately north-south, converge in the northern part of the site.

The roads are made of large smooth granite slabs above sewers designed to collect wastewater and discharge it into the Rhône.

Museum – *Near the entrance to the site.* It houses items excavated from the St-Romain-en-Gal site: ceramic vases and dishes; fragments of mosaics discovered in the wealthy villas; a stele dedicated to the Gallic god Sucellus. A scale model of the House of the Ocean Gods shows the importance of this Gallo-Roman villa.

Dwellings – At the entrance to the site is a vast residence, the **House of the Ocean Gods**, running north-south and forming a rectangle 110m/360ft long and 24m/79ft wide; its southern entrance is its only connection with the outside. The vestibule had a mosaic floor depicting ocean gods with bearded heads and long flowing hair, and marine motifs. Next is a small garden with a peristyle enclosing two pools – one U-shaped and the other rectangular. The large garden to the north, with its

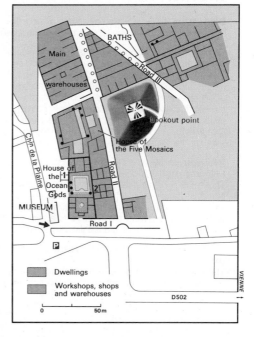

portico, occupying one third of the surface area, is slightly off-centre with regard to the other rooms. To the west can be seen a restored **hypocaust (1)** heating system *(see Introduction: Roman Architecture)*.

To the north of the House of the Ocean Gods is the **House of the Five Mosaics**, named after the different mosaic floors discovered mainly in the peristyle, the triclinium (dining room) and reception room.

Northeast of the site, on the other side of Road III, is another residential area with houses, and **baths** which follow a typically Roman arrangement: hypocaust, caldarium (hot room), tepidarium (warm room) and frigidarium (cold room).

Workshops, shops and warehouses – These are spread out irregularly over the site. Between the House of the Ocean Gods and Road III are several rooms, one of which (**2**) shows an ingenious device to preserve perishable foods: carefully arranged amphorae are fixed in the earth by their necks, thus creating an underfloor space.

Along Road II, to the northwest, stand **large warehouses** or "horrea", covering 3 000m²-32 300ft² (part of the area is covered by vegetable gardens). The eastern façade has a single entrance, large enough for carts to pass through. Around the central courtyard are compartments with a floor drained by a system of upturned amphorae *(see above)*.

The triangular block formed by Roads II and III is a craftsmen's district, bordered to the east and the west by porticoes. The rooms in the northern building contain a network of pipes; this area is followed, to the south, by a workshop consisting of nine rooms arranged around a central courtyard. The presence of basins in some of the rooms suggests that they were used by fullers or dyers. The base of the triangle, known as "the market", was occupied by workshops and shops.

The discovery of colouring products, at the corner of Roads I and II, indicates the existence of a small dyer's workshop.

Lookout point – This cleared area above the spoil from the digs gives a good overall **view** of the excavated part of the site.

Ste-Colombe (**AY**) – During Roman times this suburb was filled with luxurious residences decorated with works of art and immense mosaics. The most important discoveries were made in the Palais du Miroir (**AY**), vast thermae given this name in the 17C because one of the pools was thought to be an ornamental lake; its remains are visible at the boundary between Ste-Colombe and St-Romain-en-Gal.

Tour Philippe-de-Valois (**AY**) – The tower was built next to the Rhône by Philippe de Valois in 1343, after Ste-Colombe became part of the royal domain.

Église (**AY**) ⊘ – This ancient chapel contains a remarkable 14C **sculpture group**★ in white marble of St Anne instructing the Virgin Mary (left of the entrance).

EXCURSIONS

Boat trips (**AZ**) – Trips by *bateaux-mouches* are available in both directions between Vienne and Lyon during the tourist season.

Ternay – *Local map under Moyenne vallée du RHÔNE. 13km/8mi north. Leave Vienne on ① on the N 7 and turn left onto the D 150ᴱ.*
The 12C **church**, perched on the edge of a hillock overlooking the Rhône, is an interesting example of the Rhône Romanesque school. It belonged to a Cluniac priory and was formerly dedicated to St Mayol. The upper part of the west front, the south front and the apsidal chapels consist of alternate rows of brick and tufa. Inside, the most attractive part is the main apse, with its oven vault and blind arcade with pilasters carved with interesting capitals. South of the church can be seen the remains of the cloisters.

Beauvoir-de-Marc – *19km/12mi east. Leave Vienne on ② on the D 502 and, at La Détourbe, turn left onto the D 53ᴮ.*
The small 11C to 14C **church** with its painted, coffered ceiling consisting of 70 caissons stands on a hillside. A path leads to the top of the hillock – notice the layers of rounded pebbles in the subsoil along the slope. At the foot of the statue of the Virgin *(viewing table)* there is a **panorama**★ of the Viennois hills, dominated by the sombre mass of Mont Pilat to the west.

St-Mamert – *13km/8mi south. Leave Vienne on ④ on the N 7 south and turn left onto the D 131ᴬ.*
The **chapel of St-Mamert**, with its 11C belfry wall and 17C restored interior, is built on a terrace of pebbles which offers an extensive view of Pilat mountain range.

*The numbers ① – ② etc indicate the main routes into and out of town. They are the same on **Michelin maps** and on town plans in the guide, to make transfer from map to guide easier.*

VILLARS-LES-DOMBES

Population 3 415
Michelin map 88 fold 8 or 244 fold 15 – Local map under La DOMBES

Villars-les-Dombes was built on the east bank of the River Chalaronne, at the heart of the Dombes region.

Church ⊘ – This Gothic building with its panelled nave is decorated in the Flamboyant style. At the back of the apse *(right)* note the interesting 18C **Virgin with Child**★.

★**Parc Ornithologique** ⊘ – *1km/0.6mi south of Villars on the N 83.*
This bird sanctuary, located along one of the main migration routes in Europe, has a surface area of 23ha/57 acres, 10ha/25 acres of which are occupied by ponds. Over 2 000 birds from 400 different species live in the park, from the African ostrich to the South American fly-bird to the Australian penguin. The roof of the large heron's aviary also provides a home for wild storks which come here to nest each year. A small train takes visitors around the enclosures and the largest pond which is a refuge for thousands of ducks and coots during the hunting season.

At the entrance, the "Birds' House" provides a warm, humid atmosphere for a wonderful selection of brightly coloured exotic birds — tangaras from South America, gouras from New Guinea, toucans etc. The hangar next door presents a series of heavy vehicles from the M. Berliet Foundation, which retrace the technical development of the civil and military lorry from 1913 to 1920. The view from the terrace encompasses the park and the surrounding country-side.

Another attraction is the rock hopper or crested penguin from Australasia and Antarctica. In the same building, a Dombes pond has been reconstructed in cross-section, showing the local aquatic fauna. A tour around the enclosures will reveal vultures, pink flamingoes, ibises, pelicans, nandus, emus and ostriches in a semi-natural habitat. Bird cages contain small waders, diurnal and nocturnal birds of prey, pheasants and doves. Cranes, peacocks etc are left free to wander about the meadows.

A giant aviary provides a breeding ground for the larger birds from the Dombes area: common herons, night herons and tufted herons. White storks have built their nest on one of the metal posts.

Purple heron at the bird sanctuary

VILLEFRANCHE-SUR-SAÔNE

Population 55 249
Michelin map 88 fold 7 or 244 folds 2, 3
Local maps under BEAUJOLAIS and La DOMBES
Plan of conurbation in the Michelin Red Guide France

This busy industrial and commercial city is the capital of the **Beaujolais** region. It was founded in 1140 by the lords of Beaujeu, as part of the Anse fortress belonging to the Archbishops of Lyon, to defend the toll-house of Limans. The settlement sprang up quickly, and in 1260 Guichard IV de Beaujeu granted the town a charter, which earned it the name of "Villefranche" or "free town".

"La Vague"

"La Vague" – Every year, on the last Sunday in January, local conscripts celebrate the "**Fête des Conscrits**". Those eligible to take part are men between the ages of 20 and 80. Dress code for the occasion is a black suit and top hat, decorated with a coloured ribbon (different colour for each decade: 20s, 30s etc.). At 11am the participants form up into a procession, in which they link arms and, clutching colourful bouquets of mimosa and carnations, make their way along the Rue Nationale close on each others' heels, in what is known as the "friendship wave" *(La Vague de l'Amitié)*.

Modern Villefranche – In addition to its historical role as a wine-trading centre, Villefranche now earns its living from the manufacture of sports and work wear (Joannès Sabot founded an overalls factory here in 1887), shirts and hosiery. The metallurgy, mechanical and food-processing industries are also represented here.

SIGHTS

Old houses ⊘ – Most of the town's oldest houses built between the 15C and 18C are to be found along the **Rue Nationale** (**BYZ**). They have relatively narrow façades, because of a tax imposed on the width of house façades in 1260, to make up for the exemption from taxes and the other privileges which had been granted to the town in its charter.

VILLEFRANCHE-SUR-SAÔNE

Nationale (R.) ...... **BYZ**

Belleville (R. de) ..... **BY** 5	République (R. de la) . **AZ** 41	
Carnot (Pl.) .... **BZ** 9	Salengro (Bd Roger) . **AY** 46	
Faucon (R. du) .... **BY** 19	Savigny (R. J. M.) .... **AZ** 47	
Fayettes (R. des) ..... **BZ** 20	Sous-Préfecture (Pl.) . **AZ** 49	
Grange-Blazet (R.) ... **BZ** 23	Sous-Préfecture (R.).. **AZ** 50	
Marais (Pl. des) ...... **BZ** 32	Stalingrad (R. de) .... **BZ** 52	

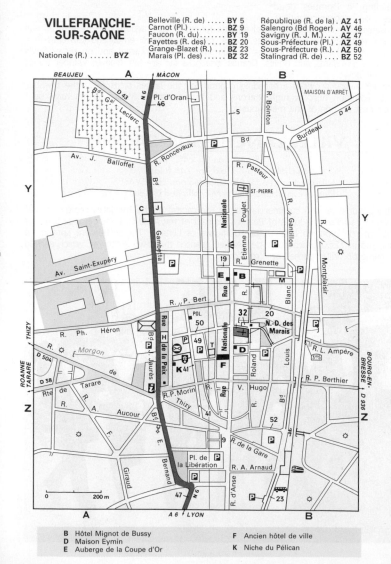

B	Hôtel Mignot de Bussy	
D	Maison Eymin	
E	Auberge de la Coupe d'Or	
F	Ancien hôtel de ville	
K	Niche du Pélican	

Odd-numbered side of the road – Note nos 375 (vaulted passageway), 401 (16C openwork spiral staircase in the courtyard), no 17 Rue Grenette (**BY**) (turret staircase with skylights) and 507 (well surmounted by a shell-shaped canopy in the courtyard). No 523, the **Hôtel de Mignot de Bussy** (**BY B**) is a lovely Renaissance building with a spiral staircase, mullion windows and shell-shaped niche containing an elegant statue. Behind the elegant 1760 façade of no 561, a vaulted passageway with sculpted supports leads to a 16C courtyard surrounded by pink-walled buildings. The **Maison Eymin** (**BZ D**) at no 761 has an 18C façade with four levels of arches in the courtyard, hammer-wrought coats-of-arms (damaged) and an elegant turret housing a spiral staircase. No 793, once the residence of the Roland de la Platière family, is indicated by a medallion and a commemorative plaque and features a monumental staircase with a beautiful wrought-iron bannister.

Even-numbered side of the road – From no 400, there is a good view of the polygonal tower and sculpted stone balustrade of the Italian Renaissance house at no 407 opposite. A 15C half-timbered house stands on the corner of Rue du Faucon (**BY**) (**19**) and the Rue Nationale (no 476). At no 486, at the back of the alley on the right, a Renaissance bas-relief depicts two cherubs with chubby cheeks holding coats-of-arms with the date 1537.

The **Auberge de la Coupe d'Or** (**BY E**) at no 528 was the oldest inn in Villefranche (late 14C) before it was transformed in the 17C. On the corner of Rue Paul-Bert, the façade on the right (no 596) with crocket gables dates from the late 15C, and that on the left with moulded mullioned windows and medallions is Renaissance. Note the Gothic corner niche at no 706. A passage at no 810 leads to a restored courtyard (well, arcade, turret).

The old **town hall** at no 816 (**BZ F**) was completed in 1660. The façade is built of beautiful warm golden Jarnioux stone and has a solid oak door decorated with cast-iron nails. The house at no 834 was built in the late 15C and has a charming courtyard with a staircase turret. The coat-of-arms is that of Pierre II de Bourbon and Anne de Beaujeu.

Rue de la Paix (**AZ**) – The façade of the building to the south of the Post Office features a "pelican niche" (**AZ K**), a Gothic sculpture decorated with finials and pinnacles. Next to it, set slightly further back, is a pretty Renaissance fountain.

Place des Marais (**BZ 32**) – This pretty square to the northeast of the church contains a fountain and is enclosed by modern houses with arcades, painted in shades of pink and ochre. On the corner with Rue Nationale, a ceramic plaque depicts Pierre de Bourbon and Anne de Beaujeu in the same pose as that on the famous triptych by the Master of Moulins.

Notre-Dame-des-Marais (**BZ**) ⊙ – In the 13C a chapel was built in honour of a statue of the Virgin Mary which had been found in a nearby marsh *(marais)*; all that now remains of it is the small Romanesque tower above the chancel. The magnificent Late Gothic (16C) façade of the church was donated by Pierre de Bourbon and Anne de Beaujeu.

Inside, the nave is surprisingly high and has pretty vaulting decorated with sculpture and pendant keystones. The organ was made by J. Callinet in 1835. Note the gargoyles on the north façade; one of them represents lust.

The numbering of houses in Villefranche is based on a metric system, calculating the distance of each house from the beginning of the street. Street numbers run from the Rue Nationale east and west, and south from the north of town.

Corniche du VIVARAIS CÉVENOL★★

Michelin map 80 folds 7, 8 or 240 folds 3, 7

This scenic crest road cuts a breathtaking course through the mountains of the Vivarais Cévenol, giving spectacular views of the surrounding countryside as it passes from one mountain ridge to the next. The beautiful natural scenery through which it travels modulates gradually during the trip, from the arid ridges running from the River Drobie up to the Tanargue massif, to the softer hills of Lower Ardèche.

FROM LA BASTIDE-PUYLAURENT TO JOYEUSE

49km/30mi – allow 2hr

La Bastide-Puylaurent – This village was founded in the 19C during construction of the railway line from Paris to Nîmes. It is a pleasant place to spend some time in summer; its charms include the clear fresh air of its site in the upper Allier valley and the soothing beauty of the surrounding hillsides covered in woodland and meadows.

Leave La Bastide east on the D 906, then turn left onto the D 4.

Corniche du Vivarais Cévenol

Meyssonnier/CAMPAGNE CAMPAGNE

Trappe de Notre-Dame-des-Neiges – This Cistercian abbey, founded in 1850, is tucked miles from anywhere amidst pine trees and beech woods, surrounded by a ring of mountains which protect it from the winds which sweep across the mountain plateaux of the Vivarais. The present buildings were built in the wake of a fire which devastated the original abbey on its hilltop site in 1912.

In 1878, on his *Travels with a Donkey* through the Cévennes, Scottish writer **Robert Louis Stevenson** spent a couple of days at the abbey, during which – as a Protestant – he had to endure the zealous efforts of two monks determined to convert him and save his soul by engaging him in lengthy religious debate *(see also Le MONASTIER-SUR-GAZEILLE)*.

Other famous inmates of the abbey include French explorer-and-soldier-turned-monk **Charles de Foucauld** (1858-1916), who did his novitiate here in the first half of 1890.

As the road drops down to St-Laurent-les-Bains, a left bend gives a stunning **view★** of the mouth of Borne gap.

St-Laurent-les-Bains – Tucked in the hollow of a narrow valley, this small spa town specialises in the treatment of various forms of rheumatism. The main street, where there is a hot spring (53°C/127°F), gives a good view of a ridge crowned by the ruins of an old tower.

The road continues downhill and crosses the Borne, before climbing steeply once more and passing through a beautiful pine forest. This eventually gives way to a rather bleak landscape of tall rocky crests.

Note, to the right, a tiny hamlet called **Petit Paris** perched in solitary splendour above granite boulders.

On a ledge shortly before Peyre, there is another good view to the right, this time of the pretty village of **Thines**★★ in its charming setting on a rocky outcrop overlooking a ravine *(see Les VANS)*.

Carry on along the D 4 through Peyre.

Beyond Peyre, the appearance of vines in the surrounding landscape heralds that of other Mediterranean plant species.

Follow the D 4 through Planzolles and Lablachère to Joyeuse.

The brightness of the limestone lowlands with their white rocks, vineyards and fragrant Mediterranean scrub *(garrigue)* is a world away from the rugged schist ridges encountered at the start of the trip.

Joyeuse – The town, with a number of interesting old houses, spreads out on terraces opposite the Tanargue massif.

VIVIERS ★

Population 3 407
Michelin map 80 fold 10 or 246 fold 22
Local map under Moyenne Vallée du RHÔNE

It was this episcopal town, created in the 5C, which gave its name to the province of Vivarais. Its location, boxed in between Jouanade hill and the rocky peak on which the upper town is built, meant that it remained almost untouched by the Industrial Revolution. Only the quarries, originally opened in about 1750 by the Pavin brothers in the hamlet of Lafarge north of the town to produce cement, are witness to the conversion of a small Ardèche business into a firm of international rank.

The ecclesiastical town, built at the foot of the cathedral, commands a view of the Rhône as it enters Donzère gorge. The contrast between the cliffs on either side of the river, the isolated peaks in the middle of the gap and the stately flowing river upstream of Châteauneuf power plant form a picturesque sight.

The bishops of Viviers – After Alba-la-Romaine, the Roman capital of the Helvia people, fell into ruins, Bishop Ausonne went to live in Vivarium, at the confluence of the Escoutay and the Rhône where the city had its port, at the foot of a rock on which a Roman *castrum* was established. The first cathedral was built on the rock. In the 5C the upper town was fortified. In 1119 Pope Calixtus III inaugurated a new Romanesque cathedral. A college of canons settled into Château-Vieux, which, enclosed by still-visible ramparts, became an ecclesiastical quarter.

Numerous donations and skilful politics gradually turned the Viviers bishops into the overlords of an immense domain east of the Rhône – the Vivarais. They fiercely defended its independence against the covetousness of the counts of Toulouse, sharing ownership with them of the Largentière mines and minting their own coins. In 1248 St Louis, leaving for the 7th crusade, was their guest at Château-Vieux.

At the end of the 13C the French monarchy wanted to expand its territory into the Rhône valley. The Bishop of Viviers finally recognised the suzerainty of the King of France in 1308; a large part of the Vivarais became "Crown" land, while the west bank of the Rhône remained "Empire" land, under the distant control of the Holy Roman Emperor.

At the foot of the rock, inside a second set of ramparts, a medieval city began to develop. All that remains of the defence towers and the main doors is a clock tower, the **Tour de l'Horloge** (**A**), which was extensively refurbished in the 19C. In 1498 Claude de Tournon, once the chaplain of Anne of Brittany, became Bishop of Viviers; he had the Romanesque cathedral destroyed and a Flamboyant Gothic chancel built.

Noël Albert, a nouveau-riche entrepreneur who had made his fortune in the salt trade and tax collection, had the Renaissance façade of the Maison des Chevaliers built. After becoming head of the Protestants, he captured the ecclesiastical city. As a result, the cathedral was partly ruined and the cloisters and canon's buildings destroyed. Albert was arrested and beheaded, but the bishop had already fled Viviers and did not return until 1731. That year, François Reynaud de Villeneuve began construction of the current bishop's palace according to the drawings of the Avignon architect J-B Franque.

On Boxing Day (26 December) Viviers, like all the towns in the south of France in the Middle Ages, organised a "Fête des Fous", or "Madmen's Festival", a highly irreverent parody of ecclesiastical customs, with actors playing members of the clergy and a "mad bishop" who "governed" the city for three days.

The general merry-making and drinking bouts led to such excesses that the bishops eventually banned the festivities, which were later resumed with a lesser degree of licentiousness until finally they came to an end in the 18C.

★OLD TOWN ⏱ 1hr

The ecclesiastical town is distinct from the lower town, built to the west on the less steep slope of the rock. They communicated via two gates, **Porte de la Gâche** (**B**) to the west and **Porte de l'Abri** (**B**) to the south. The houses in the lower town, in a tight cluster, are roofed with Roman tiles; sometimes the walls are made of calcareous quarry stone mixed with basalt. They generally consist of two upper storeys and a ground floor housing a high cellar or a shop. Most of them have kept their medieval appearance despite the many alterations which have been carried out over the centuries.

The houses in the ecclesiastical town hide their gardens and courtyards behind bare walls with semicircular openings, sometimes surmounted by a coat of arms.

*Park on Place de la Roubine (**AB**). Follow Rue J-B-Serre and Grande Rue as far as Place de la République.*

From the eastern corner of the square there is a view of the ruins of Châteauvieux tower.

Maison des Chevaliers (**A**) – The "Knights' House", also called the house of Noël Albert *(see above)*, was built in 1546. On the beautiful Renaissance façade observe the four high-relief figures on the lower part, separated by corbels decorated with acanthus leaf designs, and coats-of-arms surmounted by a helmet. The ornate window-frames on the 1st floor consist of columns and fluted pilasters with Ionic capitals; rams' heads and garlands of leaves have been carved on the lintels, between the modillions. Above are two bas-reliefs: on the left, a cavalcade of knights on horseback and on the right, a jousting tournament.

Over to the right, across Rue de la République, an archway with small Gothic openings is decorated with several carved heads.

Grande-Rue (**AB**) – This street is lined with meticulously dressed façades, some of which have ornate portals surmounted by wrought-iron balconies such as **Hôtel de Tourville** and **Hôtel de Beaulieu** (18C). Sometimes the houses are enhanced by picturesque details, such as the beautiful Romanesque twinned windows coupled together by a classical column (**F**).

Grande Rue leads to a series of little cross-streets, narrow, stepped and often spanned by arches.

Beyond the site of the former Porte Latrau lies a square planted with plane trees.

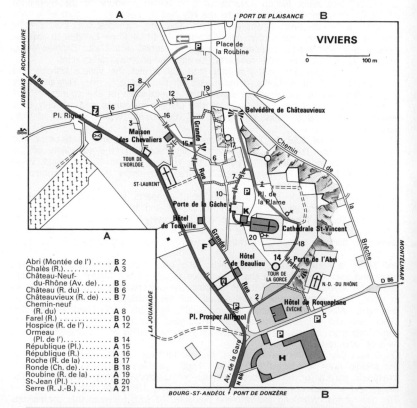

F Demeure a fenêtres romanes géminées   H Hôtel de ville   K Tour

Place Prosper Allignol (**B**) – The square is flanked by two buildings erected between 1732 and 1738 by Franque. Their classical symmetry and neat stonework makes them beautiful examples of 18C Viviers architecture: the former bishop's palace, preceded by a garden, houses the **hôtel de ville** (**H**), while the **Hôtel de Roqueplane** is the seat of the current Catholic diocese.

Walk up the steep Montée de l'Abri, which passes under Porte de l'Abri and leads to Place de l'Ormeau.

The street offers a fine view over the chapel of Notre-Dame du Rhône, rebuilt by Franque, and the mouth of Donzère gorge.

Place de l'Ormeau (**B 14**) – The square, lined with old canons' houses (17C) owes its name to a centuries-old elm tree *(ormeau)* which perished in 1976; a new tree has been planted.

From the square, the rich Flamboyant decoration of the cathedral's east end can be admired.

Take the parapet walk (Chemin de Ronde) around the cathedral; from Place de la Plaine, a passageway north leads to an enormous terrace.

Belvédère de Châteauvieux (**B**) – This belvedere, built on a natural acropolis at one time washed by the Rhône during floods, stands 40m/131ft above Place de la Roubine. The **view** from west to east embraces the old roofs of the city, the clock tower, the enormous cutting formed by the Lafarge quarries, the cooling towers of Cruas power station and the factory at Châteauneuf.

In fine weather, the view extends *(northeast)* to Trois-Becs and Chaudière pass, the first foothills of the Vercors massif.

The ruins of a medieval tower can be seen in the southwest corner of the terrace.

Turn around and go downhill via Rue de Châteauvieux (on the right) to Porte de la Gâche.

With its smooth cobblestones, covered passageways and arches, Rue de Châteauvieux has a picturesque air of the Middle Ages.

Climb the steps to the tower.

Tower (**B K**) – In the 12C this tower formed the entrance to the upper town. Only the square part of the building existed at the time, with a Romanesque chapel dedicated to St Michael on the first floor. The octagonal 14C top floor is covered with a paved platform surmounted by a watch-turret: the *Bramadière*, from which the *brameur* would sound the alarm in case of danger.

The tower, since turned into the cathedral belfry, is connected to it by a quadrangular portico with Gothic openings.

Cathédrale St Vincent (**B**) – The only remains of the 12C Romanesque building are the porch, the west front and the lower part of the nave walls.

The chancel, built at the end of the 15C by Bishop Claude de Tournon, is remarkable for its Flamboyant ribbed **vaulting**★ and the fenestration of its stained-glass windows. The nave (rebuilt in the 18C) has a meticulously dressed flat stone vault by Franque. Gobelins tapestries, after drawings by Jouvenet and Restout, decorate the nave and chancel, just above the walnut choir stalls. From left to right: the Miracle of the Loaves and Fishes, the Resurrection of Lazarus, the Scourging of the Temple, the Baptism of Christ and the Washing of the Feet.

On the left of the organ (19C) is an Annunciation attributed to Mignard.

ADDITIONAL SIGHTS

★**Viewing point** – *15min Rtn on foot. Take the path which begins opposite the bishop's palace (Évêché), west of the RN 86.*

The hill, called the "Jouanade", offers views of the old houses of Viviers clustered around the cathedral and bell tower.

From the top, on which a statue of the Virgin Mary was built in 1862, there is an extensive **panorama** over the town, then from left to right, of the Lafarge quarries, Cruas power plant, the Châteauneuf factory and Donzère gorge.

Harbour – A magnificent avenue of plane trees leads from Place de la Roubine to the little sailing harbour *(port de plaisance)* at the confluence of the Rhône and the Escoutay.

Respect the life of the countryside
Drive carefully on country roads
Protect wildlife, plants and trees

VOLVIC

Population 3 930
Michelin map 73 north of fold 14 or 239 north of fold 19

Volvic is built on the edge of the solidified lava flow from Nugère volcano. The village is not only famous for the extremely pure water of its spring, filtered through thick layers of volcanic rock and now exported throughout the world, but also for the quarrying and processing of its lava.

Volvic lava – Andesite, extracted from open quarries, is both solid and light; it has been used as building stone since the 13C and explains why many buildings in the Auvergne are black. Volvic cemetery is full of extraordinary monuments cut from this stone.

The hardness of the lava and the fact that it can be enamelled at high temperatures have made it popular for more than a century for the manufacture of signs and plaques which have to stand up to the weather: clock faces, street

Quarryman, Volvic

signs, level gauges etc. As a result of its exceptional qualities, this rock was chosen by Michelin's road sign department to make enamelled lava corner-posts, sign-posts, wall plaques etc from 1920 to 1970. Andesite is also used to make apparatus used in the chemical industry, because of its excellent resistance to acids.

SIGHTS

Church – This was part of the old priory of Mozat; its nave and façade were rebuilt during the last century. The vast 12C chancel is surrounded by an ambulatory opening onto three radiating chapels; a beautiful wrought-iron grille, from the Romanesque period, closes the axial chapel. There are interesting historiated capitals. At the entrance to the chancel, on the left, note the 14C Virgin with a Bird.

Maison de la Pierre ⊘ – A former underground quarry has been used for the "House of Stone", a centre focusing on lava and lava quarrying. Visitors travel to the heart of a **lava flow★** from Puy de la Nugère, while a soundtrack reproduces the noises during different phases of a volcanic eruption.

The result of quarrying can be seen in the uneven ceiling, supported by three enormous piers cut directly from the lava, one of which is in the form of a crescent moon. An audio-visual presentation retracing the origins of volcanism in the Auvergne, quarry work and the use of Volvic stone complete the visit.

Musée municipal Marcel Sahut ⊘ – The first rooms in this museum contain Far Eastern and African art, though the majority of the exhibitions concentrate on 19C and 20C drawings, engravings and paintings. There are many works by Sahut, who was a native of this region, including charcoal sketches, watercolours and paintings *(View of Nantes, The Tumbler)*.

Drawings★ by Daumier and Grévin show the art of the caricaturist under the Second Empire.

The last room has an unusual **collection of half-coconut shells★** which are decorated with scenes engraved by prisoners in the French penal colonies of Cayenne and New Caledonia in the 18C and 19C.

Volvic Springs ⊘ – A tour around the bottling installations is preceded by a presentation, in the reception chalet, on the collection of spring water and the bottling of mineral water and fruit drinks. The visit ends in a sampling session.

Statue of Notre-Dame-de-la-Garde – *Access via Rue de la Bannière and Rue du Calvaire, then park near the water tower.* A path *(15min Rtn on foot)* leads to the monumental statue of the Virgin, from which there is a beautiful panorama.

EXCURSION

★Château de Tournoël – *1.5km/1mi north. See Château de TOURNOËL.*

*Europe on a single sheet : **Michelin** map no 970.*

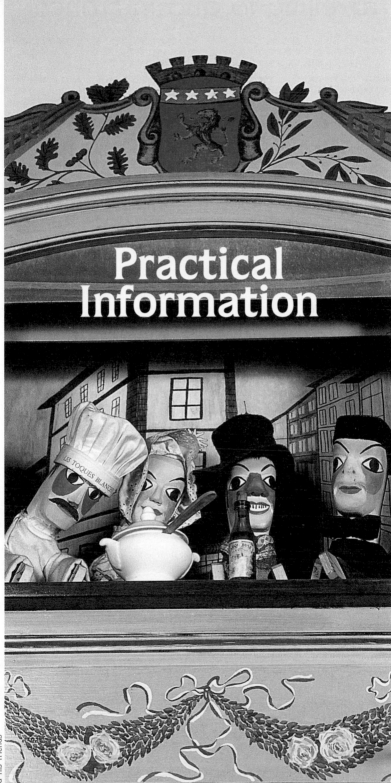

Practical Information

Ch. Delpal/EXPLORER

Travelling to and in France

Passport – Visitors entering France must be in possession of a valid national passport. Citizens of any of the European Union countries need only a national identity card. In case of loss or theft report to the embassy or consulate and the local police.

Visa – No **entry visa** is required for US and Canadian citizens whose stay in France does not exceed 3 months. Australian and New Zealand citizens should apply for a visa at the nearest French consulate. Citizens of other countries should check visa requirements with the French consulate or a travel agent.
US citizens should obtain the booklet *Your Trip Abroad* (US$1.25) which provides useful information on visa requirements, customs regulations, medical care etc for international travellers. Contact the Superintendent of Documents, PO Box 371954, Pittsburgh, PA 15250-7954, ☎ (202) 512-3238.

Customs – Apply to the Customs Office (UK) for a leaflet entitled *A Guide for Travellers* on customs regulations and the full range of duty-free allowances. The US Customs Service, PO Box 7407, Washington DC 20044, ☎ (202) 927-5580 offers a publication *Know Before You Go* for US citizens.
There are no customs formalities for holidaymakers bringing caravans into France for a stay of less than 6 months. No customs document is necessary for pleasure boats and outboard motors for a stay of less than 6 months, but the registration certificate should be kept on board.

French Government Tourist Offices – For information, brochures, maps and assistance in planning a trip to France, travellers should contact the official tourist office in their own country:

Australia – New Zealand
BNP Building, 12 Castlereagh Street, Sydney, New South Wales 2000.
☎ (61) 2-231-5244; Fax (61) 2-221-8682

Canada
30 St Patrick's Street, Suite 700, Toronto, ONT M5T 3A3.
☎ (416) 593-4723
1981 Av McGill College, Suite 490, Montreal, PQ H3A 2W9.
☎ (514) 288-4264; Fax (514) 845-4868

Eire
35 Lower Abbey Street, Dublin 1.
☎ (1) 703-4046; Fax (1) 874-7324

United Kingdom
178 Piccadilly, London W1.
☎ (0891) 244-123; Fax (0171) 493-6594

United States
France On-Call Hotline: 900-990-0040 (US$0.95/min)
for information on hotels, restaurants and transportation.
East Coast: 444 Madison Avenue, New York, NY 10022.
☎ (212) 838-7800; Fax (212) 838-7855
Midwest: 676 North Michigan Avenue, Suite 3360, Chicago, IL 60611-2819.
☎ (312) 751-7800; Fax (312) 337-6339
West Coast: 9454 Wilshire Boulevard, Suite 715, Beverly Hills, CA 90212-2967
☎ (310) 271-2693; Fax (310) 276-2835

MICHELIN GUIDES

The Red Guides (hotels and restaurants)

Benelux – Deutschland – España Portugal – Europe – France – Great Britain and Ireland – Italia – Switzerland

The Green Guides (fine art, historical monuments, scenic routes)

Austria – Belgium and Luxembourg – Brussels – California – Canada – Chicago – England: the West Country – Europe – Florida – France – Germany – Great Britain – Greece – Ireland – Italy – London – Mexico – Netherlands – New England – New York City – Portugal – Quebec – Rome – San Francisco – Scandinavia-Finland – Scotland – Spain – Switzerland – Thailand – Tuscany – Venice – Wales – Washington DC

...and the collection of regional guides for France.

Re-enactment of the first-ever flight in a hot-air balloon

Travelling by air – The various national and other independent airlines operate services to **Paris** (Charles-de-Gaulle-Roissy airport 27km/14mi north, and Orly airport 16km/10mi south) and **Lyon-Satolas**. There are also package tour flights with a rail or coach link-up as well as fly-drive schemes. Information, brochures and timetables are available from the airlines and from travel agents.

The domestic network operates frequent services: there are regular flights with Air Inter (☎ 01 45 46 90 00, Fax 01 43 22 87 23), Air Littoral (☎ 01 40 64 76 76) and TAT European Airlines (☎ 01 42 61 82 10).

Transfer buses link up with town terminals and railway stations.

By sea – There are numerous **cross-Channel services** (passenger and car ferries, hovercraft, SeaCat, Le Shuttle through the Channel tunnel) from the United Kingdom and Eire to the northern coast of France; a service from Portsmouth to Pauillac on the Gironde may also be available. For details contact travel agencies or:

    P&O European Ferries, Channel House, Channel View Road, Dover CT17 9TJ; ☎ (01304) 203-388

    Stena Sealink, Charter House, Park Street, Ashford, Kent TN24 8EX; ☎ (01233) 647-047

    Hoverspeed, International Hoverport, Marine Parade, Dover, Kent CT17 9TG; ☎ (01304) 240-241

    Brittany Ferries, Millbay Docks, Plymouth, Devon PL1 3EW; ☎ (0990) 360-360

    Sally Line, Argyle Centre, York Street, Ramsgate, Kent CT11 9AS; ☎ (0800) 636-465

    Irish Ferries, 50 West Norland Street, Dublin 2; ☎ (353) 1-6-610-511

    Le Shuttle-Eurotunnel, ☎ (0990) 353-535

To choose the most suitable route between one of the ports along the north coast of France and the regions of the Auvergne and Rhône Valley, use Michelin Motoring Atlas France, Michelin map 911 (which gives travel times and mileages) or Michelin maps from the 1:200 000 series (with the yellow cover).

By rail – British Rail and French Railways (SNCF) operate a daily service via the Channel Tunnel on **Eurostar** in a little over 3hr between London Waterloo (☎ 0345 881 881) and Paris Gare du Nord.

Fast inter-city service from Paris to **Lyon** (2hr 40min by TGV) and **Clermont-Ferrand** (3hr 20min). There are rail passes offering unlimited travel and group travel tickets offering savings for parties. Eurailpass, Flexipass and Saverpass are options available in the US for travel in Europe and must be purchased in the USA from Rail Europe Inc. ☎ (1 800) 438-7245. In the UK for information and bookings contact French Railways, 179, Piccadilly, London W1V 0BA, ☎ (0891) 515 477, or main British Rail travel centres and travel agencies.

Chemin de fer touristique de montagne

Vivarais steam railway

The French railways SNCF operates a telephone information, reservation and prepayment service in English from 7am to 10pm (French time). In France call ☎ 08 36 35 35 39 (when calling from outside France, drop the initial 0).

A good investment is the Thomas Cook European Rail timetable, which gives train schedules throughout France and Europe as well as useful information on rail travel.

Tickets bought in France must be validated *(composter)* by using the orange automatic date-stamping machines at the platform entrance. Baggage trolleys (10F coin required–refundable) are available at mainline stations.

By coach – Regular coach services are operated from London to Paris and to large provincial towns:

    Eurolines (London), 52 Grosvenor Gardens, Victoria, London SW1 0AU; ☎ (0171) 730-8235

    Eurolines (Paris), 28, avenue du Général-de-Gaulle, 93541 Bagnolet; ☎ 01 49 72 51 51

MOTORING IN FRANCE

Documents – Nationals of EU countries require a valid national **driving licence**; nationals of non-EU countries require an **international driving licence** (obtainable in the US from the American Automobile Association; US$10 for members, US$22 for non-members).
For the vehicle it is necessary to have the **registration papers** (log-book) and a **nationality plate** of the approved size.

Insurance – Insurance cover is compulsory and, although an International Insurance Certificate (Green Card) is no longer a legal requirement in France, it is the most effective proof of insurance cover and is internationally recognised by the police and other authorities.
Certain UK motoring organisations (AA, RAC) run accident insurance and breakdown service schemes for members. Europ-Assistance – 252 High Street, Croydon CR0 1NF, ☎ (0181) 680 1234 – has special policies for motorists. Members of the American Automobile Association should obtain the free brochure *Offices to Serve You Abroad.* Affiliated organisation for France: Automobile Club National, 5, rue Auber, 75009 Paris; ☎ 01 44 51 53 99.

Highway code – The minimum driving age is 18 years old. Traffic drives on the right. It is compulsory for front-seat and back-seat passengers to wear **seat belts** where they are fitted. Children under the age of ten should be on the back seat.
Full or dipped headlights (which should be correctly adjusted) must be switched on in poor visibility and at night; sidelights only should be used when the vehicle is stationary.
In the case of a **breakdown** a red warning triangle or hazard warning lights are obligatory. Drivers should watch out for unfamiliar road signs and take great care on the road. In built-up areas **priority** must be ceded to vehicles joining the road **from the right**; however, traffic on main roads outside built-up areas (indicated by yellow diamond signs) and on roundabouts has priority. Vehicles must stop when the lights turn red at road junctions and may filter to the right only where indicated by an amber arrow.
The regulations on **drinking-and-driving** and **speeding** are strictly enforced – usually by an on-the-spot fine and/or confiscation of the vehicle.

Speed limits – Although liable to modification these are as follows :
    – toll motorways *(péage)* 130kph/80mph (110kph/68mph when raining);
    – dual carriage roads and motorways without tolls 110kph/68mph (100kph/62mph when raining);
    – other roads 90kph/56mph (80kph/50mph when raining) and in towns 50kph/31mph;
    – outside lane on motorways during daylight, on level ground and with good visibility – minimum speed limit of 80kph/50mph.

Parking regulations – In town there are restricted and paying **parking zones** (blue and grey zones); tickets must be obtained from the ticket machines (*horodateurs* – small change necessary) and displayed (inside windscreen on driver's side); failure to display may result in a heavy fine (and, in extreme cases, removal of the offending vehicle!).

In some towns, there are "blue" parking zones marked by a blue line on the pavement or a blue signpost with a P and a small square underneath – in this case, you should display a cardboard parking disc which can be adjusted to display your time of arrival and which allows you to stay for 1hr 30min (2hr 30min over lunchtime). You can buy these in supermarkets or petrol stations (ask for a *disque de stationnement*).

Route planning – The road network is excellent and includes many motorways, mostly toll-roads (*autoroutes à péage*). Tolls can prove quite expensive for those driving all the way south, but it is possible to pay them by credit card (Visa, Mastercard) as well as in cash. French roads are very busy during the holiday period (particularly at weekends in July and August), and to avoid traffic congestion it is advisable to follow the recommended secondary routes (*Bison Futé – itinéraires bis*: with green signposts). During summer months there are many events and facilities (clowns, swimming, archery, classical concerts, mountain biking, sight and reflex testing etc) laid on – sometimes free of charge – at motorway service stations and rest areas *(aires)* to encourage long-distance drivers to rest. Look out for the blue signposts showing a javelin thrower which indicate these "sport stops".

Car rental – There are car rental agencies at airports, air terminals, railway stations and in all large towns throughout France. European cars usually have manual transmission but automatic cars are available on demand (advance reservation recommended). It is relatively expensive to hire a car in France, so it is worth considering booking a vehicle from home before leaving or taking advantage of fly-drive schemes operated by major airlines.
Central reservation in France:
Avis: 01 46 10 60 60   Europcar: 01 30 43 82 82
Budget: 01 46 86 65 65   Hertz: 01 47 88 51 51
Eurodollar: 01 49 58 44 44

Petrol – In France you will find four different types of petrol (gas):
super leaded *(super)*   super unleaded 98 *(sans plomb 98)*
diesel *(diesel/gazole)*   super unleaded 95 *(sans plomb 95)*

Accommodation

Places to stay – The **Places to stay map** indicates recommended places for overnight stops and can be used in conjunction with the current **Michelin Red Guide France**, which lists a selection of hotels and restaurants.

Loisirs Accueil is an officially-backed booking service which has offices in most French *départements*. For information contact Réservation Loisirs Accueil, 280, boulevard St-Germain, 75007 Paris; ☎ 01 44 11 10 44.

The **Accueil de France** tourist offices, which are open all year, make hotel bookings for a small fee for personal callers only. The head office is in Paris (127, avenue des Champs Elysées; ☎ 01 49 52 53 54 for information only) and there are offices in many large towns and resorts.

The brochure *Logis et Auberges de France* is available from the French Government Tourist Office.

Rural accommodation –
Contact the **Maison des Gîtes de France**, 59, rue St-Lazare, 75009 Paris; ☎ 01 49 70 75 75, Fax 01 42 81 28 53, or 178 Piccadilly, London W1V 0AL; ☎ (0891) 244-123, for a list of addresses of self-catering accommodation, usually in a local style cottage or apartment where you will be able to make yourself at home. Alternatively, contact the **Chambre d'agriculture d'Auvergne "Auvergne verte"** (BP 455, 63000 Clermont Ferrand Cedex 1; ☎ 04 73 43 44 45) or the **Délégation Rhône-Alpes** (1, rue Général-Plessier, 69002 Lyon; ☎ 04 72 77 17 55) for local information. Useful publications on farm accommodation (bed-and-breakfasts, camping etc) include *Bienvenue à la ferme* (published by Éditions Solar) and *Vacances et weekends à la ferme* (Éditions Balland).

Traditional Lyonnais fare

The association Stations Vertes de Vacances publishes an annual list of addresses of rural locations selected for their calm surroundings and the range of outdoor activities they offer. Details from 16, rue Nodot, 21000 Dijon Cedex; ☎ 03 80 43 49 47.

Gîtes et Refuges, France et Frontières by A and S Mouraret (published by La Cadole, 74, rue Albert-Perdreaux, 78140 Vélizy; ☎ 01 34 65 10 40) is a useful handbook in French aimed at ramblers, mountaineers, climbers, skiiers, canoeists and cross-country cyclists.

Gîtes de France also publishes a booklet on **bed-and-breakfast** accommodation *(chambres d'hôte)*.

Youth Hostels – There are many youth hostels *(Auberges de Jeunesse)* throughout France. Holders of an International Youth Hostel Federation card should apply for a list from the International Federation or from the French youth hostels association: Ligue française pour les auberges de jeunesse, 38, boulevard Raspail, 75007 Paris; ☎ 01 45 48 69 84.

Hostelling International/American Youth Hostel Association in the US (☎ 202-783-6161) offers a publication *International Hostel Guide for Europe* (US$13.95) on budget accommodation, also available to non-members.

Camping – There are numerous officially graded sites with varying standards of facilities throughout the Auvergne and Rhône Valley regions; the **Michelin Guide Camping Caravaning France** lists a selection of the best campsites. An International Camping Carnet for caravans is useful but not compulsory; it can be obtained from the motoring organisations or the Camping and Caravanning Club (Greenfield House, Westwood Way, Coventry CV4 8JH; ☎ (01203) 694-995).

Some hotels have their own tennis court, swimming pool, private beach or garden. Consult the current edition of the annual **Michelin Red Guide France**.

General information

Electricity – The electric current in France is 220 volts. Circular two pin plugs are the rule – an electrical adaptor may be necessary.

Medical treatment – First aid, medical advice and chemists' night service rota are available from chemists/drugstores (*pharmacie* – green cross sign).
It is advisable to take out comprehensive insurance cover as the recipients of medical treatment in French hospitals or clinics must pay the bill themselves. Nationals of non-EU countries should check with their insurance companies about policy limitations. Reimbursement can then be negotiated with the insurance company according to the policy held. All prescription drugs should be clearly labelled; we recommend you carry a copy of your prescriptions with you.
American Express offers its cardholders a service, "Global Assist", for any medical, legal or personal emergency – the number to call in France is ☎ 01 47 16 25 29.
British citizens should apply to the Department of Health and Social Security for **Form E111**, which entitles the holder to urgent treatment for accident or unexpected illness in EU countries. A refund of part of the costs of treatment can be obtained on application in person or by post to the local Social Security Offices *(Caisse Primaire d'Assurance Maladie)*.

Currency – There are no restrictions on the amount of currency visitors can take into France. Visitors wishing to export currency in foreign banknotes in excess of the given allocation from France should complete a currency declaration form on arrival.

Notes and coins – *See illustration on p 387*. The unit of currency in France is the French franc (F), subdivided into 100 centimes. French coins come in the following values: 5, 10, 20 and 50 centimes (all gold-coloured, except the 50-centime coin which is silver); 1, 2, 5, 10 and 20 francs (all silver, except the 10- and 20-franc coins which are silver with a gold band). French banknotes are issued to the values of 50, 100, 200 and 500 francs (the old 20-franc note is being phased out).

Banks and currency exchange – Banks are generally open from 9am to 4.30pm (smaller branches may close for lunch) and are closed on Mondays or Saturdays (except if market day); some branches open for limited transactions on Saturdays. Banks close early on the day before a bank holiday.
A passport is necessary as identification when cashing cheques (travellers' or ordinary) in banks. Commission charges vary and hotels usually charge more than banks for cashing cheques for non-residents.

By far the most convenient way of obtaining French currency is the 24hr **cash dispenser** or ATM (*distributeur automatique de billets* in French), found outside many banks and post offices and easily recognisable by the CB (Carte Bleue) logo. Most accept foreign credit cards (don't forget your PIN) and some even give instructions in English. Note that American Express cards can only be used in dispensers operated by the Crédit Lyonnais bank or by American Express. Foreign currency can also be exchanged in major banks, post offices, hotels or private change offices found in main cities and near popular tourist attractions.

Credit cards – American Express, Visa, Mastercard/Eurocard and Diners Club are widely accepted in shops, hotels and restaurants and petrol stations. If your card is stolen, call the appropriate 24hr hotline:
   American Express 01 47 77 70 00
   Visa 01 42 77 11 90
   Mastercard/Eurocard 01 45 67 84 84
   Diners Club 01 47 62 75 50
You should report any loss or theft to the local police who will issue you a certificate (useful proof to show the credit card company).

Post – Main post offices open Monday to Friday from 8am to 7pm, and Saturdays from 8am to noon. Smaller branch post offices generally close at lunchtime between noon and 2pm, and finish for the day at 4pm. Stamps are also sold in newsagents and tobacconists *(tabac)*. Stamp collectors should ask for *timbres de collection* in any post office (there is often a *philatélie* counter).

Postage via airmail:
UK – letter (20g) 3F
USA and Canada – letter (20g) 4.40F
Australia and NZ – letter (20g) 5.20F

Public holidays – The following are days when museums and other monuments may be closed or may vary their hours of admission:

1 January	New Year's Day *(Jour de l'An)*
	Easter Day and Monday *(Pâques)*
1 May	May Day
8 May	V E Day
	Ascension Day
	Whit Sunday and Monday *(Pentecôte)*
14 July	France's National Day (Bastille Day)
15 August	Assumption
1 November	All Saints' Day *(Toussaint)*
11 November	Armistice Day
25 December	Christmas Day *(Noël)*

In general, national museums and art galleries are closed on Tuesdays whereas municipal museums are closed on Mondays. In addition to the usual school holidays at Christmas and in the spring and summer, there are long mid-term breaks (10 days to a fortnight) in February and late October/early November.

Time – France is one hour ahead of Greenwich Mean Time (GMT), except between the end of September and the end of October, when it is the same (although, with plans to synchronise the switch between Summer and Winter Time across Europe, this may change).

When it is **noon in France**, it is
3am in Los Angeles
6am in New York
11am in Dublin
11am in London
7pm in Perth
9pm in Sydney
11pm in Auckland

In France, time is generally given using the 24-hour clock, and "am" and "pm" are not used.

Shopping – Department stores and chain stores are open Monday to Saturday from 9am to 6.30-7.30pm. Smaller, more specialised shops may close during the lunch hour. Food stores (grocers, wine merchants and bakeries) are open from 7am to 6.30-7.30pm, and some open on Sunday mornings. Many food stores close between noon and 2pm and on Mondays. Hypermarkets usually open until 9-10pm.

Embassies and Consulates

Australia	Embassy	4, rue Jean-Rey, 75015 Paris; ☎ 01 40 59 33 00, Fax 01 40 59 33 10
Canada	Embassy	35, avenue Montaigne, 75008 Paris; ☎ 01 44 43 29 00, Fax 01 44 43 29 99
Eire	Embassy	4, rue Rude, 75016 Paris; ☎ 01 44 17 67 00, Fax 01 45 00 84 17
New Zealand	Embassy	7 ter, rue Léonard-de-Vinci, 75016 Paris; ☎ 01 45 00 24 11, Fax 01 45 01 26 39
UK	Embassy	35, rue du Faubourg St-Honoré, 75008 Paris; ☎ 01 42 66 91 42, Fax 01 42 66 95 90
	Consulate	16, rue d'Anjou, 75008 Paris; ☎ 01 42 66 06 68 (visas) 24, rue Childebert, 69002 Lyon; ☎ 04 72 77 81 70, Fax 04 72 77 81 79
USA	Embassy	2, avenue Gabriel, 75008 Paris; ☎ 01 43 12 22 22, Fax 01 42 66 97 83
	Consulate	2, rue St-Florentin, 75001 Paris; ☎ 01 42 96 14 88

TELEPHONING

Public telephones – Most public phones in France use pre-paid phone cards *(télécartes)*. Some telephone booths accept credit cards (Visa, Mastercard/Eurocard: minimum monthly charge 20F). *Télécartes* (50 or 120 units) can be bought from post offices, branches of France Télécom, cafés that sell cigarettes *(tabacs)* and newsagents, and can be used to make calls in France and abroad. Calls can be received at phone boxes where the blue bell sign is shown.

National calls – French telephone numbers have 10 digits. In Paris and the Paris region numbers begin with 01; 02 in northwest France; 03 in northeast France; 04 in southeast France and Corsica; 05 in southwest France. The French ringing tone is a series of long tones, and the engaged (busy) tone is a series of short beeps.

International calls – To call France from abroad, dial the country code (33) + 9-digit number (omit the initial zero). When calling abroad from France, dial 00, followed by the country code, followed by the area code and number of your correspondent.

International dialling codes:		
Australia 61	Eire 353	UK 44
Canada 1	New Zealand 64	USA 1

To use your personal calling card, dial:

AT&T 0 800 99-0011	BT 0 800 99-0044
MCI 0 800 99-0019	Mercury 0 800 99-00944
Sprint 0 800 99-0087	Canada Direct 0 800 99-0016

Telephone rates from a public telephone are about 3F/min from France to the UK, and about 4.50F/min from France to the USA and Canada. Cheap rates with 50% extra time are available from private telephones on weekdays between 9.30pm and 8am, from 2pm on Saturdays and all day on Sundays and holidays. Cheap rates to the USA and Canada are from 2am to noon all week, and to Australia between 9.30pm and 8am Monday to Saturday and all day Sunday.

Toll free numbers in France begin with 0 800.

Emergency numbers:	Police 17
	Fire (Pompiers) 18
	Ambulance (SAMU) 15

Minitel – France Télécom operates a system offering directory enquiries (free of charge up to 3min), travel and entertainment reservations, and other services (cost varies between 0.37F-5.57F/min). These small, computer-like terminals can be found in some post offices, hotels and France Télécom agencies and in many French homes. **3614 PAGES E** is the code for directory assistance in English (turn on the unit, dial 3614, hit the "connexion" button when you get the tone, type in "PAGES E", and follow the instructions on screen). For route planning, use Michelin services **3615 MICHELIN** (tourist and route information) and **3617 MICHELIN** (information sent by FAX).

Cellular phones – In France, these have numbers beginning with 06. Two-watt (lighter, shorter reach) and eight-watt models are on the market, using the Itinéris (France Télécom) or SFR network. Cell phone rentals (delivery or airport pickup provided):

Ellinas Phone Rental	☎ 01 47 20 70 00
Euro Exaphone	☎ 01 44 09 77 78
Rent a Cell Express	☎ 01 53 93 78 00

International information, UK	00 33 12 44
International information, USA/Canada	00 33 12 11
International operator	00 33 12 + country code
Local directory assistance	12

Conversion tables

Weights and measures

1 kilogram (kg)	2.2 pounds (lb)	2.2 pounds
1 ton (tn)	2.2 tons	2.2 tons

to convert kilograms to pounds, multiply by 2.2

1 litre (l)	1.7 pints (pt)	2.1 pints
1 litre	0.22 gallon (gal)	0.26 gallon

to convert litres to gallons, multiply by 0.26 (US) or 0.22 (UK)

1 hectare (ha)	2.47 acres (a)	2.47 acres
1 square kilometre (km²)	0.39 square miles (sq mi)	0.39 square miles

to convert hectares to acres, multiply by 2.4

1 centimetre (cm)	0.3937 inches (in)	0.3937 inches
1 metre (m)	3.2 feet (ft) - 39.3 inches - 1.09 yards (yd)	
1 kilometre (km)	0.6214 miles (mi)	0.6214 miles

to convert metres to feet, multiply by 3.28 . kilometres to miles, multiply by 0.6

Clothing

Women								Men
	35	4	2½		40	7½	7	
	36	5	3½		41	8½	8	
	37	6	4½		42	9½	9	
Shoes	38	7	5½		43	10½	10	Shoes
	39	8	6½		44	11½	11	
	40	9	7½		45	12½	12	
	41	10	8½		46	13½	13	
	36	4	8		46	36	36	
	38	6	10		48	38	38	
Dresses &	40	8	12		50	40	40	Suits
Suits	42	12	14		52	42	42	
	44	14	16		54	44	44	
	46	16	18		56	46	48	
	36	08	30		37	14½	14,5	
	38	10	32		38	15	15	
Blouses &	40	12	14		39	15½	15½	Shirts
sweaters	42	14	36		40	15¾	15¾	
	44	16	38		41	16	16	
	46	18	40		42	16½	16½	

As sizes often vary depending on the designer, it is best to try on the articles before purchasing.

Speed

kph	10	30	50	70	80	90	100	110	120	130
mph	6	19	31	43	50	56	62	69	75	80

Temperature

Celsius (°C)	0°	5°	10°	15°	20°	25°	30°	40°	60°	80°	100°
Fahrenheit (°F)	32°	40°	50°	60°	70°	75°	85°	105°	140°	175°	212°

to convert: °F = (°C × 1.8) + 32   °C = 0.55 × (°F -32)

Notes and coins

500 Francs featuring scientists
Pierre and Marie Curie
(1858-1906), (1867-1934)

200 Francs featuring engineer Gustave Eiffel
(1832-1923)

100 Francs featuring painter Paul Cézanne
(1839-1906)

50 Francs featuring pilot and writer
Antoine de Saint-Exupéry
(1900-1944)

20 Francs

10 Francs

5 Francs

2 Francs

1 Franc

50 Centimes

20 Centimes

10 Centimes

5 Centimes

Tourist information

French Government Tourist Offices – For information, brochures, maps and assistance in planning a trip to France travellers should apply to the official tourist office in their own country *(addresses at the beginning of this chapter)*.

Local tourist offices – To find the addresses of local tourist offices throughout France contact the Fédération Nationale des Comités Départementaux de Tourisme, 280, boulevard St-Germain, 75007 Paris; ☎ 01 44 11 10 20. Useful brochures and information are available at these offices on their own region.

Comité régional du tourisme d'**Auvergne**, 43, avenue Julien, BP 395, 63011 Clermont-Ferrand Cedex 1; ☎ 04 73 93 65 50.

Comité régional du tourisme **Rhône-Alpes**, 104, route de Paris, 69260 Charbonnière-les-Bains; ☎ 04 78 42 50 04.

Comité départemental du tourisme de l'**Ain**: 34, rue Général-Delestraint, BP 78, 01002 Bourg-en-Bresse Cedex; ☎ 03 74 21 95 00.

Comité départemental du tourisme et du thermalisme de l'**Allier**: Hôtel de Rochefort, 12, cours Anatole-France, BP 1647, 03016 Moulins Cedex; ☎ 04 70 46 81 50.

Comité départemental du tourisme de l'**Ardèche**: 4, cours du Palais, BP 221, 07002 Privas; ☎ 04 75 64 04 66.

Comité départemental du tourisme et du thermalisme **cantaliens**: Hôtel du Département, BP 8, 15018 Aurillac Cedex; ☎ 04 71 46 22 60.

Comité départemental du tourisme de la **Drôme**: 31, avenue Président-Herriot, 26000 Valence; ☎ 04 75 82 19 26.

Comité départemental du tourisme de la **Haute-Loire**: 12, boulevard Philippe-Jourde, BP 332, 43012 Le Puy-en-Velay Cedex; ☎ 04 71 09 91 43.

Comité départemental du tourisme de l'**Isère**: 14, rue de la République, BP 227, 38019 Grenoble Cedex 1; ☎ 04 76 54 34 36.

Comité départemental du tourisme de la **Loire**: 5, place Jean-Jaurès, 42021 St-Étienne Cedex 1; ☎ 04 77 33 15 39.

Comité départemental du tourisme du **Puy-de-Dôme**: 26, rue St-Esprit, 63038 Clermont-Ferrand Cedex 1; ☎ 04 73 93 14 41.

Comité départemental du tourisme du **Rhône**: 29, cours Liberté, 69003 Lyon; ☎ 04 72 61 78 90.

Tourist information centres – The addresses and telephone numbers of the tourist information centres *(syndicats d'initiative)* of most large towns and tourist resorts may be found in the Admission times and charges section and in the **Michelin Red Guide France**. They can supply large-scale town plans, timetables and information on local entertainment facilities, sports and sightseeing.

Tourism for the Disabled – Some of the sights described in this guide are accessible to handicapped people and are indicated in the Admission times and charges section with the symbol &. For further information on museums which are accessible to the handicapped, contact the Direction des Musées de France, Service Accueil des publics spécifiques, 6, rue des Pyramides, 75041 Paris Cedex 01; ☎ 01 40 15 35 88. The publication *Guide Rousseau H... comme Handicaps* (published by the Association France Handicaps, 9, rue Luce-de-Lancival, 77340 Pontault-Combault; ☎ 01 60 28 50 12) provides practical information (in French) for people who suffer reduced mobility or visual or aural impairment. Information can also be obtained from the Comité National Français de Liaison pour la Réadaptation des Handicapés, 236 bis, rue de Tolbiac, 75013 Paris; ☎ 01 53 80 66 66.

The **Michelin Red Guide France** and the **Michelin Camping Caravaning France** indicate hotels and camp sites with facilities suitable for physically handicapped people.

Recreation

For visitors who are not pressed for time there are many ways of seeing the countryside from an unusual or different perspective, allowing the best possible appreciation of the local art and architecture, country life and wildlife.

Canal cruising – Boats can be hired to explore the stretch of canal between Roanne and Briennon, contact Marins d'eau douce, Port de plaisance de Briennon, ☎ 04 77 69 92 92. For cruises from the Grangent reservoir along the Loire gorges, contact Naviginter, port de St-Victor-sur-Loire, 42230 Roche-la-Molière; ☎ 04 77 90 32 38.

Canoeing – See the region from a watery perspective; information on areas in which to canoe from the Fédération française de canoë-kayak, 87, quai de la Marne, 94340 Joinville-le-Pont; ☎ 01 45 11 08 50.

Vallon Pont d'Arc

Cycling and mountain biking – Tourist offices should be able to provide lists of local firms which hire out bicycles and mountain bikes (*vélos tout terrain*, or VTT). Some SNCF stations offer bicycles for hire, and mountain bikes can be hired in season from information points within the Pilat park. A leaflet giving details is available from railway stations. Local tourist offices often have details of suggested cycle and mountain bike routes. Useful information is also available from the Fédération française de Cyclotourisme, 8, rue Jean-Marie-Jégo, 75013 Paris; ☎ 01 44 16 88 88 (leaflets showing distances and degrees of difficulty, and a *Guide des centres VTT*).

Donkeys, pony trekking and horse-drawn caravans – How about a walk with a donkey for company (and to carry the bags)? Contact the Comité départemental du Tourisme in Privas *(address above)* for the list of where donkeys may be hired, or the Fédération Nationale Anes et Randonnées, Ladevèze, 46090 Cours; ☎ 04 65 31 42 79.

Horse-drawn caravans, complete with bunk-beds and basic kitchen facilities, may be hired in some areas to follow a planned itinerary; contact the Parc régional du Pilat, ☎ 04 74 87 52 00 or local tourist offices.

For details of pony-trekking and riding holidays, contact the Délégation Nationale de Tourisme Équestre (DNTE, Ile St-Germain, 170, quai de Stalingrad, 92130 Issy-les-Moulineaux; ☎ 01 46 48 83 93) or the Fédération française d'équitation (30, avenue d'Iéna, 75116 Paris; ☎ 01 53 67 43 00), which publishes an annual handbook (*Tourisme et loisirs équestres en France* – 48F) giving details of selected riding stables and equestrian establishments throughout France.

Freshwater fishing – The abundance of rivers, streams and lakes provides anglers with many and varied opportunities to catch salmon, trout, perch, tench or carp; whatever the site, however, it is necessary to be affiliated to a fishing association and to abide by fishing regulations. Contact the local tourist office or apply to the local fishing federations or fishing tackle stores.

A folding map *Pêche en France* (Fishing in France) is published and distributed (15F) by the Conseil Supérieur de la Pêche, 134, avenue de Malakoff, 75016 Paris; ☎ 01 45 01 20 20, and from local fishing federations. Enquire here, or at local tackle shops or tourist offices, about special two-week holiday fishing permits which are available to tourists.

A brochure *(Relais St-Pierre)* gives details on the equipment you may need and the habits of fish to be found locally, as well as a list of hotels selected for their proximity to good angling waters (Maison de la France, 8, avenue de l'Opéra, 75001 Paris; ☎ 01 45 02 20 20).

Golf – For location, addresses and telephone numbers of golf courses in France, consult the map *Golfs, Les Parcours Français* published by Éditions Plein Sud based on Michelin maps.

Hot-air ballooning, hang-gliding and paragliding, helicopters – Contact local tourist offices, or:

AERO 63/Montgolfière d'Auvergne and AERO 43/Montgolfière du Velay, 63840 Sauvessanges; ☎ 04 71 03 31 83

Les montgolfières d'Annonay, BP 111,07102 Annonay Cedex; ☎ 04 75 67 57 56

L'Association des montgolfières de la Haute-Loire, 43260 St-Étienne-Lardeyrol; ☎ 04 71 03 00 42

M Cleyet-Marrel, 6, rue Rivet, 69001 Lyon; ☎ 04 78 39 50 55

Auvergne Héli-Services, 117, boulevard Clémentel, 63100 Clermont-Ferrand, ☎ 04 73 25 74 92

Chlorofeeling, Récoléine, 63210 Nébouzat; ☎ 04 73 87 17 17

Gîte des 4 vents, 63710 Le Vernet-Ste-Marguerite; ☎ 04 73 88 67 74

École ailes libres Auvergne Limousin, 35, rue du Cornonet, 63800 Cournon-d'Auvergne, ☎ 04 73 84 57 97

Vol Can, Centre Espace Volcan, route du col de Moreno, Laschamps, 63122 St-Genès-Champanelle; ☎ 04 73 62 26 00

Delta Auvergne, Chassagnoles, St-Ferréol-des-Côtes, 63600 Ambert, ☎ 04 73 82 29 16

Hydrotherapy and hot spas – There are many spa resorts in the region: Bourbon-l'Archambault, La Bourboule, Charbonnières-les-Bains, Châteauneuf-les-Bains, Châtel-Guyon, Chaudes-Aigues, Le Mont-Dore, Néris-les-Bains, Royat-Chamalières, St-Nectaire, Vals-les-Bains, Vichy.

For further information, contact local tourist offices or the Centre d'informations thermales, 48, boulevard Malesherbes, 75008 Paris; ☎ 01 44 70 74 74.

National and regional parks – *See Introduction: Flora and Fauna.* For information on the parks in this region, contact the Fédération des parcs naturels de France, 4, rue de Stockholm, 75008 Paris; ☎ 0144 90 86 20 or local tourist offices.

Rambling – Exploring the region on foot is an enchanting way of discovering the landscape and the life of the countryside. Many long-distance footpaths (*Sentiers de Grande Randonnée* – GR) cover the area described in this guide. Short-distance paths (*sentiers de petite randonnée* – PR) and medium-distance paths offer walks ranging from a few hours to a couple of days.

A collection of Topo-Guides – showing the routes and the time needed, details of access points, accommodation and places of interest en route – for footpaths throughout France is published jointly by FFRP-CNSGR (the Fédération Française de la Randonnée Pédestre and the Comité National des Sentiers de Grande Randonnée); some of the guides have been translated into English. They are on sale at the information centre, FFRP, 64, rue de Gergovie, 75014 Paris; ☎ 01 45 45 31 02.

Rock-climbing – There are numerous opportunities to explore, particularly in the Auvergne region. Information can be obtained from the Club alpin français (section Auvergne), 3, rue Maréchal-Joffre, 63000 Clermont-Ferrand; ☎ 04 73 90 81 62, or the Comité départemental de la fédération française de la montagne et de l'escalade, 17, rue Gaultier-de-Biauzat, 63000 Clermont-Ferrand; ☎ 04 73 37 94 26.

Scaling a frozen waterfall, Sancy

Skiing – Contact Ski France, an association of winter sports resorts, for their annual publication *Guide d'hiver* and a leaflet on accommodation *Hébergement* (both free), 61, boulevard Haussmann, 75008 Paris, ☎ 01 47 42 23 32.

Steam trains – These offer the opportunity of discovering some spectacular scenery, removed from busy modern communications routes. Contacts include:

Chemin de fer du Vivarais, CFTM, 2, quai Jean-Moulin, 69001 Lyon; ☎ 04 78 28 83 34;

Chemin de fer du Haut-Rhône, Maison d'Accueil, BP 36, 38390 Montalieu Vercieu; ☎ 04 74 88 49 23;

Chemin de fer touristqie du Velay, Office de tourisme de Tence; ☎ 04 71 59 81 99, or Syndicat d'initiative de St-Agrève; ☎ 04 75 30 15 06;

Chemin de fer touristique d'Anse, Association de la voie 38cm, 8, avenue de la Libération, 69480 Anse; ☎ 04 74 60 26 01;

Petit train des Monts du Lyonnais, Maison du tourisme de Brussieu; ☎ 04 74 70 90 64 (reservations).

Tourist routes – *Routes historiques* are signposted local itineraries following an architectural and historical theme, accompanied by an explanatory booklet; contact the Caisse nationale des monuments historique et des sites (CNMHS), 62, rue St-Antoine, 75004 Paris; ☎ 01 44 61 20 00.

Calendar of events

Last Sunday in January
Villefranche-sur-Saône .... Fête des Conscrits, with "La Vague" *(see alphabetical entry)*

Late January/early February
Clermont-Ferrand .... Short film festival

Spring
Clermont-Ferrand .... Clermont-Ferrand festival

Maundy Thursday
Le Puy-en-Velay .... Torchlight procession of the White Penitents in hooded robes in the streets around the cathedral
Saugues .... Procession of the White Penitents at nightfall

2nd or 3rd week in March
Clermont-Ferrand,
Mont Aigoual .... "Chamineige": 450km/280mi trek across the Massif Central, on cross-country skis, mountain bikes and on foot

Late March/early April
Lyon .... International Fair

Easter holidays
Clermont-Ferrand .... International dance festival

Eve of Ascension Day
Orcival .... Pilgrimage in honour of the Virgin Mary: torchlight procession and midnight mass

Ascension Day
Lyon .... Grand Steeple (Great Steeple Chase)

Whitsun
Lyon .... International French bowls *(boules)* tournament

Sunday following 15 May
Clermont-Ferrand .... Feast of Our Lady of the Port ending with an afternoon procession through the old town.

French Mothers' Day weekend (last Sunday in May) – in even years
Villerest .... Medieval festival: procession and tour of the ramparts

1st Sunday in June
Annonay .... Historic re-enactment of the first flight of an aerostat by the Montgolfier brothers

Sunday following 15 July
Lyon .... Horse racing: Grand prix de Lyon

3rd weekend in June
Annonay .... Hot-air balloon rally in Déomas park

Friday nearest to 24 June
Villefranche-sur-Saône .... Midsummer Night: bonfires, singers, illuminations

Late June/early July
Romans-sur-Isère .... International Folklore Festival

Late June to mid-August
Valence .... Summer festival in the old town
Vienne .... Dauphiné music festival

1st week in July
Bort-les-Orgues .... Water festival

1st fortnight in July
Vienne .... Jazz festival in the Roman theatre

Mid July to late August, on Friday and Saturday evenings
Lapalisse .... *Son et lumière* at the castle

Renaissance festival at Salers

8 September

Mont Brouilly . . . . Wine-producers' pilgrimage to Brouilly chapel

Sunday following the Feast of St Matthew (21 September)

Besse-en-Chandesse . . . . . . Return of the statue of Our Lady of Vassivière to its winter quarters in the church in Besse; fireworks

September to December

Beaujolais, Coteaux du Rhône and du Forez . . . . . . Grape harvest and wine festivals in the wine-growing regions

First weekend in October

Montbrison . . . . Fourme cheese festival; procession of flower-bedecked floats

11 November

Le Puy-en-Velay . . . . International hot-air balloon rally

8 December

Lyon . . . . Festival of light

Maturing Cantal cheese

Useful French words and phrases

ARCHITECTURAL TERMS

See the ABC of Architecture in the Introduction

SIGHTS

abbaye	abbey	**marché**	market
beffroi	belfry	**monastère**	monastery
chapelle	chapel	**moulin**	windmill
château	castle	**musée**	museum
cimetière	cemetery	**parc**	park
cloître	cloisters	**place**	square
cour	courtyard	**pont**	bridge
couvent	convent	**port**	port/harbour
écluse	lock (canal)	**porte**	gateway
église	church	**quai**	quay
fontaine	fountain	**remparts**	ramparts
halle	covered market	**rue**	street
jardin	garden	**statue**	statue
mairie	town hall	**tour**	tower
maison	house		

NATURAL SITES

abîme	chasm	**grotte**	cave
aven	swallow-hole	**lac**	lake
barrage	dam	**plage**	beach
belvédère	viewpoint	**rivière**	river
cascade	waterfall	**ruisseau**	stream
col	pass	**signal**	beacon
corniche	ledge	**source**	spring
côte	coast, hillside	**vallée**	valley
forêt	forest		

ON THE ROAD

car park	parking	**petrol/gas station**	station essence
driving licence	permis de conduire	**right**	droite
east	Est	**south**	Sud
garage (for repairs)	garage	**toll**	péage
left	gauche	**traffic lights**	feu tricolore
motorway/highway	autoroute	**tyre**	pneu
north	Nord	**west**	Ouest
parking meter	horodateur	**wheel clamp**	sabot
petrol/gas	essence	**zebra crossing**	passage clouté

TIME

today	aujourd'hui	**week**	semaine
tomorrow	demain	**Monday**	lundi
yesterday	hier	**Tuesday**	mardi
		Wednesday	mercredi
winter	hiver	**Thursday**	jeudi
spring	printemps	**Friday**	vendredi
summer	été	**Saturday**	samedi
autumn/fall	automne	**Sunday**	dimanche

NUMBERS

0	zéro	10	dix	20	vingt
1	un	11	onze	30	trente
2	deux	12	douze	40	quarante
3	trois	13	treize	50	cinquante
4	quatre	14	quatorze	60	soixante
5	cinq	15	quinze	70	soixante-dix
6	six	16	seize	80	quatre-vingt
7	sept	17	dix-sept	90	quatre-vingt-dix
8	huit	18	dix-huit	100	cent
9	neuf	19	dix-neuf	1000	mille

SHOPPING

bank	banque	fishmonger's	poissonnerie
baker's	boulangerie	grocer's	épicerie
big	grand	newsagent, bookshop	librairie
butcher's	boucherie	open	ouvert
chemist's	pharmacie	post office	poste
closed	fermé	push	pousser
cough mixture	sirop pour la toux	pull	tirer
cough sweets	cachets pour la gorge	shop	magasin
entrance	entrée	small	petit
exit	sortie	stamps	timbres

FOOD AND DRINK

beef	bœuf	lamb	agneau
beer	bière	lunch	déjeuner
butter	beurre	lettuce salad	salade
bread	pain	meat	viande
breakfast	petit-déjeuner	mineral water	eau minérale
cheese	fromage	mixed salad	salade composée
chicken	poulet	orange juice	jus d'orange
dessert	dessert	plate	assiette
dinner	dîner	pork	porc
fish	poisson	restaurant	restaurant
fork	fourchette	red wine	vin rouge
fruit	fruits	salt	sel
sugar	sucre	spoon	cuillère
glass	verre	vegetables	légumes
ice cream	glace	water	de l'eau
ice cubes	glaçons	white wine	vin blanc
ham	jambon	yoghurt	yaourt
knife	couteau		

PERSONAL DOCUMENTS AND TRAVEL

airport	aéroport	railway station	gare
credit card	carte de crédit	shuttle	navette
customs	douane	suitcase	valise
passport	passeport	train/plane ticket	billet de train/d'avion
platform	voie	wallet	portefeuille

CLOTHING

coat	manteau	socks	chaussettes
jumper	pull	stockings	bas
raincoat	imperméable	suit	costume
shirt	chemise	tights	collants
shoes	chaussures	trousers	pantalons

USEFUL PHRASES

goodbye	au revoir	yes/no	oui/non
hello/good morning	bonjour	I am sorry	pardon
how	comment	why	pourquoi
excuse me	excusez-moi	when	quand
thank you	merci	please	s'il vous plaît

Do you speak English?	Parlez-vous anglais?
I don't understand	Je ne comprends pas
Talk slowly	Parlez lentement
Where's...?	Où est...?
When does the ... leave?	A quelle heure part...?
When does the ... arrive?	A quelle heure arrive...?
When does the museum open?	A quelle heure ouvre le musée?
When is the show?	A quelle heure est la représentation?
When is breakfast served?	A quelle heure sert-on le petit déjeuner?
What does it cost?	Combien cela coûte?
Where can I buy a newspaper in English?	Où puis-je acheter un journal en anglais?
Where is the nearest petrol/gas station?	Où se trouve la station essence la plus proche?
Where can I change traveller's cheques?	Où puis-je échanger des traveller's cheques?
Where are the toilets?	Où sont les toilettes?
Do you accept credit cards?	Acceptez-vous les cartes de crédit?

Admission times and charges

As admission times and charges are liable to alteration, the information printed below is for guidance only. In cases where it has not been possible to obtain up-to-date information, details from the previous edition of the guide have been given in italics.

⊙*: Every sight for which times and charges are listed below is indicated by the symbol* ⊙ *after the title in the Sights section of the guide.*

Order: The information is listed in the same order as in the Sights section of the guide.

Dates: Dates given are inclusive. The term holidays means public holidays.

Last admission: Ticket offices usually shut 30min before closing time; only exceptions are mentioned below.

Charge: The charge given is for an individual adult. Concessionary rates may be available for families, children, students, old-age pensioners and the unemployed. Many places offer special rates for group bookings and some have special days for group visits. Large parties should apply in advance.

&. *Facilities for the disabled: As the range of possible facilities is great (for impaired mobility, sight and hearing) readers are advised to telephone in advance to check what is available.*

🚹 *Tourist offices: The addresses and telephone numbers are given for the local tourist offices, which provide information on local market days, early closing days etc. In some small towns, you will need to apply to the "Mairie" (town hall) for information.*

🔺 *: This symbol ("Ville d'Art et d'Histoire" or "Ville d'Art") indicates that guided tours are given by lecturers from the Historic Monuments Association (Caisse Nationale des Monuments Historiques et de Sites).*

A

Gorges de l'ALLIER

Blassac Church – Guided tours in July and August on Tuesdays, Thursdays and Saturdays from 4pm to 6pm. The rest of the year by appointment only. ☎ 04 71 77 43 57 or ☎ 04 71 77 40 23.

St-Cirgues Church – Guided tours in July and August at weekends from 3pm to 5pm. The rest of the year by appointment only. ☎ 04 71 77 40 36.

Aubazat Church – Guided tours in July and August on Thursdays from 10am to noon and on Saturdays from 3pm to 6pm. Otherwise by appointment only, contact M or Mme Boniface in Aubazat ☎ 04 71 77 47 38.

Arlet Church – Guided tours at weekends from 3pm to 6pm. Otherwise by appointment only. ☎ 04 71 76 41 54.

Peyrusses Church – Guided tours by appointment only, contact Mme Delaurent in Peyrusses ☎ 04 71 77 17 35.

Pébrac Abbey – Guided tours (45min) in July and August daily from 10am to noon and 3pm to 6pm. The rest of the year by appointment only. ☎ 04 71 74 01 79.

St-Arcons-d'Allier Church – Apply to the Mairie. ☎ 04 71 74 02 04.

St-Haon Church – Visit by appointment only. ☎ 04 71 08 21 43.

AMBERT
 🚹 4, place de l'Hôtel de Ville, 63600; ☎ 04 73 82 61 90

Livradois-Forez tourist railway – Scenic "Picasso" railway operates between Ambert and La Chaise-Dieu in July and August on Tuesdays, Thursdays and Sundays leaving at 2.15pm (and getting back at 6.30pm): 65F Rtn; or between Courpière, Ambert and La Chaise-Dieu from late July to late August on Wednesdays and Sundays leaving at 8.45am (getting back at 7.30pm): 100F.
Steam railway operates between Ambert and the Château d'Olliergues from mid-July to late August on Satur leaving at 2.15pm (getting back at 5.30pm): 60F.
For further information contact AGRIVAP "train touristique", La Gare, 63600 Ambert ☎ 04 73 82 43 88.

Musée de la Fourme et des Fromages (Cheesemaking) – Currently being reorganised. Details available on ☎ 04 73 82 49 23.

Musée de la Machine agricole et à vapeur (Agrivap) (Agricultural and Steam-Powered Machinery) – Open (1hr 15min guided tours available) in July and August daily from 10am to 7pm; from March to June and in September and October open from 9am to noon and 2pm to 6pm. 25F (children: 15F). ☎ 04 73 82 60 42.

Excursion

Parc zoologique du Bouy – Open daily from 10am to dusk. 37F (children: 25F). ☎ 04 73 82 13 29.

Château d'ANJONY

Tour of castle – Guided tours (45min) in July and August Monday to Saturday from 11am to noon and 2pm to 6.30pm; mid-February to June and September to mid-November daily from 2pm to 6.30pm. 30F (children: 15F). ☎ 04 71 47 61 67.

Excursion

St-Chamant Château – Guided tours (45min) in July and August daily from 2.30pm to 6.30pm. 30F (children: 20F). ☎ 04 71 69 26 85.

St-Martin-Cantalès Church – Open on Sundays for services only.

ANNONAY
🛈 Place des Cordeliers, 07100; ☎ 04 75 33 24 51

Guide tours of the town – Contact the tourist office.

Musée vivarois César-Filhol – Open on Wednesdays, Saturdays, Sundays and public holidays from 2pm to 6pm. Closed 25 December. 10.50F. ☎ 04 75 33 24 51.

Musée des Papeteries Canson et Montgolfier (Paperworks) – Open mid-July to late August daily from 2.15pm to 6pm; otherwise on Wednesdays and Sundays only at these times. Closed between Christmas and Easter. 15F. ☎ 04 75 69 88 00.

Gorges de l'ARDÈCHE

Vallon-Pont-d'Arc Mairie (Town hall tapestries) – &. *Open Monday to Friday from 10am to noon and 3pm to 5pm. Closed weekends and holidays. 10F. ☎ 04 75 88 02 06.*

Grotte des Huguenots – Open mid-June to mid-September from 10am to 7pm. Otherwise closed. 20F. ☎ 04 75 88 06 71 (in season only).

Grotte de la Madeleine – Guided tour (1hr) July and August from 9am to 6.30pm; April to June and in September from 10am to 6pm; in October from 10am to 5pm. Closed from November to March. 37F (children: 22F). ☎ 04 75 04 22 20.

Aven de Marzal – Guided tours (1hr) April to October from 11am to 5pm; in March and November, on Sundays and during school holidays at 11am, 2.30pm, 3.30pm and 4.30pm. Closed from December to February. 38F (children: 24F), combined ticket with "prehistoric zoo" 64F (children: 40F). ☎ 04 75 04 12 45.

Musée du Monde souterrain – &. Open in July and August from 10am to 7pm; from April to June and in September and October from 10am to noon and 2pm to 6pm; in March and November on Sundays, public holidays and during school holidays from 11am to 5pm. Closed December to February. ☎ 04 75 04 12 45.

Zoo préhistorique – &. Open in July and August from 10am to 7pm; from April to June and in September and October from 10am to noon and 2pm to 6pm; in March and November on Sundays and public holidays from 10am to 5pm. Closed December to February. 38F (children: 24F), combined ticket with "prehistoric zoo" 64F (children: 40F). ☎ 04 75 04 12 45.

Grotte de St-Marcel – Guided tours (45min) mid-March to mid-October from 10am to 7pm. Otherwise closed. 37F (children: 22F). ☎ 04 75 04 38 07.

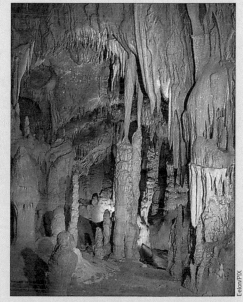

Aven de Marzal

Aven de la Forestière – Guided tours (1hr) April to September from 10am to 6pm. Otherwise closed. 32F. ☎ 04 75 38 63 08.

Labastide-de-Virac: Château des Roure – Open (45min guided tours available in July and August) Easter to late September from 10am to noon and 2pm to 7pm (5pm during last fortnight in September). Closed the rest of the year, and on Tuesdays from April to June and in September. 22F. ☎ 04 75 38 61 13.

Gorges de l'ARDÈCHE

Rambles on foot – Leaflet published by l'Association Tourena provides useful information on footpaths along the gorge; enquire about water levels from local police or the Service Départemental d'Alerte des Crues (☎ 04 75 64 54 55), before walking along the west bank.

Downstream by boat or canoe – Allow 6 to 9 hours for the descent, depending on the season and water levels (you cannot set off on your trip after 6pm). There are a number of difficult passages with rapids, so you need to have had adequate experience as a canoeist. It is essential that you are able to swim. Local canoe hire offices, town halls, tourist offices and police stations have copies of river protocol available for consultation. A useful leaflet *(Plan-Guide des Gorges de l'Ardèche)* is published by l'Association Tourena. Picnics are allowed all along the river but overnight camping is permitted only at Aire de Gaud and Aire de Gournier (25-35F per person per night), as the river flows through a nature reserve. Longer stays are possible at the campsites of Mas de Serret, Templiers (nudists) and St-Marcel caves. Boats can be hired for accompanied or unaccompanied trips downriver from companies at Vallon-Pont-d'Arc, Salavas, Ruoms, St-Martin and St-Remèze, at a cost of 120-150F per person for 1-2 days; ask for the list of hire companies (50 or so) at the tourist office in Ruoms (Rue Alphonse-Daudet, 07120, ☎ 04 75 93 91 90), Vallon-Pont d'Arc (Cité administrative, 07150, ☎ 04 75 88 04 01) and St-Martin-d'Ardèche (Rue de la Mairie, 07700, ☎ 04 75 98 70 91).

Vallée de l'ARDÈCHE

Vogüé Château – Open mid-June to mid-September daily (except Tuesdays) from 10am to noon and 3.30pm to 7.30pm; Easter to mid-June on Sundays and holidays from 2pm to 6pm. Otherwise closed. 20F. ☎ 04 75 35 76 50.

Vogüé

ARLEMPDES

Church – Apply to the Hôtel du Manoir.

Castle – Open March to late October all day. 20F. Apply to the Hôtel du Manoir. ☎ 04 71 57 17 54.

Pradelles: Musée de l'oustaou (Local museum) – Exhibitions open in July and August from 10am to noon and 2pm to 6pm. ☎ 04 71 00 80 37.

Pradelles: Musée vivant du Cheval de trait (Draught-horses) – &. Open in July and August daily from 10am to noon and 2pm to 6pm. 45F. ☎ 04 71 00 87 87.

ARS-SUR-FORMANS

Presbytery – &. Open Easter to 1 November from 7am to 8pm; otherwise from 7am to 7pm. ☎ 04 74 00 70 56.

Historial du Saint Curé d'Ars – ⅄ Open March to late October daily (except Monday mornings) from 10am to noon and 2pm to 7pm; otherwise on Saturdays and holidays from 2pm to 6pm and Sundays from 10am to noon and 2pm to 6pm. Also open on weekdays from 2pm to 5pm during school holidays between November and late February. Closed 25 December. ☎ 04 74 00 70 22.

L'ARTENSE

Lanobre: Musée de la Radio et du Phonographe – ⅄ Open (1hr guided tours available) in July and August daily from 10am to noon and 2pm to 7pm; April to June and September to mid-October from 2pm to 6pm. 20F (children: 14F). ☎ 04 71 40 32 89.

Château de Val – Guided tours (45min) mid-June to mid-September daily from 10am to noon and 2pm to 6.30pm; mid-February to mid-June and mid-September to mid-October daily (except Tuesdays) from 10am to noon and 2pm to 5.30pm. Also open at these times on 1 November and 25 December. 20F (children: 15F). ☎ 04 71 40 30 20.
Boat trips along the Dordogne – In July and August daily, leaving from the foot of the castle every 30min from 2.15pm to 5pm. 30F (children: 20F). Details from the Vedettes panoramiques (May to September). ☎ 04 71 40 30 14.

AUBENAS
🛈 4, boulevard Gambetta, 07200; ☎ 04 75 35 24 87

Château – Guided tours (45min) in July and August daily at 11am, 3pm, 4pm, 5pm and 6pm; otherwise, Tuesday to Saturday at 11am (in June and September only), 3pm and 4pm. 15F. ☎ 04 75 87 81 11.

Dôme St–Benoît – ⅄ Open in July and August from 3pm to 6.30pm. Otherwise closed. Admission free. ☎ 04 75 87 81 11.

Excursion

Aérocity – Open in July and August daily from 10am to 7.30pm; in June from 10am to 6pm; in early September from 10.30am to 6pm; in April and May on Sundays and holidays only. 62F (children: 48F, no charge for those under 1m/3ft tall). ☎ 04 75 35 00 00.

AURILLAC
🛈 Place du Square, 15000; ☎ 04 71 48 46 58

Musée de Cire (Waxworks) – Open June to September daily (except Sunday mornings) from 10am to noon and 3pm to 7pm. 25F (children: 12F). ☎ 04 71 48 64 38.

Musée des Sciences de la Maison des Volcans – Open in July and August daily (except Sunday mornings and Mondays) from 10am to noon and 2pm to 6pm; in June, September and October at same times but closed all day Sunday; January to June at same times except closed all weekend. Closed on all holidays. Admission free. ☎ 04 71 48 07 00.

Musée d'Art et Archéologie – ⅄ Open in July and August daily (except Sunday mornings and Mondays) from 10am to noon and 2pm to 6pm; mid-February to June and September to November open same times except closed all day Sunday. Closed from December to mid-February and on all holidays. 15F. ☎ 04 71 45 46 10.

Palais de Justice – *Open Monday to Friday from 9am to noon and 2pm to 4pm. Closed holidays.* ☎ 04 71 48 01 85.

Église du Sacré-Cœur – Open daily (except Sunday afternoons) from 8am to noon and from 2pm to 6pm. ☎ 04 71 48 28 51.

AUZON

Écomusée du pays d'Auzon – Guided tours (1hr 30min) June to September daily from 2.30pm to 6.30pm. 20F. ☎ 04 71 76 14 80.

Lac d'AYDAT

Château de la Batisse – Château (1hr guided tours) and gardens open in July and August daily from 10am to noon and 2pm to 7pm; in May, June and first fortnight in September daily (except Tuesdays) from 2.30pm to 6pm; in April on Sundays and holidays only from 2.30pm to 6pm. 30F (château and gardens), 15F (gardens only). ☎ 04 73 79 41 04.

Château d'Opme – Guided tours (45min) in July and August daily (except Tuesdays) from 3pm to 7pm; in June and September at weekends and on holidays only at these times. 20F (children: 10F) ☎ 04 73 87 54 85.

Olloix Church – Open July to September daily; on Sundays only in winter.

B

Château de la BASTIE-D'URFÉ

Château – Guided tours (1hr) in July and August from 10am to noon and 1pm to 6pm; April to June and in September and October from 10am to noon and 2.30pm to 6pm; November to late March daily (except Tuesdays) from 2pm to 5pm. 25F. ☎ 04 77 97 54 68.

BEAUJOLAIS

St-Julien: Musée Claude-Bernard – Open Wednesday to Sunday from 10am to noon and 2pm to 6pm (5pm between October and late February). Closed in March and on 1 January, 1 May and 25 December. 10F. ☎ 04 74 67 51 44.

Salles-Arbuissonnas-en-Beaujolais: Chapter-house museum – Guided tours (30min). 5F. Apply 48hr in advance to Mme Médal in Salles. ☎ 04 74 67 51 81.

Belleville Church – Open (30min guided tours available) July to early September on weekdays from 3pm to 6pm. Apply to the tourist office *(syndicat d'initiative)*. ☎ 04 74 66 44 67.

Belleville Hôtel-Dieu – ♿ Guided tours July to late August daily (except Sundays and holidays) from 3pm to 5pm; otherwise on the first Saturday of the month at 10.30am only. Enquire about opening times during school holidays. 15F. ☎ 04 74 69 65 85.

Château de Corcelles – ♿ Open Monday to Saturday from 10am to noon and 2.30pm to 6.30pm. Closed on Sundays and holidays. Admission free. ☎ 04 74 66 00 24.

Romanèche-Thorins: Maison de Benoît-Raclet – Guided tours (30min) on the last Saturday of October during the Raclet festival; otherwise apply to the town hall or the museum on weekdays only. ☎ 03 85 35 51 37.

Romanèche-Thorins: Le Hameau du vin S. A. Dubœuf – Guided tours (2hr) from 9am to 6pm. Closed during the first fortnight in January. 70F. ☎ 03 85 35 22 22.

Romanèche-Thorins: Musée du compagnonnage Guillon – Open in July and August daily (except Tuesdays) from 10am to 6pm; May to late June and September to late October from 2pm to 6pm. Otherwise closed. 12F. ☎ 03 85 35 22 02.

Juliénas: Cellier de la Vieille Église – ♿ Open daily from 9.30am to noon and 2.30pm to 6pm. Closed during the week in January, and on Tuesdays from October to late May, and on 1 January and 25 December. ☎ 04 74 04 42 98.

Preparation of wine casks before racking off at Juliénas

Beaujeu: Musée des traditions populaires Marius-Audin – Open July to late September daily (except Tuesdays) from 10am to noon and 2.30pm to 6pm; April to June and October to November open afternoons only (except Tuesdays); otherwise open at weekends and on holidays from 10am to noon and 2pm to 6.30pm. Closed December to late March. 8F. ☎ 04 74 69 22 88.

Beaujeu: St-Nicolas – *Church usually closed. Apply to the Mairie for guided tours.* ☎ 04 74 04 87 75.

Pays des Pierres Dorées – For information apply to the tourist office in Châtillon (Place de la Mairie, 69380 Châtillon). ☎ 04 78 47 98 15.

Marcy: Chappe telegraph tower – Open April to late November on Sundays and holidays from 2.30pm to 6pm. Admission free. ☏ 04 78 47 98 15.

St-Jean-des-Vignes: Pierres Folles – Open March to November from 8.30am to 12.30pm and 2pm to 6pm (afternoons only on Wednesdays, Sundays and holidays). 25F. ☏ 04 78 43 69 20.

Bagnols Church – *Guided tours by appointment.* ☏ *04 74 71 70 06 or* ☏ *04 74 71 80 16.*

Theizé: Château de Rochebonne – Open June to late August daily (except Tuesdays) from 3pm to 7pm; in May and September open at weekends and on holidays only. 15F. ☏ 04 74 71 29 67 or ☏ 04 74 71 26 39.

Theizé Church – Open June to August daily (except Tuesdays) from 3pm to 7pm; in May and from September to mid-October open at weekends and on holidays only. 15F. ☏ 04 74 71 26 39.

Oingt Church – Open May to late September on Sundays from 3pm to 7pm; or during the week by appointment, contact M Jean Veilloux. ☏ 04 74 71 20 88.

Oingt Tower – Open May to late September on Sundays and holidays from 3pm to 7pm. 5F. ☏ 04 74 71 20 88.

Ternand Church – Guided tours by appointment, contact the *Mairie.* ☏ 04 74 71 33 43.

Jarnioux Castle – Open during the first fortnight in July and from mid-August to late September on Tuesdays and Thursdays from 9am to noon, and on Mondays, Wednesdays and Fridays from 2pm to 6pm. Otherwise closed. 25F. ☏ 04 74 03 80 85.

Vallée de la BESBRE

Château de Beauvoir – Gardens open May to October daily from 10am to 7pm; November to April from 10am to 5pm. Castle interior can be visited by appointment. Admission free. ☏ 04 70 42 00 44.

Château de Thoury – Guided tours (1hr) June to October daily from 10am to noon and 2pm to 7pm; in April and May from 2pm to 7pm. 20F (children: 10F). ☏ 04 70 42 00 41.

Parc d'Attractions et Animalier Le Pal (Zoo and amusement park) – ♿ Open July to first week in September daily from 10am to 7pm; April to June and during the last 3 weeks of September open from 10am to 6pm (7pm on Sundays in June). 80F (children: 70F). ☏ 04 70 42 03 60.

Abbaye de Sept-Fons – Open during religious services only. ☏ 04 70 48 14 90.

BESSE-EN-CHANDESSE ◳ Place du Docteur-Pipet, 63610; ☏ 04 73 79 52 84

Musée du Ski – Open (30min guided tours given by the museum's founder) during school holidays daily from 9am to noon and 2pm to 7pm. 15F. ☏ 04 73 79 57 30 or 04 74 67 00 50.

BILLOM ◳ Place de l'Hôtel-de-Ville, 63160; ☏ 04 73 68 39 85

St-Cerneuf – Open in summer daily from 9am to 7pm; in winter from 9am to 4.30pm. Crypt open June to October from 3pm to 6pm.

Excursions

Château de Montmorin – Guided tours (1hr 30min) July to mid-September daily from 2pm to 7pm; from Palm Sunday to June and mid-September to 1 November open at weekends and on holidays at these times. 25F (children: 15F). ☏ 04 73 68 30 94.

BORT-LES-ORGUES ◳ Place Marmontel, 19110; ☏ 05 55 96 02 49

Barrage de Bort Cruisers – Operate in July and August daily, leaving every 30min from 2.15pm to 5pm from the top of the dam as far as the Château de Val. 30F (children: 20F). Further information from the Vedettes panoramiques May to September. ☏ 04 71 40 30 14.

Tourist itinerary ("Circuit visiteurs") – *Operates mid-December to mid-October daily from 9am to 6pm. No charge.* ☏ *04 55 96 02 49.*

BOURBON-L'ARCHAMBAULT ◳ 1 Place des Thermes, 03160; ☏ 04 70 67 09 79

Château – Guided tours (1hr) mid-June to mid-September daily from 10am to 6pm; April to mid-June and mid-September to mid-November from 2pm to 6pm. 20F. ☏ 04 70 67 02 30.

Musée Augustin-Bernard – Guided tours (45min) June to September daily from 3pm to 6pm; mid-April to June and the first fortnight in October on Wednesdays, Sundays and holidays from 3pm to 6pm. 10F. ☏ 04 70 67 09 31.

Excursion

Les Vignes: Musée Émile-Guillaumin – Guided tours (1hr 30min) in July and August Mondays, Wednesdays, Thursdays and weekends from 3pm to 5.30pm; May to June and September to October Thursdays, weekends and holidays from 3pm to 5.30pm. 10F. ☏ 04 70 66 30 66 (Ygrande Mairie).

La BOURBOULE 🏛 15, place de la République, 63150; ☎ 04 73 65 57 71

Grands Thermes – Guided tours (1hr) in July and August Monday to Saturday at 5.30pm; in May, June and September on Tuesdays and Fridays at 5.30pm; in April on Wednesdays at 5.30pm. 5F (shoes must be covered). ☎ 04 73 81 02 92.

Parc Fenêstre – The "Far West" miniature train operates mid-June to September daily from 10am to noon and 2pm to 6.30pm; May to mid-June from 2pm to 6.15pm: 16F Rtn. The "Théâtre Extraordinaire" is open at 4pm (contact tourist office for days when it is open): 10F (children). Mini-golf course open in season daily from 10am to 10pm: 24F.

Charlannes Plateau Cable-car – Operates July to September daily from 10.30am to 12.15pm and 2pm to 6.5pm; May to June from 10am to 12.15pm and 2pm to 6.15pm; Christmas school holidays until April from 8.45am to noon and 1.30pm to 5.15pm. 24F Rtn.

Excursions

Murat-le-Quaire: Musée de la Toinette – ♿ Guided tours (45min) Easter to 1 November daily from 10am to noon and 2pm to 7pm; Christmas to Easter from 2pm to 6pm (during school holidays 10am to noon and 2pm to 6pm). 27F (children: 14F).
☎ 04 73 81 12 28.

Cascade du Plat à Barbe
– *Entrance tickets issued at the kiosk (in season). 5F.*
☎ *04 73 65 58 55.*

BRIOUDE 🏛 Avenue Léon-Blum, 43100; ☎ 04 71 74 97 49

Hôtel de la Dentelle (Lace Centre) – Exhibition and Museum open (1hr guided tours available) April to October Monday to Friday from 9am to noon and 2pm to 6pm, weekends from 2pm to 6pm; otherwise by appointment (but not at weekends). Closed 25 December to 1 January. 25F (includes visit to workshops). ☎ 04 71 74 80 02. **Workshops** open (1hr guided tours available) Monday to Friday from 9am to noon and from 2pm to 6pm.

Musée de la Toinette, Murat-le-Quaire

Closed 25 December to 1 January. 25F (includes visit to museum). ☎ 04 71 74 80 02. Possibility of working a square of lace yourself (1hr).

Maison du Saumon et de la Rivière (Salmon and Riverlife) – ♿ Open in July and August daily from 9.30am to 1pm and 2.30pm to 7pm (last tickets sold at 6.30pm); September to June from 9am to noon and 2pm to 6pm (last tickets at 5.30pm). 30F (children: 20F). ☎ 04 71 74 91 43.

Excursion

Beaumont Church – *Open only during Sunday service every other week. Key held by M Chauvet who lives opposite Beaumont Mairie.*

Brassac-les-Mines: Musée de la Mine – Guided tours (1hr) April to October daily from 9.30am to noon and 2pm to 7pm (last tickets sold at 6pm). 20F. ☎ 04 73 54 30 88.

Blesle: St-Pierre church treasury – *Guided tours (15min) Monday to Friday. Closed on holidays. Details from the Mairie. 5F.* ☎ *04 71 76 20 75.*

Massiac: Musée-municipal Élise-Rieuf – ♿ Open (1hr guided tours available) July to mid-September daily (except Sunday and Monday mornings) from 10am to noon and 2pm to 7pm; otherwise Saturdays, Sundays and Mondays only from 2pm to 6pm. Closed 1 January and 25 December. 15F. ☎ 04 71 23 01 17.

Château de BUSSÉOL

Castle – Guided tours (45min) mid-June to mid-September daily from 10am to noon and 2.30pm to 7pm; otherwise weekends and holidays only from 2.30pm to 6pm. 25F (children: 15F). ☎ 04 73 69 00 84.

C

Monts du CANTAL

Thiézac Établissement de pisciculture (Fish farm) – *Open (30min guided tours available) daily from 2pm to 4pm. 10F.* ☎ *04 71 47 00 86.*

Tournemire Church – *Open in July and August daily from 1pm to 7pm.*

Marmanhac: Château de Sédaiges – Guided tours (1hr) July to mid-September daily from 2.30pm to 6.30pm; by appointment only in June and from the last fortnight in September to October. 25F (children: 15F). ☎ 04 71 47 30 01.

La CHAISE-DIEU

Église abbatiale St-Robert – *Open June to October daily from 9.30am to noon and 2pm to 7pm; November to May from 10am to noon and 2pm to 5pm.* ☎ *04 71 00 06 06.*

Chancel and treasury – *Guided tours late June to late September (in July and August only for the treasury) daily from 9.45am to noon and 2pm to 7pm; otherwise from 10am to noon and 2pm to 5pm. Visiting is restricted during the Chaise-Dieu Music Festival – we strongly recommend that you call in advance to check admission details. 20F.* ☎ *04 71 00 06 06.*

Historial de la Chaise-Dieu – Open in July and August daily from 9am to noon and 2pm to 7pm; Easter to June and September to mid-October daily (except Mondays which are not holidays) from 10am to noon and 2pm to 5pm (6pm on Sundays and holidays); otherwise by appointment. 15F. ☎ 04 71 00 01 88.

Le CHAMBON-SUR-LIGNON

Tour of the Lignon valley by Le Velay Tourist Train – Restoration in progress. At present operates several return trips a day between Tence and Dunières in July and August. Details from the Tence tourist office. ☎ 04 71 59 81 99.

CHARROUX

Musée de Charroux et de son canton – Open mid-June to mid-September daily (except Tuesdays) from 3pm to 7pm; April to mid-June and mid-September to mid-October on Sundays and holidays only from 3pm to 7pm. 20F. ☎ 04 70 56 80 18.

Château du CHASSAN

Château – Guided tours (30min) mid-June to mid-September daily from 2.30pm to 6.30pm. 20F (children: 10F). ☎ 04 71 23 42 20.

CHÂTEAUGAY

Keep – Guided tours (30min) May to September daily from 2pm to 7pm; otherwise by appointment 2 days in advance. 10F. ☎ 04 73 87 24 35 (Mairie).

CHÂTELGUYON

Grands Thermes (Spa) – Open early May to September Monday to Saturday from 8am to 11.30am and 3pm to 5pm (from 8am to 11am only on holidays); October to early May open Monday to Friday from 8.30am to 11.30am and 2.30pm to 5.30pm (closed weekends and holidays). Admission free. ☎ 04 73 86 00 08.

CHÂTEL-MONTAGNE

Church – Open daily except during religious services. Guided tours (1hr) available June to September on Sundays and holidays from 3pm to 6pm – send a written request a month in advance to M J Barou, 03250 Châtel-Montagne. ☎ 04 70 59 35 99.

CHÂTILLON-SUR-CHALARONNE   ⧉ Place du Champ de Foire, 01400; ☎ 04 74 55 02 27

Guided tours of the town – Contact the tourist office.

Maison St-Vincent – Guided tours on Sunday mornings; enquire at the Communauté des Soeurs. ☎ 04 74 55 26 64.

Centre Culturel de la Dombes – ♿ Also hosts cultural events (exhibitions, shows, lectures). Open Monday to Saturday from 9am to noon and 2pm to 6pm. Closed 1 January and 25 December. ☎ 04 74 55 03 70.

Apothicairerie – ♿ Guided tours (45min) June to late September Mondays and Wednesday to Friday from 3pm to 6pm; Easter to late May and during the first fortnight in October weekends and holidays only from 3pm to 6pm. Closed mid-October to Easter. 15F. ☎ 04 74 55 09 98.

CHAUDES-AIGUES

Géothermia – ♿ Open (1hr guided tours available) May to September daily from 10.30am to 12.30pm and 2pm to 6.30pm; otherwise during school holidays only daily from 10.30am to noon and 2pm to 5pm. Closed 1 January and 25 December. 12F. ☎ 04 71 23 58 76.

Château de CHAVANIAC-LAFAYETTE

Castle – Guided tours (1 hour) March to mid-November daily from 9am to noon and 2pm to 6pm; otherwise by appointment. 25F (château and grounds), 10F (grounds only). ☎ 04 71 77 50 32.

CHAZELLES-SUR-LYON

Musée du Chapeau (Hats) – Open in July and August daily from 2pm to 6pm; otherwise daily (except Tuesdays) from 2pm to 6pm. Closed 1 January and 25 December. 25F. ☎ 04 77 94 23 29. **Demonstrations by milliners,** 1st and 3rd Sundays of the month.

Château de CHOUVIGNY

Castle – Guided tours (45min) in July and August daily from 10am to noon and 2.30pm to 6.30pm; in June and September from 2.30pm to 6pm; April to May and in October on Sundays only from 2.30pm to 6pm. 20F. ☎ 04 70 90 44 95.

CLERMONT-FERRAND   🅱 69, boulevard Gergovia, 63038; ☎ 04 73 93 30 20

Notre-Dame-du-Port – Open daily, 0800 to 1900.

Cathédrale Notre-Dame-de-l'Assomption (Crypt, Treasury, Tour de la Bayette) – Guided tours July to mid-September Tuesday to Saturday from 2.30pm to 5pm; otherwise apply to the cathedral caretaker. 10F. ☎ 04 73 92 46 61 (priest).

Fontaine pétrifiantes de St-Alyre (Grotte du Pérou) – ♿ *Guided tours (45min) in July and August daily from 8am to 7.30pm; September to June from 9am to noon and 2pm to 6pm. Closed 1 January, 1 November and 25 December. 16F. ☎ 04 73 37 15 58.*

Musée du Ranquet – Open Tuesday to Sunday from 10am to 6pm. Closed 1 January, 1 May, 1 November and 25 December. 12F. ☎ 04 73 37 38 63.

Musée Bargoin – Open Tuesday to Sunday from 10am to 6pm. Closed 1 January, 1 May, 1 November and 25 December. 21F. ☎ 04 73 91 37 31.

Musée H-Lecoq – Open May to September Tuesday to Sunday from 10am to noon (except Sundays) and 2pm to 6pm; October to April from 10am to noon and 2pm to 5pm. Closed on holidays. 21F. ☎ 04 73 91 93 78.

St-Genès-les-Carmes – Open weekdays 0800 to 1800. ☎ 73 91 64 34.

Notre-Dame-de-Prospérité – Open daily, 0800 to 1200 and 1400 to 1800 (1900 in summer).

Musée des Beaux-Arts (Fine Arts) – ♿ Open (1hr 30min guided tours available by appointment on Sundays) Tuesday to Sunday from 10am to 6pm. Closed 1 January, 1 May, 1 November and 25 December. 21F. ☎ 04 73 23 08 49.

Chamalières: Galerie d'Art contemporain – ♿ Open Tuesday to Saturday from 2pm to 6.30pm. Closed on holidays. Admission free. ☎ 04 73 30 97 22.

Excursion

Maison de Gergovie – ♿ Open in July and August daily from 10am to 12.30pm and 2pm to 7pm; May to June and September to early November from 10am to 12.30pm and 2pm to 6pm; in April at weekends and on holidays only at these times. 15F. ☎ 04 73 79 42 98 or 04 73 79 40 09.

Plateau du COIRON

Château de Rochemaure (ruins) – Open July and August Mondays and Wednesday to Sunday from 3pm to 7pm; in June and September at weekends only. Otherwise closed. 15F. ☎ 04 75 49 08 07.

CONDAT

Égliseneuve d'Entraigues: Maison des Fromages – Open (1hr guided tours available) July and August daily from 10am to 12.30pm and 2.30pm to 7pm; mid-May to June and in September from 2pm to 6pm. 16F (includes visit and a little sampling session of 4 cheeses and a glass of wine). ☎ 04 73 71 92 01.

Château de CONROS

Castle – Guided tours (45min) July and August daily from 2pm to 6pm. 28F (children: 16F). ☎ 04 71 63 50 27.

La CÔTE-ST-ANDRÉ

Musée Hector-Berlioz – Open March to late December Mondays and Wednesday to Sunday from 9am to noon and 3pm to 6pm; in February from 2pm to 5pm. Closed on holidays and during January. 20F. ☎ 04 74 20 24 88.

Castle: Henry Gérard Room – Telephone in advance to arrange a visit. ☎ 04 74 20 27 00.

Musée des Liqueurs – Guided tours (1hr) July and August Tuesday to Sunday from 9am to noon and 3pm to 6pm. Closed on holidays. Admission and sampling free. ☎ 04 74 93 38 10.

COURPIERE

Livradois-Forez tourist railway – *See AMBERT.*

Excursion

Château d'Aulteribe – Guided tours (45min) July to mid-September daily from 10am to 7pm; April to June from 10am to noon and 2pm to 6pm; mid-September to March from 10am to noon and 2pm to 5pm. 28F (children: 15F). ☎ 04 73 53 14 55.

Vallées des COUZES

Farges: Troglodytic houses – Guided tours (45min) during school holidays daily from 9am to 12.30pm and 2pm to 8pm. 15F. ☎ 04 73 88 50 50.

Farges: Ferme Bellonte – ♿ Guided tours (45min) April to September daily from 8am to 10.30am and 6pm to 8pm; October to March open for one hour less at these times. Admission free. ☎ 04 73 88 50 50.

Grottes de Jonas – Open (45min guided tours available) July and August daily from 10am to 7pm; in May and June and during the first 3 weeks in September from 10am to noon and 2pm to 7pm; during school holidays between February and April and in the last week of September from 2pm to 6pm; October to mid-November Sundays and holidays only from 2pm to 6pm; otherwise during school holidays only. 26F (guided tour), 22F (no tour). ☎ 04 73 88 51 66.

Moulin-Neuf: Musée auvergnat – ♿ Open May to September daily from 9am to 7pm. 16F. ☎ 04 73 96 77 79.

St-Floret: Église de Chastel – Open mid-June to mid-September daily from 3pm to 7pm; otherwise by appointment at the Mairie in St-Floret. ☎ 04 73 71 10 39 (town hall open Mondays and Thursdays from 3pm to 6pm).

St-Floret Château – Open daily from 9am to noon and 2pm to 7pm. Admission free. ☎ 04 73 71 10 39.

Ardes Church – Open on Sundays only, before and after the service at 9.30am.

St-Alyre-ès-Montagne: Maison des tourbières et du Cézallier – *Guided tours (2hr) mid-June to late August daily from 1pm to 7pm; mid-April to mid-June on Fridays only at these times. 20F.* ☎ *04 73 65 89 36 or 04 73 71 78 98.*

CRÉMIEU
🅱 5, rue du Four-Banal, 38460; ☎ 04 74 90 45 13

Guided tours of the town 🅰 – Contact the tourist office.

Hôtel de Ville – Open all year Monday to Friday from 10am to noon and 2pm to 5pm and Saturdays from 10am to noon. Closed on Sundays. ☎ 04 74 90 45 13.

Church – *Guided tours early June to mid-September daily from 2pm to 5.30pm. Otherwise apply in advance to tourist office.* ☎ *04 74 90 45 13.*

Grottes de la Balme – Guided tours (1hr 15min) April to late September daily from 10am to noon and 2pm to 6pm; in March and October at weekends and on holidays at 11am and from 2pm to 6pm; otherwise on Sundays and holidays from 2pm to 5pm. Closed mid-December to late January. 31F. ☎ 04 74 90 63 76.

A natural underground dam in Grottes de la Balme

Hières-sur-Amby: Maison du Patrimoine – Open all year Monday to Friday from 10am to noon and 2pm to 6pm, and at weekends from 10am to noon and 2pm to 7pm. Closed 1 January and 25 December. 18F. ☎ 04 74 95 13 90.

Annoisin-Chatelans: Musée de la Lauze – Open all year daily (except Tuesdays) from 9am to 7pm. Admission free. For guided tours, apply in advance to the Maison du Patrimoine, Hières. ☎ 04 74 95 13 90.

CREST
🟦 Place du Docteur-Maurice-Rozier, 26400; ☎ 04 75 25 11 38

Keep – Open early June to late September daily from 9.30am to 7pm; otherwise daily from 2pm to 6pm; open at weekends only in January. Closed 25 December. 25F. ☎ 04 75 25 11 38.

Excursion

Upie: Jardin des Oiseaux – Open in summer daily from 10am to 7pm; in winter daily from 10am to dusk. 45F. ☎ 04 75 84 45 90.

D

DAUPHINÉ D'AUVERGNE

Colamine-sous-Vodable Church – Open July and August daily from 2.30pm to 6.30pm; in June and September from 2.30pm to 6.30pm; also on Whit Sunday and Monday at these times. ☎ 04 73 71 43 09.

La DOMBES

Abbaye Notre-Dame-des-Dombes – Only the abbey church is open to visitors, who are requested not to disturb the silence of the monastery.

Monts DÔMES

Puy de Lemptégy (Volcano) – Guided tours (2hr) July and August daily from 9.30am to 7pm (last tickets sold at 6pm); also open April to June and September to mid-October from 2pm to 5.30pm. 32F (in July and August for the guided tour), 25F (the rest of the year, no tour). ☎ 04 73 62 23 25.

Château Dauphin – Guided tours (1hr) July and August Tuesday to Sunday from 2pm to 7pm; Easter to June and September to 1 November on Sundays and holidays only from 2pm to 6pm. 25F (castle interior and grounds), 10F (grounds and castle exterior), 40F (evening visit when castle illuminated, available in July and August on Wednesdays at 9.30pm). ☎ 04 73 88 73 39.

Monts DORE

Puy de Sancy Cable-car – Operates in July and August daily from 9am to 6pm (ascent in 3min); December to April from 9am to 5pm; May to June and September to early October from 9am to noon and 1.30pm to 5pm. Closed October to mid-November. 35F Rtn, 30F single. ☎ 04 73 65 02 23.

Vallée de la DORE

Livradois-Forez tourist railway – *See AMBERT.*

Arlanc: Musée de la Dentelle (Lace) – Guided tours (45min) July to mid-September daily from 10am to noon and 3pm to 6pm; March to June and mid-September to mid-October from 3pm to 6pm. 15F. ☎ 04 73 95 00 03 (Mairie).

Marsac-en-Livradois: Musée des Pénitents blancs du Livradois – Guided tours (1hr) June to September daily from 9am to noon and 2pm to 7pm; otherwise by appointment 24hr in advance at Marsac Mairie. 15F. ☎ 04 73 95 60 08 or 04 73 95 65 03.

Olliergues: Musée des Vieux Métiers – Guided tours (1hr) mid-June to early September daily from 10am to 7pm (last tickets sold at 6pm); early April to early May from 2pm to 6pm (last tickets at 5pm); otherwise by appointment. 20F. ☎ 04 73 95 54 90.

La Chabasse Church – Enquire at Olliergues Mairie. ☎ 04 73 95 50 26.

E - F

Château d'EFFIAT

Château – ♿ Guided tours (1hr 30min) in July and August daily from 9.30am to noon and 2.30pm to 7pm, and an evening visit with illuminations every other Tuesday from 9.30pm to 11.30pm; open during the last fortnight in June and the first in September from 2.30pm to 7pm; April to mid-June and mid-September to November open on Sundays from 3pm to 7pm and holidays from 9.30am to noon and 2.30pm to 7pm. Closed 1 November and from December to March. 30F (day visit), 40F (evening visit). ☎ 04 73 63 64 01.

Monts du FOREZ

Parc naturel régional Livradois-Forez – Park information centre open Monday to Friday from 8.30am to 12.30pm and 1.30pm to 6pm (5pm on Fridays). For further information contact the head office at St-Gervais-sous-Meymont, 63800 Olliergues. ☎ 04 73 95 57 57.

Château de Boën: Winemaking Museum – Open July and August daily (except Tuesdays) from 2pm to 6pm. Otherwise closed, although it is possible to visit by appointment out of season. 15F. ☎ 04 77 24 09 10.

Pierre sur Haute Cable-car – Access to the summit by cable-car mid-July to late August and mid-December to mid-March every afternoon; June to mid-March operates on Sundays and holidays only from 9am to 5pm. Cable-car operates subject to suitable weather conditions. Rtn 35F. ☎ 04 77 24 85 09.

Chalmazel: Château des Talaru-Marcilly – Guided tours (30min) July and August daily (except Tuesdays) from 2.30pm to 5pm; in June by appointment only. Otherwise closed. 8F. ☎ 04 77 24 84 92.

Montbrison: La Diana – ♿ Guided tours (45min) on Wednesdays from 9am to noon and 2pm to 5pm, and Saturdays from 2pm to 5pm; otherwise by appointment. 18F. ☎ 04 77 96 01 10.

Montbrison: Musée d'Allard – Open daily (except Tuesdays) from 2.30pm to 6pm. Closed 1 January and 25 December. 15F. ☎ 04 77 58 33 07.

Château de Vollore – Guided tours (45min) July and August daily from 2pm to 7pm (last tickets sold at 6.30pm). 30F (day visit), 50F (evening tour with illuminations, on Tuesdays at 9.30pm). ☎ 04 73 53 71 06.

G

GANNAT 🚹 Place de la Halle, 03800; ☎ 04 70 90 17 78

Musée Municipal – Open (2hr guided tours available) June to October daily (except Tuesdays) from 10am to noon and 2pm to 6pm; 25F (children: 10F). ☎ 04 70 90 23 78.

Excursions

Veauce: Church – Open in summer daily, and in winter on Sundays only.

Veauce: Castle – ♿ Guided tours (30min) daily from 10.30am to noon and 2.30pm to 6.30pm. Open also for evening visits from 9pm to 10pm (appointments by telephone please). Closed mid-December to mid-January. 25F. ☎ 04 70 58 53 27.

Jenzat: Maison du luthier – Open (1hr guided tours available) mid-June to mid-September daily (except Tuesdays) from 3pm to 6pm. 15F. ☎ 04 70 56 81 78.

Viaduc de GARABIT

Boat trips – **Restaurant boat** (3hr 15min) operates May to October, from 168F. **Grandval reservoir** (45min) trips operate May to September daily, 41F. Trips to **Château d'Alleuze** (2hr) operate July and August daily at 3.30pm, 55F. Trips up the **Gorges de la Truyère** (45min) operate July and August at 4pm, 41F. Trips round the gorges, viaduct and road bridge (30min) operate April to October daily at 10am, 11am, 2pm, 3pm, 4pm, 5pm and 6pm, 50F (price gets lower if there are more than 6 passengers). ☎ 04 71 23 49 40.

La GARDE-ADHÉMAR 🚹 Ancienne Mairie, 26700; ☎ 04 75 04 40 10

Chapelle des Pénitents – ♿ Open April to October on Sundays and holidays from 3pm to 6pm. 15F. ☎ 04 75 04 41 21.

HAUTERIVES

Palais Idéal – Open (recorded commentary available) April to mid-September from 9am to 7pm; in January and December open from 10am to 4.30pm; otherwise open from 9.30am to 5.30pm. Closed 1 January and 25 December. 22F. ☎ 04 75 68 81 19.

HÉRISSON

Vallon-en-Sully: Vallon Arts et Traditions – ⅋ Open (1hr guided tours available) July to September Wednesday to Sunday from 3pm to 7pm; April to June and September to mid-October from 3pm to 6pm. 12F. ☎ 04 70 06 51 00.

ISSOIRE
🚹 Place Général-de-Gaulle, 63500; ☎ 04 73 89 15 90

Ancienne Abbatiale St-Austremoine: Interior – Open daily from 8am to 8pm (or dusk, out of season). Free guided tous conducted by M Raoul Ollier in July and August on Tuesdays and Fridays at 5pm (meet by the east end of the church).

Historial – ⅋ Guided tour (15min) in August daily (but not in the morning at the weekend or on holidays) from 10am to noon and 2pm to 7pm; mid-June to July from 2pm to 7pm only; otherwise by appointment. 14F. ☎ 04 73 89 12 58.

Excursions

Parentignat Château – Guided tours (45min) in July and August daily (except Tuesdays) from 2.30pm to 6pm (last tickets sold at 5.30pm); in June and September at weekends and on holidays at these times. 30F. ☎ 04 73 89 33 00 or ☎ 04 73 89 51 10.

L

LAMASTRE

Col du Buisson: Village ardéchois en miniature – Open April to October daily from 9am to 8pm. 7F. ☎ 04 75 23 14 77.

Doux Gorge by the Vivarais railway – Trips between Tournon to Lamastre in both directions by steam train or railcar operate in July and August daily; 7 May to late June and first fortnight in September daily (except Mondays); Easter to mid-May and mid-September to late October at weekends and on holidays; no more trips after 11 November. Steam train takes 4hr Rtn; railcar, 2hr Rtn. On Sundays in the summer, it is best to arrive at the station 30min in advance. Steam train: 100F (single), 79F (child), 110F Rtn. Railcar: 79F (single), 66F (child), 90F Rtn. ☎ 04 78 28 83 34 in Lyon or 04 75 06 40 14 in Lamastre (afternoons).

Château de LAPALISSE

Château – Guided tours (45min) April to early November daily from 9am to noon and 2pm to 6pm. 25F (children: 15F). ☎ 04 70 99 08 51 or 04 70 55 01 12.

LAVAUDIEU

Cloisters – Guided tours (1hr) daily mid-June to mid-September from 10am to noon and 2pm to 6.30pm; from Easter to mid-June and mid-September to October open daily (except Tuesdays) from 10am to noon and 2pm to 5pm. 20F (combined ticket includes entry to Maison des Arts below). ☎ 04 71 76 45 89.

Maison des Arts et Traditions populaires – Guided tours (30min) mid-June to mid-September daily from 10am to noon and 2pm to 6.30pm; Easter to mid-June and mid-September to October daily (except Tuesdays) from 10am to noon and 2pm to 5pm. 20F (combined ticket includes visit to cloisters above). ☎ 04 71 76 45 89.

LEZOUX

Musée archéologique – Open (1hr guided tours available) June to September daily (except Mondays) from 10am to noon and 2.30pm to 6pm. There are specially adapted facilities for blind visitors. 14F. ☎ 04 73 73 03 13.

La LIMAGNE

Aigueperse: Sainte-Chapelle – Contact the town hall: Mairie, 153, Grande-Rue, Aigueperse. ☎ 04 73 63 60 34.

Aigueperse: Hôtel de Ville – Guided tours (2hr 30min) by appointment 24hr in advance at the Syndicat d'initiative. 25F (includes tasting of local produce). ☎ 04 73 63 72 70. A tour leaflet in Braille is available for blind visitors.

Artonne: Église St-Martin – Open daily (except Sundays and holidays). ☎ 04 73 33 30 81 (priest).

Bulhon: Church – Open at weekends from 9am to 5pm. ☎ 04 73 68 72 85 (Mairie).

Maringues: Grandval Tannery – Guided tours (30min) June to September daily from 10am to noon and 2.30pm to 6.30pm. 15F. ☎ 04 73 68 70 42 (Mairie).

Pont-du-Château: Musée Pierre-Mondanel – Open (1hr guided tours available) in July and August Wednesday to Sunday from 10am to noon and 3pm to 7pm; otherwise open on Saturdays from 3pm to 5pm. Admission free. ☎ 04 73 83 20 02.

Le LIORAN

Laveissière: Maison du Buronnier – Guided tours (45min) in July and August daily from 10am to noon and 2.30pm to 7pm; mid-May to June and during September open daily from 2pm to 6pm. 16F. ☎ 04 71 48 68 68.

Le LIVRADOIS

Château des Martinanches – Guided tours (1hr) April to October daily from 1pm to 7pm; November to March open Sundays, holidays and during school holidays from 2pm to 5pm. 27F (children: 12F). ☎ 04 73 70 89 44.

Sauxillanges: Maison du Patrimoine – Open (1hr guided tours available) July to mid-September daily from 3pm to 7pm. 15F. ☎ 04 73 96 80 25.

Gorges de la LOIRE

Château de Lavoûte-Polignac – Guided tours (45min) in July and August daily from 10am to 12.30pm and 2pm to 6.30pm; in June and September daily from 2pm to 6pm. Otherwise closed. Charges not available. ☎ 04 71 08 50 02.

Lavoûte-sur-Loire Church – *Open March to 1 November, except on Sunday afternoons.*

Chamalières-sur-Loire – Guided tours on Thursdays and Saturdays from 10am to noon and 2pm to 6pm, and on Tuesdays and Sundays from 2pm to 6pm. Contact the Syndicat d'initiative, ☎ 04 71 57 44 67, or Mme Rose Ouilhon, ☎ 04 71 57 41 43.

St-Victor-sur-Loire: River cruises – Operate on the reservoir (1hr) and along the Loire gorge (1hr 30min) from early April to late October. Departures late May to late September daily at 2.30pm, 4pm and 5.30pm; in April departures at weekends only at 3.30pm. Reservoir cruise: 42F (children: 30F); Loire gorge cruise: 50F (children: 39F). Contact Navig'inter, Port de St-Victor-sur-Loire, 42230 Roche-la-Molière. ☎ 04 77 90 32 38.

St-Just-St-Rambert: Musée Le Prieuré – Open daily (except Tuesdays) from 2pm to 6pm. Closed 1 January, 1 May and 25 December. 15F. ☎ 04 77 52 03 11.

LYON ⓘ Place Bellecour et Place St-Jean, 69000; ☎ 04 78 42 25 75

A day pass carries a reduction for all the municipal museums in Lyon: Musée des Beaux-Arts, Musée de l'Hôtel de Gadagne, Musée d'Art contemporain, Musée de l'Imprimerie et de la Banque, Centre d'Histoire de la Résistance et de la Déportation and the Musée Henri–Malartre at Rochetaillée-sur-Saône.

Lecture tours 🅰 – Various walking tours are organised by the Lyon tourist office, including an exploration of the Croix–Rousse *traboules* (2hr) and Historical Lyon (2hr), among others. Apply to the tourist office in Place Bellecour, open Monday to Saturday all day, or in Avenue A. Max open every day. ☎ 04 78 42 25 75.

Bateaux-mouches river trips – Departures to Ile-Barbe (1hr) at 2pm and 5pm (and 6pm May to mid-July); to the junction (1hr 20min) at 3pm: 42F (children: 30F). Landing stage: Quai des Célestins. Reservations: Navig'inter, 13 bis, quai Rambaud, 69002 Lyon. ☎ 04 78 42 96 81.

Palais de la Miniature – Open daily from 10am to noon and 2pm to 7pm; in July and August open from 10am to 7pm. Closed 1 January and 25 December. 25F. ☎ 04 72 00 24 77.

St-Paul – Open daily from noon to 6pm. ☎ 04 78 28 34 45.

Théâtre "Le Guignol de Lyon" – Puppet shows for children are given on Wednesdays and Saturdays at 3pm and 4pm and on Sundays at 4pm. 45F (accompanying adult). 35F (children). For information on the programme and reservations: ☎ 04 78 28 92 57.

Hôtel de Gadagne – Musée historique de Lyon: Open from 10.45am to 6pm. Closed on Tuesdays and most holidays. 20F. ☎ 04 78 42 03 61.

Musée international de la Marionnette: Open from 10.45am to 6pm. Closed on Tuesdays and most holidays. 20F. ☎ 04 78 42 03 61.

A courtyard in Rue St-Jean, Old Lyon

Primatiale St-Jean – Open until 5pm at weekends. Closed afternoons on holidays. Guided tours included in the tour of Historic Lyon organised by the tourist office. ☎ 04 78 42 25 75.

Astronomical clock – *Automata at noon, 2pm and 3pm (the latter operates all year).*

Treasury – *Temporarily closed to visitors.*

Notre-Dame de Fourvière – Open daily from 7am to 7pm. Guided tours available in the afternoon from May to September. Apply to the sacristy in the morning. ☎ 04 78 25 13 01.

Musée de Fourvière – Open mid-June to early December daily from 10am to noon and 2pm to 6pm. 15F. ☎ 04 78 25 13 01.

Observatory – Open May to late October daily from 10am to noon and 2pm to 6.30pm; October to late March open at weekends only from 10am to noon and 2pm to 6pm. 10F. ☎ 04 78 25 13 01.

Parc archéologique de Fourvière – Open mid-April to mid-September from 7am to 9pm; otherwise open until 7pm. For guided tours, contact the Musée de la Civilisation gallo-romaine. ☎ 04 78 38 81 90.

Musée de la Civilisation gallo-romaine – ৬ Open Wednesday to Sunday from 9.30am to noon and 2pm to 6pm. Closed on holidays. 20F. ☎ 04 78 38 81 90.

Musée des Hospices civils – ৬ Open Monday to Friday from 1.30pm to 5.30pm. Closed on holidays. 10F. ☎ 04 78 41 30 42.

St-Nizier – Open Monday to Saturday from 7am to 1pm (except Monday mornings) and 3pm to 7pm; on Sundays from 8.30am to 12.30pm and 5pm to 6.30pm.

Musée de l'Imprimerie et de la Banque (Printing and Banking) – Open Wednesday to Sunday from 9.30am to noon and 2pm to 6pm; on Fridays open all day. Closed on holidays. 20F. ☎ 04 78 37 65 98.

Musée des Beaux-Arts (Fine Arts) – ৬ Open Wednesday to Sunday from 10.30am to 6pm. Closed on holidays. 20F. ☎ 04 72 10 17 40.

Musée historique des Tissus (Textiles) – Open Tuesday to Sunday from 10am to 5.30pm. Closed on holidays. 26F (combined ticket with Musée des Arts décoratifs). No charge on Wednesdays for individual visitors. ☎ 04 78 37 15 05.

Musée des Arts décoratifs – Open Tuesday to Sunday from 10am to noon and 2pm to 5.30pm. Closed on holidays. 26F (combined ticket with Musée des Tissus). ☎ 04 78 37 15 05.

Maison des Canuts (Silk Workers' Centre) – ♿ Open Monday to Friday from 8.30am to noon and 2pm to 6.30pm; on Saturdays from 9am to noon and 2pm to 6pm. Closed on Sundays, Mondays during August, and holidays. 10F. Guided tours (1hr) available; apply in advance to the Service des Visites, Maison des Canuts, 10, rue d'Ivry, 69004 Lyon. ☎ 04 78 28 62 04.

Ateliers de Soierie Vivante (Silk workshops) – Guided tours on Wednesdays at 2.30pm, 4pm and 5.30pm; other workshops can be visited on certain Thursdays and Saturdays at 3pm. 15-60F depending on tour. We recommend that you book in advance. ☎ 04 78 27 17 13.

Parc de la Tête d'Or – Open all year daily from 6am to 9pm (until 11pm April to September). Admission free.

Jardin botaniqe – Open all year daily from 8am to 11.30am and 1pm to 5pm.

Grande Roseraie – Open early April to late September daily from 6am to 11pm; otherwise from 6am to 9pm.

Jardin zoologique – Open April to late September on weekdays from 9am to 5pm, weekends and holidays from 9am to 11am and 2pm to 5pm; otherwise on weekdays from 9am to 4.30pm, weekends and holidays from 9am to 11am and 1.30pm to 4.30pm.

Musée d'Art contemporain – For details of admission times and charges, call: ☎ 04 72 69 17 17.

Musée Guimet d'Histoire naturelle – Open Wednesday to Sunday from 1pm to 6pm; during local school holidays open Monday to Sunday from 10.30am to 6pm. Closed on holidays. 20F. ☎ 04 72 69 05 00.

Centre d'Histoire de la Résistance et de la Déportation – Open Wednesday to Sunday from 9am to 5.30pm. Closed on holidays. 20F. ☎ 04 78 72 23 11.

Musée des Moulages d'Art antique – ♿ Open on Wednesdays from 2pm to 6pm or otherwise by appointment Monday to Friday. Closed during August and on holidays. 20F (guided tour). ☎ 04 72 73 33 20.

Musée africain – Open Wednesday to Sunday from 2pm to 6pm. Closed 1 January, Easter and 25 December. 20F. ☎ 04 78 58 45 70.

Château Lumière – Open Tuesday to Sunday from 2pm to 7pm. Films shown in the afternoon. Closed 1 January, 1 May and 25 December. 25F (27F including film show). ☎ 04 78 78 18 95.

Le Furet tourist train – Guided tour of Lacroix-Laval park by train (30min) daily during school holidays; otherwise on Wednesdays, at weekends and on holidays only. Departures from the museum entrance in front of the château. 22F. ☎ 04 78 42 88 70.

Château de la poupée (Dolls) – Open mid-February to mid-November daily from 10am to 5pm; mid-November and mid-February on Wednesdays and Sundays. Closed 1 January, 1 May and 25 December. 25F. ☎ 04 78 87 87 00.

Rochetaillée: Musée Henri-Malartre – Open in July and August daily from 9am to 7pm; otherwise from 9am to 6pm. Last tickets sold 1hr before closing time. Closed 1 January and 25 December. 20F. ☎ 04 78 22 18 80.

Neuville-sur-Saône Church – Open on Sunday mornings only. ☎ 04 78 91 32 03.

La MARGERIDE

Tour de Ruynes – Open (1hr 30min guided tours available) mid-June to August daily from 10am to 7pm; during the first fortnight in September from 2pm to 6pm; otherwise by appointment (1 day in advance). 22F. ☎ 04 71 23 42 96 or 04 71 23 42 22.

Domaine de Longevialle – Open (1hr 30min guided tours available) mid-June to August daily from 10am to 7pm; during the first fortnight in September from 2pm to 6pm; otherwise by appointment (1 day in advance). 22F. ☎ 04 71 73 72 43 or 04 73 23 42 96.

Inside Pierre-Allègre farm, Loubaresse

Ecomusée de la Margeride – Ruynes-en-Margeride

La MARGERIDE

Ferme de Pierre-Allègre – Open (1hr 30min guided tours available) mid-June to August daily from 10am to 7pm; during the first week in September from 2pm to 6pm; otherwise by appointment (1 day in advance). 22F. ☏ 04 71 73 70 04 or 04 71 23 42 96.

École de Clémence Fontille – Open (1hr guided tours available) mid-June to August daily from 10am to 7pm; during the first fortnight in September from 2pm to 6pm; otherwise by appointment (1 day in advance). 22F. ☏ 04 71 23 42 22 or 04 71 23 42 96.

Mont Mouchet Resistance Movement Museum – ♿ Open May to mid-September daily from 9.30am to noon and 2pm to 7pm; mid-September to mid-October weekends and holidays from 10am to noon and 2pm to 6pm. 25F. ☏ 04 71 74 11 28.

MAURIAC   🛈 Place Georges-Pompidou, 15200; ☏ 04 71 67 30 26

Monastère St-Pierre – Guided tours (30min) in July and August daily from 10am to noon and 2pm to 6pm; mid-May to June and in September open daily (except Tuesdays and Sunday mornings) at these times. Closed 1 May and 14 July. 10F. ☏ 04 71 68 07 24.

Musée – Open (1hr guided tours) in July and August daily from 10am to noon and 2pm to 6pm; Easter to June and in September daily (except Tuesdays and Sunday mornings) at these times; by appointment October to December. Closed 1 May and 14 July. 12F. ☏ 04 71 68 07 24.

Excursions

Château de la Vigne – Guided tours (45min) in July and August daily from 2pm to 7pm; otherwise by appointment only. 25F (castle); 30F (castle and model vehicle collection). ☏ 04 71 69 00 20.

Salon de l'automobile miniature – Combined ticket with Château de la Vigne above.

Anglards-de-Salers: Château de la Trémolière – Open mid-July to August daily from 10am to noon and 2.30pm to 7pm; mid-June to mid-July and the first fortnight in September from 2.30pm to 7pm. 15F. ☏ 04 71 40 00 02 (town hall).

Le MONASTIER-SUR-GAZEILLE   🛈 Mairie, 43150; ☏ 04 71 08 37 76

Abbey Church Treasury – Guided tours (2hr) mid-June to mid-September on Tuesdays from 10am to noon; otherwise by appointment. ☏ 04 71 08 31 88.

Musée municipal – Open July and August Tuesday to Sunday from 10.30am to noon and 3pm to 7pm; in September from 10.30am to noon and 2.30pm to 5pm; in June and October from 2.30pm to 5pm. Closed November to late May. 10F. ☏ 04 71 03 94 08.

Le MONT-DORE 🛈 Avenue de la Libération, 63240; ☏ 04 73 65 20 21

Établissement thermal (Pump Rooms) – Guided tours (45min) mid-May to early October Monday to Saturday at 3.15pm, 3.30pm, 4pm, 4.15pm, 4.45pm and 5.15pm; early October to mid-May Monday to Friday at 10am, 11am, 3pm and 4pm 10F. ☏ 04 73 65 05 10.

Salon du Capucin – **Funicular** operates mid-May to September from 10am to 11.45am and 2pm to 6.45pm. 18F (single), 23.20F (Rtn). ☏ 04 73 65 01 25.

"Les Chanteurs" pump room, Mont-Dore spa

Excursion

Fontaine pétrifiante – Guided tours (30min) mid-May to September daily from 9.30am to noon and 2pm to 6.30pm; early April to mid-May from 2pm to 6.30pm. 16F. ☎ 04 73 81 08 34 or 04 73 65 24 03.

Le MONT-D'OR LYONNAIS

Poleymieux: Maison d'Ampère – Open daily (except Tuesdays) from 9am to noon and 2pm to 6pm. Allow 45min for two audio-visual presentations. 18F. ☎ 04 78 91 90 77.

MONTÉLIMAR

🛈 Avenue Rochemaure, 26200; ☎ 04 75 01 00 20

Guided tours of the town – Contact the tourist office.

Château – Open from 9.30am to 11.30am and 2pm to 5.30pm (6pm in July and August). Closed on Tuesdays from November to late March, and on 1 January and 25 December. 12F. ☎ 04 75 01 07 85.

Excursions

Tricastin nuclear power plant – Guided tours (2hr 30min) weekdays only by appointment. Closed weekends and holidays. Contact the Centre nucléaire de production d'éléctricité du Tricastin, BP 9, 26130 St-Paul-Trois-Châteaux. National identity card required. Minimum age limit is 10 years. ☎ 04 75 50 37 10.

MONTLUÇON

🛈 1ter, avenue Max-Dormoy, 03100; ☎ 04 70 05 05 92

Château des Ducs de Bourbon – Currently being reorganised. Contact the tourist office for details.

Musée des musiques populaires – Currently being reorganised. Contact the tourist office for details.

Excursions

Château de la Louvière – *Open July to September daily (except Tuesdays) from 10am to noon and 2pm to 6pm; during the weekends of Easter, Ascension and Whitsun open at these times also. 20F.* ☎ *04 70 05 04 91 or 04 70 05 00 16.*

Huriel: Keep – Open on weekdays from 8am to noon and 1.30pm to 6pm. Weekends and holidays open by appointment only, contact M. Duperat, 8, Grand'Rue, 03380 Huriel. Admission free. ☎ 04 70 28 60 08 (town hall); ☎ 04 70 28 61 35 (M. Duperat).

MORESTEL

Excursions

Centrale nucléaire de Creys-Malville (Nuclear Power Station) – Guided tours (3hr) all year Monday to Saturday. Apply at least 15 days in advance, by telephone to E.D.F., Centrale de Creys-Malville, Service des Relations Publiques. ☎ 04 74 80 27 30. Identity card required. Minimum age: 10 years.

Parc d'Attractions Walibi Rhône-Alpes (Leisure Park) – ♿ Open in July and August daily from 10am to 7pm; second fortnight in June from 10am to 6pm; late April to mid-June open Wednesdays, weekends and holidays only from 10am to 6pm; in September open weekends only from 10am to 6pm. Closed October to mid-April. 120F (children: 105F). No charge for those under 1m/3ft tall. ☎ 04 74 33 71 80.

MOULINS

🛈 Place de l'Hôtel-de-Ville, 03000; ☎ 04 70 44 14 14

Cathédrale Notre-Dame – Triptych by the Master of Moulins: Guided tours (15min) April to September daily from 9am to noon and 2pm to 6pm (last tickets sold at 11.40am and 5.40pm); on Sunday mornings there is one tour only at 11am. October to March tours daily (except Tuesdays) from 10am to noon and 2pm to 5pm (last tickets at 11.40am and 4.40pm); on Sunday mornings there is one tour only at 11am. Closed 1 January, 1 May and 25 December. 10F. ☎ 04 70 20 89 65.

Musée de Folklore et du Vieux Moulins – *Guided tour (1hr 15min) April to September daily (except Thursday mornings) from 10am to noon and 2pm to 6.30pm; October to March daily (except on Thursdays and on Sunday mornings) from 10am to noon and 2pm to 5.30pm. 20F.* ☎ *04 70 44 39 03.*

Musée d'Art et d'Archéologie – Open daily (except Tuesdays) from 10am to noon and 2pm to 6pm. Closed 1 January, 1 and 8 May, 15 August and 25 December. 20F. ☎ 04 70 20 48 47.

MOULINS

Mausolée du Duc de Montmorency – Guided tours (45min) Monday to Saturday from 3pm to 5.30pm; otherwise by appointment, contact the tourist office. Closed on Sundays, holidays and during November and December. 16F. ☎ 04 70 44 14 14.

Excursions

Yzeure: St Pierre – *Contact the Mairie for details.* ☎ *04 70 20 57 73.*

Arboretum de Balaine – ♿ Open (2hr guided tours available) March to November daily from 9am to noon and 2pm to 7pm; otherwise by appointment. 35F. ☎ 04 70 43 30 07.

MURAT
 Hôtel-de-Ville, 15300; ☎ 04 71 20 09 47

Maison de la Faune – Open in July and August daily (except Sunday mornings) from 10am to noon and 3pm to 7pm; May to June and September to October open at these times, but until 5pm; open until 6pm during school holidays. Closed 1 January and 25 December. 25F (children: 15F). ☎ 04 71 20 00 52.

Excursion

Albepierre-Bredons Church – Guided tours from the third week in June to early September daily (except Mondays) from 10am to noon and 2pm to 7pm.

MUROL

Murol Castle – *Open mid-April to September daily from 10am to 6pm. Guided tours with people in period costume early July to mid-September daily (except Saturdays). 20F, 40F (guided tours).* ☎ *04 73 88 67 11 (Compagnons de Gabriel).*

O

ORCIVAL

Excursion

Château de Cordès – Guided tours (15min) daily from 10am to noon and 2pm to 6pm. 20F (children: 10F). ☎ 04 73 65 81 34.

Château de Cordès

Aven d'ORGNAC

Underground chambers – Guided tours (1hr) July and August daily from 9.30am to 6pm; April to June and in September from 9.30am to noon and 2pm to 6pm; in March and from October to mid-November from 9.30am to noon and 2pm to 5pm. Closed from mid-November to late February. 38F (combined ticket with museum: 49F). ☎ 04 75 38 62 51.

Rando' souterraine – Guided tours (3hr) March to mid-November. Reservations must be made at least a week in advance. 120F (children: 108F). ☎ 04 75 38 62 51.

Musée de Préhistoire – ♿ Open in July and August from 10am to 7pm; April to June and in September from 10am to 1pm and 2pm to 6pm; in March and from October to mid-November from 10am to noon and 2pm to 5pm. Closed from mid-November to late February. 28F (combined ticket with tour of underground chambers: 49F). ☎ 04 75 38 65 10.

P

Lac de PALADRU
🖂 Maison du Pays d'art et d'histoire, Charavines, 38850; ☎ 04 76 55 77 47

Guided tours of the lake – *In July and August (2hr); contact the Maison du Pays at Charavines.*

Charavines: Musée du Lac de Paladru – Open July and August daily from 10am to noon and 3pm to 7pm; in June and September daily from 10am to noon and 2pm to 6pm; in May, October and November open weekends and holidays only from 2pm to 6pm. 18F. ☎ 04 76 55 77 47.

Silve bénite tithe barn – Open in July and August at the same times as the Musée du Lac above. 10F.

Château de Virieu – Guided tours (45min) July to late September daily (except Mondays) from 2pm to 6pm; in May, June and October weekends and holidays only. Otherwise closed. 30F. ☎ 04 74 88 27 32 or 04 74 88 20 10.

Puy de PARIOU

Access – Since the Puy de Pariou is on a shooting range, access is only possible on Monday mornings (until 1pm), Wednesdays and Thursdays between 1 April and 30 September; otherwise on Monday, Wednesday and Thursday mornings (until 1pm). It is open at weekends all year round. Additional restrictions may occasionally be applied.

PÉROUGES
🖂 01800; ☎ 04 74 61 00 88

Maison des Princes de Savoie – Combined ticket with the Musée du Vieux-Pérouges below.

Musée du Vieux-Pérouges – Open Easter to late October daily from 10am to noon and 2pm to 6pm. Closed during winter. 15F, ticket gives access to the Maison des Princes de Savoie (art exhibitions) and the Hortulus. ☎ 04 74 61 00 88.

Ste-Marie-Madeleine – Open from 10am to 6pm. Entrance through the side door facing the town hall.

Château de PESTEILS

Château – Guided tours (45min) in July and August daily from 10am to noon and 2pm to 7pm; Easter to June and in September from 2pm to 7pm. 30F. ☎ 04 71 47 44 36.

Mont PILAT

Parc naturel régional du Pilat – **Main headquarters** at Maison du Parc, Moulin de Virieu, 42410 Pélussin, ☎ 04 74 87 52 00. Open Easter to 11 November during the week from 8.30am to 12.30pm and 2pm to 6pm (5pm on Fridays), weekends and holidays from 9am to 12.30pm and 2pm to 6.30pm; otherwise open during the week only at the above times.
For **guided rambles**, contact the guides two weeks in advance.

Maison-de-l'Eau – *Temporarily closed to visitors.* ☎ *04 77 51 82 31.*

Maison des Arts et Traditions La Béate – Open mid-July to late September on Sundays and holidays only from 2.30pm to 6.30pm. ☎ 04 77 51 24 70 or 04 77 51 20 33.

Maison de la Passementerie (Trimmings) – Visit by appointment from early May to late September. ☎ 04 77 39 91 92 or 04 77 39 91 10.

Maison des Tresses et Lacets (Braids and Ribbons) – ♿ Open in July and August daily from 2.30pm to 6pm; April to late June and September to late December open on Wednesdays, Fridays and Sundays only. Otherwise closed. 15F. ☎ 04 77 20 91 06 or 04 77 20 95 59.

POLIGNAC

Château – Open (45min guided tours available) June to September daily from 10am to 7pm; Easter to May and October to 1 November from 2.30pm to 6pm. Otherwise closed. 12F. ☎ 04 71 02 46 57.

PRIVAS
🖂 3, rue Elie-Reynier, 07000; ☎ 04 75 64 33 35

Musée de la Terre ardéchoise – *Open July and August daily from 9am to noon and 3pm to 7pm; September to June Wednesday to Sunday from 2pm to 6pm. Closed on holidays. 18F. ☎ 04 75 64 43 69.*

Le Bouschet de Pranles Protestant Museum (Pierre and Marie Durand's birthplace) – Open July to mid-September daily (except Sunday mornings) from 10am to noon and 2.30pm to 6.30pm; April to late June and mid-September to late October daily (except Fridays) from 2.45pm to 6pm. Closed November to late March. 15F. ☎ 04 75 64 22 74.

PUY DE DÔME

Grotte du Puy de Dôme – Guided tours (30min) Palm Sunday to September daily from 10am to 7pm. 20F. ☎ 04 73 62 17 41.

Ascent via the toll road – The road is open (weather permitting) May to September daily from 7am to 10pm; in April and October open from 8am to 8pm; in March and November open from 8am to 6pm; during December and the Christmas school holidays open at weekends from 9am to 5pm. Toll: 22F (car), 15F (motorbike). In July and August visitors must travel up in the shuttle buses provided between 11am and 6pm. Access prohibited to pedestrians and two-wheeled vehicles under 125cc. ☎ 04 73 62 12 18.

Reception and information centre – Open May to 1 November (weather permitting). ☎ 04 73 62 21 46.

Le PUY-EN-VELAY

🛈 Place du Breuil, 43000; ☎ 04 71 09 38 41

Guided tours of the town 🅰 – Contact the tourist office.

Atelier conservatoire de la dentelle du Puy (Lace workshop) – Open Mondays, Tuesdays, Thursdays and Fridays from 10am to 11am and 2pm to 3pm. Closed on holidays. Admission free. ☎ 04 71 09 74 41.

Centre d'enseignement de la dentelle au fuseau (Bobbin lace centre) – Open in July and August Monday to Saturday from 9am to 7pm; mid-May to June and second fortnight in December open Tuesday to Saturday from 10am to noon and 2pm to 7pm; January to mid-May and mid-September to mid-December open from 10am to noon and 3pm to 7pm; first fortnight in September open from 3pm to 7pm. Closed on holidays. Admission free. ☎ 04 71 02 01 68.

Tourist train – Departures from Place Michelet, opposite the tourist office, May to October on the hour from 9am to 7pm (until 9pm in July to August). 30F (children: 20F). ☎ 04 71 02 70 70.

Cathédrale Notre-Dame – **Guided tours** available: apply to the sacristy or M. le Recteur. ☎ 04 71 05 44 93. **Fresco of St Michael:** Guided tours available in season; apply to the sacristy. **Treasury:** Open from 9am to 6pm in season; otherwise, from 9am to noon and 2pm to 6pm.

Chapel of Relics, Cloisters, Religious Art Treasury – Open (45min guided tours available) July to September daily from 9.30am to 6.30pm; early April to June from 9.30am to 12.30pm and 2pm to 6pm (no midday break on Sundays and holidays); October to March from 9.30am to noon and 2pm to 4pm (no midday break on Sundays and holidays). Closed 1 January, 1 May, 1 and 11 November, 25 December. 22F. ☎ 04 71 05 45 52.

Prior's Lodgings – Open in July and August from 9am to noon and 2pm to 6pm. 6F.

Rocher Corneille – Open July and August daily from 9.30am to 8pm; May, June and September from 9am to 7pm; mid-March to April from 9am to 6pm; October to mid-March from 10am to 5pm. Closed December and January, except for during local school holiday periods and on Sunday afternoons. 10F. ☎ 04 71 09 38 41.

Chapelle St Michel d'Aiguilhe – Open mid-June to mid-September daily from 9am to 7pm; first fortnight in June from 10am to noon and 2pm to 7pm; mid-September to mid-November from 9.30am to noon and 2pm to 5.30pm; mid-March to May from 10am to noon and 2pm to 5pm; mid-February to mid-March and during Christmas school holidays from 2pm to 4pm. Closed mid-November to mid-February (including 1 January and 25 December). 10F. ☎ 04 71 02 71 32.

Musée Crozatier – Open (1hr 15min guided tours available) May to September daily (except Tuesdays) from 10am to noon and 2pm to 6pm; October to April daily (except Tuesdays and on Sunday mornings) from 10am to noon and 2pm to 4pm. Closed 1 January, 1 November and 25 December. 12F. ☎ 04 71 09 38 90.

Atelier Chaleyé – Guided tours (30min) by appointment; apply to workshop. Admission free. ☎ 04 71 09 31 38.

Excursions

Château de St-Vidal – Guided tours (30min) in July and August daily from 2pm to 7pm (last tickets sold at 6.30pm). 20F.

Espaly-St-Marcel: Rocher St Joseph – Access to the statue and diorama in July and August daily from 2pm to 7pm; September to June daily from 9am to 5pm. 10F. ☎ 04 71 09 16 71.

Michelin Maps which cover the area described in this guide are nos 69, 73, 74, 76, 77, 80, 81 and 88.

R

RAVEL

Château – Guided tours (45min) July to September daily from 10am to noon and 2pm to 7pm; Easter to June and Ocotber to 1 November daily from 2pm to 6pm, Sundays and holidays from 10am to noon and 2pm to 6pm. 35F. ☎ 04 73 68 44 63.

Les RHUES

Apchon: La Font-Sainte chapel – Open July to September daily from 9am to 7pm. ☎ 04 71 78 90 40.

Château du RIAU

Castle and tithe barn – Guided tours (1hr) April to September daily (except Tuesdays) from 2.30pm to 6.30pm (last tickets sold at 6pm). 25F. ☎ 04 70 43 34 47.

Moulin RICHARD-DE-BAS

Mill – Guided tours (1hr 15min) July and August daily from 9am to 8pm (last tour starts at 7pm); otherwise from 9am to noon and 2pm to 6pm (last tours start at 11am and 5pm). Closed 1 January and 25 December. 23F (children: 16F). ☎ 04 73 82 03 11.

RIOM

🛈 16, rue du Commerce, 63200; ☎ 04 73 38 59 45

Guided tours of the town ◪ – Contact the tourist office.

Sainte-Chapelle – Guided tours (1hr) July and August Monday to Friday from 10am to noon and 2.30pm to 5.30pm; in June and September Wednesday to Friday from 3pm to 5pm; in May on Wednesdays from 3pm to 5pm (last tickets at 4.30pm). Closed 1 and 8 May, 14 July and 15 August. 15F. ☎ 04 73 38 99 94.

Musée régional d'Auvergne – Open (1hr 30min guided tours available once a week in July and August) June to September daily (except Tuesdays) from 10am to noon and 2.30pm to 6pm; October to May from 10am to noon and 2pm to 5.30pm. Closed on holidays and during the Cendres (Ash Wednesday) and St-Amable fairs. 18F (admission free on Wednesdays), 25F (guided tours). ☎ 04 73 38 17 31.

Musée Mandet – Same conditions as the Musée régional d'Auvergne (guided tours last 2hr). ☎ 04 73 38 18 53.

Hôtel de Ville – Open daily from 9am to noon and 2pm to 5pm. A special guide is available to blind visitors. Admission free. ☎ 04 73 33 79 00.

Excursion

Château de Chazeron – Guided tours (1hr) May to September daily from 3pm and 6pm; Easter to April and October to mid-November open Sundays and holidays from 3pm to 6pm. 25F. Evening visit with illuminations in July and August on Mondays at 10pm: 50F. ☎ 04 73 86 66 12.

Sources pétrifiantes de Gimeaux – ৬ Open April to third week in December daily from 9.30am to noon and 2pm to 6.30pm; in February and March daily (except Wednesdays) at these times. Closed from the last week in December to late January. 16F. ☎ 04 73 63 57 59.

Château de Davayat – ৬ Guided tours (45min) mid-June to mid-September daily (except Saturdays) from 2.30pm to 6.30pm (last tickets at 6pm). 25F (children: 13F). ☎ 04 73 63 30 27.

RIOM-ÈS-MONTAGNES

🛈 Place Charles-de-Gaulle, 15400; ☎ 04 71 78 07 37

Maison de la Gentiane – Open in July and August daily from 10am to 12.30pm and 2.30pm to 7pm; in June and September from 2pm to 6pm. 17F. ☎ 04 71 48 68 68.

ROANNE

🛈 Cours de la République, 42300; ☎ 04 77 71 51 77

Barge trips – Half-day, full-day or longer trips can be organised to or from Roanne. A variety of options is on offer, principally for group excursions.
For trips on the *Prospérité*: contact the youth hostel, Auberge de la Jeunesse, 4, rue de Fontenille, Roanne, ☎ 04 77 72 52 11;
on *L'Infatigable*: contact Marins d'Eau Douce, Port de plaisance de Briennon, ☎ 04 77 69 92 92;
on the *Palombe*: contact the Fédération des Œuvres Laïques, 12, avenue de Paris, Roanne, ☎ 04 77 7125 81.

Musée Joseph-Déchelette – Open daily (except Tuesdays) from 10am to noon and 2pm to 6pm. Closed on holidays. 10F. ☎ 04 77 70 00 90.

Écomusée du Roannais – ♿ Open daily from 3pm to 7pm. Closed 1 January and 25 December. 15F. ☎ 04 77 71 31 88.

Musée de la Maille – ♿ Guided tours (1hr 15min) Tuesday to Sunday from 2pm to 6pm. Closed on first and third (and fifth) Sundays of month, holidays and between Christmas and the New Year. 5F. ☎ 04 77 70 02 42.

Excursions

Villerest: Boat trips – Not operating at the time of going to press. For information, call the Roanne tourist office or the Villerest sailing base. ☎ 04 70 31 35 99.

Villerest: Musée de l'Heure et du Feu – Open July and August Tuesday to Sunday from 3pm to 7pm; Easter to late June and first fortnight in September open at weekends only. Otherwise closed. 15F. ☎ 04 77 69 66 66.

St-Marcel-de-Félines Château – Open July and August on Sundays and Mondays from 2pm to 6pm; Easter to 1 November open Sundays and holidays at these times. 28F. ☎ 04 77 63 23 08.

Dining room, St-Marcel-de-Félines château

Château de l'Aubépin – Open all year Mondays, Fridays, weekends and holidays from 11am to 6pm. Admission free.

St-André-d'Apchon Church – *Contact the presbytery.* ☎ 04 77 65 80 47.

Ambierle: Musée Alice-Taverne – Open February to late November from 10am to noon and 2pm to 6pm; otherwise by appointment. Closed December and January. 20F. ☎ 04 77 65 60 99.

Château de la ROCHE

Medieval manor – Guided tours (45min) daily from 9am to noon and 2pm to 7pm. 25F. ☎ 04 73 63 65 81.

ROMANS-SUR-ISÈRE   🚹 Place Jean-Jaurès, 26100; ☎ 04 75 02 28 72

Guided tours of the town – Contact the tourist office.

Collégiale St-Barnard: Chapel of the Holy Sacrament – Guided tours (1hr) mid-June to mid-September Monday to Saturday from 10am to noon and 3pm to 6pm; on Sundays from 3pm to 6pm only. Closed out of season. 15F.

Musée International de la Chaussure (Shoes) – Open July and August Monday to Saturday from 9am to 6pm; January to late June and September to late December open Tuesday to Saturday from 9am to 11.45am and 2pm to 5.45pm. Open on Sundays all year round from 2.30pm to 6pm, as well as certain holidays at these times. Closed 1 January, 1 May, 1 November and 25 December. 25F. ☎ 04 75 05 81 30.

Excursion

Mours-St-Eusèbe: Musée diocesain d'Art sacré – Guided tours (1hr 30min) May to late October daily (except Saturdays) from 2.30pm to 6.30pm. Otherwise closed. 15F. ☎ 04 75 02 01 26.

ROYAT
🚹 Place Allard, 63130; ☎ 04 73 35 81 87

Taillerie de Pierres Fines (Stone-cutting Workshop) – ♿ Guided tours (30min) July and August daily (except Sundays) from 2.30pm to 5.30pm. 15F. ☎ 04 73 35 81 25.

S

ST-ANTOINE

St Antoine Abbey Church and Treasury – Guided tours March to late November daily (except Tuesdays and on Sunday mornings) from 10am to noon and 2pm to 7pm; otherwise open to visitors not wanting guided tours. Closed December to late February. 20F. Apply in advance to the tourist office. ☎ 04 76 36 44 46.

Musée Jean Vinay – Open July and August daily (except Tuesdays) from 11am to 12.30pm and 1.30pm 7pm; mid-March to mid-April, mid-May to late June and September open from 2pm to 6pm. Closed November to March and on 1 May. 15F. ☎ 04 76 36 40 68.

STE-CROIX-EN-JAREZ

Church – Guided tours daily every hour from 10am to noon and 2pm to 6pm. ☎ 04 77 20 20 81.

Former sacristy (frescoes): ♿ Guided tours (15min) daily from 10am to noon and 2pm to 6pm. 10F. Apply to L'Association de Sauvegarde de la Chartreuse, 42800 Ste-Croix-en-Jarez. ☎ 04 77 20 20 81.

ST-ÉTIENNE
🚹 3, place Roannelle, 42000; ☎ 04 77 25 12 14

Musée d'Art Moderne – ♿ Open daily from 10am to 6pm. Closed on most holidays. 26F. ☎ 04 77 79 52 52.

Grand'Église – *Closed Sunday afternoons.* ☎ *04 77 32 22 36.*

Musée du vieux St-Etienne – Open Monday to Saturday from 2.30pm to 6pm. Guided tours (1hr 30min) available Wednesdays. 10F. ☎ 04 77 25 74 32.

Musée d'Art et d'Industrie – Closed for restoration. Scheduled for re-opening in 1998. Contact the tourist office for details.

Puits Couriot, Musée de la Mine – Guided tours (1hr 30min) during school holidays daily (except Monday mornings) from 10am to 11.30am and 2pm to 5.30pm (6pm at weekends); otherwise from 10am to 11.15am and 2pm to 4.30pm (6pm at weekends). Closed during first fortnight in January and on certain holidays. 35F (children: 25F). ☎ 04 77 43 83 26.

ST-FLOUR
🚹 Cours Spy des Ternes, 15100; ☎ 04 71 60 22 50

Musée de la Haute-Auvergne – Open (1hr guided tours available) mid-April to mid-October daily from 10am to noon and 2pm to 6pm; mid-October to mid-April Monday to Saturday at these times. Closed Sundays and holidays out of season and 1 May. 20F. ☎ 04 71 60 22 32 or 04 71 60 61 20.

Musée A-Douët – Guided tours (45min) mid-April to mid-October daily from 9am to noon and 2pm to 6pm; mid-October to mid-April Monday to Saturday at these times. Closed 1 January, Easter Day, 1 May, 1 November and 25 December. 20F. ☎ 04 71 60 44 99.

Musée postal d'Auvergne – ♿ Open (1hr guided tours available) June to September daily from 10am to noon and 2pm to 7pm. 20F (children: 8F). ☎ 04 71 60 38 03 or 04 71 60 08 55.

ST-NECTAIRE
🚹 Mairie, 63710; ☎ 04 73 88 50 86

St-Nectaire – Open (guided tours available by appointment) June to mid-September daily (except Tuesdays and on Sunday mornings) from 10am to noon and 2.30pm to 6pm; Easter to May and mid-September to mid-October open Mondays, Wednesdays, Fridays, Saturdays and Sundays from 2.30pm to 4.30pm. Closed mid-October until Easter. ☎ 04 73 88 50 86 or 04 73 88 50 67 (guided tours).

Grottes du Cornadore – Guided tours (45min) May to the third week in September daily from 10am to noon and 2pm to 7pm; from the February school holidays until April, during the third week in September and during the other school holidays open from 2pm to 6pm; October to mid-November open Sundays and holidays from 2pm to 6pm. Closed 1 January and 25 December. 22F. ☎ 04 73 88 51 66.

ST-NECTAIRE

Maison du St-Nectaire – Guided tours (30min) May to third week in September daily from 10am to noon and 2pm to 7pm; from the February school holidays until April, during the third week in September and during the other school holidays open from 2pm to 6pm; October to mid-November open Sundays and holidays from 2pm to 6pm. Closed 1 January and 25 December. 16F. ☎ 04 73 88 51 66.

Fontaines Pétrifiantes – Open (30min guided tours available) June to September daily from 9am to noon and 2pm to 7pm; February to May open daily (but not on Mondays in March) from 9am to noon and 2pm to 6pm; October to January open Tuesday to Sunday from 9am to noon and 2pm to 5.30pm. Closed mid-November to third week in December. 18F (children: 9F). ☎ 04 73 88 50 80.

ST-PAUL-TROIS-CHÂTEAUX

Maison de la Truffe et du Tricastin – Open May to September daily (except Monday mornings) from 9am (10am on Sundays) to noon and 3pm to 7pm; in April and October open daily (except Monday mornings) from 9am (10am on Sundays) to noon and 2pm to 6pm; November to late March open Monday to Saturday at these times. Closed on holidays. 15F. ☎ 04 75 96 61 29.

ST POURÇAIN-SUR-SIOULE   🛈 35, boulevard Ledru-Rollin, 03500; ☎ 04 70 45 32 73

Musée de la Vigne et du Vin – Open (1hr guided tours available) mid-June to mid-September daily from 10am to noon and 2.30pm to 6.30pm; March to mid-June and mid-September to December. Closed 1 November, 25 December and from January to February. 22F. ☎ 04 70 45 62 07 or tourist office.

ST-ROMAIN-LE-PUY

Eglise du Prieuré – Open (guided tours available) mid-April to mid-September. Enquire at the town hall. ☎ 04 77 76 60 55.

ST-SATURNIN

Ste-Madeleine Chapel – Exhibitions open mid-June to August daily from 2pm to 6pm.

Castle – Guided tours (45min) mid-June to mid-September daily from 10am to noon and 2pm to 7pm; Easter to mid-June and mid-September to October on Sundays and holidays from 2pm to 6pm. 22F. ☎ 04 73 39 39 64.

SALERS   🛈 Place Tyssandier-d'Escous, 15410; ☎ 04 71 40 70 68

Ancien Bailliage – Guided tours (30min) daily from 9.30am to noon and 2pm to 7pm. 15F. ☎ 04 71 40 70 59.

Maison de Bargues – Guided tours (30min) May to September daily from 10am to noon and 2pm to 7pm. 15F. ☎ 04 71 40 73 42.

Maison des Templiers – Open daily (except Tuesdays) from 10.30am to 12.30pm and 2.30pm to 6.30pm. Closed January to mid-February. 20F. ☎ 04 71 40 75 97.

Maison du Bailliage

SAUGUES

Tour des Anglais – Open July and August daily from 10am to noon and 2pm to 6.30pm. 16F. ☎ 04 71 77 81 22.

Diorama de St Bénilde – Open April to November daily (except on Sunday mornings) from 10am to noon and 2pm to 6pm. Closed in the morning on holidays. Admission free. ☎ 04 71 77 82 53.

SERRIÈRES

Musée des Mariniers du Rhône – *Guided tours (1hr) April to late October weekends and holidays from 3pm to 6pm. Otherwise closed (and closed on 1 May). 12F.* ☎ *04 75 34 01 26.*

SOUVIGNY

Église prieurale St-Pierre-et-St-Paul – *Open daily from 9.30am (but not during religious offices); guided tours (1hr) of the sepulchral chapels, sacristy, cloisters and chapter-house from mid-July to late August daily (1 tour at the end of the morning, tours at regular intervals during the afternoon).* ☎ *04 70 43 60 51 (Communauté Saint-Jean).*

Musée de la Grange Nord – Open April to mid-November daily from 10am to noon and 2pm to 6pm. 20F. ☎ 04 70 43 60 38.

T

THIERS
🛈 Château du Pirou, 63300; ☎ 04 73 80 10 74

Maison des Couteliers and Musée de la Coutellerie – Open (1hr 30min guided tours available) June to September daily from 10am to noon and 2pm to 6.30pm (last tickets sold at 5.45pm); October to May Tuesday to Sunday from 10am to noon and 2pm to 6pm (last tickets at 5.15pm). Closed 1 January, 1 May, 1 November and 25 December. 20F. ☎ 04 73 80 58 86.

Église du Moutier – Church is closed other than during religious services. Key can be obtained from the presbytery behind the church. ☎ 04 73 80 02 30.

Creux d'Enfer contemporary art centre – Open Mondays, Wednesdays, Thursdays and Fridays from 10am to noon and 2pm to 6pm, weekends from 2pm to 7pm. Admission free. Closed 1 January, 1 May and 25 December. ☎ 04 73 80 26 56.

Château de TOURNOËL

Château – Open (30min guided tours available) mid-July to mid-August daily from 10am to 7pm; April to mid-July and mid-August to September open daily (except Thursdays) from 10am to 6pm; mid-February to March and October to mid-November open from 1.30pm to 5pm. 20F. ☎ 04 73 33 53 06.

TRÉVOUX
🛈 Place du Pont, BP 108, 01600; ☎ 04 74 00 36 32

Guided tour of the town – Contact the tourist office.

Palais du Parlement – Open mid-June to mid-September Monday to Friday from 9am to noon and 2pm to 6pm, weekends from 2pm to 6.30pm; otherwise open during the week only. Closed in August and on holidays. ☎ 04 74 00 36 32.

Hôpital – ♿ Open mid-June to mid-September Mondays, Fridays, weekends and holidays from 2pm to 6.30pm. ☎ 04 74 00 36 32.

Forêt de TRONÇAIS

Guided tours of the forest – These are organised during 1 or 2 months in the summer, leaving from the Rond de Tronçais crossroads; contact the Office National des Forêts at Moulins. For further information on activities for tourists, contact the Association du Pays at Cérilly, ☎ 04 70 67 55 89.

Cérilly: Charles-Louis Philippe's Birthplace – Guided tours (1hr) May to October Thursdays, weekends and holidays from 3pm to 6.30pm. 15F. ☎ 04 70 67 52 00.

V

VALENCE
🛈 54, rue Denis-Papin, 26000; ☎ 04 75 44 90 44

Guided tours of the town 🄰 – Contact the tourist office or the Maison des Têtes (☎ 04 75 56 95 82).

Musée des Beaux-Arts – Open Wednesdays and weekends from 9am to noon and 2pm to 6pm; otherwise, during the week, open afternoons only. Closed holidays. 15F (admission free on Sundays). ☎ 04 75 79 20 80.

Maison Dupré-Latour – Guided tours included in tours of the old town. Contact the tourist office or call ☎ 04 75 56 95 82 (Maison des Têtes, "Valence ville d'art".)

Excursion

Tournon-sur-Rhône Château – Open June to late August daily (except Tuesdays) from 10am to noon and 2pm to 6pm; in April, May, September and October open afternoons only (closes at 5pm during October). Otherwise closed. 20F. ☎ 04 75 08 10 23 (Tournon tourist office).

River boat trips – Operate in season from Valence to Vienne, Avignon and the Camargue. For bookings contact Société RestoRhône, quai de l'Epervière, Valence, ☎ 04 75 41 43 15.

Les VANS

Gravières Church – Open Fridays only in summer from 5.30pm to 6pm and in winter from 4.30pm to 5pm. Contact the priest. ☎ 04 75 37 30 22.

VERNOUX-EN-VIVARAIS

Boffres: Château des Faugs – Open mid-July to late August daily (except Tuesdays) from 2.30pm to 6.30pm. Otherwise closed. 25F. ☎ 04 75 58 24 29.

Source des Célestins, Vichy

Le VEURDRE

Château de St-Augustin – *Open June to mid-September daily from 2pm to 7pm; otherwise Wednesdays, weekends, holidays and during school holidays from 2pm to 7pm. 37F.* ☎ *04 70 66 42 01.*

VICHY 🚩 19, rue du Parc, 03204; ☎ 04 70 98 71 94

Maison du Missionnaire – *Open mid-May to mid-September Monday to Saturday from 3pm to 6pm. Closed on holidays. Admission free.* ☎ *04 70 98 34 29.*

VIENNE 🚩 Cours Brillier, 38200; ☎ 04 74 85 12 62

Guided tours of the town 🅰 – Contact the tourist office.

St-André-le-Bas – Apply to St-André's cloisters.

Cloître St-André-le-Bas, Théâtre Romain, Musée des Beaux-Arts et Archéologie, Ancienne Église St-Pierre – Open April to late October daily (except Tuesdays) from 9.30am to 1pm and 2pm to 6pm; otherwise, we advise checking the opening times in advance. Closed 1 January, 1 May, 1 and 11 November and 25 December. 10F per monument (joint ticket for all four: 26F). ☎ 04 74 85 50 42.

St-Martin – Apply to the presbytery, 6 place St-Martin. ☎ 04 74 85 18 43.

Gallo-Roman city of St-Romain-en-Gal – For guided tours, apply to the tourist office in Vienne. ☎ 04 74 85 12 62.
Archaeological museum – This new museum was inaugurated in late 1996. It is open Tuesday to Sunday from 9.30am to 6.30pm. Closed on holidays. 30F. For guided tours contact the museum (☎ 04 74 53 74 00) or the Vienne tourist office.

Ste-Colombe: Église – Open during services only. Otherwise, apply to the presbytery, 2, rue du Salin, 69560 Ste-Colombe. ☎ 04 74 53 11 55.

VILLARS-LES-DOMBES

Church – Open during the week, but no sightseeing during services. ☎ 04 74 98 06 29.

Parc Ornithologique (Bird Sanctuary) – Open daily in summer from 9am to 7pm and in winter from 9am to 5.30pm. 35F (children: 17F). ☎ 04 74 98 05 54.

VILLEFRANCHE-SUR-SAÔNE

🛈 290, rue de Thizy, 69400; ☎ 04 74 68 05 18

Guided tours of the town – Contact the tourist office.

Old houses – Guided tours (2hr) in July and August on Saturdays from 10am to noon, leaving from the tourist office. 15F.

VIVIERS

🛈 07220; ☎ 04 75 52 77 00

Old Town – *For guided tours, contact the tourist office or the Association Patrimoine Vivarois.* ☎ *04 42 21 05 11.*

VOLVIC

🛈 Mairie, 63530; ☎ 04 73 33 50 38

Maison de la Pierre – Guided tours (45min) May to September daily at 9.15am, 10am, 10.45am, 11.30am, 2.15pm, 3pm, 3.45pm, 4.30pm, 5.15pm and 6pm; otherwise, tours daily (except Tuesdays) at these times, starting at 10am and 5.15pm. Closed mid-November to mid-March. 20F (children: 10F). ☎ 04 73 33 56 92.

Musée municipal Marcel-Sahut – ♿ Open daily (except Sunday mornings) from 10am to noon and 2pm to 5pm. Closed 1 January, 1 May and 25 December. 10F (admission free). ☎ 04 73 33 57 33.

Volvic Springs – ♿ Open May to September daily from 9am to noon and 2pm (2.30pm at weekends and holidays) to 6pm; in April open Monday to Friday (not holidays) at these times; October to first week in November open from 2pm to 6pm. Guided tours (1hr) to see the bottling process of Volvic mineral water June to early September Monday to Friday (not holidays) from 2pm to 4.30pm by appointment (children under the age of 7 not admitted). Admission free. ☎ 04 73 63 20 19.

Index

Annonay *Ardèche*   Towns, sights and tourist regions followed by the name of the *département*.

Berlioz, Hector   People, historical events and subjects.

MANUFACTURE FRANÇAISE DES PNEUMATIQUES MICHELIN
Société en commandite par actions au capital de 2 000 000 000 de francs
Place des Carmes-Déchaux - 63 Clermont-Ferrand (France)
R.C.S. Clermont-Fd B 855 200 507

© Michelin et Cie, Propriétaires-Éditeurs 1997
Dépôt légal Juin 1997 – ISBN 2-06-130402-8 – ISSN 0763-1383

Printed in the EU 03-99/2

Cover illustration by Jean-Luc ROYER/Lorenzo TIMON